Andean Tragedy

Andean Tragedy

Fighting the
War of the Pacific,
1879–1884

William F. Sater

University of Nebraska Press
Lincoln and London

Library of Congress Cataloging-
in-Publication Data
Sater, William F.
Andean Tragedy: Fighting the war of the
Pacific, 1879–1884 / William F. Sater.
p.   cm.— (Studies in war, society,
and the military) Includes bibliographical
references and index.
ISBN-13: 978-0-8032-4334-7 (cloth : alk. paper)
ISBN-10: 0-8032-4334-0 (cloth : alk. paper)
ISBN-13: 978-0-8032-2799-6 (paper : alk. paper)
1. War of the Pacific, 1879–1884
2. Chile—History, Military—19th century.
3. Bolivia—History, Military—19th century.
4. Peru—History, Military—19th century.
I. Title.
F3097.S264   2007
983.06′1—dc22
2006029929

To John M. Dixon, my son-in-law,
and Milo Joseph Dixon, my grandson.

To those men and women who sacrificed
their health, their lives, and their youth
protecting their respective *patrias*.

Contents

Maps

Tables

Acknowledgments

This book, like many scholarly works, is the result of a collaborative effort. My close friends Professors Christon Archer and Jaime Rodriguez mercilessly harassed, hectored, and hounded me in order to present the reader with a study that purports to be a volume of objective scholarship. I think their collective efforts have successfully restrained my natural exuberance, although the churlish might disagree.

The list of Chilean colleagues to whom I owe a great deal grows longer with each year. Professor Patricia Arancibia Clavel, her brother, Gen. Roberto Arancibia Clavel, Ret., and his daughter Claudia Arancibia Floody provided me with much assistance, as did Capitán de Navio Carlos Tromben, Ret., and Sr. Gilles Galté. Dr. Ricardo Couyoumdjian and his wife, Mabel, have always made a place for me in their home, as well as at their dinner table, which I deeply appreciate. I have also benefited from works of Professors Gonzalo Vial, Alejandro San Francisco, and Angel Soto. My *mispocha*—the late Nana Bronfman and her children and Lucy and her husband, Claudio, son Eduardo, and daughter Irene—have generously welcomed me whenever I visited Santiago. Gonzalo Mendoza and his wife, Veronica, have made me feel at home be it Los Angeles, Madrid, or Santiago, and I have spent some delightful hours with them and their children. Peru's general counsel to Los Angeles, Ambassador Liliana Cino, and her husband, Ambassador Gustavo Silva, as well as Jorge Ortiz Sotelo facilitated my research in Peru, as did the director and the staff of that country's national library. The interlibrary loan section of the California State University, Long Beach, also helped me enormously.

Introduction

When asked to define "armed conflict," George Ives, an 111-year-old veteran of Britain's struggle with the South African Boers (1899–1902), relied on the same logic that the thief Willy Sutton employed to explain why he robbed banks: "You went to war to kill someone," Ives observed, "and they tried to kill you back."[1] In this sense the War of the Pacific is not unique; it is just one more of the countless blood baths that characterized the nineteenth century. And it is perhaps for that reason that many scholars never heard of the War of the Pacific or that the few who may vaguely recall it confuse that conflict with the Pacific theater of the Second World War. In fact, the War of the Pacific did not occur in the twentieth century. Beginning in 1879 and lasting until 1884, it pitted the Republic of Chile against the combined forces of Bolivia and Peru. This struggle would dramatically alter not merely these nations' boundaries but their collective memory as well. A triumphant Chile would annex the Bolivian province of Atacama, thereby making La Paz the capital of a landlocked nation and Santiago the owner of its guano beds and nitrate (salitre) mines. (Chileans did not know at that time that the Atacama also contained some of the world's richest copper deposits.) Thanks to its victory, Chile also incorporated the Peruvian province of Tarapacá, thus endowing Santiago with almost complete control of the world's nitrate deposits. The export of salitre, used to manufacture explosives and fertilizer, would fund various Chilean governments until the early 1920s. Conversely, the loss of the salitreras stunted Peru's economic growth. Long after the fighting had ended, the Peruvians and Bolivians threatened to unleash a revanchist war on Chile. Santiago, however, tenaciously retained two Peruvian provinces, Tacna and Arica, until an agreement in the late 1920s returned the former to Peru. Bolivia, although allowed to use the port of Arica duty free, still yearns, not for a place in the sun, but for one by the seashore.

The International Context

The War of the Pacific was not only one of the longest struggles of late-nineteenth-century Latin America; it was one of the few large-scale conflicts to afflict the world at that time. After 1871 the normally pugnacious countries of western Europe ceased to annihilate each other with their customary zeal. These nations did not suddenly beat their swords into ploughshares nor their spears into pruning hooks; on the contrary, they spent enormous sums keeping their weapons well honed. They had simply shifted the venue for slaughter to Asia, Africa, or Europe's fringes, the land separating Russia and Turkey, central Asia, or the Balkans. Thus, the British battled the Pathans of Afghanistan in the late 1870s; what some derisively dismissed as the Fuzzy Wuzzies or Dervishes of the Sudan in 1885 (who despite the patronizing name broke the British square); the Zulus of Natal (1879); and the Boers of the South African veld. Other European nations also participated in imperial struggles: the French finally triumphed over the Vietnamese in the early 1880s, although they had to use melinite shells to vanquish the Hova people of Madagascar between 1883 and 1885 and, after 1898, some of the island's other tribes. We should not be completely surprised that the Germans, anxious to seize land in southwest Africa, waged a genocidal war that killed 90 percent of the region's pastoral Herero people by 1908. Even the smaller European powers indulged colonial impulses: King Leopold oversaw Belgium's post-1884 brutal occupation that annihilated millions of Congolese; his Dutch neighbors found it somewhat harder to fight the sultan of Achin in Indonesia in 1873. The Italians fared the worst, suffering a humiliating loss to Menelek's Ethiopian legions at the 1896 Battle of Adowa.

Alexander III, unlike his western European neighbors, did not have to travel overseas to continue Russia's inexorable push into central Asia or to fight the Turks in 1877–78. Apparently success in these two arenas encouraged Alexander's heir, Nicholas II, to battle the Meiji emperor's newly modernized armed forces in 1904–5. Simple good judgment should have curbed the czar's imperial appetites, but as Kaiser Wilhelm had earlier concluded, wisdom was not Cousin Nicky's long suit. Thus, the czar blundered into a conflict that proved far more costly than Russia's earlier adventures: by 1905 the Japanese armed forces had eradicated most of Nicolas II's Far Eastern and Baltic fleets and a substantial portion of his army, forcing the czar to rein in his imperial urges.

With the exception of the Russian encounters with the Turks and Japanese, most late-nineteenth-century struggles were short-lived, low-level conflicts. Given this lack of "modern wars," military historians have had few case studies to analyze. Thus, not without reason did some scholars devote their efforts to studying the American Civil War and the Franco-Prussian War. These contests proved highly instructive because they were the first encounters where the contestants used the breech-loading rifle, which permitted troops to load their weapons from a prone position, thereby reducing their exposure to enemy counterfire. The new small arms, when rifled and employing metallic cartridges, doubled the soldiers' rate of fire while increasing their range by up to 400 percent. Thanks to this new technology, entrenched infantry could, in the words of one military thinker, turn into "food for gunpowder" any formation of closely packed men or cavalry squadron who foolishly entered what various American military officers dubbed "the danger zone" or the "deadly space," the open terrain in front of a defensive position. Henceforth, units would abjure attacking in compact formations. Instead, small clusters of men would advance in leaps and bounds, a technique that some called "swarming." Once the attacking troops came under fire, they were to dig in and use their small arms to suppress the enemy fire while a second wave of attackers passed through the first unit, toward the objective. If necessary, a third wave could follow in the footsteps of the second. These leapfrogging waves of men would alternate digging in or advancing until they could finally close with their enemy. Such tactics, by presenting fewer and more widely separated targets, minimized casualties.[2]

Despite these maneuvers' clear advantages, many skeptics still doubted the efficacy of the new battlefield techniques. A British officer, Capt.

C. B. Brackenbury, admitted, "It is a very ugly thing to attack against breech-loaders, but it has to be done . . . it is moral force which will prevail."[3] The czar's army embraced precisely that philosophy in mid-July 1877, when its massed formations assaulted fortified Turkish positions at Plevna. The well-entrenched Ottoman troops, equipped with top-of-the-line Peabody-Martini breechloaders, repelled the Russians, slaughtering or wounding 25 percent of the czar's officers and 23 percent of his men. These horrific losses did not deter the czarist generals. Another massed assault, this one preceded by six hours of shelling, also failed, again at a cost of 25 percent of the Russian troops. The Russians ultimately succeeded in taking Plevna but only after abandoning massed frontal assaults in favor of a five-month siege.

Regrettably, the European armies seemed impervious to the lessons of the American Civil War and the Franco-Prussian War. During the initial stages of the Zulu War in 1879, Gen. Frederick Thesiger, commander of the British expeditionary force and recently named Lord Chelmsford, committed two cardinal military errors: he divided his command and, worse, he underestimated his adversary. Leading a column consisting of two battalions of the Twenty-fourth Regiment of Foot plus local auxiliaries and some artillery, Chelmsford entered Zulu territory on 11 January 1879. Within nine days his column reached Isandlwana, a tall mountain that loomed over a plain spacious enough to accommodate the invading forces and their mounts. Ordering six companies of the Twenty-fourth, about eight hundred men, plus nine hundred auxiliaries and a few artillery pieces to remain at the base of Isandlwana under the command of Lt. Col. Henry Pulleine, Chelmsford moved out in hopes of finding the Zulu legions.

Chelmsford's enemies found his command first: on 26 January 1879, twenty thousand assegai-wielding Zulus attacked. The one-armed British commander valiantly tried to rally his men, and, equipped with the Martini-Henry .45 caliber rifles and artillery, they did constitute a formidable force. But rather than dig in, which would have afforded them cover, the British formed the "long red line." Although sometimes overused, that description proved quite accurate in this case because the English troops at Isandlwana did in fact wear red tunics, as well as blue trousers, topped off with white helmets. The line may have repelled an "onslaught of a fanatical horde" at Khartoum, but it failed in the Natal.[4] The Zulu *impis* attacked in their classic Horns of the Buffalo formation: one group, representing the animal's body, assaulted the English frontally while two other columns, the horns, enveloped the British flanks. Although equipped with modern rifles and artillery-firing canisters at point-blank range, the red line fell back. They formed squares but for naught: the Zulus overran them, first killing and then eviscerating over thirteen hundred officers and men.

The Zulus repeated this tactic a second time. Within days of the Isandlwana debacle, 4,000 Zulus attacked a 140-man contingent, also of the Twenty-fourth Regiment, stationed at a missionary station in nearby Rorke's Drift. These soldiers, unlike their unfortunate brothers, did not make their stand in the open. Instead they took cover behind hastily erected sandbag parapets and in the stone mission building. Thus, despite the overwhelming odds, the British, protected by their makeshift fortifications, repulsed wave after wave of the Zulus, forcing them to retreat, and only losing 17 dead and 43 wounded. The two lessons that emerged from these contests reinforced those of the American Civil War and the Franco-Prussian contest: that the rifle bullet, not the bayonet—which Gen. William Sherman dismissed as superfluous—had become the battlefield's most efficient killer and that troops should fight behind cover.[5]

Those weapons that elevated the infantry to battlefield preeminence limited the artillery's role. Although some armies, including the British, continued to favor smoothbore, muzzle-loading bronze cannons, these guns simply could not compete against the new steel breechloaders, particularly those produced by Krupp. The rifled artillery piece, like the rifle, had a greater range—up 400 percent from one thousand yards—superior accuracy, and a higher rate of fire.

But even with such improvements, these field guns suffered from certain limitations. During earlier conflicts, generals moved their artillery forward, close to the front line, so its grapeshot could shred the massed enemy formations. Now the gunners faced new perils: the superior range of the breech-loading rifle forced the gun crews either to pull back their weapons or die at their cannons. More significantly, as the U.S. Civil War and the Russo-Turkish conflict indicated, artillery had little impact on entrenched infantry. Henceforth the big guns had to occupy a more discreet role.

And the same technology that allowed the infantry to displace the artillery as the preeminent presence on the battlefield virtually doomed the cavalry. The futile August 1870 charge of Gen. A. Michel at Morsbronn and Gen. Jean Margueritte's failed attempt to break the Prussian lines at Sedan painfully demonstrated that the cavalry might have retained its panache but had lost its shock power. Again the combination of the breech-loading rifle, the Gatling gun, and shrapnel-firing artillery relegated the cavalry to serving either as mounted infantrymen or reconnaissance units, certainly not the hard-charging force of yesteryear.

Hereafter, the defense, particularly if hunkered down and equipped with the new small arms, trumped the offense. In August 1871 Prince Augustus of Württenberg ordered his troops, marching in dense columns and preceded by regimental bugles and drums, to assault the French at St. Privat. Within twenty minutes, eight thousand troops, 25 percent of the prince's corps, lay dead or wounded.[6] As Helmuth von Moltke concluded, "Little success can be expected from a *mere frontal* attack, but very likely a great deal of loss. We must therefore turn towards the flanks of an enemy position" (italics in original).[7] Ironically, had he studied the lessons of the American Civil War, the German general would have already learned that lesson. But von Moltke disdained the U.S. Civil War, supposedly dismissing the conflict as "two armed mobs chasing each other around the country from which nothing could be learned."[8] The War of the Pacific would provide the same opportunities for strategists to test their theories and weapons, but again, few bothered to study it. Thus, the Russian and Japanese armies would have to relearn this lesson in 1905, as would all the belligerents in the First World War.

Clearly the waging of war had evolved. Men no longer marched into battle expecting to live off the land. Armies needed railroads to transport their greater numbers, artillery, equipment, and provisions to the front. They also required the newly invented telegraph to allow headquarters to communicate with units in the field. In short, to satisfy the increasingly complex needs of so many troops, the military had to create the quartermaster elements to feed and clothe their soldiers, a medical corps to maintain their health in garrison as well as on the battlefield, plus signal and transportation units. And standing far above these disparate elements stood the general staff, consisting of the army's intellectual elites, which ensured that the activities of the supply and support units amplified the combat arms' efforts.[9]

A few nations assimilated some of the technological lessons of the U.S. Civil War as well as the Franco-Prussian conflict. Even Russia, for example, created and used a telegraph service, railroad units, as well as a medical corps in its 1877–78 encounter with Turkey. Ironically, the French did not establish a railroad bureau in the Ministry of War until 1877.[10] But the developed nations seemed to ignore the tactical implications of these earlier disputes.

Given the paucity of European wars, those interested in the evolution of warfare should have analyzed other, non–western European and non-U.S. conflicts, in this case, the War of the Pacific. This struggle incorporated many of the same weapons that were so important in the earlier battles in Europe and the United States and would prove equally influential in subsequent wars. Indeed, because the combatants also fought for control of the seas, the South American struggle, unlike the Franco-Prussian War, provided a unique opportunity to study the progress of naval warfare, including the use of the ram, the armored warship, and the torpedo. Unfortunately, while some countries belatedly acknowledged some aspects of the War of the Pacific, they did not assimilate any of the tactical lessons; they would pay dearly for this oversight.

The Warring Nations

None of the three belligerents appeared ready for the war that enveloped them in 1879. Peru, with the largest population and land mass, stretched from approximately 3 to 21 degrees south as well as due east from the Pacific, across the Andes, and into the Amazon Basin. As in the case of Bolivia and Chile, the Andes dominated Peru's geography. Three branches of the mountain range—the Cordillera Occidental, the Cordillera Central, and the Cordillera Oriental—had twisted much of Peru into series of troughs or mountain valleys running in all directions. The Cordillera Occidental, which hugged Peru's coastline from its border with Ecuador south, often flowed literally into the Pacific Ocean. Normally, this coastal strip could not sustain agricultural activities, but centuries of the runoff from the Andes had dug east-west running gorges and alluvial plains that could be farmed. Unfortunately, only thirty valleys reached the ocean on Peru's fourteen hundred miles of coastline. The Andes' tendrils, moreover, so isolated some of the fertile valleys that they had to communicate with the rest of the nation via the sea rather than overland routes.[11] Pushed upward, sometimes by volcanic activities, the coastal mountains rose inexorably eastward, often fourteen thousand feet in height, before forming a coastal high desert and a series of basins separated from the coast by the Cordillera Occidental and from the Amazon Jungle by the often twenty-thousand-foot, snow-covered peaks of the Cordillera Oriental. Although some of these basins could sustain agriculture—generally only below fourteen thousand feet—the higher altitudes precluded most pastoral activities except for the raising of alpacas or llamas on *ichu*, a local grass.[12]

In 1879 Peru covered 1.5 to 1.6 million square kilometers. Of its nearly 2.5 to 2.7 million inhabitants, 23 percent resided either in the port of Callao, the capital of Lima (100,000–120,000), and coastal cities such as Arica, Pisagua, Ilo, and Iquique or in those alluvial valleys that emptied into the Pacific Ocean. Almost three-quarters of Peru's overwhelmingly Indian population resided in Andean highland settlements, and not surprisingly, given their distance from the coast as well as from other *altiplano* settlements, they spoke Aymara or Quechua, not Spanish.[13]

Although mountains covered a large portion of Peru, it enjoyed certain advantages over its similarly configured neighbor Bolivia. Peru's proximity to the sea facilitated the sale of its agricultural and mineral exports to the North Atlantic world. By 1879, moreover, Peru possessed a relatively developed transportation system: numerous railroads moved commodities from inland plantations or mines to the nearby ports. One rail line, the Central—an engineering marvel created by the genius of the American Henry Meiggs and the sweat of countless workers—connected the capital to the Andean city of Chicla, a railhead at thirteen thousand feet above sea level.[14] Clearly hoping to facilitate the export of its cotton and sugar, the Peruvian government had invested a small fortune in its rail system. But the agrarian sector did not generate as much revenue as did Peru's mines. Indeed, since the 1850s exports of guano—

ossified bird droppings found in Peru's arid south and on the Chincha Islands offshore—financed the national government, its various public works, and, of course, its burgeoning bureaucracy. Fortunately for Peru, just as the deposits of guano began to disappear, prospectors discovered nitrates in the southern province of Tarapacá. Anxious to extract maximum profits from the sale of this commodity, the Peruvian government, in 1875, expropriated the largely foreign-owned mines. Thereafter the mining corporations dug out and processed the nitrates for a fee while the nation received most of the profits, part of which it used to pay off the debt Peru had incurred by nationalizing the mines and to fund the government.

Developing the nation's resources proved difficult in no small part because of demographic problems: most Peruvians lived in the altiplano, where they eked out a frugal existence as subsistence farmers, not on the coastal plantations that produced commercially important crops such as sugar or cotton. The entrepreneurs' need for a workforce to tend the nation's rich valleys eventually prompted them to import slaves from Africa or "indentured servants"—quasi slaves, if there is such a condition—from China. The Asians, often chained together, also labored in the *guaneras*, where some preferred suicide to scrapping desiccated avian feces from the sunbaked and fetid Chincha islands. Further to the south, some nine thousand Chileans sweated in Peru's salitreras in Tarapacá.[15]

Southeast of Peru's most southern province lay Bolivia's Pacific littoral, a two- to three-hundred-mile stretch of cliffs, some fifteen to eighteen hundred feet high, that fronted on the Pacific Ocean. These coastal bluffs abutted the Atacama Desert, approximately seventy-two thousand square miles of uncharted, arid wasteland whose soil consisted either of sand and small stones or sand mixed with small seashells. Neither one provided a welcoming environment for agriculture, although happily for Bolivia, its miners had discovered substantial deposits of guano and nitrates both atop and beneath the desert floor. While five ports—Cobija, Mejillones, Antofagasta, Tocopilla, and Huanillo—provided access to the desert, only one, Antofagasta, enjoyed good connections to the Bolivian hinterland.

Traveling the 750 miles from Bolivia's capital of La Paz, located over thirteen thousand feet high in the Andes, to the Pacific Coast required enormous effort and time in the post-1850 period. In 1879, for example, the army of Gen. Hilarión Daza spent twelve to thirteen days marching the 280 miles from La Paz to Tacna, an inland city in the southwestern corner of the Atacama Desert, and an additional eleven days trudging from Tacna to Pisagua, a port on the Pacific.[16] The Bolivian soldiers would still have had to march south 250 more miles before reaching Antofagasta, a town that bordered on Bolivia's Pacific Coast. In short, any traveler using the most direct route, which was not the one the soldiers followed, required almost a month to cover the distance to the Pacific from La Paz. Given these geographic limitations, Antofagasta looked to the sea for its water, which it desalinated, and sustenance.

Traversing the Atacama, while difficult, was perhaps the least of the many problems Bolivians had to surmount. As one moves inland from the coast, the hills become the Cordillera de la Costa, or the Andes' Cordillera Occidental, a chain of mountains that juts upward thousands of feet into the air. East of the Cordillera Occidental but west of the Andes' Cordillera Oriental lies a valley some twelve to thirteen thousand feet above sea level and approximately four hundred miles wide that contains the world's highest inland body of water, Lake Titicaca. On the eastern side of Bolivia's altiplano stands another chain of mountains, many more than twenty thousand feet high, which eventually subside into the tropical lowlands that comprise Bolivia's eastern borderlands. Clearly, the Andes constitute Bolivia's defining feature: offshoots of the mountain chain do not simply split the country along a north-south axis but also divide it east to west into a series of often isolated valleys. From the air, Bolivia resembles a Byzantine maze of intersecting mountains that in the late nineteenth century left the nation's population cut off from each other, let alone the world.

Containing little arable land, Bolivia could, at best, manage to feed itself. Happily for the country, beneath its soil lay enormous reserves of silver and industrial minerals.[17] The discovery of nitrates and guano in Bolivia's littoral seemed to open new possibilities for generating wealth, although the stench from Mejillones de Bolivia's guaneras assailed the seaborne visitor's nose long before he laid eyes on the city.[18] This aesthetic limitation did not inhibit the miners from flocking to the littoral. Nor did the vagaries of nature: the earthquakes, fires, and tidal waves that periodically ravaged Bolivia's coastal cities, casting oceangoing vessels over a mile and a half into the desert and, in 1877, literally erasing Antofagasta's hospital. Even three years after the disaster, "scarcely a house remain[ed]" in nearby Cobija, which looked as if the port "had been exposed to a severe bombardment." One observer wrote, "We initially imagined that we were viewing the effects of the war."[19] Despite the potential danger to life, limb, and olfactory organs, so many foreigners moved to the Atacama that a Frenchman, Charles Weiner, calculated, "Of every twenty inhabitants, seventeen are Chilean, one a Peruvian, one a European, and one a Bolivian colonel." There was, according to Weiner, a rough division of labor: "The Chileans work, the Europeans trade, and he [the Bolivian colonel] commands."[20] What Weiner either tactfully failed to mention or did not know is that so many of the Atacama's Chilean residents resented the Bolivian colonel's heavy hand that they formed "patriotic societies" such as La Patria, which sought to fuse the desert province with Chile; others appealed to their countrymen for relief from what they perceived to be Bolivia's arbitrary misrule.[21] In 1879 these Chilean groups' petitions seeking relief from Santiago would help precipitate the War of the Pacific.

Bolivia encountered difficulties administering its littoral because it lacked the infrastructure to do so. As a French engineer reported, "What is called a road in this country is not more than a trail without bridges, passable only for those who walk, ride atop a horse, or a beast of burden."[22] Without all-weather roads and domestic railroads, moving items within Bolivia proved extraordinarily difficult, if not impossible: if a visitor in the 1870s required five to six days to travel from Sucre to Cochabamba, a distance of approximately 150 miles, the export of raw materials proved substantially more complicated and expensive.[23] Thanks to the 1874 completion of a railroad in nearby Peru, goods could flow from the La Paz in northwest Bolivia into Peru's Puno region, then west to the port of Mollendo and from there to the port of Valparaíso or to the port of Callao. Bolivian merchants also managed to send their exports into Argentina. But the nation needed more than these few paltry outlets. Logically, Bolivia should have developed rail lines to carry its goods from its highlands to harbors such as Arica. But as Henry Meiggs had demonstrated, constructing railroads in the Andes required great expertise and greater amounts of money. Regrettably, Bolivia lacked both. And since few foreign creditors appeared willing to invest in such a politically volatile nation, Bolivia's economic future did not seem particularly bright. Bolivia, in fact, would not develop railroads until the late nineteenth century, and it would be approximately twenty years more until rail lines would connect its important cities. This same lack of domestic roads or rail lines restricted the government's authority to La Paz and its immediate environs. Indeed, a simple equation seemed to govern Bolivian politics: the greater the distance from the capital, the more dubious the state's authority.

Sadly, Bolivia's political institutions were as underdeveloped as it infrastructure: since the government conducted its last census in 1854, no one knew how many citizens La Paz ruled nor where they lived. One geographer reckoned that 2.3 million Bolivians, 80 percent of whom were Indians, inhabited a nation that covered 1.3 million square kilometers.[24] An Italian visitor refined these population statistics, estimating that seven-eighths of the population resided in La Paz, Oruro, Cochabamba, Sucre, and Potosí. These provinces, plus the more lightly populated Cobija, Tarija, Santa Cruz, and Beni, covered about 801,000 square kilometers.[25] The same natural barriers that divided Bolivia into regions also split the nation into separate linguistic and cultural groups: the Aymara Indians, who populated the area south of Lake Titicaca, and the Quechua, who resided to the southeast. Predictably, this unhappy convergence of geographic obstacles and language differences fostered a strong sense of identification with a region rather than with the nation-state.[26]

The same topography that stunted Bolivia's economic growth, fomented regionalism, and undermined the central government's authority also starved the state of the revenues it required to govern. As late as 1846 Bolivia's government gleaned 51 percent of its income from Indian tribute and the impost on coca. The discovery of the Caracoles silver deposits, located in the mountains ten thousand feet high and about 160 miles northeast of Antofagasta, and the Huanchaca mine appeared to offer new hope to the Bolivian economy. Still, although the taxation of Bolivia's silver mines ultimately replaced the levy on the Indians and coca, the regime's 1879 income—adjusted for inflation—remained at the same level as that of 1825.[27] Worse, as more countries turned from bimetallism to the gold standard, the international price for silver contracted, and therefore so did Bolivia's revenue. Clearly, the nation needed to develop a more reliable source of income, preferably in a geographical region that enjoyed access to transportation, thus reducing the cost of production.

The discovery of the guano and nitrates located in its littoral, promised to cure Bolivia's economic anemia. Perhaps for the first time geography would not stunt Bolivia's development: not only did the nation's vast deposits of nitrates lie close to the surface of the Atacama Desert, but only a few miles of flat pampa stood between the salitreras and the port of Antofagasta. Bolivia did not have to wait long to savor the economic fruits: by 1879 La Paz derived approximately 50 percent of its revenue from the taxes on the Atacama's mines. Clearly, Bolivia had finally found the Atahualpa's ransom it required to end its economic underdevelopment.[28] Unfortunately, Bolivia's leaders had committed, inadvertently, a dangerous sin of omission: as Adolfo Ballivián, Bolivian envoy to Britain, noted, "The nation for who [sic] there is opened by chance at the edge of the sea, a wide door on incalculable riches and future fortune should either close it or guard it well against the envy and rapacity [sic] of violence. He who cares for coasts, ports, and railways should not neglect the responsibilities which they entail."[29] But the Bolivian government failed to heed Ballivián's caution: attracted by the allure of jobs in the mining industry, more than ten thousand Chileans had flooded into the Atacama. In many respects, Bolivia replicated Mexico's folly vis-à-vis Texas: by permitting large numbers of foreigners to settle in its territory, La Paz had created a demographic imbalance that favored the Chileans. And although a Santiago newspaper, *El Ferrocarril*, warned that various Bolivians living in the Atacama might prefer Chilean rule, "Chile," wrote the *Chilian Times*, "would never take their [the Bolivians'] territory at the price of war; and it is doubtful if she would take its turbulent inhabitants at any price."[30] Both journals proved egregiously wrong.

Of the three participants, Chile was, if not the poorest, then certainly the smallest in terms of area and population: its approximately 2.25 million residents populated 362,000 square kilometers. Some argued that only whites comprised Chilean society, but as an American schoolteacher unkindly retorted, the "Araucanian Indians have, by intermarriage, disseminated their blood, as well as their slovenly habits, among the lower classes largely throughout the nation." Doubtless, the truth about Chile's racial composition lay somewhat between those extreme statements.[31]

Although the smallest in area, Chile's land mass was not more compact than its neighbors. An elongated sliver of territory, approximately 880 miles separated Chile's northern frontier with Bolivia from its central valley, the area where most of that nation resided and that produced most of the country's food, consumer goods, and services. Theoretically, Chile's sovereignty included the Strait of Magellan, but Santiago's hold on the land between Punta Arenas and the Bio Bio River was tenuous and intermittent.

Rail lines connected the capital, Santiago, with some of the southern wheat-producing provinces. And a separate spur linked Santiago to Valparaíso, one of the Pacific Coast's principal entrepôts and Chile's premier port. But no railroads extended from Santiago to the north. (There were some in what came to be called the Norte Chico, but these connected the mining camps of the interior with ports such as Caldera, not with Chile's heartland.) Although the country possessed a network of roads, these were too few, generally in wretched condition, and too underdeveloped to reach Chile's Norte Chico, let alone the Atacama Desert miles to the north. Thus, the Chileans used the Pacific Ocean as the most efficient and least costly form of transportation.

Initially, the Chilean government received most of its revenues from a levy on imports. Eventually, the nation began to export wheat to South America's Pacific Coast nations as well as to the United States and Great Britain. The discovery of silver in the Norte Chico shifted the economic locus to the mining sector. While initially exporters of raw materials, Chilean miners began to refine the ores they prized from the earth, thereby creating the beginning of heavy industries located in the capital, the extreme south, and the north. The majority of Chile's population, however, inhabited the countryside, where they labored as tenant farmers, or *inquilinos*, on the large landed estates.

Chile's political system appeared almost as developed as its economy. Like all the former Spanish colonies, the Captaincy General endured years of war. By 1830 two competing factions—the liberals and the conservatives—had emerged. Building upon their victory at the Battle of Lircay, the conservatives, led by their *eminence gris*, Diego Portales, visited upon Chile what came to be known as the "weight of the night," a highly centralized authoritarian constitution that limited government office and the franchise to a handful of wealthy, literate, older men. Despite its deficiencies, the system worked: having submitted themselves to the rule of law, as embodied by the Constitution of 1833, the nation's elites elected four men, who managed the nation for the next forty years.

These decades were not without strife: Portales would perish at the hands of rebellious troops in 1837, and two civil wars, both abortive, erupted in 1851 and 1859. Over the years, however, the republic's political climate became more benign: an increasingly well educated elite created new parties that, by 1879, numbered four, including some seeking to create a more open and secular society. In 1870 the legislature amended the constitution to prohibit presidential succession. Henceforth the chief executive could serve only a single five-year term, and two men—Federico Errázuriz (1871–76) and Aníbal Pinto (1876–81)—did so largely without incident. In fairness, the legislative and presidential elections were not honest—they would not be so until well into the twentieth century—but they were not so wicked that they inspired the political opposition to resort to force. On the contrary, Chile's elite engaged in an baroque charade: elections occurred as prescribed by the Constitution of 1833; the press could and did spew its political invective upon those it loathed, while each party, including splinter groups, employed a variety of tactics—stuffing ballot boxes, purchasing votes, miscounting, and the occasional use of force—to ensure their access to power. What resulted was not a true democracy but a political accommodation that permitted the peaceful transfer of power from one candidate to another.

If flawed, the Chilean political system still seemed preferable to that of either of its neighbors. Between 1823 and 1830, for example, Peru adopted and then rejected six different constitutions, and before 1836, when Peru and Bolivia temporarily merged into a confederacy, eight men ruled during a single ten-year span. Not until 1845 did a Peruvian president complete a full four-year term. The country embraced yet another constitution in 1856 that lasted for only four years. The political instability did not hurt the nation's economy, which prospered thanks to the exports of guano. Unfortunately, the easy wealth encouraged the government to invest in extravagant public works projects, including the building of railroads, to pacify its friends and win allies. As Heraclio Bonilla observed, "the source of each caudillo-president's power lay in the military capability of his followers," who constantly vied for "power in order to plunder the resources of the state," which, as the duke of Newcastle said of the old parliament, became "a pasture for the beasts to feed on." The country's first political party, the Civilista, did not appear until 1872, when its leader, Manuel Pardo, became president. Four years later another Civilista president, Gen. Mariano Prado, would make the fatal decisions that led Peru into war in 1879.[32]

Bolivia's political life was, if possible, more rudimentary than that of its ally, a predictable result, since as one of the nation's founding fathers, Antonio José Sucre, observed, "the ground we are working is mud and sand, and on such a base no building can exist." Rather than parties that, however imperfectly, espoused some ideology, personalist bands predominated. "Politics in Bolivia," noted an English visitor, "are best described as purely personal, for the different political parties seem to spring up, change, and die out accordingly as some ambitious leader comes to the front, and soon gives place to a newer man." Reflecting this situation, few presidents managed to complete their elected term of office. Indeed, between 1839 and 1876 eleven men served as chief executive, overseeing a nation that suffered more than one hundred revolutions. These upheavals, which consumed the nation's civil leaders as well as its officer corps and military equipment, undermined Bolivia's ability to defend itself.[33]

The Casus Foederis

While the former Spanish colonies may have rejected Madrid's rule, they accepted the doctrine of *uti possidetis juris de 1810*, the notion that newly minted republics would accept as their frontiers the boundaries that Spain had used to delineate its former colonies. Agreeing on boundary lines proved quite complicated because over the years various military, religious, and political organizations had created often conflicting versions of the same maps. As Chile's *Diario Oficial* noted, the cartographers often had only a vague idea where the boundaries lay.[34] The frontier separating Bolivia and Chile, for example, ran through the Atacama Desert, one of the world's more desolate territories. During their early years neither Bolivia nor Chile had disputed too vigorously the precise location of their common border: the ownership of a few feet of an arid wasteland simply could not excite even the most avid jingo. But thanks to the discovery of guano and, later, nitrates, both highly prized sources of chemicals needed to manufacture fertilizer and explosives, the Atacama suddenly became alluring. Consequently, beginning in the 1860s Santiago and La Paz began to press their claims to this potential economic bonanza: Bolivia demanded the land down to the twenty-fifth parallel south latitude, and Chile, the territory north to the twenty-third parallel south latitude. Anxious to assert its sovereignty, Santiago's minions occupied Mejillones in 1861, replacing the ousted Bolivian officials with Chileans who issued rights to mine the guano in the disputed area. In 1863 Bolivia's legislature, eager to assert its claim to the desert, gave the president, Gen. José María de Acha, permission to use force if Chile refused to recognize Bolivian sovereignty over the disputed land.

The border issue might have plunged the nations into a war but for an unexpected revival of imperialism: an 1864 Spanish scientific expedition, in fact a naval task force, used the supposed maltreatment of its citizens as an excuse to seize Peru's Chincha Islands. The incident so inflamed both Chile and Bolivia that they set aside their own squabbles to repel the Spanish invasion. Pending a final solution, the border was drawn on the twenty-fourth parallel. Eventually, Peru's coastal batteries in Callao drove Madrid's fleet from South American waters but only after it had seriously damaged Chile's principal port, Valparaíso. With peace restored to the Pacific, a new Bolivian government under Gen. Mariano Melgarejo tried again in 1866 to solve the boundary issue. Santiago, perhaps in thrall to the spirit of "Americanism," agreed to accept the twenty-fourth parallel as the border. Chile, however, retained the right to share equally in the revenues generated by anyone exploiting those minerals mined in the territory located between the twenty-third and twenty-fifth parallels.

By the early 1870s numerous Chile-based companies mined not only guano but also, increasingly, nitrates from the Atacama. Similarly, Chilean interests also extracted from Bolivia's Caracoles mines silver ore, which they sent to Chile, where it was smelted, processed, and then exported to Europe.[35] Believing itself to be the victim of greedy Chilean capitalists, the Bolivian legislature decided to protect their nation's economic future by seeking more control of its desert resources. It began by nullifying Melgarejo's 1866 pact.

Normally, the Chileans would have responded aggressively, but the Chilean government, feeling threatened by Peru's recent naval rearmament program and Argentine territorial demands, considered it prudent to resolve peacefully its dispute with Bolivia. Thus, Chile's new president, Federico Errázuriz, sent Santiago Lindsay north to La Paz with orders to settle the boundary issue. The resulting 1872 accord, the Lindsay-Corral pact, seemed almost a repeat the 1866 agreement, although La Paz did agree to include nitrates as one of the minerals that Chileans could mine duty free in return for some financial concessions. Not surprisingly, many Bolivians feared that the Lindsay-Corral pact would not truly inhibit Chile from attempting to control the contested area: obviously Bolivia needed more than words to keep its territory out of Chile's clutches. Bolivia quickly discovered an anti-Chilean soul mate in Peru, which viewed Errázuriz's decision to acquire two armored warships as jeopardizing its maritime interests. Thus, in February 1873 Bolivia and Peru signed a secret military agreement pledging to aid each other if Chile threatened either signatory.

Perhaps emboldened by this alliance, the Bolivian congress refused to ratify the Lindsay-Corral accord. Errázuriz, fearful that Bolivia and Peru might entice Argentina to join their anti-Chilean coalition, again compromised: in August 1874 Bolivia and Chile again set the boundary between their territories at the twenty-fourth parallel. Chile surrendered its territorial claims and its right to share any revenues derived from taxing enterprises mining the Atacama, and in return the Bolivian government vowed not to raise taxes on any Chilean corporation mining the desert for a period of twenty-five years. Some Bolivian deputies wanted to reject the treaty, but the threat of the then president, Tomás Frías, to resign forced the legislature to acquiesce.[36]

Regrettably, the 1874 treaty did not end the friction. Chile's miners, who had long complained about the rough treatment they received at the hands of the Atacama police, continued to carp. And following the murder of their countryman Eliseo Arriagada, whom the local police had shot, the Chilean miners begged the Pinto government to protect them.[37] Although this matter came to the attention of the Chilean Chamber of Deputies, the abuse did not cease, much to the dismay of many Chileans who still considered the Atacama to be theirs. What particularly galled some Chilean journalists was the fact that the Errázuriz government's concessions to Bolivia had accomplished nothing: Bolivia continued to maltreat its Chilean workforce. In short, just as Christ died on the cross, "to redeem humanity," wrote a Copiapó newspaper, "Chile in the name of American solidarity, had given its land to Bolivia." Yet Chile still suffered from "offenses which daily wound its sons."[38] Thus in 1879, after years of not-so-silent suffering, Chile responded to Bolivia's newly "elected" president Hilarión Daza's latest insult—the unilateral imposition of higher export taxes—by seizing the land it had earlier ceded to Bolivia, thus causing the War of the Pacific, a contest that would soon involve Peru as well.

The Course of the War

The War of the Pacific can be divided into six periods. The first, and shortest, began with Chile's capture of the Bolivian seaport of Antofagasta in February 1879 and ended a few days later when Santiago had occupied the rest of the Atacama Desert. During the second stage, which lasted from April to October 1879, the Chilean and Peruvian fleets fought for control of the sea-lanes. Both sides desperately needed to dominate the waters adjacent to southern South America: if Peru's navy triumphed, its ships could have attacked Chile's exposed garrison in Antofagasta as well as its ports, particularly Valparaíso, the nation's transportation and commercial nerve center. A victorious Peruvian armada could also have prevented the Moneda, the Chilean presidential palace, from importing supplies and moving troops, equipment, and pack animals north to the war zone. Peru, of course, was just as vulnerable to a seaborne attack as Chile. Santiago's fleet hoped to stop Lima from reinforcing its garrisons in Arica and Tarapacá. It also wanted to hobble Peru's economy by limiting its exports of nitrates and to curtail the importation of war materiel. Finally, without dominance of the sea, Chile could not invade Peru. The Chilean navy resolved the issue of naval supremacy when, in October 1879, it captured Lima's last ironclad off Punta Angamos on Peru's southern coast; within a month Peru's fleet almost ceased to exist.

Building on its victory at Angamos, Chile invaded the province of Tarapacá. After landing troops at Junín and Pisagua, Santiago's legions enlarged their beachhead by marching inland. Chile's triumph at Dolores, or San Francisco, in November 1879 gave it virtual control of the region. A few days following their loss at Dolores, the Allies won a victory, preventing a Chilean force from capturing the city of Tarapacá. The Allied success, essentially its only military victory, did not significantly alter the course of the war: without access to supplies, the Peruvian and Bolivian troops had to evacuate the district they had fought so tenaciously to hold. The conquest of the Peruvian territory proved a godsend to Santiago: control of the nitrate mines provided Chile the means to finance its war effort. Alternately, the loss of the export tax on salitre crippled Peru's finances and thus its ability to obtain the weapons it needed to fight the war.

A Chilean invasion and conquest of the provinces of Tacna and Arica brought them closer to their goal, Lima. This campaign, which ended in May 1880, forced Chileans to fight first at Los Angeles and then to march through a singularly inhospitable desert in order to assault the Peruvian and Bolivian troops holding the southern portion of the province. The Chileans paid a heavy price to vanquish the Allied army at the Battle of Tacna, or Campo de la Alianza, but this triumph, plus the capture of the Peruvian naval bastion of Arica, opened the way for Santiago to attack Lima. The conclusion of this, the fourth segment of the war, also marked the virtual eradication of the Allies' regular armies: henceforth Peru would have to rely mainly on raw recruits to fight the war. Peru also lost its ally: after May 1880 Bolivia ordered its surviving troops back to the capital, where they hunkered down and waited.

Approximately six months after Arica fell, Chile launched its last and most ambitious offensive: its ships transported approximately thirty thousand men, along with their mounts and equipment, five hundred miles to the north in order to attack Lima. The Chileans, despite suffering heavy casualties, managed to capture the Peruvian capital in January

1881. Many expected, or perhaps hoped, that the seizure of Lima would have ended the struggle. But Chile's failure to snare the remnants of the army defending the capital allowed the vanquished Peruvian troops to flee to the Andean highlands, from where they would harass the Chileans.

When no Peruvian politician would cede territory to the Chileans in return for a peace treaty, the war degenerated into a ferocious guerrilla struggle, not unlike that which beset Napoleon in Spain. The campaign to eradicate the last vestiges of Peruvian resistance became the conflict's most difficult, most savage, and most prolonged period of fighting. Certainly the two-year battle against the irregular forces consumed Santiago's resources and slowly sapped its determination. Fortunately for Chile, Peruvian resistance collapsed first: the newly minted Chilean government of Miguel Iglesias signed a peace treaty with Lima in October 1883. Months later the threat of a Chilean invasion forced Bolivia to accept an armistice and end the war.

The Nature of the War

Superficially, the War of the Pacific resembled the American Civil War and the Franco-Prussian conflict. The competing armies used modern muzzle-loaders, or breech-loading rifles, Krupp steel field and mountain artillery, and Gatling guns; their fleets' ironclads contested the control of the sea. Indeed, the world's second encounter between armored ships occurred off Point Angamos in October 1879. Later, the navies manufactured and deployed a variety of torpedoes and naval mines, as well as the newly created torpedo boat. The belligerents also relied upon the telegraph and railroads to communicate and to transport their troops, while their medics tended to the sick and the wounded.

While perhaps puny when compared to the size of the armies involved in U.S. or western European conflicts, the War of the Pacific proportionately consumed a relatively large number of the three belligerents' male populations. By early 1881 the Moneda's army had under arms about forty-two thousand men, who, in conjunction with two to three thousand sailors and marines, constituted about 2 percent of Chile's male inhabitants. Calculating how many Peruvian and Bolivian men served in the war is more difficult, in part because these nations did not know precisely how many of their citizens resided in isolated settlements in the Andes.[39] Still, we calculate that Bolivia sent an army of at least eight thousand troops west to drive the Chileans from Tarapacá. Later La Paz raised other units containing at least another two thousand men. Thus, more than 1 percent of Bolivia's male population served in its army. Peru's Army of the South, which numbered approximately nine thousand, when taken in conjunction with the twenty-one thousand troops defending Lima, represented more than 2 percent of its population. This figure, moreover, does not include the soldiers garrisoning positions in the north of Peru. In short, these wars significantly impacted on the male inhabitants of both sides. As we shall see, women also participated in the war.[40]

Although historians from each of the three nations have described these armies as the products of *leveés en masse*, in fact, they were not. At the war's onset, the patriotic or naive immediately volunteered for military service, but once the martial fever broke, the respective governments reverted to the traditional practice of press-ganging the unwary, the unimportant, and the unlucky. Traditionally the press-gangs harvested first the criminals, the idlers, and the beggars. And after they had exhausted this source, the recruiters focused on the Indians of Peru and Bolivia as well as the three nations' rural and urban working class and their artisans; the *gente decente* (those with money) appeared exempt from the draft.

Since most of the Allied officers gained their military experience not in waging foreign wars but in trying to protect or upend an existing government, few had learned anything resembling formal military tactics. Nor had most of Chile's regular officers, many of whom had graduated from its Escuela Militar, studied the recent wars in the United States or western Europe. Ironically, while the constant fighting against the Araucanian Indians provided Chilean officers with military experience, these encounters did not prepare them to fight a set-piece war. Thus, like their enemies, Chilean commanders would continue to use the tactics of the Napoleonic period—attacks in massed columns—in preference to the open formations employed during the final years of the U.S. Civil War or Prussia's tactics of maneuver.

If the opposing armies were unaware of or unwilling to adopt the most recent wars' tactical lessons, they did incorporate some of their technology. Chile and Peru used the telegraph while simultaneously trying to deny their opponents access to this instrument. Railroads also played a role but not to the same degree as in North America or western Europe, in part, because neither Santiago nor Lima possessed extensive rail systems. Chile's railroad transported men and supplies from its Central Valley to the capital and then to Valparaíso, where they embarked to sail north. Peru's main rail line, which ran from the seaport of Callao to Lima and then to the foothills of the altiplano, would not prove as useful because it did not reach the heavily populated Andean area. Chile would also use Peruvian railroads to move men and supplies to Tarapacá, to shift troops from Tacna to Arica, and to transport men and materiel from the coast to the altiplano during the conflict's final phase. At no time did the armies actually staff these services, which remained the purview of hired civilians.

Peru's military, perhaps because it was fighting essentially in its own territory, did not have to create a supply corps; instead it relied on sutlers or foraging parties. Although in some cases it too depended upon foraging, Bolivia primarily used its prewar institutions, the *prest*, to feed the troops. But since Chile had to operate in foreign territory, the Moneda had to establish quartermaster units. These new organizations, however, relied upon civilian manpower and technical skills to function. The same was true of various ambulance companies: all three countries had to depend upon civilian physicians and charities to staff, fund, and equip their units just as they had come to rely upon civilians for transportation, communications, and sometimes provisioning.

When compared to many European conflicts, the War of the Pacific might appear a backwater, but it nonetheless advances our knowledge of the history of warfare. Chile became one of the few nations to launch amphibious operations, not merely invading Peruvian territory, but using its fleet to engage in naval warfare as well as secure its supply lines. The struggle to win naval supremacy provided some lessons for maritime strategists: although the Peruvian fleet used its submerged rams, it quickly became evident that, in the age of heavy naval guns, these had a very limited future. Similarly, the deployment of naval mines and the spar as well as Lay torpedoes revealed that these weapons needed fine-tuning. (Ironically, in an 1891 civil war the Chilean navy would be the first to use the Whitehead torpedo to sink a capital ship.) The battle between the Peruvian ironclad *Huáscar* and the Chilean *Almirante Cochrane* and *Almirante Blanco Encalada* provided naval engineers an opportunity to study the effect of heavy guns on armored warships.

The armies that fought the War of the Pacific appear to have employed the most modern weapons but in the service of traditional tactics. With rare exceptions, none of the participants' formations or tactics differed dramatically from those used in earlier wars. True, the adversaries utilized the railroad and the telegraph when these existed, but since none of the combatants had an extensive transportation network, the impact of the railroad was limited, though the telegraph system, because of the area it covered, proved more useful. Nor did the competing armies immediately realize that war had become so complex that they needed a general staff to direct the combat arms as well as the technical services. In fact, none of the armies contained functioning general staffs at the onset of the war. And when the various armies finally created these units, few if any of those officers serving in them had attended anything remotely resembling a staff college. In short, the armies may have acquired modern weaponry but not the knowledge that would have allowed them to use these armaments more fluently. These had to be improvised.

Imports and domestic arms industries allowed Chile, Peru, and Bolivia to provide their armies with weapons and ammunition. None of the belligerents possessed organizations capable of providing the armed forces technical services. Since they lacked the organic organizations to supply logistical support, they privatized the war effort: they rented telegraph lines and railroads and transport, and they appealed to the public for financial and technical support as if supporting the military were a volunteer hospital or public charity. Fortunately for these nations, their civilian populations provided not just leadership and technical expertise in the areas of supply, transportation, medicine, and communication but even nursed the wounded and sometimes buried those who succumbed to their wounds.

As we shall see, the warring sides committed various errors in the War of the Pacific, largely as a consequence of failing to assimilate the lessons that the wars of the United States, Europe, and Russia offered. These failures, however, do not prove that the Latin American armed forces were innately incompetent. The armies of Europe, even when battling supposedly inferior foes in Africa and Asia, also ignored or failed to assimilate these same lessons. Even after Britain's war with the Boers had demonstrated the folly of massed attacks, Brig. Gen. Launcelot Kiggell still argued, "Victory is now won actually by the bayonet, or by the fear of it."[41] The French army, which in 1870 learned firsthand not to launch massed assaults, would also have to relearn the painful lesson, at great cost, during the First World War.

The South American countries, at least, had an excuse for not assimilating the most modern military theory: since these nations were at different stages in the process of modernization than their European or North American counterparts, they lacked the intellectual training and infrastructure of the more modern societies. More significantly, neither Peru nor Bolivia were nations in the traditional sense: as the Bolivian Roberto Querejazu observed, the two countries' size and the separation of their populations by economic activity, by cultural differences, and by geographic barriers fomented regionalism while undermining the concept of a nation-state.[42] Eventually, all the combatants, not just the Peruvian and Bolivian governments, recognized they had to restructure their institutions, including their armed forces. But they would never have realized this pressing need until the guns of the War of the Pacific had fallen silent.

1. The Prewar Maneuvers

Fat Tuesday in 1879 fell on 25 February, less than a month before the end of the Bolivian summer. The next morning, La Paz's newly penitent revelers exchanged their carnival masks for the cross of ashes, thus marking the onset of Lent. As these faithful trudged to church they learned some disquieting news: on 14 February, the Chilean ironclads *Almirante Cochrane* and *Almirante Blanco Encalada*, plus the corvette *O'Higgins*, had put ashore two hundred troops. The Chilean contingent commanded by Col. Emilio Sotomayor quickly occupied Antofagasta, the principal city and port of Bolivia's littoral. Within hours of landing, the *Blanco Encalada* and the *O'Higgins* took up positions off Bolivia's ports of Cobija, Tocopilla, and Mejillones. By the end of the month, two thousand Chilean soldiers, some of them militiamen from newly mobilized guard units, garrisoned Antofagasta, Cobija, and Tocopilla. It quickly became clear to Colonel Sotomayor that if he wished to defend Antofagasta against a possible Bolivian counterattack, he had to occupy some of the towns located in the interior. Thus, some six hundred regular troops marched 125 miles east from Antofagasta, through one of the world's most desolate deserts, to Calama, a key road junction that controlled the overland approaches to the coastal cities, reaching the city by 23 March.

Sotomayor, who did not scout the Bolivian position prior to the battle, divided his men into three groups, sending the first two to capture the city. Logically, the approximately 135 Bolivians, almost all poorly armed civilians, should have made some token show of resistance and then either surrendered or fled.

Instead, they ambushed the Chilean cavalry unit that led the assault, killing seven and wounding six. Properly chastised, Sotomayor's men redoubled their efforts. One Bolivian, Eduardo Abaroa, however, proved obstinate. When called upon to surrender, he supposedly replied, "Me surrender? Shit, let your grandmother surrender." Taking Abaroa at his coarsely expressed word, the Chileans killed him. Abaroa's act won him a place in Bolivia's pantheon of war heroes; in another sense, his heroic martyrdom became emblematic of Bolivia's plight: men dying in a war that should not have occurred. By the time the mourners buried Abaroa, Bolivia had become a landlocked nation.[1]

La Paz did not supinely accept the loss of its seacoast: some eight to ten thousand of its residents massed in one of the capital's main plazas demanding weapons so they could expel the Chilean filibusters who had seized their coast. In truth, these enthusiastic but utterly unprepared volunteers could do nothing. Even President Hilarión Daza had to limit himself to symbolic gestures: two weeks after the Chilean occupation of Antofagasta, he declared that Chile had imposed "a state of war" on Bolivia. Apparently this decree did not constitute a formal declaration of belligerence, which he announced on 18 March. Only on 5 April did Santiago reciprocate, plunging South America's west coast into what became known as the War of the Pacific, a conflict that lasted until 1884.[2]

The Chilean seizure of its seacoast should not have surprised Bolivia. For days one of Santiago's man-of-war, the *Blanco Encalada,* had hovered off Antofagasta. Chile's President Aníbal Pinto had sent the ship north to demonstrate his concern about one of Bolivia's recent acts. On 14 February 1878, President Daza had increased, by ten cents per quintal, the taxes levied on the export of nitrates.

In truth, the surcharge on the tax was inconsequential. Nor, given Bolivia's history of threatening the "property, the liberty, and life itself of foreigners," was this arbitrary levy utterly unexpected.[3] But its imposition upset the Compañía de Salitres y Ferrocarril, a Chilean-owned corporation extracting salitre from the Bolivian littoral. The company reacted predictably: citing the 1874 treaty, which explicitly prohibited the Bolivian government from taxing Chilean companies exploiting the Atacama Desert, the miners demanded that Daza rescind the impost. And to give its complaints more gravitas, the mining company also appealed to Santiago to support its claims. Since the shareholders of the Compañía de Salitres y Ferrocarril constituted some of Chile's most powerful political and economic elites, President Pinto could ill afford to ignore their plight; he too joined the chorus of naysayers.

For the Chilean president the dispute became a morality play. Chile, Pinto argued, had surrendered its claim to the Atacama in return for a Bolivian promise not to increase taxes on any Chilean corporation extracting salitre. Now, only four years later, Daza's imposition of the ten-cent tax nullified the 1874 pact. As far as Pinto was concerned, both nations had returned to their pre-1874 boundaries, which gave Chile the legal right to retake—or, to use Pinto's phrase, "revindicate"—the contested territory.

Casus Belli

Daza might have selected a more felicitous moment to involve his nation into a diplomatic crisis; in 1879 Bolivia was a country battered by disaster. Earthquake and plague had devastated the nation's population; a drought so seared the wheat and potato crops that people had to eat bark or insects in order to survive. Daily the police trolled the nation's streets collecting the remains of those who had starved to death during the night. In one two-month period, Cochabamba's authorities picked up an average of a dozen bodies a night; in Sucre more than twenty died in four days.[4] Regrettably, Bolivia had few assets to attend to its citizens' needs. Since he had already dissipated his country's limited economic resources, Daza hit upon the idea of raising revenues by increasing the tax on the Compañía de Salitres y Ferrocarril.

Daza's decision to increase taxes also came at a particularly sensitive moment for Chile's president. Since Pinto's 1876 inauguration, Chile's economy had contracted drastically: inclement weather slashed agricultural output; the adoption of the gold standard dampened the world's need for Chilean silver; and the economic depression of the 1870s reduced Europe's demand for the country's copper. Because it had to export its specie to pay for its imports, Chile slowly began to run short of hard money. Worse, the local banks did not have the bullion to convert their own commercial paper into specie. In mid-1878 the nation learned that all of its credit institutions, save one, lacked the funds to redeem their bank notes. The government had no choice but to permit the banks' paper to circulate and to empower the state to print its own paper notes to keep the economy functioning.

Regrettably for Pinto, this economic downturn constituted but one of his problems. Across the Andes, the Argentine Republic questioned Chile's claims to Patagonia and the Strait of Magellan. And as if to give its rhetoric more substance, Buenos Aires began to acquire naval vessels. The Moneda could survive without the arid pampa to the east, but the strait afforded Chile its best link to the North Atlantic economy. Hence, the Pinto government sent an historian, Diego Barros Arana, to Buenos Aires to negotiate some arrangement that would surrender Patagonia in return for Santiago's control over the waterway. In a moment of exceedingly poor judgment, Barros Arana not only bargained away Patagonia but gave Buenos Aires joint control over the strait.

Upon hearing the news, Pinto disavowed Barros Arana's actions, demanding to reopen negotiations. Buenos Aires complied, sending Manuel Bilbao, a Chilean-born naturalized Argentine, to represent its interests. Writing in the Santiago daily *El Ferrocarril,* Bilbao managed to malign most of the Chilean political elite and the nation that they governed. Rioting ensued in which a Santiago mob defaced a statue erected in honor of Argentina and threatened Bilbao's person.

Pinto faced a serious dilemma: the economic depression of the 1870s had forced him to reduce substantially the size of the army as well as decommission various warships. Hence the president lacked the economic as well as military means to prosecute a war with Argentina. With Daza making menacing noises to the north, the Moneda wanted to avoid fighting on two fronts: Pinto offered to strike a deal with the Argentines. Fortunately, Buenos Aires, also suffering economically, backed away from its harsh words and authorized its consul in Chile, Mariano Sarratea, to settle the dispute before both sides stumbled into war. The Argentine diplomat and Alejandro Fierro, Pinto's foreign minister, could not decide upon a permanent border, but on 6 December 1878 the two men agreed that both Argentina and Chile would control the strait pending a final resolution to the boundary question. Having temporarily resolved the Argentine issue, Pinto could deal with Daza's seemingly arbitrary, if not illegal, decision to increase the levies on the Compañía de Salitres y Ferrocarril.

Unfortunately for Chile, its focus on Argentina had diverted its attention away from the tax that Daza had imposed in 1878. Initially, the impost did not seem so serious: the Bolivians tried to defuse the situation by verbally promising that they would not enforce the measure. Given Chile's history of diplomatic problems with its northern neighbor, however, Pinto's representatives spurned the Bolivian oral undertaking; the Chileans wanted the Daza government to state, unambiguously and in writing, that it would not to try to collect the levy.[5] While the Bolivians pondered the Chilean demand, Pinto's envoys also sought to convince Daza to abandon the idea of raising the tax. Pedro Videla, Chile's minister to Bolivia, warned Daza that enforcing the tax decree might push the Compañía de Salitres into bankruptcy, which would throw more than two thousand workers onto the labor market. The discharged miners, the Chilean warned, might riot, thereby threatening internal order. And if that prospect did not dismay Daza, Chile's foreign minister, Fierro, cautioned that a Bolivian refusal to cancel the tax would force Pinto to "declare null the [1874] treaty."[6] What exactly that meant was not immediately clear.

In December 1878, rather than debate whether the 1874 treaty with Chile prohibited Bolivia from levying or increasing taxes, the Bolivian authorities adopted a new tactic. The Daza regime now argued that the Compañía de Salitres, although incorporated under Chilean law, headquartered in Valparaíso, and largely owned by Chileans, could not legally seek the protection of the 1874 treaty because the corporation operated under a concession that derived from a "purely private contract" with the Bolivian government. The Daza administration observed, moreover, that Bolivia's constitution also stipulated that such concessions required legislative approval before they became law. In short, since the Bolivian congress had never endorsed the 1874 agreement, the Chilean corporation had no legal right to operate in Bolivia. Fortunately for the Chilean capitalists, the Bolivian government observed, there was a way out: the congressional passage of the law of 14 February 1878 did confirm the Compañía de Salitres's right to mine the Atacama but only on the condition that the company accept the primacy of Bolivian law *and* pay the ten-cent tax.[7] Two weeks later, Daza's foreign minister, Martín Lanza, reaffirmed the notion that the "tax that [the Chilean government] protests derives from a private contract between the Compañía de Salitres y Ferrocarril de Antofagasta and my government" and that, as such, it remained subject to the purview of Bolivia's courts and government.[8] And at the end of December the Bolivian government demonstrated its intent when it presented the head of the Compañía de Salitres a bill for ninety thousand pesos.[9]

While distressed, the Chilean government did not initially overreact: Fierro, of course, rejected the notion that the Compañía de Salitres's right to mine was conditional upon the Bolivian legislature's approval. That nation had earlier promised not to tax the company in exchange for the Chilean government abandoning its claims to the Atacama.[10] On 3 January 1879 Fierro wrote Videla suggesting that he try to convince the Bolivians to submit the tax question to mediation. Fierro insisted, however, that the Daza government suspend enforcing the 1878 law while the negotiations proceeded. If Daza refused, Fierro instructed Videla to demand his passports and to inform the Bolivian leader that the Chilean government would no longer consider itself bound by the 1874 treaty's provisions. The import of this statement quickly became clear: the day before Videla relayed Fierro's call for calm, Chile's president ordered the *Blanco Encalada* to Antofagasta.[11] The arrival of the vessel on 7 January certainly made Lanza pause: when the Bolivian foreign minister questioned Videla about the warship's purpose, the Chilean envoy disingenuously responded that the vessel was merely paying a courtesy visit to the port.[12]

One day before the *Blanco Encalada* arrived, 6 January 1879, Severino Zapata, a Bolivian functionary administering the Atacama province, had given the Compañía de Salitres three days to pay its ninety-thousand-peso back tax bill. It refused, and on 11 January Zapata seized the nitrate company's property and threatened to sell it in order to liquidate the company's tax debt. Videla protested: Daza, he argued, could not urge Santiago to submit the dispute to discussion while refusing to curtail his minions' actions; for mediation to proceed both nations had return to the status quo ante. Daza's government responded by rescinding the original concession that allowed the Compañía de Salitres to operate in Bolivia and announced that the government would, on 14 February 1879, liquidate the company's tax bill by auctioning off its assets.[13]

An exaggerated sense of amour propre may have inspired Daza to confiscate the Compañía del Salitres's property. In a private letter to Zapata, the president reported that in order "to prove to Chile that . . . the *Blanco Encalada* does not frighten us, the Cabinet has annulled the contract with the English house [the Compañía del Salitres], so that the government will have the freedom of action to exploit it or rent it, whatever best satisfies the interests of the nation."[14] Publicly, Daza's foreign minister tried to put the situation in the best light: by annulling the Compañía de Salitres's concession, Lanza wrote, Bolivia had effectively cut the diplomatic Gordian knot. Indeed, having extracted the bone of contention, Chile and Bolivia could put the matter behind them and resume amicable relations.[15]

Daza had no such illusions about returning to the good old days. He expected problems from Chile, especially after Videla asked for his passport. Because he considered Lanza too conciliatory on the tax issue and because he had opposed his policies, Daza fired Lanza and replaced him with the more tendentious Serápio Réyes Ortíz.[16] As one of his first acts, Réyes Ortíz departed La Paz, not for Santiago in order to seek peace, but for Lima, where Daza prayed Réyes Ortíz could reach "an accord with the Peruvian government so that Chile, in case of war, will have an enemy whom it will respect, and that it will strike its colors as it had done with Argentina."[17] Pinto did not react as Daza hoped or predicted. On 14 February the *Blanco Encalada* landed enough sailors and troops to capture Antofagasta. None of the belligerents realized it yet, but the War of the Pacific had begun.

The Leaders

Of Hilarión Daza much has be written, little of it complimentary. The Sucre-born bastard child of an Italian immigrant and a local woman, Daza spent a hardscrabble childhood in the care of his maternal uncle. Leaving school after completing the third year of *humanidades*, Daza apparently devoted himself to playing *curipata*, a Bolivian version of handball. One historian alleges that he turned to crime to support himself.[18]

His vocational epiphany came in 1857: witnessing a parade of the army's Third Battalion, Daza followed the troops as they marched back to their barracks, where he enlisted as a seventeen-year-old private soldier.

By consistently choosing the winning side in Bolivia's numerous revolutions, Daza rose quickly, first to sergeant and then, in 1861, to the commissioned ranks; in three years he ascended from sublieutenant to captain. As a reward for riding the four to five hundred miles separating Sucre and La Paz to warn President Mariano Melgarejo of a coup, Daza became a major. Three years later Daza received a promotion to colonel for helping depose the same Melgarejo he had earlier saved. By 1876 he was both a general and the minister of war under President Tomás Frías. He decided to seek the presidency, but apparently fearing that he would lose the forthcoming election, Daza overthrew Frías, claiming that in so doing he had saved the nation from civil war. Not without reason did some claim that the career of the thirty-six-year-old Daza epitomized "the autocracy of the saber," which had mismanaged Bolivia virtually from its inception. As a Chilean journalist presciently predicted, Daza's tenure would doubtless end should he preside over any defeat.[19]

If Daza lacked in formal education, he certainly was not deficient in his sense of self: that the dictator decreed that Bolivians celebrate his birthday at Easter indicated the almost limitless boundaries of his egotism. This custom continued into 1879. Thus, the same year that municipal authorities removed the bodies of scores of Bolivians who starved to death on the nation's streets, Daza commemorated his birthday with bullfights, fireworks, military parades, cannon salutes, and various concerts, all of which finally culminated in a grand, formal party.[20] Witnessing these activities, one English visitor noted, "Of all the adventurous careers recorded in the annals of South American republics, Daza's . . . will perhaps stand out as the most glaring instance of successful perfidy and audacity," a man so narcissistic that he believed only in himself.[21]

Daza's administration rested upon his relationship with the army's First Battalion, the Colorados, so named for their red jackets. Described as "men of great height, almost all bearded as their commander with high boots, shining cuirasses, plumed hats and long capes," they seemed a combination of the Grenadier Guards and "a company of the Duke of Alba on the fields of Flanders." Although the Colorados had a reputation for being "insolent, willful, conceited, without discipline, [and] corrupted by alcoholism," they adored Daza, who rewarded them with high salaries and daily visits.[22] Acutely aware of how he achieved power, Daza worked to ensure that no one else could follow the same path: he often rotated the members of the officer corps, encouraging them to feud against each other; he dispersed favors and rank only to those brother officers who "demonstrated political loyalty to his regime."[23]

Daza's rationale for the tax increase still appears somewhat clouded. Clearly the Bolivian government always needed money, in part because Daza had a history of being a big spender. But in addition to funding normal government services, the president also hoped to develop the nation's littoral, as well as to finance a railroad that would link the altiplano with the Pacific Ocean. Both projects would require large capital investments, which Daza hoped the export tax on salitre would finance.[24]

The general's goals may have been laudable but not his judgment or sense of timing. Some contemporaries, not all of them Bolivian, have argued that Daza was well within his legal right to levy the surcharge on the Compañía de Salitres. But even if he were, Daza recognized full well that imposing this tax might trigger Chilean reprisals. Still, he may also have believed that he had selected the most propitious moment to act so recklessly: with the Moneda fearfully looking fearfully over its shoulder toward Argentina, Bolivia, he believed, could strike from the north with impunity. Indeed, based on Pinto's earlier capitulation to Argentina on the issue of ownership of Patagonia and the Strait of Magellan, which demonstrated Chile's "weakness and impotence," Daza was sure that Santiago would "not use force to intervene in this matter [the dispute with Bolivia]." Obviously Daza felt he could act with abandon, as he exultantly boasted, "I have really stuck it to the gringos [the owners of the Compañía de Salitres y Ferrocarril]," and "the Chileans can only bite their tongues and stop protesting." And if for some reason Pinto did not cravenly submit as Daza expected, Bolivia, he noted, "can count on the support of Peru."[25]

Lima and Santiago had few reasons to like each other: Peru had not repaid Chile for its financial support in the wars of independence in the 1820s. Later, Chilean fear that Andrés Santa Cruz's newly created Peruvian-Bolivian confederation would jeopardize its existence inspired

Santiago to invade Peru in the 1830s. Although the destruction of the confederation supposedly restored the balance of power to the Pacific, Chile and Peru still sparred with each other by engaging in a naval arms race. It was fear of Chile's purchase of warships that encouraged Lima to enter into a defensive alliance with Bolivia in 1873. This agreement called for either nation to assist the other in case of a confrontation with Chile. Theoretically, the 1873 treaty was hush-hush, but Santiago learned of its existence within months of its ratification. Chile tactfully chose to ignore the pact's existence, in part because it did not anticipate that either party would invoke it.

At first glance, Chile's discretion appeared sound: the same economic downturn that ravaged its Pacific Coast neighbors blighted Peru. By 1878, notes one author, "Peru's situation was one of an acute fiscal crisis," a nation burdened with a large foreign debt that it could not service and a burgeoning population trying to live on a shrinking supply of foodstuffs.[26] President Mariano Prado, moreover, was a friend of Chile. He had lived there while in exile and apparently still had investments in the Chilean economy. Prado also recognized the folly of war, complaining to the Bolivian foreign minister, Réyes Ortíz, that "Peru has no navy, has no army, has no money; it has nothing for a war."[27] But if Prado feared confronting Chile, many of his countrymen did not. Certainly the Peruvian foreign ministry regarded Pinto's invocation of the doctrine of revindication as utterly absurd. Chile, a minister argued, could not now reassert its claims to territory that it had earlier, and repeatedly, acknowledged as Bolivian. Still, President Prado wanted to contain the damage, and in an attempt to defuse the crisis he sent José Antonio de Lavalle to offer Peru's good offices to resolve the Bolivian-Chilean quarrel. Unfortunately, Peru insisted that Chile withdraw from the recently seized Bolivian littoral as a precondition for starting discussions with La Paz.[28]

Pinto's situation became increasingly precarious. The Bolivian crisis had come to a head immediately after the resolution of the Argentine boundary dispute and weeks before Chile's congressional elections. Not surprisingly, those elements who earlier denounced the president's capitulation to Buenos Aires's demands now warned that Pinto would submit again, this time to Bolivia, a nation that they regarded as populated by ingrates and savages. Pinto could only neutralize his domestic political enemies, and help his fellow liberals win seats in the forthcoming congressional election, by standing firm vis-à-vis Bolivia and Peru.[29]

Regrettably, Prado's actions worsened Pinto's situation. Even as de Lavalle was en route to Santiago, the Peruvian president ordered his fleet to prepare for war while mobilizing and equipping his army. By late March, most of Santiago believed that Peru had thrown its support to Bolivia and that it would declare war on Chile as soon as it had readied its armed forces. The Chilean public demanded that Pinto ask de Lavalle directly and officially two questions: Did a defensive alliance exist that committed Peru to assist Bolivia in case of a war with Chile? And if so, did Lima plan to honor this agreement? Confronted with these queries, de Lavalle could prevaricate no longer: he answered yes to both. Given this response, Pinto sought and received legislative approval to declare war, which he did on 5 April 1879.[30]

Seeking the Origin of the War

Over the years, the War of the Pacific became one of those conflicts whose origins moved from the simple to the sinister. A widely held interpretation argues that a coterie of well-placed and affluent Chileans—sometimes but not always, depending on the theorist, acting in consort with their English masters—bulldozed Pinto into declaring war in order to protect the owners of the Compañía de Salitres y Ferrocarril. These allegations possess a mote of truth: the stockholders of the nitrate company did include some of Chile's economic and political elite. And they did buy the services of at least one of the country's newspapers to argue their case to the Chilean public.[31]

But the advocates of economic determinism, building on a flimsy combination of facts, advance a bolder argument: Chile, they claim, its economy devastated by the economic depression of the 1870s, saw salitre as a replacement for its silver, copper, and wheat, commodities that the world no longer wished to purchase. Consequently, local capitalists pushed Pinto to find an excuse to seize Bolivia's salitreras, thereby providing the Chilean state, and themselves, a new source of income. These same elements also had economic reasons for attacking Peru. Since 1873, they noted, nitrates from Peru's southern province of Tarapacá had become

Lima's principal export and its premier source of income. In 1875, anxious to guarantee itself a steady stream of revenues, the Peruvian government had nationalized the salitreras. Henceforth, although the former owners might operate Tarapacá's mines, the salitreras belonged to the Peruvian government, which, working through a consortium of banks, set prices as well as production quotas.[32] Peru had created a nitrate monopoly that virtually dominated the world market.

Obviously Chile's nitrate miners, even those exploiting the recently annexed salitreras of the Bolivian littoral, could not compete against the Peruvians. Thus, if Santiago wanted to assure its economic future, it had to seize not only La Paz's salitreras but those of Lima as well. Hence, rather than negotiate a peaceful settlement with Daza, Pinto used Peru's 1873 defensive alliance with Bolivia as a pretext to declare war both on Lima and La Paz. In short, some theorists argue, Chile precipitated the 1879 conflict not to protect its treaty rights or uphold its national honor but to win control of the world's nitrate supply.

Unfortunately, this interpretation overlooks certain important facts. Many Chileans, such as Melchor Concha y Toro, the politically powerful president of Chile's Cámara de Diputados, had invested large sums in Bolivia's Huanchaca silver mine. Clearly he and other Chileans wished to protect their Bolivian assets. Indeed, *Las Novedades*, a Santiago daily, claimed that Concha y Toro, fearing that Daza would use the war as an excuse to expropriate his investments, offered Pinto two million pesos to end the dispute and return to the 1874 boundary line. Lorenzo Claro, a Chilean founder of the Banco de Bolivia and a prominent member of the National Party, also wrote Pinto strongly defending Daza's tax increase.[33] In other words, there were as many powerful interests opposed to helping the Compañía de Salitres as there were those seeking to aid the corporation.

From the onset, various contemporary observers dismissed the economic conspiracy theory. Germany's minister to Santiago argued that the conflict between Chile and its enemies would "have erupted sooner or later, [and] on any pretext." The root causes of the struggle, he suggested, were not economic but geopolitical: a struggle between Chile and its neighbors for control of the southwestern portion of the Pacific. The minister even opined that Bolivia and Peru, victims of countless corrupt administrations and incessant revolutions, had developed a "bitter envy," which ripened into a hatred of Chile's material progress and good government. In sum, as the minister noted, "To attribute the origin of the present war to the nitrate interests reminds me of my youth, when people laughed at those who sought the origin of the revolution of Belgium against Holland in the presentation of the 'The Deaf of Portici.'"[34]

Curiously, few have studied what inspired Peru to honor the 1873 treaty. Prado, it must be remembered, could have legally refused to enlist in Daza's anti-Chile crusade. And given Lima's wretched economy and the potential for political unrest, he would have been well advised to remain neutral. But some have also found an economic motivation undergirding Prado's decision to go to war. According to the English envoy to Santiago, Peru "desired to monopolize and appropriate the nitrate works [and] to strengthen [its] nitrate monopoly." Initially, Prado did not have to fear that Chileans exploiting their domestic salitreras could challenge Peru's nitrate cartel: the mines of Taltal and Aguas Blancas, located in Chile's north, simply did not produce enough nitrates. The Atacama, however, did contain vast reserves of nitrates, and it appeared in early 1879 that Chile would annex this Bolivian province. Thus, as an Italian visitor noted, if Peru wanted "to protect its own monopoly of nitrates," it had stop "the competition of Chilean nitrates extracted from the Bolivian littoral."[35] Thus, Daza's declaration of war was a godsend: it gave Prado an excuse to declare war and crush Chile before its investors, capitalizing on the Atacama's resources, could rival Peru's domination of the nitrate market. As the Chilean press, and even the Lima daily *La Tribuna,* charged, Peru went to war to defend "a foreign country that might be an ally of cartels."[36] In other words, Chile did not precipitate the conflict; Peru did. "In the final analysis," wrote England's envoy to Chile, "the Peru-Bolivian convention was for Peru the cold calculation of a trader; and for Bolivia a vote of indemnity which covered the previous violations and future infractions of the agreement of 1866."[37]

Other contemporary sources saw Prado's declaration of war as the product of domestic forces. As early as March 1879, Britain's minister in Lima, Spencer St. John, warned that "the rival parties may try to make political capital out of jealousy for the national honor, and His Excellency [President Prado] may be forced to give way to the popular sentiment."[38] St. John proved tragically prescient: within weeks Peru's political factions, its military, particularly those who wished to come off the inactive list, avaricious business men, the proponents of cheap money, and virtually all of Lima's press called for war.[39] As an American visitor reported, when "a furious mob appeared before the doors of the municipal palace and demanded his [the president's] intentions, Prado saw that he must renounce Chile or lose his life."[40] Prado chose life.

Pinto labored under similar pressures. As the French minister to Chile, Baron d'Avril, observed, "In order to avenge the concessions made to the Argentine Confederation and to win popularity on the eve of the [congressional] elections, the Cabinet in Santiago imprudently launched itself into an adventure which will require great effort to get out of if not take a step back, . . . [and] which has excited the ardor of the masses." The American minister to Santiago concurred with his French colleague, noting, "It is doubtful, indeed, if the administration could have taken another course and sustained itself," an opinion seconded by José Manuel Balmaceda, who served as Chile's foreign minister under Pinto and became president in 1886.[41] Even de Lavalle, along with other prominent Chileans, observed that if Pinto had not declared war, he would have fallen from power and the war would still have erupted. Perhaps Antonio Varas, a leading political figure, best summed up the prevailing climate of opinion in Chile. Writing to Pinto, he noted, "Either we occupy all of Antofagasta or they [the war proponents] will kill you and me."[42] Varas need not have worried: officially aware of Peru's duplicity, Pinto declared war.

It is one of the peculiarities of scholarship that debate about the war's cause has gone on longer than the conflict itself. After a while, however, the argument becomes superfluous: we may dispute the cause or causes of the War of the Pacific, but its most important part, its resolution, is not a subject for discussion. In short, while we might not know with complete certainty who precipitated the war, we do know who won it.

Curiously, President Daza's decision to raise taxes on the Compañía de Salitres did not roil unduly the diplomatic waters. On the contrary, Chile and Bolivia acted as if it were business as usual. In late July 1878, for example, Daza confirmed Chile's right to use Antofagasta as a port to export nitrates mined from the area south of the twenty-fourth parallel. More significantly, Chile's diplomatic representative in La Paz informed his minister that Belisario Peró, who ran the Huanchaca Mining Company, and Aniceto Arce, that corporation's principal shareholder, had arrived in La Paz to arrange the financing of a railroad that would connect Bolivia's littoral with its capital. Significantly, the Chilean envoy described the railroad proposal as a project that would be good for "the Government, commerce, and the people of Chile." Once completed, he enthused, the rail line could not only increase Bolivian exports but also forge a "new commercial and social tie" between Chile and Bolivia. And by creating a community of financial "interests and sentiment," the project would distract "attention from the last remnants of discord, . . . the long debated question of the border, which still divided the two peoples."[43]

Other events transpired that encouraged those who believed, or hoped, that Chile and Bolivia would remain friends and thus avoid war. In late August the Chilean and Bolivian governments cooperated to arrange publicity for an auction of guano from Mejillones, which would take place in early 1879. It is noteworthy that in October 1878 the two nations also clarified the terms of an 1874 trade agreement. Nor did the volume of trade between the two nations, especially of nitrates, significantly decline.[44] Thus, both countries seemed to act as if the tax increase was in limbo, which was not unusual, since, as noted earlier, in July, Bolivia's diplomats had orally promised not to collect the export levy. Conceivably, Daza, never the most constant of men, might have changed his stance on the tariff. Alternatively, an anti-Daza coup, certainly not improbable given Bolivia's turbulent history, could have deposed the president. If so, Bolivia's congress might have repudiated Daza's nitrate policy just as it had undone Melgarejo's. In other words, the situation remained in flux until the end of 1878, when Bolivia announced it would auction off the Compañía de Salitres's assets. This decision pushed Santiago into a corner.

Ironically, one of the most proximate causes for the War of the Pacific was to be found not in La Paz or Santiago but in Buenos Aires. For years, Chile and Argentina had wrangled over their common border. Preserving its rights to the Strait of Magellan as well as Patagonia, not the nitrate issue, became Chile's obsession. A study of the Chilean press in 1878, for example, reveals that the various newspapers saw Argentina as their nation's principal foe; few journalists noticed, let alone complained about, Daza. The rioting that erupted in Santiago during the negotiations with a representative of the Argentine government demonstrated the Chileans' depth of feelings. Thus, Pinto's decision to accede abjectly to the *porteño* demands had unexpected consequences: it convinced Daza that the Moneda, having surrendered once, would do so again. Thus, three weeks after the proclamation of the Fierro-Sarratea agreement, Daza announced that his government would seize the Compañía de Salitres's assets if the corporation did not pay its delinquent taxes.

This ultimatum, described by the Chilean press as "the result of our humiliation" at the hands of Buenos Aires, forced Pinto to reoccupy the disputed territory.[45] It was one thing for Chile to back down before the Argentines; the prospect of yielding to Bolivia, a nation many Chileans regarded as peopled by "cholos" and roiled by revolution, however, proved simply too mortifying to contemplate. Facing an angry opposition, already excited by the forthcoming congressional elections, Pinto either had to call Daza's bluff or suffer the electorate's wrath either at the polling place or, worse, in the streets. Consequently, he ordered the occupation of the littoral.

Having miscalculated, Bolivia's President Daza had no choice but to brazen it out: in March he suddenly declared war on Chile. He also appealed to Peru to honor its treaty obligations. The Peruvian leader, regardless of personal feelings, had to abide by the 1873 treaty with Bolivia. As de Lavalle observed, failing to assist Daza would not only "arouse the most intense indignation in the Bolivians and the most profound disdain in the Chileans . . . [but it] would double our enemies, throwing Bolivia into the arms of Chile and doing precisely what they hoped to avoid by the signing of that pact."[46] In short, the Peruvian president, like Pinto, fell victim to a pro-war public opinion that threatened "either to push Prado into war or overthrow him."[47]

Thus the War of the Pacific, like the First World War after it, appeared to begin by accident, with one unrelated act knocking over the first domino that in turn upended others. Before they realized it, Chile, Peru, and Bolivia were at war. In the end, Chile emerged victorious, while its foes lost substantial portions of their territory, thousands of their youth, and millions in treasure. By the war's close, Chile controlled Bolivia's entire seacoast and three of Peru's southernmost provinces. None of the men who ruled the nations in 1879 did so in 1884: following an 1881 election, Pinto turned over the Moneda to his successor; rebellions overthrew Daza and Prado. Indeed, after five years of conflict, little of the Andean nations' geography or political life remained the same.

2. Comparing the Armies

E ven the most nationalistic Chilean might have questioned the wisdom of the Moneda's decision to declare war on the Allies. The population of Peru and Bolivia exceeded by 100 percent that of Chile, and the combined Allied armies could field almost three times as many troops as Santiago. If one were to consider the Allied militias, which numbered almost 120,000, compared to Chile's 7,000-man *guardia nacional*, the disparity appears even more overwhelming. But contrary to Napoleon's dictum, victory does not always go to the big battalions.

Chile's prewar army might have been smaller, but the quality of its officer corps more than offset its fewer numbers. Generally composed of graduates of the Escuela Militar and bloodied by years of fighting a low-level war against the Araucanian Indians on its southern frontier, Santiago's commanders were better trained and more experienced than their Allied counterparts. But the War of the Pacific presented certain problems. First, Chile had to carry the battle north, to the Peruvian heartland. To accomplish this goal, Aníbal Pinto's regime had to create, virtually from scratch, organizations to transport the army to its ports of embarkation; establish a communications network to link the expeditionary force to the army's headquarters; clothe, equip, as well as feed its troops; and finally, provide medical support to those who fell either from disease or battlefield injuries.

Although Pinto could count on a cadre of trained commissioned and noncommissioned officers, he still lacked enough troops to guard the nation's southern frontier from an Indian rebellion and protect its eastern flank from a possible Argen-

Table 1. Peru's prewar army

Unit	Strength	Prewar Garrison
Infantry		
Btn. Pichincha N. 1	529	Lima/Callao
Btn. Zepita N. 2	578	Cuzco
Btn. Ayacucho N. 3	813	Lima/Callao
Btn. Callao N. 4	421	Lima/Callao
Btn. Cuzco N. 5	421	Lima/Callao
Btn. Puno N. 6	312	Lima/Callao
Btn. Cazadores N. 7	400	Lima/Callao
Btn. Lima N. 8	450	Lima/Callao
Cavalry		
Rgt. Húsares de Junín	232	Lima/Callao
Rgt. Lanceros de Torata	435	Lima/Callao
Rgt. uías G	166	Lima/Callao
Artillery		
Rgt. Artillería de Campaña	333	Lima/Callao
Rgt. 2 de Mayo 30 guns	467	Cuzco
Total	5,557	

Sources: Cáceres, *Guerra del 79*, 13–16; Paz Soldán, *Narración histórica*, 110.

tine threat in addition to fighting the war in the north. To accommodate these manpower needs Chile, like Peru and Bolivia, would rely upon press-gangs to recruit men forcibly. Sadly, once inducted, these troops suffered from a host of afflictions: poor rations, wretched clothing, lack of medical care, and brutal discipline. That the men from the three belligerent nations fought as long as they did, and under such difficult conditions, is a tribute to them as soldiers and a testament to their integrity.

The Peruvian Military

The declaration of a state of belligerence caught the Peruvian and Chilean armies in various stages of military unpreparedness. In Peru's case, this condition partially resulted from bad luck: in 1875 the Lima government embarked on a project to reorganize the army using its noncommissioned officers recently graduated from the newly created Escuela de Clases as the core of the new formations. Economic as well as domestic political considerations, however, delayed the proposal's completion. Thus, once the conflict erupted, Mariano Prado's government had to abandon its efforts at restructuring and revert to the army's old table of organization—seven infantry battalions, three cavalry squadrons, and two artillery regiments—to fight the war.[1]

As part of its abortive reform proposal, between 1869 and 1878 Lima sent two missions abroad to acquire small arms. The first purchased two thousand Belgian Comblain II rifles. When Peru sought to buy more of these weapons three years later, it learned that the factory could not fill its order. (Deliveries to Brazil and Chile absorbed most of the plant's capacity.) The second mission compromised, acquiring five thousand of the less effective French Chassepots, which it modified to accept the same cartridge as the Comblain. This weapon became known as El Peruano, or as the Castañón, in honor of Col. Emilio Castañón, who led the delegation.

The arrival of these new rifles, however, still could not satisfy completely the needs of Peru's newly expanded army. Consequently, the government had to equip its troops with the obsolescent weapons, generally of different calibers and national origin, that clogged Lima's arsenals. The Pichincha, Zepita, and Ayacucho battalions carried American-made Sniders, while the Dos de Mayo and Cazadores de Cuzco battalions toted Chassepots. The administration later claimed that by September 1879 it had standardized its weapon systems to the point that at least each division used the same firearms. Yet, on the eve of the Battle of Tacna in May 1880, a provincial prefect informed President Nicolás Piérola that the army was equipped with 5,873 rifles and carbines produced by twelve different manufacturers. As Segundo Leiva of the Second Army of the South noted, relying on such a heterogeneous mélange of rifles caused enormous logistical problems. It proved so difficult to provide ammunition that in some units troops had weapons but no bullets.[2] Predictably, the government fobbed off its most out-of-date equipment, the Austrian or Prussian minié guns, on the various guardia nacional units; others carried the old Peabody.

Peru's artillery park consisted of four eight-centimeter Krupp M/67 guns, twelve six-centimeter Krupp M/73 mountain guns, four Gatling guns, as well as some very heavy and very obsolete bronze cannons. During the war Peru purchased additional small arms, ammunition, as well as forty to fifty Gatling guns plus artillery. Local foundries, moreover, manufactured over 650,000 cartridges for the Chassepots, Castañóns, and 688,000 minié balls. These same factories also produced sixty artillery pieces constructed of fused railroad tracks that they encased in bronze and reinforced with iron rings. Called the Grieve cannon to honor its designer, it fired the same shells made for the Krupp mountain gun and had a range of five thousand yards.[3]

Of all its combat arms, Peru's cavalry seemed the most ill equipped. Although all mounted units were supposed to use Winchester carbines, they did not. Col. Manuel Zamudio reported, for example, that one of the Lanceros de Torata's two squadrons, clad in body armor, carried lances as well as sabers; the other received Henry carbines that often malfunctioned because it proved difficult to extract spent cartridges.[4] Another curious fact distinguished Lima's mounted units: while Quechua- and Aymara-speaking Indians constituted the bulk of the infantry, and indeed the country's population, the authorities prohibited them from serving in the cavalry in the belief that Indians did not know how to ride horses. This honor fell only to blacks and mestizos, who apparently had a genetic predisposition to serve in the cavalry as well as the artillery.[5]

Curiously, while we know a great deal about the Peruvian army's equipment, its size remains uncertain because the 1878 *Memoria de Guerra* did not provide the number of its enlisted soldiers. Nor do contemporary and secondary sources agree on these figures. Peru's statistical service noted that in January 1879 Peru's army contained slightly more than fifty-six hundred men, a number that later military scholars have challenged. Some observers' estimates ranged between forty-five hundred and nine thousand soldiers.[6] J. G. Clavero seemed to compromise: in March 1879 he stated that Lima's peacetime army numbered seven thousand.[7]

Though the number of the enlisted personnel remained unclear, the 1878 *Memoria* did publish exact information about the size of the officer corps: 2,613 men, including 26 generals, held commissions in Lima's army. Peru's military, in short, contained six times as many officers as the Chilean army, and in fact, the number of Peruvian officers was only slightly less than the entire Chilean army, which totaled about 2,800 men. Not all of these officers served with units; approximately 959 were identified as *licencia indefinido*, men who, although on leave, still drew a reduced salary. An anonymous writer, presumably a Chilean, claimed that the figure of 2,613 was incorrect, that the Peruvian army's register contained an additional 1,257 names, thus making for a total of 3,870 officers, many holding senior ranks. Not surprisingly, an Italian described these colonels as "more numerous and damaging than locusts."[8]

Peru's officer corps had become so bloated because of the military's involvement in politics. According to Tomás Caviano, Lima's army, which he dubbed Peru's *partido sui generis*, consisted of two factions: those in power and those who yearned to displace them. Like some Hegelian forces, these two elements constantly vied for control. The victors enjoyed the perks of dominance: rank and higher salaries. The vanquished, who became known as the *indefinidos* or the *caidos*, had to subsist on a small pension while conspiring to launch a coup that would permit them to regain control, advance up the chain of command, and pension off their enemies, who, in turn, would repeat the process.[9] One crucial result of this game of military musical chairs was that regardless of which faction won, the state lost revenue and equipment. Despite these obvious problems, the process continued until the cost of maintaining such a bloated bureaucracy had become so great that the minister of war noted, "it threatens to absorb a large portion of the State's income." The Lima government annually had to spend over 1.6 million soles just to service the pensions.[10]

The quality of many of Peru's officers remained doubtful. Although Lima opened its first military academy in 1823, the school, as well as its successors, operated only sporadically. The most recent reincarnation, the Colegio Militar, had only begun to function in 1875, and it did not graduate its first class until 1877.[11] Consequently, most of those who received their commission directly did so by choosing the winning side of one of Peru's numerous revolutions. Not surprisingly, the results of this system dismayed the nation. The officers' performance during the war, particularly those at the company grade level, was so wretched that it had been, according to one British officer, the cause of the army's defeat. Indeed, the Peruvian intellectual Ricardo Palma said of the officer corps that "for every ten punctilious and worthy officers, you have ninety rogues, for whom duty and motherland are empty words. To form an army you will have to shoot at least half the military." Curiously, scores of officers from Uruguay and Argentina volunteered to serve under Peruvian colors. One of these was future Argentine president Roque Saenz Pena, who managed to survive the Battle of Arica and return to Buenos Aires to fight in the only marginally less bloody battles of Argentine politics.[12]

Given the harsh living conditions, recruiting and retaining enlisted men proved a daunting task, even in peacetime.[13] Theoretically, the army had a ready source of manpower: an 1872 decree mandated military service for all men twenty-one or older. (The affluent could buy a replacement.) Once inducted, a soldier would serve three years on active duty plus two in the reserves. In practice the draft system failed because the government could not overcome "the serious difficulties" reconciling "the respect due to a citizen's liberty with the fulfillment of a [citizen's] obligation [to serve]." Thus, rather than rely upon conscription, the army decided to entice men into enlisting for specific periods—two years for the infantry, for example. Once the soldier fulfilled his obligations he would receive a bonus that he could use to begin his civilian life.[14] The army hoped to alter the plan so that it would have more time—three years—to train those serving in the artillery or in the cavalry.

The onset of war dramatically increased the need for troops. As a Chilean reporter cynically observed, though the University of San Marcos's students clamored for war, they seemed reluctant to fight.[15] Thus, the Peruvian army resorted to a traditional method to fill its ranks: press-ganging Indians "in the interior . . . [who were] sent tied together to the capital; [and who] at the first opportunity . . . will desert and return home." Apparently, the burden of military service fell upon people of color; whites avoided it by hiding in their homes or using great caution when venturing outside—yet "another example," noted a foreign resident, "of Peruvian justice."[16]

The Indians apparently accepted the dragooning as just another natural disaster to endure, but not so Lima's *El Comercio*, which argued that drafting the heads of family impoverished their families.[17] A Chilean agent operating in Peru said that the government's promise not to employ force to conscript men was simply a ploy to lure the naive out into the streets where the press-gangs would seize them.[18] As the Italian naval surgeon Felice Santini wrote, the press-ganged Peruvian Indians, "poorly clad, wretchedly shod, and smelling so terribly that they repelled people, entered into battle not inspired by the notion of fulfilling their duty of conscience or by patriotism, [but] by their fear of the truncheon."[19] Regrettably, these practices did not end: in 1880 Lima's *El Nacional* complained that press-gangs had seized the son of one of the capital's best families, shaving his head and beard before placing him in a cavalry unit.[20] The result of such tactics was that for the overwhelmingly Indian army the cheer "Viva el Perú" had absolutely no meaning. Nor did they understand the cause for which they fought. One officer even informed a British observer that he had heard his men say that "they are not going to be shot for the benefit of white men."[21] For this reason a foreign diplomat concluded, "The Peruvian people . . . are not, have not been, and never will be in the present conditions a warrior people."[22]

Occasionally recruiters illegally grabbed foreign nationals. In one case the military impressed at least three Ecuadorian citizens, whom they held for a year. Only repeated complaining by Quito's diplomats secured their release, although in one instance a Peruvian colonel still refused to free the man.[23] Any able-bodied citizen who managed to escape the recruiting sergeant had to serve in the national guard. The authorities enforced these regulations by stopping men on the streets of Lima and sending those without proof of membership in the militia to the active army.[24]

Bolivia's Army

Peru was not the only nation whose army contained too many officers commanding too few men. Bolivia created its first military academy in 1823. Like its Peruvian counterpart, the school functioned only intermittently. Indeed, in 1847 the military institute for the third time closed its doors. Not until 1872 did these reopen when President Tomás Frías entrusted the Colegio Militar and its cadets to the care of a French general and a veteran of the Franco-Prussian War. (The defeat sustained by the French in the Franco-Prussian War should have given the Bolivians pause.) Regrettably, this school did not meet its founders' expectations, and even if it had, it never trained enough officers to change dramatically the tone, or level of skills, of Bolivia's officer corps. Just before the War of the Pacific ended, the Bolivian government called for the creation of both another academy and a school to train noncommissioned officers.[25] Reform of any kind proved difficult: the constant diet of "revolutions, mutinies, mob unrest," which one scholar calculated had convulsed Bo-

Table 2. Bolivia's prewar forces

Bolivian army

Unit	Authorized number	Actual strength
Infantry		
Btn. Daza 1 de la Guardia (Colorados) Col. Ildefonso Murguia	500	598
Btn. Sucre 2 Granaderos de la Guardia (Amarillos) Col. Niño de Guzmán	539	273
Btn. Illimani 1 3 de Linea Cazadores de la Guardia (Verdes) Col. Rámon González	500	536
Cavalry		
Rgt. Bolívar 1 de Húsares Col. Julián María López	250	280
Artillery		
Es. Ametralladoras		

Source: Bolivia, Ministry of War, *Memoria, 1878*.

Bolivian national guard units, by branch and location

Department	Unit
Infantry	
La Paz	Btn. La Paz
	Btn. Omasuyos
	Btn. Pacajes e Ingaví
	Btn. Yungas
	Btn. Sicasica
	Btn. Inquisivi
	Btn. Larecaja
	Btn. Muñecas
Oruro	Btn. Pária y Carángas
Cochabamba	Btn. Cochabamba
	Btn. Tapacarí
	Btn. Gliza
	Btn. Tarata
	Btn. Totora
	Btn. Arque
	Btn. Caparé

Table 2. (*cont.*)

Department	Unit
Potosí	Btn. otosí P
	Btn. Porco
	Btn. Chayanta
	Btn. Colquehaca
	Btn. Chorolque
	Btn. Chicas
Chuquisaca	Btn. Sucre (Cazadores)
	Btn. Cinti
	Btn. Yamparaez
Tarija	Btn. arija T
	Btn. Tomayapo
Cavalry	
Cochabamba	Es. unata P
	Es. Mizque
Chuquisaca	Es. adilla P
	Es. Azero
Tarija	Reg. San Lorenzo
	Reg. Concepción
	Reg. Salinas
	Reg. San Luis
Santa Cruz	Reg. Santa Cruz
	Reg. Valle Grande
	Reg. Cordillera
Artillery	
Oruro	Btn. ruro O

Source: Hilarión Daza, Circular, La Paz, 28 February 1879, in Ahumada Moreno, *Guerra del Pacífico*, 1:106.

livia at least three times each year since it had won its independence, eroded the army from within.[26] As recently as 1876, Andrés Ibáñez had led a revolution in Santa Cruz that roiled Bolivia for five months, consuming the army's scarce resources and costing the lives of some of its best leaders. The next year the army had to deal with unrest in Potosí as well as repress yet another rebellion, this time in Antofagasta.[27] It should come as no surprise that by 1879 many doubted the army's capacity.

Still, Hilarión Daza's legions managed to impress Lima's envoys. Just prior to the war, a Peruvian diplomat observed how Bolivia's army "has demonstrated its military skill in various parade formations that it performed in the public plaza." Indeed, another of Lima's representatives concluded that its military's "training, discipline, weapons and troops" were superior to those of Peru.[28] Both men misspoke. As Bolivia's President Narciso Campero noted, La Paz's officer corps "not only do not know their own obligations but they have not been educated in the duties of a soldier, [and] have not seen the regulations or tactics of their branch of service."[29] In short, Bolivia's officers lacked the education or training to fight a conventional war. True, a few officers, such as Gens. Pedro Villamil and Guillermo Villegas, had studied in France; Campero not only attended military schools in France and Spain but even served with the French army in Algeria. With these few exceptions, lamented the minister of war, the officer corps was educated, if at all, "in the school of Frederick the Great which was transmitted by our Spanish masters, [and] it knew nothing of the advances which have been made in the wars since 1866 to now."[30] One anonymous wag cruelly summed up the ethos of Daza's army this way: "After victory, loot. After the rifle, beer. This is the most complete synthesis of Bolivian military history."[31] An English resident of Bolivia earlier sounded even more pessimistic: "Bolivian military tactics consist in making a great noise and show, in order to see which party will get first to the running-away point; then the least frightened take courage, charge desperately and 'devil take the hindmost.' The army is . . . tolerably well armed with rifles but with no artillery worth mentioning, and their officers and discipline are simply contemptible. They have no notion of strategy or tactics, and the Generals principally distinguish themselves by their feats in running away from danger."[32]

The military, additionally, lacked the institutions of a modern army: when it existed the general staff, rather than consisting of the army's intellectual elite, had become a dumping ground for officers considered too untrustworthy to command troops in the field; it had even lost most of its copies of its own *Código Militar*. The general staff did supervise uniform changes and, more significantly, called for a court-martial and, if necessary, the forced retirement of officers found drunk on duty. In 1858 the José María Linares government (1858–61) merged the general staff with the Ministry of War, where it remained, its staff unchanged for eighteen years. Although General Daza apparently revived and reorganized the general staff in the early months of the War of the Pacific, it did not actually function until 1880.[33]

Since the Bolivian army lacked a mechanism to evaluate its officers' performance, most of the commissioned ranks won their promotions like the barely literate Indian Maj. Juan Réyes: "by vanquishing a large part of the officers of his class."[34] The result, according to Benjamín Davlos, was an army ruled by "the autocracy of the saber"; what Alcídes Arguedas described as "a praetorian guard, that defends today one *caudillo* and tomorrow another, who in order to reward their services, has no recourse other than to award them prizes at the cost of the state's funds."[35] Another Bolivian minister of war concurred, opining that this problem "originated or was fomented by the constant turmoil or stupid domination of *caudillaje*."[36] Certainly the career of General Daza, who shot his way into the presidential palace, provided living proof for this allegation.[37] But, as a minister of war so haplessly admitted, Bolivia would never progress until the government purged the army and ended its involvement "in the nation's domestic politics." Only then could the military become "a social institution beloved and respected by the people."[38]

The organization of Bolivia's army, like that of its ally, seemed to be in a state of flux when the war erupted. In 1876 some 1,911 men served in five infantry battalions, three squadrons of cavalry, plus an artillery unit. The next year, Minister of War Carlos de Villégas's *Memoria* placed the number of troops at 1,598 men, more than the authorized figure but still fewer than in 1876. Adding the staffs of various administrative units, such as the attachés assigned to the government, Bolivia's army consisted of between 1,655 and 1,675 men, of whom 228 were officers, 688 were noncommissioned officers, and 661 were private soldiers. What Bolivia's officers lacked in training they made up in numbers, approximately one for every three privates or noncoms.[39] *El Mercurio*'s La Paz correspondent believed that officers would regard the onset of the war as providential because "it would employ hundreds of colonels, generals, and other rogues who populate the nation, without damaging the economy since this type of people neither work nor speculate."[40] The Bolivian army of 1877 included not only a smaller number of men but fewer units as well: three battalions of infantry, the Daza Granaderos 1 de la Guardia, the Sucre Granaderos de la Guardia, and the Illimani Cazadores de la Guardia; one cavalry detachment, the Bolívar 1 de Húsares; and a mobile squadron of four Gatling machine guns. The Regimiento Santa Cruz de Artillería also contained four cannons, purchased in 1872, as well as ten to fifteen older weapons. In 1880 Bolivia organized the Bolívar 2 de Artillería, which consisted of sixteen artillery field and mountain guns.[41]

Although few in number, Bolivia's soldiers could endure enormous hardship. One Chilean educator noted, for example, that Daza's men managed to survive on "a little coca, toasted corn or cooked potatoes, [and] after long marches, naked and in need, fight in battle providing his officers and leaders set an example."[42] (Given the description of the officers, such models seemed unlikely to emerge.) In addition to their stamina, Bolivia's troops were certainly the most colorful: each infantry received unit jackets of a different color. The five hundred men of the First Battalion, popularly known as the Colorados, wore red; since the Second and Third battalions, which numbered three hundred men each, sported yellow or green coats, they became known as the Amarillos and the Verdes, respectively. As other units, such as the Batallón Loa or the Aroma, came on line, they too adopted different colored uniforms so that La Paz's army always brought different tints to the battlefield.[43]

The small arms that these troops carried—ranging from Martini-Henrys to flintlocks—proved as varied as their uniforms. Worse, not one unit carried the same weapons into battle. La Paz's minister of war attributed this problem to the countless *cuartelazos* that had consumed so many weapons that there was no uniformity of small arms within each of the army's units. This lack of standardization not only led to supply problems but, according to the 1877 *Memoria*, "caused many, grave troubles in practical training as well as in their use." Of the three combat arms, only the infantry seemed marginally acceptable. Certainly the artillery appeared blighted: it possessed two heavy and two light machine guns, and three three-inch artillery pieces. But the unit lacked the horses to transport them to the field and the technical skills needed to fire them accurately. Thanks to a lack of decent mounts, the product of the constant civil unrest, one minister called the cavalry the least efficient branch.[44]

In fairness, Bolivia tried to remedy these problems. Unfortunately, its attempt to improve the troops' living conditions, increase junior officers' salaries, purchase draft animals, and acquire small arms plus four

Krupp cannons foundered due to a lack of funds.[45] In 1878, with war in the offing, Bolivia had requested and received permission from Peru to import, duty free, fifteen hundred Remington rifles plus some other military items. And in mid-1879 it received another two thousand Remingtons to add to the approximately three thousand rifles of the same make. By 1881, thanks to shipments from Panama, Bolivia acquired six modern Krupp artillery and enough rifles that it could to lend some to Peru, though it still continued to carp about the lack of ammunition. La Paz, however, had yet to standardize its arsenals' contents.[46]

Procuring weapons proved far easier than recruiting soldiers. La Paz had a conscription law, but, like many of Bolivia's edicts, it was honored more in the breach than in fact.[47] Even before the war, the government admitted that the recruiting methods it employed were not only "absolutely unwise and violent" but also unjust, because "only the roughest class" performed military service.[48] In part this problem arose because of the regime's inability to enforce fairly the law. In some cases, provincial officials, inspired by favoritism and slowed by sloth, simply grabbed the first warm body they could, even if the law exempted that hapless soul from conscription. Not surprisingly, some areas refused to apply the law; other officials selected recruits by lot, a system that appeared less capricious.[49]

The onset of the war magnified existing flaws: "The aggressive and violent capture of a citizen by armed force" still underpinned Bolivia's conscription process, a system "which tears its victim from the lowest social stratum . . . which starts, almost always with the criminal class, and which beneath the beautiful uniform of the defender of justice, hides a rotten heart or a stupefied conscious."[50] According to the newspaper *El Civilista*, a government minister would release any press-ganged recruit in return for a payment or bribe of either fifty Bolivianos or a horse. Not surprisingly, President Campero discovered that Bolivia's workers fled "to the forests and other impenetrable places, abandoning their houses and plots of land that are ready for harvest," rather than enter the military. Apparently, civilian protests against the dragooning of soldiers briefly ended that government practice, but in 1880 the authorities, in violation of existing laws, again began seizing men.[51] Predictably, many of those whom the recruiter snared were unfit for military services; those who were suitable tried to desert. In one case 69 privates of the Batallón

Ayacucho managed to run away during the course of one three-league march.[52] Of Bolivia's 9,000-man army in Peru, 2,000 had decamped. To limit their losses one officer had to station one battalion behind another. Despite such problems, the army of 1881 numbered 422 officers and 3,665 soldiers, indicating that the military had partially made up for the losses it suffered in the first months of the war.[53]

Bolivia, like Chile, used its regional militia as the basis of the expanded army, although apparently race and class, as well as geography, determined membership: the *gente decente* (a euphemism for "white") from the capital, Oruro, Cochabamba, Sucre, Potosí, Camargo, Santa Cruz, Trinidad, and Tarija entered the Batallón Murillo, the Vanguardia, the Libres del Sur, the Escuadrón Velasco, or the Escuadrón Méndez.[54] Daza placed the first four units in the Legion de Bolivia, which had the reputation of being for the *hijos de bien*, those affluent enough to pay for their own weapons and mounts.[55] (Batallón Chorolque, according to one Peruvian diplomat, also consisted of Bolivia's elites.)[56]

The less exalted artisans, teachers, bureaucrats, and apprentices, who tended to be mestizos, enlisted in La Paz's Victoria, Illimani 2, Paucarpata, and Independencia; those from Cochabamba entered the Aroma, Viedma, and Padilla; the men from Chuquisaca joined the Olañeta; while the *cholos* of Oruro, Tarija, and Potosí signed on in the Batallones Dalence, Bustillo, Ayacucho, Tarija, and Chorolque.[57] Those who rejected the notion of creating an army consisting solely of the lower class, particularly Indians, who "lacked sufficient culture to learn and practice their responsibilities to the motherland," found the composition of Bolivia's army refreshing: the entry into the military of artisans, noted José Ochoa, "has invigorated our army, enlisting in it with the satisfaction of fulfilling a grateful duty to their heart and an unavoidable one for his conscience."[58]

Some units did not fit into the various racial or class categories: General Daza used the police of Sucre and Potosí as the nucleus to establish the Batallón Sucre 2 de la Guardia.[59] The Bolivians also created units from exile communities; the troops in the Escuadrón Franco-Tiradores, for example, came from the littoral. The Columna Loa consisted of Bolivians who lived in the Peruvian province of Tarapacá. These men accompanied Peruvian troops as they retreated to Tarapacá, where they fought a rearguard action against the Chileans.[60]

Rather than depend on the provincial authorities who sometimes did not cooperate, the Campero administration ordered all men over eighteen to enroll in the active army, the mobile reserve army, or the passive territorial reserve. To avoid well-founded charges of favoritism or political influence, draftees would be selected on the basis of a lottery. Only bachelors or childless widowers under the age of thirty-five had to serve in the active army. The new decree mandated the induction into the army of any man who failed to enlist in the reserves.[61]

Apparently Campero's reforms came to naught, because in 1883 the authorities attributed their nation's defeat to the fact that the press-gangs filled the army with men who were too young, too old, too ill, too uneducated, or simply too neurotic to defend their motherland. Fortunately, Bolivia's vulnerable were not without their own resources: when the recruiters of the Escuadrón Méndez and the Granaderos tried to enlist recruits in the Potosí region, they discovered that all the able-bodied men had already abandoned both field and home.[62]

Bolivians had ample reason to avoid military service, even in wartime. Housed "like sardines in a metal can," a Peruvian diplomat noted, "the Bolivian soldiers ceases to live under the protection of the laws. His commander is the owner of his life. For the smallest flaw or on a mere caprice he can take his life, ordering that he be lashed 1,000 times." To ensure complete fidelity, the officers did not allow soldiers to communicate with civilians. Deliberately estranged from family and friends, a recruit considered the unit to be home and family. But after years of mind-numbing drills and alienation, one minister of war noted, soldiers became "licentious, poor, and useless."[63] By 1881 La Paz had improved the lot of its troops by providing food and clothing, as well as a general education. It also created various militia units such as the Guardia Republicana and hoped to train another ten thousand militiamen.[64]

The Bolivian soldier's stolid endurance, his stoicism, and his ability to endure privation did not make a skilled soldier. As Campero observed, training an illiterate Indian, "who does not know how to hold a rifle, [and who] has a very little idea of the motherland or of its elevated ends," proved extremely difficult.[65] Before the army could make these men into soldiers, it had teach them to be citizens, "to impart notions of civilization" or culture for the soldier "to know and to practice his duties to the

Table 3. Chile's prewar army, 1878

Unit e Nam	Strength	Garrison ation Loc			
		Upper Indian Frontier	Lower Indian tier	Santiago	Valparaíso Fron
Infantry					
Btn. Buin 1 de Linea	300	302			
Btn. 2 de Linea	300		152		169
Btn. 3 de Linea	300	300			
Btn. e e4 d Lin	300			304	
Btn. apadoreZ	300	334			
Cavalry					
Reg. Cazadores a Caballo	320	121			283
Reg. Granaderos a Caballo	210	230			
Artillery					
Reg. de Artillería N. 1	410			217	183
Totals	2,440	1,287	152	521	635

The 3 January 1878 authorized the army to have a strength of 3,316.
Sources: Estado Mayor General, *Historia*, 4:177; Chile, Ministry of War and the Navy, *Memoria, 1878*, 96.

motherland."[66] Blissfully unaware of these deficiencies, one La Paz newspaper pronounced that "the Bolivian army never has been so brilliant, superb, and proud as it is today . . . with such brave soldiers there is no question of our victory and our triumphant occupation of Santiago."[67]

The Chilean Army

Chile's military differed from its enemies in a variety of ways. On the most superficial level, Santiago's troops dressed rather drably, at least when compared to Bolivia's colorfully clad hosts. A few of Chile's militia units did design some regalia that rivaled in hue those of La Paz, but the Ministry of War, doubtless anxious to ensure uniformity—always a cardinal military virtue—quickly stifled such originality. Instead, Santiago's troops, aping the French army's fashions as well as its tactics, marched into battle wearing blue or red kepis and jackets, red trousers, and sometimes brown puttees or leggings.

Another, and certainly a more significant distinction, was that Chile's prewar army was composed of volunteers: those who served as private soldiers or noncommissioned officers had enlisted, generally in return for a bonus. The enlisted men did not constitute the elite of the Chilean nation. Indeed, one foreign writer described them as "the very lowest scum of society." Thus, we should not be surprised if these sunshine soldiers often deserted, taking their bonus and their new uniforms with them. Curiously, while Chilean men did not have to serve in the army, they did have to enroll in the national guard, the territorial militia. These organizations had so atrophied over the years that the unlucky members who had to waste their Sundays drilling, received little training. In 1876 one deputy, describing the guard as without military value, called for its abolition.[68]

Legally, the government could not require guardsmen to serve abroad. But once the war began, the Moneda ignored this law, as well as the protests of the militia, sending the mobilized guard units into the war zone. Similarly, when Chilean patriots ceased enlisting in the regular army, the authorities, as well as individual military unit commanders, unleashed the press-gangs. In their search for cannon fodder, the recruiters first emptied the jails; then they picked up the vagrants or invaded the bars, where they seized the drink-sodden idlers. Once they exhausted this rather coarse niche of Chilean society, the press-gangs concentrated on the honest farmers, the *inquilinos*, the miners, and the artisans. On the streets of Santiago, the military chased men down and, after trussing them up like animals, marched them off to the barracks. The legislators occasionally protested this grotesque violation of the citizens' rights, but it took solace in the fact that these recruitment drives reduced Chile's crime rate.[69]

The urgent need for recruits caught the Pinto government by surprise. Indeed, suffering from the same economic woes that afflicted its foes, the Moneda had gutted its military. In just one year, the army dismissed 700 infantrymen and cavalry troopers and abolished an artillery regiment. When the purge ended, Chile's army consisted of but 2,841 officers and enlisted men, serving in five battalions of infantry, including one called the Zapadores, a regiment of artillery, plus two of cavalry, the Cazadores a Caballo and the Granaderos a Caballo. The infantry battalions consisted of four companies, the cavalry regiments of three squadrons—except for the Granaderos a Caballo, which contained only two—and the artillery regiments of two batteries. With the exception of the artillery, two infantry battalions, and the Regimiento de Cazadores—which garrisoned either Santiago or Chile's main seaport, Valparaíso—more than half of the army consisted of smaller units that manned the nation's unofficial southern boundary, "watching Araucanian Indian cattle lifters that occasionally commit depredations along it."[70]

Unlike the Allies, the Chileans had standardized the regular army's weapons. The infantry carried Comblain II rifles, and artillerymen used Winchester carbines, while the cavalry's Regimiento de Cazadores a Caballo dangled Spencer carbines from their saddles. Increasing the size of the army, however, forced some units to use less modern small arms. The newly created Atacama and Concepción battalions used Beaumont rifles, some of which exploded each time the troops used them for target practice; the Regimiento de Granaderos a Caballo employed both types of carbines plus some percussion rifles. Santiago began the war with four Gatling guns as well as forty-four field pieces and mountain guns, including sixteen six- and eight-centimeter cannons purchased from the House of Krupp. Unfortunately, Chilean gunners had little experience deploying these weapons: in two years they had fired their field pieces only once. It does not appear that the infantry had much more experience using their small arms.[71]

While the active army had adequate weaponry, the same could not be said for the national guard. The seven-thousand-man militia—which tumbled from eighteen thousand in 1877—had to make do with 3,868 ancient minié guns and "old French flintlock rifle[s], converted into percussion weapons, which through use and long time in service, are now found in bad state." Unsurprisingly, the guard's artillery, or cavalry guard units, also had to make do with outdated equipment.[72]

A few factors distinguished Pinto's army from that of the Allies. Thanks to Diego Portales, who had purged the army officer corps, the nation had managed to avert some of the more grievous sequela of unbridled militarism. Chile, however, was not immune to internal unrest: in 1851 and 1859 the army had to subdue rebellions. The Moneda sometimes called upon the military—but more so the national guard—to guarantee the "correct," not necessarily honest, outcome of an election. Officers who demonstrated a lack of enthusiasm for this task or who vocally espoused a different political ideology than the government's favorites sometimes had to resign their commissions.

Table 4. Small arms

Peruvian and Bolivian small arms

Weapon	Caliber in millimeters	Length in meters	Rate of fire (rounds per minute)	Weight of rifle in kilos	Initial muzzle velocity in meters per second	Range in meters	Weight of bullet in grams
Remington	11–12.7	1.3	8	4.2	390	914	26
Remington M/1871	11	1.32	16	4.2	410	914	25
Bonmmuller	11	1.35	6	4.5	432	1,200	32
Castañon	11	1.3	6	4.1	375	1,100–1,200	25
Comblain II	11	1.3	10	4.3	430	1,200	25
Chassepot	11	1.3	6–8	4.0	375	1,100–1,600	25
Gras	11	1.3	9–10	4.2	430	1,200–1,800	25
Snider	14.6	1.4	10	4.3	380	540–2,500	31
Spencer Carbine	13.2	.94	15–20	3.8	360	250–1,000	20.8–22
Peabody	10.4–11	1.3	10	4.2	435	457	19.1
Martini-Henry	11.43	1.2	20	4.2	400	540–2,500	31.1

Chilean small arms

Weapon	Caliber in millimeters	Length in meters	Rate of fire (rounds per minute)	Weight of rifle in kilos	Initial muzzle velocity in meters per second	Range in meters	Weight of bullet in grams
Comblain II	11	1.3	9	4.3	430	1,200	26
Gras	11	1.3	10	4.5	375	1,200–1,800	25
Kropatschek	11	1.24	9	4.5–5.1	430	2,900	25
Beaumont	11	1.32–1.8	9	4.4–4.7	405	200–1,800	44
Winchester Carbine	7.5–9	1.17	20–25	3.9	360	300–1,000	1,300

Sources: Grieve, *Historia*, 330–33, 335, 337–38, 386; Ekdahl, *Historia militar*, 1:43–45, 47, 56–57; Smith and Smith, *Book of Rifles*, 253, 274–75, 350, 361–62; Johnson and Lockhoven, *International Armament* 1:199, 201, 212, 218, 230–32, 236.

Table 5. Artillery

Chilean artillery

Model	Number	Caliber in millimeters	Weight in kilos	Initial muzzle velocity in meters per second	Range in meters	Weight of shell in kilos
Krupp Mountain Gun M1873 L/21	12–16	60	107	300	2,500	2.14
Krupp Field Gun M1867 L/25		78.5		357	3,000	4.3
Krupp Mountain Gun M1879 L/13	38	75	100	294	3,000	4.5
Krupp Mountain Gun M1879–80 L/24	24	87	305	465	4,600	1.5
Krupp Field Gun M1880 L/26	29	75	100	465	4,800	4.3

Model	Number	Caliber in millimeters	Weight in kilos	Initial muzzle velocity in meters per second	Range in meters	Weight of shell in kilos
Krupp Field Gun M1873	12	87	450	465	4,800	6.8
Armstrong M1880	6	66	250	550	4,500	4.1
BRONZE Model 59 Emperador	12	87		313	323	11.50
La Hitte Field Gun M1858	4	84		342	342	4.035
La Hitte Mountain Gun M1858	8	86.5		225	225	4.035

Table 5. (*cont.*)

Peruvian artillery

Model	Number	Caliber in millimeters	Weight in kilos	Initial muzzle velocity in meters per second	Range in thousands of meters	Weight of shell in kilos
White Mountain Gun	31	55			2.5	2.09
White Field Gun	49	55			3.8	2.09
*Grieve Steel	42	60	107	300	2.5	2.14

*Grieve artillery pieces were produced by local Peruvian foundries. Grieve, *Historia*, 354.

Bolivian artillery

Model	Number	Caliber	Weight in kilos	Initial muzzle velocity in meters per second	Range in thousands of meters	Weight of shell in kilos
Krupp Mountain Gun M1872 L/21	6	60	107	300	2.5	2.14

Gatling guns

Model	Caliber in millimeters	Length in meters	Rate of fire (rounds per minute)	Initial muzzle velocity in meters per second	Range in meters	Weight of of bullet in grams
Gatling	11.4	.90	200–400	384	1,200–1,900	31

Sources: Boonen and Körner, *Estudios*, 1:291; William A. Acland, R.N., qtd. in Tauro, "Defensa de Lima," 79; Grieve, *Historia*, 350–57; Ekdahl, *Historia militar*, 1:45; Tarnstrom, *French Arms*, 85, 207; Le León, *Recuerdos*, 85, 207; Private correspondence with Giles Galté, 2004.

In short, although flawed, the Chilean system nonetheless differed from that of Bolivia, where the chain of command was supplanted by cronyism, where "the intimate friends of the commander take turns sharing the command with him."[73] These facts do not mean that some Chilean officers did not call upon their *santos en la corte* to influence promotions, to arrange a coveted assignment, or to obtain protection from official retribution. Indeed, precisely because some officers served as government bureaucrats or sat in the legislature as elected representatives their acquaintance with politicians gave them some clout. But Chilean army officers also realized that the congress not only authorized the military's budget but also set limits on its size, that if the minister of war was a professional officer he served at the pleasure of a civilian president and legislature, and that a promotion law required that officers spend a certain number of years in grade in order to ascend in the army's hierarchy. Compare this requirement to Daza, who in thirteen years rose from the rank of private to lieutenant colonel.

Additionally, Chile's officer corps, unlike that of the Allies, was professionally educated. True, a few of the army's most senior officers, such as Gens. Justo Arteaga and Manuel Baquedano, received their commissions directly, but they were in a minority. Most of Chile's officers entered the army only after completing a course of study in the Escuela Militar. Founded by Chile's first national leader, Bernardo O'Higgins, the school at times seemed more like a refuge for juvenile delinquents than an institute for aspiring officers. A cadet riot, for example, forced the authorities to close the school in 1876, but it reopened in late 1878 with the expectation that it would graduate its first class in five years.

Even attending the Escuela Militar or unit-level postgraduate seminars did not prepare Chile's officers for modern war. The lessons of the later years of the American Civil War and the Franco-Prussian conflict—that rapid-fire rifles and breech-loading artillery devastated massed troop formations—did not seem to influence Chile's infantry, which continued to use the tactics outlined in a translated edition of a 1862 French military text. Unfortunately, as Jay Luvaas noted, "The infantry regulations of 1862, which had been described as a 'faithful reproduction of the regulations of 1831' [varied] little in spirit from the Ordinance of 1791."[74] Thus Chile would go to war in 1879 using the tactics of the

Napoleonic era. As Emilio Sotomayor observed, "A soldier, especially the Chilean, because of his nature has to be watched and overseen constantly by his officers. Otherwise—as practical experience has shown us on many occasions—the soldier obeys the tendency to disperse and to fight alone."[75] This habit might have developed as a consequence of a situation unique to Chile: for decades the Araucanian Indians were Santiago's major enemy. Whatever their deficiencies, Chile's army acquired more military skills fighting the Indians than the Bolivian army did from "promoting or suffocating revolutions or mutinies."[76] Ironically, the foot soldiers seemed no more backward than Chile's cavalry, which still followed some early-nineteenth-century Spanish regulations. The infantry employed tactics modeled on those of the Spanish for muzzle-loading weapons, not techniques adapted to the use of modern firearms. The artillery perforce demanded a higher level of education: in 1874 Gen. Luis Arteaga wrote a manual to teach the army's gunners how to master their newly acquired Krupp artillery and Gatling guns.[77]

Perhaps these faults did not appear so egregious in peacetime. After all, as one colonel sarcastically observed, some still believed that "to be a good officer [one] only has to learn the Regulations, know how to fulfill his obligations in the barracks, to command Sunday drill and tactical maneuvers, [and] to wear the uniform with a certain elegance." Instead, the colonel noted, the officer "should have a profound and detailed knowledge of the weapons of war, of military organization, of supply troops in the field, tactics for the battlefield, attack and defense of positions, study of topographical maps, military reconnaissance and the other branches [of knowledge] which constitute the art of war."[78] Unfortunately, many did not.

While some argued that the Chilean army did not need to incorporate the new tactics, a few officers nonetheless tried to modernize training. The army did contain a small coterie of European-educated officers.[79] Two of these, Diego Dublé Almeida and his brother Baldomero, sought and received permission to teach their brother officers the latest tactics, particularly the notion of advancing in open formations in order to minimize casualties. Their lecture fell on largely deaf ears. One colonel objected to utilizing such techniques: "Dispersed order was not needed," he pronounced, just "being a Chilean soldier is sufficient to triumph."

Only two commanders, Ricardo Santa Cruz of the Zapadores and Domingo Toro Herrera of the Chacabuco, absorbed the lessons, which they later demonstrated during maneuvers. Their efforts, while not converting other commanders, convinced a few to adopt the maneuver of having their companies advance in skirmish lines; regrettably, the rest of the army, an American naval officer observed, did not embrace the new tactics, devoting its efforts to "mechanical precision and too little to skirmishing. Open-order fighting did not seem to form part of the system of tactics."[80]

In addition to the gaps in their education, Chile's officers often lacked practical experience. The army's more senior commanders did not know how to maneuver large units. Col. Marco Arriagada complained that most officers did not possess the knowledge to train the infantry and cavalry how to use their new rifles. Even when they acquired new Krupp field pieces, Chile's gunners did not understand their value because they had fired them but once in past two years.[81]

In sum, Chile's army seemed ready to fight the war against Peru and Bolivia in 1879 using the same tactics it had employed when it had battled against the armies of the Peruvian-Bolivian Confederation in 1836. Happily for the Moneda, its enemies' military proved equally rooted in the past: just as the Bolivians still resorted to Napoleonic squares to repel cavalry charges, the Peruvians continued to follow Spain's only slightly more modern 1821 military regulations, which, many officers sadly acknowledged, seemed appropriate only for a "distant epoch."[82]

Manpower

The onset of war forced the three nations to modify, in some cases drastically, their armies' tables of organization. In early 1879, a Chilean infantry battalion consisted of 300 men serving in four companies.[83] In late February, doubtless in anticipation of the conflict, the Chilean minister of war, Cornelio Saavedra, increased by 50 the complement of each company, regardless of branch. A month later, the regular army transformed the Battalions of the Line 1, 2, 3, and 4, the Santiago, and the Zapadores—not an engineer battalion but a regular infantry unit originally charged with the mission of developing and guarding Chile's southern provinces—into regiments.[84] Henceforth each of these contingents consisted of two battalions, containing eight companies of 149 enlisted men plus 5 officers.[85] Since the minister of war added only two companies to the Zapadores, this battalion possessed 400 fewer men than regular infantry regiments.[86] In addition to altering the size of existing elements, the minister of war formed a new infantry battalion, the Santiago, in March 1879; he also militarized the police forces of Santiago and Valparaíso, creating two new battalions, the Bulnes and the Valparaíso.[87]

The Chilean government did not concentrate solely on beefing up the infantry: the minister of war used a battery taken from an existing artillery unit to create the nucleus for the Brigada de Artillería de Antofagasta, which subsequently became the Regimiento de Artillería Num. 2. This artillery regiment was divided into five brigades—four to serve with the army and one to man coastal defenses—each containing two batteries of four guns staffed by a complement of 250 men. The Regimiento de Artillería Num. 1 was reorganized in early 1880, so it consisted of three brigades of two companies of 300 men.[88] Similarly, the authorities elevated an already existing unit, the Batallón de Artillería de Marina, initially created in 1866 to service coastal artillery as well as naval guns, to the status of a regiment. The new organization consisted of two battalions containing four companies, numbering approximately 1,000 men.[89] In his attempt to expand his nation's forces, Saavedra also attached an additional squadron to the Cazadores a Caballo so that it and the Regimiento Granaderos de Caballo each consisted of five 160-man squadrons.[90] Thus, by mid-June 1879 Chile's Army of the North was composed of six regular infantry regiments, two battalions of recently mobilized infantry militia, plus the militarized police battalions Bulnes and Valparaíso. There were also two artillery units: the Regimiento de Artillería de Marina and the Batallón de Artillería de Linea. The cavalry had expanded to two regiments (the Cazadores and the Granaderos), and by mid-August there was a company of engineers.[91]

Because Chile managed to shift its regular troops north quickly, it did not initially depend so heavily on the militia. In February 1879 the authorities formed two guard battalions, the Antofagasta 1 and 2, as well as units in Caracoles and Carmen Alto.[92] Within a few months, Chilean authorities in the littoral had raised a force of approximately 2,700 men, while the Army of the North numbered 9,127. In mid-July 3,600 militia-men, comprising six battalions and a brigade of infantry, a squadron of cavalry, and brigade of artillery, served in the littoral's guard units. By June 1880 the Santiago government called up eighteen battalions of infantry as well as three squadrons of cavalry. Thus, by mid-June the sedentary militia consisted of forty battalions, twenty-four brigades, and five companies of infantry; a battalion, thirteen brigades, and a company of artillery, plus a regiment, ten squadrons, and two companies of cavalry.[93] Increasingly, the militia assumed a more active role in the war. The Chilean government sometimes assigned mobilized guard formations to garrison Chile, particularly its southern frontier, or to occupy recently captured territory. In late 1880, for example, the Chilean minister of war stationed 6,600 men to guard Tacna, 1,500 to garrison Tarapacá and Antofagasta, 2,400 to protect the capital, Curicó, and San Felipe, and another 4,400 to defend the southern border against Indian raiders. Most of the guard, approximately 18,000 men—two thirds of the expeditionary army—serving in twenty-one militia battalions or regiments, stormed Lima in early 1881. And after the minister of war, José Francisco Vergara, demobilized sixteen of these contingents, seven remained in the army of occupation. Even in 1884 some 13,000 guardsmen remained on active duty, including some serving in Peru.[94] Chilean citizen soldiers, not the regular army, did much of the fighting in the War of the Pacific.

Theoretically, the Peruvian and Bolivian armies retained their prewar formations with each infantry battalion consisting of four companies. Curiously, neither of the Allied high commands managed to standardize their weaponry or their tables of organization: Peruvian units numbered between 80 to 100 men per company and the Bolivians, 120. In fact, the size and strength of units varied considerably. In 1880, for example, the Batallón Loa, contained 360 men who served in five companies while the Batallón Sucre consisted of six companies.[95] As a consequence, Allied infantry units were much smaller than their Chilean counterparts.

One Peruvian military historian claimed that Allied cavalry regiments contained two squadrons, but this statement appears to be incorrect. Bolivia's Regimiento de Caballería Bolívar, for example, consisted of four companies numbering eighty-six men. Its replacement, the Húsares del Rocha, created in 1880, numbered almost three hundred officers and men. The third, the Escuadrón Junín 3 de Coraceros, which used the same organizational table as the Regimiento 1 de Caballería, disappeared after the Battle of Campo de Alianza. While the Bolivians created another unit, the Escuadrón Libertad 4 de Coraceros, consisting of ninety-eight officers and men, it too vanished.[96] A lack of weapons limited the size of allied artillery units: Peruvian artillery units consisted of two or three batteries of eight guns apiece; Bolivia's gunners, who began the war with only four modern and ten to fifteen outmoded pieces or Gatling guns, expanded when their government acquired newer weapons.[97]

Although for different reasons, Bolivia, Peru, and Chile all came to rely heavily on their militias: the Allies because they needed replacements after their regular armies had disappeared into the maw of war and the Chileans because a long string of victories forced them to use their guard both to fight and to serve as occupation forces. Initially, the Allied high commands sent troops to the war zone in the south. Thanks to its naval victory at Angamos in October 1879, Chile enjoyed almost complete control of the sea-lanes. Hence the Prado administration dared not force transports carrying troops, and to a lesser extent its materiel, to run a Chilean naval gauntlet. Increasingly, the Peruvians turned to its supposedly sixty-five-thousand-man-strong national guard to defend their southern provinces. Fortunately for Peru, although a large portion of these troops were concentrated in the Lima-Callao area, substantial numbers of militia still operated in the Sierra and elsewhere.[98] The elements defending Los Angeles, as well as Piérola's Second Army of the South, which numbered close to three thousand men, consisted mainly of activated militia units.[99] To reinforce these components, the commanders of southern garrisons also created new contingents. Col. Alfonso Ugarte, for example, established and funded the Batallón Iquique, a unit that consisted of local workers. The port's stevedores joined the Columna Naval, while the city's elites, along with its police, formed the Columna de Honor.[100]

Given his army's small size, General Daza had to rely heavily upon its militia. When Bolivia's army took to the field in April 1879, it contained seventeen infantry battalions, of which fourteen were either mobilized guardsmen or newly created outfits. Keeping track of these units sometimes proved difficult. A few, like Batallón Victoria N. 1 or most of the

Bolivian cavalry units, fell in battle. Some were reincarnated—the Columna Loa, for example, which became the Batallón Loa, 3 de Linea,
replacing another unit bearing the same name that was annihilated in
the Battle of San Francisco. The Bolivians also rechristened some units:
los Colorados de Daza, for example, became the Batallón Alianza Num.
1 only to return to being the Colorados in mid-1880. Sometimes commanders reshuffled the various units, disbanding one, such as the Escuadrón Méndez, and distributing the men to other elements.[101] The
Daza regime disbanded a few formations because they had been founded
by the president's political enemies.[102] With more reason, insubordination or participation in the abortive March 1880 rebellion, commanded
by Colonels Silva and Guachalla, forced the government to disband the
Victoria Num. 2, Oruro, and Bustillo, which subsequently reappeared as
the Batallón Grau.[103]

The Chilean army suffered from similar problems: in September 1880
the Cazadores del Desierto, formed in 1879, apparently mutinied. The authorities disbanded the unit, sending its troops to other outfits.[104] Elements
such as the Escuadrón de Abaroa, Méndez, Albarracin, and Luribay existed
only for a short time.[105] The Peruvians also changed units' names or recast
them: the Batallón Ayacucho became the Pisagua; the Provisional de Lima
joined with the Guardia Civil de Iquique, emerging as the Tarapacá.[106]

By mid-1880 Bolivia's prewar army virtually ceased to exist; within
months the Peruvian forces suffered a similar fate. That Allied armies
suffered such high casualties demonstrates that these troops, despite being press-ganged, inadequately fed, and indifferently led, gave a disproportionately higher measure of devotion to their nations than they received. Ironically, no longer having to participate actively in the war, the
Bolivian government could completely restructure and reconstitute its
military.[107] The Peruvians, who wished to resist Chilean occupation, had
to rely on the few troops who survived the battles for Tarapacá, Tacna,
and Lima, plus those forces it recruited in the altiplano. Each Chilean
victory in the north increased the burden on its national guard: the army
employed its militia not simply to fight the war but also to provide occupation forces. Bolivia and Peru, however, used their guard to substitute
for the regular units the Chileans had destroyed in its conquest of the
Atacama, Tarapacá, and Tacna.

The Logistics of War

The belligerents' logistical organizations were more primitive than the tactics they employed on the battlefield. Bolivia's supply system was, in the words of Nataniel Aguirre, the minister of war, "so neglected in the last years . . . that it could be said not to exist."[108] The bureaucrat may have only slightly exaggerated. Prior to the onset of the conflict, the government had devised a process, albeit a wretched one: it simply forced local populations, particularly the Indians, to provide the army with transportation and food. Once the war began and the army expanded, La Paz adopted another technique, the *prest*; it paid each soldier a daily ration allowance: 1.60 Bolivano for commanders, 80 centavos for officers, and 40 centavos for the enlisted personnel.[109] Generally, the soldiers would turn over this stipend to their *rabonas*, "these famous inseparable companions of the Bolivian soldiers of other times; these extraordinary women, the genuine incarnation of all the virtues and all the vices." Cooks, mistresses, nurses, laundresses, porters, comrades, and fellow warriors, these women shared their soldier-lovers' load, even carrying their rifles on long marches and occasionally, as in the example of La Fiera Claros, fighting in battle. The rabonas of the Batallón Colorados had great affection for Daza, who had so cosseted the women that they too begged for rifles to defend his regime. In sum, as *La Patria* noted, the rabona performed for the soldier from the "most elevated jobs of an intendant of the army or a sutler to the most humble and indispensable tasks of domestic life."[110]

Besides rabonas, another class of women, the *vivanderas*, also accompanied the troops. These ladies worked as caterers, preparing food for those men who did not have rabonas. In May 1880, a few days prior to the Battle of Tacna, Bolivian vivanderas offered, for ten centavos a serving, a breakfast that included broth, roasted fish, eggs, or beef steak. Even the morning of May 26, the day of the Battle of El Campo de la Alianza or Tacna, Bolivian troops received an advance of eighty centavos, which they used to buy breakfast. Curiously, even the onset of shooting did not stop the vivanderas' activities. A *cochabambina* named Lorenza was hawking bread, cigarettes, and matches when a Chilean shell burst, covering her with dirt. Clearly a woman of probity as well as monumental calm, she nonchalantly rubbed her eyes and, turning to her clients, admonished them not to forget their change.[111]

Despite the rabonas' virtues, many Bolivians disdained the army's ad hoc supply system. *La Patria* of La Paz complained that the "Bolivian soldier easily forgets that he has to eat the following day, [and instead spends the money] in order to give himself the pleasure of a shot of *aguardiente* or to satisfy the whim of his rabona."[112] The minister of war shared this opinion, complaining about the "lamentable number" of rabonas. While he hoped to replace the rabona-based supply system with either a traditional army quartermaster or a bonded sutler, the minister recognized that "the special conditions of our land and the inveterate customs, which are difficult to uproot, are opposed to the adopting of a more rational system for provisioning and the service of food of an army."[113]

Bolivia's makeshift quartermaster system, unsteady in the best of times, collapsed during any crisis: a government failure to pay the men their *prest* allowances caused problems; in one case, the troops mutinied, resulting in the execution of eight men whose bodies the authorities left unburied as a graphic warning to other malcontents.[114]

Even when the authorities provided funds, they failed to adjust allowances to meet the demands of the market.[115] When units took to the road, it became quite difficult to obtain supplies, often because the authorities did not establish or stock caches of food.[116] During its wanderings, the Fifth Division, for example, ran out of bread, sugar, and rice, forcing the soldiers to subsist on one day's ration of half a pound of flour and meat every other day. Their mounts and pack animals suffered as well, in one case going days without forage. Desperately hungry troops, reduced to eating watercress and insect larva, sometimes slaughtered their mounts to survive. General Campero, commander of the Fifth Division—called the Israelites because they spent weeks wandering in the desert—lamented that he faced a terrible choice: "It is impossible to move forward . . . or remain here because there is not enough forage for the animals which serve the division."[117] To feed its men and their animals, the army borrowed or cadged money from civilians. On other occasions the military, through the use of force, commandeered supplies from towns in the guise of requisitions. Sometimes they did not even pretend: the Fifth Division simply demanded that the towns of Poopo, Cuancani, and Hurmiri feed them. Occasionally, civilians or private corporations contributed provisions, although it is likely they did so more to avoid looting or to limit their losses than as an act of charity. When these methods failed, some troops did sack civilian stores or homes to feed themselves and their animals.[118]

Problems developed even when provisions were available: although Col. Francisco Benavente pooled his unit's per diem allowance to acquire food, the sutlers sometimes distributed it uncooked to the troops. Miguel Birbuet, for example, complained that he and his comrades received a pound of raw llama, or alpaca meat, plus four ounces of rice, which they had to prepare. Only with the arrival of some Italians and Spaniards, who opened a small hotel, did the men have access to better food.[119] Predictably, some Peruvian merchants took advantage of the scarcities to gouge "Bolivian soldiers who were dead from hunger and thirst."[120]

The rabonas might have served as caterers or laundresses, but even they could not do everything: if the newly recruited troops expected the army to supply uniforms, they quickly learned otherwise. More than one soldier received a piece of cloth accompanied by orders that he had to sew the material into an article of clothing. Either the men did not possess the requisite skills or the locally manufactured products could not withstand the rigors of the field. Whatever the reason, army commanders incessantly carped that their men lacked uniforms, hats, cloaks, overcoats, blankets, or shoes. Doubtless to dramatize their plight, they even described their troops as nearly or completely naked.[121]

Peru also had rabonas. Manuel González Prada noted how these Indian women "faithfully followed them [their men] to the slaughterhouse" of Lima. When asked their motives, each replied that she had come "to kill a Chilean." A French naval officer, M. de León, noted the Peruvian rabona, like her Bolivian counterparts, improvised or substituted for the supply system: she prepared the camp, purchased food with her lover's ration allowance, and carried his children on her back. "They are true beasts of burden who endure with resignation their wretched fate. Their presence gives a strange aspect to the Peruvian armies, especially at meal time." Watching some rabonas laboring under the weight of children, clothing, cooking utensils, and firewood, an Italian tourist gallantly noted that these women provide "all the services of a good servant and a good mule."[122]

Some Peruvian rabonas actually fought. A woman, Dolores, accompanied her sergeant husband in the assault on San Francisco. When he fell, she is reputed to have picked up his weapons and shouted, "Cowards, climb faster; run as I do to avenge the sergeant." Dolores subsequently fought at Tarapacá but apparently perished as the troops retreated to Arica. Women even accompanied the irregular forces during the guerrilla campaigns of 1881 and 1882. Gen. Andrés Cáceres's wife, Antonia—who, with her children, had to flee to the mountains to escape Chilean reprisals—accompanied her husband during the extremely arduous Sierra campaign. Idolized by the Indians, she became known as Taita, Quechua for "mother," or Mama Grande, perhaps in part because she was pregnant.[123] Women also fought in the various battles in the altiplano: Valentina Melgar and Rosa Peréz battled and died as irregulars in the Battle of Chupaca; Joaquina Avila apparently led a guerrilla band at Sicaya. Other women—Paula Fiada, Maria Avila, and Candelaria Estada—also participated in the mountain encounters.[124]

Lima had an enormous advantage over its ally and certainly its adversary: since it was fighting on its home soil, its forces had fewer supply problems because they could work with existing provisioners like Gomez y Cía. This did not mean, however, that it did not encounter difficulties with its sutlers.[125] Like Bolivia, Peru had to requisition draft animals to move weapons and ammunition inland. Unfortunately, the animals' owners preferred to hide these beasts. Lima also had difficulties providing clothing. Segundo Leiva complained that only one battalion of the First Division, apparently the Batallón Huancané, had uniforms. "In the other units," he noted, the "nudity of the soldier is complete, only those troops who had belonged to the First Division kept their uniform; the rest wear the ill fitting clothes that they wore when they left the nation, and these are still in very bad condition." Additionally, the men lacked ammunition pouches and decent shoes. "The only thing they have is lots of weapons, but these are of so many different types, including miniés, that it causes numerous problems." It was precisely to avoid confusion when supplying units in combat that the Peruvians painted ammunition boxes different colors to match them.[126] Invariably, it became a question of priorities. Having spent funds producing cloaks, bandoliers, clothing, and shoes, nothing remained to purchase shirts.[127] Given these financial problems, the Peruvian government resorted to "forced loans" or, as in the case of a provincial official, José Jiménez, appealed to the women of Cuzco to contribute money. The situation became so bad that Col. Augustín Gamarra had to beg Piérola for six hundred soles to acquire a horse.[128]

Men also suffered from a lack of rations, a situation that worsened when local merchants used the excuse of scarcity to cheat troops, charging one sol for a cracker and ten for a pound of sugar. Desperate men in search of food often looted areas; others ate their pack animals and mounts. Later in the war, the Peruvian resistance forces took steps to purchase enough coca for its highland troops operating in Huanta and La Mar.

Chile's prewar army, like that of its opponents, did not include a unit to feed or clothe its troops. It too used the *prest* system of giving the men an allowance they could use to purchase provisions. Occasionally the troops received food that they had to prepare. Of the three belligerents it had the most difficulty provisioning its men, largely because of the distance separating the nation's heartland from the front. Initially, Santiago's army hired the services of civilian sutlers. The Pinto government quickly tired of the dishonest provisioners, who shamelessly "delivered rations consisting of worm-eaten beef jerky, old beans, and nitrate instead of salt, which caused illness."[129] Hence, in May 1879 the Moneda authorized the creation of a supply corps, the Intendencia General del Ejército y Armada en Campaña. Under the leadership of a civilian, Francisco Echaurren, this organization achieved a variety of objectives. It created two sets of rations: those for troops in garrisons and those for men in the field. Both included jerked meat, toasted flour, hardtack, garlic, and onions; those in a camp for more than one day received field rations plus beans, fat, and salt. Later the intendant changed the diet: men in garrison ate meat, potatoes, porridge or rice, fat, garlic, salt, hardtack or flour, toasted flour, onions, sugar, and coffee. Dry field rations consisted of beef jerky, beans, porridge or rice, hardtack, toasted flour, onions, fat, garlic, salt, sugar, and coffee.[130] The navy sometimes received the same rations as the army: bread, some vegetables, fat, as well as spices and coffee. As an alternative to beef jerky, the authorities delivered an ox to the crew of the *Cochrane*. Rather than slaughter the animal for meat, *La Patria* reported, the sailors made it their mascot, "El Negro, whom they kept tethered to the deck even during battles." The newspaper never explained who cleaned the deck.[131]

Thanks to the fleet and the merchant marine, the supply system functioned relatively well but only as long as the expeditionary force remained in Antofagasta. When Chile invaded Tarapacá, the army had to push inland, thus cutting the troops off from the sea and their lifeline to the south. To cure this problem, the Intendencia created and stocked a series of warehouses that supplied troops in the interior with food and ammunition. Providing the men and animals food and water was not an easy task, particularly during the initial campaigns, which were fought in the desert or the arid highlands.[132] Just feeding the approximately three thousand soldiers of the First Division for one day required 120 mules to carry twenty thousand liters of water, 50 to transport food, and 30 with forage. But the supply corps became increasingly proficient, eventually feeding its troops canned rations and even baking ten thousand pieces of bread in field ovens.

When the troops moved north, first to Tacna and then to Lima, the distance strained the capacity of the supply corps' transport and staff to fulfill their mission. To relieve the stress, the Moneda decided to revert to the sutler system in rear areas, such as Antofagasta and Iquique, where such businesses already existed. Ironically, Santiago hired the infamous Adolfo Carranza, the same Argentine provisioner who supplied flour, beef jerky, and corn to the Bolivian troops. The army initially purchased their meat from another Argentine, who may not have had such a conflict of interest. Apparently returning to the sutler system had men like Abel Rosales and his comrades complaining about being "tormented by the provisioner and his protectors."[133]

The two-year Sierra campaign, fought in the Andes far from the sea, complicated Chile's supply problems. The authorities tried to send provisions and clothing via the railroad, but the Peruvian irregulars would ambush and destroy the trains, while keeping items, such as boots, for themselves.[134] When the supply routes were open, the troops received "worm-eaten jerked beef" and hardtack with the consistency of concrete; when their supply lines were cut, troopers like the Second of the Line's Marcos Ibarra subsisted on coca tea and lard-flavored fried dough, potato stews, or noodles. The men ate llama meat most of the time and beef but four times per month. Not surprisingly, when given a pass, the soldiers foraged in the countryside, stealing the Indians' poultry and pigs. The situation reached such a point that Private Ibarra, his shoes disintegrating, took a dead soldier's boots. Just before returning to Lima, however, the men received new shirts and underwear as well as orders to shave: their commander did not want his men to enter Lima looking disreputable.[135]

Even at its most efficient, the supply corps could not sate the troops' need for female companionship. Happily, the soldiers had their own solution: hordes of compliant ladies accompanied Chilean troops into the field. It would be churlish, as well as incorrect, to characterize as prostitutes all those women who followed their men; many, perhaps even a majority, were the soldiers' common-law wives. Additionally Chile's legions did not have to import harlots because, as the troop commanders complained, so many local prostitutes infested the recently captured towns that they constituted "a plague in all senses of the word." One of these demimondes, a teenage Chilean, became famous for being the mistress of the Peruvian general Juan Buendía. Regardless of their nationality, these ladies quickly passed on to Chilean troops what Arturo Benavides Santos's mother had called "shameful infections." Indeed, within two months of the onset of the war, the minister of war complained about the "lamentable" manner in which venereal disease had spread through the expeditionary force. Roberto Souper, an officer serving in the north, complained that sixty "damned whores are infecting the soldiers, including the officers for good measure." The Chilean army would quickly discover that they could vanquish the Allied hosts but not syphilis or gonorrhea.[136]

Because physicians lacked the skills to cure these infections, all the authorities could do was emulate Benavides Santos's regimental surgeon: caution the soldiers about these ailments and, more significantly, tell them how to avoid them. To limit the spread of the infection, the minister of war suggested that the authorities perform weekly medical inspections on all prostitutes, either isolating the infected until they were cured or expelling them from the war zone. Realizing that the troops might carry the disease from Chile to the north, he also suggested that the army screen the recruits, prohibiting the infected from traveling to the front.[137] These warnings failed. Of the 199 Chilean troops with illnesses during the last two weeks of December 1879, 56 percent suffered from venereal diseases.[138] Although the authorities tried to enforce the health regulations—Dr. Guillermo Castro, for example, received an order stating that no single woman could remain in camp unless she possessed a certificate of good health—they failed. In the last three months of 1882, 120 men of the Batallón Talca contracted venereal disease while garrisoning the port of Callao.[139]

Whatever their status, women became so ubiquitous among the troops that a scandalized chaplain tried to expel them from the barracks as well as prohibit them from bathing with the men. The administration even attempted to stop ladies from accompanying their husbands or lovers, but these efforts, like those attempting to limit venereal disease, more often than not failed. Women often donned uniforms to slip aboard troop transports. Authorities discovered twenty females accompanying the troops sailing on the *Copiapó*, while Concepción's *Revista del Sur* complained that when a local national guard left for the north, the city lost eight to nine hundred people, including various women. Exasperated authorities ordered a military court to try one of the stowaways, a punishment that at least one newspaper considered inappropriately harsh. Since Chileans apparently made friendships with various Peruvian women, any effort to stop the flow of women north would fail.[140]

It seems that the army eventually came to accept, however grudgingly, some female presence. The camp followers and their families accompanied Chile's legions' march on Lima, although their presence sometimes caused disturbances. Chilean women even remained with their men during the singularly harsh Sierra campaign. In one case, a sergeant's pregnant wife began to experience contractions during a prolonged trek through the Andes. The troops continued to lead her horse until she alighted, lay down on a bed of blankets, delivered her child, and then remounted her horse to continue the journey.[141]

Some Chilean women actively participated in the war. Dolores Rodríguez fought at her husband's side at Tarapacá, where she suffered some wounds while apparently inflicting not a few on the enemy. She would later admit that she missed the hurly-burly of combat. "It is so pleasant to help a wounded man," she noted, "to give a glass of water or brandy to a tired companion, above all, to fire a rifle from time to time and to kill a *cholo*." Apparently slaying Allied soldiers did not faze Doña Dolores, nor did the prospect of her own death. "I have the consolation," she noted, "that I have already sent ahead some *cholos* so that they can prepare the road to the other life for me."[142]

In addition to the sometimes unappreciated soldier's wife or lover, the Chilean army created a special niche for the *cantineras*. Unlike the rabonas, cantineras were granted an official status by the government and assigned to a specific unit. The integration of these women did not come easily. Some questioned the policy of allowing cantineras but prohibiting wives from joining their men. Initially, the Chilean authorities, such as the physician Wenceslao Díaz as well as Francisco Echaurren, opposed the cantineras, fearing that they might slow the pace of a march, consume additional rations, and precipitate fights between men seeking their favor. But eventually, the authorities accepted their presence, assigning two ladies "of acknowledged morality" to each regiment. Even individual commanders, such as the commander of the Second of the Line, who had earlier expelled most of the women, permitted ladies of "recognized wisdom and good customs" to remain as nurses.[143]

Generally the cantineras served as battlefield medics. María Ramírez, for example, brought water to the wounded. When the men were too weak to drink, she filled her mouth with water before squirting it directly from her mouth to theirs. But Ramírez, as well as other cantineras such as Cármen Vilches, sometimes would seize a weapon from a wounded soldier to join the battle. Others shouted encouragement: "Forward boys!" screamed the cantinera of the Regimiento Coquimbo, "Be brave, and God will help you." Although officially noncombatants, the cantineras nonetheless suffered the same fate as their comrades. Three cantineras, for example, perished alongside the men at the disastrous Battle of Tarapacá; others died at La Concepción. Juana López enlisted in a mobilized Valparaíso guard unit while her husband and three sons joined others. Though she managed to survive all of the war's battles, her family did not: all perished. She retired from the war with a handful of medals, an Allied army officer's sword—which she carried in a victory parade in Lima—and a baby.[144] Not surprisingly, cantineras enjoyed such prestige that Victor Torres Arce wrote *The Cantinera of the Second of the Line*, a novel that described one of the women who died at Tarapacá. The press also praised the cantineras' patriotism, although the departure of so many women left Lota, a coal mining center in the south, with a short-age of housemaids. After 1881, with a reduction in the size of the army, the need to recruit cantineras diminished. Later white slavers trying to entice women into the brothels of Valparaíso preyed upon Lota's female population.[145]

In addition to food and clothing, the belligerents' armies also needed to acquire small arms, artillery, and ammunition to make up for losses sustained in battle and to equip new recruits. Peru tended to purchase weapons from American manufacturers who devised a variety of ruses to avoid American neutrality laws. Charles Flint, who had served as Pe-ru's consul and financial agent in New York, dispatched ten Pratt Whit-ney torpedoes, wrapped in oilcloth, as well as torpedo boats, which he shipped, dismantled, in boxes marked as carriages.[146] The Grace Broth-ers, another U.S. supplier of Peru's needs, sent five Gatling guns, fifty thousand rifles, almost one million bullets, including some in barrels marked "lard," as well as ten Lay torpedoes.[147]

The trade routes from Europe or the United States to Lima were com-plicated and hence more subject to interruption than shipping materiel to Chile. Placed on vessels bound for Panama, the contraband had to be off-loaded and then shipped across the Isthmus of Panama, via train, to Bilbao, where it was placed on ships for the voyage to Callao. Clearly the Colombian authorities could have embargoed the arms traffic but often did not do so thanks to the efforts of Peru's agents who also greased the palms of local officials, railroad employees, as well as newspaper own-ers publishing pro-Peruvian propaganda. Colombian political instability, however, often produced abrupt changes in its neutrality policy, causing the Peruvians no end of heartache and the payment of additional bribes. In 1880 Panamanian authorities forbade this traffic, although they sub-sequently changed their policy.

Connivance on the part of Panamanians did not always work. On more than one occasion, crates splintered, spewing out their contents. When this occurred, or when they believed Chilean representatives tried to prevent the Peruvians from transferring their weapons, Peruvian agents arranged for weapons to be loaded on coastal ships and then transferred, on the high seas, to other vessels that made the trip to Callao. In order to avoid being duped, which happened more than once, Lima's agents demanded the right to examine the military weapons before sending them south. To prevent the Chileans from discovering what they were doing, Peruvian agents had to enter the bonded warehouses at night to complete the inspections.[148]

Even after the destruction of Peru's navy, foreign flag transports occasionally managed to off-load military supplies in one of Peru's numerous unguarded ports. The Chilean blockade of Peru's major ports made it so difficult to import items that the Peruvian authorities offered their citizens a bounty for surrendering any Peabody, Remington, or Comblain rifle, a horse, or one hundred rounds of ammunition. Those who refused to sell their weapons or ammunition to the authorities would be fined two hundred soles and spend six months in jail. In order to encourage compliance, the government offered a hundred soles to any informer. These problems became more acute following the capture of Lima. Gen. Andrés Cáceres, who led resistance to Chile, promised a reward—apparently payable in interest bearing promissory notes—to anyone who delivered their firearms to the authorities.[149]

Chile, like its foes, encountered problems purchasing weapons, ammunition, and war materiel from foreign manufacturers. Great Britain, for example, refused to allow Chile to take delivery of military or naval supplies on English soil. Peruvian diplomats also tried to stop these shipments. Sometimes they failed when, for example, English trade officials argued that they could not differentiate between an unarmed torpedo boat and a civilian launch. Normally, Santiago's envoys had to send what the English considered contraband of war first to the European mainland, generally to Belgium or Germany, where it could be transshipped to Chile. American officials proved almost as hidebound as their British counterparts. Pinto's minister to the United States sometimes had to send weapons to England and from there to Germany.

Chile, unlike Peru, normally did not have as many problems transporting the arms shipments that reached Valparaíso via the Strait of Magellan. Although once, in winter of 1879, the Peruvians unsuccessfully attempted to intercept a weapons shipment, Peru's agents also tried, again without success to convince Platine diplomats to prohibit boats carrying armaments to Chile from stopping in Argentine or Uruguayan ports. Peruvian authorities even suggested that some agents, operating under a Bolivia's letter of marque, try to capture the vessels.

As the Chileans' army expanded, so did the military's appetite for small arms, artillery as well as ammunition. Since the Belgian manufacturers of the Comblain II could not satisfy the Moneda's hunger for weapons or cartridges, Chilean authorities had to find substitutes. Naturally, the variety of different rifles carried by the troops greatly complicated the supply process. Eventually the Chilean authorities bought Chassepot, Peabody, Gras, or Beaumont rifles that they rechambered to accept the same size cartridge as the Comblain. Sometimes this compromise worked, but just as often it did not. In 1880 Santiago acquired another sixteen thousand Gras rifles that had been modified to accept the Comblain bullet. At the same time, a diplomat, Alberto Blest Gana, purchased some twenty-four million cartridges, fifteen million of which were packed with powder.

Acquiring ammunition constituted but one obstacle; finding a transport company, such as the Kosmos Line, to carry these bullets or shells proved quite difficult. The fear of a shipboard fire on an ammunition ship would make the bravest sailor or greedy ship owner hesitate. Curiously, sailing vessels, perhaps because they were less valuable, were willing to carry ammunition, but these voyages took three months to reach Chile.[150] Ultimately one steamship company agreed to transport this dangerous cargo, but only if the Chileans paid four thousand British pounds for insurance. When the war erupted, the insurance costs rose. To minimize the expenses, some shipping companies suggested sending the cartridge casings, the bullets, and the gunpowder separately. In the end, most of the arms shipments arrived safely, but one vessel, the *Alwick-Castle*, did blow up, apparently the victim of combustible coal dust, not overheated ammunition. Happily for the crew and the nearby residents, the vessel did not carry gunpowder.[151]

Of the three nations, Bolivia seemed the most tortured by logistical problems. Weapons generally could reach La Paz only after passing first through an Argentine port, generally Buenos Aires or Rosario, before making the long trip across the pampas. Normally, La Paz had to hire the services of an agent, often the infamous Adolfo Carranza, to act as a middle man. In August 1879, despite unrest in Argentina, which disrupted travel, and despite Chilean attempts to stop it, a shipment of three thousand rifles reached Bolivia. But Carranza was not dependable. Daza, no stranger to deceit, denounced the Argentine arms merchant as "a speculator and guilty of bad faith," in part because he sometimes sold the Bolivians faulty ammunition. Daza's claims did not lack merit: Narciso Campero complained that of forty-four thousand bullets the Argentine supplied, forty-two thousand jammed the rifles. Carranza had his own set of grievances: he refused to deliver materiel to the Fifth Division until Daza paid him. Believing that Carranza was cheating them, the Bolivians rejected his demands, confident that its troops could survive without the Argentine's assistance.[152] They could not.

Rather than wait for arms shipments, the belligerents tried to manufacture their own weapons and ammunition. Bolivia, for example, established a foundry in Cochabamba as well as a saddle factory in Oruro; its mint fabricated bullets. Peru's *maestranza* could and did make shells for its artillery. Lima also had a powder factory, which produced higher quality explosives less expensively than imports and operated at a profit. In Chile, various foundries produced weapons, cannons, or repaired firearms. But Aurelio Arriagada complained about the lack of a facility to manufacture powder and another to produce bullets. Such a plant, he noted, would allow Santiago to acquire ammunition for less than imported items and would guarantee that the state would have these items in time of war.[153] In fact the army's workshops did manage to produce small arms ammunition, sometimes using spent cartridges. But they did not obtain a machine to turn out cartridge cases until 1882.[154]

None of the competing armies created transportation or signal units. In fact, Bolivia began the war without a domestic telegraph or rail system—losing its few miles of track when the Chileans conquered the Atacama. Although Peru and Chile relied upon the railroad to prosecute the war, these did not play as important a role as they did in North America or western Europe. In part, this occurred because neither the Chileans nor the Peruvians possessed as an extensive rail systems as did Prussia,

France, or the United States. In Chile's case, the state-owned railroad system, which covered about 1,000 miles, transported men and supplies from its Central Valley to Santiago and then to Valparaíso, the port of embarkation for the north. About 674 miles of privately owned railroads existed in Chile's north, but these lines generally transported ore from nearby mines to nearby ports for export. Peru's rail system consisted mainly of approximately 1,000 miles of government-owned track. One of the nation's more important lines ran 87 miles from the seaport of Callao to the capital and then into the Andean foothills; another line connected Arequipa and the Puno region with Mollendo, a port 400 miles south of Lima. Like Chile, Peru had a series of regional rail lines linking agricultural or mining centers with nearby ports.[155]

Neither side tried to incorporate the railroads into the military by creating special units to direct the transportation network. In part this may have reflected a lack of technical personnel. By 1870, for example, the Universidad de Chile had graduated but one civil engineer.[156] Perhaps the tradition of respecting property proved too ingrained. When Chile's military needed to move troops outside of Chile, it did not requisition the enemy's rail system but chartered them.[157] Chileans, led by the European-trained engineer Federico Stuven, also used Peruvian railroads, when they had the good fortune to capture them intact, to move supplies into Tarapacá, to shift troops from Tacna to Arica, and to transport men and materiel from the coast to the altiplano during the war's final phase. But even when Chile's Adm. Patricio Lynch was the de facto viceroy of occupied Peru, he still paid the freight bill, albeit at a 50 percent discount, to the owners of the Callao to Lima rail spur, the Ferrocarril Inglés, and the Central Transandino to send men and materiel on their trains.[158]

Both Chile and Peru also had access to a telegraph system, with Chile's being the largest, consisting of about thirty-five hundred miles of wire. Again, neither belligerent created a signal corps to operate the telegraph system.[159] Instead they patronized the civilian-owned communications companies as they did the railways. Thanks to the bankruptcy of the Compañía Nacional Telegráfica in 1875, the Peruvian government became owner of the nation's domestic telegraph system. Only in December 1880 did the government appoint Carlos Paz Soldán, who had been the *director general de telégrafos civiles* to head the telegraphic section of the general staff.[160] Following the capture of Lima, Chileans turned to the telegraph service much as it patronized the rail lines. Santiago even continued to employ Peruvian telegraphers, who, of course, compromised the system's security. Bolivia, as noted earlier, had no telegraphs operating inside the country.

Medical Service

Given the delay in creating a supply system, it should come as no surprise that the competing armies also initially failed to establish a medical corps. Although the tables of organization of Bolivia and Peru included berths for surgeons as well as a surgeon general, these armies did not possess medical units when the war began.[161] In May 1879, however, Prado's administration managed to field an ambulance unit that helped the *Independencia*'s wounded; it would also attend to the wounded of the Battle of San Francisco. Not until 1881, however, did the Peruvian army try to promulgate various regulations governing its medical service.[162] The Bolivian government also published regulations creating a medical service in June 1879, although it was not until December 1879, after having learned that their injured "were left abandoned on the battlefield [of San Francisco] dependent upon the charity of the victor," that Bolivians formally organized the Cuerpo de Ambulancias. The first medical unit, consisting of three ambulance companies and staffed by civilian physicians, arrived in time to participate in the Battle of Tacna in May 1880.[163] The Peruvians enjoyed some of the same advantage in providing medical care as it did supplying its men: since almost the entire war occurred within its territory, the government could utilize existing civilian medical personnel and hospital facilities to render help to the motherland's wounded and ill.

The Chileans did not enjoy this luxury. When their troops occupied Antofagasta, for example, the local civilian hospital demanded that Chile pay for the care provided to its military men.[164] In truth, Chile's army contained no physicians until after the onset of the war. Those soldiers who had the bad luck to fall ill sought care from a civilian physician, a charity hospital, or a sympathetic comrade. Perhaps because this jerry-built system seemed to function well on the Indian frontier, the army neglected to include a physician or ambulances when its forces invaded the Bolivian littoral. Only in early May 1879, when scores of his five-thousand-man expeditionary force began to fall prey to a variety of ailments, did General Arteaga ask the minister of war to send medical instruments, drugs, and the doctors to use them. The request pushed the government into creating a medical service corps, whose command it eventually entrusted to the leadership of Dr. Ramón Allende Padín.

The combatants' medical services, like their supply services, were a mixture of state involvement and private enterprise.[165] Chile's medical units, for example, which came under the authority of the Intendencia General del Ejército y Armada en Campaña, were staffed by civilian physicians. Private and public philanthropy provided the ambulances, instruments, and drugs. Bolivia, like Chile, depended to some extent on public charity and civilian doctors to give care.[166] This reliance upon donations persisted throughout the war: the Bolivian representatives had to seek funds from Archbishop Juan de Dios Bosque to pay for the repatriation of its wounded. Unfortunately the cleric's donation of two thousand dollars did not suffice. In one case, Chile's General Baquedano had to arrange passage.[167] Even the Peruvian medics had to borrow money after the Battle of Dolores or San Francisco, to defray the costs of caring for the wounded.[168] Regardless of its deficiencies, some Chileans considered that Bolivia's medical service, as well as Peru's, functioned better than that of Chile.[169]

Happily for the wounded, the three warring nations adhered to the Geneva Conventions. And to their credit, the belligerents' medical units often cared for the enemy wounded as well as their own. This generosity of spirit proved quite lucky for Chile: in November 1879 Gen. Erasmo Escala neglected to include ambulances or physicians in the expedition that invaded Tarapacá, thus forcing his men to seek help from their foes. In fairness, Escala returned the favor, lending the Peruvian medics some blankets and stretchers and also caring for the wounded until his staff could arrange to evacuate them via the Red Cross.[170]

Despite the best of intentions, disputes erupted: the Peruvians accused Chileans of firing on their corpsmen as they retrieved the wounded from the field and of stealing supplies from their ambulances.[171] Bolivians complained that the Chileans treated their medics as ordinary prisoners of war rather than as noncombatants. The Chileans, however, agreed to repatriate these men as soon as possible.[172] As we shall see, the Chileans acted more brutally during the battle of Tacna, stealing medical supplies and even water as well as ruining equipment.[173] Apparently Peru lost many of its medical units while defending the south, forcing the government to ask civilians to create additional medical companies and to establish a hospital in a hall leftover from a public exposition.[174]

Atrocities

Sadly, an almost febrile brutality came to characterize the War of the Pacific. An American, noting the disproportionately large number of battlefield deaths among the Peruvian troops—six hundred at the battle of Huamachuca alone—concluded that most had died *after* surrendering or sustaining a wound. He was not alone in making this assertion. Another anonymous American observed, "Most of these battles were sanguinary, and all of them were horribly brutal. In the figures of loss it is common to find the *number of the killed equaling the number of the wounded*, a fact which proves that cold-blooded butchery was practiced upon the wounded on the battle-field. The proportion of killed to wounded in our battle of Gettysburg was less than one to five" (italics in original).[175] The admittedly pro-Peruvian Clements Markman reported that Chileans gave no quarter, bashing in their foes' skulls or, in some cases, throwing them off the side of a mountain.[176] Markman agreed with the American critic, noting that the Peruvians lost seven hundred dead at the battle of Arica and only one hundred wounded.

Many Chileans carried a *corvo*, a knife peculiar to them. Apparently Chilean troops employed these deadly weapons to cut the throats of the captured and the wounded as well as to disfigure the dead. In one case a Chilean soldier supposedly entered a Peruvian aid station, where, after stating that "today not even one *cholo* will be left alive," he beheaded the enemy wounded. Some foreign witnesses reported that 90 percent of the Allied dead were found with their throats cut. The "Chilianos [*sic*] took no prisoners, except when a whole army capitulated. The knowledge of this characteristic, and the fear of the Chiliano [*sic*] knife, was a powerful factor in the subjugation of the more humane Peruvians," behavior which inspired the Argentine D. E. Uriburu to describe Chileans as "cannibals" and a Peruvian contemporary to compare their behavior to the savagery of the Spanish conquest. Apparently some Chileans took pride that they employed the corvo to "take revenge without mercy or pity." Curiously, according to a supposedly neutral observer, Chilean soldiers did not hesitate to turn these weapons against their compatriots when disputing the ownership of looted property.[177] No matter how terrible, some might argue that perishing from a slashed throat was perhaps a more humane death than being slowly devoured by a gangrenous wound.

Both sides charged the other with using explosive bullets. A Chilean medic as well as an officer with the unlikely name of Moltke submitted evidence indicating that Peruvians used explosive bullets, a charge subsequently repeated.[178] But rather than explosive charges, it is more likely that the bullets' high velocity caused the damage.

The Allies also committed atrocities. Highland Indians proudly told the wife of General Cáceres that they liked cutting off the heads of Chilean soldiers and using them to decorate the entrance to their villages. Peruvians, of course, argued that such conduct was justified, that it was the Chilean habit of raping Indian women during the war of the Sierra that inspired Indians to mutilate sexually the Chilean wounded and dead. These acts of savagery in turn led to the Chileans hanging dead *montoneros* from telegraph poles. This cycle of violence seemed to deepen, particularly during the guerrilla battles of 1881 and 1882.[179]

Crime and Punishment

The belligerents all seemed to favor the same methods to keep their troops in line: the lash and, for more extreme violations, execution. While draconian, these penalties possessed a certain logic. The Chilean army did not possess a stockade to house the recalcitrant, and the commanders would not wish to send troublesome soldiers back to their homeland. Thus, corporal punishment or the firing squad represented the only alternatives.[180]

Not surprisingly, in the warring parties the punishment varied with the nation, the commanding officer, and the offense. When one Bolivian soldier, whether intentionally or not, fired at his commander, Col. Castro Pinto, the authorities ordered him flogged two hundred times. Bolivia's Gen. Narciso Campero was particularly bloodthirsty. In one case, he sentenced troublemakers or deserters to five hundred lashes. When the whip did not inspire enough fear, Campero ordered the execution of any deserter, including Francisco Álvarez, who did not simply run away but did so while on guard duty.

Desertion plagued all the armies. In August 1879 the authorities discovered two Bolivian soldiers missing after a pass in review. A lieutenant sent to capture these men stopped anyone who looked Bolivian and who spoke only Quechua. Finding a man who met these criteria, the officer forced him to enlist, then ordered him beaten before sending him to the barracks.[181] President Piérola ordered two men executed for killing an officer and fomenting a mutiny but sentenced their accomplices to only twenty lashes. Ironically, the Peruvian ordered the whipping of some of his fellow countrymen when they threatened to harm some Chilean POWs.

Drunken Chilean soldiers normally received twenty-five lashes, thieves fifty, and anyone striking a noncommissioned officer one hundred. Alberto del Solar saw one soldier endure fifty strokes. His screams might not have fazed the noncommissioned officer wielding the whip, but del Solar confessed that he would have preferred to resign his commission rather than witness another similar beating. He subsequently changed this opinion, ordering the ringleader of a riot protesting poor food to be lashed fifty times. When the troublemaker, one Francisco Canchú, rashly observed that the punishment would not alter his behavior, del Solar ordered another fifty. Unfortunately for Canchú, the regiment's colonel arrived and called for yet another fifty, promising to shoot the next barrack room agitator. Apparently harsh punishments were quite common. An English officer was appalled to see delinquent Chilean troops receive up to two hundred lashes on their bare buttocks. The Chileans also punished Francisco León with two hundred lashes; when finished he was given a shot of *pisco*. Curiously Estanislao del Canto, who once ordered his men to show no quarter to captured Peruvians, opposed the lash, claiming only animals should be beaten. After seeing one man's back wet with blood and his buttocks in "covered in wounds," the journalist-soldier Justo Rosales agreed with this judgment.[182]

While generous with the whip, the belligerents only infrequently applied the death penalty. The Chilean authorities sentenced José Romero to death for insubordination. He was standing on the edge of a cemetery, surrounded by the men from the Regimiento de Artillería, the Melipilla, and the Aconcagua, waiting to be shot when he learned that the government reduced his sentence to six years in jail. The news delighted his comrades, who demonstrated their approval by rattling their bayonets in their scabbards.[183]

Such generosity did not characterize the Chilean occupation of Peru: the Chilean authorities executed three civilians for each Chilean soldier the Peruvian resistance might have killed. The word of a single eyewitness was enough for the authorities to sentence to death anyone convicted of murdering a Chilean soldier. To force a Peruvian to denounce *franc-tireurs* or *montoneros*, Chilean commanders ordered the man to be lashed between two and five hundred times. If the guilty party did not come forward, his captors would execute the hapless spectator.[184] Obviously such cavalier punishments did not endear the Chileans to their temporary hosts. This behavior, however, would characterize the war for the duration.

Often commanded by officers of limited aptitude, composed of largely press-ganged troops, and equipped with a variety of outmoded arms, the vying armies appeared largely unprepared for a war. Lack of a military infrastructure—a quartermaster, medical, signal, and transportation corps—seriously hobbled their capacity to fight. Indeed, the War of the Pacific quickly became a logistical and medical nightmare in which the belligerents had to do battle with each other while simultaneously improvising solutions to solve their technical problems. Lacking the expertise, the warring nations had to turn to the civilian sector for financial support and technical assistance, particularly in the case of skilled health providers and equipment.

As we shall see, the Allies and Chile not only declared war for different reasons but they also pursued different objectives. Furious at what they perceived as Bolivian duplicity, the Chileans occupied the Atacama. And in order to insulate this newly seized territory from future Allied aggression, Chile needed to drive President Prado's army from his nation's southernmost province, Tarapacá. Bolivia, of course, longed to retake its seacoast, while Peru hoped to ensure its own territorial integrity by maintaining a buffer zone between it and its warlike neighbor. Achieving these contrasting goals shaped each belligerent's behavior: to win, Chile had to mount an expedition to capture Peru's land. These campaigns would test the mettle of the belligerents' armies, which, although manned by soldiers with little understanding of notions such as the nation-state, performed heroically on the fields of battle. But before these competing armies would meet, Chile's fleet first had to sweep the Peruvians from the sea.

3. Comparing the Navies

Evaluating the relative strengths of the belligerents' fleets just prior to the outbreak of the War of the Pacific is a vexing task. Chilean and Peruvian historians, for example, traditionally pronounced their nations' ships as barely seaworthy and belittled their crews' professional skills, while exaggerating their opponents' prowess. This rite of self-effacement had a clear purpose: by depreciating their prewar flotillas, and those who served in them, the writers could rationalize their nations' defeats while elevating their victories to the level of the miraculous.[1] Real problems did exist. But although budgetary problems forced the Chilean government to reduce naval expenditures, it was the questionable judgment and misguided priorities of Juan Williams Rebolledo, the Chilean navy's commander, not material deficiencies, that limited his flotilla's performance. Conversely, the skill and dedication of Adm. Miguel Grau, the commander of the Peruvian fleet, allowed his nation's fleet to compensate for the loss of some its equipment and hold back the Chilean armada for the first six months of the war.

Learning the Lessons of Sea Power

Chile's navy first took to the seas in 1818, when an embryonic fleet, under the command of the Scotsman Lord Thomas Cochrane, sailed north from Valparaíso to liberate Peru and Bolivia from Spanish rule. Some of the British naval officers who served in Cochrane's armada remained in Chile's fleet, thus explaining the presence of so many sailors with English surnames: John Williams, Santiago Bynon, Roberto Forster, Roberto Henson, Guillermo Wilkinson, Robert Simpson, Jorge O'Brien, Raimundo Morris (a few Americans, such as Charles Wooster, also served in Chile's navy). Some, like Robert Simpson and Juan Williams Wilson, even sired a second generation of Chilean naval officers, including three who rose to the rank of admiral.[2]

Recognizing the vulnerability of the nation's economy and its coastal population to a seaborne attack, Chile's leaders early realized the need for a strong fleet. The government used this navy to vanquish the Peruvian-Bolivian Confederation in 1836. Domestically, the fleet helped suppress the abortive 1851 and 1859 revolutions. But after 1860, perhaps lulled by the lack of foreign and local enemies, Chile neglected its navy. The error of this policy became painfully apparent in the mid-1860s, when Chile and Spain went to war and a Spanish naval squadron subjected Valparaíso to a three-hour bombardment that inflicted fourteen million pesos in damage to the port. This Spanish incursion taught the Moneda that it needed a strong navy, especially since Peru's fleet, reinforced by some recently purchased ironclads, now dwarfed that of Chile. In furtherance of this policy, Santiago bought two British-built corvettes, the *Chacabuco* and the *O'Higgins*, in 1866 and 1867. Two years after Peru responded by acquiring the *Oneota* and the *Catawba*, surplus U.S. riverine monitors, the Chilean government ordered two oceangoing ironclads from British shipyards. It also obtained two additional wooden corvettes, the *Magallanes* and the *Abtao*, as well as a transport.

Anxious to achieve naval parity with Chile, the Peruvians wanted to buy more armored ships. Its legislature even allocated approximately four million soles for their purchase. The onset of a worldwide economic recession in the mid-1870s forced Lima to abandon its naval expansion program. Infected by the same economic malaise, Chilean officials became so desperate that they even considered selling the fleet's ironclads for four million British pounds. Fortunately for the Chileans, their government could find no takers. Consequently, until onset of the War of the Pacific, the composition of the Peruvian and Chilean navies remained relatively stable.[3]

The Belligerents' Ships of the Line

Chile

Chile's newest, and clearly most powerful, warships were its British-built central battery ironclads: the *Almirante Cochrane* and the *Almirante Blanco*

Encalada. Two compound, horizontal trunk engines and double screw propellers powered the sister ships—designed by England's premier naval architect, Sir Edward Reed—at a speed of almost thirteen knots per hour. In addition to the coal-fired engines, the ironclads carried three masts whose bark-rigged sails could either increase their speed or provide an alternative if the ship began to run out of coal.

Belts of ebony or teak sandwiched between armor plates reinforced the ships' iron hulls: a center strip nine inches thick running between two more, each six inches thick, formed a girdle protecting the ironclads at their waterline. These panels of armor narrowed to about four and one half inches thick at the vessels' stern and bow. Three inches of armor, which also thinned out to two inches at the bow and the stern, reinforced the upper deck near the gun casements. Two strakes of armor, one eight inches and the other six inches thick, tapering off to four and half inches toward the aft end, protected each gun battery.

Chile's ironclads carried six nine-inch, muzzle-loading, electrically fired, rifled Armstrong guns (MLRs). Two of these cannon were mounted on either side of the ship's forward sections; the remaining four amidships, two to each side, were housed in sponsons, barbettes that bulged out from the hulls like a fat man's belly protruding over his belt. While the vessels appeared somewhat ungainly, the location of the six guns provided the warships almost overlapping fields of fire.[4] The ironclads mounted three additional cannon firing twenty-pound, nine-pound, and seven-pound shells. Both vessels carried Nordenfelt machine guns, on either side of the bridge in the *Blanco Encalada* and forward in the *Cochrane.*[5] Typical of the time, each ship's crew included twelve marines who, during a battle, would take up firing positions in the tops of masts in order to snipe at the enemy sailors below. To complement naval cannon, both ironclads possessed a submerged armored ram that presumably could eviscerate an enemy warship by tearing an enormous hole beneath the waterline. They also mounted spar torpedoes, although these did not play a significant role in the early stages of the war.

The Chilean navy also included four wooden corvettes, two of which were the sister ships the *O'Higgins* and the *Chacabuco.* Powered by a combination of sail and steam engines, these vessels could make between eight and ten knots per hour. The corvettes mounted three seven-ton

Armstrong muzzle-loading rifled carriage guns. Located in their broad-sides stood two 70-pounder and four 40-pounder Armstrong MLRs.[6] The third corvette, the *Abtao*, also English-built and the sister ship of the former Confederate raider the *Alabama*, used a combination of sail and steam engines for propulsion. Slower than the *Chacabuco* and *O'Higgins*, the *Abtao* cruised at between five and six knots per hour, mounting six Armstrong MLRs: three 150-pounders on pivot carriages and three 30-pounders, two mounted broadside and one on a pivot carriage.[7] The newest corvette, the bark-rigged *Magallanes*, was one of the navy's fastest ships, capable of reaching about eleven knots per hour, and carried three cannon, all Armstrong MLRs—a seven-inch (115-pound) weapon, a 64-pounder, and a 20-pounder—each resting on a pivot carriage.

Two more warships rounded out Chile's prewar fleet: the sloop *Esmeralda* was the squadron's oldest, built in 1854; the slowest, capable of steaming at only three knots per hour; and perhaps the most lightly armed, with twelve to fourteen forty-pound muzzle-loading Armstrong rifles. The *Covadonga*, a schooner captured by the Chileans in the war with Spain, appeared only marginally better than the *Esmeralda*. The three-masted ship, launched in 1858, cruised at five knots and carried two seventy-pound muzzle-loading Armstrong rifles. In truth not only was neither ship seaworthy, both the *Covadonga* and the *Esmeralda* were disarmed hulks, riding on fouled bottoms in Valparaíso's harbor.[8]

Once the war erupted, the Chileans tried to acquire some additional warships, but foreign neutrality laws often made this difficult. When it could not obtain weapons, the Aníbal Pinto government improvised: Chile purchased the *Angamos*, originally the *Belle of Cork*, a British-built fast transport, on which the navy mounted an eight-inch Armstrong cannon. Chile also bought the *Loa* from the Compañía Sudamericana de Vapores, converting it into a fast, albeit unarmored, cruiser by installing a seventy-pound cannon, as well as four smaller ones.[9] Later in the war, Chile acquired eleven torpedo boats. In addition to its warships, the Chilean navy owned two relatively fast transports, the *Toltén*, a side-wheeler, and the *Amazonas*. The navy subsequently mounted a seven-inch cannon on the *Amazonas*, transforming it into an armed merchantman; it also lightly armed the *Toltén*. In case of emergency, the Chilean government could legally seize the transports of the Pacific Steam Navigation

Company. Fortunately for the nation, the Cousiño family, which owned coalmines in Chile's south, lent some of its colliers to the navy.

Peru

Peru, like Chile, learned well the lessons of the Spanish incursion. By late 1878 Peru acquired two British-built vessels—a central battery ship, the *Independencia*, and a turret ship, the monitor *Huáscar*. Like the Chilean ironclads, the *Independencia* and the *Huáscar* relied upon a combination of sail and steam engines for their power. The *Independencia* carried one muzzle-loading 150-pounder Vavasseur cannon, which was mounted on a pivot carriage in the bow, and one 150-pounder muzzle-loading Parrot gun at the stern. In addition to a submerged ram, the *Independencia* also mounted twelve 70-pounder, four 32-pounder, and four 9-pounder muzzle-loading Armstrong rifles on the ship's broadside. A strake of armor four and a half inches thick backed by ten inches of teak protected the ship's sides, but it did not alter the fact that the Peruvian ironclad closely resembled the earlier wood-hulled screw frigates.

The *Huáscar* was clearly Peru's most heavily armed ship and its premier naval asset. A product of the Laird Brothers, it mounted two ten-inch three-hundred-pounder Armstrong MLRs, seated on rollers in a single armored turret. The *Huáscar* also possessed a protected ram plus three Armstrong MLRs: one forty-pounder and one twelve-pounder on the starboard and port quarter deck and a forty-pounder in the stern. A belt of armor, reinforced by a combination of teak and iron, protected the shallow draught *Huáscar*. A girdle of side armor five and a half inches thick also buttressed by teak shielded the turret's sides, while iron plates two inches thick covered its roof and the deck. One of the vessel's two masts and its funnel stood atop the superstructure, which extended from the rear of the turret to the stern, as did an armored screen behind which the ship's commander could direct fire and command the vessel during battle. Unlike any of the vessels in either fleet, the *Huáscar* had recently participated in a naval campaign. In May 1877 it became the flagship of Peru's political gadfly, Nicolás de Piérola, who had launched a coup against the government of Mariano Prado. Prado ordered three naval vessels that remained loyal to his regime to capture or destroy the

Huáscar, but they failed either to sink the ironclad or to prevent it from fleeing.

No sooner had the *Huáscar* escaped than it had to deal with a more formidable enemy: the Royal Navy ships the *Shah* and the *Amethyst* commanded by Adm. Algernon de Horsey. Furious that the *Huáscar* had supposedly damaged British shipping and property, de Horsey decided to teach the Peruvian raider a lesson. Catching the rebel ship off the southern port of Ilo (or Pachoca) on 29 May 1877, the British admiral first offered the insurgents safe passage to a neutral port if they surrendered; if they would not, he threatened to hang them as pirates. It remains unclear what most outraged Piérola: the patronizing tone of de Horsey's letter or his impudent meddling in a domestic matter. Whatever his motivation, Piérola rejected the Englishman's offer, and a battle began.

For three hours the HMS *Shah,* an unarmored iron frigate, and the HMS *Amethyst,* a wooden frigate, bombarded the *Huáscar.* But this encounter, like the earlier confrontation with the Peruvian navy, proved inconclusive: the *Huáscar* held off the British ships and then, capitalizing on its shallow draught, escaped into the night. The British crowed that their navy had won a strategic victory, but the *Huáscar* certainly demonstrated its worth by absorbing with little effect some eighty hits from the British ships. As one contemporary observer noted, if only the *Huáscar*'s gunners could have matched the skill of their commander, the English vessels, not the Peruvian, would have taken flight.[10]

Although the *Huáscar* had proven itself in battle, it nonetheless suffered from grave defects: its superstructure limited the main turret's field of fire so that its three-hundred-pound guns could shoot only at targets that fell into two narrow 135 degree arcs extending from the monitor's sides; worse, it could not fire directly fore or aft. Additionally, because the *Huáscar*'s main turret used human rather than steam power to move the carriage on which the heavy guns rested, it sometimes took as long as fifteen minutes for the crew to hand-crank the machinery before the gunners could load or aim their weapons. This primitive technology severely limited the *Huáscar*'s ability to respond to any naval threat.

Following the tradition of giving Incan names to their naval vessels, the Peruvians christened their two American-built monitors the *Manco Cápac* and the *Atahualpa.* These vessels mounted two muzzle-loading Dahlgren fifteen-inch five-hundred-pounder smoothbore cannon, which rotated in a steam powered armor turret. Originally designed for riverine warfare, the *Manco Cápac* and *Atahualpa* lay so low in the water that other vessels could see only their masts, funnels, and turrets.[11] While this feature lowered the monitors' silhouettes and thus reduced their vulnerability, during storms the high seas could pour through the gun turrets and sink the ships. Consequently, the monitors had only limited utility, particularly on the open ocean.[12] Although much slower than the *Huáscar*, the lumbering monitors' guns could fire in almost every direction except aft.

While the Peruvian navy possessed more armored vessels than Chile, it contained fewer auxiliary ships. The *Unión*, a French-built wooden corvette, mounted twelve seventy-pound and one nine-pound cannon. Thanks to its speed, and good fortune, it would become the last surviving unit of the Peruvian fleet. A less heroic fate would befall the *Pilcomayo*, another wooden corvette, built in England in 1873, which carried six muzzle-loading Armstrong rifles, two seventy-pounders, four forty-pounders, and four twelve-pounders. Lima's fleet also possessed four transports, two of them lightly armed—the *Chalaco* and the side-wheeler *Limeña*—plus the *Oroya*, also a side-wheeler, and the *Talismán*. By early 1879, when the war erupted, the Peruvian government had revamped its fleet.[13]

Bolivia's Virtual Navy

As late as 1878 five Bolivian vessels sailed or steamed from their country's coast cities to Chilean ports; another two or three engaged in coastal traffic (*cabotaje*) within Chilean waters. Up to 1878 Bolivia possessed both a merchant marine and a war fleet. By 1879, however, these ships either no longer existed or, if they did, they no longer flew the Bolivian tricolor.[14] La Paz nonetheless hoped to participate in the naval war, but without "a single ship at sea," Bolivia's foreign minister, Serapio Reyes Ortiz, admitted that his nation could contribute little to help its ally. Reyes Ortiz, however, devised a way to join the maritime war: he announced that his government would deploy the poor man's navy: a fleet of privateers. On 26 March 1879 President Hilarión Daza formally offered letters of marque to anyone willing to sail under Bolivia's colors.[15] Although objectionable, Daza's actions were not illegal: since Bolivia had not signed the

1856 Treaty of Paris, which outlawed privateering, it still possessed the right to use corsairs.

Of course, the prospect of privateers preying upon neutral merchantmen upset U.S. diplomats. Even the normally laconic English became livid at the thought of corsairs plundering neutral vessels. The international community's complaints notwithstanding, Bolivia argued that it had a perfectly legal right to use letters of marque. If technically correct, the United States, England, and France refused to recognize the legality of Bolivia's position. Even Peru, realizing that La Paz was causing more problems than providing help, tried to discourage its ally.[16]

Happily, reason prevailed. After some study, the British Foreign Office's lawyers decided that Daza's threat to use privateers utterly lacked credibility: the Chilean army's early 1879 occupation of Bolivia's littoral denied La Paz any seacoast from which its ships could operate. Nor could Bolivian privateers legally operate out of a Peruvian port: since the Prado government, unlike La Paz, *had* signed the Treaty of Paris, it could not allow Bolivian privateers to enter its ports.[17] But in the unlikely possibility that Daza decided to proceed with his plans, the British government stated that "HMG will not recognize letters of marque and hence will resist, by force, any interference in British flag vessels" and that it would treat privateers as pirates.[18] While the U.S. and French governments did not use those precise words, they made it clear that they expected Bolivia's privateers to respect their flags.[19] Thus, Daza's threat to unleash a wave of freebooters, like many of his pronouncements, never materialized: Bolivia, which contributed troops to the Allied war effort, could not contribute meaningfully to the naval conflict.[20] Bolivia, however, did try: it dismantled the steamship *Sorata*, which normally sailed on Lake Titicaca, sending it to the Peruvian port of Mollendo, where the authorities refloated it. Apparently, the ship cruised around the Isla de los Alacranes before disappearing into the mists of history.[21] Thus the naval side of War of the Pacific became a match between Peru and Chile.

Comparing the Fleets

Chile

If in 1879 Chileans carped about their navy's plight, they had ample reasons: budget cuts forced the navy to sell the *Independencia* and to disarm the *O'Higgins* and the *Covadonga*. As a consequence of the loss of these vessels, the fleet also dismissed twenty-two officers and slightly more than four hundred enlisted personnel. The following year, arguing that they were in such poor condition that they did not justify repairs, the Ministry of War and Marine sold the *Ancud* and, after numerous attempts, finally auctioned off the *Abtao*. (As luck would have it, the government managed to sell the *Abtao* just prior to the war. Once the struggle began, the need for shipping became so great that Pinto's minister of war and marine had to repurchase the vessel.) The Chileans had also disarmed the clearly decrepit *Esmeralda* and *Covadonga*.

Rather than thin the naval cadre's ranks, the navy tried to retain as many essential personnel as it could. Thus, instead of discharging the few remaining *guardia marinas* (midshipmen) who served as junior deck officers, the Chilean government sent them to complete their training in the navies of Great Britain, France, and Germany. Surplus line officers received assignments to the maritime administration of ports, thus allowing the government to reduce their budget by dismissing civilian bureaucrats while retaining as many officers as it could.[22] The Pinto government also closed the Escuela Naval, which had trained Chile's naval officers, in part to save money and in part because the much smaller fleet did not need many officers. Of course, once the war began, the navy seemed willing to enroll anyone, even foreign merchant marine officers, in a crash program to train more junior officers.[23] It also created a new rank, *aspirante*, a junior officer who took the place of the midshipman.

At the beginning of the conflict the navy's ward rooms did contain fewer men, but below decks there was, in the words of the future admiral Luis Uribe, "a disorganization that augured nothing good and that was the cause of serious mishaps in the beginning and for much time after the opening of the naval campaign."[24] The navy's enlisted ranks suffered, perhaps more than their officers, when the economies of the late 1870s forced the fleet to reduce crews' rations and to deny them adequate clothing, even when serving in the cold duty stations of the south. These budget cuts lowered morale in a fleet where widespread drunkenness already reduced the sailors' efficiency. Forced to live in cramped quarters, wear tattered uniforms, and subsist on sparse rations, the navy liberally dispensed only one commodity: the lash, which it applied in accord with the draconian rules as stipulated by the colonial Spanish *ordenanzas.* Not surprisingly, naval enlisted men deserted in large numbers, and the fleet issued a variety of orders, all largely futile, to limit the effects of this flight.

The staff reductions lowered efficiency. Since the crewmen of the *Blanco Encalada* labored seven days a week, simply to maintain their ships, they did not have time to perfect their military skills.[25] Oscar Viel, captain of the smaller *Chacabuco,* denounced the navy's policy of rotating men every three months, which, he claimed, adversely affected their training.[26] Throughout the fleet there were so few sailors that most vessels could not engage in maneuvers without cannibalizing the crews from other units. For years the navy continued to deteriorate. The boundary dispute with Argentina forced the Chilean fleet to remain on alert. In November 1878 Pinto despatched his ironclads to the southern coal mining town of Lota so that they could be within easy striking distance of the Argentine Patagonia, an order that taxed the fleet's manpower. One Chilean official even suggested that the government send the *Chacabuco,* not its ironclads, to the Strait of Magellan because the navy simply did not have enough sailors to man them.[27]

Chile's navy also needed ships' engineers. Early in the war it became apparent that the Pinto government could not find enough Chileans to operate or maintain to its fleet's engines and boilers. A few men acquired technical training from Santiago's Escuela de Artes y Oficios, but many lacked practical experience. Those who were still apprentices needed years of seasoning before they would acquire the necessary technical skills.[28] Obviously the fleet could not wait for this process of maturation; instead, the navy began to hire foreigners whom it enticed to enlist by offering them a higher salary than that authorized by law. This tactic did not always work: in 1883 the fleet could not fill slots for thirteen third engineers because it paid so little that experienced men refused to enlist.[29] By the war's end, non-Chileans constituted 53 percent of the first engineers; 20 percent of the second engineers; 8 percent of the third engineers; and 5 percent of the apprentices. The presence of so many foreigners understandably worried the minister of war, who recognized that Chileans would have preferred that the nation rely on its own sons' unquestioned "patriotism and abnegation" rather than trust the uncertain loyalty of foreign mercenaries.[30]

Similar personnel shortages affected the navy's medical service, which lacked enough physicians and, in some cases, the facilities to care for the fleet's wounded or ill. Happily, some doctors enlisted, but many of these men lacked experience; others resigned either to pursue additional education or because they were so poorly paid.[31] Even the navy's chief surgeon publicly asked that the volunteer physicians' "sacrifices and risks . . . be worthily compensated."[32] Clearly, if something were not done, the surgeon general worried, "the ships of the fleet will lack the necessary personnel to fulfill this service [providing medical treatment]."[33] The situation did not deteriorate to that point, but, discouraged by the poor pay and lack of professional advancement, the exodus of doctors accelerated, particularly once they had gained experience in dealing with "the illness of the sailor."[34] In 1882 the navy's chief surgeon observed that the number of the medical personnel was "inadequate, even in the passive state of the maritime war" to supply support for blockading fleets, for troops in transit, as well as for army units occupying garrisons.[35] Providing assistance to the land forces often exacerbated the problem. Chile's fleet exhausted its medical resources caring for the soldiers wounded in the Battles of Chorrillos and Miraflores. Consequently, this wholesale flight of doctors "notably damages the care of the ill on board, the good organization of the ship's pharmacy, and the infirmary."[36]

If possible, the vessels of Chile's battle fleet were in worse condition than the personnel who manned them: the *Chacabuco* and the *O'Higgins* needed such an "extensive and radical repair," including careening and a change of boilers, that the minister of war and navy suggested that they should be used as sailing ships. The *Chacabuco*, for example, could generate less than a third of its required steam pressure.[37] Even the newest ships suffered from neglect: the navy had to order the *Cochrane* to England to replace the zinc amour plate, and if the government wanted to save the *Blanco Encalada* from suffering more extensive damage, it too should have been sent to Britain, but the nation's treasury simply did not have the funds to pay even for the most urgently needed repairs. The fleet's condition deteriorated so much that the annual report of the *comandante de arsenales* concluded that of the navy's seven warships, only the *Magallanes* and the side-wheeler transport *Toltén* were "in a perfect state of service."[38]

The Bolivian crisis forced Pinto to order his ironclads to Antofagasta, but stationing its armored ships in the north not only strained the navy's manpower resources but damaged its ships. After late 1878 the ironclads' engines, boilers, and hulls began to suffer from the constant wear and tear of steaming. Thus, Chile's navy began the war with its capital ships, and most of its ancillary vessels, in various stages of disrepair. These flaws, plus the lack of training, compromised Pinto's maritime forces. As Commander Boys of the HMS *Pelican* sadly noted, "The Chilean ironclads are . . . handy and efficient vessels, but owing to want of practice, some doubt may be felt to their power of maneuvering with rapidity and skill sufficient to enable them to avoid or parry the attack of the *Huáscar* ram."[39]

Peru

While the Chileans whined about their navy's wretched condition, a Peruvian government pamphlet, *Le Perou en 1878*, modestly described Lima's fleet as "the best organized and disciplined of all the Pacific."[40] The 1878 report of Peru's minister of the marine reinforced this optimistic assessment, stating that since the *Huáscar* "has new boilers, and its engines have recently been worked on . . . it is in perfect condition and ready to undertake whatever military commission it might have to fulfill." The same official stated that the *Manco Cápac* was "in the best condition and ready for any task for which it might be selected" and that the *Pilcomayo*'s "hull, engine, masts, and spars are in perfect condition."[41] Not all the squadron's units, however, were in such marvelous shape: *La Unión*, despite two overhauls in 1873 and 1877, still needed some repairs, but these, the *Memoria de Marina* noted, were not crucial. The *Atahualpa* required mending, while the *Independencia*, with its engines extracted, appeared to be a large jigsaw puzzle waiting to be assembled. While he would have liked to have purchased another warship, on the whole, President Prado, was satisfied with his fleet.[42] What Peru needed was time to prepare its navy, and thanks to Prado, time is what it got.

In February 1879, while publicly offering to mediate the Bolivian-Chilean dispute, President Prado, with his council of ministers' consent, secretly ordered his subordinates to ready the fleet as well as to purchase new equipment and, if possible, to acquire additional vessels.[43] The authorities used this time wisely: during the last week in February, the *Manco Cápac,* following a stay in a Callao dry-dock, where laborers cleaned and painted its bottom, was pronounced seaworthy. And by early March Lima's *El Comercio* reported that the *Independencia's* dismantled engines had not only been reassembled but functioned so well that the ship's new boilers could steam at between 11.5 and 12 miles per hour, a speed that would doubtless increase after its bottom had been scraped. The *Independencia* had also received a four-hundred-millimeter Blackley cannon, which the Callao shipyard mounted on its prow; later the authorities sited a 250-pound muzzle-loading Vavasseur rifle on its bow and a 150-pound muzzle-loading Parrott rifle on its stern. Even while the *Pilcomayo* and the *Unión*—which each received two 100-pound muzzle-loading Parrott rifles—waited for their turn for the dry-dock to complete repairs, they began ferrying troops and equipment to Peru's southern cities of Arica and Iquique.[44] In the interim both the *Chalaco* and the *Limeña* also installed new naval artillery Thus, perhaps the Peruvian minister of war and navy did not indulge in puffery when he stated that with the exception of the indolently slow-moving *Atahualpa* and "the soon to be ready" *Independencia,* "all the rest [of the fleet] is ready, presently performing the services of this institution."[45] Not without reason did Chile's minister to Peru note, "It is clear that Peru is hostile to us and that at the end of a more or less brief time, perhaps in the course of this week, war with that nation will break out."[46] He missed the mark by four days.

Prado's navy appeared better prepared for war than its officers. While some of the Peruvian officers demonstrated great skill and even panache fighting de Horsey's flotilla, not all the fleet's leaders possessed such virtues. Still, what the Peruvian officers lacked in skill, they made up for in numbers. In truth, Lima had enough officers to staff as many as three navies. To command a flotilla of six warships Peru employed 375 officers; in comparison, Chile required only 120 officers to direct its seven ship squadron. Many of the surplus Peruvian officers performed tasks of distinctly non-naval-type tasks: seven, including two *capitánes de navío* (naval captains), served in the Ministry of Foreign Relations, and thirty-two, including eighteen *capitánes de navío,* labored in the Ministry of Treasury and Commerce.[47] Apparently there were two reasons for this administrative bloat. One was that Peru's Escuela Naval produced too many officers. Another was that the Peruvian navy apparently refused to retire its officers. Instead, the navy department continued to carry many of these men, albeit at reduced pay rates, on their officers' roster. Appropriately called *indefinidos* (indefinites), these officers lived in an administrative limbo, marking time, waiting to be recalled to service. Many, such as Capt. Aurelio García y García, eventually returned to active duty.[48]

Favoritism complicated Peru's personnel problems. Just prior to the war, for example, Capitán de Fragata Nicolás Portal replaced Juan Bautista Cobian as commander of the *Unión*: Portal's powerful friends clearly trumped Cobian's superior naval skills. While the Lima newspaper, *El Comercio* seemed distressed, *La Opinión Nacional* did not, publishing a letter that included list of additional personnel changes.[49] As we shall see, Chile's navy was not immune to these same problems.

The tendency to retain officers on the active list produced a navy whose senior ranks resembled more the roster of a retired seamen's home than a seagoing navy: for example, Capitanes de Navío José María Salcedo and Pedro Carreño, who entered the fleet as midshipmen in 1821 and 1828, respectively, had twenty-eight and twenty-six years in grade; Pedro Santillana, the most senior *capitán de fragata* (lieutenant commander) with twenty-five years of service at that rank, had joined the navy in 1830. Granted, some of Chile's senior naval officers were hardly callow youths, but few of them served for as many years as their Peruvian counterparts. Only one, the British-born former Royal Navy officer Rear Adm. Santiago Bynon, had been in the navy for fifty years, while only Rear Adm. José Goñi and Capitánes de Navío Miguel Hurtado and Ramón Cabieses spent forty or more years with the fleet. In their cases, moreover, all but Cabieses served on the navy's Junta de Asistencia, which appears to be more of an honorific sinecure than a real command.

Even if not in their dotage, numerous Peruvian naval officers lacked the requisite naval skills because their nation had not created the facilities to prepare officers for war. The first educational institution was the Escuela Central Militar, which trained the commissioned ranks for both the army and the navy. Later it would be replaced by the Escuela Central Naval. Gaining admittance into this training institution did not seem particularly demanding: to matriculate a candidate had to be literate, healthy, and the son of decent parents. The school suffered from a variety of problems: political upheavals forced its closure in 1854 and in 1856, and an 1866 midshipmen mutiny closed it again from 1867 to 1870. Even when the school functioned, it sometimes graduated men who had not completed certain courses.[50] Other problems developed: *guardias de marina* normally had to spend a year at sea on a naval vessel in order to be promoted to *alférez de fragata.* In 1877, because Peru had no warship available, three midshipmen completed their training by serving on merchantmen; others served with foreign navies. These men still received their promotions. Miguel Grau, Peru's preeminent naval figure of the war, received much of his training in the merchant marine.[51]

Once they graduated, officers enjoyed few, if any, opportunities to put to sea or to practice gunnery, in part because the government, fearing the fleet's participation in a mutiny or rebellion, hid parts of the ships' engines, thus rendering them useless. Some Peruvian naval historians have praised the fleet's officers, in part because they served in the British Royal Navy. Others, like Ensigns Fermín Diez Canseco and Jorge Velarde, had sailed with the French fleet. Lt. Theodorus Mason, an officer in the U.S. Navy, doubted these assertions: most of Lima's naval officers, he concluded, gained their "professional experience, merely [by] living aboard ships which they were not taught to handle, and rarely drilled at their guns."[52]

If possible, the enlisted ranks of Peru's armada appeared more wanting than their officers. As Lima's *El Comercio* noted, "Almost all the sailors who man our warships lack the necessary skill to maneuver them; a fault that, if dangerous in the peaceful operation of a ship, is much greater on having to perform the different maneuvers and evolutions that a naval battle demands."[53] The newspaper had little faith that these malnourished and poorly clad crews would "fulfill their obligations in a satisfactory manner, particularly because it was their stomachs," not patriotism, that inspired them.[54] *El Comercio*'s harsh commentary did not miss the mark. Indeed, even prior to the outbreak of the war, it appears that a good portion of the lower deck, was populated by the "deserters and runaways from nearly every marine in the world, the best of whom were Chilians [*sic*]."[55]

Replacing the foreign sailors with Peruvians, however, failed to solve

the navy's personnel problems. Those who entered the Escuela de Grumetes "came from the lowest stratum of society," the most "marginalized:
[the] criminals, vagabonds," the alcoholics, the tubercular, the venereal,
the rejects of the army's Escuela de Clases or, worse, of Lima's jails. The
result, according to Capitán de Navío Camilo Carrillo, one-time head of
the Escuela de Grumetes, was that the enlisted men entering the fleet
were "defective . . . without knowledge of the profession, . . . without habits of morality, obedience, or discipline." The authorities tried to coerce
already brutalized men into "giving respect and even to fulfilling their
responsibilities," but they failed: worse, by menacing their officers, the
new sailors undermined the fleet's efficiency.[56] The navy's resort to its
traditional recruiting tool, the press-gang, proved equally unrewarding
since impressed sailors usually jumped ship at their first opportunity.
Indeed, in May 1878 Lima's *La Opinión Nacional* complained that more
than half of the *Unión*'s two-hundred-member crew had deserted.[57]

The quality of the lower deck degenerated even further after April
1879. Once war erupted, the Peruvian navy had to replace its Chilean
mariners with foreign sailors who served as petty officers and ordinary
seamen.[58] The lowest ranks of navy, however, remained the domain of
"the native cholos," at best "greenhorns" and at worst the utterly unquali-
fied dregs of Peru's jails, of whom an American naval officer noted even
the "best officers in the world could not have made anything out of such
material."[59] This assessment proved sadly true. Juan Moore, captain of
the ill-fated Peruvian *Independencia* would rue the quality, or lack of it, in
the raw sailors who became hysterical their first time in combat.[60] Worse,
he came to fear his own men: in April he had to surrender to the naval
authorities some crew men whom he suspected of either deliberately or
accidentally starting a shipboard fire.[61] A captured Peruvian document
revealed that as late as June 1879 none of the *Huáscar*'s crew knew how
to fire the ship's cannon. To remedy this problem, at least partially, Adm.
Antonio de la Haza recommended that the navy hire up to thirty foreigners who had experience as naval gunners.[62] This solution, while perhaps
wise, converted gun turrets into naval Towers of Babel where the various
crewmen did not understand each other.[63]

Staffing the lower decks constituted only one part of the personnel
problem. The Peruvian navy had come to rely almost exclusively upon

foreign engineers, particularly British or American. The *South Pacific Times*, Peru's principal English-language newspaper, urged the government to recruit and to train Peruvians to work the engine rooms.[64] Still, personnel records indicate that six of the *Huáscar*'s eight engineers and machinists were foreigners. Among the monitor's crew were thirteen Englishmen, three Greeks, two Germans, a Norwegian, a Frenchman, and a Dane. Only one of the twenty-one *artilleros contratados* was Peruvian.[65]

An official observer of the War of the Pacific, Theodorus B. M. Mason, a U.S. Naval Academy graduate and one of the American navy's leading intellectuals, considered the Chilean fleet to have good ships and "a corps of young officers well suited to handle them," a judgment seconded by another young American naval officer, Lt. J. F. Meiggs. While noting the presence of foreigners in the fleet, particularly in the engine room staff, he remarked that Chile's Indians who served in the lower ranks, unlike their Peruvian counterparts, came from provinces with a seafaring tradition. In short, he concluded that the Chilean navy's "discipline and instruction of the men were very fair," unlike the Peruvian fleet, whose "discipline was very lax, and [where] drill were [*sic*] almost unknown."[66] Some, like the U.S. Navy's Lt. J. F. Meigs, would later attribute Santiago's subsequent victory to the superior quality of Chile's officers and men.[67] Not so Luis Uribe, one of Chile's heroes in the War of the Pacific, who caustically noted that "the enemy fleet was found equally or even more disorganized than ours in respect to discipline."[68]

The onset of the War of the Pacific caught Chile's fleet, and to a lesser extent that of Peru, off guard. A world economic recession had forced both nations as part of an austerity program to disarm their flotillas. Ironically, although it had to refurbish some of its ships, Peru's fleet was in better condition, or at least no more deficient, than that of Chile. The constant steaming, initially to meet the threat of an Argentine attack and then to revindicate the Bolivian littoral, had taxed Chile's naval assets. Now it would have to confront what might be considered one of the area's most powerful fleets. Fighting a maritime war with ships in dire need of repair would test Chile's navy and complicate its prosecution of the war. Peru's fleet also required repairs, but Lima possessed the resources, including a dry-dock, to prepare its armada for war. The distance separating Lima from its southern provinces was not as great as that which Chilean vessels had to journey from Valparaíso to the war zone. Chile's better officers and men, however, would prove essential in conducting the naval side of the War of the Pacific.

Table 6. A comparison of Chilean and Peruvian naval vessels

Chilean navy: Ironclads

	Date of construction	Tonnage	Horsepower	Speed in knots	Armament
Almirante Cochrane	1874	3,560	2,000	9–12.8	6 (9-inch) 2 50-pounders 1 0-pounder2 1 -pounder 9 1 enfelt Nord MG
Almirante Blanco Encalda	1875	3,560	3,000	9–12.8	6 (9-inch) 2 50-pounders 1 20 pounder 1 -pounder 9 2 enfelt Nord MG

Chilean navy: Wooden vessels

	Date of construction	Tonnage	Horsepower	Speed in knots	Armament
Abtao	1864	1,050	300	6	3 150-pounders 3–4 0-pounder4
Chacabuco	1866	1,670	1,200	8–10	3 115-pounders 2 0-pounder7 4 0-pounder4
Covadonga	1858	412	140	5	2 70-pounders 2 -pounders9
Esmeralda	1854	850	200	3	12 40-pounders
Magallanes	1872	950	1,200	11	1 115-pounder 1 4-pounder6 1 0-pounder2
O'Higgins	1866	1,670	1,200	8–10	3 115-pounders 2 0-pounder7 4 0-pounder4
Amazonas	1874	1,970	2,400	11	1 6-inch
Angamos	1876	1,180	480	14	1 8-inch
Toltén	1875	240	270	9	

Table 6. (*cont.*)

Chilean navy: Torpedo boats

	Date of construction	Tonnage	Horsepower	Speed in knots	Armament
Colo Colo, Tucapel,	1879	35	40	19	2–3 par S torpedos 2 machine guns
Janequeo (Sunk)	1879	35	400	20	2–3 par S torpedoes 1 machine gun
Rucumilla, Teguelda, Glaura, Guale, Janequeo	1880–81	35	400	20	2 par S torpedoes 1 machine gun
Lauca, Quidora	1880–81	70	400	20	2 par S torpedoes 1 machine gun
Guacolda	1879	30	100	16	2 par S torpedoes

Peruvian navy: Ironclads

	Date of construction	Tonnage	Horsepower	Speed in knots	Armament
Huáscar	1865	1,130	1,200	10–11	2 300-pounders 2 40-pounders
Independencia	1865	2,004	1,500	12–13	2 150-pounders 12 70-pounders 4 32-pounders 4 4-pounders
Atahualpa	1864	1,034	320	6	2 500-pounders
Manco Cápac	1864	1,034	320	6	2 500-pounders

Peruvian navy: Wooden ships

	Date of construction	Tonnage	Horsepower	Speed in knots	Armament
Pilocmayo	1873–74	600	180	10–11	2 70-pounders 4 40-pounders 4 12-pounders
Unión	1864–65	1,150	450	12–13	12 70-pounders 1 12-pounder
Limeña	1860	1,163	350	12	2 40-pounders
Oroya	1873	1,159	400	12	2 40-pounders
Chalaco	1863	1,000	300	12–14	4 70-pounders 2 12-pounders
Talismán	1871	310	90	10–11	
Mayro	1861	671	250	5–6	2 12-pounders

Peruvian navy: Torpedo boats

	Date of construction	Tonnage	Horsepower	Speed in knots	Armament
República, Allay	1879		100	16	2 Spar torpedoes

Sources: Mason, *War on the Pacific Coast*, 14–16, 18; Fuenzalida Bade, *Armada de Chile*, 3:721–27, 947; "Armada de Chile," 1 April 1882, in Chile, Ministry of the Navy, *Memoria, 1882*; Conways, *Fighting Ships*, 411–15, 418–19; Clowes, *Modern Naval Campaigns*, 77; López Martínez, *Historia marítima*, 252–62. There are numerous differences of opinion as to the ships' speed and armament. Some of these differences can be attributed to the fact that the various sources may have been evaluating the ships at different times.

4. Chipana to Iquique

Sloth characterized Chile's navy during the first weeks of the War of the Pacific. Chile's Adm. Juan Williams Rebolledo, overruled his civilian masters and instituted a blockade of the Peruvian port of Iquique in early April. Though it had been virtually eradicated by earthquakes and tidal waves in 1868, 1875, and 1877, the discovery of salitre had revived Iquique. The newly rebuilt city, now containing more sumptuous buildings and wider streets, had become the principal exporting center of Lima's burgeoning nitrate industry.[1] After quarantining the Peruvian port, the Santiago squadron appeared utterly paralyzed. Conversely, Peru's fleet fluttered with activity: renovating its ships, completing their rearming, importing war materiel from Panama, and reinforcing its southern garrisons. Almost by default, Peru, if not controlling the sea-lanes, at least enjoyed the freedom to use them with impunity.

Chile's passive, if not utterly supine, policy did not require that its fleet seek out and destroy the enemy. Indeed, for weeks it looked as if the Chilean navy had no strategy other than waiting for the Peruvian fleet to do something. Of course, the Peruvians were doing something. Meanwhile, Williams Rebolledo seemed content to consume his fleet's scarce coal, wear out his ships' engines, and dissipate the energy of his shipmates, doing virtually nothing.

Two naval contests did occur in the first months of the war: the first encounter, which transpired off the Peruvian port of Chipana, happened by chance, not as part of Williams Rebolledo's overall strategy. Eventually, Chileans tired of Williams Rebolledo's passive policy. The admiral, anxious to become president, realized he had to do something to break the stalemate. After his fleet sortied north, the Peruvians attacked Iquique. This utterly unexpected encounter had far-reaching implications. Thanks to a combination of Chilean cunning and Peruvian ill fortune, Pinto's fleet accidentally won a significant strategic victory. Unfortunately, Chile's naval leaders, particularly Williams Rebolledo, failed to alter their approach to conducting the maritime war; instead Williams Rebolledo reimposed a blockade of Iquique, giving the Peruvians ample opportunity to cause mischief. This inaction effectively delayed not only Chile's prosecution of the naval side of the conflict but perhaps its land offensive as well.

Grau versus Williams Rebolledo

Two personalities dominated the maritime campaign during the early months of the War of the Pacific. The first was Chile's naval commander Adm. Juan Williams Rebolledo (1826–1910), and the other, his rival, Peru's *capitán de navío* and later admiral Miguel Grau (1838–1879).

Grau's father was a Colombian army officer who helped liberate Peru from Spanish rule, and his mother was the daughter of a Spanish colonial official. Grau, who initially went to sea at nine, abandoned his plan of a maritime career when his first ship sank. At his mother's insistence, he returned to school but performed so poorly that his parents allowed him, now eleven, to reenlist in the merchant marine.[2] These years proved a formative experience as he sailed on a variety of vessels flying different flags and plying the waters of the Atlantic and the Pacific oceans. Returning to Peru, he entered the navy as a midshipman in 1854. He did not last long, losing his commission when he chose the wrong side of one of the many revolutions that roiled his homeland. Grau returned briefly to the merchant marine, only to rejoin the navy in 1863 as a second lieutenant. He would be court-martialed again, this time for insubordination. Although found innocent, Grau nonetheless resigned. Briefly commanding the *Puno*, a merchant vessel belonging to a British steamship company, he rejoined the fleet in 1872. Four years later, he again quit, this time to serve in Peru's legislature as a deputy representing Paita. When the War of the Pacific erupted, he relinquished his congressional seat, returning to active service at his former rank, *capitán de navío*. He would serve first in the Ministry of the Navy before taking command of the *Huáscar*.[3]

Williams Rebolledo, like Grau, came from a mixed ethnic background: the son of an English naval officer who had served in the wars for independence and a local Chilean woman. The eighteen-year-old Anglo-Chilean entered the fleet in 1844 as a midshipman, cruising the Strait of Magellan on the tiny *Ancud*. Within two years he received his commission as a second lieutenant. By 1850 First Lieutenant Williams Rebolledo commanded the brigantine *Meteoro* and in that capacity aided the government in quelling an 1851 revolution. The following year, he helped restore order in Magallanes when a group of prisoners seized control of Chile's southern penal colony. In 1854 he sailed to England, where he served as the executive officer of the newly built *Esmeralda*. Williams Rebolledo's return trip proved unexpectedly turbulent: he had to crush a mutiny by the British crew hired to sail the ship to Chile. After 1856 Williams Rebolledo charted Chile's waters, repressed Indian uprisings, and cruised his nation's coast. When the Spanish fleet attacked Peru, Williams Rebolledo was a *capitán de fragata* in charge of the *Esmeralda*, which under his leadership managed to penetrate the Spanish blockade. In November 1866 off Papudo, he captured the *Covadonga*, thereby winning a promotion to *capitán de navío*. As an officer in the Peruvian-Chilean squadron he successfully defended Abtao and Huito from Spanish attacks. He subsequently took command of the Chilean flotilla during the Argentine crisis of late 1878, and in that capacity he supervised Chile's seizure of Antofagasta.[4]

The Naval War's First Weeks

Just reaching Antofagasta taxed the endurance of those Chilean vessels that had to sail from Valparaíso. The *Esmeralda* and the *Chacabuco*, for example, arrived spewing such large amounts of steam that they more resembled locomotives than warships; when the rest of the fleet captured the remaining ports of the Bolivian littoral, the *O'Higgins* had to remain in Antofagasta to undergo repairs to its decrepit engines.[5] The voyage north, moreover, consumed so much of the squadron's scant fuel that its ships could not do much once they had reached Antofagasta. Not until the end of March, when the flotilla received needed supplies and coal, could it consider any more aggressive action.

As commander, Williams Rebolledo became the architect of his nation's naval strategy during the first months of the struggle. His superior in more than mere rank, Chile's mild-looking and -acting President Aníbal Pinto, as well as many civilian advisers, urged Williams Rebolledo to blockade the Peruvian fleet while it lay at anchor in Callao. Once it had bottled up the enemy flotilla, Pinto argued, the Chilean navy could at its leisure support an invasion of Peru's southern provinces or, more audaciously, attack the capital, Lima.[6] The fifty-three-year-old Williams Rebolledo haughtily rejected Pinto's suggestion. Rather than risk his ships in Callao, which was defended by some impressive coastal artillery batteries, he wanted to blockade Iquique, a nitrate port located 180 miles north of Antofagasta. Williams Rebolledo's strategy, like his imagination, smacked of the banal. If Chile's fleet quarantined Iquique, he averred, Peru could not export nitrates, the commodity that had replaced the more noxious guano as the country's principal revenue source. Threatened with losing the economic resources he needed to finance the war, Peru's President Prado would have to order his fleet to lift the blockade. Then, when Prado's squadron sailed out of the shadow and range of Callao's coastal guns, Williams Rebolledo would annihilate it.[7]

Williams Rebolledo carried the day: on 3 April his squadron, consisting of the *Cochrane*, the *Blanco*, and the three corvettes *Chacabuco*, *Magallanes*, and *Esmeralda*, sailed from Antofagasta for the north. Two days later the admiral superfluously informed Iquique's civilian and military authorities what any fool could see: that the Chilean navy had blockaded their port. But Williams rarely deviated from his defensive strategy. He had once, in the 1860s, bedeviled the Spanish fleet, but the combination of age, fear, which bordered on irrational, and ill health—either syphilitic or psychogenic in origin—turned Williams into a most reluctant warrior of the 1870s.[8] With his first objective secured, the admiral divided his flotilla into two divisions: the first consisting of the *Blanco*, the *Magallanes*, and the *O'Higgins*, which he commanded; the second, the *Cochrane*, the *Chacabuco*, and the *Esmeralda*, under the control of the alcohol-sodden Capitán de Navío Enrique Simpson. Thus, having vanquished Bolivia's nonexistent navy, captured the virtually defenseless port of Antofagasta, and blockaded Iquique, Williams Rebolledo rested.

The admiral's decision to isolate Iquique failed to achieve its objectives. Quarantining Iquique while permitting the nearby port of Pisagua to remain open demonstrated the Williams Rebolledo's lack of imagination, if not his utter ignorance of geography. Since both a railroad and coastal highway connected Pisagua to Iquique, the Peruvians easily circumvented the blockade by landing men and materiel first at Pisagua and then moving them overland. Williams Rebolledo's selection of Antofagasta as a forward base of operations also proved extremely ill advised: located eight hundred miles north of Valparaíso, it lacked sufficient resources, including an ample water supply and repair facilities. Thus, any time Chilean ships patrolling Iquique's waters required a substantial refit, they had to leave the theater of war for Valparaíso. Extended supply lines and poor communications posed additional problems: the fleet had only one collier, the *Matías Cousiño*, which the Cousiño family, owners of numerous coalmines, had loaned to the navy. Consequently, Chile would have to improvise a means of getting fuel north. The most glaring error in Williams Rebolledo's naval plan, however, was that it fundamentally condemned his fleet to utter inaction: the admiral had made Chile's navy into the equivalent of a wallflower at a cotillion awaiting the pleasure of someone, in this case Miguel Grau, before joining the activities.

Thus, Williams Rebolledo's misguided strategy granted the Peruvians ample time to upgrade Callao's defenses and completely refit their navy. Worse, as the bottoms of Williams Rebolledo's ships accumulated barnacles in Iquique's harbor, Grau's fleet used the freedom of the sea-lanes to send troops and equipment to its southern garrisons. During the war's first days, for example, Peruvian transports like the *Talismán* and the *Chalaco*, impudently ferried men, weapons, and munitions south to Arica and Mollendo, while other vessels sailed north to Panama to procure arms and materiel.

The Battle of Chipana

Like the blinded and shorn Samson, the Chilean commander flailed about the theater of operations. Williams Rebolledo ordered the *Magallanes* and the *Cochrane* to intercept a Peruvian flotilla, which he mistakenly believed was en route to destroy Antofagasta's water distillation plant. While in Antofagasta, he also expected the *Magallanes* to refuel. The Chilean flotilla never encountered the Peruvian ships, and after the *Magallanes* had recoaled, it received new orders to proceed north to reconnoiter the area off the port of Huanillos, a center of guano mining, and, if possible, to destroy its loading facilities. Antofagasta's military commander, Col. Emilio Sotomayor, also requested the *Magallanes* to deliver an important letter to the fleet blockading Iquique.

The *Magallanes*'s trip to Iquique inadvertently triggered the war's first naval encounter. Grau, learning that the Chilean transport *Copiapó* was carrying fifteen hundred men, supplies, and coal to the north—information the Peruvians gathered simply by reading the Chilean press, which invariably published ships' sailing dates and their destinations—sent the *Unión* and the *Pilcomayo* to intercept it. The Chilean merchantman *Copiapó*, however, had already docked in Antofagasta. Thus, on 12 April, while they were searching for the Chilean transport, the Peruvian vessels ran into the *Magallanes*. Initially, the Peruvians thought that the ship they sighted was the transport *Copiapó*. They were not the only ones to err: the *Magallanes*'s commander, Juan Latorre—the son of a Peruvian father and the brother of a Peruvian officer commanding a coastal artillery battery in Callao—mistakenly concluded that two smoke trails he spied belonged to the *Esmeralda* and the *O'Higgins*.[9] Only after an hour of steaming toward each other did both sides realize their errors. (In part, the Peruvian mistake seems explicable: the *Unión*'s Capt. Nicolás Portal claimed that the *Magallanes* displayed the Chilean tricolor only after the battle began.)

The Peruvian fired the first salvo, but thanks to his inexperienced gunners, it became clear that Portal would have to close with his enemy to inflict damage. Maneuvering became crucial because although the *Pilcomayo* had guns located in its prow, the *Unión* did not; it could only fire those cannon that were mounted amid ship. To use its naval rifles to the maximum advantage, the *Pilcomayo* first crossed the *Magallanes*'s wake and then turned north. This maneuver sandwiched the Chilean vessel between the two enemy ships. For a brief time both Peruvian warships subjected the *Magallanes* to a punishing crossfire. But when the *Pilcomayo* developed boiler problems, it had to drop out of the engagement. This unexpected mishap left only the *Unión*, which the faster *Magallanes* easily outran, thus ending the battle.

The Battle of Chipana, unlike subsequent naval encounters, spilled no blood and took no lives. A Peruvian near miss, which drenched the crew of the *Magallanes*'s number four gun, came the closest to injuring anyone. Nor did the ships sustain more than minor damage. But for a few Peruvian shells, which scored its side, the *Magallanes* would have emerged from the battle unscathed.[10] Capitán de Fragata Juan Latorre, who admitted that his gunners' "accuracy . . . did not shine," nonetheless claimed that the *Magallanes*'s shells must have struck the *Unión* because its funnel began to belch steam. Midshipman Vicente Zegers sounded even more positive, writing his father that his shipmates scored as many as ten hits on their foe. But Latorre and Zegers were wrong: whatever damage the *Unión* and *Pilcomayo* suffered occurred as a consequence of unrelated engine problem, not Chilean gun fire.[11]

In one sense, Chipana was the ideal encounter, a splendid opportunity for both sides to indulge in jingoistic puffery: neither side lost; both won. The Peruvians, for example, crowed that in their first naval action in forty-five years, they had chased off the *Magallanes* without sustaining any harm because "the Providence that protects the justice of our cause will not permit them [the Chileans] to cause us the slightest injury."[12] Simultaneously, the Chileans proclaimed that the outgunned *Magallanes* first damaged its foes and then repulsed them, proving, in the words of the Santiago daily *El Independiente*, that "the true force of Chile's sailors is not found in its ironclads or its cannon but in the breasts of its valiant defenders."[13] While the proud citizens of Santiago sent a gold watch to Latorre in gratitude, Rafael Sotomayor, a high-ranking government official, seemed more cynical: "The battle of the *Magallanes* has been deformed in such a way that it is considered a great triumph. . . . The truth is that it has no importance: Latorre used all his power to escape . . . he had little choice to do what he did."[14] Rather than celebrate, Sotomayor seemed disconcerted that the Peruvian navy "should show more audacity than our [fleet]."[15]

The Return to the Stalemate

To vindicate his original strategy, Williams Rebolledo occasionally launched some half-hearted ventures to entice not only the *Unión* and the *Pilcomayo* but also the *Huáscar* to attack. Sometimes the admiral ordered specific ships to quit the blockade of Iquique in order to harry the Peruvian coast. On 15 April, for example, the *Cochrane* and the *Magallanes*, under the command of Capt. Enrique Simpson, sortied north to Mollendo with orders to destroy its harbor facilities. As part of his overall strategy to prevent the Peruvians from exporting salitre and to force them to attack, Williams Rebolledo also sent the *Blanco*, the *Chacabuco*, and the *O'Higgins* to demolish loading equipment, distillation plants, and railroads in the ports of Pabellon de Pica and Huanillos.[16]

When the Peruvians still refused to take the bait, the Chilean admiral redoubled his efforts to scorch the Peruvian coastline. Williams Rebolledo's attack on Pisagua marked the high point of his war on the Peruvian economy. The admiral, aboard the *Blanco* and accompanied by the *Chacabuco*, reached the Peruvian port on 18 April. The two ships sent landing parties ashore to capture any launches they might find. (Williams Rebolledo's ships, however, would burn or capture only the boats that belonged to the ports and that were used to load or unload items; the foreign ships, which normally carried the nitrates, remained off limits.)

The Peruvian garrison, to Williams Rebolledo's acute distress, opened fire on the Chilean fleet. The admiral, apparently infuriated because the Peruvians had the poor taste to fight back, ordered his guns to bombard not just Pisagua's coastal fortifications but the entire city. After a brief cannonade, Williams Rebolledo dispatched a second landing party. When the Peruvians again ungraciously opened fire, the Chileans unleashed a massive bombardment.[17] The results were outstanding: by the time Williams Rebolledo departed, he left a "defenseless city in flames [he destroyed about one million pesos in property], killing three women, an infant, and a Chinese," while wounding a handful of soldiers. Even the admiral allowed that he might have overreacted, but he nonetheless believed that he had taught the Peruvians a well-deserved lesson.[18] After his victory at Pisagua, the Chilean admiral continued to raze Peru's southern coastal cities, confident that these raids "would provoke the enemy to a naval battle."[19]

Captain Simpson also tried to increase the pressure.[20] Between mid-April and 1 May, the *Cochrane* and the *O'Higgins* entered the southern Peruvian harbors of Mollendo and Mejillones del Perú to check for contraband and devastate whatever took their fancy. In both ports the local garrisons, which in Mejillones numbered as many as five soldiers, fired on the Chileans when they began to destroy some launches. In both cases, a distressed Simpson decided that he had to "take energetic steps": the *O'Higgins*, beginning with its smaller cannon but eventually including its bigger guns, bombarded Mollendo for twenty minutes. Simpson also attacked Mejillones, leaving that port aflame without launches or wharves. While doubtless Simpson considered this retribution as deserved, one Peruvian official described his actions as the equivalent to "the greatest outrage of the filibusters."[21]

By mid-May it had become increasingly clear that blockading Iquique while simultaneously harassing Peruvian cities and shipping had failed to achieve its purpose. Consequently, some Chileans began to question Williams Rebolledo's strategy. Antonio Varas, the minister of the interior and thus Chile's second most powerful politician, complained about the admiral's refusal to attack Callao.[22] Some of the press also joined the chorus of naysayers.[23] While Williams Rebolledo arrogantly ignored the government, he could ill afford to alienate the public. The admiral hoped to compile a brilliant war record that he planned to use in 1881, when he would run for the presidency.[24] Recognizing that the failure of his Iquique policy might disenchant the electorate, Williams Rebolledo decided that he had to act boldly to regain his popularity. Thus, the admiral, who six days earlier had refused to attack the Peruvian fleet at its Callao anchorage, radically changed his strategy.[25] On 15 May, without informing the government of his destination, Williams Rebolledo's flotilla sailed for the north.

The Battle of Iquique

The addled Williams had concocted a plan so complex it verged on the baroque. The entire fleet, with the exception of the corvette *Esmeralda* and the sloop *Covadonga*, would, as unobtrusively and as surreptitiously as possible, leave Iquique for Callao. The two corvettes *Chacabuco* and *O'Higgins* sailed out of the harbor first. The *Cochrane* and collier *Matías Cousiño* followed, while the gunboat *Abtao* and the *Blanco* departed after dusk fell. Once at sea, the fleet was to meet some forty miles off Pisagua and then steam for Callao.

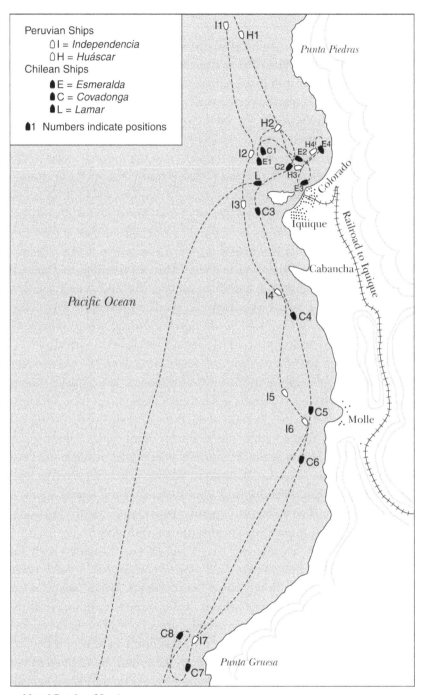

Peruvian Ships
 I = *Independencia*
 H = *Huáscar*
Chilean Ships
 E = *Esmeralda*
 C = *Covadonga*
 L = *Lamar*

 1 Numbers indicate positions

Punta Piedras

Colorado

Railroad to Iquique

Iquique

Cabancha

Pacific Ocean

Molle

Punta Gruesa

1. Naval Battle of Iquique

Williams Rebolledo's attack plan divided the squadron into three sections. The first, including the two ironclads and the *Abtao*, its hold filled with sixty *quintales* of gun powder, were to slip into Callao's harbor. Then the gunboat would insinuate itself among the enemy warships. Once in place, its small volunteer crew would attack the Peruvian fleet, set the vessel afire, and then evacuate before the ship's magazines and boilers simultaneously exploded. Using the fire from the burning *Abtao* to illuminate the harbor, the *Blanco* and *Cochrane* could then shell the enemy's ships. As the Peruvian ironclads struggled to fend off the Chilean boarding parties—selected from the *Blanco*'s crew—three makeshift torpedo boats, consisting of the launches from the ironclads and one of corvettes, would attack the enemy. Meanwhile, the *Chacabuco* and the *O'Higgins* were to begin firing either on the enemy fleet or preferably on Callao as the *Magallanes* entered the harbor to pick up the *Abtao*'s survivors and any other Chilean sailors who might have fallen overboard. The collier *Matías Cousiño* would not join in the fighting: its task was to remain far out at sea, safeguarding the coal needed for the fleet's return trip.

Nothing went according to Williams Rebolledo's plan. The two corvettes and the gunboat suffered mechanical breakdowns, substantially slowing the convoy. Once the Chileans arrived off Callao on 21 May, technical problems delayed the preparation of the three torpedo boats, forcing Williams Rebolledo to reschedule the attack for dawn of the following day. Daybreak of 22 May brought Williams Rebolledo great sadness: the Peruvian ironclads, the objects of Williams Rebolledo's exercise, were not lying at anchor; they had sailed south. Rather than attack the remaining Peruvian warships, Williams Rebolledo petulantly set his course for Iquique, a course of action that the Peruvian government ridiculed.[26]

The return trip became the navy's *via dolorosa*. Problems with the *Abtao*'s engines or boilers drastically slowed the convoy. A more pressing issue emerged: the flotilla could not locate the *Matías Cousiño*. (The admiral did not know it, but because its personnel could not read the fleet's signals, the collier had remained at the original rendezvous point, off Pisagua, rather than accompany the expedition on its trip to Callao.) With its only collier hundreds of miles to the south, the Chilean squadron began to run out of coal. In order to ensure that the *Blanco* and the *Cochrane* reached port safely, Williams Rebolledo ordered the *O'Higgins* and the *Chacabuco* to transfer their coal to the ironclads and then to proceed south under sail: the first to Valparaíso to repair its engines, and the second either to Iquique or to Antofagasta. Williams also commanded the *Cochrane* to take the gunboat *Abtao* in tow.

While Williams Rebolledo was planning his ill-fated attack on Iquique, President Mariano Prado had consulted with some of the nation's leading political and naval officers to determine what his fleet should do to counter the Chilean threat. According to Mariano Paz Soldán, a government minister, Capt. Miguel Grau informed Prado that the *Huáscar* was not the equal of either of Chile's ironclads. Worse, his crew consisted of raw recruits, men who "scarcely understand their principal obligations," let alone possessed "the discipline and . . . practice" needed to man a ship and fire its cannon. Captain Moore of the *Independencia* also complained of discipline problems. Grau, claiming that it was "dangerous" to undertake any serious mission, urged the government to wait.

Unfortunately, Prado could not: the Peruvian public demanded action, a yearning that the president had to gratify if he wished to remain in power. Second, if Lima did not act quickly, its garrison in Arica, which Prado considered essential to the nation's defense, would starve to death. In mid-May, after consulting first his civilian advisers and then the navy's senior officers, Prado ordered his two ironclads, his monitors, and three transports carrying needed supplies, ammunition, and reinforcements to sail for Arica. If all went well, the monitors were to buttress the defenses of Arica while permitting the rest of the fleet to attack Chile's fleet or its coastline. This squadron never made it out of Callao: one of the monitor's boilers malfunctioned. Consequently, the flotilla returned to its moorings, departing on 16 May, this time without the *Manco Cápac* or the *Atahualpa*.[27]

En route, one of the Peruvian transports, the *Limeña*, broke off from the main fleet, heading for nearby Mollendo, where it briefly anchored before steaming for Pacocha. The remaining vessels reached Arica on the morning of 20 May. After docking Prado learned that the Chilean fleet, with the exception of the *Esmeralda* and the *Covadonga*, had sortied for Callao. Their unexpected absence would provide the Peruvians the opportunity to reinforce and resupply not just Arica but also Iquique, whose garrison also began to suffer from the effects of the Chilean blockade.

Faced with a new situation, Prado convened another meeting. It was agreed that the two transports, after unloading the heavy cannon needed to fortify Arica, should depart for Pisagua in order to deliver weapons and reinforcements, including the Bolivian Olañeta Battalion.[28] In the meantime, the *Huáscar* and the *Independencia* were to take advantage of Williams Rebolledo's absence by attacking the Chileans at Iquique at dawn of 21 May. Following the destruction of any Chilean ships found in Iquique, the Peruvian ironclads would assault Antofagasta, sinking any Chilean vessels it might find, bombard the port's defenses, and cut the submarine cable connecting it to Valparaíso.

Ideally, the Peruvian ships would also attack Chilean shipping further south. Eventually these naval movements would culminate in a Peruvian-Bolivian land offensive that would drive the Chileans from La Paz's littoral. This strategy would succeed, Prado concluded, "thanks to the stupidity of Admiral Rebolledo, who on undertaking his operation on Callao, in search of the Peruvian squadron either to fight it or blockade it in the port" did not take the precaution of determining whether or not the enemy fleet had sailed or not from Callao.[29] Thus, the Peruvians sailed for Iquique on 20 May, the same day that Williams Rebolledo had originally planned to destroy the *Huáscar* and the *Independencia*.

Three Chilean ships occupied Iquique's bay on 21 May 1879: a transport, the *Lamar*; the corvette *Esmeralda*, commanded by the thirty-one-year-old Capitán de Fragata Arturo Prat; and the faster *Covadonga*, captained by the half-Peruvian half-English Capitán de Corbeta Carlos Condell. The *Covadonga*'s lookout first spotted the enemy, which the crew quickly identified as the Peruvian ironclads. Condell, awakened from his sleep, verified the information, and then signaled Prat about the enemy's presence. Prat, who had already heard the news, ordered general quarters.

Both officers must have known that their wooden and lightly armed ships had virtually no chance of sinking their ironclad enemies; simply surviving would be an accomplishment. Thus, acutely aware that they doubtless would not live to the afternoon, they prepared for battle. After destroying his ship's correspondence, buckling on his sword, Prat—perhaps believing that dying required formal dress—put on a pair of gloves before going up on deck.

Well aware of his predicament, Prat positioned the *Esmeralda* to take full advantage of its shallow draught. After ordering the *Lamar* to abandon Iquique—which it did, flying the American flag from its mast—and signaling Condell to follow in his wake, Prat told his crew that no Chilean naval vessel had ever struck its colors and that the *Esmeralda*'s crew would not become the first to betray that tradition. Informing his men that he expected them, and their officers, to fulfill their duty, he closed by shouting, "Viva Chile!" Below decks, two of his officers had a final drink together.

The battle began badly for the Chileans. The *Esmeralda*'s fragile boilers malfunctioned, reducing the ship's speed to about two knots per hour. Luckily for Prat, the captain of the port, Capitán de Corbeta Salomé Porras, informed Grau that since a ring of mines protected the corvette, he should approach the *Esmeralda* with a certain prudence.[30] Porras was mistaken: while the Chileans had experimented building some rudimentary explosive charges, these never progressed beyond the initial stages.

Prat, in the interim, wisely positioned himself between Iquique and the *Huáscar*, expecting that Grau would be reluctant to fire at the almost inert *Esmeralda* because an overshot might strike the city. In retrospect, Prat need not have moved: after almost ninety frustrating minutes, the Peruvian ironclad's guns still had not hit the virtually immovable *Esmeralda*. Iquique's military commander, Gen. Juan Buendía, ordered his artillery units to shoot at the Chilean corvette. The army's gunners, unlike their brothers at sea, began inflicting casualties on the Chileans, when finally one of the *Huáscar*'s shells crashed into the *Esmeralda* at its waterline.

Aware that he was caught in a punishing crossfire, Prat tried to move away from shore, but his vessel lacked the power to do so. Meanwhile Grau, discovering that a string of mines did not protect the *Esmeralda* and painfully aware of his crew's poor marksmanship, decided to ram Prat's ship. The Chilean commander could do little to stop the Peruvian monitor: his forty-pound guns obviously could not even dent the *Huáscar*'s armor, and when his last boiler exploded, the *Esmeralda* remained incapable of avoiding the Peruvian attack. On its first try, Grau's ironclad drove its ram deep into the corvette's side.

At that moment Prat, hoping to capture the monitor, screamed "Board it, boys!" and accompanied by a petty officer, Juan de Dios Aldea, jumped aboard the *Huáscar.* Grau reversed his engines to withdraw his ram, leaving Prat and Aldea stranded on the *Huáscar*'s decks. Their deaths were the stuff of epic poems: Prat was cut down while advancing on the armored bridge. And as he lay wounded and helpless on the deck, a Peruvian sailor apparently administered a coup de grâce; Aldea fell nearby, riddled with rifle bullets.[31] Although the *Huáscar* continued to fire, the *Esmeralda*'s second in command, Lt. Luis Uribe, tried to outmaneuver Grau. Another ramming, however, ripped open the *Esmeralda*'s hull, leaving the ship motionless. The Chileans still continued to resist. Indeed, inspired by Prat's example and led by Lt. Ignacio Serrano, twelve sailors boarded the *Huáscar*, where they too were quickly cut down.

Grau waited, perhaps hoping that the *Esmeralda* would strike its colors. When it did not, another ramming apparently split the ship in two. As the vessel began to sink, spewing its dead and wounded into the ocean, a teenaged midshipman, Ernesto Riquelme, managed to fire a largely symbolic final defiant salvo from his dying ship. At 12:10 P.M. the *Esmeralda* slipped beneath the waters, its flag still fluttering. Prat and his men may have lost the battle, but they had not broken a venerable tradition: they had not struck their colors.

If Grau's performance borderded on the embarrassing, that of the *Independencia*'s captain, the well-mannered Anglo-Peruvian and former Royal Navy officer Juan Guillermo Moore, would soon validate an earlier Chilean assessment that he lacked the skills and character to command a ship.[32] Initially the *Covadonga* had, as ordered, followed in Prat's wake. But sandwiched between the *Independencia* and some thirty smaller boats, which tried to place boarding parties on the Chilean ship, Condell fled the harbor. Prat wondered why the *Covadonga* had disobeyed his orders, but as he was otherwise occupied with the *Huáscar*, there was little he could do but speculate about Condell's motives.

Condell wisely used his shallow draught to advantage, clinging as close to shore as possible while all the time under attack by the *Independencia.* The Peruvian ship's untrained gunners repeatedly tried to hit the *Covadonga*, but it proved too elusive. Moore's men also had to contend with another factor: Chilean sharpshooters firing from the *Covadonga*'s rigging prevented the *Independencia*'s gun crews from using the ship's prow cannon. The same Chilean snipers also managed to pick off or wound three of Moore's best helmsmen. In the long run the loss of these skilled quartermasters may have proved decisive to the battle's outcome.

With two of his cannon dismounted, and disheartened by his gunners' lack of skill, Moore had no choice but to use his ram. Sailing off Punta Gruesa, south of Iquique, the adventurous Condell, with Moore in hot pursuit, managed to steam over a submerged reef. Although without a skilled helmsman to steer through the shallow water, the *Independencia* nonetheless plunged forward, only to run aground on some uncharted rocks. Moore reversed his engines in hopes of escaping, but the ship, caught "as if a hand of steel had nail[ed] it to the rock," could not move. As seawater poured into the ironclad, extinguishing its boilers, the *Independencia* heeled over, allowing even more water to enter through the gun ports. Although Moore's cannon ceased to function, his men heroically continued to resist, firing their machine guns, rifles, and even pistols at the *Covadonga*.[33]

Recognizing that his command was literally sinking beneath him, the Peruvian captain ordered his men to scuttle the *Independencia* by igniting the ship's stores of gunpowder. Unfortunately for Moore, so much water had flooded the magazines that the crew could not detonate the explosives. The Peruvian officer faced another problem: if he scuttled his ship, most of his crew, which consisted of raw conscripts who could not swim, would drown. As Moore tried to get these helpless men ashore in boats, Condell circled back to lacerate the *Independencia*. Stuck on a reef like a skewered cocktail sausage, under fire by the *Covadonga*, and with most of its guns inoperable, the Peruvians struck their colors.[34] Although the battle had theoretically ended when his flag was lowered, Moore and a handful of officers remained on board frantically trying to destroy his ship's correspondence or indeed anything that the Chileans might find useful. He had earlier ordered his men to jettison their weapons and to spike the ship's cannon. (The Peruvians subsequently did raise two heavy cannon from the *Independencia*, using these to defend Iquique.)[35] Once Moore capitulated, Condell had planned to return to Iquique either to rescue the *Esmeralda* or, given its opponent's power, to pick up the ship's survivors. But en route to the south, the Chilean saw the *Huáscar* steaming toward him. Perhaps appreciating the fact that he had stretched the limits of his luck, Condell fled, leaving the *Huáscar* to rescue Moore and his shipmates.

Although chastened, Grau did not slink back to Callao. On the contrary, he tried to fulfill at least a portion his original mandate by attacking Chilean coastal shipping. After obtaining additional coal in Pisagua, the *Huáscar* turned south again. Near Tocopilla, south of Iquique, Grau unsuccessfully pursued the transport *Itata*. If that vessel escaped him, the brigantine *Recuperado*, a Peruvian pilot's boat, which the Chileans had taken as a prize, did not. Unable to spare a crew, Grau destroyed the ship as well as the Peruvian sloop *Clorinda*, another Chilean prize that the Peruvian commander recaptured at Mejillones. The *Huáscar* even came within a hair of catching the Chilean transport *Rímac*, which had the speed and good fortune to escape.[36] Grau then entered Antofagasta's harbor, the home base of the Moneda's expeditionary force, in hopes of shelling the port's precious water distillation plants. Instead, he exchanged volleys with the local gun batteries and the *Covadonga*, which initially had tried to hide among a cluster of neutral ships, before leaving during the night. The *Huáscar* returned the following morning, tarrying long enough to cut the submarine cable connecting Antofagasta with Valparaíso before departing.

On 28 May Grau managed to elude Williams Rebolledo's dispirited flotilla as it steamed south. Steering clear of the Chilean warships, the Peruvian fleet destroyed some launches in Cobija as well as recapturing the former Chilean prize the schooner *Coqueta* and seizing the Chilean bark *Emilia*, which was illegally sailing under false registry papers. Since he was on the homeward bound portion of his trip, Grau sent these vessels back to Peru as prizes rather than sink them. He finally turned to the north, stopping en route to leave some of his booty in Iquique and recoaling at Ilo before steaming for Callao, which he reached in late May.[37]

As Grau plundered Chile's northern shipping lanes, the government in Santiago still had no idea of Williams Rebolledo's location. One of the Chilean agents found Grau's latest escapades particularly distressing and noted that if Peru had not lost the *Independencia*, Lima's ironclads could have fallen upon Antofagasta, "captured all our transports . . . burned [first] Antofagasta and then our entire coast." "If we continue being so stupid," he feared, "how much longer, [before] God will stop protecting us."[38]

The survivors of the Battle of Iquique enjoyed different fates. Predictably, Prat became the premier hero: Chileans named their streets, their children, even a beer in honor of the dead officer. The Chilean press became caught up in the same wave of emotion, elaborately praising Prat and comparing his self-sacrifice and sense of duty to the Spartans at Thermopylae or Nelson at Trafalgar.[39] If initially a hero, Condell did not remain so, particularly among his brother officers, who quickly tired of his boasting.[40] Moore had his own reasons for questioning Condell's self-aggrandizing version of the encounter off Punta Gruesa. The Chilean, Moore observed, owed his victory not to his skill but to "a fatal accident that ensured his salvation and that of his boat."[41]

The Peruvian public desperately tried to understand the sinking of the *Independencia*. Many blamed local pilots, who, although aware of the reef's existence, failed to warn the *Independencia*'s captain of its existence.[42] Others, while criticizing Moore's "reckless imprudence" and patriotic "temerity," tried to downplay the loss of the ironclad.[43] "The present conflict," noted the *South Pacific Times*, "will be decided on land, not on the sea."[44] A few, like "Celso," a correspondent for *El Comercio*, concluded that the Battle of Iquique demonstrated the Chileans' "negligent and stupid lack of care, the lack of foresight and reasoning, and military myopia." President Prado refused to indulge in hypocrisy or fantasies: the destruction of the *Independencia* not only was "a regrettable event which we can never lament enough [but it] has short circuited the plan that I had proposed."[45] Thus, the Peruvians had to console themselves with Grau's "victory" over the *Esmeralda*. Some compared his humanitarian treatment of the *Esmeralda*'s survivors with that of Condell, whom they accused of not aiding Moore's crews after they had abandoned ship.[46] Indeed, Grau became the Peruvian public's hero, receiving a promotion to rear admiral.

Neither Moore nor Grau survived the war: the admiral, still in command of the *Huáscar*, died five months later. Moore, although exonerated by a court-martial, apparently felt so belabored with guilt that he contemplated suicide. Finally, rather than take his own life, he constantly accepted the most dangerous military assignments, ultimately perishing in a vain attempt to repel the Chilean 1880 assault on Arica's main defenses.[47]

Iquique's Impact

Once the Chilean public finished feting Prat and Condell, they slowly began to realize that Williams Rebolledo's Callao expedition was a complete fiasco. The admiral had squandered his nation's scarce naval assets on a foolhardy venture that, according to Roberto Souper, a Chilean army officer, had brought Chile "almost to the door of a disaster." With Williams Rebolledo's fleet absent, he noted, the *Huáscar* could have easily destroyed the transports carrying men and supplies to the north. Alternatively, it could have attacked Antofagasta, which lacked enough coastal defense batteries to repel the Peruvian monitor.[48] The more charitable might have blamed Williams Rebolledo's abortive mission on an unusual run of bad luck. But empathy quickly yielded to analysis and then to anger. Williams Rebolledo, one critic subsequently noted, should have had enough wit to determine the whereabouts of Peruvian fleet before trying to engage it.[49] But Williams Rebolledo had not acted without knowing beforehand his foe's location. On the contrary, he knew exactly what he was doing.

On the evening of 15 May, the admiral, his chief of staff, Capitán de Corbetta Domingo Salamanca, and another officer spoke with a Captain Potts, an English merchant marine officer who supposedly informed them that the Peruvian fleet was preparing to leave Callao for the south.[50] If this allegation is true, and Williams Rebolledo admitted that he met Potts, why did the admiral sail to the Peruvian navy's home base when he knew the ironclads would not be there? Alternatively, why did Williams Rebolledo not try to ambush the Peruvians as they were approaching Arica, when they no longer enjoyed the protection of the heavy guns of either Callao's or Arica's forts?

Williams Rebolledo, it appears, never seriously planned to attack the Peruvian fleet at its Callao anchorage. The admiral was a man who had become increasingly protective of his own health and reputation, refusing to undertake any act that jeopardized either. Williams Rebolledo, as earlier noted, hoped to capitalize on his war record in order to become president of the republic. By mid-June it had become increasingly clear that his strategy of loitering in Iquique's harbor had started to antagonize the public. Williams Rebolledo therefore had to do to save his budding political career.[51]

The attack on Callao served two purposes: it permitted Williams Rebolledo to depict himself as aggressive without actually exposing either his person or his fleet to danger. It also burnished his reputation as a war hero. In short, the Callao foray was a public relations ploy designed to seduce the nation into believing that Williams Rebolledo was actively pursuing the war when in fact he was not. These same reasons explain why he did not attack the *Unión*, the *Pilcomayo*, or the *Atahualpa* as they lay at anchor in Callao: Williams Rebolledo did not really want to put himself in harm's way.

But Williams Rebolledo's elaborate charade went awry. The admiral obviously did not expect the Peruvian ships to sail south from Arica to attack Iquique. When the Peruvians did so, albeit at great cost to themselves, Williams looked the fool. Initially, he escaped criticism in the patriotic delirium that followed the Battle of Iquique. Eventually, however, some of the press turned away from praising Prat to questioning the admiral's strategy and his motivations. "Why," inquired José Alfonso, a civilian assigned to work with the army, "were those two ships [the *Esmeralda* and the *Covadonga*] left alone" in Iquique's harbor?[52] Other than consuming the fleet's fuel and scant resources, what had Williams Rebolledo's foray achieved? And why had the return trip from Callao taken so long? The more temperate newspapers urged the public not to prejudge the admiral without learning his side of the tale.[53]

But President Pinto and his advisers had neither the reason nor the desire to be so charitable. The government was still furious because Williams Rebolledo had acted not only without its permission but without its foreknowledge. The admiral had simply sent the Chilean president two communications: the first message stated that he was sailing north to Arica; the second told Pinto to ignore the first message.[54] As much as Williams Rebolledo's conduct outraged Pinto and his advisers, they could do nothing: the admiral's political allies in congress insulated him from government retribution. Eventually, however, even Williams Rebolledo's luck would run out.

Williams Rebolledo's blockade of Iquique had produced two lamentable results: he had squandered any early advantage Chile might have had while foolishly putting his fleet on the defensive. In a sense, the admiral had forgotten the lessons of Chile's own history: that it had triumphed over the Peruvian-Bolivian Confederation in the late 1830s by sending its fleet to attack Callao directly. Had Williams Rebolledo done so in 1879, he would have caught the Peruvian coastal defenses unprepared and perhaps some of its ships dismantled. The blockade had given the Peruvian government time to complete its coastal defenses, overhaul its ships, as well as rush reinforcements, ammunition, and supplies to its southern garrisons. Later, when they had to capture these ports, Chileans discovered how much Williams Rebolledo's inaction would cost them in blood and treasure.

Neither the blockade nor the attacks on Peru's coastal towns and shipping enticed Grau to attack. Belatedly recognizing that his defensive war, if continued, would foreclose his presidential aspirations, Williams Rebolledo concocted his bizarre plan to attack Callao. Paradoxically, this foray inadvertently achieved the admiral's goal: enticing the Peruvian ironclads to steam south. Perhaps his foray on Callao justified Williams Rebolledo's original strategy, but unfortunately, by the time the Peruvians arrived, the heaviest units of Chile's navy had left and with them sailed the possibility of engaging Grau in some decisive battle. In short, the Williams Rebolledo–Grau ballet provided a metaphor for the first months of Chile's naval war: two forces seeking the other but invariably missing.

Chileans may still celebrate Prat's moral example at the Battle of Iquique, but it was at Punta Gruesa where their nation took its first steps toward winning the naval war. With the loss of the *Independencia* went "all rational hope of equaling the material advantage that the enemy unquestionably enjoyed."[55] After 21 May 1879 the naval balance of power had definitely shifted in Chile's favor. But sinking the *Independencia* proved much easier than dislodging Williams Rebolledo from his command. Until that was done, which would not be for several more months, Chile did not control the sea-lanes.

5. Angamos and Beyond

The destruction of the *Independencia* cost Peru 40 percent of its fleet's offensive power. All that remained of Peru's once mighty flotilla was the *Huáscar*, its two ponderously slow monitors, two corvettes, the *Unión*, and the *Pilcomayo*, plus a few armed transports. The Chilean navy should have capitalized on its superior firepower and numerical advantage by hunting down and destroying the rest of Peru's armada, but Adm. Juan Williams Rebolledo seemed incapable of realizing that he enjoyed, if not supremacy, then at least superiority over Peru's navy. Thus, instead of seizing the offensive, Williams Rebolledo and his men simply returned to doing what they knew best: blockading Iquique's harbor. While the battle off Punta Gruesa had forced President Mariano Prado to tailor his naval strategy to conform to the country's new strategic reality, the Peruvians were not without resources, particularly Adm. Miguel Grau, who still commanded the Peruvian fleet. Ironically, Grau was ably assisted by Williams Rebolledo, who by stationing almost his nation's entire fleet in Iquique Bay, gave the audacious Peruvian naval officer complete freedom to reinforce and resupply Lima's southern outposts as well as attack Chile's shipping. Henceforth, Grau's men would avoid engaging the Chilean armada unless the Peruvians outnumbered or outgunned them. And thanks to this strategy and Grau's skills, the Peruvian fleet managed to fend off the Chilean navy until October 1879.

Two changes would have to occur before the Chilean fleet finally acted as if it had the upper hand. First, President Aníbal Pinto had to replace the sclerotic Williams Rebolledo. But politics made it difficult to make this personnel change. It would require months of costly mistakes before the public become so angry at Williams Rebolledo that even his conservative allies could not save him. Once rid of the admiral, the government could address the fleet's material needs. Its ships would have to undergo a substantial refit so that they could generate enough steam to drive the *Huáscar* from the seas. Eventually the president and his cabinet had to take an active role in conducting the naval war in order to cure the fleet's problems and to set its agenda. The participation of government ministers, advisers, and delegates in the decision making process proved crucial to Chile's winning naval supremacy, which in turn would allow its army to invade Peru.

The Afterglow of Iquique

Rather than seizing the offensive during the months after 21 May, Williams Rebolledo returned to his misguided strategy of blockade. The admiral's decision perplexed even the Peruvians, who obviously benefited from the Chilean officer's confusion. "Only an occlusion or constant cerebral congestion, of which it is said Williams was a victim," noted Rosendo Melo, a Peruvian naval historian, "could prolong the easy mobility of the Peruvian ships, throwing away Chile's incontestable naval superiority, which even children or the very ignorant in matters of the sea, could not deny."[1]

But the passage of time, and perhaps neurasthenia, may have impaired Williams Rebolledo's clearly limited mental capacity. Those who knew him during the war with Spain were struck by how dramatically the admiral had declined: his once black beard had turned white; he had become "shaky in his movements" and temperamental, if not clinically depressed; and he reeked of alcohol.[2] Yet, in the opinion of Roberto Souper, an army officer stationed in Antofagasta, it was not age that caused the admiral's inaction but the fact that he was "a coward, no more no less," and until the Moneda dismissed him, Souper believed, the "enemy, who has more intelligence, and drive, and even valor," would dominate the sea.[3]

Souper's charge, while harsh, did not lack merit. Williams Rebolledo steadfastly refused to acknowledge that his squadron had not only more ships but also better ones, that his ironclads possessed six guns to the *Huáscar*'s two, that two propellers powered each of Chile's vessels, while the *Huáscar* had but one, and that the Chilean gunners possessed a much greater field of fire than that of *Huáscar*. But instead of utilizing these advantages, Williams Rebolledo seemed paralyzed either by fright or an overdeveloped sense of caution.

After the Peruvian defenders of Iquique presumably deployed either a torpedo or a naval mine in an attempt to sink his flagship, Williams Rebolledo became almost pathologically afraid that they might try a second time. Consequently, much to the amusement of the Peruvians, he, as well as most of his squadron, nightly fled Iquique's harbor for the supposed safety of the high seas.[4] Williams Rebolledo became neurotically sensitive. When confronted with the news that his inaction or a Peruvian offensive distressed the public, the admiral retreated to his stateroom to nurse either his numerous, and sometimes imaginary, ailments or his bruised ego.[5]

In an attempt to appear dynamic, Williams Rebolledo sometimes overacted. Apparently, the admiral believed that the residents of Iquique should accept his blockade with easy grace, if not good cheer. But once the port's authorities had the gall to unleash a torpedo in Iquique's harbor, Williams Rebolledo responded hysterically, issuing such contradictory orders that had they been obeyed, the *Cochrane* would have opened fire on the *Abtao*. This episode, noted Domingo Santa María, a leading figure in Pinto's administration, "indicates to you the degree of confusion and bewilderment of our sailors." Souper added, "I am now more disenchanted than ever with the navy under the command of Williams; it will never do anything because it does not dare."[6]

Happily for Peru, Grau seemed free of his adversary's neurosis. As the Chilean flotilla lurked in Iquique's harbor, he reinforced his nation's southern garrisons, bringing in fresh troops, weapons, and artillery, generally imported from Panama; he destroyed Chilean port facilities and harried its merchant ships as they tried to transport men and materiel north.[7] By early June the *Huáscar*, although still suffering from some structural damage, largely the result of ramming the *Esmeralda*, once again headed south to ravage Chilean coastal shipping.[8]

Williams Rebolledo devoted himself to more mundane tasks. In late May the collier *Matías Cousiño*, which had remained at sea since it became separated from Williams Rebolledo's flotilla, finally sailed into

Iquique's harbor. The admiral, who reinstituted the blockade of Iquique on 31 May, must have been delighted because his squadron finally had access to coal.[9] Williams Rebolledo, still involved in housekeeping duties, had divers scrape the *Blanco*'s bottom.[10] Once ready, and believing that Grau would attack again, the recently scrubbed *Blanco* and the *Magallanes* sailed on 2 June for Huanillos. On that same day, the *Huáscar* almost captured the *Matías Cousiño*, which used the cover of darkness to flee south.[11]

Around dawn of 3 June a lookout spotted a ship that Williams Rebolledo correctly guessed was the *Huáscar*. Upon sighting the Chileans, Grau reversed his direction—he was still under orders not to engage superior forces—while Williams Rebolledo's flotilla poured on the steam. Slowly, the Chilean ship began to close the almost nine-thousand-yard gap separating the two vessels. And after four hours of steaming, it seemed that the *Huáscar* might come within range of the *Blanco*'s guns. Discovering that his engine room staff was burning low-grade coal, which he had taken on in Ilo and Pisagua, Grau switched it for a higher quality English fuel. The monitor quickly accelerated. To increase its speed, Grau's men jettisoned everything expendable, such as lifeboats, as well as the large quantities of poor quality coal, which it carried on its decks. (Among the items the crew got rid of was a Peruvian journalist, Antonio Cucalón, who presumably fell overboard and was not deliberately discarded as excess baggage. Henceforth, Chileans used his name as a synonym for a bumbling civilian who unwisely meddled in military or naval matters.) Once the range narrowed to four thousand yards, the *Huáscar* opened fire. When the *Blanco* responded, its shells fell close but did not strike the Peruvian ship. Hence, Williams Rebolledo ordered his gunners to increase the powder charge and to elevate their sights, but this time his salvos overshot the *Huáscar*. Grau returned fire with equally dismal results.[12]

At this point, Williams Rebolledo committed a crucial error. Initially, the *Blanco* had only fired its forward guns. Due to the ship's architecture, the ironclad could not train all its cannons on the Peruvian ship. Consequently, Williams Rebolledo altered the *Blanco*'s course so that he could bring more of its weapons to bear on the Peruvian vessel. Although the admiral had provided the Chilean gunners a better field of fire, they still kept missing their target. Worse, by changing the *Blanco*'s angle of fire on the *Huáscar*, Williams Rebolledo had inadvertently increased the distance between the two vessels. The combination of the Chilean navigational error and the high quality English coal being used by the Peruvians proved too much. By the early morning of the next day, Williams Rebolledo discovered that the *Magallanes*, which began the battle fighting alongside the *Blanco*, had disappeared and that the *Huáscar* had dramatically widened the gap between the two ships. A dejected Williams Rebolledo, falsely claiming that he had run out of coal, quit the chase. Within less than an hour, he encountered the *Magallanes*, and together they skulked back to Iquique.[13] Grau, running out of artillery shells, fearful that he could not obtain more high quality coal, and aware that the *Huáscar*'s engines, hull, and riggings needed repair, sailed to Callao.[14]

In some ways, this futile encounter resembled the Battle of Chipana: a desultory exchange of cannon fire followed by a chase that accomplished absolutely nothing. Williams Rebolledo's memoirs, of course, make the encounter sound thrilling. He also indicated that he cut short his pursuit because he did not wish to risk the *Magallanes*. Whether true or not, this decision was a wise precaution. The sinking of the *Esmeralda* had already incited the public's anger; losing the *Magallanes* might have made Williams Rebolledo a pariah.

The encounter, which began off Huanillos, a port south of Iquique, produced an unexpected dividend: the *Huáscar* entered a Callao drydock, where it remained for the month of June undergoing extensive repairs.[15] Grau had a lot to do: in addition to overhauling the monitor's engines, which he claimed malfunctioned thanks to "the incompetent personnel who oversee them," he also needed trained seamen, particularly gunners' mates. Consequently, Grau combed the rooming houses of Callao, hiring any foreign sailor, especially those with experience as a naval gunner or helmsman.[16] Thanks to his efforts, the number of *Huáscar*'s foreign *artilleros de preferencia* rose from five in May to twenty-five in August 1879.[17] The admiral's temporary absence did not reduce the level of conflict: the Peruvian navy remained on the offensive, but at least its principal protagonist was absent.

Williams Rebolledo's already tattered reputation further unraveled in the late May or early June. Increasingly tired of the admiral's incompetence, so amply demonstrated at Iquique, forces within the government began to call for his replacement.[18] Even the future minister of war in the field, Rafael Sotomayor, who had once praised the admiral's caution, sought his resignation. But powerful conservative legislators and newspapers still managed to shield Williams Rebolledo from Pinto's well-deserved retribution. Indeed, realizing that he enjoyed such protection, Williams Rebolledo sadistically toyed with the government's ministers. Citing his supposed ill health—he suffered from some chronic throat ailment, which a fleet surgeon diagnosed as "gangrenous diphtheria" but that might have been a misdiagnosis for *gumma*, a venereal ailment—he volunteered to resign his command.[19] As much as it despised Williams Rebolledo, the Moneda had to reject the admiral's cynical offer: the government feared the political repercussions that might result; it also had no one who could replace him. One of the most logical choices, Capitán de Navío Enrique Simpson, drank so much that Pinto's minister of the interior, Antonio Varas, dared not place him in charge of the fleet. (Why the minister left him in command of the *Cochrane* is a mystery.) Thus, as much as Pinto and his aides yearned to call the admiral's bluff, they could not: Williams Rebolledo retained his command.[20] The government, however, did dismiss some officers, like Capitán de Fragata Domingo Salamanca, Williams Rebolledo's chief of staff, who spent more time bolstering the admiral's fragile ego than supervising the fleet.[21] Salamanca's replacement was a seasoned regular, Capitán de Navío Galvarino Riveros.

In late June, to allay the army's fears about the safety of its forces in Antofagasta and to protect the southern route to the heartland of Chile, Williams Rebolledo reorganized the fleet. One division, comprising the *Cochrane*, the *Magallanes*, the *Abtao*, and the *Matías Cousiño*, maintained the blockade of Iquique, while the rest of the ships, under the ever-audacious Williams Rebolledo, sailed to Antofagasta.[22] The admiral's inaction confounded even the Bolivians, who noted, "His squadron can scarcely take care of the *Huáscar*'s incidents and maintain the derisive quarantine of Iquique."[23]

The admiral's behavior had become increasingly confused: while freely acknowledging that Chile enjoyed naval supremacy, paradoxically he still urged restraint. The speed of the *Huáscar* and the *Unión*, he claimed, precluded a "decisive battle." If the government wanted him to annihilate the "Ghost of the Pacific," he needed complete freedom to devise and execute a plan. His last charge, like many, was untrue: the Moneda had earlier given him a free hand, but it did insist that he not undertake any significant mission without first informing the Moneda.[24] Pinto need not have worried: Williams Rebolledo's "new plans" of early July consisted of destroying the water supplies of the guano ports of Huanillos and Pabellon de Pica. Having achieved this objective, he returned to Iquique, where, in the words of a La Paz newspaper, "[he did] nothing more than make [his] presence known."[25]

While the Chileans dithered, the Peruvians acted. The *Pilcomayo*, after escorting the transport *Oroya* to Pisagua on 6 July, attacked Tocopilla and Duende, destroying coastal installations, launches, and sinking the Chilean bark *Matilde de Ramos*. Only the fortuitous arrival of the *Blanco* and the *Chacabuco*, which recently returned to the fleet following a refit in the south, forced the *Pilcomayo* to flee. The *Blanco* pursued it but again with the same result: after a 180-mile chase the Peruvian ship escaped and eventually made its way to Arica.

On 10 July, the *Huáscar* indicated that it had returned to the war by attacking the fleet blockading Iquique. Grau did not have many targets because most of Williams Rebolledo's flotilla was not in Iquique's harbor. Following a Peruvian torpedo boat's earlier abortive assault on the *Matías Cousiño*, a significant portion of Chile's blockading squadron adopted the custom of departing Iquique's bay for the safety of the high seas. Hence, Grau had to settle on destroying the warship *Abtao*, which had the responsibility of patrolling the bay at night.

Having wired ahead to request that the garrison and civilian population of Iquique black out the city, Grau easily slipped into the port just after midnight on 10 July. The *Huáscar* did not find the *Abtao*, which normally guarded the port's entrance. It did, however, encounter the *Matías Cousiño*, which Grau ordered to surrender. The collier's crew was in the process of obeying his order when the *Huáscar*, not realizing that the Chileans had capitulated, fired a shot across its bow. The warning, while designed to energize the *Matías Cousiño*'s crew, inadvertently alerted the rest of the Chilean fleet. Thus, just as Grau was in the process of sending a prize crew to capture the collier, he saw an enemy ship bearing down on him. Realizing that he could not capture the *Matías Cousiño* as a prize, he would have destroyed it had the enemy not begun to steam toward his vessel.[26]

The first Chilean ship to reach the *Matías Cousiño* was the *Magallanes*, commanded by Juan José Latorre, who had decided to investigate after his crew heard cannon as well as rifle fire. Although obviously outgunned, Latorre did not hesitate to attack. The *Huáscar* and *Magallanes* exchanged salvos and small arms fire, but, as usual, the *Huáscar's* gunners missed. Frustrated by "the impressive uncertainty of our cannon fire," Grau repeatedly tried to ram the *Magallanes*, a tactic that Latorre skillfully evaded.[27] One of *Magallanes's* heavy guns even managed to get off a round that penetrated the *Huáscar's* armor, damaging the vessel. Grau, realizing that things had gone awry, abandoned Iquique's harbor with Enrique Simpson of the *Cochrane* in hot pursuit. After more than seven hours, the Chileans gave up the chase. Thus ended what some naval historians grandiosely call the Second Battle of Iquique, an encounter that did not directly affect the war, although, as one observer hinted, the *Cochrane's* poor performance may have later contributed to the removal of the alcoholic Simpson from the ironclad's command.[28]

Given the nature of the skirmish, the Second Battle of Iquique brought little joy to Lima. The Peruvians took some solace from Grau's "sense of simple humanity," his willingness to allow the collier's crew to abandon ship before opening fire. The captain of the *Matías Cousiño*, Augusto Castleton, grateful to be alive, clearly shared this sentiment: he sent Grau a case of wine, which the admiral acknowledged by promising to drink to Castleton's continued good health and good fortune.[29]

Williams Rebolledo learned of the *Huáscar's* attack on Iquique and its exchange with the *Magallanes* while en route to the north from Antofagasta. Reaching Iquique on 16 July, his flagship, the *Blanco*, plus the *Magallanes*, the *Abtao*, and a transport, the *Limarí*, became the new blockading force. Meanwhile, he ordered the *Cochrane* first to recoal at Antofagasta and then to sail to Valparaíso for a refit.

On 16 July, in what had become the trademark of the war, the *Cochrane* inadvertently encountered the *Pilcomayo*, which was then attacking Chilean merchantmen in the harbor of Tocopilla. A familiar scenario unfolded: as the *Pilcomayo* headed south, it spied smoke that turned out to be Simpson's ship. The smaller Peruvian ship fled, of course, pursued by the *Cochrane*. And after hours of futile steaming, Simpson broke off the chase, permitting the *Pilcomayo* to return to its home port.

Those who championed the old admiral finally began to regret their choice. On the evening of 16 July, the Peruvians supposedly launched a torpedo at the Chilean fleet blockading Iquique. Few actually saw the missile, and those who did disagreed about its shape and size. Indeed, the information was so scant that some cynics wondered if the Peruvians had in fact attacked. Williams Rebolledo, however, was adamant and, in an act described by the Peruvian Col. Santiago Contreras, an official in the Iquique government, as "worthy only of the Vandals of the Middle Ages," ordered his ships to bombard Iquique's sleeping citizens.[30] Approximately fifty-five Chilean shells landed, damaging a few buildings and killing one soldier and three infants. Even some Chileans questioned the wisdom, let alone the humanity, of Williams Rebolledo's retaliatory actions. "A ridiculous cowardice makes us appear like curs," wrote Domingo Santa María, "we are capable of killing in the late hours of the night, women, sick old people, and children. We do not fight ships, but we are audacious enough to disturb the dreams of defenseless people and surprise them with death."[31]

For the remainder of July and all of August, Grau humiliated Chile's navy by ravaging its coastal towns and preying upon its merchant marine. The *Huáscar* and the *Unión*, for example, entered Chañaral, four hundred miles south of Antofagasta and off Chile's coast, where on 19 and 20 July they captured two Chilean ships flying the Nicaraguan flag, the coal-laden frigate *Adelaida Rojas*, and the ore carrier *Saucy Jack*. The Peruvians also sank various small boats in Chañaral, Huasco, and Carrizal Bajo. On their return trip, Grau and Capitán de Navío Aurelio García y García, commander of the *Unión*, destroyed launches in Carrizal and Pan de Azúcar and captured another merchantman carrying copper, the *Adriana Lucía*, which they sent to Callao as a prize.[32] The *Huáscar*'s bold forays first infuriated and then frightened the Chileans. Domingo Santa María, who would replace Pinto as president, plaintively wondered how the supposedly inferior Peruvian navy so successfully harried Chile's coastal cities. After listening to Captain Simpson's excuses, Santa María realized that the admiral's defeatism had infected the entire fleet.[33]

The *Rímac* Fiasco

The Peruvian just missed scoring an enormous coup. Learning from the *Chala* of the Compañía Inglesa de Vapores that a group of high-ranking military and civilian officials, including Domingo Santa María, had sailed on the transport *Itata*, which was in Antofagasta, Grau and García decided to cruise off that port in hopes of capturing them. Instead, the Peruvian sailors bagged an even bigger prize.[34]

Grau's daring forays occurred at precisely the time when the Chilean high command planned to order two merchantmen, the *Rímac* and the *Paquete de Maule*, to convey troops, weapons, and horses to Antofagasta. Rather than risk the *Huáscar* seizing these vessels, the naval minister directed the two transports to remain in Valparaíso until the danger passed. On 20 July, upon receiving news that the sea-lanes were again safe, a local official, Eulogio Altamirano, the intendant of Valparaíso, authorized the ships to depart. In anticipation of the arrival of the *Rímac* and the *Paquete de Maule*, Chilean authorities in the north also took special precautions. Santa María, one of President Pinto's advisers, ordered the *Blanco* to return to Tocopilla to unload needed coal and then to cruise off Antofagasta in order to protect the merchantmen, which were expected to arrive on 22 July.

The plan miscarried. On 21 July in the mid-morning, Altamirano wired Santa María, warning him that the *Unión* and the *Huáscar* were in Caldera, a port west of Coapiapó, and that he should direct the *Cochrane* to steam south from Antofagasta in order to safeguard the Chilean transports. Capt. Enrique Simpson, unfortunately, had already sailed, and Santa María had no idea of the *Cochrane*'s location, and even if he had, he lacked the means to reach him. Similarly, since the authorities in the south did not know the whereabouts of the *Rímac* and the *Paquete de Maule*, neither could they warn them of the imminent danger they faced. In hopes they could alert them, the authorities ordered the *Itata* to sail from Antofagasta to caution the transports.[35] The officials had two alternatives: wait for Simpson to return to Antofagasta so they could send him south to convoy the transports or pray that the *Rímac* and the *Paquete de Maule* aborted their trip.

On 22 July, Santa María received a telegram informing him that two transports had returned to Valparaíso. Believing that these ships were the *Rímac* and the *Paquete de Maule*, Santa María concluded that the cause for anxiety had passed. In fact, the Chilean official had misread the telegram: the two vessels that the wire mentioned were the *Copiapó* and the *Toltén*; the *Rímac* and the *Paquete de Maule* were still steaming north. Simpson, incorrectly deciding that he was no longer under any obligation to protect the *Rímac* and the *Paquete de Maule*, sailed to Caldera, where he hoped to engage the *Huáscar*. He did reach Caldera but not in the way he would have wished. The *Cochrane* ran out of coal, and the *Itata* had to tow the ironclad into port. Simpson's attempt to attribute his failure to a lack of fuel did not wash: the head of the supply service claimed that the *Cochrane* had more than enough coal to make the trip. "No pretext," he noted, "is admissible for someone to claim that they could under any circumstance lack coal . . . since it is provided in such profusion and abundance."[36] Gen. Basilio Urrutia, Minister of War and Marine, agreed: Simpson should have taken proper precautions "to ensure the good success of any commission he is assigned, and particularly to avoid the possibility of being attacked by enemy forces, without having the indispensable elements of resistance."[37]

If the Chilean government had no idea of the whereabouts of the *Rímac* and the *Paquete de Maule*, Grau did. The *Huáscar* intercepted the *Colombia*, an English transport whose captain informed the Peruvians that the *Rímac*, carrying a cavalry detachment, the Carabineros de Yungay, departed from Valparaíso on 21 July. Grau quickly capitalized on the opportunity.[38] Calculating the ship's speed, the Peruvian admiral concluded that his target should reach Antofagasta on 23 July. Thus, the *Unión* and the *Huáscar* sailed south to wait for their prey.

The Chilean transports, however, were no longer traveling together: the *Paquete de Maule*'s captain, who had decided to make the trip north by sailing close to the coast, did reach Antofagasta. The *Rímac*, which opted to go north by traveling far out to sea, had almost arrived at its destination when it stopped. The transport's civilian captain, Pedro Lathrup, fearing that Antofagasta's defenders might fire on his ship if it entered the port at night, deliberately reduced the *Rímac*'s speed. Thanks to this decision, the merchantman arrived in the morning, in time for the *Huáscar* and *Unión* to capture it.

At dawn on 23 July, the slow-moving *Rímac*'s passengers saw an ironclad that they erroneously identified as the *Cochrane*. When he realized that it was the *Unión*, Lathrup, following his orders, relinquished command to Capitán de Fragata Ignacio Gana. In the interim, the *Unión* closed to within a few hundred yards, where it began to rake the *Rímac* with its cannons. Gana's situation was desperate: his ship had neither the speed to outrun the Peruvians nor the weapons to outshoot them—it carried only four thirty-two-pound smoothbore guns. The Chilean could attempt to scuttle his ship. The *Rímac*, however, carried only enough lifeboats for a third of the 250 cavalrymen of the Carbineros de Yungay. Gana, in truth, faced a Hobson's choice: destroy the transport, thereby depriving the Peruvians of a prize, but at the cost of a substantial number of the Chilean troops. The naval officer could also have followed the far-fetched suggestion of Gonzalo Bulnes, the commander of the Carabineros, and ordered the cavalrymen to board the Peruvian man-of-war.

The *Huáscar* quickly resolved the issue: a three-hundred-pound shell fired across the *Rímac*'s bow quickly convinced Gana to capitulate. The Chilean, however, did try to minimize the Peruvian's victory: while he destroyed the *Rímac*'s code books, the Carabineros jettisoned their weapons and equipment. (Some claim that many of the soldiers also drank up the ship's store of alcohol, which led them to vandalize the vessel.)[39] Gana also ordered the *Rímac*'s engineers to open the seacocks in hopes of scuttling the ship.[40] Unfortunately for Gana, Peruvian sailors boarded the vessel in time to close the valves. The *Rímac* was taken back to Peru, where it became part of Grau's task force. Gana was subsequently court-martialed but was exonerated when the tribunal decided that the naval officer was the victim of faulty instructions and an incompetent civilian crew that had become so drunk it would not obey his orders.[41]

The *Rímac*'s capture unleashed a firestorm in Chile. Riots erupted in Santiago as mobs surged through the streets threatening the congress and the president. Pinto's government had to use the army to quell the disturbance. The upheaval forced Antonio Varas to resign as minister of the interior. As his replacement, Pinto selected the violently anticlerical Domingo Santa María. Curiously, Williams Rebolledo managed to escape censure although even the Peruvians believed that his days were numbered.[42] Some concluded, however, that simply dismissing the admiral would not turn around the situation. According to Roberto Souper, a dry rot permeated the entire fleet: the government needed to discharge not just Williams Rebolledo, whose "imbecility and cowardice" caused these problems but his "decayed, lazy, and timid" compatriot, Enrique Simpson, that "mass without life, without heat, without ideas."[43] Disgust with the naval high command even surfaced within the fleet. Latorre despaired that while the navy did nothing, "Our enemies, who possess fast boats, have really taken over our coasts in the north." Chile, Latorre noted, should "suspend the blockade and assign one of our ironclads, accompanied by a transport, to pursue the *Huáscar* and the *Unión* until they finish them off." The government, the officer succinctly noted, needs "to bite so that we will not be bitten."[44]

Grau, who considered the capture of the transport "a moral triumph," launched another series of raids.[45] In early August, accompanied by the newly seized *Rímac*, the admiral sailed out to attack again Chile's sea-lanes. When the transport's engines acted up, the *Huáscar*, after taking as much of the *Rímac*'s coal as it could carry, continued on its mission alone. Twice in early August, Grau entered Caldera's harbor but, seeing nothing worth demolishing or capturing, withdrew. After an unsuccessful skirmish with the *Cochrane* and the transport *Lamar*, he stopped at Taltal, where he was in the process of destroying some launches when he was discovered by the *Blanco* and the transport *Itata*. Both gave chase but to no effect: the *Huáscar* easily outdistanced them, the Peruvian ironclad reaching Arica on 10 August.[46] Besides wreaking havoc, Grau's mission had achieved another goal: as the Chilean fleet obsessed about the *Huáscar*, a Peruvian transport, the *Talismán*, towed the monitor *Manco Cápac* from Callao to Arica, where it became part of that port's defenses.

The Punta Arenas Raid

In August the Peruvians opened a new theater of operations when the *Unión* boldly sailed to Punta Arenas, a port located in the middle of the Strait of Magellan, well over thirty-four hundred miles south of Callao. The trip south proved arduous for the Peruvians, who en route encountered some of the Indians of Tierra del Fuego, a tribe that would soon become extinct.[47] Initially, on 16 August when Capt. Aurelio García y

García entered Punta Arenas, few Chileans paid much attention because the *Unión* flew a French tricolor that did not arouse any suspicion. Only after he captured a coal-carrying lighter, the *Katie Kellok*, did Captain García y García unfurl the Peruvian banner. By then, of course, the local officials could do nothing. In addition to the coal he had already captured, García y García also demanded fresh provisions. The Chileans initially refused to accede to his wishes, but when the Peruvians threatened to shell the city, the local government officials reconsidered their position. Happily, the local British consul arranged a compromise: foreign merchants would sell the *Unión* the provisions it demanded in return for a promise not to bombard the port. García y García agreed.

The *Unión* had not steamed so far simply for free food and the opportunity to terrorize the burghers of Punta Arenas. Utilizing documents found aboard the *Rímac*, García y García hoped to capture the British freighter *Gleneg*, which was transporting weapons and supplies from Europe. His efforts proved fruitless: the English ship, escorted by the *Loa*, had already passed through the strait. Reprovisioned and carrying substantial stores of coal, the *Unión*, as well as a prize ship, the *Luisita*, sailed north on 18 August. García y García may not have achieved his original mission, but the Punta Arenas raid forced the Chileans to send two ships to the south to protect the transport *Genovese*, another vessel carrying needed weapons. The government warned all future transports to take precautions, such as sailing on the high seas without lights, when making the trip north.[48]

The End of the Beginning

Clearly something had gone terribly wrong with Chile's naval war. The supposedly crippled Peruvian fleet had seized the offensive, while the manifestly superior Chilean squadron was commanded by a man who spent most of the winter sulking in his stateroom. The admiral's behavior had become so bizarre that a rumor spread that in July Williams Rebolledo had temporarily suspended pursuing the *Pilcomayo* in order to hunt for an enormous sea turtle.[49] (If the tale is true, one can only presume he wanted fresh meat.) Whether true or not, the tale seems to indicate that Williams Rebolledo's behavior had passed from the eccentric to the irrational.

In late July Williams Rebolledo, lamenting that his ships lacked fuel and that their "engines and boilers" had become worn out steaming "in order to avoid torpedoes," told the government that he wanted to abandon the blockade he once so vigorously championed.[50] When the Moneda did not respond, he unilaterally ordered his ships, with the *Abtao* in tow, back to Valparaíso.[51] This was the second and the last time that he would act without informing the government. Upon his arrival in Valparaíso, he received orders to report immediately to Santiago, where on 17 August Pinto dismissed him.[52] The news of his humiliation delighted the Peruvian press, which, forgetting Moore, derisively noted that Williams Rebolledo had "passed into the pantheon of the incompetent."[53] Henceforth, the man charged with obtaining, in the words of Lytton Strachey, the "maximum of slaughter at the minimum of expense" would be Rafael Sotomayor, who as minister of war in the field served as Pinto's eyes and ears and the military's brains.[54] (Sotomayor's government post was created specifically to deal with the problems of the War of the Pacific.)

The Peruvians, as usual, were busy. By the end of August, Grau conceived a more brazen tactic. He planned to use some newly acquired Lay torpedoes to destroy the *Blanco* while it was undergoing repairs in Antofagasta.[55] The *Huáscar* sailed from Arica in the predawn of 22 August, reaching Antofagasta three days later. Although the *Blanco* had already departed, Grau decided to unleash his Lay torpedoes either at the warships the *Abtao* and the *Magallanes* or at the transports the *Limarí* and the *Paquete de Maule.*

If Grau hoped to insinuate his vessel among more than a dozen foreign merchantmen lying at anchor in Antofagasta's bay, his ruse failed: a transport, spotting the *Huáscar*, fired a signal flare alerting the Chilean fleet. Having come this far, the admiral did not hesitate. Grau's men immediately fired their torpedo. Evidently someone had inadvertently damaged its steering mechanism. Whatever the cause, once launched, no one could guide the weapon to its target. Worse, the missile doubled backed toward the *Huáscar.* Supposedly, were it not for a young Peruvian lieutenant, Fermín Diez Canseco, who jumped into the water and diverted the rogue torpedo, Grau might have sunk his own flagship.[56] Although he still had a variety of targets available, a frustrated

Grau departed Antofagasta the morning of 25 August. President Prado, not sure whom to blame for the erratic Lay torpedo, refused to pay for the weapon. Meanwhile Grau, upset by the Antofagasta fiasco, test fired another torpedo, again with poor results. The Peruvian admiral, apparently intent on demonstrating his disdain for the Lay torpedoes, ordered them buried in an Iquique cemetery.[57]

On 26 August Grau attacked Taltal, a nitrate port almost two hundred miles south of Antofagasta, capturing some launches and a barge. Two days later he again raided Antofagasta in hopes of cutting the submarine cable. When the immobilized *Abtao* impudently opened fire on the monitor, the *Huáscar* responded in kind, shooting at the gunboat, the *Magallanes*, and various Chilean coastal batteries. In an exchange with the *Abtao*, the *Huáscar*'s gunners hit the Chilean ship twice—not a particularly difficult task since it could not move—killing nine and wounding twelve. The *Huáscar*, however, did not escape unscathed: a shell from one of the fort's guns struck the warship, obliterating Carlos Heros, a young Peruvian officer who had distinguished himself on the earlier attack on Antofagasta. Grau retreated, but en route to Arica he almost encountered the *Blanco*, which was in the process of sailing south. This time, however, the Peruvian vessel escaped under the cloak of darkness. The trip home was not without profit: Grau managed to destroy or capture some small vessels in Mejillones, Cobija, and Tocopilla, ports located between Iquique and Antofagasta, reaching Arica on 31 August. This foray, however, would be Grau's last cruise.[58]

The Battle of Angamos

Purging Williams Rebolledo was the first step in reorganizing Chile's navy. The command of the fleet went to the career officer Capitán de Navío Galvarino Riveros, the "newspaper hero" disparaged by the official journal of the Peruvian government as "improvised by the minister of the Antofagasta Company [a sarcastic remark hinting that the nitrate interests controlled the government]."[59] Riveros, unlike Williams Rebolledo, burned with a certain *elan vital.* "My plan," he wrote Eusebio Lillo, a novelist and government official, "is to search out the enemy, even if he hides in a cave, because I am old, ill, poor, and I wish to leave

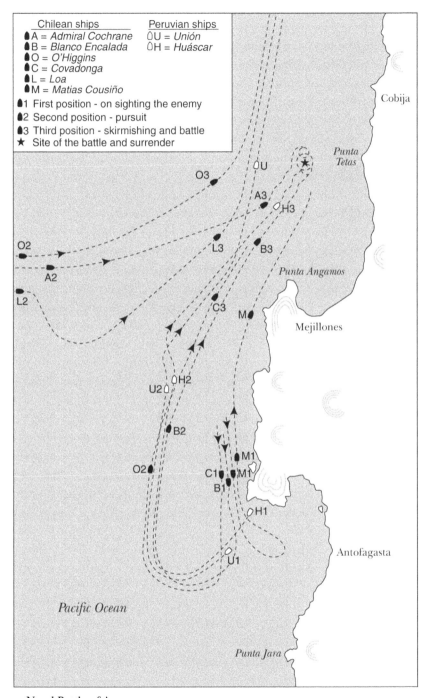

Chilean ships
🌑A = *Admiral Cochrane*
🌑B = *Blanco Encalada*
🌑O = *O'Higgins*
🌑C = *Covadonga*
🌑L = *Loa*
🌑M = *Matias Cousiño*

Peruvian ships
◗U = *Unión*
◗H = *Huáscar*

🌑1 First position - on sighting the enemy
🌑2 Second position - pursuit
🌑3 Third position - skirmishing and battle
★ Site of the battle and surrender

Cobija

Punta
Tetas

Punta Angamos

Mejillones

Antofagasta

Pacific Ocean

Punta Jara

2. Naval Battle of Angamos

my family the honor of having died on the field of battle."[60] The government seemed to have learned its lesson from the Williams Rebolledo debacle. This time the Moneda issued a variety of suggestions, really orders, telling Riveros to destroy the *Huáscar*.[61] As part of what Domingo Santa María called the government's wish to play the game "with new cards," the minister replaced the *Cochrane's* commander, Enrique Simpson, with the far more competent and dynamic Juan José Latorre, formerly captain of the *Magallanes*.[62]

The new ministry and the fleet commander finally paid some attention to improving the condition of the navy. Thanks to Eulogio Altamirano and others, Chile's fleet began to rotate its ships so that their engines could be repaired and their hulls scraped. Working on the ironclads proved particularly troublesome. Divers had to clean the bottom of the *Cochrane* by hand because Valparaíso's facilities could not accommodate the ironclad. The vessel also received new, locally made boiler tubes to replace most of the originals, which carbon had fouled. The combination of repairing the ship's engines and cleaning its hull permitted the *Cochrane* to steam at approximately twelve knots per hour.[63] The *Blanco's* engines and boiler tubes—some stopped up with small clams—were repaired in Mejillones. But because it was in worse condition and the repair facilities more primitive, the refurbished *Blanco* could not achieve its maximum speed. In addition to the ironclads, the *O'Higgins*, the *Chacabuco*, the *Loa*, and the *Covadonga* all underwent repairs and, in some cases, received additional armament.[64] The newly refurbished fleet consisted of two divisions: the first, under Riveros, included the *Blanco*, the *Covadonga*, and the *Matías Cousiño*; the second, commanded by Latorre, included the *Cochrane*, the *O'Higgins*, and the *Loa*. Once its squadron was ready, the government ordered Riveros to pursue the Peruvian ships while Latorre's contingent remained in Antofagasta to support the army.[65]

Instead of passively lying in wait for the Peruvian ship, which had been Williams Rebolledo's tactic, Minister of War in the Field Rafael Sotomayor set an elaborate trap to destroy Grau. Forewarned by the captain of the merchantman *Bolivia* that the *Huáscar*, and perhaps the *Unión*, might attack Antofagasta, the civilian plotted a response.[66] First, he ordered the *Blanco* to sail south, supposedly to Coquimbo, where he would leave the transport *Lamar*, which was undergoing repairs, as the bait. He then directed officials in the north to tell the captain of a mail boat, whom he suspected of spying for Peru, that the *Lamar* was defenseless because the Chilean fleet had left it alone. Unbeknownst to Grau, the *Blanco* would double back, shadowing the mail boat. When the latter rendezvoused with the *Huáscar*, the *Blanco* would attack. The somewhat baroque plan failed, apparently because the Chilean cruiser arrived too late.[67]

The Chileans tried again, this time hoping to destroy the ironclads as they lay in Arica's harbor on 3 October. Riveros and his squadron improvised a squadron of torpedo boats, in fact, the steam launches taken from the *Cochrane* and the *Blanco*, which they rigged to fire their torpedoes at the enemy's ironclads. These makeshift torpedo boats were to be towed into position so that they could attack early in the morning. After they launched their torpedoes, the rest of the Chilean squadron would commence firing on the *Huáscar*.

Unfortunately, an accident delayed by a day the torpedo attack. Then, just as Riveros's squadron was ready to put its plan into action, the commander learned from some Italian fishermen that the *Huáscar* and the *Unión* had already sailed. Deciding it was futile to waste their resources on any remaining targets, the attackers separated: the *Blanco* and the *Covadonga* returned to Antofagasta, while the *Cochrane*, the *O'Higgins*, and the *Loa* turned north to search for the *Huáscar*. Later, these three ships received new orders to sail to Mejillones.[68]

Meanwhile, the *Huáscar*, after escorting the *Rímac* so it could land troops and equipment in Iquique, had joined with the *Unión*, trolling for targets in Chile's northern harbors. After capturing the transport *Coquimbo* in Sarco, a port south of Huasco, Grau sailed south to Tongoy. On 5 October, the Peruvian monitor reversed direction, temporarily anchoring off Coquimbo to permit its crew to repair its engines before again moving north. In the early minutes of 8 October, the *Huáscar* and the *Unión* could see the lights of Antofagasta. The *Huáscar* reconnoitered the harbor and, discovering little of value, joined the *Unión* to continue their voyage home.

Sotomayor, in the interim, had devised a simple but effective stratagem to neutralize Grau: the two Chilean squadrons would bide their time until the *Huáscar* and the *Unión*, whose movements the government would carefully monitor, began their trip north. Then Riveros's First Division, the *Blanco*, the *Covadonga*, and *Matías Cousiño*, would wait near Antofagasta to defend it against a possible Peruvian attack. If Grau bypassed Antofagasta and simply headed directly north, Riveros's First Division would pursue the Peruvian vessels. Meanwhile Latorre's Second Division would have taken up a position twenty miles west of Antofagasta. Like a beater at a bird shoot, Riveros would drive the *Huáscar* forward; then the Second Division would move to cut off Grau's escape route. Once caught between the jaws of a Chilean naval nutcracker, the two squadrons could finally destroy the *Huáscar*.

Beginning in early October, the Chileans tracked closely the *Huáscar*'s movements after it left Arica. Relying on telegrams from its officials in the ports of Vallenar, Copiapó, Ovalle, and Tongoy, the Moneda determined that the Peruvian squadron, after having sailed as far south as Tongoy, had finally turned north to return to Peru. By late 7 October, Grau's ships had taken up a position, slightly north of Antofagasta at a promontory inelegantly named Punta Tetas.[69]

At approximately 3:30 a.m. on 8 October, lookouts aboard Riveros's ships, then sailing due south, sighted the Peruvians. Upon recognizing the Chileans, Grau reversed direction so that the *Huáscar* and the *Unión* were proceeding north. At 4 a.m., Grau ordered the ship's engineer, Samuel MacMahon, to give him full power. The engineer complied, pushing his engines to move at about sixty revolutions per minute, or 10.75 knots per hour. At approximately 5:40 a.m., Grau, sure that he had out distanced the Chileans, ordered MacMahon to reduce speed to slightly more than 9 knots per hour.

The *Huáscar* and the *Unión* had been steaming north, with Riveros still in pursuit, when, at approximately 7:15 a.m., Grau's men spotted Latorre's flotilla, led by the *Cochrane*, closing in from the northwest. Doubtless believing that he could easily outrun the Chileans, Grau initially did not react. But after almost an hour, the Peruvian captain, realizing that Latorre was closing the distance, again ordered MacMahon to give him full power. Closing the safety valves in order to raise more steam, the engineer pushed his engines almost to their limits. Unfortunately, the marine growth on the monitor's hull reduced its speed to less than that of the Chilean ironclads.[70] Grau's situation was virtually hopeless: the more he opened the distance between the *Huáscar* and the *Blanco*, the closer his ship came to the *Cochrane*; the Peruvian monitor was caught in a vice. When Latorre's ship approached to within thirty-three hundred yards, the *Huáscar* opened fire but to no effect. A second Peruvian salvo hit its target, but it still did not stop the *Cochrane*.

Latorre's maneuvering of his ship was masterful. He deliberately refrained from approaching Grau at any angle, which might have allowed the Peruvian to use his ram. Instead, Latorre positioned his ship so that he was following the same course as the *Huáscar*. Although steaming roughly parallel to Grau, Latorre cleverly kept his vessel slightly astern of the Peruvian warship. This tactic permitted the Chilean to bring the *Cochrane*'s forward guns to bear on Grau, while the *Huáscar*'s main turret, due to the ship's architecture, could not retaliate.

At 9:40 a.m., after slowly closing the gap to twenty-two hundred yards, Latorre's men finally opened fire. One of these shells penetrated the *Huáscar*'s main gun turret, killing some of the crew and jamming the mechanism that rotated its gun turret. Henceforth, the Peruvians could not quickly reload and aim their main batteries. As Grau's men struggled to repair the damage, another shell severed the cables that the helmsman needed to maneuver the monitor. The *Huáscar*, which earlier experienced steering problems when the helm was transferred from the wheelhouse to a more protected position, now veered erratically starboard. Meanwhile, the *Cochrane* adjusted its course and fired another salvo. This time a shell struck the armored bridge, obliterating Grau, leaving only his feet and some teeth. The shell's concussion also killed Lt. Diego Ferré.[71]

Although the *Huáscar*'s executive officer, Capt. Elías Aguirre, assumed command, he could do little: the same shell that killed Grau had also penetrated the ship's turret, first killing more of the gun's crew and then annihilating or wounding the sailors who struggled to steer the ship. Again the *Huáscar* temporarily veered off course, permitting Latorre, who still feared the Peruvian monitor wanted to ram it, to unleash another salvo. These shells killed many of the crewmen trying to operate the *Huáscar*'s jerry-rigged steering mechanism. The ironclad's mariners attempted to return fire, but their weapons, now manned by the less experienced gunners, generally missed the target. The *Cochrane* tried to ram the *Huáscar*, and when that maneuver failed he unleashed another salvo. This volley, which again disrupted the steering system, penetrated the monitor's armor, slaying more crewmen, including the ship's doctor. The *Cochrane* unsuccessfully tried to ram the *Huáscar* a second time.

In the midst of the monitor's death throes, the *Blanco* also tried to ram the burning Peruvian warship. By interposing his ship between the *Cochrane* and the *Huáscar*, however, Riveros gave the Peruvian vessel a few yards of breathing space as well as a brief respite from the battering of the Chilean ships. Latorre, who had to veer off to avoid being stuck by the *Blanco*'s ram, circled back and managed to steam parallel to the *Huáscar*, using his guns to devastate the burning hull while slaughtering many of the remaining crewmen. Meanwhile, the *Blanco* also doubled back so that it, as well as the *Cochrane*, sailed parallel to the *Huáscar*'s port side.

Around 10:20 a.m., the Peruvian flag disappeared for a few moments, leading the Chileans to believe that the *Huáscar* had struck its colors. But when the Peruvian bicolor reappeared, the Chilean ships, sometimes but five yards from the *Huáscar*, opened fire yet again. Even the *Covadonga*, somewhat unfairly perhaps, joined in shelling the once proud Peruvian monitor.

By now most of the *Huáscar*'s officers, including Aguirre, had perished. Command of the monitor fell to Pedro Gárezon, a mere first lieutenant, who ordered the *Huáscar*'s flag struck. While willing to save his crew's lives, Gárezon did his best to deny the Chileans a trophy: he commanded Chief Engineer MacMahon to open the seacocks in order to scuttle the ship. In a more melodramatic gesture, the surviving Peruvian officers threw their swords overboard rather than deliver them to the Chileans. Gárezon's plan to sink the monitor failed. The *Cochrane* dispatched a boarding party that included engine room personnel to seize control of the heavily damaged vessel, whose bilges held some four feet of water. By the time they arrived, however, the engine room crew already had opened the seacocks. The English engineer hoped that by disguising himself as a common stoker, the Chileans would have ignored him while they frenetically looked for the valves to stop the flooding. The plan might have worked, but Lt. Juan Simpson, who commanded the boarding party, recognized MacMahon. Grabbing him by the collar, he said to him, "Look, gringo: you are going to close seacocks; if not, I will shoot you six times." Convinced by the clarity of Simpson's threat, MacMahon secured the valves. Thanks to this act, in conjunction with extinguishing the various fires, the Chileans saved the *Huáscar*. Latorre humanely also sent some of his medical personnel and a chaplain to minister to the wounded and give the last rites to the dying.[72]

The Battle of Punta Angamos proved a complete success for the Chileans. The *Blanco*, having arrived only at the end of the struggle, suffered no damage; the *Cochrane* sustained five hits, which killed one sailor and wounded nine. The *Huáscar* did not fare so well, absorbing nineteen nine-inch shells, which perforated the monitor's armor, jammed its aiming mechanism, and partially disabled its steering apparatus. The Peruvian's casualty rate was high: thirty-five of the two-hundred-man crew dead, including five officers. Many of those had perished because the *Huáscar*'s armor, when struck by the *Cochrane*'s heavy shells, shattered into shards of iron, not unlike shrapnel, thereby devastating the monitor's crew.

Although the *Huáscar*'s hull and gun turrets sustained heavy damage, its engines still functioned. Thus, the victors towed the monitor to port, where it underwent repairs, eventually joining the Chilean fleet. In an uncharacteristic understatement, Sotomayor noted that the *Huáscar*'s capture "has put us in a brighter situation."[73] As Chile rejoiced, the Allies mourned. Even in Bolivia's altiplano a Peruvian envoy feared that the news of Angamos might precipitate a rebellion. "All hope has died," noted another envoy, "since Chile won clear naval preponderance. A bad result is expected. Nothing is expected from anyone."[74]

Chile's reaction, of course, was joyously ecstatic. Crowds assembled in ports like Chañaral to greet the newly captured *Huáscar* as it made its way down the coast. Once it put into Valparaíso for repairs, the new prize attracted such crowds of admirers that the railroad company ran special trains to carry the happy visitors from the interior to the port. The government also promoted Riveros to the rank of rear admiral and Latorre to *cápitan de navío*.[75]

In less than six weeks, the Peruvians would endure another, only slightly less catastrophic, loss. In early November, near Mollendo, Riveros's flotilla spied the *Unión*, the *Chalaco*, and the *Pilcomayo* sailing north. As the

Chileans moved to attack, the *Unión*, sighting Riveros's flotilla, alerted its cohorts before using its superior speed to escape. When the *Blanco*'s captain, Luis Castillo, decided to pursue the *Pilcomayo*, the *Chalaco*'s captain, Manuel Villavicencio, managed to escape by sailing close to shore. Firing as it went, the *Pilcomayo* tried to elude the Chilean ship until the *Blanco*'s big guns began shooting. Realizing that the Chileans could easily destroy his vessel, the Peruvian commander, Capitán de Navío Carlos Ferreyros, planned to command his crew to abandon ship. But first, hoping to ensure that the Chileans would not profit from their victory, he ordered his officers to open the *Pilcomayo*'s seacocks, flood its magazines, and set fires in various cabins. Just to make sure the man-of-war would not survive, the Peruvians also destroyed its pumps and used their cannons to shoot holes in the warship's bottom. Only after the *Pilocmayo*'s engineers informed him that his vessel would soon sink did Ferreyros tell his men to take to the lifeboats. He and his officers remained aboard.

A boarding party under Lt. Oscar Goñi took charge of the *Pilcomayo*, forcing its engineers to reveal the location of its seacocks. After closing these, the Chileans began to fight the fires. Goñi tried to enlist the Peruvian officers in his mission, warning them that if they did not help the ship might explode. Ferreyros and his brother officers nonetheless chose to not to abet the Chileans. Even without them, Goñi's men managed to extinguish the fires and, using pumps from the *Blanco*, prevented the *Pilcomayo* from sinking.[76] Transferring the Peruvian wounded to the *Blanco*, a prize crew brought the *Pilcomayo* into port, where after some repairs it, like the ill-fated *Huáscar*, joined the Chilean navy. Peru now had but one seaworthy warship: the *Unión*.

The Stealth War

Chile may have won almost complete naval supremacy, but this did not mean that the naval war had concluded. On the contrary, in 1880, when Nicolás Piérola's armada hardly existed, Chile's fleet would suffer its heaviest losses, due almost exclusively to the Peruvian's adroit use of torpedoes and trickery. The torpedo had become part of the naval arsenal only recently. The most primitive of these weapons, the spar torpedo, was essentially a bomb tethered to a long pole, which was either towed or attached to the side or bow of a ship. At the appropriate moment, the sailors of the attacking vessel would swing the explosive-tipped spar, not unlike a baseball player trying to hit a pitched ball. Ideally, the submerged charge would detonate when it struck below the enemy ship's waterline, thereby destroying the ship and its crew. In some cases, an electrical charge triggered the explosion.

Because it required so little technical expertise to use, the spar torpedo enjoyed great popularity. Nonetheless, its range limited its potential. Separated from its foe by only the length of the submerged spar, the aggressor had to use great skill in order to attack his enemy. If his foe spotted the attacking ship before it drew near enough to detonate the torpedo, the putative assailant suddenly became the unhappy recipient of "an overwhelming storm of lead and steel from the quick-firing machine guns and would stand little or no chance of approaching within an effective distance."[77] Deploying the spar torpedo, in essence, became an almost suicidal act.

Some of the self-propelled torpedoes resembled modern-day wire-guided weapons. Traveling either on the surface or slightly below the waterline, this type of torpedo remained tethered by an electrical cable to a gunner who guided the naval missile as well as detonated it upon command. One of the foremost examples of this model was the American-made Lay torpedo that the Peruvians had employed in their unsuccessful attack on Antofagasta in August.

Not surprisingly, the Peruvian navy tried desperately to obtain torpedoes, the ships to launch them, and the technicians to operate these weapons, because, as El Peruano noted, "the strongest armored ship, with the biggest cannons, the best officers and crew, . . . can disappear in any given moment . . . when such a vessel is attacked by torpedo boats."[78] Indeed, within days of the outbreak of the conflict, Charles Flint, an American who served as a Peruvian agent and diplomatic representative in New York, sent ten Pratt Whitney dirigible torpedoes as well as two American-made Herreshoff fifty-foot torpedo boats to Peru. Other shipments of arms would follow.

The Peruvians also employed another device, which it called a torpedo but that was, in fact, a naval mine. Indeed, these highly sophisticated and dangerous devices became Lima's favorite weapon. In early May 1880 sailors from the Chilean armed transport *Amazonas* sighted two copper tubes containing three hundred pounds of explosives and armed with a chemical detonator floating in Callao's harbor. The fact that the Peruvians had set these infernal machines adrift so that the tide could carry them into the bay where they might damage any ship infuriated the commanders of the Chilean flotilla. The fleet became even more distressed when the Peruvians fired on any Chilean ship that attempted to neutralize these weapons. Eventually Riveros had to order one of his newly arrived torpedo boats, the *Guacolda*, to use its machine gun to destroy one of the mine-torpedoes. The second was towed to San Lorenzo Island in Callao Bay, where it exploded when it hit the beach.[79] The following month a Lay torpedo detonated harmlessly near the *Blanco* and the *Huáscar*.[80]

Peru's attempts to manufacture mines sometimes proved as futile as their efforts to deploy them. In late April Maj. Pedro Ruiz, a watchmaker turned bomb maker, tried to fabricate a torpedo. Apparently the first model worked well, but the second prematurely exploded with such force that it shook many of the ships in the harbor. It also tore the flesh from Ruiz's bones, killing another four Peruvians while simultaneously damaging six buildings. Such accidents, of course, delighted the Chileans. Valparaíso's principal newspaper, *El Mercurio*, crowed that these mistakes "confirm what we already knew: that the *cholos* were not born to manage torpedoes and other infernal machines." Clearly such weapons required "dexterity and skills," which their "clumsy and coward[ly]" enemies lacked.[81]

Obviously, the newspaper either did not know about, or had tactfully forgotten, an earlier abortive attempt that involved the Chilean navy using dynamite bombs to destroy the *Huáscar*. A Chilean technician had plastered some dynamite with tar. The *Magallanes* then hoped to place some pitch-coated explosives in a barge, which it would then cast adrift. Clearly the Chileans planned that the Peruvians would capture this launch, transfer the coal to the *Huáscar*'s bunkers, and then one day a Peruvian stoker would toss the tar-covered dynamite into the boilers, where it would explode, destroying the monitor. This scenario never occurred because, as we know, the *Huáscar* succumbed to more conventional tactics.

The dynamite bombs almost achieved an unintended consequence.

Following the battle of Angamos, the captain of the *Magallanes* returned the coal, still containing the explosives, to his ship's bunkers. The *Magallanes*'s black gang was burning this fuel, when, just in time, someone noticed that a few chunks of coal had begun to melt: the stokers had almost destroyed the *Magallanes* with the bombs the navy created to destroy the *Huáscar*. Apparently the Chileans preferred to spread the news that the Peruvians had tried this ruse rather than let the nation know "the truth of the case, which is not funny and which the enemy might ape in similar nasty tricks."[82]

The Peruvians did indeed adopt this tactic: with its fleet destroyed, the torpedo became the Peruvian navy's weapon of choice or necessity and certainly the only one that the Chileans realistically had to fear. Consequently, Admiral Riveros ordered all his torpedo boats to remain on alert, so they could defend against Peruvian mines or torpedoes.[83] Riveros's warning was not misplaced. Late in the afternoon of 4 July 1880, Chile's armed transport *Loa* sighted a small sailboat floating unattended in Callao's harbor. On closer inspection, the Chileans discovered that, although unmanned, the boat contained enormous quantities of fresh fruits, rice, vegetables, as well as some live poultry. The *Loa*'s commander, Capitán de Corbeta Juan Guillermo Peña, ordered his crew to bring his vessel alongside the boat and then directed Midshipman Manuel Huidobro to conduct a search. Several officers, including 1st Lt. Leoncio Señoret and a pilot, Pedro Stabell, warned Peña that they suspected a ruse, but he dismissed their concerns. He ordered his crew, which had few opportunities to eat fresh food, to transfer the sailboat's cargo to the *Loa*. After unloading most of these provisions, the crew started to shift some sacks of rice, when a three-hundred-pound dynamite bomb, apparently secreted in the launch's false bottom, detonated.

The blast killed or wounded some forty crewmen, including Peña, who lost most of his uniform as well as a good portion of an ear. Many of the officers, who had been relaxing in the wardroom, rushed topside to find their ship rapidly sinking beneath them. The situation quickly disintegrated into chaos. Discovering that the explosion had destroyed all but two of the *Loa*'s lifeboats, some crewmen, particularly the newest recruits, panicked. In their zeal to flee, so many sailors crowded into one of the remaining lifeboats that it quickly sank. Fortunately, another lifeboat, the *Loa*'s last, was not swamped. Regrettably, there were no other lifeboats available and too few life preservers so that those crewmen who did not know how to swim drowned. Worse, Peña's crew did not have enough time to fire a signal gun indicating their distress. Two hours elapsed before nearby vessels, some of them French and British warships, rescued those few who survived by clinging to floating debris.

Many questioned how Chile could suffer this humiliation. Certainly such an attack was not completely unexpected. Rumors had circulated earlier that a young Peruvian named Manuel Cuadros had built a torpedo mine that would be placed in a large sailboat filled with fresh provisions.[84] Apparently the Peruvians had earlier tried the same stratagem in a vain attempt to sink the *O'Higgins*. The captain of that ship, unlike the *Loa*'s, refused to take the bait.[85] Given these facts, many believed that the *Loa*'s captain knew, or certainly should have known, about the Peruvian ploy. But even if Peña had not learned of the earlier attempt on the *O'Higgins*, Lt. Leoncio Señoret as well as various high government officials specifically reminded him of the potential danger. Despite these warnings, Peña and his crew "fell for the trap."[86] As the pilot Pedro Stabell noted, however, Peña was stubborn man who regarded as an "enemy . . . anyone who contradicted him in the slightest."[87]

The *Loa*'s loss outraged the Chilean public. Unfortunately, the debate on the disaster became partisan. Peña's brother charged that Admiral Riveros had not informed the fleet that the Peruvians might use a ruse to destroy a Chilean man-of-war.[88] Others also blamed the navy, not for failing to warn Peña, but for permitting such a flawed officer to command a ship of the line.[89] Peña's critics described him as barely competent, while others considered his death as providential. Had he lived, the government would surely have subjected him to a court-martial.[90]

Critics found Chilean claims of outrage at the use of torpedoes to be hypocritical. It was the Chileans, noted *La Estrella de Panama*, who were the first to use torpedoes in May 1879: Williams Rebolledo's attack on Callao called for three steam launches, all carrying torpedoes, to participate in the raid. That Williams Rebolledo's attempts failed did not matter; he had prepared a torpedo assault. The Peruvian journalist José Ulloa echoed these sentiments, seeing the *Loa*'s destruction as retribution for Santiago's tendency to bombard indiscriminately Peruvian cities.[91]

Predictably, but somewhat belatedly, Riveros took countermeasures. To protect his flagship, he ordered the *Magallanes* and the *Abtao* to position themselves so that they, and not the ironclad, would absorb any stray torpedo. He also required all Chilean vessels to leave Callao at 5 p.m. The only exceptions to this rule were the transports and the *Abtao*, which had the task of alerting the fleet in case of another torpedo attack.[92] Perhaps as an additional precaution, the Chileans occupied San Lorenzo Island, a small speck of land in Callao Harbor, so the garrison could provide early warning of a possible raid.[93]

Two months after the *Loa* fiasco, the *Covadonga* was blockading the port of Chancai. While in the process of attempting to disrupt rail communications, a lookout spotted a launch and a sailboat approximately two hundred yards away. The *Covadonga* destroyed the launch but then became captivated by the sailboat, which was newly painted, with full sails and leather seats. After some crewmen checked the deserted boat, the *Covadonga*'s captain, Capitán de Corbeta Pablo de Ferrari decided to bring it alongside his warship. Ferrari must have realized that his action might prove dangerous because he instructed his crew to inspect the sailboat with great care, even checking under the hull for an explosive charge. When the crew could find nothing amiss, Ferrari ordered a second search that, like the first, uncovered nothing. Finally convinced that the boat constituted no threat, Ferrari ordered his executive officer, 1st Lt. Enrique Gutiérrez, to supervise the raising of the ship. Gutiérrez, following hallowed tradition of the armed forces, delegated this job to the officer of the watch, Sblt. Froilan González. Before González could do anything, a crewman discovered some boxes located in the sailboat's stern and prow. The ship's carpenter examined these but declared them no danger to the ship. Despite his assurances, some officers still urged caution. González, following the chain of command, ordered the work party to raise the boat. When the crew complied, the skiff exploded with tremendous force.

As in the case of the *Loa*, the *Covadonga* quickly began to sink. Unfortunately, only two of the ship's five lifeboats, the smallest, survived the blast, and so many of the terrified crew tried to board these that they almost swamped them. As one boat tried to move away from the sinking the ship, Gutiérrez distributed lifebelts to the men. (A Peruvian paper, *La Patria*, claimed that the *Covadonga*'s officers used their side arms to keep the lifeboats and lifebelts for their exclusive use.)[94] Happily for Chile, the sinking of the *Covadonga* did not cause as many casualties as the *Loa* disaster, in part because the *Covadonga* went down in relatively shallow water close to shore. The survivors, moreover, found enough floating wreckage to keep them afloat until help arrived.

A court of inquiry blamed the *Covadonga*'s loss on the two crewmen who had failed to search the boat properly. Others had their own pet theories. One of Chile's leading journalists, Benjamín Vicuña Mackenna, charged that it was not negligence of the *Covadonga*'s crew but a Lay torpedo, detonated from the shore, that destroyed the Chilean corvette. Other journalists attributed the disaster to "Riveros's lack of foresight and the government's leniency and hesitation."[95] The ultimate responsibility, of course, was that of Captain Ferrari, who should have known better, particularly after the sinking of the *Loa*. Ferrari, like the star-crossed Peña, managed to avoid the indignity of a court-martial: he too went down with the ship.[96] Antigovernment elements, however, attributed the debacle to the government's ineptitude.[97]

Emboldened by their recent successes, the Peruvians tried the same trick again. In October 1880 the *Toltén* came across a small launch. The flotilla commander, Captain de Navío Juan José Latorre, not wishing to share the fate of the late and unlamented Juan Peña and Pablo Ferrari, commanded his crew to destroy the skiff. But after an hour of sporadic and obviously inaccurate shelling, the boat was still afloat. Enraged at the ineptitude of the *Toltén*'s gunners, Latorre ordered them to cease fire. Seconds later the suspect vessel blew up. Although his flotilla had escaped any damage, Latorre was still furious: he wanted to take reprisals but could not do so because the ship's guns lacked the range to hit any significant target. A month later, the Peruvians tried to use an electrically detonated submerged charge. This attempt failed because they could not get the makeshift weapon to remain underwater.[98]

Had the war lasted a little while longer, the Chileans might have had to confront Peru's new superweapon: a submarine. Federico Blume, a German-trained engineer and resident of Peru, had constructed a steam-powered, submersible warship that managed to negotiate Callao's waters without drowning its volunteer crew. Ideally, Blume hoped that his forty-eight-foot-long boat might come close enough to a Chilean ships that he could destroy it with either a Lay torpedo or a dynamite bomb before escaping. Blume had completed his submarine when the Chileans captured Lima. Rather than permit it to fall into Chilean hands, Lima's garrison destroyed the putative submarine, as well as what remained of the Peruvian fleet.[99]

Riveros's flotilla ultimately triumphed but at a heavy price. The destruction of the *Loa* and the *Covadonga*, in conjunction with the other attacks, infected Chile's fleet with a fear, if not a phobia, about torpedoes, which one ship's surgeon sarcastically diagnosed as "torpeditis."[100] These fears were reasonable: the Peruvians had sown so many torpedoes in Callao's waters—one source claimed as many as 150—that the Chilean fleet dared enter only certain parts of the harbor when they wished to bombard their enemy. Even the normally blasé English minister, as well as the commanders of the British, German, and American fleets stationed in Callao, complained about the danger that Peruvian mines posed to neutral shipping.[101] This anxiety about mines also infected Chilean commanders, who feared to interdict Peru-bound ships even while they were still in Panamanian waters.[102] Not surprisingly, since they did not have to suffer the consequences, some government officials wondered if the navy was not being too cautious.[103]

Around the time that they had destroyed the *Covadonga*, the Peruvians tried to dislodge the Chileans from San Lorenzo Island. On the evening of 15 September 1880, seven boats filled with Peruvian troops attempted to recapture the island, while some other launches fired on a nearby ship, the tender *Princesa Luisa*. The assault failed: San Lorenzo's garrison repelled the invaders, while the Chilean torpedo boat *Fresia* made its maiden appearance by rushing to the aid of another Chilean launch. The *Fresia* would have destroyed an enemy vessel if one of its torpedoes functioned properly and a mechanical failure had not prevented it from attacking a second time.[104]

The Chilean public, outraged over the loss of two ships and angry that Peru's armed forces dared to attack San Lorenzo Island, called for the fleet to take reprisals. The Moneda happily complied. Its new minister of war and marine in the field, José Francisco Vergara, ordered Riveros to demand that Peru return the *Rímac*, which it had captured in July 1879, and surrender the *Unión*. If Peru elected not to comply within twenty-four hours, Vergara empowered Riveros to shell the nearby ports of Chorrillos, Ancón, and Chancai on 22 September 1880. When Callao's diplomatic community learned of Riveros's demands, they vigorously protested: the sinking of the *Covadonga*, they noted, was an unfortunate result of war and certainly not an act that would justify such a barbarous response such as shelling defenseless cities. Riveros dismissed their arguments, noting that Chorrillos and Chancai were hardly defenseless because their garrisons had fired on his ships.

Riveros's shelling did not gratify his wishes: the fleet's guns did not ignite a firestorm that the admiral hoped would devour the cities. Worse, the shore batteries insolently returned the fire, striking but not damaging the *Cochrane*. Certainly the results did not justify the expenditure of approximately three hundred cannon shells.[105] Clearly, even the most skilled fleet could not take and hold Lima; that task would fall to the army.

Since May, Grau had conducted a brilliant naval campaign under extremely adverse conditions. From the onset, the Peruvian commander recognized that his flagship lacked the armor, armament, and maneuverability of the Chilean ironclads. Worse, the scarcity of experienced gunners forced him to use the *Huáscar's* submerged ram like an infantryman employed a bayonet—not a weapon of choice, but one born of desperation.[106]

Eventually, Grau's luck ran out: over the course of the war, the *Huáscar's* bottom became as fouled as those of the Chilean ironclads at the onset of the conflict. The admiral begged President Prado to allow his ship to undergo repairs before setting out on another raid. If not, Grau warned, its barnacle-encrusted keel would so slow the *Huáscar* that the Chileans might easily overtake and destroy it. Prado would hear none of it. Perhaps a victim of over-optimism, he insisted that Grau sail south. The admiral complied but reportedly said, "I obey because my duty requires me it, but I know that I am leading the *Huáscar* to sacrifice." So sure was he that he would not survive that before leaving Arica he sent to a Señor del Rio of Lima a package containing documents and family mementos that he wanted saved. Grau's prophecy came true: he, like Prat, fulfilled his duty, dying a hero's death.[107]

Grau, of course, emerged Peru's principal hero, still revered to this day. García y García, captain of the Peruvian corvette *Unión*, however, became the object of some scorn. An anonymous critic complained that García did not help Grau but instead fled the harbor, pursued by two wooden warships. The unknown critic went further, claiming that the *Unión*'s officers, crying in frustration, demanded that the government punish García y García. Worse, the critic warned that the *Unión*'s crew might mutiny or desert and that one of the ship's officers had written a statement condemning García y García but that he feared to submit it to higher authorities. García y García demanded a court-martial that eventually exonerated him.[108]

Chile triumphed at Angamos for a variety of reasons. The Moneda owed its victory in no small part to the fact that the defeatist Admiral Williams Rebolledo no longer commanded its fleet. Substituting Riveros for Williams Rebolledo and Latorre for Simpson transferred control of the nation's most important ships from a neurasthenic hypochondriac and an alcoholic to more capable hands. It also permitted the authorities to address some of the fleet's more glaring problems: correcting the wear and tear caused by almost a year of steaming and providing the fleet with some leadership. One cannot underestimate the role of Rafael Sotomayor, the civilian appointed to implement the government's will. Thanks to him, the navy finally formulated an overarching strategy to neutralize the *Huáscar* rather than fighting the war, as Williams Rebolledo had done, on a day-to-day basis.

Ironically, the victory at Angamos opened a Pandora's box of injured egos. Most observers believed that Latorre alone deserved the credit for vanquishing Grau.[109] But Adm. Galvarino Riveros tried to claim a large portion of the glory for the victory while denying the allegation that one of his shells had inadvertently hit Chile's other ironclad, the *Cochrane*.[110] As the supporters of the two officers squabbled, it became clear that the Chilean government had little, if anything, to fear on the seas. Now it must face the daunting task of attacking Peru.

6. The Land War Begins

The Pinto government had to delay invading Peru, perhaps the only way to force Mariano Prado to the peace table, until after October 1879, when Galvarino Riveros virtually swept Lima's navy from the sea. Fortunately for Chile, its army had used the months since April to mobilize various national guard units, to import weapons as well as equipment, and to train its new recruits. But the army's leadership, like that of the navy, seemed frozen in the past. The expeditionary force's commander, the seventy-four-year-old Gen. Justo Arteaga Cuveas, was sclerotic, listless, easily confused, and incapable of independent thought. And just as Juan Williams Rebolledo's dithering slowed the naval war, Arteaga Cuveas's inability to formulate some overarching strategy delayed the prosecution of the land campaign. Fortunately for Chile, Arteaga Cuveas possessed neither Williams Rebolledo's hubris nor his lust for public office. On the contrary, in a brief moment of patriotic lucidity in July 1879, the quasi-senescent Arteaga Cuveas, recognizing his declining condition, resigned his command. To replace him, Pinto and his advisers selected Gen. Erasmo Escala, a soldier known more for his piety than for his military skills. Escala, who initially seemed reluctant, accepted the post, promising to bring the war to Peru.[1] He would enjoy only limited success.

But before the general could do anything, his masters still had to decide where to strike. Earlier, in June, government advisers Domingo Santa María, Rafael Sotomayor, José Francisco Vergara, and José Alfonso met General Arteaga Cuveas to plan some strategy. While all favored an assault on Peru, Pinto's advisers devisers debated whether the army should attack Tarapacá, Moquegua, or Lima. They reached a general consensus that Tarapacá offered the best possibility for success: its proximity to Chile and its naval base at Antofagasta would not tax Santiago's supply lines, and the capture of Peru's salitreras would generously fund the Moneda's war effort. Chile's seizure of Peru's nitrate mines, moreover, would deprive Lima of its principal source of revenue and thus hobble its war effort and force Peru to capitulate. And finally, the Chilean conquest of Tarapacá would perforce mean it had annihilated some of the Peruvian army's premier units, thereby weakening Prado's ability to wage war.[2] Given these attractions, the government selected as its principal target Iquique.

The Desert Campaign

Once cursed by Christian missionaries as the Sodom and Gomorrah of the Pacific, Iquique had become the principal port through which Peru exported its nitrates to Europe. Thus, the capture of that city and the nearby salitre mines would constitute an economic and strategic victory. Opting to invade the arid province of Tarapacá, however, posed a serious problem for the Chileans. Rather than directly besiege the well-defended Iquique, Rafael Sotomayor called for two landings to the port's north. A small contingent would create a diversion by going ashore at Junín Bay, while the main body of troops would disembark at Pisagua. Once the Chileans captured these targets, they would link up, drive inland due east, and then, following the local railway line, strike southwest to isolate Iquique from the east. Blockaded from the sea and without overland access to either Peru or Bolivia, the port's defenders would have to capitulate.

Since the navy had to transport the expeditionary force as well as its mounts, equipment, and provisions, the fleet played a crucial role in the invasion of the north. The officer selected to command the flotilla of transports was Patricio Lynch, a Chilean-born, red-haired lieutenant who served as a junior officer in the British navy during the Opium Wars. Lynch's flotilla consisted of nine steam transports—the *Itata*, the *Lamar*, the *Limarí*, the *Matías Cousiño*, the *Santa Lucía*, the *Copiapó*, the *Toltén*, the *Huanay*, and the *Paquete del Maule*—the tender *Toro*, and the sailing ship

Elvira Alvárez. Escorted by the *Cochrane*, the *Magallanes*, the *O'Higgins*, the *Covadonga*, the *Amazonas*, the *Angamos*, the *Abtao*, and the *Loa*, the fleet had to carry northward some ninety-five hundred troops, plus more than 850 animals. The invasion plan called for these ships, each separated by 440 yards, to sail west from Antofagasta, where, once well out to sea, they would rendezvous and then steam north. By departing on 28 October, they hoped to attack Pisagua on 2 November 1879.[3] But problems developed: the shortage of boatmen and longshoremen, many of whom had been drafted into the militia, delayed the loading. While Isiodoro Errázuriz blamed many of these failures on the lack of trained staff officers, the process went better the next day, when the authorities, using specially built large barges, managed to put twenty-five hundred troops aboard the transports. Errázuriz, who likened the movement of so many to "emigration of a tribe," felt justifiably proud.[4]

On 1 November, as planned, most of the fleet rendezvoused for a final briefing. Although the navy had planned to begin the assault on Pisagua on 2 November at 4:00 a.m., it had to postpone the opening bombardment. Thanks to some navigational errors on the part of Capt. Manuel T. Thomson, the flotilla assembled at a site twelve miles north of its intended target.[5] It took two hours for the fleet to double back to Pisagua. Finally, at approximately 7 a.m., led by the *Cochrane*, the *O'Higgins*, the *Magallanes*, and the *Covadonga*, the Chileans opened fire at the enemy's coastal positions.

The Pisagua Landing

Pisagua sat atop some palisades that soared upward, approximately 330 to 450 yards above the waterline. It was not a vertical drop from the heights down to the ocean: a small stretch of rocky beach separated the coastline from the cliffs' escarpment. Toward the southern end of the bay stood some structures as well as the terminal of a rail line that zigzagged its way from the shoreline up the mountainside to the top of the bluffs. The Bolivian and Peruvian forces defending Pisagua had erected two forts, imaginatively named North and South, each mounting a one-hundred-pound Parrot gun. Although these weapons could not alone repulse a naval assault, they certainly could cause mischief for anyone

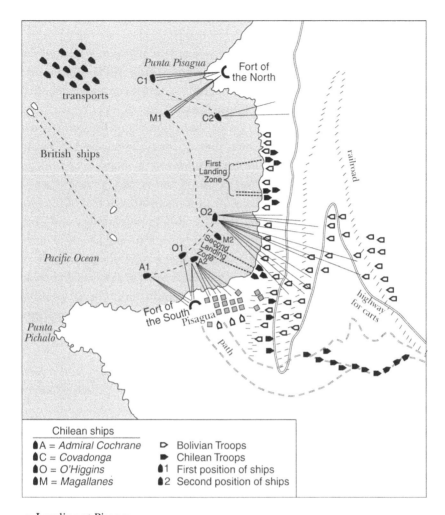

3. Landing at Pisagua

trying to land. The Bolivian command supplemented these forts by having twelve hundred soldiers, mainly from the Batallones Victoria and Independencia, dig in behind the railroad track that snaked its way up the coastal mountain.

Chile had to confront a more intractable enemy: geography. Pisagua's half-moon bay afforded only two sites where there was just enough beach for the troops to land: Playa Blanca, a 330- to 550-yard stretch of sand located almost in the middle of the bay, and, to the south, Playa Huanai, another strip of seaside, approximately 550 yards long, positioned near

Pisagua's customs house and the beginning of the rail spur. While not too rocky for troops to go ashore, bad tides and strong winds complicated the landing. This combination of natural obstacles and an entrenched enemy should have given the Chileans pause.

On 2 November 1879 at 7:15 a.m., the residents of Pisagua felt the impact of some explosions, which they erroneously believed to be involved with mining salitre. In fact, the authors of the blasts were Chilean navy warships that fired on Pisagua's forts and troops' positions while the transports remained well back, close to the northern end of the bay. The Chileans first zeroed in on the coastal defense batteries: the ironclad *Cochrane* and the corvette *O'Higgins* concentrating on the Fuerte del Sur, the corvette *Magallanes* and the schooner *Covadonga* focused on the northern gun. The Chileans made quick work of neutralizing these batteries—decapitating one of the battery's commanders in the process. Once the coastal defense batteries were silenced—a feat that required less than an hour—the ships shifted their guns to fire on the enemy troops dug in on the mountain's side and in the city.[6]

At 9:30 a.m. the Chilean merchantmen *Copiapó*, *Limarí*, and *Lamar* moved to within twenty-three hundred yards of the beach to offload men from the Regimiento Buin, the First of the Line, two companies from a mobilized militia unit, the Batallón Atacama, and one from the Zapadores, plus two batteries of mountain artillery. These troops climbed down ladders flung over the transports' sides, crowding into a variety of small craft, either some built specially for the invasion or simple long boats, all powered by oars.

Thanks to an error, the initial landing party numbered but 450 troops and not 900 as the invasion plan specified. The initial wave of Chilean troops paid a high price for the honor of being first. As the boats proceeded toward the beaches, they came under heavy enemy fire. Not just the troops but also the ratings and officers who manned these landing barges started to suffer casualties, sometimes as high as 50 percent before they reached the beach. (Although they were not supposed to do so, sometimes the naval personnel joined in the fighting. Lt. Amador Barrientos of the armored transport *Loa*, for example, helped seize a position and became the first to plant the Chilean flag on enemy soil.) Sometimes being a spectator proved lethal: sixteen soldiers of the Fourth Line Regiment were shot, three fatally, as they watched the invasion from the deck of the *Tolten.*[7]

Once ashore, the Chileans had to take and hold a beachhead while the landing boats returned to the transports for reinforcements. In the intervening hour that the launches took to return, the seriously outnumbered soldiers of the first wave sustained heavy losses.[8] Constantly under fire, the Chilean troops found it difficult to make headway, in part because sand filled their boots and because they began to run out of ammunition. Unfortunately, Capitán de Navío Enrique Simpson, charged with supervising the disembarkation of the troops, performed this task as poorly as he had commanded the *Cochrane;* apparently drunk, he could not be found in time to carry out his orders. Replacing him cost the invaders an hour that the Bolivians efficiently used to regroup.[9] Fortunately for the Chilean infantry, its navy's warships utilized the time to shell the enemy's defenses. Consequently, by the time the second wave—the remainder of the Atacama and Zapadores, plus troops from Buin and Second of Line—started to land, the fleet's guns had forced many of the Bolivian defenders to abandon their positions.

The combination of heat and the intensity of the enemy's resistance slowed the attackers struggling to ascend the heights. But the Bolivian defenders faced their own problems: the naval bombardment ignited heaps of nitrate and coal, producing thick clouds of smoke that masked the Chilean invaders as well as suffocated the defenders, making it difficult for them to fight. Almost asphyxiated and having consumed their ammunition, the outnumbered and exhausted Bolivians fled into the desert, allowing Escala's men, supported by a third wave of reinforcements, to capture Hospicio, a town that stood atop the escarpment, by early afternoon.

The Bolivians had fought well. Even the Peruvian commander, Gen. Juan Buendía, praised the outnumbered troops' "courage and serenity," while a journalist claimed that "the filibusters of America have received an eternal and bloody lesson of heroism and valor that they will have to remember always." But Bolivia's men paid a high blood tax for these words of praise: the Batallón Victoria lost 298 of 498 enlisted men; the other unit lost almost as many. The Chilean army and navy suffered less:

55 dead and 142 wounded. The vanquished Bolivians fled into the desert with only the clothes on their back."[10]

Meanwhile, the *Magallanes*, the *Amazonas*, and the *Itata*, carrying the Third Regiment of the Line, the Batallón Naval, the Batallón Valparaíso, and two batteries of mountain artillery, had left the main invasion fleet to attack Junín. These troops encountered little resistance because the defenders had apparently fled upon hearing the guns of the *Amazonas*. Although spared having to overcome the same amount of opposition as the men who landed at Pisagua, the combination of an extremely rocky shore and high seas so delayed the Junín landing that by the time two thousand Chilean soldiers had scaled the cliffs, the rest of the expeditionary force had already captured Pisagua.[11]

Seizing Pisagua established a Chilean beachhead in the province of Tarapacá, but much remained undone. More troubling, the landing revealed many flaws in the Chilean armed forces: infighting within the army as well as that between the officers and civilians, Thomson's faulty navigation, and Simpson's botched landing, deeply troubled the Ministry of War and Marine. The authorities would be horrified to learn that Escala had forgotten to include medical units in the invasion, forcing one of his chaplains, Father J. Valdés Carrera, to organize a hospital, which a naval surgeon from the *Magallanes*, Dr. David Tagle, staffed and equipped.[12] But the man who seemed to arouse the most anger was Col. Emilio Sotomayor, first for picking such a bad landing site and then for refusing to modify the plan when it became clear that the weather and the rocky shoreline would complicate the landing.[13]

Given this inauspicious beginning, Pinto did not want his troops rushing pell-mell into the arid wasteland of Tarapacá. Instead, he hoped to use Pisagua as a base from which Chilean cavalry would launch a series of raids that the president prayed would goad the Allies into counterattacking. Only if the Peruvian and Bolivians did not react to this provocation would the Chileans invade the desert, cut the enemy's supply lines, and thus force Iquique to surrender.[14]

Pinto's hope that the Chilean presence at Pisagua might provoke an Allied response quickly foundered: the Peruvian and Bolivian troops simply would not take the bait. Worse, within four days of the landing, it became clear that the fleet's condensers could not produce enough water to sustain the ten-thousand-man expeditionary army, their mounts, as well as Hospicio's civilian population. The nearest source of water was Quebrada de Pisagua, two leagues east of the seacoast, but this well, which produced just a little "brackish and noxious water" every three to four hours, obviously could not slake the Chileans' thirst.[15] Initially the authorities chose to ignore this problem, but when the water shortage drove some soldiers to suicide, the commanders realized that they had to do something. Lt. Col. José Francisco Vergara, a national guard officer and future minister of war, volunteered to lead a reconnaissance mission into the interior, where, given the number of still functioning salitreras, he was sure he could find ample water supplies. Although the regular army's most senior officers initially opposed his suggestion, eventually he received permission.

Following the railroad line and moving at night, Vergara's men pushed east, arriving first at San Roberto and then Jazpampa, where they found a functioning locomotive and rolling stock. They also discovered supplies, coal, and three large tanks containing sweet water. Vergara's men then turned southeast from Jazpampa, reaching the salitrera of Dolores on 5 November, where once again they found more wells as well as enormous stores of water, pumps, more rolling stock, and a railroad repair facility. The next day, after dispatching a train carrying water to Pisagua, Vergara's men moved further south to Agua Santa, another salitrera, where they learned that most of Iquique's garrison had withdrawn into the interior, leaving the port virtually defenseless.

Vergara continued to follow the railway as it moved toward the southeast. Aware that he might encounter some retreating Allied troops, the Chilean ordered a detachment of cavalry under Lt. Gonzalo Lara to scout ahead. Near Germania on 16 November, Lara rode into an Allied ambush that forced the outnumbered Chileans to flee with the Bolivian and Peruvian cavalry in deadly pursuit. Unfortunately for the Allied horsemen, they ran into the main body of Vergara's cavalry, which counterattacked, killing more than fifty to sixty cavalrymen, whose unburied bodies the Chileans left to rot on the nitrate pampa.[16] Perhaps realizing that he might be tempting the fates, Vergara retreated first to Negreiros and then to Dolores.

As Vergara retreated along the railroad line, Presidents Hilarión Daza

Table 7. Bolivian army, 1 April 1879

	Number	roopsof T
Lejión Boliviana		
Es. Rifleros el ed Nort	283	
Es. Vanguardia/Murillo, Rifleros del Centro	227	
Es. Libres del Sur	225	
1a. División - Comandante, Jeneral de División Cárlos de Villegas		
Btn. Daza, Granaderos 1 de la Guardia	588	
Btn. Paucaparta, 2 de la Paz	434	
Btn. Olañeta, 2 Cazadores de la Guardia	469	
Rgt. Bolívar, 1 de Húsares	280	
2a. División – General de Brigada Castro Arguedas		
Btn. Sucre 2, Granaderos de la Guardia	540	
Btn. Víctoria, 1 de la Paz	537	
Btn. Dalence, Carabineros 1 de Oruro	538	
Rgt. Santa Cruz de Artillería	226	
3a. División – General de Brigada Pedro Villamil		
Btn. Illimani, Caza 1 de la Guardia	536	
Btn. Independencia, 3 de la Paz	435	
Btn. Vengadores, 3 de Potosí	533	
Es. Escolta, 1 de Coraceros	58	
4a. División - General de Brigada Luciano Alcoreza		
Btn. Oropeza, 1 de Cochabamba		
Btn. Aroma 2 de Cochabamba		
Btn. Viedma, 3 de Cochabamba		
Btn. Padilla, 4 de Cochabamba		
Es. Junín, 3 de Coraceros		
Es. Libertad, 4 de Coraceros		
5a. División – General de Brigada Narciso Campero		
Btn. Bustillo, 1 de Potosí		
Ayacucho, 2 de Potosí		
Chorolque, 4 de Potosí		
Tarija, 3 de Granaderos		
Es. Mendez, 2 de Coraceros		
Lejión de Bolivia		

Calls were made for Bolivians living in Atacama who had taken refuge in Peru to form a division composed of the Batallones Antofagasta, Mejillones i Caracoles, Rifleros de Atacama. Bolivia, Ministry of War, *Memoria*; La Paz, 1 April 1879, in Ahumada Moreno, *Guerra del Pacífico*, 1:107–8. Divisions Four and Five had not arrived, and as such did not belong to the Army of Tacna; they did, however, later fight.

Those units in **boldface** composed Bolivia's prewar regular army.

Table 8. Peruvian forces stationed in Tarapacá Province, 5 November 1879

División de Esploración	Col. Bustamanate	
	Btn. 1 Ayacucho, N. 3	908
	Btn. Provioncia Lima, N. 3	355
	Columna Voluntarios de Pasco,	185
División de Vanguardia	Col. Justo Pastor Dávila	
	Btn. Puno, N. 6	438
	Btn. Lima, N. 8	443
	Rgto. Guías, N. 3	173
	Es. Castilla	81
Primera División Peruvian	Colonel Velarde	
	Btn. Cazadores del Cuzco N. 5	468
	Btn. Cazadores de la Guardia, N. 7	458
	Rgt. Husáres de Junín	343
Segunda División	Col. Andrés Cáceres	
	Rgt. 2 de Mayo	476
	Btn. Zepita, N. 2	636
Tercera División	Col. Francisco Bolognesi	
	Btn. 2 de Ayacucho	441
	Btn. Guardia de Arequipa	498
Quinta División	Btn. Iquique N. 1	417
	Cazadores de Tarapacá	171
	Columna Loa (B)	343
	Columna Tarapacá	246
	Columa Artesanos de Costa	93*
	Brig. de Artillería	91*
Total including divisional general staffs:		6,453

Sources: Ochoa, *Semblanzas*, 101; J. M. Cevallos Ortiz, "Estado de las fuerzas del ejército aliado el 5 de Noviembre de 1879," in Ahumada Moreno, *Guerra del Pacífico*, 2:101.

*Dellepiane, *Historia militar*, 2:130, claims that in first months of the war, the Peruvians lost 1,174 in Pisagua from wounds, death, desertion, or illness.

and Mariano Prado met in Tacna to discuss how to respond to the Chilean invasion. The Bolivian leader had arrived in Tacna at the end of April, his eight thousand troops completing the taxing 380-mile march from La Paz in twelve days. Daza subsequently sent his First and Third divisions, south to Tarapacá; the Second and Fourth divisions remained in Tacna. After some discussions, the two generals agreed that Daza's three thousand men would march sixty-two miles south to Tana, a town ap-

Table 9. Bolivian army in Tarapacá, 5 November 1879

1a. División	
Btn. Illimani - Col. Ramón González	539
Btn. Olañeta - Col. Eloi Martínez	483
Btn. Paucarpata - Col. Pablo Idiaquez, N. 1	456
Btn. Dalence - Col. Donato Vazquez, N.1	545
Es. Franco Tiradores - Col. Napoleón Tejada	150
Rgt. Bolívar 1 de Húsares - Col. Julian María Lopez	280
2a. División	
Btn. 1 de Aroma - Col. Beslario Antesana, N. 1	558
Btn. Independencia - Col. Pedro Varas, N. 1.	433
*Btn. Loa - Col. Detelino Echazu T.	300
Btn. Vengadores - Col. Federico Murga, N. 1	528
Btn. Víctoria - Col. Juan Granier, N. 1	427
Nacionales de Bolivia	N/A
Total	4,699

*Composed of Bolivians residing in Peru, the *Loa* served with the Peruvian forces.

Sources: Hilarión Daza, "Manifesto del Jeneral Hilaríon Daza a sus conciudadanos," Paris, 5 July 1881, 4:151, 155, 160–61, José Manuel Cevallos Ortiz, Iquique, 28 October 1879, 2:101, *La Democracia* (La Paz), 7 November 1879, 2:102, in Ahumada Moreno, *Guerra del Pacífico.*

proximately forty-four miles northeast of Pisagua. At the same time, Juan Buendía's nine thousand Bolivian and Peruvian troops would advance fifty-five miles north, paralleling the La Noria to Tana railroad. Once Daza's and Buendía's troops linked up, they would veer west to Hospicio in order to drive the Chileans into the sea.

Although initially leery, the Chileans had found good reasons for moving inland. Capturing Tarapacá's salitreras as well as Iquique would give Santiago not only an economic bonanza but also a diplomatic asset that it could barter in return for Peru ending the war.[17] Thus, on 5 November Sotomayor ordered thirty-five hundred troops, under the command of Col. José Domingo Amunátegui and consisting of the Fourth Regiment of the Line, the Buin, and the Atacama and Coquimbo battalions, as well as a battery of mountain artillery, to depart Pisagua for Dolores and Negrieros. Three days later, Col. Martiniano Urriola's twenty-five hundred men of the Third Regiment of the Line, the Navales and Valparaíso battalions, and a field artillery contingent also left for the interior. By 10 November these six thousand men had assembled at Dolores to initiate their offensive to capture Pozo Almonte, which, if successful, would sever Iquique's supply lines with the interior and thus force the port's garrison to capitulate. Curiously, even as his troops marched south, Escala's attention still seemed riveted on the north. On 11 November spies informed him that Daza's legions were heading south from Arica and that all that stood between the Bolivians and Pisagua were thirty-five hundred men. The Bolivian dictator had departed Tacna with great ceremony. A La Paz newspaper correspondent reported that the assembled bands played both the Peruvian and Bolivian national anthems as Daza's troops, their ears ringing with the cheers of a hat-waving crowd, disappeared into the desert.[18] The intelligence reports proved correct, but Escala need not have worried: Daza may have departed for Tana, but he never arrived. His failure to link up with the Peruvians would have an enormous impact on the war.

Were the consequences not so tragic, Daza's trek through Tarapacá's hinterland might provoke coarse laughter. From the onset of his campaign, the general demonstrated an almost monumental incompetence: he refused to hire guides to lead his forces through the unforgiving and unknown wasteland. Rather than travel at night, and thus spare his men from the searing desert sun, Daza instead advanced during the day. (Apparently he feared, with good reason, that his troops might desert under the cover of the darkness.) The Bolivian general rejected a Peruvian offer of ambulances, and he ordered his artillery to remain in Arica. Perhaps one of Daza's most criminally negligent acts was that his refusal to bring sufficient water with him. Worse, he permitted his men to fill their canteens with wine or raw spirits, a disastrous mistake given the fact that the nearest supply of water was a substantial distance away from Arica. Col. Narciso Tablares, alerted by a commissary official that Daza's expedition would carry only eleven water skins, warned the Bolivian general that his men might run out of water. When Daza haughtily dismissed these fears with the words "You do what you are told," Tablares had little choice but to obey. Thanks to this decision, anyone wishing to chart the progress of Daza's army only had to follow the string of dehydrated and sometimes dead Bolivian soldiers who had succumbed to thirst, "altitude sickness, exhaustion, and hunger." Three tortuous days later, Daza's exhausted and parched troops reached Camarones, about fifty miles south of Arica, where he planned that they rest before renewing their drive south to Tana.[19] But when the Bolivians finally broke camp, they marched not to Tana but north to Arica.

On 16 November at Camarones, Daza discussed future strategy with his senior officers. Following the meeting, the dictator abruptly cancelled the offensive, instead ordering his men to return to Arica. Daza's motivations still confound scholars today. Some have suggested that Chilean officials bribed Daza into canceling his offensive.[20] While Santiago had few qualms about employing such a ruse, no proof exists to substantiate this charge. Others aver that the dictator, learning that his opponents within the army planned to overthrow him, cancelled the offensive in order to return immediately to La Paz to secure his hold on the presidency. Certainly it would not be out of character for the narcissistic Daza to conclude that he, not Bolivia, should have first call on the army's services, particularly his beloved Colorados.[21]

Daza subsequently argued that he had aborted his Tacna campaign for two reasons: first, he could not move south because President Prado failed to equip his army with the necessary artillery, supplies, water, and mounts; second, his most senior commanders had begged him to return to Arica. Either allowed Daza to proclaim self-righteously that he was "not therefore the author of the retreat at Camarones, [that] I acceded only to the sadly famous accord of this council . . . [that] wanted to diminish my authority [and that] sought a reason to supplant me."[22] Daza's subordinates, however, insisted that the caudillo had "told various officers, in secret, *that from this place* [Camarones] *the army will countermarch* [to Arica]" (italics in the original). Few of his officers dared to disagree because, as the Peruvian journalist Juan José Pérez, once noted, the caudillo did not tolerate anyone "who does not think or say except what Daza wants."[23] The Bolivian troops, of course, did not care what motivated their commander's decision. Throwing their hats into the air and heartened by band music, they happily marched north. Daza, however, did not join them: stating that he wished to meet Buendía, he rode south, escorted by a small band of cavalry.[24]

Unaware of Daza's decision to return to Arica, General Escala still feared that the Bolivian officer would lead his men south. Consequently, Escala ordered his cavalry to the north, to Tiliviche near Tana, where the warhorses could graze on the ample pasture, while his men would provide an advance warning of a possible Bolivian move. On 17 November, news reached both Escala and Vergara that pickets had sighted the Bolivian vanguard at Tana. To confirm this rumor, Escala ordered Lt. Col. Feliciano Echeverría to scour the area. Unaware of Escala's order, Vergara also led a band of horsemen to the north to accomplish the same mission. Sighting enemy cavalry, both men spread the alarm.

What Vergara and Echeverría spied was not Daza's cavalry but the Bolivian president and his escort. If either of the Chilean units had attacked, they could easily have captured the Bolivian. They failed to do so, however, owing to a crucial mistake: uninformed that another Chilean unit was operating in the Tana area, Echeverría and Vergara mistook the other's scouting party for the vanguard of Daza's legions. Hence, rather than engage what they believed was the entire Bolivian army, they hastily retreated to warn Escala.

Unaware of this crucial mistake, Escala immediately moved to block Daza's putative southern advance. On 18 November, he ordered Lt. Col. José Echeverría to move the Batallón Bulnes from Hospicio to Jazpampa, a key junction standing astride the road from Arica to the south. He also commanded Col. Emilio Sotomayor to transfer part of Dolores's garrison to Jazpampa. Colonel Sotomayor complied, delegating to Lt. Col. Ricardo Castro the task of leading north the Third Regiment of the Line, the Batallón Coquimbo, and some artillery. Although he had dispatched some of his men to Jazpampa, Sotomayor continued to comply with Escala's orders to move south in order to besiege Iquique. To scout ahead, Sotomayor sent Capt. Manuel Barahona south toward Santa Catalina. There the Chileans ran into Buendía's advance party.

While Daza's army fled north, the unsuspecting General Buendía faced the difficult problem of massing his forces. First, he led the survivors of Pisagua away from the seacoast and then south into the wastes of Tarapacá. Then he merged these troops with any Allied soldiers stationed either on the coast or in the interior in order to concentrate his force, so they could repel a possible Chilean incursion. By 8 November Buendía managed to collect these men in Pozo Almonte. Eight days later Buendía, still following Prado and Daza's original plan, ordered his nine-thousand-man army north. By 18 November they had reached Agua Santa. As his infantry rested, Buendía sent a cavalry unit north to Negreiros to gather intelligence. It was this unit that collided with Barahona's cavalry.

Table 10. Chilean expeditionary force invading Tarapacá,
2 November 1879

Gen. Erasmo Escala		
Lt. Col. Luis José Ortiz	Rgt. Buin, 1 de Linea	1,100
Lt. Col. Eluterio Ramírez	Rgt. 2 de Linea	1,117
Lt. Col. Ricardo Castro	Rgt. 3 de Linea	1,100
Lt. Col. Domingto Amunátegui	Rgt. 4 de Linea	1,076
Lt. Col. Ricardo Santa Cruz	Rgt. Zapadores	400
		(1 brigade)
Lt. Col. Domingo de Toro Herrera	Btn. Chacabuco	600
Lt. Col. José Echeverría	Btn. Bulnes	500
Col. Jácinto Niño	Btn. Valparaíso	300
Lt. Col. Alejandro Gorostiaga	Btn. Coquimbo	500
Lt. Col. Juan Martínez	Btn. Atacama	590
Col. Martiniano Urriola	Btn. Navales	640
Col. Ricardo Santa Cruz	Btn. Zapadores	400
Lt. Col. Pedro Soto Aguilar	Rgt. Cazadores a Caballo	395
Capt. Rodolfo Villagrán	Rgt. Granaderos a Caballo	125
		(1 company)
Lt. Col. José Velásquez	Rgt. 2 de Artillería	625
Lt. Col. José Rámon Viadurre	Rgt. Artillería de Marina, Ponteros	400
Total		9,868

Sources: Chile, "Plan Mayor," in Ahumada Moreno, *Guerra del Pacífico*, 2:64–68; Chile, Ministry of War and the Navy, *Memoria, 1880*, 22–23.

The news of Barahona's sighting of Buendía's forces doubtless shocked Sotomayor, who suddenly realized that unless he acted, his men could be crushed between the armies of Daza and Buendía. Deciding to make his stand at the Santa Catalina salitrera, Sotomayor desperately recalled the troops he had just sent to reinforce the north. As Castro's men retraced their steps, Sotomayor shuttled the Fourth Regiment of the Line, 220 cavalrymen, and four artillery pieces to Santa Catalina, where the Batallón Atacama later joined them. Escala also acted, ordering the Artillería de Marina, an artillery battery, the Second of the Line, and the Zapadores and Batallón Chacabuco to move from Hospicio to reinforce the Chileans in the south.

At the suggestion of Bernardo de la Barra, the same savant who had urged Escala to land at Junín, Sotomayor decided to dig in at Santa Catalina. Happily for Chile, Vergara, after a heated exchange, managed to convince Sotomayor to abandon Santa Catalina in favor of taking a stand on San Francisco, a large hill rising two hundred yards above the nitrate pampa. Unfortunately, Sotomayor's change of heart required his troops

Table 11. Allied forces defending Pisagua

Pisagua Garrison	Peruvian National Guard	240
	Peruvian Artillerymen	45
	Btn. Víctoria (B)	498
	Btn. Independencia(B)	397
Mejillones de Peru		
	Btn. Aroma (B)	490
Germania		
	Btn. Vengadores (B)	489

B = Bolivian

Sources: Dellepiane, *Historia militar*, 2:94–100; Estado Mayor de la Segunda Division Boliviano, Agua Santa, 4 November 1879, in Ahumada Moreno, *Guerra del Pacífico*, 2:86.

to abandon their newly prepared defensive positions at Santa Catalina, to race about four miles to the north, and to dig in yet again. Obeying this order proved particularly taxing for the men of the Atacama Battalion, who arrived at Santa Catalina at 2 a.m. of 19 November only to learn that they had to return immediately to Dolores, a taxing assignment that they still managed to accomplish just before daybreak.

As Buendía's army lumbered north, Sotomayor frantically prepared his defenses. Cerro San Francisco really consisted of two peaks: the lowest, called either San Francisco Norte or Cerro Dolores, provided the defenders a vista of the pampa to the west and southwest, and the taller of the two hills, San Francisco Sur, overlooked the south, the east, and the west. Colonel Sotomayor placed the Fourth of the Line and Batallón Coquimbo on the lower slopes of San Francisco Sur.

Slightly to the rear and to the northeast, Colonel Sotomayor positioned eight field guns under Maj. José Salvo. He also placed the Batallón Atacama and an artillery unit, consisting of four mountain guns and two machine guns, to the north of these units in order to protect the Chilean left, or eastern, flank. Twelve artillery pieces, whose fields of fire covered sectors on the west and south, stood on the right flank of San Francisco Norte. Sprawling slightly below these guns, the First Line Regiment and the Batallones Valparaíso and Navales faced southwest. To defend the Chilean rear, as well as the crucial water wells of Dolores, the Chileans sited eight more artillery pieces atop Tres Clavos, a rock outcropping slightly north of Cerro Dolores. These guns could also stop any enemy unit that might try to move north in an attempt to outflank the Chilean position. A mixed force of infantrymen drawn from other units,

Table 12. Battle of San Francisco/Dolores, 19 November 1879

Allied Forces (Authorized Strength)

Allied Right Wing
4a. División - Peruvian - Col. Justo Pastor Dávila

Btn. Puno, N. 6	452
Btn. Lima, N. 8	456
Rgt. Guías, N. 3	173
Es. Castilla	81

6a. División - Peruvian - Gen. Pedro Bustamante [Esploradora]

Btn. Ayacucho	702
Btn. Lima, N. 3	355
Col. Pasco	185

1a. División – Bolivian - Gen. Carlos Villegas

Btn. Paucarpata	457
Btn. Dalence	546
Btn. Illimani	530
Btn. Olañeta	484
Rgt. Bolívar, N. 1 Húsares	281
Es. Franco-Tiradores	147

Allied Left Wing
1a. División – Peruvian – Colonel Velarde

Btn. Cazadores del Cuzco	482
Btn. Cazadores de la Guardia	472
Rgt. Húsares de Junín	343

3a. División – Peruvian – Col. Francisco Bolognesi

Btn. Ayacucho, N. 2	460
Btn. Guardias de Arequipa	498

3a. División – Bolivian – Gen. Pedro Villamil

Btn. Aroma	559
Btn. Vengadores	529
Btn. Independencia	434
Btn. Victoria	537

Allied Center
2a. División – Peruvian - Col. Andrés Cáceres

Btn. Zepita	477
Btn. 2 de Mayo	636

Additional Allied Infantry

Btn. Iquique 1	410
Btn. Voluntarios de Pasco	
Btn. Cazadores de Tarapacá	171
Col. Navales	
Col. Loa	303
Col. Tarapacá	196

Allied Artillery
    Col. Artillería de Costa   65
    Brigada de Artillería   200

Allied Artillery	
Col. Artillería de Costa	65
Brigada de Artillería	200
Total	11,662
Chilean Forces	
Chilean Left, or Eastern, Flank – Col. Ricardo Castro	
Rgt. 3 de Linea	700
1 battery of 4 artillery pieces	
Chilean Center –Col. José D. Amunátegui	
Btn. Atacama	500
Btn. Coquimbo	500
Rgt. 4 of Line	1,000
2 batteries of artillery (14 guns) plus 2 Gatling guns	
Chilean Right, or Western, Flank - Col. Martiniano Urriola	
Btn. Navales	600
Btn. Valparaíso	300
Rgt. Buin	1,000
2 batteries of 6 pieces	
Chilean Infantry	
Various elements taken from other units, some engineers	
Chilean Artillery	
Scattered to flanks and rear	106
Chilean Cavalry	
Rgto. Cazadores a Caballo – 1 squadron	
Es. Granaderos a Caballo	

Sources: Buendía, *Guerra con Chile*, 153–54; Dellepiane, *Historia militar*, 2:129–30; Machuca, *Cuatro campañas*, 1:304–7; Toro Dávila, *Síntesis histórico militar*, 256–57; Pinochet U., *Guerra del Pacífico*, 163–64. General Escala's report to the Minister of War indicates that men from Bulnes fought, but he is the only one to mention that unit. Erasmo Escala to Minister of Navy and War, Partes oficiales chilenos, in Ahumada Moreno, *Guerra del Pacífico*, 1:135.

two cavalry squadrons and the Zapadores, protected the nearby artillery as well the rear of the San Francisco and the Dolores water well.[25]

The Battle of Dolores

As the Chileans rushed to take up their positions atop Cerro San Fran-cisco, seventy-four hundred troops, thirty-two hundred of these Bolivi-ans, marching in three parallel columns, divided into three components, and led by a line of skirmishers, advanced northward. The first, under

4. Battle of Dolores/San Francisco

the command of Gen. Pedro Bustamante, consisted of Col. Justo Dávila Pastor's Fourth Peruvian, or Vanguardia, Division (Batallones Puno and Lima Num. 8), Col. Pedro Bustamante's Sixth Peruvian, or Exploradora, Division (Batallones Ayacucho, Lima Num. 3, and Columna Pasco), and the First Bolivian Division under Gen. Guillermo Villegas (Batallones Paucarpata, Dalence, Illimani, and Olañeta). The second group was composed of Baltasar Velarde's First Peruvian Division (Batallones Cazadores del Cuzo and Cazadores de la Guardia), the Third Peruvian Division of Col. Francisco Bolognesi (Batallones Ayacucho Num. 2 and Guardias de Arequipa), and the Third Bolivian Division, commanded by Gen. Pedro Villamil (Batallones Aroma and Vengadores, plus the remnants of the survivors of the Battle of Pisagua). The third wave was Col. Andrés Cáceres's Second Peruvian Division (Batallones Zepita and 2 de Mayo). As they moved forward, the columns peeled off from the main body of troops, each taking a different path: the first wave forming the Allied right, the second constituting its left. Part of the third detachment, stationed in the rear, became the reserve. The Allied cavalry and artillery units took up positions slightly forward of Col. Andrés Cáceres.[26]

Running back and forth between Santa Catalina and San Francisco may have weakened the Chileans, but they were in far better condition than their foes. Rather than use the road north, Buendía had ordered his men to travel overland. This decision proved disastrous: during their night march, Allied units stumbled into each other, fell into the deep holes that miners had dug to extract nitrate, or collided with the heaps of salitre awaiting refining. Not surprisingly, the units lost their cohesion, forcing them to stop periodically in order to re-form. Worse, these men reached San Francisco not simply exhausted but starving and dehydrated: during the preceding twenty-four hours their rations consisted of but four ounces of beef jerky and a few drops of water. Buendía and Suárez's "shoeless, naked" men, so destitute that they did not have "money even to buy cigarettes," seemed only slightly superior to their Bolivian comrades, who had gone without water for two days.[27] Buendía desperately wanted to feed his men, but without government funds to pay for provisions, he could not do so. Eventually he had to sign a personal note to borrow the money to purchase supplies.[28]

Despite these problems, at least according to Col. Andrés Cáceres, the

Allied troops enthusiastically moved toward Cerro San Francisco, anxious to strike before more Chilean reinforcements arrived from Hospicio. But as the bands played martial tunes and the officers harangued their troops, Buendía ordered his men to halt, to build shelters, and to rest: the Peruvian had postponed the offensive to await Daza, who would command the ten thousand troops. As the Peruvian commander would learn, neither Daza nor his men would arrive as planned on 19 November 1879. If this news depressed Buendía, it must have demoralized the Bolivian soldiers who not only lost heart but became the butt of coarse Peruvian jibes. Suddenly, thanks to Daza's defection, Buendía had to assume command of the Allied troops.[29]

Some of Buendía's brothers-in-arms doubted that the Peruvian officer was suited for his command. Although known as a man of breeding and culture, he reputedly lacked a personality "that commands respect and obedience in the army, or the professional skill that inspires in his subordinates a blind confidence in his aptitudes."[30] Ill-prepared and elevated by a fluke to command a rag-tag army plagued by unrest, Buendía may have been the wrong man at the wrong time.

Not surprisingly, Buendía devoted a good portion of the morning to playing catch-up, studying the situation to determine if he should act and then, after concluding that he must, devising a strategy to capture San Francisco. At approximately 11:00 a.m., he presented to his senior officers his plan, which called for a portion of his expeditionary force to attack the Chilean troops dug in at the southern end of Cerro San Francisco. While the enemy defended against this assault, the Allied right would first proceed northeast and then veer north, paralleling the rail line, so it could capture Dolores's water well. Meanwhile, as the Peruvians inched toward the oasis, his left wing would move northwest, along Cerro San Francisco's western flank and then wheel east until it reached La Encañada located at the rear of Cerro Dolores. If successful, the Allies would have encircled the Chileans while simultaneously depriving them of access to water, leaving Sotomayor with the unpalatable choice of either capitulating or attempting to break through the Allied lines.

Some of Buendía's officers opposed, if not his plan, then its timing. As Gen. Pedro Villamil observed, with most of the Bolivian troops hungry, thirsty, exhausted, and demoralized by Daza's defection, that afternoon was not the most propitious moment to launch an offensive. Instead, he suggested that Buendía postpone the attack until the following morning, a recommendation that Suárez seconded. Apparently, Buendía initially ignored their objections, ordering the assault at approximately 3:00 p.m. Indeed, Colonel Cáceres was in the process of leading his men toward the Chilean positions when suddenly his bother officer Colonel Suárez galloped over to inform him: "Happily, I have succeeded in convincing the commander in chief to abandoned the attack, postponing it until the early hour of tomorrow morning." It appears that Buendía, just prior to the attack had unexpectedly run into some of his officers, who argued so convincingly that he canceled the offensive for a second time. Instead, he told his subordinates to distribute rations to the men, so they could spend the afternoon eating and resting; they could always die tomorrow, when at dawn they would assault Cerro San Francisco.[31]

Some less obvious forces perhaps inspired Buendía's decision. Clearly Daza's defection changed the situation for the worse: left in the lurch by the dictator, Buendía and his chief of staff, Colonel Suárez, worried about the trustworthiness of their Bolivian brothers-in-arms. This was not the first time that the Peruvians questioned their allies' capabilities: after Pisagua one bureaucrat complained to Buendía that the Bolivians were "a major disappointment, disobedient or disrespectful of everyone."[32] Buendía also had ample cause for concern: high-ranking Bolivian officers, including Generals Villamil and Villegas, blandly announced that their duty lay not in trying to wrest San Francisco from the Chileans but in overthrowing Daza. Upon overhearing these remarks, the Peruvian Col. Justo Pastor Dávila muttered that "useless officers such as these can land us in hell." Worse, some Peruvian commanders reported that a few Bolivian officers, citing Daza's defection, had encouraged their men to desert, so they could return to La Paz to depose the dictator. Apparently the enlisted men intended to heed their officers' advice: a Quechuan-speaking Peruvian colonel, Victor Fajardo, eavesdropping on some Bolivian soldiers learned that these troops, not wishing to die for Peru, planned to fire their rifles a couple of times and then bolt for La Paz. Clearly, the Peruvians would have been wise to reconsider their attack until they were more certain of their Bolivian comrades.[33]

Meanwhile, the men of the Allied army rested. Using their blankets to shade them from the hot sun, some of the soldiers ate; others, particularly the desperately thirsty Bolivians, lined up to drink and to fill their canteens from a well near the salitrera of El Porvenir. According to a Bolivian eyewitness, Miguel Armaya, the Bolivian soldiers requested and received Buendía's permission to have the units from the two nations take turns at the well. Either Buendía's subordinate commanders did not receive the order or they chose to ignore it. Whatever the reason, around 3:00 p.m. the supposed allies began bickering over the water; words escalated into blows when a Peruvian struck a Bolivian. An angry Bolivian soldier then stabbed a Peruvian with a bayonet while urging his comrades to open fire on their allies.[34] When someone discharged his rifle, at what the bystanders were not sure, others also began firing their weapons. The trigger-happy soldier's identity was unknown. The Peruvians, although not positive, predictably blamed their Bolivian comrades; one source even identified the culprit as a Bolivian sergeant serving in the Batallón Illimani. Just to complicate matters, a Chilean artillery officer subsequently admitted that his men, interpreting the Bolivian presence at the water well of Porvenir as the preamble to an assault on their positions, had opened fired.[35] This act, in turn, inspired the troops gathered at the water hole to edge forward. The sudden appearance of a mounted Peruvian officer, who ordered the men to move ahead, converted their tentative advance into a charge. Intentionally or not, the Battle of Dolores had begun.[36] Meanwhile, the other Peruvian troops, hearing the gunfire and believing that the battle had started, joined the impromptu attack. Their officers tried to halt the charge, but the Bolivians, as Belisario Suárez discovered, "deaf to the bugle, indifferent to gunfire, to threats, to exhortations, and to everything," pressed forward. It quickly became evident that the Allied commanders had no choice but to attack, following the battle plan that Buendía had hoped to employ the next morning.[37]

As prearranged, the closed columns of the Peruvian Lima Num. 8, Puno, and Zepita battalions, as well as the Bolivian Illimani and Olañeta, led by skirmishers, attacked the Chileans dug in at the southern end of Cerro San Francisco. Initially, the Allied troops enjoyed some success because they had managed to find a dead zone where the Chilean artillery shells could not strike them. Unfortunately, as Dávila's and Bustamante's men started to scale the hill, a difficult task made worse by the heat, dust, clay soil, and the hill's steep angle of ascent, some of the troops of the Olañeta and Illimani, operating in small disorganized groups, opened fire. Tragically, because their rifles lacked the range, the Bolivian troops shot not the Chilean defenders but instead savaged their comrades.[38]

Caught in a deadly crossfire, which Remijo Morales of the Batallón Lima called "a fatal error that not surprisingly produced a calamity," the assault stalled. Still, some of the men of the Zeptia and Illimani surmounted the high ground, silencing a Chilean gun battery. For one brief moment, it appeared that the Peruvians would triumph: a few soldiers actually captured two Chilean field pieces.[39] But Salvo's artillerymen, fighting as infantry alongside the Atacama and Coquimbo, launched a series of bayonet charges that repelled the attackers.[40] The Allied troops counterattacked three times, but eventually the casualties inflicted by Chilean artillery, small arms, and machine guns, as well as exhaustion and a lack of ammunition proved too much: demoralized by Bolivian friendly fire, the Allied soldiers retreated.[41]

As the Bolivian and Peruvian troops tried to seize the Chilean positions at the southern end of Cerro San Francisco, the Allies launched their enveloping movements. Buendía's force—composed of the Batallones Lima Num. 3 and Ayacucho, plus the Bolivian Batallones Paucarpata and Dalence—moved on Cerro San Francisco's eastern flank, while Suárez's men pushed toward the hill's western side. Neither commander succeeded. Martiniano Urriola, who commanded the Chilean artillery located on Cerro Dolores's forward slope, opened fire with, as the Chilean officer modestly noted, "superb results." On the other side of Cerro San Francisco, the men of the Aroma and the Vengadores in addition to the survivors of Pisagua tried to push north to take the Chilean artillery, but they failed thanks to the recently arrived Valparaíso and Bulnes battalions, which, having sprinted from the train station to join the battle, repulsed the attack.[42] Buendía's men suffered a similar fate: although his troops managed to reach the railroad line and to advance toward the water wells of Dolores, the Chilean artillery located on San Francisco's eastern slope and atop Tres Clavos so severely shredded them that their commander ordered a retreat. Buendía tried to rally his men, but each time the Chilean guns stopped them. And when the Allies fell back, the Chileans counterattacked.[43]

Meanwhile, under heavy artillery fire, some Bolivian troops first wavered and then, chanting "to Oruro, to Oruro," threw down their weapons and ran into the desert.[44] These soldiers not only fled but did so in front of the entire Allied expeditionary force, igniting a defeatist panic that spread in their wake. Although Cáceres would later demean the Bolivians for being feckless, not all lost their nerve. The Dalence may have retreated, but it did not bolt. Some Peruvian units, moreover, did not behave any more valiantly: Buendía's cavalry, which had been held in reserve, also funked. Once the flight began neither "threats nor appeals to patriotism and soldiers' obligations had any effect." By 5 p.m., with no cavalry or Bolivian allies, the remaining Peruvian units fled "in complete disorder into the nitrate fields." Discipline had collapsed, and some troops appeared on the verge of mutiny.[45]

The defeat at Dolores, coming as it did on the heels of the loss of its navy and the Chilean landing at Pisagua, severely wounded the Peruvian psyche. Lima's *El Nacional* chronicled the terrible consequences: "Through all our body's pores flows the blood of our shame and of the contempt that an inept handful of functionaries spread over the Republic."[46] *El Comercio*, a Peruvian daily, blamed the loss on Buendía, noting "it is inexplicable the temerity of a general who, having the responsibility for the welfare of 10,000 soldiers, could have decided to attack without the slightest possibility of triumph and with the complete security that it would be a sterile and painfully costly sacrifice for the country." The paper hoped that the generals involved, having lost 37 percent of their troops, would learn from their mistakes.[47] Their supposed allies proved equally critical. One Bolivian noted, "Buendía's brain was confused. In this immense mass of men, his [Buendía's] was the only head that did not think." Suárez fared no better, being described as someone confronting a labyrinth "that he could neither order nor understand."[48]

The defeat at Dolores, of course, was not unexpected. The untrained, exhausted, undisciplined, barefoot, and wretchedly equipped Bolivian troops fighting alongside allies who denigrated them and commanded by unprepared officers whom they did not know had virtually no chance of success. What else could be expected, asked Miguel Armaza, from generals "incapable of commanding troops" who only knew how to spill "their blood uselessly"?[49] A leading Bolivian politician, Ladislao Cabrera, noted, "There was not one error that was not committed, from the most transcendental to the smallest detail. . . . There was no battle plan, there was no General in Chief, there was no division commander who received a decisive order." While some attributed the loss to Daza's flight, Buendía, whom one Chilean depicted as someone "who talks about everything without knowing anything," also came up short. One Bolivian attributed Buendía's failures to the fact that he was so besotted with romancing his mistress, a thirteen- or fourteen-year-old Chilean, that he paid scant attention to directing the war.[50]

Although victorious at Dolores, the Chileans also had ample cause for concern. Gen. Erasmo Escala revealed himself as a man so ultramontane that he appeared more concerned about his officers' fulfilling their religious obligations than with protecting his troops' health: he forgot to attach ambulances or medical units to the invasion force, thus condemning many of his wounded troops to an agonizingly slow death. The litany of Escala's errors did not stop: the general had waited until 3:00 a.m. of 19 November before sending urgently needed reinforcements to San Francisco. He failed to order his cavalry, which sat out the battle, to hunt down the Allied stragglers. Indeed, Escala, accompanied by his personal chaplain, only arrived at Dolores after his men had finished mopping up the battlefield. Not without reason, some argued that the general contributed little, if anything, to the battle.

Still, Escala did have flair: instead of ordering his troops to pursue and exterminate the fleeing enemy, the general benignly watched as his clerical companion—whom Williams Rebedollo had expelled from the fleet—proudly unveiled a banner bearing the visage of the Virgin of Carmen. Perhaps forgetting that the Bolivian army also claimed the Virgin of Carmen as its patron saint, Escala exclaimed to Vergara, "This, although you do not believe it, Señor Secretary, is what has given us our triumph." For once the general, whose acuity the "Señor Secretary" legitimately questioned, proved correct: Vergara—a grand master in Santiago's Masonic Lodge—emphatically rejected Escala's pious assertion. The Chileans, the official responded, owed their victory "more to our valor and bayonets" than to any saintly intercession. *El Mercurio* also shared Vergara's anticlericalism. Critical of the general for substituting a religious banner for Chile's tricolor, the newspaper argued that Escala rarely led his troops: "In Pisagua, he was at Junín; in Dolores at Hospicio, in Tarapacá in Iquique, and today where will he lead them?" The ultrareligious *beatos*, however, saw the hand of God in the Chilean victory. Chaplain Ruperto Marchant quoted Escala as saying that neither cannons nor bayonets mattered: "It is the God of the Armies Who knows how to award victories to whomever and whenever He wants." The same priest also saw a direct correlation between the troops' attendance at mass and Chile's victories.[51]

Despite the reports redolent with patriotic gore, Dolores's casualty rate was not that high. Ladislao Cabrera estimated that the Bolivians lost 400 to 500 dead and wounded. Buendía put the figure for the Peruvians at 488 (slightly more than 10 percent). The Chileans indicated that 61 of its men had died, with the Batallón Atacama suffering the heaviest losses; another 176 sustained wounds. The Chilean death rate would subsequently rise: Escala's failure to include medical personnel and ambulances forced the Chileans to evacuate their wounded. By the time the survivors of the Battle of San Francisco reached Chile, many of their wounds had become gangrenous.[52]

The relatively low body count should not obscure the ferocity of the contest: José Martínez, the Atacama's commander reported coming across a Chilean and Peruvian soldier who, having impaled and shot each other, remained locked by rigor mortis in a final deadly embrace. Modesto Molina, a Bolivian journalist, noted that many bodies of the Allied dead at Germania bore wounds inflicted by a *corvo* as well as signs of being mutilated. Worse, Vergara's men had left their lifeless enemies on the pampa, where birds of prey tore apart their bloated bodies.[53] The Chileans, of course, had their own complaints: one officer, for example, insisted that their foes used explosive bullets.[54] (They were not explosive but high-velocity missiles that inflicted heavy damage.)

Disorder and confusion marked the Allied retreat. Intent only upon surviving, the demoralized, ill, and homesick Bolivians simply ran into the high desert. Once on their own, these troops degenerated into a horde of looters and marauders that supposedly rivaled Attila's Huns: "not men but wild beasts of Senegal who only wished to satiate their limitless appetite."[55] Buendía's legions behaved only marginally better, shedding their equipment as they ran. The Chileans, as they mopped up, found the enemy's battle flags, supplies, and twelve disabled field pieces.[56] The Peruvians at least had the presence of mind to spike their cannons when they discovered they lacked the livestock to pull their artillery.[57]

Incompetence and the suffering it caused became the leitmotif of the Allied trek across the desert. The fleeing troops spent their first night not moving east but wandering in circles. Only good fortune and a thick fog prevented them from stumbling into a Chilean encampment. None of the Allied commanders, who had orders to lead their men to Arica, knew its location or how to get there. Nor, apparently, did they have maps to consult. Regrettably, their guides seemed only slightly better informed. A lucky few rode mules that had been used to pull the Allied artillery. The Bolivian march across the desert almost replicated the disorganization that had characterized Daza's abortive journey from Arica to Camarones. The supply train collapsed. Forced to plod long distances under a hot sun without water, some soldiers drank their own urine, and the troops' only food consisted of two to three live goats, which the men had to slaughter.[58] Somehow the Allied survivors managed to straggle into Tarapacá on 22 November.

As the survivors of Dolores staggered east, Buendía wired Col. Miguel Rios, ordering him to join the remnants of the Allied force at Tarapacá, seventy miles from the port. But before surrendering Iquique, Rios disarmed his coastal guns and destroyed anything that his men could not carry. Thus, on 22 November, after first turning over the city to the local consular corps, Rios led his men, mainly national guardsmen, into the desert. The following day sailors from Chile's blockading squadron occupied the port until troops from the Regimiento Esmeralda assumed control. Three days later, after getting lost twice and then marching the last eighteen leagues without food or water, 900 of Rios's original 1,034 men—"a band of men made desperate by the heat of the sand, by hunger and above all by the thirst, in complete disorder . . . the strongest in the front and the weakest remain lagging behind entrusting themselves to the designs of Providence"—stumbled into Tarapacá.[59]

Tarapacá

Believing that San Francisco was only a preface for another, more titanic battle, this time with the entire Allied army, Escala refused to pursue his fleeing enemies.[60] But once the *camanchaca*, the desert fog, cleared and the Chileans could see the dust cloud kicked up by their retreating foes, they realized that the Allies had no intention of launching another assault. Col. Emilio Sotomayor, Rafael's brother, confirmed this view when some captured teamsters informed him that Buendía had selected Tarapacá as the assembly point for his scattered troops, intelligence that the officer relayed to Escala. The general also received news that the Allied army was "in terrible condition, overwhelmed by exhaustion, lacking in resources, and completely demoralized, caused in great part by its shameful flight and by the profound dissention that is felt by the Allies and that has already revealed itself in scandalous and very serious events."[61] This information greatly underestimated the Allied army's condition.

Upon hearing this report, the unbearably enthusiastic Vergara requested and received Escala's permission to lead an expedition toward Tarapacá. Hence, on 24 November Vergara, at the head of a squadron of the Granaderos a Caballo, 250 Zapadores, and two field guns, departed for the south. The following day a Peruvian prisoner informed Vergara that Tarapacá contained 1,500 enemy troops. Aware that his task force lacked the manpower to confront such a large force, Vergara requested that Escala send additional troops. The general complied, ordering Col. Luis Arteaga to lead 1,900 fresh soldiers—the Chacabuco and Second of the Line regiments, the Artillería de Marina, and the Unidad de Artillería, as well as a section of the Cazadores a Caballo—to reinforce Vergara's small party. Perhaps because he had not fought at Pisagua or Dolores, Arteaga did not understand the importance of ensuring that his men carried adequate supplies of food, forage, and particularly water for themselves and their pack animals. His troops would pay dearly for this oversight.

On 25 November Arteaga's men moved by train and foot from Santa Catalina to the salitrera of Negreiros, where they were supposed to rendezvous with Vergara. The national guard officer, however, had already left for Tarapacá. Although he had more experience in desert warfare, Vergara sadly committed the same crucial error as Arteaga: he too failed to ensure that his men brought enough supplies, especially water. Furious that Vergara had not waited for him, Arteaga managed to catch up with him and presented the militia officer with two choices: return to Negreiros or remain at Iluga, where he was presently resting. Vergara accepted the latter alternative and spent 26 November waiting for Arteaga's troops to arrive. Anxious to do something, Vergara sent out some scouts who spied Rios's bedraggled contingent, the troops who had earlier garrisoned Iquique, staggering into Tarapacá. On the basis of their appearance and numbers, Vergara incorrectly concluded that the enemy garrison consisted of no more than twenty-five hundred exhausted men. But Arteaga, rather than wait for the supplies that General Escala promised to send, instead ordered an officer and some men to lead the promised supply column to the rest of the unit while he set off into the desert. Nine taxing hours after he departed from Negreiros, he caught up with Vergara. Unfortunately, having consumed all their rations and water en route, the colonel's men arrived empty-handed. This news devastated Vergara, who had expected Arteaga to bring supplies for his starving and dehydrated men. The Chileans faced an unpalatable choice: either attack Tarapacá, which had water wells, or perish in the desert. Hence, Arteaga, still believing that their foes were few in number and in worse condition than they, decided to attack before the Peruvians evacuated the city.[62]

The Battle for Tarapacá

Tarapacá was a small town located at the bottom of a deep ravine, 330 to 650 yards wide and approximately nine miles long. Normally a river flowed through the gorge, although during droughts it turned brackish and stagnant. Initially, the town contained approximately forty-five hundred Allied troops—triple its normal population—but by the time the Chileans arrived, fifteen hundred men of Colonel Dávila's Vanguard Division and Lieutenant Colonel Herrera's First Division had already reached Pachica en route to Arica, their ultimate destination. Remaining were four units: Cáceres's Second Division, Francisco Bolognesi's Third, the Fifth Division (Rios's militia from Iquique), and Francisco Bedoza's Exploradora. Additionally, Colonel Castanón commanded an artillery unit without its guns as well as Ramón Zalava's infantry unit, the Provisional de Lima Num. 3.

Arteaga's plan of attack called for Lt. Col. Ricardo Santa Cruz at the head of 500 men from the Zapadores, First of the Line, some artillery,

Table 13. Peruvian forces participating in the Battle of Tarapacá, 27 November 1879

Commander - Gen. Juan Buendía

En route to Pachica

División de Vanguardia	Col. Justo Pastor Dávila	
Btn. Puno, N. 6	Col. Rafael Chamarro/ Ramírez	438
Btn. Lima, N. 8	Col. Remijio Morales	443
Rgt. Guías N. 3	Col. Juan González	173
Es. Castilla	Col. Santiago Zavala	80
Primera División	Col. Alejandro Herrera	
Btn. Cazadores del Cuzco, N. 5	Col. Víctor Fajado	470
Btn. Cazadores de la Guardia, N. 7	Col. Mariano Bustamante	473
Rgt. Husáres de Junín	Col. Rafael Ramírez	200

In Tarapacá

Segunda División	Col. Andrés Cáceres	
Rgt. 2 de Mayo	Col. Manuel Suárez	487
Btn. Zepita, N. 2	Col. Andrés Cáceres	640
Tercera División	Col. Francisco Bolognesi	
Btn. 2 de Ayacucho	Col. Andrés Moreno	439
Btn. Guardia de Arequipa	Colonel Carrillo	498
Quinta División	Col. Miguel Rios	
Btn. Iquique, N. 1	Col. Alfonso Ugarte	391
Btn. Caz. de Tarapacá	Col. Joaquin Carpio	171
Col. Loa (B)	Colonel Echazú	290
Col. Tarapacá	Col. José Santos Aduvire	201
Es. Gendarmes de Iquique	Maj. P. Espejo	N/A
Col. Navales	Com. Carlos Richardson	297
Col. de Honor	Col. Juan Hidalgo	200
Col. Artillería de Costa		61
Brig. de Artillería	Col. Emilio Castañon	188
División de Esploracion	Col. F. Bedoya	
Btn. 1 Ayacucho, N. 3	Col. Melchor Ruiz	898
Btn. Provisional Lima, N. 3	Col. Ramón Zavala	355
Col. Voluntarios de Pasco		185
Total		7,578

Sources: Cáceres, *Guerra del 79*, 33–34; Juan Buendía to S.E. Supreme Dictor, "Parte del Jeneral en Jefe," 2:195–96, "Relacion de las planas mayores," 2:241, "Estado jeneral del ejéricto del Perú," 2:242, in Ahumada Moreno, *Guerral del Pacífico*; Buendía, *Guerra con Chile*, 153; Dellepiane, *Historia militar*, 2:130.

Table 14. Vergara's Column

Granaderos a Caballo		
1 Squadron	Cpt. R. Villagrán	115
Btn. Zapadores		
2 comps	LC. Santa Cruz	270
Artillery Mtn. guns,		
2 pieces	Lt. J. Ortúzar	27
	Total	412
Chilean Forces Attacking Tarapacá		
Col. Luis Arteaga		
Rgt. Artilleria		
de Marina – 4 guns	LC. Vidaurre	358
Btn. Chacabuco	LC. D de Toro	450
Art. Section,		
Bronze guns,		
Rgt de Art. 2		39
		847
Col. of LC. R. Santa Cruz		
Granaderos a Caballo		86
Btn. Zapadores		
2 comps.	LC. . Santa Cruz	289
2 of Line,		
1 company	Capt. R. Villagrán	110
4 Krupp guns,		
Art. de Marina	Maj. E. Fuentes	57
		532
Col. of LC. E. Ramírez		
2 of Line, 7 comps. LC. Ramírez		820
2 French mtn. Guns, Art. de Marina		40
1 Cavalry picket		
		866
Total		2,286

Dellepiane, *Historia Militiar*, II, p. 155; Letter to Ed. *El Mercurio,* Santa Catalina, 2 Dec. 1879, AM, II, 210–11; F. Machuca, *Las cuatros campañas de la Guerra del Pacífico* (4 vols.; 1926–1930, Valparaiso), I, p. 329. "Partes oficiales chilenos," AM, II, 186–95. The Chilean sources do not agree about the size of the units attacking Tarapacá.

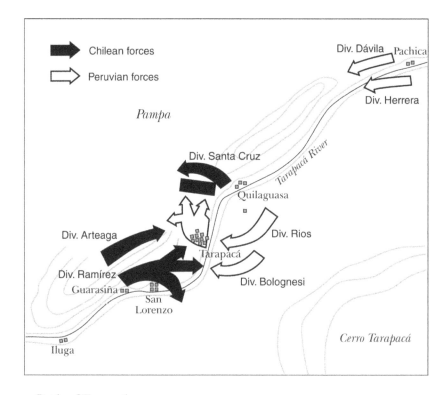

5. Battle of Tarapacá

and a few cavalrymen to leave before the other units in order to reach and capture Quillahuasa, a town located a mile away at the narrow end of the ravine. Meanwhile, Lt. Col. Eleuterio Ramírez would lead a second column of 880 men from the Second of the Line, a squadron of cavalry, and two artillery batteries to attack the Allied troops located at least 330 yards below on the floor of the ravine. At the same time, Arteaga's 850 soldiers from the Chacabuco, Artillería de Marina, supported by two guns, would advance on Buendía's western flank and then assault Tarapacá from the west. If all went according to plan, Arteaga and Ramírez would drive the Allied troops to the northeast up the Tarapacá Gorge, allowing Santa Cruz to bottle them up at Quillahuasa. Arteaga's plan suffered from serious flaws: he had no idea about the geography of his target, the location of his enemies, or their number. Perhaps the Chilean commander believed that he and his men had a chance, but not Lieutenant Colonel Ramírez, who presciently observed, "They are sending me into a slaughterhouse."[63]

Just as Ramírez feared, Arteaga's plan completely unraveled. Santa Cruz's exhausted and thirsty men, who started their trek northeast at 3:30 a.m., became lost in the camanchaca and wasted two hours wandering in circles. By the time the fog lifted, they realized that they had not reached their destination. Sending the cavalry ahead to Quillahuasa, Santa Cruz planned for the infantry to follow. Unfortunately for Arteaga, the Peruvians sighted the Chileans, and this loss of surprise fatally compromised the Chilean offensive. Alerting the entire garrison, Cáceres ordered his men to scale the western side of the ravine to engage Santa Cruz's forces. At this point, the Chilean could have saved the situation: although outnumbered, his guns held the high ground, and they could have easily devastated the Allied forces below them. Regrettably, Santa Cruz refused to improvise: Arteaga had ordered him to Quillaguasa, and to Quillaguasa he would go. Thus, as he continued to follow the ravine to the northeast, troops of Zepita and 2 de Mayo stormed the heights and attacked Santa Cruz's rearguard. Within thirty minutes, the fifteen hunderd men from Bolognesi's Ayacucho and Zavala's Provisional de Lima joined in the assault, overrunning Santa Cruz's artillery and inflicting heavy casualties. The Chileans' position became desperate.[64]

Hearing the sounds of the battle, Arteaga abandoned his original plan, racing instead to help Santa Cruz. Unfortunately his men, "exhausted by the trip, their heavy packs, and swooning from thirst," could not save their comrades. Running out of ammunition and unable to repulse the fresh Peruvian reinforcements with their bayonets, the Chileans had to retreat. As the men began to withdraw, Vergara sent a messenger to beg Escala to send help. Suddenly, for a brief moment it seemed that the Chileans' luck had turned: Santa Cruz's cavalry, which had reached Quillaguasa, doubled back upon hearing the gunfire. Briefly held up by enemy fire and the terrain, the Granaderos a Caballo charged the rear of the Peruvian infantrymen, forcing them back and giving the Chileans a brief respite.[65]

Meanwhile, most of Ramírez's men entered the valley, while two of his companies began to scale the ravine's eastern flank. Earlier, the Peruvians had shifted Rios's and Bolognesi's men to the quebrada's eastern wall, in essence placing the attacking Chileans in a deadly crossfire. Thus, when the main body approached the town of Tarapacá, they ran into a wall of bullets as their foes opened fire from cover, catching the Chileans in the open. Ramírez ordered two companies to hit the Allied flank while he advanced into the town itself. Unfortunately, the enemy pulled back, enticing Ramírez's men to move deeper into the valley, where they even reached Tarapacá's main plaza. Still, the entrenched Peruvian defenders began to take their toll. When it became clear that the Chileans were too exhausted, Ramírez ordered his men to retreat south to Guarasiña, a small hamlet at the mouth of the Tarapacá Gorge, where the troops from the two companies joined them. By then, the street battle had consumed half of Ramírez's men as well as most of their ammunition.

Following Santa Cruz's cavalry charge and Ramírez's retreat, an unexpected lull becalmed the battlefield. The Chileans, believing that they had triumphed, took advantage of the quiet to draw water, feed their horses, and scavenge for food. This bucolic scene—if one ignored the dead bodies—ended when the Allied forces, reinforced by the troops of Cols. Juan Pastor Dávila and Alejandro Herrera, who had rushed back from Pachica, launched another assault. Advancing across both flanks as well as the valley floor, the Allies' broad attack forced back the Chileans, some of whom by then were reduced to fighting with bayonets or entrenching tools.[66]

By 3:30 p.m. it became clear that the Chileans could not stem the Peruvian advance. The twice-wounded Ramírez, whose only remaining weapon was his revolver, tried to lead his beleaguered men in another bayonet attack. Wounded a third time and with his unit suffering heavy casualties, Ramírez took refuge at the side of a house, where he perished. The leaderless Chilean troops continued to use their sabers to resist until they too fell.[67] Meanwhile, other Chileans either scaled the ravine's face or slowly retreated. It was a complete rout: only the lack of Allied cavalry prevented Buendía's exhausted men from finishing off the few remaining survivors.[68]

Baquedano, who finally received Vergara's request for help, sent a relief column to Tarapacá, where they found the remnants of Arteaga's expedition. By then, however, the Chileans had experienced heavy losses: 546 dead and 212 wounded. In Ramírez's Second of the Line, 45 percent of the complement were wounded or killed; the Zapadores lost 37.5 percent of its strength.[69] The Peruvians also suffered—236 slain and 261 wounded—leading one Allied soldier to describe the battlefield, covered with the dead rotting in the desert heat, as another Waterloo. Trinidad Guzmán, a Bolivian, depicted Tarapacá not as a battle but "a series of duels to the death."[70]

The battle was, in fact, unusually cruel. The Chilean wounded, including two cantineras and Lieutenant Colonel Ramírez, had taken refuge in a house near the gorge's entry. When the Chileans supposedly killed a Peruvian subaltern who offered to take their surrender, the Peruvian forces set fire to the ranch, immolating those defenders who did not have the good fortune to succumb first to smoke inhalation. These were not the only Chileans to perish. A Chilean officer, Liborio Echanes, alleged that the Allied forces also killed the Chilean wounded, bludgeoning them to death with their rifles or bayoneting them. Indeed, had their officers not intervened, the Bolivians of the Batallón Loa would have annihilated all the Chilean wounded or prisoners.[71] Months later, a Chilean army patrol revisited Tarapacá to bury those corpses that still littered the battlefield. The commander discovered and verified the remains of Ramírez, placing the charred body in a coffin with disinfectant.[72]

The Peruvians captured the Second of the Line's standard as well as eight artillery pieces, but without oxen to pull the heavy guns, the Peruvians had to bury them in the sand. Thanks to some informers, the Chileans found these cannons, putting them to good use later in the war. These same field pieces might well have supported the Chilean troops at the Battle of Tacna, when the Second of the Line recaptured its colors.[73]

The Peruvians may have won the battle, but their victory did not alter the course of the war. Isolated in the desert, without access to supplies or food, their situation became so bad that Peruvians ghoulishly stripped the Chilean dead and wounded not simply of their weapons but also of their ammunition, clothing, boots, and eating utensils. The victorious troops had no choice, as Colonel Suárez ruefully admitted, but to abandon Tarapacá to the Chileans.[74] Unable to proceed by the shortest route for fear the Chileans might attack them, the Allied survivors fled into the desert. The 195-mile trek from Tarapacá north to Arica constituted yet another Allied *via crucis*: dodging the Chileans, "an immense caravan of the starving [and] tattered" troops survived by eating their mules and horses and drinking water from stagnant pools. The wounded, marching shoeless on rocky paths, their "fingers rotting from gangrene," left bloodstained footprints on the pampa floor. Only as the army approached Arica, which they reached on 18 December, did they receive some hardtack, beef jerky, and rice. During this odyssey three to four hundred soldiers, "whose end only God knows," disappeared.[75]

The suffering of Buendía, Suárez, and countless other high-ranking Allied officers did not end when they reached Arica: they still had to explain their earlier conduct to a court-martial. The military judges subsequently faulted Buendía for inadequately preparing for the Battle of Dolores and for not saving his equipment once the Chileans routed him. The same tribunal condemned Suárez, Bustamante, and Col. Manuel Velarde for leaving their men on the battlefield without leadership and called for punishing Col. Rafael Ramírez, whose cavalry bolted without firing a shot, for fleeing the battle "in an unusual manner." Although many of these crimes were capital offenses, the judge suggested that the government simply strike these commanders' names from the officers' registry and dismiss them.[76] Many blamed Buendía for the defeats at Pisagua and Dolores and the "victory" at Tarapacá. Apparently some of his critics hoped he would publicly confess the error of his ways. Instead, the general "buries himself in the mutism of the very guilty. He has not had even today enough breath to stammer an excuse in his favor."[77]

For the Chileans, the campaign was a mixed blessing. The conquest of Tarapacá and the capture of the nitrate mines brought Chile enormous benefits. Henceforth, the Pinto government controlled a resource that, when taxed, would generate enough revenue to fund Chile's war effort. Conversely, the capture deprived Lima of its major source of funding. But the Pisagua invasion, the encounter at Dolores, and particularly the abortive attack on Tarapacá revealed serious flaws in the Chilean army.

The Politics of Defeat

Although he did not participate in the Tarapacá campaign, the Bolivian President Daza had not been idle. Unlike his counterparts Pinto and Prado, Daza had to fight on two fronts: to protect Bolivia from the Chilean hordes and to defend himself against his increasingly numerous domestic enemies. In just the first months of 1879, the president's enemies unsuccessfully launched three coups. His lackluster conduct of the war did not dilute this discontent: in September unrest erupted in Cochabamba. Although the authorities repressed it, a Peruvian diplomat predicted yet another coup.[78] Clearly Daza's paranoia about retaining power was not without cause.

Turning tail at Camarones effectively destroyed Daza's regime, as Zolio Flores, Bolivia's minister to Peru noted, by converting him "from a hope into a disappointment, from a colossal figure into someone common, from a brave man into a coward, from an object of envy into one of disdain, from a guarantor of victory to the cause of our disaster, and what is most grave still, from a loyal subject into a traitor, from a sign of national glory into an instrument . . . of humiliation and shame for the nation."[79] *La Reforma* saw Daza's decision to retreat as one "that places his own interest and personal security" over the needs of the nation and asserted that Daza's "only political aspiration is a wish to dominate Bolivia for ten or more years," even at the cost of brutalizing the nation.[80] Col. Juan Granier wrote of "this criminal inertia that has for the past nine months consumed the vital forces of Bolivia [and] has, in the satisfaction of personal passions, weakened its leadership."[81]

Clearly Daza's hold on power was tremulous. In late November a Peruvian diplomat reported that a group of *cholos* ran through La Paz's streets screaming, "Viva Chile!" By then even Daza's presidential escort had turned against him.[82] The anti-Daza forces, which seemed to multiply, became more openly critical: recalling the general's flight at Camarones and the disaster at San Francisco, one citizen denounced Daza for lacking "public and private virtues and qualities that [he does] not possess [n]or could ever possess." In Tacna a group of soldiers shot an effigy of Daza. To commemorate the place where he betrayed the Bolivian army, the firing squad attached a drawing of shrimp (*camarones*) to the dummy's chest. La Paz's *El Comercio* was more explicit: Bolivia had but "one choice . . . the degradation of the author of our dishonor, his removal from the undeserved power he has assumed, and the selection of a new Director." Sensing that their own days were numbered, some of Daza's ministers resigned their offices, either taking refuge in a diplomatic embassy or disappearing. While a few of these men drifted back, others, fearing what might befall La Paz when its humiliated soldiers returned, demanded that someone preserve order.[83]

Since Daza's power rested in large part on the bayonets of his indulged Colorados, any anti-Daza coup had to begin by neutralizing this unit. The rebels, led by Gen. Eliodoro Camacho—who would denounce Daza as "the Judas of Bolivia"—achieved this feat by ordering Colorados to march to a nearby river to bathe and to wash their clothes. Not needing their weapons, the soldiers left these at their camp. When these troops returned from their ablutions, they discovered that the conspirators had surrounded their barracks after first removing all their ammunition; the Colorados could do nothing but surrender.[84]

Daza, in the meantime, boarded an Arica-bound train on 27 December to confer with Adm. Lizardo Montero about the future conduct of the war. The Bolivian never returned: after his meeting, Daza received a telegram from Camacho, informing him that the army no longer recognized his authority. When Montero refused to help Daza crush the conspiracy, the ex-dictator, apparently bellowing obscenities, departed into a European exile.[85] Fortunate to have escaped with his life, and with the not inconsiderable sum of five hundred thousand pesos, Daza did not seem to suffer unduly while living in Europe. In 1894 he unwisely returned to Bolivia, ostensibly to clear his name. This time he was not so lucky: on a provincial Bolivian train station's platform, an obscure army officer murdered him.[86] Daza had returned to stay. Ironically, Camacho, who led the conspiracy to overthrow Daza, did not become president. Following a series of provincial *cuartelazos*, the public selected Gen. Narciso Campero to rule Bolivia.[87] He would remain in power until the end of the war.

Manuel Prado also lost his post, albeit less violently. Saddled with the responsibility for the capture of the *Pilcomayo*, the loss at San Francisco, and the bittersweet victory at Tarapacá, the president—"who has given no triumphs only defeats . . . [and] has brought us always from fall to fall to a certain shipwreck"—became the *bete noire* of Lima's mob.[88] Some of the press called for a reshuffling of his cabinet. *La Tribuna*, for example, wanted a new minister of war, ideally someone who possessed the skills of von Moltke and Kaiser Wilhelm.[89] Others demanded a more radical political change, although *El Comercio* opposed a return to a dictatorship that it considered the root of the nation's problems. Peru, it argued, should never stray from the path of constitutional order. The *South Pacific Times*, on the other hand, offered a third alternative. Peru, the paper argued, had already lost the war. Instead of persisting in this madness, the nation should negotiate "not 'peace at any price,' be it understood, but Peace with Honor," a not impossible feat. With the war over, Peru could devote itself to restoring the nation. In short, "The greatest victory that Peru could now achieve would be to conquer itself."[90]

Prado tried to avert a crisis by inviting his principal political rival, Nicolás Piérola, to join his government. Piérola refused: why serve, he might have asked, when he could lead? It had become clear, moreover, that replacing the cabinet would not save Prado. Indeed, public anger became so palpable that the authorities stationed troops around the president's home to protect him. Rather than thrust the country into a political maelstrom, Prado boarded a ship sailing to Panama. Claiming that he left to purchase weapons, he turned over his office to his constitutional successor, the aged General La Puerta. The old warrior inspired even less public confidence than Prado. Hence, when Piérola led the men of his militia unit into rebellion, he had few foes. Shooting spread through the capital causing casualties among the competing factions. On 23 December 1879, supported by the army as well as various civilian organizations, Piérola became the head of state.[91]

Some Peruvians saw Piérola as a savior. Within days of his accession to power, one newspaper praised the changes he had made: thanks to him, it noted, "there is a formidable, skilled, disciplined and enthusiastic army. Arms and equipment are in the depots. Cannons are being forged in the foundries. In the barracks [men] are working, . . . there is life, vigor and activity." The dictator, on whom *El Nacional* urged a "more rapid, more impulsive, more efficient" war effort, did, in fact, accomplish certain things. He reorganized the military, creating one army in the center, another in the north, and two in the south. (Piérola's motives for forging the Second Army of the South were not purely military: at the end of December 1879 he clearly sought to ensure that Adm. Lizardo Montero, who commanded the First Army of the South, could not challenge him politically.) Piérola also created two reserve components, which supposedly would include all able-bodied men: the active, consisting of men aged thirteen to thirty, and the sedentary, those aged thirty-one to fifty.

As befitting a class society, the exemptions proved generous: public employees, teachers, university students, attorneys, physicians, hospital employees, only sons of widowed mothers, owners or employees of printing companies, surviving brothers of someone killed in combat, the physically unfit, and finally, those who contributed fifty soles per month to the war effort.[92] Piérola would quickly learn that wielding power required more than reorganizing the army and promulgating decrees.

In contrast to his rivals, Pinto completed his term of office in 1881. It is a tribute to Chile's political system that during the War of the Pacific the government conducted two elections for congress as well as one for the president. It is also noteworthy that neither President Pinto nor his successor muzzled either the Chilean press or the legislature, although both sometimes gave ample reason for doing so. Conversely, Bolivia prohibited the publication of material that, by favoring peace, undermined the national war effort.[93] Cynics might argue that Chile may have owed its success more to luck than political maturity. We do not know, for example, how long the nation would have tolerated a stalemated war or what would have happened if Riveros had failed to vanquish the Peruvian fleet or if he had committed other errors. The riots following the capture of the *Rimac* indicate that Chilean democracy had its soft underbelly. On the other hand, the country did survive more tragic events, such as Battle of Tarapacá. Whether it was a matter of timing or good fortune, Pinto's government, unlike that of Prado or Daza, had to battle only the Allies, not its own citizens.

Chile's military offensive, its first since the 1859 civil war, gave Santiago control of Tarapacá's lucrative salitreras. It had also changed the Bolivian and Peruvian political landscapes: the defeats at Pisagua and Dolores forced the venal Daza and the hapless Prado from power. As Prado's successor, Nicolás Piérola, came to discover, without access to the sealanes and the income from its salitreras, Peru would find it more difficult to pursue the war. Land-locked Bolivia's situation became more tenuous: isolated in the Andes, its political and demographic heartlands separated by great distances from the battlefields and without either a transportation or communication network, La Paz's participation in the war became more tentative, if not problematic.

Pinto surmounted the *Rimac* crisis and thus was the only prewar leader who remained in power. He too, however, had to overcome his own demons. Recognizing that sclerotic leadership of the army and navy had jeopardized Chile's land and sea campaigns, and thus his regime's stability, he moved to assert civilian authority over the nation's armed forces. Clearly, he could not tolerate another botched landing or a "glorious defeat," such as Tarapacá. Henceforth civilians would create and largely man the armed forces' medical and supply corps. Similarly, private citizens like Sotomayor and then Vergara would play important roles in the planning and direction of the war's next phase: invading Tacna.

7. The Tacna and Arica Campaigns

The surrender of Tarapacá Province only briefly appeased Chile's war hawks, who demanded that the army continue northward. Alas, much as it might wish, the high command could not respond immediately: the Tarapacá campaign had pruned the army's ranks, consumed its supplies, equipment, clothing, footwear, and transport, while revealing flaws in the newly created supply and medical services. Thus, before the military could launch another offensive, it needed to find fresh recruits, restock its supply depots, and purchase new equipment as well as transport, including three to four thousand pack mules. It also had to reorganize the army's technical branches, particularly the medical corps. Thus, while the army restored itself, the country's civilian and military leaders pondered their options.[1]

The Aníbal Pinto government considered two possible targets: Lima, Peru's capital, or Arica, its most important port south of Callao. Given the existence of numerous possible landing sites, as well as their access to the sea, and thus the support of the fleet's big guns, Gen. Erasmo Escala advocated assaulting Lima. Rafael Sotomayor, however, raised a criticism that even Escala acknowledged as valid: besieging Peru's capital without first eradicating Arica's garrison would expose the Chilean rear to an Allied army that could attack the recently captured Tarapacá. Other government advisers concurred, warning that an enemy presence in Arica threatened Chilean supply lines. Conversely, capturing this harbor guaranteed Chile's access to an adequate supply of water and forage while allowing it to threaten the enemy's supply lines to the troops stationed in the highland cities of

Arequipa and Moquegua. Once seized, moreover, the Chileans might offer to cede Arica to Bolivia in return for its promise to end its participation in the war.

But assaulting Arica also had its drawbacks: the Peruvians had built numerous coastal strong points to defend the harbor. And rising more than 670 feet above the oceanfront loomed El Morro, a slab of mountain atop which stood various forts mounting heavy artillery with a clear view of the sea. Anchored below, the Peruvian monitor *Manco Cápac* still remained on guard. Obviously an amphibious landing on the port itself would have been costly, if not suicidal. If the Chilean military hoped to capture what Benjamín Vicuña Mackenna called "the Sebastapol of the Pacific," it would first have to land its army elsewhere, then move the troops, their artillery, and supplies overland in order to assail the strategically important fortress from the east, not unlike what the Japanese did to Singapore in 1942.[2] Eventually a council of war selected Ilo, a port approximately seventy miles to the north of Arica, as its invasion site. But before it could strike north, the army had to amass supplies and manpower; it also had to coordinate its plans with Chile's navy to procure the shipping, to transport its units to Ilo, and to protect them en route from the remnants of Peru's fleet. Once these tasks were complete, Chile's army would be ready to attack Tacna and Arica, thus moving closer to its ultimate destination: Lima.

Blockading Peru's Coast

As of October 1879, Peru's navy consisted of two monitors and a few torpedo boats, none of which dared venture into the open sea. Only the oceangoing *Unión* could still cause substantial mischief. Rather than prowl the sea-lanes in search of the enemy corvette, the Pinto government decided to order its ships to close Peru's ports. By effectively entombing the *Unión*, the Chileans could, moreover, curtail, if not completely stop, Peru's importation of needed war materiel.[3] Thus, by November 1879 the *Cochrane*, the *Covadonga*, and the *Magallanes* were already blockading Iquique and Mollendo while watching over the less important harbors of Chucumata and Patillos. Following Iquique's capture, the Chileans shifted their focus to the north, quarantining the ports north of Pisagua and south of Callao. (The Chilean fleet still needed to patrol Iquique and Pisagua for fear that the *Unión* might attack these undefended places. Hence, the *Abtao* remained off Pisagua and the *Magallanes* off Iquique until these coastal cities possessed enough artillery or mines to defend themselves.)[4]

On 28 November the *Chacabuco*, the *O'Higgins*, and the *Magallanes* sailed into Arica's harbor. Proclaiming its formal blockade of that port, the Chilean fleet gave neutral shipping ten days to sail. Four days later the *Covadonga* and the transport *Lamar* arrived. Finally, on 5 December Juan José Latorre, captain of the *Cochrane*, assumed command of the Chilean squadron. At the same time, the navy increased its area of control when at the end of December 1879 it sent units to cruise off Ilo.[5]

For the first weeks the besieged and their foes peacefully coexisted. In February 1880 the Chilean navy rotated some of its ships, ordering the newly refitted *Huáscar* to Arica. The monitor's captain was Manuel Thomson, an officer who managed to combine a sensitive ego and an abrasive personality with an unseemly thirst for publicity.[6] In an attempt to gain the attention of the Chilean public, Thomson provocatively steamed around Arica's bay like some adolescent boy looking for a fight. On 28 February, perhaps tired of what they considered Thomson's insolent behavior, the Peruvian forts, as well as the *Manco Cápac*, opened fire on the *Huáscar* and its escort, the *Magallanes*. For less than an hour the Chilean ships and their land-based assailants traded salvos without inflicting much damage on one other.

The exchange of cannonades had begun to subside when Thomson opened fire on a railroad train carrying soldiers to Arica. Immediately the *Manco Cápac* and the nearby forts began shooting at the Chilean ship. This time the Peruvian gunners found Thomson's range: four shells struck the *Huáscar*, killing six sailors and wounding another fourteen. These losses did not discourage Thomson. On the contrary, when the *Manco Cápac*, earlier described as a "floating battery," ponderously began to move out into the bay, Thomson responded, planning to fire his cannon while simultaneously skewering the Peruvian monitor with his ram. The Chilean officer had already committed his ship when he discovered a Peruvian torpedo boat huddling at the *Manco Cápac*'s side. Fearful of being torpedoed, Thomson ordered his engine room to increase speed, so he might escape. Unfortunately, the *Huáscar*'s engines malfunctioned, preventing the monitor from moving.[7] The *Manco Cápac* might have been slow, but it gunners were not: the Peruvian ship, taking advantage of Thomson's temporary lack of mobility, opened fire. One of the five-hundred-pound shells struck the *Huáscar*, virtually obliterating Thomson. All that remained of his once impressive presence was a piece of his skull and his heart, which was found dangling from a lifeboat.

Although unable to return the fire because the monitor's main battery turning mechanism had jammed, Thomson's executive officer, Emilio Valverde, managed to extricate the wounded Chilean ship. As the squadron's most senior surviving officer, Carlos Condell assumed command of the *Huáscar* and ordered Lt. T. Rogers to take over as captain of the *Magallanes*. The navy sent Thomson's remains, as well as some of its wounded, back to Chile. And as the nation mourned, its fleet retaliated: the *Angamos* and the *Huáscar* bombarded Arica for hours, concentrating on its population centers.[8]

In March the Chileans had an opportunity to neutralize the *Unión*. The Peruvian corvette carrying the torpedo launch *Alianza* managed to slip past the Chilean blockade and reach Arica. Although the Peruvian vessel had humiliated the blockading fleet, some Chileans viewed the presence of the *Unión* as a godsend: if the blockaders could bottle up or destroy the ship while it lay in Arica, the Peruvian fleet would effectively cease to exist.

Adm. Galvarino Riveros quickly marshaled his forces, ordering the *Pilcomayo*, the *Angamos*, and the *Blanco* to Arica. In addition, he requested that the *Cochrane* and the *Amazonas* rejoin the fleet. Rather than wait for reinforcements, the *Huáscar* began to exchange fire with the Peruvian corvette, the *Manco Cápac*, as well as some of the naval forts. The *Cochrane*, which arrived with the *Amazonas*, joined Condell in a second round of firing, again focusing on the *Unión*.

Both the *Cochrane* and the *Huáscar* suffered hits, including a few from the *Manco Cápac*'s heavy guns. Although they had incurred some damage, Latorre and Condell took comfort from the fact that their gunners also struck the *Unión*: more than six artillery rounds hit the Peruvian ship, destroying its launch, damaging its boiler, and injuring or killing some of the crew.

After almost two hours of shelling, Latorre called a meeting with the commanders of the *Huáscar* and the *Amazonas* to discuss how they could prevent the *Unión* from slipping away under the cover of night. As they discussed this issue, the Peruvian ship, cheered on by the crews of the nearby European men-of-war, fled the harbor for the south.[9] The *Cochrane* immediately began a pursuit, as did other elements of the Chilean fleet, but for naught: the *Unión* had escaped yet again. It appeared impossible that the Peruvian corvette could have evaded the blockade, but it had. Having sighted plumes of steam rising from the *Unión*, apparently the Chileans concluded that the Peruvian ship could not get up a good head of steam. This assumption was wrong: the *Unión*'s boilers were fine. But the Chileans, operating on this misconception, relaxed their vigilance, allowing the Peruvian ship to bolt.[10]

Rafael Sotomayor, Chile's minister of war in the field, decided to act decisively: rather than trying to destroy piecemeal each of Peru's few remaining vessels, he called for Riveros to bottle them up in Callao. Such a quarantine would have numerous ancillary benefits: by demonstrating Lima's inability to protect itself, the blockade might destabilize the government; it would also damage Peru's already crippled economy. Depriving Lima of export income, moreover, would also diminish Peru's creditworthiness among its foreign creditors, making it difficult to float war loans abroad. Finally, a blockade would permit Chile to raid Peru's entire coast, disrupting communications and commerce while isolating the north from the south. Sotomayor generously admitted that his was an ambitious agenda, but, in the words of one who did not have to obey his own orders, he stated that his suggestions were "easy to implement, immediate, and useful."[11]

Trying to bottle up the *Unión*, however, also severely strained the Chilean navy's limited resources. In addition to the Chilean ships patrolling Peru's major port, the *Cochrane* and the *Magallanes* still cruised off Arica, the *Chacabuco* loitered near Mollendo, while the *Abtao* and the *Covadonga* protected various transports that supplied the troops who had invaded Arica Province.[12] The blockade absorbed not only war ships but also supplies. José Gandarillas estimated that it would take three colliers just to keep the Callao squadron steaming. Unfortunately, the fleet did not have enough of these vessels available. In addition, the navy needed to buy better quality coal.[13]

With the *Unión* and the various transports imprisoned in Callao, Peru's fleet remained effectively neutralized. Other than releasing mines or, alternatively, ordering its coastal batteries to fire on the Chilean ships, Peru's navy had two options: remain tethered to Callao's coastal defenses or attempt some suicidal dash for the sea. As we shall discover, Peru's squadron preferred to immolate itself rather than fall into Chilean hands.

Although without ships, the Peruvian sailors quickly discovered flaws in the Chilean naval cordon. Rather than try to run the naval gauntlet, the Peruvian transport *Talismán* would dock at Quilca, the main port of entry for Arequipa, or Mollendo, where it offloaded its cargo onto launches before speeding their contents to Arequipa via the local railroad.[14] Weapons and supplies destined for Lima and Callao arrived via the ports of Chancay, Chira, or Lurin.[15] Meanwhile, ships, some unflagged, continued to bring in cannon, rifles, and torpedoes from Panama.[16] Unfortunately for the Chileans, Peru possessed more potential landing sites than Pinto's fleet had patrol boats.

The Tacna Invasion

As Chile's navy tried to eradicate Peru's fleet, Chile's army dedicated itself to accumulating men and supplies. By mid-February Pisagua's bay filled with ships, as the authorities began loading a new expeditionary force and its artillery and cavalry on transports for the invasion of Arica. As the troops boarded their respective vessels, the navy tried to complete the construction of rafts capable of carrying 250 men. On 24 February the authorities finished loading nineteen ships carrying between 10,500 and 11,000 soldiers of the First, Second, and Third divisions plus their equipment. The Fourth Division would remain in Pisagua. At 4:00 p.m., protected by the *Blanco Encalada*, the *Toro*, and the *Magallanes*, as well as the torpedo boats *Guacolda* and *Janequo*, the convoy sailed, conveying the recently completed barges.

As before, the navy used the technique of pairing a sailing boat to a steam-driven transport because it relieved the fleet's warships of any responsibilities other than guarding the convoy and pursuing the enemy. It also guaranteed that weather or sea conditions would not in any way prevent the sailing ships from fulfilling their orders.[17] To maintain the convoy's formation, and to avoid collisions, each ship sailed at a speed of six miles per hour while keeping three cable lengths between vessels.

When the invasion force neared its destination, Chile's torpedo boats left the convoy to conduct a reconnaissance of the beach. The Chilean armada arrived off Punta Coles, near Pacocha, where the ships anchored at 9 a.m. on 26 February. After learning from the *Magallanes* and the torpedo boats that there would be little opposition, the disembarkation began. The various vessels, each following a certain predetermined order, dropped ladders that the troops descended before climbing into the longboats or lighters for the trip to the shore.

The Rejimiento Esmeralda started offloading at 4:30 p.m., approximately the same time that some of the Artillería de Marina went ashore and captured Pacocha, a port at the mouth of the Monquegua Valley. Encountering no resistance, the expeditionary force decided to utilize Ilo's dock rather than rely upon the slower lighters. Hence, by 8 p.m. five thousand men had gone ashore. The Chileans devoted the following day to emptying the rest of the ships. Once completed, Riveros ordered the *Amazonas*, the *Loa*, the *Matías Cousiño*, and the *Toro* to return to Pisagua to transport the Fourth Division to Ilo.[18]

While President Pinto supported the plan to attack Arica, he was under great pressure to avoid the bungling that characterized Escala's earlier expedition. Hence, rather than have his troops march into the interior, a tactic that had proved so disastrous in the Tarapacá campaign, the president directed his army to dig in after going ashore at Ilo. Again, Pinto and his advisers were hoping that their presence would inspire the Peruvians into trying to drive the Chileans from their beachhead. It did not. Thus, when Adm. Lizardo Montero, the local Peruvian commander, refused to take the bait, Pinto ordered his cavalry to raze the area around Ilo. If that tactic failed to spur the Peruvian admiral into action, Sotomayor planned to up the ante: he would send an infantry unit to destroy loading facilities and railroad equipment in the nearby port of Mollendo. Ideally, this raid would goad Montero to attack, because severing Arequipa's communications and supply lines to the coast would threaten the existence of the Peruvian stronghold. The assault on Mollendo, moreover, might also scare Montero into shifting the soldiers defending Tacna, another of Chile's objectives, to protect Arequipa.[19] Hence, on 8 March the *Blanco*, the *Amazonas*, and the *Lamar*, carrying the Third Regiment of the Line, the Batallón Naval, and the Zapadores, as well as a small number of cavalrymen, left Pacocha. In order not to alert Mollendo's authorities, the navy dropped some two hundred soldiers from the Batallón Naval near the port of Islai, where they cut the telegraph wires. Having achieved this objective, the rest of the men landed and began their march on Mollendo.

The landing, while ultimately successful, did not begin auspiciously. The minister of war, José Gandarillas, complained that the navy had intentionally put the army ashore where the water was so deep that the invading troops almost drowned.[20] The expedition further unraveled once the men reached Mollendo. Many of the Chilean soldiers were miners who had labored in Tarapacá's salitreras and who had suffered at the hands of Peruvian citizens once war erupted. These troops used the opportunity to avenge past slights and settle old scores. Discovering a cache of liquor, the miners turned soldiers soon became drunk and, joined by some of their officers, began to pillage the city. This burst of rapine excess supposedly included rape, sacking a church, and even desecrating the Host. The rioting, which inflicted more than two million pesos in damage, lasted for more than a day and eventually required the Chilean officers to use force to restore discipline before the men returned to Ilo on 11 March.[21]

The lawlessness manifested at Mollendo reinforced Pinto's belief that the army's commanders could not control their troops. Worse, if his soldiers disobeyed their officers in Mollendo, they might again ignore their superiors when ordered to attack an armed enemy. But the government eventually decided it had no other choice than to advance inland: Montero, his power undercut by Nicolás Piérola and believing that he could best utilize his limited resources by massing his men in Tacna, refused to react to the Chilean incursion. Thus, however reluctantly, Pinto had to order Gen. Manuel Baquedano, commander of the cavalry, to advance on Moquegua, a town located deep in the desert. The general's battalions would make the fifty-four-mile trip in stages: the cavalry would depart first, and the infantry and artillery would leave a day later. After linking up at Conde, forty-two miles east of Ilo, the task force would assault Moquegua.

Moving into the Interior

Although the Chileans had the good fortune to capture four locomotives as well as some rolling stock, including a tanker car carrying water, Baquedano's expedition began inauspiciously. His cavalry reached Hospicio, where, as expected, they found an enormous vat filled with water. After the general's men and their mounts virtually drained the cistern, Baquedano ordered a train to bring more water from Conde for the infantry and artillery units that were scheduled to arrive the following day. Unfortunately, the train derailed before it could complete its mission. Unaware of this fact, the troops had already left Ilo. Worse, apparently the soldiers' fifty-pound packs contained everything but adequate supplies or water: their officers did not require it, believing that the troops would find these items in Hospicio. (Sotomayor had tried to remedy this deficiency by forcing the departing units to include iron rations and water in their packs, but many soldiers could not obey his orders because they lacked knapsacks or, in a quarter of the cases, canteens.)[22]

The infantry and artillery units, commanded by Col. Maríano Muñoz, departed Ilo on the evening of 12 March. Reaching Estanques on the following day, they rested before resuming their trek. Suffocated by the desert dust, blistered by the sun, and numbed by the weight of their packs, the men managed to reach Hospicio by mid-morning on 14 March. Inspired by the prospect of finally slaking their thirst, many of the troops, their water all but exhausted, literally sprinted the remaining yards. The water tank was, of course, empty.

Muñoz should have ordered his soldiers to march though the night, when it was cooler, in hopes of finding water at the next stop. Instead, he allowed them to rest. The following dawn brought with it the scalding sun, which made the journey almost unbearable. Men collapsed, some, like a Lieutenant Navarro, perishing from sunstroke. The desperate commander of the Second of the Line, Estanislao del Canto, devised a novel way to revive his troops: using a bayonet, he prized open the unconscious soldiers' jaws and revived them by spraying some wine into their mouths. These makeshift cures could not obscure the failures of those higher up the military hierarchy. "The lack of foresight," noted one officer bitterly, "is victimizing us, and it is clear that it will do more damage to us then the enemy. In truth, there are people who never learn and who are incapable of learning."[23]

Each day brought news that reinforced Pinto's fears and undermined his confidence in Escala. Spying the Ilo River, the distraught soldiers began fighting to reach the water first. Muñoz only avoided a complete breakdown of discipline by threatening to order his artillery to fire on anyone who broke ranks to get to the river. Having staved off a mutiny, he organized a rudimentary system to extract and distribute the Ilo's water to his men and their animals. The sated troops then continued on to Condes, where they discovered vineyards whose tanks held enormous quantities of wine. The Chileans indulged in an orgy of drink and excess—one soldier even drowning in a wine vat—which Baquedano barely managed to quell. To prevent a reoccurrence, he ordered the vats emptied, which unleashed so much wine that the rivers ran red and the mules, which drank from them, staggered drunkenly from one place to another.[24]

Anxious to avoid another breakdown in discipline, the Chilean civilian functionary, Rafael Sotomayor, vowed to supervise more carefully the campaign and to take a more active role in directing the war. But his involvement, while quite justified, exacerbated the already wretched relationship that existed between Sotomayor and his general in chief. Eventually, the dispute between the two erupted into an open break. Officers, despairing of a general who seemed to trust more to faith than good works, called for the government to fire him. The Pinto administration had also tired of the ultramontane commander, "whose lack of prestige was so frightening" and whose demoralizing policies threatened to spread through the army like gangrene.[25] Thus, when Escala petulantly tendered his resignation, the regime, much to his surprise, accepted. In his stead, the Pinto government appointed Gens. Manuel Baquedano and José Velásquez as commander and army chief of staff, respectively. The sixty-seven-year-old Baquedano, who entered the army at fifteen, would remain the army's commander until early 1881.

The Battle for Los Angeles

The Hospicio fiasco notwithstanding, Baquedano captured Moquegua. His victory was not an impressive feat since the defenders, commanded

Table 15. Battle of Los Angeles, 22 March 1880

Peruvian side

Andrés Gamarra		
Col. Julio C. Chocano	Btn. Grau	300
Col. Manuel Gamarra	Btn. Granderos de Cuzco	300
Col. Martin Alvarez	Btn. Canchis	350
Col. Manuel Velasco	Btn. Canas	300
Lt. Manuel Jiménez	Col. Gendarme de Moquegua	50
	Total	1,300

Chilean Side

Mayor Manuel Baquedano		
Mayor Juan Martínez	Btn. Atacama	590
Col. Mauricio Muñoz	2nd of Line	1,000
Mayor Estanislao Leon	Rgt. Santiago	1,000
Mayor José Echeverría	Btn. Bulnes	500
	1 Comp. Rgt. Buin	155
Lt. Col. Tomas Yávar	Granaderos a Caballo	100
Lt. Col. Pedro Soto	Cazadores a Caballo	200
Lt. Col. José Novoa	Rgt. 2 de Artillería	97
Total		3,642

Sources: Dellepiane, *Historia militar*, 2:208; Andrés Gamarra to Commander, Second Army of the South, Omate, 4 April 1880, 2:440–41, Manuel Baquedano to Chief of Army, Moquegua, 27 March 1880, "Partes oficiales chilenos, Muertos i heridos durante la espedición sobre Moquegua i acción de Los Ánjeles," 2:433, 438–39, in Ahumada Moreno, *Guerra del Pacífico*; Paz Soldán, *Narración historica*, 845.

There is no source, primary or secondary, that gives the exact size of the Chilean forces attacking Los Angeles. The figures for the artillery and cavalry can be verified in various reports. We do know that the contingent that landed at Moquegua consisted of approximately 3,250 infantrymen, 840 cavalrymen, and 290 artillerymen. Machuca, *Cuatro campañas*, 2:133.

by Col. Andrés Gamarra, had already abandoned the town, taking refuge on Los Angeles, a mesa looming sixty-five yards over the valley floor. Unfortunately, Baquedano could not simply bypass the Peruvian troops, whose presence threatened Moquegua as well as the communications network extending southeast across the Locumba Valley to Tacna and northwest to Arequipa and northeast Bolivia. Clearly, Baquedano had to destroy the enemy position, but to do so he would have to evict an entrenched Peruvian garrison from a position that seemed impregnable.

Sandwiched between the Torata and the Moquegua rivers, which had clawed deep gorges on either side of the plateau of Los Angeles, Gamarra's thirteen hundred men—three battalions of infantry, the Grau, Ca-

nas, and Chaquis, plus one of cavalry, the Granaderos de Cuzco, supplemented by fifty men from the Gendarmes de Moqeugua—appeared
invulnerable to attack. Convinced that no one could scale the ravine on
his right flank, Gamarra concentrated on defending his center and his
left. Thus, he ordered the Batallón Grau to dig in on the mesa's forward
edge. This position gave the Peruvians a clear field of fire over the zigzag
road that tortuously climbed up the hill to the Pampa del Arrastrado, the
plain overlooking Los Angeles, and from there to Arequipa. To protect
his eastern flank, he placed most of the Granaderos de Cuzco as well
as an artillery unit on Quilinquile, a mountain located on the pampa.
The Canas and the Chaquis occupied positions toward the rear of the
Pampa de Arrastrado, from which they could easily move to reinforce
any threatened defenses. The night before the battle, Gamarra ordered
the Canchi to replace the Granaderos de Cuzco on Quiliquile.

Baquedano's strategy was simple: skirmishers drawn from the Batallones Bulnes and Santiago and, supported by two artillery batteries would
launch a feint on the Peruvian center. As Gamarra's men concentrated
on repulsing this assault, the Batallón Atacama, under Colonel Martínez,
would try to find a way up the Torata Gorge on the Peruvian right, while
Colonel Muñoz, at the head of seven companies of the Second of the
Line, a battalion from Regimiento Santiago, a battery of mountain guns,
and three hundred cavalry, would scale the Quiliquile heights on the
Peruvian left. If all went according to plan, the two Chilean columns
would converge on the Pampa de Arrastrado, attack Gamarra's rear, and
capture the Peruvians before they could retreat.

On the evening of 21 March, Martínez's men, carrying one hundred
rounds of ammunition, water, and various improvised mountaineer-
ing tools, began their ascent of the Quiliquile Ravine. A combination
of poor roads, the mountains, and the river prevented Muñoz's troops
from locating a place from which they could begin their ascent. Supposedly, the colonel became so distraught that he sought assistance from
the local inhabitants, who generously pointed him in the right direction. These same Peruvians also informed Gamarra what had happened.
This intelligence not only delayed the Chilean sortie but confirmed what
Gamarra had earlier learned from some captured Chilean prisoners: that
Baquedano's units would attack his left flank. Consequently, Gamarra

moved the Granaderos and Canchis to reinforce his positions along the Quiliquile Gorge. At 5:00 a.m., as the Chileans came into view, the Canchis and the Granaderos, plus the Jendarmes on Púlpitos, opened fire. Muñoz's men and their horses were caught in a murderous crossfire as they struggled to climb in single file up a steep slope. Unable to retreat because the cavalry could not turn around, the Chileans tried to take cover. Fortunately, Muñoz's gunners manhandled a Krupp artillery piece to a fold in a nearby mountain facing Quiliquile. Once in place, the Chilean gunners drove the Peruvians back from their center and left flank, giving the Chileans the cover to inch forward.

Martínez's plans also appeared to have gone awry. As per arrangement, his unit departed its camp after midnight. Sending a company under Capt. Rafael Torreblanca to scout ahead, the rest of the battalion waited fifteen minutes before beginning its march. But as the Atacama had reached its jump-off place for its climb, the Chileans heard gunfire. Fearing that he had lost the element of surprise, Martínez did not know if he should proceed or abort his mission. Seeking guidance from Baquedano, he was informed that a firefight had indeed erupted earlier but that Martínez should nonetheless obey his original orders.

At 4:00 a.m. the troops of the Atacama, advancing in single file and using their bayonets to gain a foothold, successfully scaled the ravine on the Peruvian right. After two hours, they managed to reach the high ground above and to the defenders' rear undetected; the Chileans then advanced down the hill. Initially, Gamarra believed that these soldiers were his own soldiers coming to reinforce his position. But when the Atacama, screaming "Viva Chile!" launched a bayonet charge, the Peruvian officer realized his error. Meanwhile, Muñoz's men also arrived at the top of the plateau's left flank, and they too charged the Peruvian positions. Battered by artillery on their left and from the valley below, squeezed from the center and their flanks, the Peruvian defenders imploded. Leaving the Granaderos as a rearguard, the Grau pulled back. Although the exhausted men of the Atacama did not have the strength to pursue the fleeing Peruvians, Baquedano's cavalry did try to capture them. A good portion of Gamarra's forces successfully escaped, reaching the safety of Arequipa. The Peruvians lost between 100 and 134 dead and wounded; the Chileans suffered 4 or 5 killed plus no more than 40 wounded.[26]

Advancing on Tacna and Arica

Lima's *Opinión Nacional* exaggerated when it labeled the Battle of Los Angeles "one more disaster for Peru." While clearly not cause for rejoicing, Gamarra's defeat changed little: the garrisons of Tacna and Arica remained intact; the Chileans would still have to annihilate these forces if they wished to secure the province.[27] Rather than assault Arica directly, which might prove extremely costly, the Chileans planned to advance inland from Ilo first to Tacna, a city that sat astride various roads linking the interior to the coast some forty miles distant, and then attack the port from the east. Capturing these strong points required the Chilean forces first to cross a desert, seemingly devoid of resources and about which they knew virtually nothing.[28]

Baquedano's strategy called for Mauricio Muñoz's Second and José Amunátegui's Third divisions to march from their respective bases in Ilo and Moquegua to Hospicio, where they would turn southeast into the desert. If all went well, they would link up with other Chilean units at Buenavista. Even after completing this fifty-six mile odyssey, the Chileans would still be some twenty-six miles short of Tacna. Meanwhile, elements of Col. Santiago Amengual's First Division would leave Ilo, trudge south, paralleling the coast until it reached Ite, where it too would move inland, to the northeast, to join the rest of the army at Buenavista. Since the desert roads could not support the expeditionary forces' artillery, the high command decided to transport the heavy guns, as well as Barboza's Fourth Division, by sea to Ite another port that provided access to a road to Buenavista. In early May, the army's Fourth Division, its artillery, and its supply train landed at Ite, marching inland to rendezvous with the rest of the expeditionary force at Buenavista and Yaras. The high seas complicated the unloading of the heavy guns, which did not arrive in camp until 11 May.

Beginning on 8 April, some of Amengual's units began their long trek; Amunátegui's troops followed two weeks later. The crossing taxed the men: the treacherous roads delayed the supply trains; mosquitoes devoured the hapless troops, while disease—fevers of unknown origin, dysentery, and a hemorrhagic small pox, which killed as many as 70 percent of the infected—ravaged the soldiers before they ever saw the enemy. Soldiers who fell ill in the morning did not live to see sunset. Dr. Ramón Allende Padín, head of Chile's medical service, had to evacuate two thousand to twenty-five hundred soldiers suffering from the fever as well as treat an additional one thousand of the troops marching overland toward Tacna. In one case, a unit that survived the Battle of Los Angeles almost intact lost half of its complement in the trek across the desert. These problems were not un-expected. Baquedano's chief of staff earlier complained about the lack of medicine and "the alarming scarcity of doctors."[29]

March discipline deteriorated as the troops, sometimes at their offi-cers' instigation, discarded their equipment, retaining only their weap-ons and ammunition; soldiers became drenched with sweat after strug-gling up the sandy hills during the day and suffered when the cold night air converted their perspiration sodden uniforms into frozen mantles.[30] Dehydration drove desperate men to embrace desperate measures. A teenage soldier in the Lautaro, Arturo Benavides, mixed unrefined sugar with his urine, but though he was extraordinarily thirsty, he still could not bring himself to drink this concoction. A good comrade, he offered his sugar-laced urine to another soldier who had no scruples about swallow-ing it. Apparently, this was not an uncommon experience: as Sgt. Manuel Salas noted in a letter to his father, the situation had become so terrible that "even the officers drink urine." When the thirst and fatigue became unbearable, some soldiers killed themselves: a Corporal Cordero shot himself, some of his companions slashed their wrists, and others also died, albeit with less flair.[31] Poorly victualed, the starving troops ate sugar cane, an offense punishable with the lash.[32] Somehow, the three Chilean divisions managed to overcome their various trials to reach Locumba: Amunátegui's Third Division made the trip in eight days.

Forewarned by the Chilean press, which provided almost daily reports on the progress of Baquedano's army, the Allies had to decide where to make their stand. Two schools of thought evolved: Col. Eliodoro Ca-macho and Gen. Juan José Pérez wanted to march the Allied army to the Sama Valley to surprise the Chilean forces while they were crossing the desert in stages and before they could mass. The Peruvians, Admiral Montero and Colonel Latorre, however, favored digging in at Tacna and Arica.[33] Thus, it fell to Narciso Campero, who only reached Tacna in late April, to make this crucial decision.

Taking command of an Allied army about which he knew very little, the Bolivian commander spent his first days trying to learn about his troops and their ability to complete their mission. Apparently in order to test their proficiency and stamina, Campero ordered his troops to undertake a desert march. After covering but 1.5 leagues, the Bolivian directed his men to return to their base. The Allied force, he concluded, lacked sufficient transport to move into the field its artillery as well as its rations and, more significantly, its supplies of water. Consequently, Campero had to abandon any hopes of attacking the Chilean army while it was en route to Tacna; instead his troops would have "to wait for the enemy in its position."[34]

After studying the terrain, Campero decided for reasons of logistics to make a stand at Alto de la Alianza, a plain about five miles northwest of Tacna. A wide pampa, it progressively narrowed at its base, like a keystone, until it collided with a twenty-two-hundred-yard-long hill that ran perpendicular, on an east-to-west axis, to the valley. Flanked by mountains, the hillock controlled the high ground to the south, overlooking the Caplina Valley and the city of Tacna as well as the Chilean encampment to the north. These heights were not simply large mounds of earth; they contained a series of dips paralleling one other and also running on a east-to-west axis. The Allied troops improved on these natural depressions, converting them into rifle pits that measured ten feet in diameter, six to seven feet wide, and less than three feet deep. When completed, this berm effectively concealed the Allied forces and their reserves from Chilean view. Buttressed with sandbagged redoubts, which sheltered emplacements for seventeen cannon and two Gatling guns, and reinforced by three squadrons of cavalry, the position might have given von Moltke pause.[35]

Campero divided his forces into three groups, assigning each a sector to defend: an artillery position consisting of six new Krupp field pieces and two machine guns anchored the line's extreme right. To its west, on the left, Adm. Lizardo Montero commanded the First and Sixth divisions of the Peruvian army, consisting of the Lima Num. 11, Cuzco, Lima Num. 21, and Cazadores del Rimac infantry battalions. The Bolivian Third and Fourth divisions—the Batallones Colorados, Aroma, Murillo, and Zapadores—stood behind the Peruvian units, prepared to

Table 16. Allied forces, Battle of Campo de Alianza/Tacna, 26 May 1880

Rear Adm. Lizardo Montero

Right Wing	Col. Adolfo Flores
Btn. Murillo (B)	
Btn. Lima, N. 11	C. Remigio Morales B.
Btn. Cuzco, N. 19	Valetín Quintanilla
Btn. Lima, N. 21	C. Diaz
Btn. Cazadores del Rimac	Col. Víctor Fajardo
Center	Col. Miguel Castro Pinto
Btn. Loa, N. 3	Col. Raimundo González
Btn. Grau, N. 9	Col. Lizandro Penarrieta
Btn. Chorolque, N. 8	Col. Justo de Villegas
Btn. Padilla, N. 6	Col. Pedro Vargas
Left Wing	Col. Narciso Camacho
Btn. Pisagua	Mayor Pedro Matiz
Btn. Arica	Col. Belisario Barriga
Btn. Zepita	Mayor Carlos Llosa
Btn. Misti	Col. Samuel Lara
Reserves of the Right Wing	
Btn. Nacionales	Prefecto Pedro del Solar
Btn. Colorados, N. 1	Col. Ildefenso Murguía
Btn. Aroma, N. 2 (Amaraillos)	Col. Juan Aramayo
Btn. Zapadores	
Reserves of the Center	
Btn. Arequipa, N. 7	Col. Martín Rimachi
Btn. Ayacucho, N. 3	Col. Nicanor de Somocurcio
Btn. Sama	
Reserves of the Left	
Btn. Huáscar	Col. Belisario Barriga
Btn. Víctoria	Col. José Godines
Btn. Viedmam N. 5	Col. Ramón González
Btn. Tarija, N. 7	Col. Miguel Estenssoro
Btn. Sucre, N. 2	Col. Juan Ayala
To the rear of the Right Wing	
Es. Husáres de Junín	Col. A. Salcedo
Es. Guías	Col. Pedro Nieto
Es. Flanqueadores de Tacna	Col. Pedro del Solar
Es. Gendarmes de Tacna (Nacionales)	
To the rear of the Left Wing	
Es. Coraceros	Col. Octavio la Faye
Es. Vanguardia de Cochabamba	
Es. Libres del Sur	
Es. Escolta	

Sources: Dellepiane, *Historia militar*, 2:247–49; Díaz Arguedas, *Historia*, 206, 216–17, 275–76, 318–21; Machuca, *Cuatro campañas*, 2:264–65; Ahumada Moreno, *Guerra del Pacífico*, 2:560.

offer assistance if needed. Another artillery redoubt, containing a cannon and two machine guns, separated the Allied right from its center, which Col. Miguel Castro Pinto commanded. This sector, like that on the right, consisted of two lines: the most forward, the Bolivian Loa, Grau, Chorolque, and Padilla battalions, controlled by Col. Claudio Acosta, and the center's reserve, which consisted of the Peruvian Fifth Division, the Batallones Arequipa and Ayacucho and the Columna Sama. A third artillery redoubt holding a cannon and two machine guns separated the center from the Allied left. The first row consisted of the Peruvian Pisagua, Arica, Zepita, and Misti battalions, backed up by the reserve Huáscar and Victoria battalions. Another artillery position, containing nine cannon, as well as the Bolivian Batallones Viedma, Tarija, and Sucre, stood at the extreme western end of line. These units held the high ground, which veered off at about a forty-five degree angle from the main line of the defense. At the eastern edge of this line and sited to the rear stood the Peruvian cavalry Jendarmes de Tacna, Flanqueadores de Tacna, and Nacionales, while the Guías and Junín served as their reserve. Similarly, backing up the westernmost point stood the Bolivian Coraceros, Vanguardia de Cochabamba, Libres del Sur, and Escolta. In terms of manpower, the Bolivian forces numbered about 5,150 officers and men, the Peruvians 8,500. They would face 14,147 Chileans.[36]

Thanks to their intelligence reports, the Allies knew that the Chileans intended to march on Tacna. Indeed, by 22 May they could even see the smoke rising from Baquedano's campfires. What the Allied officers did not know was the size of their opponent's army, its composition, and its weaponry.[37] The Chilean chief of staff, Col. José Velásquez, attempting to discover what confronted his troops, dispatched a mixed force of fifteen hundred to two thousand men to probe Tacna's defenses. Before dawn on 22 May this contingent left the main base for the Quebrada Honda, a deep gully located approximately midway between the Chilean camp at Yaras and the Peruvian encampment near Tacna. Once there, some Chileans broke into smaller groups to study the area; Velásquez's gunners also fired a few rounds at the Allied position in order to get some idea of the range.

The Chilean incursion appeared to arouse more Allied curiosity than angst: the Peruvian and Bolivian troops calmly observed the Chilean ac-

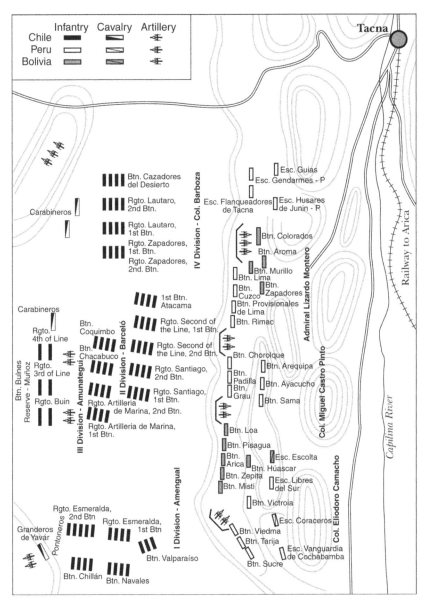

6. Battle of Tacna/Campo de la Alianza

tivities while devouring huge breakfasts of cooked beef, potatoes, soups, roasted fish, tongue, and eggs.[38] General Campero appeared equally blasé: initially he was unsure if the enemy's incursion was a raid or a reconnaissance mission. But after consulting his watch, he concluded that the Chileans would not attack: "It is two o'clock in the afternoon," he noted, "and no battle begins at this time."[39] Campero was right, although the late hour did not stop the two sides' artillery from intermittently shelling each other.

In the evening of 25 May, Campero tried initiate the battle, if not at a more reasonable time, then at least on more advantageous terms. Upon learning that the Chileans had camped at Quebrada Honda, the Bolivian convinced his colleagues that the Allied units should attack Baquedano's forces prior to daybreak, before the Chileans could deploy their artillery or cavalry and when, of course, the Allies had the advantage of surprise. His associates agreed, and at midnight Campero led his troops into the desert night.

The tactic failed abysmally. Not untypically, the camachaca descended on the desert, cloaking Baquedano's troops. And since the Chileans had ordered their men to forgo any campfires in order to hide their position, the Allied force had no way to locate its foes. (This restriction forced Col. Estanislao del Canto to resort to the teenager's ploy of furtively smoking his hand-rolled, corn-leaf cigarettes under a blanket.)[40] After two hours of aimless meandering, the Allies realized they had lost their bearings in the night mists. Indeed, Campero's forces became so confused that one Peruvian unit almost stumbled into a Chilean position. Clearly, Baquedano's sentinels must have heard Campero's troops because they gave the alarm, triggering a search for the interlopers. Recognizing the futility of lurching through the darkness, and with a Chilean unit in pursuit, the exhausted Allies aborted their attack. Although they did not know it at the time, some of Baquedano's men awoke early enough to see the dawn breaking on their enemies' backs.

Very early on 26 May both sides began their preparations for the imminent battle. During the previous evening, Father Ruperto Marchant, a Chilean army chaplain, converted his tent into an improvised chapel, where he heard confessions and prayed with those who requested it. He then made the rounds of the men on guard duty. Just prior to daybreak,

Table 17. Chilean forces, Battle of Campo de Alianza/Tacna, 26 May 1880

1a. División	Col. Santiago Amengual
Rgt. Esmeralda	Lt. Col. Adolfo Holley
Btn. Navales	Col. Martiniano Urriola
Btn. Valparaíso	Col. Jacinto Niño
Btn. Chillán	Lt. Col. Juan Antonio Vargas
2a. División	Col. Francisco Barceló
Rgt. Santiago	Lt. Col. Ladislao Orrego
Rgt. 2 de Linea	Lt. Col. Estanislao del Canto
Btn. Atacama, N. 1	Lt. Col. Juan Martínez
3a. División	Col. José Amunátegui
Btn. Chacabuco	Lt. Col. Domingo Toro Herrera
Btn. Coquimbo, N. 1	Lt. Col. Alejandro Gorostiaga
Btn. Artillería de Marina	Lt. Col. José Ramón Vidaurre
4a. División	Col. Orizimbo Barboza
Btn. Zapadores	Lt. Col. Ricardo Santa Cruz
Btn. Cazadores del Desierto	Lt. Col. Jorge Wood
Btn. Lautaro	Lt Col. Eulojio Robles
Reserve	Col. M. Muñoz
Rgt. Buin	Lt. Col. José Ortiz
Rgt. 3 de Linea	Col. Ricardo Castro
Rgt. 4 de Linea	Lt. Col. José San Martín
Btn. Bulnes	Lt. Col. José Echeverría
Cavalry and Artillery	
Rgt. Granaderos de Yungai	Lt. Col. Manuel Bulnes
Rgt. 2 de Artillería	Lt. Col. José Francisco Vergara
Rgt. Granaderos a Caballo	Lt. Col. Tomás Yavar
Es. Carabs de Maipú	Lt. Col. Rosauro Gatica

Sources: Machuca, *Cuatros campañas*, 3:257–59; "Partes Oficiales chilenos," Arica, 11 June 1880, in Ahumada Moreno, *Guerra del Pacífico*, 4:560–77.

Marchant celebrated a mass as well as gave general absolution to the troops of the Regimientos Esmeralda, Navales, Valparaíso, and Chile. At the conclusion of the religious service, the troops threw their kepis into the air while offering a "deafening 'Viva Chile' from God to the motherland."[41]

At daybreak bands playing Chile's national anthem, and the more martial "Himno de Yungay" awaked those of Baquedano's troops who had managed to sleep through the din. The soldiers had a great deal to do: many entrusted their bedrolls and personal gear to bandsmen, like the Regimiento Coquimbo's drummer Gococillo, retaining just their weapons and bayonets to carry into battle.[42] The troops also drew a basic load of ammunition—130 rounds per man, with the exception of the soldiers of the Esmeralda, who received only 100 rounds, a fact that would have some significance later in the day—as well as dry rations and water. Supposedly, these would carry the troops through the day, providing, of course, that they lived that long. Those unfortunates carrying the Grass rifle had to perform a singularly unaesthetic, if not bizarre, task: because the fine desert dust jammed their weapons, the men urinated on their rifles' firing mechanisms to free up the breech block.[43] Unlike the Allied troops who wandered into their camp at daybreak, most of the Chileans managed to eat a hot breakfast. Hipólito Gutiérrez, who slept sitting up with his rifle cradled in his arms, had time to make coffee for himself and his lieutenant.[44] Typical of all armies, long waits interrupted the minutes of frantic activity. Arturo Benavides, after consuming a breakfast omelet, was either extremely tired or very blasé because he used this downtime to nap.[45]

By 7:20 a.m. the troops had lined up in their formations. Some heard words of encouragement from their officers. Del Canto, for example, reminded his troops of the heavy loss of life that the Second of the Line had sustained at Tarapacá. Claiming that the Peruvians had supposedly burned alive Lt. Col. Eleuterio Ramírez, the unit's commander, as well its cantineras, he ordered his troops to spare no enemy soldier, including the wounded. In fairness, the colonel treated his men only slightly less harshly, suggesting that his troops shoot any comrade who behaved in a cowardly fashion.[46] Doubtless this scene occurred throughout the Chilean army. Finally, to the sounds of more martial music, the crash of artillery fire, and the collective benedictions of the army's chaplains, Baquedano's legions marched off to do battle.

At the other end of the pampa, the Allied troops performed many of the same rituals as their enemies. But the bands' playing of "happy reveilles and even marineras" could not dissipate an air of general anxiety that enshrouded the Allied camp. Awakened at 6 a.m., the Bolivians drew ammunition as well as their per diem food expenses. They did not have long to wait to spend their money: a *vivandera* circulated among them selling soup, roasted meat, and a shot of cognac for those who needed an early morning bracer.[47] Some of the more fortunate Bolivians enjoyed more personalized care. Sergeant Olaguibel's faithful rabona, carrying their child on her back, brought his meal in a clay pot. While she prepared his breakfast, the soldier played with his son. Then the sergeant embraced her perhaps for one last time, kissing his boy goodbye. She disappeared into a cloud of dust kicked up by a Chilean shell. Happily, she survived, although we are not sure about the fate of her lover.[48]

Apparently this scene repeated itself on that day. An Argentine officer, Florencio del Marmól, noted that as he rode his mule toward the battle he saw three to five hundred rabonas, babies on their backs, pots in their hands, and "their eyes full of tears, heartsick grief on their lips," leaving what would soon be a battlefield.[49] The Allied soldiers, like their enemies, tried to tie up the loose ends of their lives: Lt. Col. César Moscoso asked a comrade to take care of his mother for him; another officer, Julian Vargas Machicado, gave some money to a friend, begging him to deliver it to his sister should he perish.[50]

Allied officers also tried to inspire their men. As the various units' bands played, Maj. Juan Reyes steadied his Colorados. "Don't worry," he counseled, "bullets do not kill, fate does."[51] Quiet acts of patriotism also occurred: Juanito Pinto, a twelve- or thirteen-year-old drummer boy of the Alianza grabbed ammunition and a rifle from a civilian to join the battle, and General Acosta and Colonel Miguel Estensorro rose from their sick beds join their units.[52] Another officer came upon a girl about fourteen or fifteen years old moving not toward the rear but to the battlefield. Motherless, she preferred to share the fate of her father, without whom, she observed, "I would have no one in my life, if I outlive him." We do not know what happened to her, but Campero tried to order Estensorro and Acosta off the battlefield. They refused but promised "to return to see if we survived [the battle]." Acosta never made it: a Chilean artillery shell struck him. In one of war's many ironies, after killing the Bolivian in battle, the Chileans buried him with all the pomp of a full military funeral, including an honor guard from the Regimiento Buin.[53]

Campo de la Alianza resembled the Battle of San Francisco except that this time the Chileans had to attack the Allied contingents entrenched on the high ground. Thanks to good luck, the Chileans captured an enemy document indicating how many units opposed them and the lo-

cation of those units. This knowledge only seemed to make them painfully aware of what they had to accomplish. Confronting such a dug-
in enemy, Col. José Francisco Vergara earlier suggested that a portion
of the Chilean forces should launch a feint to divert the Allied forces
while the main body enveloped the enemy's right, thereby cutting off
Tacna and its defenders from their water supply, an essential resource
in the arid plain. If implemented, Vergara's plan would also prevent the
Allied troops from fleeing either to Tacna or, in the case of the Bolivians, to their homeland. Ironically, even a Bolivian officer subsequently
criticized Baquedano for not adopting Vergara's plan at Tacna. Had he
done so, the Chileans would either have trapped the town's defenders or
forced them to try to flee to Arica, a taxing endeavor.[54]

But Baquedano and his chief of staff, Velásquez, vehemently rejected
the civilian's plan: enveloping the Allied line, they argued, would be too
complicated, reduce Baquedano's ability to control his troops, and expose the Chilean forces' flank to an enemy counterattack. As would occur at Lima, Baquedano favored the simpler, if not simplistic, frontal
assault. Aware of the high casualties that his decision would cause, he
believed that his troops would still triumph, simply because they were
Chilean. A laconic man, apparently he stuttered and was reputed to have
dismissed Vergara's proposals with the words "Chilean soldier, forward,
forward."[55]

Baquedano's plan called for Amengual's First Division, consisting of
the Batallones Valparaíso, 1 and 2 Esmeralda, and Chillán, and Barceló's
Second Division, composed of five battalions from the Atacama, the Second of Line, and Santiago, first to shatter the Allied left, piercing the
defensive line, and then attack the remaining troops from the rear. As
the enemy concentrated on defending its left flank, Amunátegui's Third
Division, comprising the two battalions of the Naval Artillery Regiment,
as well as the Coquimbo and Chacabuco, stood ready to reinforce either
the First or Second Division, while Colonel Barbosa's Fourth Division,
consisting of battalion-size units of the Zapadores, the Lautaro, and the
Cazadores del Desierto, would assault the enemy center and right. A reserve, commanded by Col. Mauricio Muñoz, composed of the Third and
Fourth of the Line and the Bulnes in addition to the Carabineros, stood
directly behind the Third Division.

Chile's tactics, advancing "in solid columns, only light companies being deployed as skirmishers, and . . . firing . . . executed in close formations of double ranks," were, as an American naval officer noted, worthy
of any Napoleonic army.[56] Worse, Baquedano's decision to attack frontally not only minimized the Chilean army's numerical edge but "was an
act of heroic lunacy, the worst strategy we could have adopted," converting the task facing his battle-hardened veterans from the dangerous to
the homicidal: his men would have to cross approximately thirty-eight to
forty-two hundred yards in sometimes ankle deep sand, which slowed the
movement of both the infantry and the artillery, without cover, seared
by a burning sun, and under fire the enemy's field guns before they
could even begin the deadly task of assaulting the Allied troops dug in
on the high ground. Worse, as Amengual observed, "I had no idea of
the purpose of the march nor did I have instructions from either you
[Baquedano] or the Chief of Staff on the plan of attack, or the enemy's
location." Amengual even slowed his advance hoping to receive instructions that never arrived.[57] Essentially, Baquedano, always generous with
the blood of others, threw his units into a battle with no more direction
than pointing a finger at the Allied forces.

Chile's artillery park, which consisted of thirty-eight cannon and six
Gatling guns, was divided into sections and distributed to protect the
advance. At the rear of the Fourth Division, Gumercindo Fontecilla commanded a battery of six Krupp mountain guns. Ten cannon and two
machine guns under Santiago Frias stood behind and to the left of the
First Division. Eleven cannon, including five Krupp mountain guns, under José Errázuriz and Exequiel Fuentes, trailed behind the Second and
Third divisions.[58] The Chilean cavalry hovered at Baquedano's rear and
flanks: the Cazadores del Desierto stood to the rear and left of the Fourth
Division, the Cazadores a Caballo and Second Escuadrón Carabineros
de Yungay to the rear of this division. The Granaderos a Caballo, under
Colonel Yávar, were located between First Division's rear and Salvo's artillery battery.

When the Allied artillery opened fire at approximately 9:00 a.m., the
Chilean guns replied in kind. Neither side's cannon inflicted much damage: the Chileans fired shrapnel, which could not penetrate the Allied
defenses, and those shells that landed sometimes sank into the sand

without detonating. The Allied gunners failed to zero in on Baquedano's units, and even when their shells ran true, they did not inflict substantial casualties. Thus, after two hours of futile artillery exchanges, both sides' batteries ceased firing, while Amengual's First Division and Barceló's Second Division began their advance. The advance had all the precision of a minuet: the Chileans advancing "maneuvering as if on a parade grade. And the enemy watching."[59] The attackers would have a long walk.

As the Chileans approached, the Allied troops began to sing their national anthems and to shout encouragement to one other. In truth, there was little else for Campero's soldiers to do except pray that the trek across the pampa would so exhaust the Chileans that they would not have the strength to assault the Allied positions. Still, it must have been unnerving for Campero's men to watch passively as that "black and dusty line" of Chilean troops slowly came both into focus and rifle range. But, as one Bolivian officer noted, thanks to his troops' "proverbial obedience and unalterable discipline," they held steady.[60]

By approximately 10 a.m., when Amengual's men had moved to within thirty-five hundred yards of the Allied line, they halted to allow the Chilean artillery to soften again the enemy positions. Once the barrage lifted, Amengual ordered the units to form up into a column of battalions and his gunners to move their weapons forward. By then the Allies had formed a skirmish line atop the first ridge, which masked the location of the main body of the Peruvian-Bolivian troops. At approximately 11:30 a.m. Amengual, still about eleven hundred yards short of the enemy, ordered the Valparaíso to form a skirmish line, followed by another line consisting of the First Esmeralda, the Navales, and, behind them, yet a third from the Second Esmeralda and the Chillán. When they neared the Allied position, the troops in the second file broke into companies to begin an assault.

As the Chileans, who had already sustained heavy casualties just crossing the open ground, charged the high ground, the Allied infantry suddenly appeared and, without waiting for orders, opened fire. Their first volley stunned the attackers of the Valparaíso and the Esmeralda's First Battalion, killing or wounding eighty to one hundred Chileans.[61] The fighting became increasingly brutal as Amengual's men began using their bayonets or corvos to dispatch their enemies. Capturing the next

line of dugouts proved particularly troublesome: the Allies had sent in
fresh reinforcements, who, backed by two cannon and a machine gun,
tore holes in Amengual's division. When the Chileans tried to outflank
the Allied left in order to envelop it from the rear, the defenders extended their front, thus thwarting Baquedano's forces. Still, despite the
terrible barriers and the heavy fire, Amengual's troops managed to take
the second line of trenches and even captured some artillery.

On Amengual's left, Barceló seemed to fare no better. Led by three
companies of skirmishers—the soldiers of the Santiago and Second of
Line regiments and the Atacama Battalion—the Second Division advanced in a single line. In order not to exhaust either the men or their
ammunition supply, Barceló had ordered his troops to rest briefly before
launching an all out assault on the Allied position. But Col. Estanislao
del Canto of the Second of the Line disobeyed his commander's order:
presumably anxious to avenge his unit's honor for the loss at Tarapacá,
he called on his troopers to assault the enemy line. Barceló, fearing that
the Second of the Line would be annihilated, had little choice but to direct the rest of his men to follow del Canto's lead. His division, forming
an elongated skirmish line, threw themselves at their enemy.

The intense enemy rifle fire temporarily stalled the attack. The Bolivian Col. Eleodoro Camacho, realizing that Amengual hoped to outflank
or smash him, ordered his artillery to pull back to reduce its vulnerability
to the Chilean riflemen, placing it in a location from which it could still
fire at the enemy fieldpieces. But when he changed his guns' location,
Camacho created a hole in his line, which he ordered the reserve battalions Huáscar and Victoria to plug. He also directed his Bolivian reserves—the Viedma, Tarija, and Sucre—to move toward the left, thereby
extending his flank and thwarting a possible Chilean envelopment. But
these maneuvers left Camacho with only four squadrons of Bolivian cavalry to reinforce his extended front.

Having consumed his sector's reserves, Camacho asked for and received as additional reinforcements the Batallones Arequipa and Ayacucho, which were taken from forces originally designated as the reserves
for the Allied center. When these units proved unable to contain the
Chileans, Gen. Narciso Campero sent the troops from the Batallones
Alianza (the Colorados) and the Aroma (the Coloraditos, so called be-

cause, like the Colorados, they too wore red jackets but with gray pants) to help Camacho. The transfer of these soldiers, while buttressing the Allied left, so seriously weakened its center and right that it ultimately made them vulnerable to an attack by the Chilean Third and Fourth divisions.

The fierce battle began to take its toll of the defenders. Campero's "blood turned to ice in his veins" when he saw the Peruvian Batallón Victoria first buckle and then disintegrate. Campero, as well as the Victoria's commander, tried to stanch the flight by waving Peruvian flags. When that stratagem failed, he ordered the newly arrived Colorados and one of his Peruvian units to fire on the fleeing men in hopes of forcing them to return to the front. Neither the bullets nor the fluttering standards, however, could rally the demoralized troops.

After an hour's bitter fighting, the Chilean First and Second divisions had captured the second line of Allied trenches, but an assault on the third row of dugouts stalled as Amengual and Barceló learned that their units were running out of ammunition. Although a captain managed to manhandle two boxes of bullets forward, these were inadequate: the Chilean commanders begged Baquedano for more munitions and reinforcements. Outmanned, exhausted, and with their ammunition almost depleted, Amengual and Barceló ordered their men to retreat. Fortunately for them, the withdrawal did not degenerate into a rout: the Chileans withdrew slowly, often pausing to fire volleys at their enemy.

Seeking to press his advantage, Camacho ordered the Colorados and the Aroma to attack. The Colorados' commander, Col. Ildefonso Murguia, and his executive officer, Lt. Col. Felipe Ravelo, immediately mounted their horses to lead their troops into the maw of battle. "'Cowardly Rotos,'" the bald, thinly bearded Murguia screamed out in an "imposing voice, . . . 'cinch up your underpants because the Colorados of Bolivia are coming.'"[62] But before they could close with their enemy, the Colorados and Coloraditos first had to step over three rows of inert bodies, each wearing "yellow jackets, white pants, and white hats," lying in 820-foot-long files and separated by intervals of 650 feet. These corpses were those of the Amarillos, or the Sucre Battalion, men who faithfully maintained in death the same formation in which they marched into battle.

Firing in disciplined volleys, the Aromas and Colorados drove the Chileans back, recapturing some Peruvian heavy guns, which Baquedano's people earlier had seized, as well as some Chilean field pieces and a machine gun. Barceló's division also came under pressure from the center, as Castro Pinto's troops joined the Allied counterattack. In brutal hand-to-hand fighting, Campero's soldiers slowly retook the ground that the Chileans sacrificed so dearly to capture.[63] Sure that they had vanquished the Chileans, the Colorados began waving their rifles in the air. Their rejoicing was premature.

Spying a cavalry unit, the Granaderos a Caballo, commanded by Tomás Yávar, the Esmeralda's desperate commanding officer, Adolfo Holley, begged for their help. Yávar complied, ordering his men to charge the Allied lines. This tactic failed for two reasons: first, because the smoke and dust of battle obscured their vision, the Granaderos inadvertently killed some of the very troops they rode to rescue. The Chileans also underestimated their foes: the Colorados did not panic but instead quickly formed infantry squares. Waiting until the Chilean cavalry were within twenty yards, the Bolivian squares opened fire, stunning Yávar's horsemen and blunting their attack.[64] But if the Granaderos could not drive the enemy from the field, they managed to occupy the Allied troops long enough for Amengual's and Barceló's beleaguered infantry to regroup. Using the bullets they scrounged from their dead and wounded comrades, they held out long enough for additional ammunition to arrive— it came in sealed boxes that required an ax to open—and for Baquedano to order his Third Division under Amunátegui to advance.[65]

It had taken approximately ninety minutes for the Chilean Third Division to advance. But once it did, the Chacabuco Infantry Batallion, led by the cigar-smoking Lt. Col. Domingo de Toro Herrera, and the Coquimbo smashed the Allied center, while the Artillería de Marina, advancing at a fast trot, struck Camacho's left. Under enormous pressure caused by the arrival of these fresh troops, the units that Camacho and Castro Pinto previously ordered to attack the Chilean right had to retreat back to their fortified positions.[66] As Murguia ruefully noted, he would have annihilated the Chileans if he could have called upon the reserves, but he had none: Campero had already folded these men into the battle.[67] To complicate matters for the Allies, the Chilean Lautaro

Infantry Battalion, carefully aligning itself on the standard carried by Lieutenant Benavides, advanced in a closed formation. Finally hearing the bugle sound charge, the battalion along with the rest of the Fourth Division attacked Montero's undermanned right.[68]

General Campero watched as the Chilean and Allied soldiers fought in such close quarters that they congealed into "a dense dark mass, impenetrable to sight, but illuminated from moment to moment, like when a ray of light crosses the space of a tempestuous night." El Campo de la Alianza became a field of "desolation and death, disguised by dazzling clothes," as "victims who fell were replaced immediately by others."[69] Blinded by "gunpowder, smoke, and sand clouds," the opposing soldiers became so entwined that neither side dared fire its artillery for fear of hitting its own troops.[70] For the same reason, the troops hesitated to discharge their weapons: instead they resorted to bayonets and their corvos or wielded their rifles as clubs. Occasionally, the hand-to-hand combat became personalized. When the Batallón Buin went into action, its members yelled out, demanding to know the whereabouts of the Colorados. The Bolivian infantry responded first by firing a salvo and then launching a bayonet attack. One Colorado managed to skewer a Buin with his bayonet before the Chilean impaled him.[71] The sound of war, what Campero called "an indefinitely prolonged thunder," became increasingly louder. Miguel Claros, another Bolivian, noted that the bullets that whizzed over his head sounded like mewing cats; his Chilean foe Abraham Quiróz, who served with the Lautaro, characterized the gunfire as the roll of a drum.[72] Either way, the sounds killed.

As the late morning blurred into the afternoon, the situation turned increasingly bleak for the Allies: the men of Batallón Padilla, their ammunition exhausted, fought back with Comblains taken from the Chilean dead. Capitalizing on their machine guns and their superior numbers, the Chileans turned the Allied left flank—costing the Peruvian Batallón Zepita its commanding officer, Col. S. Luna, who fell leading a counter-attack—while hammering the undermanned defenses of the Camacho's center.[73] At the same time, the Allied right, whose reserves had been sent to bolster Camacho's troops, collapsed before Barboza's Fourth Division. Campero, shouting threats and waving a battle flag, called on the men to hold. But pouring through the massive gaps in the Allied line, the Chileans sent the enemy reeling back while capturing an enormous amount of booty, including some 1879 Krupp cannon, five Gatling guns, plus five thousand rifles of mixed manufacture.

Within hours of their collapse, the Allied troops and officers, "covered in powder, bathed in sweat, and many bloodstained," began to fill Tacna's streets. But if various civilians offered the vanquished troops water and even beer, some of town's lower class, including a few women, chased the exhausted Bolivian troops down the street, coarsely shouting that they had caused the rout. As José Ochoa observed, "For us there is no other choice than to begin the trip to our unfortunate motherland." Thus, with the cries of "On to Pachia," the vanquished Allies abandoned the battlefield.[74]

Upon reaching Pachia the fleeing soldiers had two options: one road led to the mountains and the Peruvian cities of Arequipa and Puno, the other to Tacora and the altiplano. The trek to Bolivia killed many troops, some of whom froze to death. The lucky few survived by devouring *chancaca* (partially refined sugar) and corn; many of those who had nothing to eat died. Florencio del Marmól sat next to a man who spent his last night on earth spitting up blood from a mortal wound.[75] Claros, fearful that he might become a prisoner, had the foresight to put on two suits under his uniform. Although his compatriots laughed at him, he could better survive the Andean cold on the long march for La Paz.[76] Like others, however, he would endure great hardships, traveling without much water and forced to eat almost raw llama and alpaca meat.

The Chilean officers declared captured Tacna off-limits to their men. This decision infuriated soldiers like Hipólito Gutiérrez, who claimed that Gen. Manuel Baquedano had promised them the freedom of the city if they vanquished the Peruvians. Thus, instead of pillaging the vanquished town, Gutiérrez and his mates had to spend the night in the field, hungry, thirsty, and cold.[77] The Allies would later accuse the Chileans of looting Tacna as well as despoiling its citizens, but this version of the city's fate differs sharply from that of Gutiérrez and the Chilean high command. An eyewitness, an officer in the Buin, indicated that Tacna and its residents had indeed suffered but at the hands of their erstwhile defenders, not the Chileans.[78]

The battle for Tacna had been brutal. Baquedano triumphed, but his tactics cost Chile dearly: his four divisions sustained 689 dead and 1,509 wounded, or approximately 15 percent of its forces.[79] Many of the 80 to 100 wounded would die from shock because the surgeons had to operate on some of them without chloroform.[80] Certain units were more than decimated: the Atacama lost 24.9 percent of its complement, and 11.2 percent of the Santiago Regiment fell. Heaps of amputated limbs grew outside of the aid stations. Clearly, the American military attaché's dictum for the Russo-Turkish war—that "the breech-loader is no respecter of persons"—applied to the encounter at Tacna.[81] Only the Fourth Division, which served as a reserve, emerged almost unscathed. The cold statistics obscure the battle's real personal tragedies. The commander of the Atacama's Fourth Company, Major Martínez, for example, lost two sons, Melitón and Walterio. Their father's only response was "What God gave me, the motherland has taken." Martínez did not have to spend much time mourning the deaths of his warrior children: he would perish in the attack on Lima.[82]

The Chileans certainly gave at least as good as they got: Dr. Zenón Dalence, the head of the Bolivian medical unit, put the Allied dead at fifteen hundred, one thousand fewer than reported by a Bolivian general staff officer. (Dalence also observed an interesting phenomenon: Peru lost more officers but fewer enlisted men than the Bolivians.)[83] Many of the often-denigrated Bolivians fought until their units almost ceased to exist: the Chorolque, the Amarillos, and the Colorados battalions suffered between 80 to 81.7 percent casualties; the Padilla lost 67 percent. The Sucre Battalion's executive officer, who had two horses shot out beneath him and who sustained a bad leg wound, told his nephew that his unit simply no longer existed. Fate, as Major Reyes had earlier predicted, proved fickle: the Bolivian chief of staff, Gen. Juan José Pérez, sustained a mortal head wound, while Colonel Camacho, who had prayed for "nothing more than that a bullet would kill me," survived.[84] Overall, it is believed that 45.6 percent of the Bolivian troops perished defending Tacna.[85]

The Peruvians also sustained heavy losses: battered by Chilean artillery, rifle, and machine gun fire, slightly more than 30 percent of the Batallón Ayacucho survived Tacna; the Provisional Batallón Lima 21, which retreated fighting, lost 200 of its 480 soldiers. One unit, the Columna de

Artesanos, was so completely destroyed that the high command could not report accurately on the number of its casualties. Officers suffered disproportionally: Cáceres suffered two wounds, and Col. Carlos Llosa of the Zepita as well as the commanders of the Arica and the Cazadores de Rimac perished.[86] Clearly, few could accuse the Allies of cowardice.

Like brief bursts of light, acts of heroism emerged from the carnage: officers like the Bolivian Col. Francisco Solis, as well as his staff, for example, battled as simple infantrymen.[87] Lt. Daniel Ballivián's superiors in the Colorados ordered him to carry a message to a cavalry squadron. Realizing that by the time he returned the Chileans would have overrun his unit, the young officer tried to disobey. Go, his commanders insisted, go where "you can do something. There are enough of us here, veterans for whom life is no more important than a plug nickel, to write this last page of glory." Ballivián departed. His last view of the battlefield was that of a wounded officer, his shattered leg leaking blood, advancing toward the still raging battle lines, waving his sword while calling out in a voice that "still rings in my ears: forward, boys, forward! Forward, forward!"[88] Clearly, too few troops remained to heed his plea. Still, the long casualty lists allowed Lieutenant Colonel Ravelo, the Colorados' executive officer, to declare that at Tacna Bolivia had "lost all except [its] honor."[89]

Like the Bolivians, many Peruvians also rose to the occasion: Col. Andrés Cáceres continued to fight after having lost two horses, his executive officer, two aides, his standard bearer, and 80 percent of his Zepita Battalion. As usual, the soldiers displayed their best and worst: the unit fighting alongside the Zepita plus the Jendarmes de Tacna may have bolted, but members of the general staff, Cols. Manuel Velarde and Agustín Moreno, fought with absolutely no "hope of triumph . . . [but] in search of a glorious death."[90] In the end, of course, Allied heroism made no difference except to the vanquished: by 2:00 p.m. the Chileans owned the battlefield.

Some of the triumphant soldiers seemed to have followed del Canto's advice—he had urged his men to murder Peruvian wounded in reprisal for the losses they inflicted upon their comrades at Tarapacá—and, in fact, they took no prisoners. Indeed, a Chilean soldier, Alberto del Solar, alleged that the Chileans butchered twenty-five hundred Allied troops, in part because they were still angry at the ferocity of their resistance. An officer of the Batallón Santiago reported that one soldier threatened his commander when he tried to prevent him from killing a wounded Allied soldier, just one example of "this fever to kill that possessed the victors, particularly those of the Second of the Line."[91]

Regrettably, first aid stations did not provide sanctuary. Chilean troops apparently invaded a Peruvian hospital unit, stripped a Colonel Barriga of his uniform, and then shattered his face by firing bullets into his head at close range. The Bolivian physician, Dr. Zenón Dalence, also charged that the Chileans frequently slit the throats of the wounded. Stealing from the enemy casualties became common: Col. Agustín López lost his riding boots and his insignia of rank. Chilean soldiers also looted Dalence's ambulance unit's supplies, taking its brandy and using its stretchers for firewood. Nevertheless, the Chilean authorities, including Dr. Ramón Allende Padín as well as some officers, tried to protect the Bolivian field hospital and even shared some medicines with them.

Moving the wounded from the battlefield to aid stations constituted the medics' biggest problem. Delays occurred due to a lack of corpsmen, stretcher-bearers, and ambulances. The more fortunate, the walking wounded, managed to stagger into field stations, sometimes helped by a friend. The large number of casualties following the Campo de Alianza appeared to overwhelm Chile's medical units. Dr. Allende Padín's corpsmen created makeshift hospitals in a Tacna warehouse. When this proved inadequate, he sent the wounded to a school, a theater, as well as a marketplace, where apparently the doctors worked for hours performing amputations, the traditional "cure" for bullet-shattered limbs, a task made more grisly when the surgeons ran out of chloroform. Fortunately, surgeons serving aboard Chile's naval vessels as well as foreign warships anchored in Arica's harbor helped care for the wounded.

The Chileans attempted to clean up Tacna and disinfect its facilities. Lamentably, even the best of intentions could not improve the situation: the wounded often succumbed to septicemia and gangrene, as well as a host of other fatal infections. The only solution was to evacuate them to proper hospitals. Baquedano possessed both the ships and facilities, although unsanitary conditions on the transports sometimes killed these men before they reached Chile. And while the Peruvians used the Red Cross to bring its wounded home by sea, Bolivia could not and had to send their casualties overland.[92]

The news of the debacle of Tacna greatly saddened the Allies. As before, some of the press blamed the defeat not on Chilean skills but "almost exclusively on the lack of skill, the incompetence and the inertia of the senior officers that we have the misfortune of placing at the head of such brave and loyal soldiers."[93] Still, some of the Peruvian press valiantly tried to convince its readers that because Chile had also sustained heavy losses, the garrison at Arica might defeat Baquedano's hosts.[94] *La Tribuna*, a La Paz daily, describing victory as "the infamous prostitute of chance," urged its readers to take heart: a nation, it observed, does not commit suttee because it has lost a battle. Instead, Bolivia's citizens should draw inspiration from their army's "martyrdom" and continue the war.[95] But the government and its vanquished troops ignored *La Tribuna*'s posturing: the Bolivians might remain a belligerent, but Tacna marked their nation's last battle of the War of the Pacific. Still, the landlocked country could take pride in its soldiers' fierce, almost suicidal, resistance.

Logic and prevailing military thought indicated that the Chileans should not have triumphed at Tacna. The two armies were roughly equal in size: the Peruvian-Bolivian forces numbered about 10,000. Theoretically, Baquedano's 14,000-man army dwarfed its foes. In fact, excluding the reserves, only four Chilean divisions—between 9,600 and 10,500 men—fought at Tacna. Thus, the difference between the two sides was not so significant. On the contrary, since the standard military texts specified that any attacker should have a three-to-one majority to capture a fortified position, theoretically the Chileans needed 32,000 soldiers to vanquish their foes. The Allied troops, many equipped with breech-loading rifles, Krupp field artillery, and holding a well-fortified high ground, should have annihilated the Chileans long before they had covered the forty-three-hundred-yard-long stretch of open sand separating them. As a Peruvian colonel, Justo Pastor Dávila, observed, "Neither the numerical superiority of the invaders, nor the superiority of their weapons would have caused our defeat if the lines had been fought in accordance with the unbreakable rules dictated by tactics and strategy; unfortunately, this did not happen, and for this reason the bravery of the division and the blood that has so liberally spilled, while it glorified its name, . . . [it] also produced a tragic result for our arms."[96]

Clearly Baquedano had not learned the lesson so bloodily demonstrated by the American Civil War and the Franco-Prussian War: that frontal assaults on entrenched infantry equipped with rapid-fire rifles was a murderous business. Happily for Chile, its foes, while possessing enough Gatling guns and breech-loading rifles, lacked the skill to deploy them efficiently. Nor did their artillery bombard the advancing Chileans with shrapnel. Had they done so, Baquedano's tactics most likely would have failed. Similarly, the general's rejection of fighting in dispersed order or open cost his nation dearly. The Fourth Division's Colonel Barboza, who had learned this tactic from Santa Cruz, applied this method. It proved successful: the Regimiento Esmeralda, which attacked in the traditional mass formation, lost 248 men; the Zapadores, which followed Barboza's plan, only 77.[97]

The Taking of Arica

Tacna's fall did not end the campaign; Arica's garrison still remained intact. While some politicians questioned the value of trying to capture that port, others believed that Chile needed its harbor to resupply its forces, who had begun to run short of food, ammunition, and equipment. Arica, moreover, served as the principal port for supplying the Allied garrisons in the interior as well as Bolivia's principal cities; thus, its capture might allow Chile to starve its enemies into submission. Curiously, some Peruvians, at least after the loss at Tacna, saw no logic in trying to defend the port. A Peruvian bureaucrat, Pedro del Solar, for example, urged Col. Francisco Bolognesi, Arica's Peruvian commander, first to destroy the port's military equipment and then lead his men into the mountains.[98] But from his base high in the altiplano, Admiral Montero made defending Arica a matter of Peru's national honor: the port's garrison, he ponderously intoned, "should blow itself up with all its defenders and all its assailants" rather than capitulate.[99]

The port was a formidable target. Not unlike Gibraltar, Arica's defenses rested on a mountain, El Morro, which towered 670 feet above the ocean before sloping gradually toward the Andes, melting into the pampa floor 5,500 yards to the east. North of El Morro, the Lluta, or Azufre, River cascaded west from the Andes into the Pacific Ocean. Almost perpendicular to the river, a rail line and a road connected Arica with Tacna. In addi-

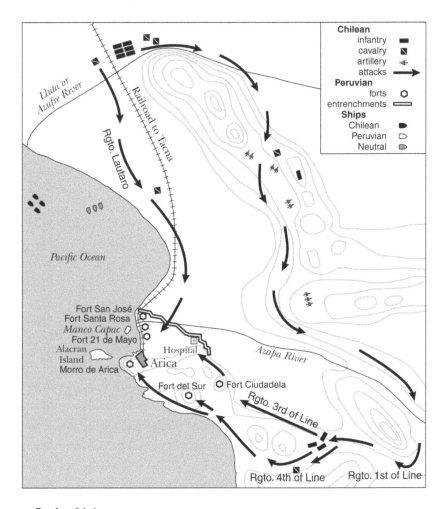

7. Battle of Arica

tion to anchoring the monitor *Manco Cápac* at El Morro's base, Bolognesi constructed numerous strong points, including three gun batteries, at ground level on the mountain's northern flank. These installations, Forts San José, Santa Rosa, and 2 de Mayo, which together mounted two Parrot and two Vavasseur cannon, became collectively known as the northern guns. Arica's defenders had also dug a three-kilometer-long trench, which ran southeast from the water's edge until it melted into El Morro, to protect the northern forts' rear from an infantry assault. Atop the port's heights stood three strongholds that housed various large-caliber guns: Fuerte Ciudadela, located on the mountain's northern side; Fuerte

Table 18. Battle of Arica, 7 June 1880

Allied commander - Col. Francisco Bolognesi	
7a. División	Col. Joaquin Inclán
Btn. Artesanos de Tacna	Major Varela
Btn. Granaderos de Tacna	Col. Justo Arias
Btn. Cazadores de Piérola	Lt. Col. Francisco Cornejo
8a. División	Col. Alfonso Ugarte
Btn. Tarapacá	Lt. Col. Ramón Zavala
Btn. Iquique	Lt. Col. Roque Sáenz Peña
Coastal Defense Forts	
Norte	Col. Juan Ayllon
Este	Lt. Col. Medardo Cornejo
Morro	Capitán de Navio Juan Moore
Chile	
Chilean commander - Col. Pedro Lagos	
Rgt. Buin, 1 de Linea	Lt. Col. Luis Ortiz
Rgt. 3 de Linea	Lt. Col. Ricardo Castro
Rgt. 4 de Linea	Lt. Col. Juan San Martin
Rgt. Lautaro	Lt. Col. Eulojio Robles
2 Rgt. de Artillería	Lt. Col. José Novoa
Es. Carabineros de Yungai	Lt. Col. Rafael Vargas
Rgt. Cazadores a Caballo	Capt. Alberto Novoa

Sources: Dellepiane, *Historia militar*, 2:277; Manuel de la Torre, "Primer Ejército de Sur, Plaza de Arica," 5 June 1880, 3:186, "Partes oficiales chilenos," 3:176–84, in Ahumada Moreno, *Guerra del Pacífico*.

Este, which curiously was west of Ciudadela; and at the northern most end of El Morro, Fuerte El Morro, consisting of two gun emplacements, the Alta and the Baja, mounting five and four guns, respectively.[100] The commander of the Alta was the beached naval captain Juan Moore, who was still doing penance for driving the *Independencia* aground during the Battle of Iquique.

In addition to the coastal artillerymen, the Peruvians created, almost from scratch, two divisions: the Seventh Division, 805 troops enrolled in the Batallones Artesanos de Tacna, Granaderos de Tacna, and Cazadores de Piérola, and the Eighth Division, the 518 men of the Batallones Tarapacá and Iquique. Together with the crews of the forts, El Morro's garrison numbered approximately 1,858.[101] Drawn from local militia, these units were poorly armed and only partially trained; their officers, many recently commissioned, lacked experience. The Chilean-educated Col. Alfonso Ugarte, for example, had been a merchant and the mayor of

Iquique before receiving command of the Seventh Division. Ugarte, with all of his deficiencies, at least remained at his post: many of his brother officers, including a Colonel Belaunde, chose to flee long before the onset of the battle.[102]

The Peruvians introduced a new weapon to the battlefield: the land mine. An engineer, Teodoro Elmore, had used some 250 quintales of dynamite to manufacture electrically or pressure-detonated mines, each weighing from one and a half to thirty pounds, which he planted atop El Morro, in the northern forts, and in other crucial locations. The Chileans first discovered these weapons on 2 June, when a scouting party's horse inadvertently triggered an explosive device, injuring three soldiers. Fortunately for the Chileans, they managed to capture Elmore, who, after being threatened with death, "quickly understood his situation": he surrendered a map indicating not only the various minefields' locations but also the places from which they could be electrically detonated.[103]

Beginning on 2 June, General Baquedano used two locomotives and various rolling stock, "liberated" after Tacna's fall, to rush troops and supplies to the coast. By 3 June, forty-four hundred soldiers from the First (Buin), Third, and Fourth line regiments, the Batallón Bulnes, four artillery batteries, and some cavalry arrived in Arica, where they camped at Chucalluta, on the northern side of the Lluta, or Azufre, River. The one-thousand-man Regimiento Lautaro reached the port two days later.

On the evening of 4 June, the First, Third, and Fourth infantry units, three batteries of field artillery, and a cavalry squadron sneaked across the Lluta, taking up positions on the Lomas de Condorillo, a chain of low hills paralleling the seacoast east of El Morro. The next morning, the Chilean artillery opened fire on the northern batteries and the entrenched infantry. Having earlier discovered the location of the Peruvians guns, the Chilean gunners learned to their regret that their artillery lacked the range to hit the enemy batteries, some fifty-five hundred yards distant. Indeed, because the more powerful Peruvian artillery had a greater reach, the Chilean gunners had to move their own field pieces around to avoid suffering damage.[104]

Hoping that the demonstration of Chilean firepower had cowed the Peruvians, Baquedano sent Maj. José de la Cruz Salvo to suggest that Bolognesi capitulate.[105] But after consulting his subordinates, the Peruvian refused. "Arica," he noted, "will not surrender: I have sacred duties to fulfill, and I will fulfill these until I have fired my last cartridge." Thus, on 6 June a battalion from the Lautaro and some troops from the Buin launched a sortie probing of the Peruvian defenses near the northern forts. Although Bolognesi's soldiers easily repelled the raiders, the Peruvians became convinced that the Chileans would make these gun batteries the focus of their offensive. Consequently, Bolognesi ordered his Eighth Division to bolster the defenses of the northern forts.[106]

Meanwhile, Baquedano, still hoping to intimidate the Peruvians, ordered another artillery display, this time requesting his naval colleagues join in bombarding Arica. On 6 June the *Loa*, the *Magallanes*, the *Covadonga*, and finally the *Cochrane* began firing on El Morro. For approximately four hours, the Peruvian coastal artillery and the *Manco Cápac* traded salvos with the gunners of the Chilean army and navy. The Chilean fleet got the worst of the exchange: the *Cochrane* sustained a hit that destroyed a gun and killed nine sailors. The Peruvian gunners also managed to strike the *Covadonga*, but they did not kill any of ship's crew.

Although the artillery had not truly dented the Peruvian defenses, Baquedano nonetheless hoped that the second artillery display might convince Bolognesi to capitulate. Thus, he sent Teodoro Elmore to ask the colonel to surrender, which he again refused to do. Col. Marcelino Varela, who served in the Arica garrison, subsequently observed that the Peruvians seemed to reject the Chilean offer more because of its form than its substance. "We were," he noted, "disposed to receive an official flag of truce, sufficiently authorized and that he [the delegate] offer proposals that would be in accord with military honor and the laws of war." But apparently because a civilian delivered the ultimatum, "the meeting was concluded, saying goodbye to Señor Elmore and directing each of us to our posts."[107]

Rather than lead the assault, Baquedano delegated this responsibility to Col. Pedro Lagos. The new commander's plan to capture Arica called for the First, Third, and Fourth of the Line to attack El Morro from the southeast. At the same time, the Lautaro would cross the river and frontally assail the sandbagged infantry positions, seizing the northern forts. The Batallón Bulnes would remain in the mountains to protect the artillery, while the cavalry, at the onset of the offensive, would clear the valley of Peruvians.

Fearing that a protracted battle might prove too costly in terms of men and supplies—and there was an ammunition shortage—Lagos ordered his troops to attack at dawn, when, he hoped, his soldiers could seize the key forts before the defenders reacted. Thus, on 7 June at between 6:30 and 7 p.m., Lagos's soldiers—the First, Third, and Fourth of the Line as well as Bulnes—left their mountain positions, stealthily crossing the valley floor before establishing themselves on the mountains located southeast of El Morro. By 11 p.m. the Chilean units were approximately one to two miles away from the enemy. The next day at 3:00 a.m. the Lautaro quietly crossed the Lluta River so that by 6:00 a.m. it too was within rifle shot of the Peruvians. To deceive Bolognesi into believing that the Chilean units had not moved during the night, Lagos ordered the cavalry, which remained at the original encampment, to keep the campfires burning.

Before dawn on 7 April, the Chilean troops began their ascent of El Morro. After an hour they had crept to within 330 to 450 yards of the first strongpoint. The Seventh Division troops manning Fuerte Ciudadela awoke to see a "a black line that could barely be distinguished," only to realize that one thousand troopers of the Third of the Line had inched close enough, as one colonel noted, to be "within range of his Peabody rifles."[108] Once the Peruvians opened fire, the Chilean Fourth of the Line rushed to take Fort Este, while the Third charged the Ciudadela.

The outnumbered Peruvian infantry immediately began shooting, but the Chileans closed with Bolognesi's gunners before they could depress their cannon in time to open fire.[109] Aided by electrical mines planted on the approaches to the mountain forts and bolstered by reinforcements, the Peruvians resisted fiercely. Yet, the Chileans managed to penetrate the front lines and had begun fighting inside Ciudadela when two mines exploded. According to the report of Ricardo Castro, commander of the Third of the Line, the concussion blew Lt. Ramón Toribio Arriagada into the air, landing him deaf, bruised, and naked in a pile of corpses. Despite this mishap, Toribio Arriagada, presumably still unclothed, immediately joined the struggle to capture another fort. Lt. José Poblete lost more than his dignity: the blast decapitated him. The triggering of these devices had two unexpected consequences: they killed more Peruvians than Chileans and, by destroying the defenses, they made it easier for the

Chileans to press the attack on the fort.[110] Within minutes, the Peruvians abandoned the Ciudadela, fleeing toward El Morro, all the while under the devastating fire of the Chilean infantry, who also captured Forte Este. Exalted by their comrades' feat, the Buin ignored Lagos's order to serve solely as the reserve and instead spearheaded an assault that overran Forts Alta and Baja.

Once the battle began, the Peruvians realized that Lagos had duped them: the sortie of 6 June was merely a feint; the main Chilean thrust did not focus on the northern forts but on those gun batteries located on El Morro. Apparently at the same time that Col. Alfonso Ugarte ordered the Eighth Division to bolster El Morro's defenses, the Lautaro launched its offensive. With the Peruvians already in the process of retreating, the Chileans, supported by Lagos's field artillery, easily pierced the Peruvian defensive line. Despite taking fire from the Peruvian forts and the *Manco Cápac*, Lagos's men captured Fort San José. The gun crews of the Forts Dos de Mayo and Santa Rosa either deliberately detonated their mines or they exploded accidentally. Whatever the cause, to the men of the Lautaro, the explosion resembled a strong earthquake, leaving them deaf and covered with dirt.[111] Meanwhile, elements of the Tarapacá and Iquique retreated to El Morro, where, exhausted by their run up the mountain's side, they joined the Seventh Division trying to fend off the Chileans.[112]

The defenders were now desperate. An attempt to destroy themselves and their forts had miscarried when a mechanical problem prevented them from destroying the forts' powder magazines. The Peruvians could retreat no more: the survivors, including Bolognesi, with the Peruvian flag flying overhead, made their stand on a two-hundred-meter plain at the edge of El Morro. Obviously, the battle had ended, and admission of defeat did not seem inappropriate. But the Chileans, supposedly livid that the Peruvian mines had inflicted so many casualties, seemed loath to offer their adversaries an opportunity to surrender. Instead, the Chileans launched, by all accounts, a ferocious attack on the remaining men. Bolognesi died firing his pistol at a Chilean soldier who literally cleaved his skull in two. Moore finally atoned for Iquique by perishing at Bolognesi's side. Col. Alfonso Ugarte, the mayor turned division commander, wrapped himself in the Peruvian colors before spurring his horse to leap off El Morro into the ocean.

Although he did not realize it, Capt. José Sánchez Largomarsino of the *Manco Cápac* became Arica's last defender. He had heard the sounds of cannon and small arms' fire, and when he saw the Chilean fleet entering Arica's harbor, he realized that the final assault had begun. The *Manco Cápac* immediately opened fire on the Chilean forces attacking Fort San José. When he spied the other citadels explode, he turned south in the hope that he could assist the land forces. Sighting the Chilean flag atop El Morro, and under fire from its cannon, Sánchez tried to engage the Chilean fleet but to no avail: his ship's boilers could not generate sufficient steam either to fight or to flee. It became clear, moreover, that but for the monitor, the Chileans had captured Arica. Not wishing to endanger his crew, Sánchez ordered his sailors to sabotage the ship's engine and spike its guns. Then he directed the crew to open the seacocks. When the water had flooded the machine room and the powder magazine, Sánchez transferred his shipmates to waiting ships, abandoning the *Manco Cápac*.[113] The remaining Peruvian vessels, including the torpedo boat *Alianza* dashed for the port's entrance in a vain attempt to escape. By 9 a.m. the battle had ended: Chile now controlled not only the provinces of the Atacama and Tarapacá but Tacna as well.

From the Peruvian perspective, Arica became the abattoir of its youth. Most historians put Chilean losses at 474, of whom 120 died and 354 were wounded. Depending on the sources, of the approximately 1,800 to 2,000 Peruvian defenders, approximately 700 to 900 perished, a death rate of between 35 and 47 percent. An additional 200 suffered wounds, and the Chileans captured about 1,300 men.[114] The Chilean practice of tossing the bodies of the dead Peruvians from atop El Morro into the ocean came back to haunt them: the tides spewed many of these cadavers back on Arica's beaches, where they began to rot. (In some cases, Peruvian dead remained unburied for up to ten days.) Eventually, the Chileans had to burn some of the corpses to prevent the spread of infection.[115]

But Arica became synonymous not so much with death but atrocities. Baquedano's soldiers, some claim on his orders, made a practice of killing enemy wounded, particularly the officers, whom they sometimes first stripped of their clothes and then mutilated. Maríano Paz Soldán, a Peruvian, stated, "The motto of the Chilean army in this battle was *today there will be no prisoners* and this was accomplished with a savagery not seen in America since the conquest" (italics in the original). The killing, moreover, did not end with the capture of El Morro: Chilean troops murdered some seventy to ninety survivors of the Batallones Iquique and Tarapacá who had fled into Arica,[116] where supposedly "drunk on [a concoction] alcohol mixed with blood, they continued to sack houses, where they respected neither modesty nor the aged . . . [and] whatever man they met, be he a soldier or not, fell beneath the blade of the treacherous corvo."[117]

The Chileans might disagree with these appraisals, but even one of their own, Máximo Lira, described the slaughter as "horrible": "The blood down ran from the top of the mountain to the plain and the mountain is composed of sand. . . . I cannot tell you what our soldiers did there until we see each other."[118] A Chilean cavalry officer, upon viewing the Fourth of the Line's handiwork, noted that "the blood [had] formed rivulets," while pieces of human bodies—including a decapitated officer—were "scattered in a horrible confusion and the stench of blood makes one dizzy."[119] Compassion became a scarce commodity atop El Morro. An anonymous officer observed, "Voices of mercy are heard here, heartbreaking cries of those who fall, run through by the bayonets of our soldiers." But sometimes Chileans had ample reason to act so harshly: when Col. Justo Arias y Arragüéz, commander of the Granaderos de Tacna, cleaved the head of a Chilean soldier who offered to accept his surrender, the remaining troops shot and bayoneted the ungracious officer.[120] Arias y Arragüéz was not the only ingrate: Captain Moore tried to shoot Maj. Luis Solo de Zaldívar when he suggested that the Peruvian concede defeat. Zaldívar may have been forgiving but not to the point of masochism: he returned fire, killing the naval officer.[121] Happily, even in the midst of this carnage, occasionally some Chileans did act humanely, even at risk to themselves: Ricardo Silva had to hold his troops off at sword point in order to save a future president of Argentina, Roque Saenz Peña, as well as Lt. Colonel Manuel de la Latorre from his vengeful men.[122]

The Peruvians interpreted such actions as some atavistic throwback demonstrating a traditional Araucanian hatred of the superior Incan culture.[123] Even American and British eyewitnesses remarked about the large numbers of Peruvian dead; one Argentine likened the Chileans to cannibals.[124] While perhaps emotionally gratifying, this interpretation fails to explain the orgy of death. Apparently the Chilean army regarded mine warfare in much the same light that its fleet viewed the naval torpedo: a sneaky or a cowardly way of fighting. As Arturo Benavides Santos noted, the mines were "contrary to the Chilean way of being, who attacks frontally and openly." For Rafael Vargas of the Cazadores a Caballo, the decision to take no prisoners possessed a certain logic: once the Peruvian used mines, "our soldier gave no quarter."[125] Eloy Caviedes, a correspondent for *El Mercurio*, seemed to revel in Lagos's war to the death: "There is no quarter. Blood demands blood. Mines, the corvo. And all their throats are cut. No one escapes. The soil becomes wet with the hot torrents. Pools of blood are formed. . . . The ridiculous gentlemanly behavior has ended. Against the mines, corvos." Still, the correspondent of the *Estrella de Panama* feared that the supposed slaughter and rape of Arica was merely a prelude to what the Chileans would do when they captured "the City of the Kings, whose population includes seventy to eighty thousand women and children."[126]

Chile's capture of Tacna and Arica marked a significant moment in the War of the Pacific. For all intents and purposes, the Peruvian and Bolivian prewar regular armies ceased to exist. Only a handful of seasoned officers and noncoms survived the abattoirs of the Campo de la Alianza and El Morro. That the Allied armies had suffered such losses is a testament not to their skill but to their sense of duty. Often poorly armed, many of the Peruvian and Bolivian troops fought with great tenacity. Clearly, leadership proved crucial: some units continued to struggle as long as their commanders could lead. When these officers succumbed either to wounds or death, troops sometimes lost heart and fled the battlefield; others remained to fight to the last. But even the best of officers and most exalted sense of duty could not overcome the sheer weight of the well-equipped and better-led Chileans.

Those Peruvians who survived the first year and half of the war would face the enormous task of raising, equipping, and training yet another army. Curiously, few blamed Piérola for their nation's wretched situation. On the contrary, the disaffected concluded that "the oligarchy, with whom the political party of Prado governed, has been fatal for Peru." Conversely, Piérola has preserved Peru's "*Civilization*, its *Christian* nature, and its *Liberty*" (italics in the original). Indeed, thanks to this man who has the "heart of a Spartan and the constancy of Brutus. The Republic . . . is saved."[127]

The Peruvian press seemed equally strident. Peru, noted *La Patria*, still had the resources to continue to fight, and hence it was "the duty of all and the obligation of each . . . to organize for victory." Indeed, according to *El Nacional*, Chile supposedly lacked the manpower and the funds to bring the war to Lima.[128] Heeding his compatriots' call to action and aware that his own tenure depended upon actively prosecuting the war, Piérola dedicated himself to preparing the capital's defenses. Although the Chileans eventually captured Lima, the nation would fight an irregular war for an additional two years. This phase of the conflict, which occurred in Peru's heartland, cost Lima dearly in terms of its infrastructure, its treasure, and its youth.

Bolivia confronted a different problem and fate. While the battle of El Campo de la Alianza had eradicated most of Bolivia's remaining soldiers, a few surviving regular officers returned to the altiplano in hopes of raising a new army. But President Campero would not send these men west to fight against Chile. Instead, he adopted a brilliant, albeit cynical, policy: as Chile and Peru strained to exterminate each other, Bolivia would sit by the sidelines. Perhaps by the time it had bludgeoned Peru into suing for peace Chile would have lost interest in the war and would negotiate a generous peace with Bolivia.

8. Investing Lima

The capture of Tarapacá's salitreras and the destruction of Peru's regular army at Tacna and Arica should have given President Nicolás Piérola pause. By December 1879 Peru had lost the economic resources it needed to fund its war effort. And after the first six months of 1880 Peru no longer possessed the skilled military manpower required to defend itself or its interests. Clearly, Lima would be the next target, and Peru appeared almost helpless. Had Piérola sued for peace in June 1880, he would have saved countless Peruvian lives and the nation's treasure. But Piérola, whom some Chileans called "El Loco de Lima" would instead continue the struggle: perhaps the heroic deaths of Miguel Grau, Juan Moore, and Francisco Bolognesi had established a standard of behavior—of battling to the end—that the president simply could not ignore. But by promising to resist the Chileans "to the last bullet," Piérola had fashioned a golem that threatened to destroy him and his nation.[1]

Paradoxically, Chile, its string of victories notwithstanding, also faced an unappetizing future. Its heroic war dead called out for vengeance as well. If an angry public had pushed Aníbal Pinto into declaring war in 1879, it would now demand, perhaps this time with more justification, that the president finish the job by defeating Piérola and force him to sign a draconian peace treaty. To achieve this end, the Chileans would have to invest Lima, whose capture many expected would end the conflict.

Launching this phase of the campaign posed even greater problems for Chile than its earlier expeditions: at Lima the Chilean army would have to confront virtually the entire male population of the capital. Worse, the Peruvians would be defending prepared positions, supported by a formidable collection of coastal guns and heavy artillery. Just to mount such an ambitious expedition, Chile would have to accumulate thousands of men, hundreds of horses, and tons of materiel before chartering enough transports to travel the thousand miles from Valparaíso to Callao. The Peruvians, conversely, were not only fighting on their home ground but within a few miles of the capital's arsenals and supply depots.

Thus, the struggle for Lima promised to be a titanic battle, an Armageddon, that the Chileans had to win to triumph. For the Peruvians, this contest offered the last chance to inflict a telling loss upon their foes. If Piérola's legions succeeded, Peru would gain months before the Chileans could field another expedition. Both sides, therefore, approached the forthcoming struggle with no little anxiety, well aware that the encounter might prove to be the crucial one. Not surprisingly, the belligerents redoubled their efforts: the Peruvians to buttress their defenses and the Chileans to amass the resources to launch what they hoped would be the final campaign. The Chileans, moreover, faced yet another problem: how to maintain the morale and fighting edge of the troops garrisoning Arica and Tacna while its high command prepared for the attack on Lima.

Lynch's Foragers

Within a month of Arica's fall, Capitán de Navío Patricio Lynch wrote Pinto suggesting that he authorize a series of raids on the coast north of Lima.[2] These forays, Lynch argued, would hone the soldiers' martial skills, boost Chilean morale, increase the pressure on Piérola, collect taxes that President Pinto could use to defray the costs of the war, so ravage the countryside that Peru's rural rich would beseech their government to capitulate, and finally, oblige Piérola to divert some if his men from defending Lima to protect Peru's littoral.[3] Conversely, inaction, Lynch warned, gave Lima more time to prepare its defenses and uselessly consumed Chile's limited military and naval assets while eroding the troops' discipline and degrading their skills.

Logically, Pinto should have rejected Lynch's request and instead used his resources for the push on Lima. But just as the government had to acquire the men and equipment for its invasion of Tacna, it needed time to prepare for what it hoped would be the war's final offensive. Lynch's proposed raids promised to placate public opinion, which demanded the active prosecution of the war, while giving the government time to recruit and equip additional troops. Thus, in August 1880 the president authorized the punitive expedition.

To avoid a repetition of the Mollendo fiasco, Pinto set some strict ground rules: Lynch could not tax property "that does not yield a direct profit" to the government, and he had to guarantee that his men would not commit acts of "arson or vandalic destruction." The naval officer, moreover, could destroy Peruvian property only if its owner refused to pay a war tax, either in cash or in kind; of course, neutral possessions remained off-limits. And just to ensure that the expedition would adhere to these legal niceties, Lynch even appointed an attorney, Daniel Carrasco Albano, to adjudicate issues involving the ownership of property.[4] Having made its position clear, in early September the Chilean government authorized Lynch to command a punitive expedition.

Lynch's brief would range from Paita in the north, close to the border with Ecuador, to Quilca in the south. His orders to his commanders were simple: attack any vulnerable enemy strong point, seize supplies or materiel that the Peruvian army might find useful, destroy the enemy's rail assets as well as its weapons, collect taxes, and punish those who do not cooperate.

On 4 September 1880, Lynch's raiding party, composed of two thousand troops from the Batallones Colchagua and Talca, the Regimiento Buin, plus engineers, artillerymen, and cavalry and their horses and guns as well as ammunition, boarded the *Itata* and the *Copiapó*, which sailed north from Arica. Upon reaching Mollendo the convoy picked up its escort, the *Chacabuco*; the *O'Higgins* joined the squadron a few days later. At dawn of 10 September, the *Itata* and the *Copiapó*, as per Lynch's instructions, landed at Chimbote. Immediately the Chileans demanded some one hundred thousand soles in silver from a local *hacendado*, the politically well-connected Dionisio Derteano, whose Palo Seco sugar plantation and refinery were estimated to be worth one million British pounds. It seemed particularly appropriate for Derteano to suffer this fate since he had backed the war and in 1880 commanded a military unit defending Lima.[5] But Derteano's mayordomo faced an unpleasant choice: if he did not pay Lynch, the Chilean would surely destroy Palo Seco. Alternatively, if he acceded to the Chilean officer's demands, an act the Peruvian government had declared as treasonous, Lima would confiscate his master's land.[6] Curiously, Lynch tried to cajole the manager into cooperating, arguing that since Lima did not control Derteano's property the Peruvian government could not prohibit him from paying the tax. But realizing that the Chileans would eventually leave Peru, Derteano opted to suffer the temporary inconvenience of Lynch's wrath rather than the permanent loss of his *hacienda*.[7]

Normally, Lynch encountered little meaningful resistance. José M. Aguirre, commanding some 250 volunteers and gendarmes, dramatically vowed that he would defend the city of Monsefú to the death. When the Chileans arrived, though, Aguirre and his men fled, but not before they had turned the town over to the care of some foreigners.[8] Some Peruvian officials preferred bargaining to bluster. One prefect, Adolfo Salmon, tried negotiating with Lynch, requesting an extension of a deadline so that the local hacendados could raise the funds that the Chilean demanded. The naval officer agreed, but, he warned, if the locals failed to come up with the money, the entire community would suffer. Happily, a German national, Luis Albrecht, offered Lynch sixty thousand pesos to leave, a proposition that the local American consul urged the Chilean to accept. The news of this cooperation infuriated Lima, which demanded that Salmon investigate. Unbeknownst to the Piérola government, however, Salmon and Lynch had earlier struck up a kind of friendship, the Peruvian referring to the Chilean as "my dear friend"; Lynch reciprocated, indicating that Peru would have been better served and governed if it had more functionaries like Salmon.[9]

On the whole, Lynch fulfilled his mission. His sometimes draconian methods did embroil his government in a series of incidents that distressed the local European and American consuls. But almost as often the diplomats' demands for protection were excessive: some envoys complained that since English and French financial interests owned the mortgage to Palo Seco, for example, Lynch should not have attacked it.[10] In his defense, the naval officer pointed to the testimony of the British consul in Paita as well as others who noted how respectfully the Chileans treated neutral property.[11]

Peruvian property, however, did not fare well. Lynch's men captured and destroyed large caches of ammunition as well as the haciendas that housed them. In mid-September they wrecked Chimbote's railroad. During that same month Lynch levied and collected fines from the towns of Lambayaque and Monsafú. When the elites of Eten or the owners of individual properties resisted the naval officer's demands, his men simply destroyed government buildings, railroads, and rolling stock, as well as the privately owned machines used in refining sugar; they also torched state owned buildings in Paita and entire plantations like Palo Seco and San Nicolás.[12]

For some Peruvians, Lynch's most barbarous act was not the imposition of a war tax but his freeing the Chinese who had labored on Peru's haciendas. Somehow these supposedly indentured, but in reality enslaved, workers aroused the compassion of Lynch, who released them from their bondage. Predictably, the Asians fled from the countryside, much to the distress of their former owners, who feared that some of them might take advantage of their new freedom. Although Lynch's actions antagonized the Peruvians, they inspired the gratitude of the Chinese, who faithfully served the Red Prince, as they came to call him, as well as the Chilean army for the remainder of the war.[13]

When all the damages were totaled, Lynch's raid destroyed some $4.7 million in Peruvian property.[14] On the positive side, the Chilean expedition captured foodstuffs—sugar, rice, and spices—as well as industrial goods, bronze, matches, concrete, textiles, tubes, and railroad signal equipment. The Chacabuco also found an unexpected bonanza: while searching the merchant ship *Islay*, the Chileans seized approximately 7.3 million soles in Peruvian bank notes, as well as $375,000 in postal stamps. In addition, the soldiers collected £29,000, and $11,000 in silver.[15] Having turned a net profit, Gen. Manuel Baquedano recalled Lynch's men, so they could participate in the attack on Lima.

The Drive for Lima

When in late 1880 the Chilean government finally decided to launch an expedition to invest Peru's capital, it did so hesitantly and with few expectations. True, the enemy capital constituted one of the few remaining targets. But as early as July, Pinto concluded that Chile could ill afford the cost of assaulting Lima. Additionally, the president and many of his advisers also doubted that capturing the Lima would push Piérola to the peace table.[16] Still, as the harried president acknowledged, he had no choice: his government could not resist attacking Lima "without exposing the nation to disturbances."[17] Thus, with great trepidation and few hopes, the Pinto regime began to mount its most ambitious offensive to date.

By the spring of 1880 Chile's army numbered approximately forty-one thousand. About half of these men—twenty-seven thousand—served under Baquedano, an additional eight thousand occupied the recently conquered territories in Tarapacá and Tacna, and the remainder garrisoned Chile's heartland or patrolled its southern frontier. The proposed expeditionary force consisted of three divisions, each containing two brigades of infantry, two brigades of artillery, and a regiment of cavalry. Earlier the army had established a *parque general*, a centralized quartermaster depot, as well as three division-level branches that would provide supplies to the units in its respective divisions.[18] In addition to its own storage area, each division also had a *cuerpo de bagaje* that provided transportation.[19]

Pinto's military might have possessed the manpower to launch its Lima offensive but little else. Indeed, according to the chief supply officer for Chile's armed forces, the intendant Hermójenes Pérez de Arce, the army had "no supplies, no forage, no clothing, and no equipment. . . . In a word, there has not been any preparation for this expedition."[20] Clearly the soldiers seemed to need almost everything: eight hundred mules plus their tackle; six million cartridges of assorted ammunition—enough to provide four hundred rounds per man—as well as thirty-eight shells per artillery piece; fifteen hundred Winchester carbines; four hundred sabers; bayonets; canteens; one thousand kilos of sugar; uniforms, as well as shoes for twenty thousand; forage for four thousand animals; sufficient water wagons to prevent the soldiers and their pack animals from dying of thirst; and oceangoing ships and special launches to transport the men north and to offload them when they reached Lima.[21]

Amassing these items required time and, in some cases, a certain arbitrariness: to satisfy the military's needs for pack animals and mounts the authorities simply began confiscating mules and horses off the streets of the capital as well as those of provincial cities. Procuring the riding tackle proved more difficult.[22] Satisfying the army's daily food needs also seemed daunting. Approximately fourteen thousand officers and men daily consumed 3,200 kilos of dried meat, 4,900 of beans, 1,680 of grain, 2,800 of hardtack, 2,800 of toasted grain, and 700 of fat. Normally the men also drank or used 2 to 3 liters of water; their animals, 30. Thus, the expedition's approximately four thousand animals daily consumed 120,000 liters of water per day plus 600 quintales of forage; the soldiers consumed another 50,000 liters per day.[23]

A shortage of shipping seriously handicapped the government's attempts to feed and equip its army. At the onset of the war, Chile leased the vessels of the Compañía Sudamericana de Vapores to transport men and materiel. It also used three vessels belonging to the Lota Coal Company and the fleet's three transports. While enormously helpful, these were not sufficient, forcing the Moneda to purchase fifteen sailing boats; it also constructed thirty-five specially designed launches capable of ferrying three thousand men or twelve artillery pieces from their transports to the shore. The Office of the Quartermaster had to modify most of the newly acquired transports by installing galleys, water tanks, and ventilation systems, so they could carry soldiers.[24] Altering the ships to accommodate the three divisions' four thousand horses or mules proved a more complicated task. Just the animals' daily water allowance, for example, absorbed enormous space. Indeed, the authorities dedicated the *Santa Lucia* solely to producing and carrying water. In anticipation of the attack on Lima, the minister of war acquired the steamships *Chile*, *Paita*, and *Pisagua* and chartered another. Unfortunately, the addition of these vessels still did not solve the army's transportation problems: as José Francisco Vergara observed, the government needed ships to move troops and supplies not only from Arica to the war zone but also from Valparaíso to Arica. Since Chilean merchantmen could not transport the entire invasion force and its supplies at one time, the drive on Lima would have to take place in stages.

On 6 November, while the military and civilian bureaucracy labored to resolve its logistical problems, Minister Vergara and his civilian advisers—Eulogio Altamirano, Esubio Lillo, and Máximo Lira—met Gens.

Manuel Baquedano, Marcos Maturana, and Cornelio Saavedra and the three divisional chiefs to plan the next phase of the war. Acknowledging that they lacked the vessels to move the entire expedition at one time, the leaders decided to send the eight thousand men, three hundred horses, and four hundred tons of supplies of General Villagrán's First Division to secure a bridgehead at Pisco, a port about halfway between Arica and Lima. To defend against a possible Peruvian counterattack, Vergara suggested, and the council concurred, that they should also order the Second Division's First Brigade, commanded by Col. José Francisco Gana, to reinforce Villagrán's men.[25] Once they had achieved a foothold in Pisco and captured Ica's provincial capital, Villagrán's men were to dig in and wait. In the interim, the transports would return to Arica, where they would first pick up Gana's brigade for its trip north.

Having agreed upon the plan, Lynch's brigade, which constituted Villagrán's vanguard, entrained for Arica, where on 12 November it began filing aboard the fleet's transports. It required two full days to load the First Division's eighty-eight hundred men, their twenty cannon, and their supplies. As in previous expeditions, the steamships towed the seven sail ships and four launches carrying the expedition's supplies.[26] To avoid repeating the logistical mistakes of the past invasions, each vessel bore a number that the authorities used to identify the ship's cargos. This artifice permitted Villagrán's staff to unload first the expeditionary force's most essential items; the rest it stockpiled. As a precaution, Admiral Riveros ordered the *Pilcomayo* and the *Magallanes* to accompany the convoy in the very unlikely occurrence that the *Unión* or any of Peru's five torpedo boats tried to attack the convoy. On 15 November, bolstered by the cheers of the soldiers and Baquedano's promise that this would be "the third and last campaign of the motherland against her enemies," the fleet departed, reaching Pisco without incident on 19 November.[27]

Most of the Chilean fleet could be found blockading Callao, a particularly onerous task for the crews that had to subsist on a diet of monotony and dried rations. On 7 and 8 October Minister Vergara ordered Riveros to leave the *Huáscar* and the *Cochrane* to guard Callao while the rest of the blockading squadron—the *O'Higgins*, the *Pilcomayo*, the *Angamos*, the *Magallanes*, and two transports—sailed for Arica. The *Blanco* would subsequently follow, and at Arica it received orders to go to Iquique for careening.

On 19 November, five days after it sailed, Villagrán's division reached Pisco. Predictably, most of the officers, who received better rations as well as more spacious quarters, enjoyed the trip north. The lower ranks, who lacked these amenities, did not. Arturo Benavides, a subaltern serving with the Latauro, for example, complained that his sleeping space on the *Mateo Murzi* was so cramped he could barely lie down, and even if he could, the heat was so oppressive that if he could not spend the night above deck, he would have to sleep naked. Still, he noted, his comrades' spirits improved, perhaps in part because they had managed to smuggle some women aboard the ship.[28]

Rather than blunder ashore, Villagrán wisely ordered some of his ships first to reconnoiter the harbor. When a party of four hundred infantry and artillerymen landed, they learned that three thousand Peruvian men garrisoned Pisco and that the authorities had also mined the harbor and coastal approaches.[29] Hoping to frighten the Chileans, the Peruvian commander, Col. Manuel Zamudio, detonated two mines in Pisco's harbor. His ploy to scare Villagrán only partially succeeded: rather than chance a possibly dangerous landing in Pisco, the remaining Chileans simply disembarked at Paracas, ten miles to the south, the same harbor where Chilean and Argentine troops had landed in 1820 to help liberate Peru from Spanish rule.

Although apparently calm, a combination of reefs, sandbars, and shallow waters made Paracas's bay a potentially dangerous port for most of the transports. Consequently, many of the ships, particularly the sailing vessels, anchored well off shore. But thanks to the efforts of Francisco Alvaro Alvarado and Pacífico Alvarez, two civilian experts, as well as 102 stevedores specially brought from Valparaíso, the offloading and ferrying of men went smoothly. Once ashore, the Chilean vanguard advanced on Pisco, intent on seizing the port's steel pier, thereby facilitating the unloading of the rest of the convoy.[30]

Pisco's defenders were few in number, singularly unenthusiastic, and, thanks to their refusal to attend the mandatory drills, utterly unprepared.[31] Paradoxically, as the Chileans approached, the Peruvians voiced increasingly more bloodthirsty threats, promising that they would scorch the earth, wage a guerrilla war, and poison the local wells rather than surrender. A group of hacendados even asked for explosives, which they

promised to use to mine their homes and estates, plus rifles, so their agricultural workers could fight as irregulars.[32] The arrival of the Chileans,
however, quickly cooled the Peruvians' patriotic ardor. Juan José Pinillos,
the Peruvian officer who served as Zamudio's chief of staff, became livid
when he discovered that not just the enlisted men but some of his most
senior officers had "without permission abandoned their units or companies to the enemy."[33]

Before attacking Pisco, the Chileans offered Colonel Zamudio a
chance to surrender. The Peruvian melodramatically spurned the suggestion: "Not a single Peruvian," he intoned, "will quit this position that
I have the duty of defending against the invading hordes." Indeed, in-
voking Bolognesi's example, Zamudio grandiosely promised that Peruvians preferred "to die, defending the national honor" rather than surrender.[34] Clearly the port's civilians did not share his sentiments: they
fled, leaving Zamudio's troops planting mines—including one containing 120 kilos of explosives—and preparing defensive positions in Pisco's
Plaza Central.

Pisco, however, was no Arica, and Zamudio was certainly no Bolognesi. Once under fire from the Chilean fleet's guns a "panic dominated
everything," stilling Zamudio's voice. And rather than fight to the last
bullet, the four-hundred-man local garrison funked. Indeed, his band of
soldiers did not stop running until they reached Humai, thirty-five miles
to the north.[35] In his haste to flee, Zamudio also forgot to detonate the
mines that he had so diligently sowed. Watching this spectacle led one
provincial subprefect to conclude, "All is a farce, it's as if we were not
Peruvians."[36] After General Villagrán entered Pisco on 20 November at 2
p.m., his engineers disarmed the remaining explosive devices, allowing
the rest of the division to land unhindered and then to occupy various
coastal cities as well as Ica's provincial capital.

Meanwhile, the Second Division's First Brigade, consisting of thirty-
five hundred men from the Esmeralda, the Chillán, and the Buin, and
the artillery, medical, and supply units—and their 416 horses—began
boarding the merchantmen in Arica. After two days of loading, six transports as well as three sailing vessels departed Arica on 27 November. They
reached Pisco on 2 December, unloading Gana's brigade and Villagrán's
field artillery before sailing south to pick up the remainder of the army.

When José Francisco Vergara, who had accompanied the fleet to Pisco, returned to Arica to supervise the embarkation of the rest of the expedition, he discovered that the remaining units were not prepared to leave. General Maturana, Baquedano's chief of staff, reported that his men still urgently needed thirty-five hundred pairs of undershorts, over one thousand pack animals, fifteen thousand canteens, one hundred thousand rounds of small arms ammunition, and additional artillery shells, plus spare parts for their Armstrong cannon, as well as their Gatling and Hotchkiss machine guns. Ironically, even if Hermójenes Pérez Arce, the head of the supply corps, could have immediately filled Maturana's orders, he lacked the ships' bottoms to send the supplies north: Baquedano had diverted scarce transports to perform tasks not directly related to the invasion. Thus, while the minister of war frantically scoured Chile for twelve hundred horses and mules, riding gear, and even drovers, twelve thousand of its sons squatted in Pisco.[37]

On 7 December, as the authorities began collecting the needed supplies, Baquedano and his subordinates met with various high-ranking civilians, including Vergara. The general proposed that the Third Division, plus the Second Division's Second Brigade, sail for Chilca, a port thirty-eight miles south of Lima, where the bulk of the army would land. En route to the north, the convoy would stop at Pisco, where it would pick up Villagrán's artillery and José Francisco Gana's brigade, which had arrived earlier. As the ships shuttled back and forth, Villgrán's division would depart Pisco no later than 14 December to march overland in order to reach Chilca on 22 December, the same day that the rest of the army would land. Once reunited, the soldiers would proceed north through the Lurín Valley to Lima. Although Vergara did not strongly endorse Baquedano's plan, he nonetheless accepted it.[38]

On 15 December General Baquedano's fourteen thousand men and approximately twenty-four hundred horses and mules departed Arica for the north. But for a galley fire aboard the *Elvira Alvarez* that almost spread to the ship's powder magazine, the trip was as calm as was the sea. Still, the invasion fleet's passengers suffered: packed like sardines, Sblt. Justo Rosales and fifteen hundred of his comrades made the trip on deck. Many soldiers who were fed "bread of an unknown type" and a *puchero* (stew) flavored by rotten potatoes and beef bones either vomited up these inedible rations or simply flung them overboard. On 18 December, as planned, the convoy reached Pisco to pick up the First Division's artillery plus Gana's brigade.[39] Baquedano, however, became furious upon learning that Villagrán's men had only managed to reach Tambo de Mora, a scant twenty miles from Pisco and that, although Lynch's men were in Cañete, they were still fifty miles short of their objective. Complaining that a combination of poor roads and a lack of water handicapped him, Villagrán refused to proceed to Chilca unless Baquedano would first assume the responsibility for any mishap that might occur en route to the north.[40] Baquedano, doubtless trying to keep to the original timetable, acceded to Villagrán's wishes: he agreed to accept the blame for any misfortune that might arise. But, he noted, Villagrán's behavior might cause a "grave risk, if not a calamity, [then] at least the sterile sacrifice of a considerable number of lives." Not surprisingly, Baquedano also informed Villagrán that if any resulting "fault" developed, it would not be his.[41]

The government distrusted Baquedano, who it correctly believed was trying to position himself to run for president in 1881. But Pinto could ill afford to allow a squabble between Villagrán and Baquedano to paralyze what he hoped would be the war's last campaign. Thus, the president, with Vergara's enthusiastic support, sacked Villagrán, ordering him to return to Santiago.[42] Baquedano, now the most senior military authority, issued new orders: the First Division's artillery and its Second Brigade as well as that of Gana would travel by sea to Chilca. Only Lynch's brigade would march the approximately fifty-five miles north to Chilca. The trip was uneventful, although Lynch had more problems finding ample supplies of water than in overcoming limited Peruvian resistance.[43]

On 22 December the troops of the Second Brigade of Gen. Emilio Sotomayor's Second Division and of Col. Pedro Lagos's Third Division were poised to go ashore at Chilca. When the authorities realized that they knew nothing about the bay as a possible landing site, they decided to let the infantry disembark at Curayaco, slightly north of Chilca. After a scout reported that nearby deep sand would complicate the landing of the artillery, the expedition's leaders decided to offload the cannon at another port south of Lurín. By 23 December Chilean soldiers occupied Lurín itself, where they enjoyed a well-deserved rest.[44]

The Heavenly City of Lima

In 1879 Lima, the object of Chile's desires, contained between 120,000 and 130,000 residents, about a third of whom a Peruvian, Héctor Valenzuela, characterized as unemployed *lumpen*. Though harsh, his description proved quite accurate: these jobless masses would happily join in the rioting that destroyed parts of the Peruvian capital. During its initial years, the war did not seem to inconvenience the local population. The cost of essential provisions may have increased, at least for the city's poorer residents, but consumption of foreign imports continued unabated. Indeed, the more affluent seemed almost blissfully unaware of the war. As the Peruvian Manuel Zanutelli tartly noted, "While in our hospitals soldiers died of gangrene or tuberculosis . . . the sale of North American or European articles continued as in the best of times."[45]

President Piérola realized that Baquedano would next attack Lima. If the Peruvians feared their enemies, they had ample reason. An officer in the Chilean expeditionary force supposedly told the British naval commander that if the Peruvians continued to resist, Lima would be "erased from the map." Should that not give Piérola pause, the British consul in Valparaíso informed his colleagues in Lima that the Chilean authorities were holding out the prospect of looting Lima, and raping its female inhabitants, as an incentive to enlist.[46]

In June, after losing the best units of his army at Tacna and Arica, the Peruvian leader mobilized the capital's active and sedentary reserves. Henceforth, all men aged sixteen to sixty had to report for daily military training between 10 a.m. and 2 p.m. And to ensure that all able-bodied reservists attended, the government ordered the *limeños* to suspend commercial life for those four hours. As usual, the government excused certain occupations—physicians, pharmacists, clergy, health or charity workers, as well as employees of the ministry of war or government—from the exercises. To ensure that people would not flee, Piérola's government required a passport from anyone wishing to leave the province, except those involved in the transportation of foodstuffs.[47]

Less than a month later, the government ordered all men to register to serve in a newly created reserve army composed of ten infantry divisions, as well as some artillery and cavalry units. Interestingly, the administration organized these formations on the basis of the recruits' civilian employment: Division One consisted of bachelors as well as men involved in the legal system or legal professions; Division Two included property owners and men of commerce or finance. Professors and students belonged to Division Three; architects and those in the construction trade composed Division Four. Those who worked in leather or millinery trades enrolled in the Fifth Division. Division Six consisted of metal workers or millers. Men involved in printing and government or charitable employees joined the Seventh Division. Bakers, domestic servants, and tavern employees made up the Eighth Division. The Ninth Division consisted of painters, paperhangers, upholsterers, barbers, and salesmen. Finally, the Tenth Division included transportation, municipal services, plumbing, and railroad employees. Individuals providing livery services were assigned to the cavalry; for some reason, firemen and carriage men were placed in the artillery. Viewing these organizations from afar, a German-language Chilean newspaper sarcastically suggested that Piérola organize his army not by class but by color.[48]

The government made it clear that it expected all Peruvian men, regardless of class or social position, to share equitably in the burden of defending Lima. And to ensure compliance it threatened to levy a fine of up to one thousand incas on anyone who either did not show up for training or who failed to enlist. In mid-July, the government ordered all commercial establishments or businesses to close at 3:00 p.m., when a church bell would ring, signaling that the reservists had thirty minutes to report to their units for daily training. Men who did not obey the summons or who failed to register could be arrested and inducted immediately into the active army.[49]

Had Baquedano attacked in July, one diplomat expected that he would "shatter the opposing army to pieces and take the capital in a few hours." But luckily for Piérola, the Chileans did not launch their invasion until December. The Peruvian dictator promised that he would use that five-month respite to raise an army of as many as forty thousand men. Britain's envoy to Lima was unimpressed, forecasting that the new army would consist of about 50 percent Indians, who "at the first opportunity, will desert and . . . [and] another large body . . . of imperfectly drilled citizens—commanded by civilians," which would "degenerate into an armed mob, without a general or any efficient leaders."[50] The envoy's prophesy proved true.

Still, the Peruvians soldiered on, the authorities mobilizing the nation's reservists on 6 December. Henceforth citizen-soldiers would live in a barracks in order to drill between 6 a.m. and 8 a.m. before leaving for work. At 8 p.m. the men returned to their quarters to spend the night. The police would patrol the city during the evening, arresting any men found on the streets without an excuse. The authorities could confine any reservist absent without permission to quarters for three days; they sent chronic absentees to the active army. To finance this new citizen reserve army, the Peruvian government imposed a special tax upon the propertied classes, "whose rights and interests [this army] is called upon to defend and to protect." It is interesting to note that the government did not collect this tax: instead, the authorities hired a tax farmer, who, in return for a 5 percent commission, contracted to amass the funds, which the government promised to use solely to provide equipment to the military.[51]

The threats of punishment notwithstanding, many men, particularly the most affluent, simply refused to attend drills. One official lamented that the upper class, who should set an example of patriotism, "are the same ones who remained closeted in clubs, cafes, and pool halls during the hours when good citizens are using their time preparing themselves to defend the motherland." Not surprisingly, the functionary suggested that the authorities should raid these establishments and arrest any able-bodied man discovered loitering in the neighborhood. In fairness, sunshine soldiers did not reside solely in the capital. In Humai, local officials also complained that reservists failed to attend the drills scheduled for Sundays and holidays.[52]

Rather than depend exclusively on Piérola's makeshift defenses and their rag-tag protectors, various Peruvians turned to God. The army paraded its newly formed battalions before priests to receive a benediction plus a silver medallion on which was engraved "Death or Victory." Women, according to a Panamanian correspondent, particularly mothers or those of the lower class, loudly prayed to various religious artifacts. Lima's archbishop urged his parishioners to make a novena to Santa Rosa de Lima to seek the intercession of the saints, and to make the Stations of the Cross. To console the faithful, the cleric promised to make the Host available for a month beginning on 26 December. He also urged the physically fit to fast on 28 December—when the church commemorated the deaths of the innocents whom Herod had ordered slain—so that God would help them face "this grave tribulation that has come to afflict us."[53]

Curiously, even the secular press embraced some of the bishop's imagery, if not his piety. "Providence," one journalist observed, "will not deny us this merited compensation for our faith in its justice and our effort." Another columnist argued that Peru would never perish, that a newly resurrected nation would arise to punish the invaders. Lima, he promised, would become a Chilean cemetery: "We will die, but so will all the Philistines."[54] "The rifle, the maneuver, the barracks: here is, from now on, our idol, our cult, our temple. The God of the armies, who is also the God of the nations, will bless our efforts and reward our sacrifices," converting the road from Pisco to Lima into Chile's *via crucis*.[55] Neutral observers cynically dismissed these remarks as puffery. "No city," observed the British minister, "could be more unsuited to street warfare and no people less likely to make a desperate defense than the inhabitants of Lima."[56]

Not surprisingly many Limeños began to flee. Lamentably, the men assigned to defend the approaches to the capital joined this spontaneous exodus. In some cases, they had ample reason for bolting: one southern commander, Col. Pedro José Sevilla, described his 310 men as "unshod, unclad, and unhappy."[57] Since so many of his troops deserted, he might have added "unenthusiastic" to his description. Given this situation, the colonel suggested that he save his weapons and his men by pulling back northeast to the towns Chincha or Cañete.

The authorities, however, encouraged Sevilla to "resist, to harass the enemy, even if but ten men remained, and if the only alternative is waging a guerrilla war."[58] The eyes of the entire nation were watching the colonel, observed Paz Soldán, and noting that the country would reward those who fought, he begged Sevilla to ensure that "our flag will emerge with honor and that he should proceed with the prudence and skill that we all are delighted to recognize in him." Privately, a Peruvian statesman admitted that he expected little from Sevilla, just a show of symbolic resistance to counteract what had most depressed the public: "the shameful retreats [that occurred] without firing a single shot." Sevilla did manage to satisfy these minimal expectations: after waylaying some Chilean patrols and supposedly killing two men, he bolted. Although the Chileans ultimately captured Sevilla, his ambushes, which one Chilean journalist denigrated as beyond the pale of "civilized war," delighted one Peruvian official, who noted, "Let the blood flow, since thusly regeneration becomes real."[59]

Some Peruvians observed their soldiers' retreat from Pisco and General Baquedano's approach to Lima with an almost glacial calm. The journalist José Casimiro Ulloa became convinced—on what evidence remains unclear—that the Pisco invasion had consumed Chile's resources, that the Peruvian defenses would work, and that hence the nation could await Baquedano's hosts with serene confidence.[60] Another journalist compared Peru's "discipline, obedience, union between the governors and the governed" with Chile's army, which was a barbarous horde.[61]

Toward the end of December, the pace of preparations for Lima's defense quickened. President Piérola created the approximately twenty-five- to thirty-two-thousand-man-strong Army of Lima by melding two units, the Army of the Center and the Army of the North. The newly created Army of Lima was divided into two components: the approximately sixteen to twenty-four thousand soldiers of the Army of the Line consisted of four corps. The authorities assigned these corps to defend the city: the First, under Col. Miguel Iglesias, consisted of Divisions One, Two, and Three from the Army of the North; the Second Corps, commanded by Gen. Belisario Suárez, contained the Army of the North's Fourth and Fifth divisions. The Army of the Center's Third Corps, led by Col. Justo Pastor Dávila, included Divisions three and five; Col. Andrés Cáceres led the Fourth Corps, also from the Army of the Center, consisting of Divisions One, Two, and Four. The Army of the Reserve, some six to ten thousand troops, consisted of the First and Second corps, which included the new recruits.[62]

Over the next few days, the army absorbed Lima's police, leaving the foreign volunteers of the urban guard to patrol the city. Military authorities also began requisitioning horses, thus effectively stopping Lima's urban trolley system while reserving to the army, with few exceptions, the

Table 19. Peruvian defenders

1 Company of Engineers – Col. Francisco Paz Soldan 10 companies of engineers, each commanded by a captain
Artillery – Col. Adolfo Salmón 2 regiments, each commanded by a colonel and, consisting of 6 companies
Flying Squad – Col. Manuel Zevallos 4 companies
Cavalry – Col. Juan Francisco Elizalde 2 squadrons, each with 2 companies
Infantry Each division with 6 companies commanded by a captain 1a. División – Brevet Col. José Unánue Batallones 2, 4, 6, 8, 10, and 12
3a. División – Brevet Col. Serapio Orbegozo Batallones 14, 16, and 18
4a. División- Brevet Col. Juan Aliaga Puente Batallones 20, 22, and 24
5a. División – Brevet Col. Manuel Benavides Batallones 26, 28, and 30
6a. División – Brevet Col. Ramón Montero Batallones 32, 34, and 36
7a. División – Brevet Col. Dionisio Dertano Batallones 38, 40 and 42
8a. División – Brevet Col. Juan Arrieta Batallones 44, 46, and 48
9a. División – Brevet Col. Bartolmé Figari Batallones 50, 52, and 54
10a. División – Brevet Col. Antonio Bentín Batallones 56, 58, 60, and 61

Source: Peru, Ministry of War, Permanent Commission, *Gesta de Lima*, 63–123.

use of rail trains.[63] Businesses were to remain open, if for no other reason than to ensure that Lima's residents could purchase food.[64]

These preparations seemed to galvanize the capital's citizens. The press reported that Lima throbbed with pro-war sentiment. Individuals who earlier refused to attend drill suddenly volunteered. Supposedly,

even the ill begged for weapons. Like many, one journalist invoked Bolognesi's image, likening Peru to Sparta. Just prior to the final battles, another newsman described the Chileans as cowardly, while Peru's soldiers
confidently predicted victory.[65]

Yet no one expected a Peruvian triumph. By December, an observer
reported, Lima's fate depended on a "simple agglomeration" of approximately thirty thousand men, at least half of them Quechua-speaking Indians "with no military training" augmented by a handful of veterans
or men recruited from other parts of the nation. Untrained, equipped
with different small arms, shoeless, and clad in the same ragged civilian
clothes that they wore when impressed into the army, these hapless troops
were led by officers whom President Piérola had selected on the basis of
their loyalty to him, not their military expertise. Having first struck those
with experience and training from the army's active list, he subsequently
purged the *guardia nacional.* Although these fledgling officers tried to
improve their skills by meeting in private homes for seminars on military
tactics, the classes had little effect. Some of the best professional officers, particularly those who opposed Piérola, found themselves assigned
to a replacement depot. If they wished to serve in line units, they had
to do so as enlisted men. Piérola's policies made one Italian cleric lament that Peru could perhaps successfully protect its capital but only if it
"could have put at its head of government a man only partially endowed
with good sense." Instead, Lima had selected Piérola, who "instead of
devoting himself to defending the capital," used the opportunity to ride
around the city in order to show off his uniforms.[66]

Piérola ordered the construction of two parallel lines of breastworks,
dotted with strong points, to shield Lima's southern flank. The first of
these barriers, a ten-mile-long defensive position, was located at San
Juan, near the town of Chorrillos—a bathing resort patronized by Lima's
elites—where ninety-five hundred men had burrowed into the ground.
Piérola had placed heavy cannon, including some raised from sunken
ships like the *Independencia,* in the fortifications overlooking the capital.
Not surprisingly, one of these defense batteries, Ciudadela Piérola, bore
the dictator's name. Regrettably, the Peruvians could not fire these guns,
fearing that their shells would hit the city rather than the enemy. Smaller
artillery pieces, including those forged in Lima's foundries, guarded the

various redoubts. Additionally, the defenders could call upon the guns of the *Atahualpa*, the ill-fated *Manco Cápac*'s sister ship.[67]

Viewed from above, the chain of hills anchoring Chorrillos's defenses resembled a lopsided *W* with the letter's western side extending to the north. They were aptly named the Zigzag Mountains, with the highest point being the approximately one-thousand-foot-tall Morro del Solar. The Peruvians had wisely placed their first line of defensive positions along a mountainous ridge, approximately 165 to 180 feet high, on which they emplaced various cannon. With its western edge abutting the ocean and numerous mountain gun batteries dug in atop the peak, the Morro del Solar's defenders had a clear field of fire to the east and southeast. Lima's defenders had also dug in on the eastern and southeastern approaches to the Morro del Solar, allowing them to concentrate their fire on any unit attacking from the south alongside the ocean.

Piérola divided his defensive line into three sectors, each manned by one of his four divisions. Col. Miguel Iglesias, head of the First Corps' fifty-two hundred soldiers, forty-eight guns, and twenty machine guns, defended the zone that covered the area from the Pacific Ocean to the western flank of the Zigzag Mountains, including the Morro del Solar. Col. Andrés Cáceres's Second Corps' thirty-five hundred troops, supported by twenty-three guns, protected the center that extended east from the westernmost side of the Zigzag Mountains to a hill dubbed Mount Viva el Perú. Col. Justo Pastor Dávila's corps' forty-three hundred men anchored the Peruvian left, the westernmost side of Mount San Francisco. The twenty-eight hundred fighters of Col. Belisario Suárez's corps stood to the rear, between the center and the extreme left, ready to deploy where and when needed.[68] Piérola's defenses might have appeared imposing to a civilian, but Colonel Cáceres described it as unfinished, undermanned, unimpressive, and a half-century out of date.[69] Fortunately, Piérola had backup: if the Chileans managed to penetrate the San Juan line, another string of breastworks constructed near the town of Miraflores still protected Lima.

For months, Chile's sailors tried to isolate Peru's coast. This essentially passive strategy undermined the navy's morale: eyewitnesses reported that the ships' crews occupied their idle time in self-abuse, sodomy, or drinking the alcohol that they smuggled on board.[70] Chile's fleet, however, played a substantial role in the final assault of Lima. Admiral Riveros earlier dispatched his ships to reconnoiter the area in order to discover the whereabouts of Peru's troops and to locate their forts and artillery positions. The fleet also planned to use their naval guns to support the attackers. To avoid the hazards of friendly fire, Riveros sent a team ashore to advise the vessels of the army's positions and to coordinate its shipborne heavy guns with the advancing infantry movements. Juan José Latorre, commander of the invasion fleet, stationed his torpedo boats near the mooring of the *Unión* in the unlikely possibility that it should try to escape and to inform the rest of the flotilla when the land battle began.[71]

On 13 January 1881, when the Chilean infantry began their assault, the *Blanco*, the *Cochrane*, the *O'Higgins*, and the *Pilcomayo* had already taken up positions allowing them to shell the Morro del Solar's western flank, particularly those gun emplacements that enjoyed a clear field of fire. Although it violated orders, the navy sometimes fired on targets of opportunity when it believed that this action would not endanger the Chilean troops. In addition, one of the *Blanco*'s launches patrolled the coast, its machine guns raking Peruvian coastal positions. Even after the battle ended, the fleet continued to serve: Riveros sent his naval surgeons to care for the wounded, while the ships provided supplies and water for the exhausted victors.

The First Assault: The Battle of Chorrillos

The Zigzag Mountains were not a solid range but a chain of discrete hills. As one approached the Peruvian left, gaps appeared through which ran the various roads that connected the Lurín Valley with the capital and Callao. Consequently, Piérola's supposedly impressive line was quite porous. As the Chileans probed the Peruvian defenses to discover the number, location, and armament of Piérola's contingents, Baquedano met his more senior commanders to discuss how to attack Lima. The commanding general himself visited what would become the battlefield three times. After some consideration, he decided that his troops would launch a frontal assault along the entire Peruvian line and that once they created or discovered a weakness they would call upon his reserve division to punch through the line to Chorrillos.

Gen. Marcos Maturana, Baquedano's chief of staff, advocated a different stratagem. Unlike his supposed superior, Maturana realized that seizing Lima, although symbolically important, would not necessarily end the war; eradicating the Peruvian army, however, might. Thus Maturana placed a premium on the strategy of maneuver: avoid the frontal attack in preference to outflanking Piérola's fixed defenses. This tactic would allow the Chileans to capture not only the enemy capital but also its defenders before they could flee into the altiplano, where they might regroup. To achieve this goal, Maturana wanted one division, supported by the navy's guns, to feign an attack on the Peruvian front while Chile's other divisions veered north-northwest and then west, through the mountains, not emerging until they had outflanked Lima's defenses. Then the Chileans would drive northwest, pushing the Peruvian defenders into the Surco Valley and denying them access to the Oroya Railroad and surface roads, the principal routes out of the city into the Andes. If Maturana's plan succeeded, the Peruvians would be trapped in a box, their backs to the sea, surrounded on three sides by the Chileans.[72]

Minister Vergara seconded Maturana, also favoring outflanking Piérola's forces. Tacna, Vergara noted, should have taught the general that while infantry could attack and defeat an entrenched enemy, the butcher's bill would be high. Instead he argued that if the Chilean army marched to the northeast and then moved slightly northwest at Manchay, it would emerge east of Rinconada, from where it could outflank not merely Chorrillos's defenses but those of Miraflores as well. Sandwiched between the sea and Baquedano's men, Peru's army could not escape because the Chileans controlled access both to the Oroya Railroad and the highways to the altiplano. Hence, Piérola would have to capitulate.

Baquedano understood completely what Maturana and Vergara advocated. He had even ordered Col. Orizmbo Barboza to lead a two-thousand-man force that had, by following the same path that Vergara and Maturana suggested, successfully reached Rinconada.[73] Although he had to retreat, Barboza had demonstrated that an army including heavy artillery could easily outflank Piérola's defensive line. But Baquedano, invariably generous with the blood of others, would have none of it. Worse, the other military members attending the meeting—Generals Sotomayor and Saavedra, Capitán de Navio Lynch, and Colonel Velásquez—duti-

Table 20. Battles of Lima, 13, 15 January 1881

Chilean Contingents	
1a. División	Col. Patricio Lynch
1a. Brigada	Col. Juan Martínez
Rgt. 2 de Linea	Lt. Col. Estanislao del Canto
Rgt. Atacama	Lt. Col. Diego Dublé Almeida
Rgt. Colchagua	Lt. Col. Manuel Soffia
Rgt. Talca	Lt. Col. Silvestre Urizar
Btn. Melipilla	Lt. Col. Vicente Balmaceda
2a. Brigada	Col. Domingo Amunátegui
Rgt. Artillería de Marina	Lt. Col. José Rámon Vidaurre
Rgt. 4 de Linea	ol. José Amunátegui
Rgt. Chacabuco	ol. Domingo Toro Herrera
Rgt. Coquimbo	Lt. Col. José Soto
Btn. Quillota	Lt. Col. José Echeverría
2a. División	Brig. Gen. Emilio Sotomayor
1a. Brigada	Col. Francisco Gana
Rgt. Buin, 1st of Line	Lt. Col. Juan García
Rgt. Esmeralda	Lt. Col. Adolfo Holley
Rgt. Chillán	Lt. Col. Pedro Guiñez
2a. Brigada	Col. Orozimbo Barboza
Rgt. Curicó	Lt. Col. Joaquín Cortés
Btn. Víctoria	Maj. Exequiel Soto
3a. División	Col. Pedro Lagos
First Brigade	Col. Martiniano Urriola
Btn. Artillería Naval	Lt. Col. Francisco Fierro
Rgt. Aconcagua	Lt. Col. Rafael Díaz
2a. Brigada	Lt. Col. Francisco Barceló
Rgt. Santiago	Lt. Col. Demofilo Fuenzalida
Btn. Bulnes	Lt. Col. José Echeverría
Btn. Valvidia	Lt. Col. Lucio Martínez
Btn. Caupolicán	Lt. Col. José del Canto
Rgt. Concepción	Lt. Col. José Seguel
Reserve	Lt. Col. Arístides Martínez
Rgt. 3 de Linea	Lt. Col. José Gutiérrez
Rgt. Zapadores	Lt. Col. Guillermo Zilleruelo
Rgt. Valparaíso	Lt. Col. José Marchant
Regimiento de Artillería	Lt. Col. Carlos Wood
First Brigade	Capt. Ansenio de la Torre
Second Brigade	Lt. Col. Antonio González
Regimiento 2	Lt. Col. José Novoa
Cavalry	
Rgt. Cazadores	Lt. Col. Pedro Soto
Rgt. Granaderos	Lt. Col. Tomás Yavar
Rgt. Carabineros de Yungai	Lt. Col. Manuel Bulnes

Sources: Chile, Ministry of War, *Partes oficiales.*

fully lined up behind their commander. Velásquez, for example, argued that trying to envelop the enemy's left would compel the army to plod through an additional sixteen miles, sometimes in deep sand, before the Chileans could attack. Pursuing this course of action, moreover, would expose the Chileans' flank and rear to a Peruvian counterattack, cut them off from naval support, and require them to trek through an arid desert without adequate supplies. At a second meeting, held on 11 January, Vergara, Baquedano, and other high-ranking officers met again to discuss the minister's plan. Vergara could have saved his breath: Baquedano's toadies supported their commander.

Baquedano's strategy was so simple it bordered on the primitive: Lynch's First Division would attack the Peruvian right, controlled by Iglesias; the Second Division, under Gen. Emilio Sotomayor, would assault the Peruvian middle and left, defended by Cáceres and Dávila. The Chilean Third Division, led by Col. Pedro Lagos, would support Lynch and Sotomayor as well as prevent Dávila from reinforcing the units to the south. As Baquedano noted, "I believe that this will be the last action that will give us the keys to Lima; it is necessary, then, to have a firm hand."[74]

On 12 January at 6 p.m., Baquedano's men, serenaded by their bands, left their bases in the Lurín Valley for jump-off points from which they would attack Lima. On the Sunday before the battle, some Chileans attended church services, listening to sermons, and participating in a Te Deum. Observing these rites, a British officer, doubtless a Protestant, cynically concluded that since the men were either too far away or the priest's voice too low, "I am afraid that the soldiers benefited little by the religious ceremony." Baquedano attempted to speak to the men, but apparently emotions so overcame him that he could not.[75]

On their last evening, the French military observer attached to Baquedano's army noted that a sense of melancholy seemed to settle on the assembled Chileans.[76] After wrapping their bayonets and canteens in rags—to muffle the sound—the troops entrusted to their friends those items they wanted passed on to their families in case they died in battle. Others gave their unit's sutler letters to be mailed in case of their death. Thanks to the generosity of one of their officers, each trooper of the Coquimbo received two cigarettes. Another officer spent one hundred pesos for two bottles of bad *aguardiente.* We do not know if he shared

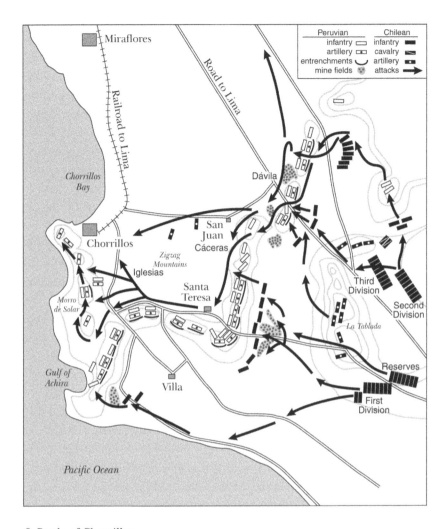

8. Battle of Chorrillos

the liquor. Captain José de la Cruz Reyes told his commander that he was sure that he would perish because he saw his unlucky number everywhere. He proved sadly prescient.[77]

On the other side of the battlefield, a Bolivian journalist watched a Col. Montero Rosas raise his glass to "those who will be able to eat tomorrow." When no one joined him, the colonel observed, "I will be the only one." He was not. The Chileans who would kill him as well as many of the colonel's troops who left their equipment in the care of their respective

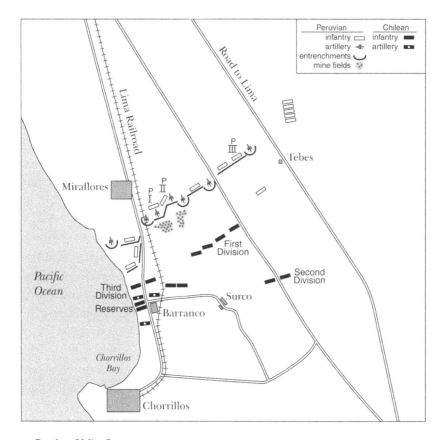

Legend:
Peruvian		Chilean	
infantry	⬜	infantry	▬
artillery	⬞	artillery	◼
entrenchments	⌣		
mine fields	✺		

Road to Lima

Lima Railroad

Miraflores

P III

Tebes

P II
P I

First Division

Second Division

Pacific Ocean

Third Division

Reserves

Surco

Barranco

Chorrillos Bay

Chorrillos

9. Battle of Miraflores

bands and drew their ammunition load of 150 rounds per man as well as two days' iron rations.[78]

Baquedano's decision to attack the Peruvian lines simultaneously caused certain problems: he had to preposition his troops at different locations and stagger their departure times so they could reach their respective jump-off points in time to launch a coordinated assault. Lynch's troops, followed by the reserves under Col. Arístides Martínez, crossed the Lurín River at Santa Lucía, heading northwest until the road divided, when one element continued on the Conchán Road west to the Morro del Solar; the second veered also northwest, leading the Chileans toward the Hacienda de Villa and the Santa Teresa Pass. Gen. Emilio Sotomayor's Second Division crossed the Lurín River to the northeast, at Palmas and Venturosa, before veering off to the northwest following the

Otocongo Road until it reached its jumping off point north of Mount Tablada and facing the Pamplona Plain, from which it would attack the San Juan Pass. Since Lagos's division, followed by the field artillery, followed the same path as the Second Division, it too ended up on the Plain of Pamplona but took up a position in front of Sotomayor's division. Baquedano's reserves, under Lieutenant Colonel Martínez, shadowed Lynch's division. Both the artillery and the cavalry followed. Once the troops reached their designated positions, about midnight, they could rest until 3:30 a.m., when they would begin to move north, this time toward the Peruvian defenses at Chorrillos.

Lynch divided his First Division into four columns: the first, consisting of the Second Regiment of the Line and the Colchagua, would attack the mountains guarding the Hacienda Santa Teresa; the Second of the Line, the Regimiento Atacama, and the Talca would assault the mountains south of the pass; the Third and the Fourth Regiments of the Line and the Chacabuco would drive on the Hacienda de Villa, which lay in a cul de sac bordered on three sides by Peruvian artillery. The fourth column, the Batallón Melipilla and Regimiento Coquimbo, had the shortest distance to march, but it faced the greatest challenge: these men had to advance down the beach road to attack frontally the Morro del Solar, whose garrison along with fifty-six cannon and twenty machine guns awaited them. Sotomayor's Second Division would concentrate on smashing through the Peruvian line to the north to take San Juan. The Third Division of Colonel Lagos would assault the northernmost part of the W, pinning down the Peruvian defenders, thereby preventing them from reinforcing the line to the south and southwest. If necessary, Lagos would help the Second Division break through the center.[79] If all went as planned, the Chilean infantry, supported by artillery located on the forward slope of a hill to the north of the ocean, would attack simultaneously, smash through Piérola's defenses, and capture Chorrillos.

The Chilean experience at Chorrillos lived up to the military theorists' dictum that prearranged battle plans invariably go awry once the fighting begins. Baquedano's divisions did arrive at their jump-off positions around midnight, thereby giving his men only a few hours to rest and, for the most fatalistic, a chance to sleep. At around 3:30 a.m., the men awoke to discover that fog covered the battlefield. This did not stop the troops, who, under instructions to be silent in order to not alert the enemy, moved out. In truth, a drum and bugle corps could have preceded the Chilean legions: thanks to a deserter and some reports from troops in the field, Piérola knew that Baquedano's men were on the move. And although the fog obscured the Peruvian position, Piérola's troops began firing a series of colored flares, tracking the Chileans' position. At 5 a.m. the Peruvian batteries began firing. Baquedano's artillery did not respond until the guns were within one thousand yards of the Peruvians; his advancing infantrymen held their fire until they were three to four hundred yards from their objectives.

Lynch's units assaulting the Hacienda de Villa, the high ground to the east, as well as the Peruvian trenches immediately began to take heavy casualties, some caused by mines and booby traps. One unit, the Chacabuco, lost its commander, its executive officer, and its third in command. Clearly hurting, Lynch requested help from the Second Division, only to learn that Sotomayor's men had yet to reach their assigned jump-off place. Lynch's assault faltered and might have stalled had Baquedano not ordered Martínez's reserves to join the battle. Thanks to these elements and some of the Second Division that had arrived, the Chileans managed to capture Hacienda de Villa as well as take the high ground to the west. By 9 a.m. Lynch's men held Santa Teresa Pass, as parts of the Second and the Third divisions wheeled to attack the Morro del Solar's eastern flank.[80]

While some of Iglesias's men decamped for Chorrillos, others retreated to the west, reinforcing the already heavily fortified Morro del Solar. Thanks to moving some of their artillery forward, thereby allowing them to fire on the Morro del Solar's defenders, the Coquimbo and the Melipilla captured the Peruvian positions located on the southernmost end of the Morro del Solar. By early morning, however, the strain of the battle, the effects of plodding three and one half miles through sand, high casualties, and a shortage of artillery shells slowed Lynch's advance. Seeing the Chileans hesitate, the Peruvians counterattacked, driving back Lynch's severely mauled division and threatening to overrun the Talca as well as those serving the mountain guns. Meanwhile, a lack of ammunition almost compelled the Second and Fourth regiments, the Atacama, and the Chacabuco to retreat until Col. Estanislao del Canto, promising to shoot those who hesitated, ordered his men to fix their bayonets and charge.[81] Suddenly, the course of the battle changed: Lynch's men received additional supplies of bullets, allowing them to restart the offensive, while Lagos's division, after piercing Dávila's defenses, pivoted west behind Piérola's defensive line to attack the Morro del Solar's northernmost position. Running low on ammunition, their machine guns and artillery malfunctioning, and without infantry to protect them, Col. Miguel Igelsias's gunners pulled back but not without first detonating their powder magazines. Eventually joined by Chile's Regimiento Santiago, the Batallones Bulnes and Valdivia, and their comrades of the Regimientos Caupolicán and Concepción, Lynch, Urrutia, and Amunátegui managed to capture the high ground, taking more than one thousand prisoners, including Iglesias. Lynch's victory was impressive, but so were his casualties: 22.4 percent of his men either suffered wounds or died.[82]

About an hour after the Chilean offensive began, the Chilean Buin, Esmeralda, and Chillán regiments of Sotomayor's Second Division joined the battle against the Peruvian Second and Third Corps, commanded by Colonels Cáceres and Dávila, respectively. Apparently claiming that he had to rest his exhausted Second Brigade or that he had lost his way in the fog, Sotomayor did not get his men on the move until 4:30 a.m., an hour after Lynch had departed. Not only did these troops begin their trek late, they literally ran into the Lagos's formations, who, having to cover a greater distance before attacking, had departed earlier. Happily, Lagos ceded his place to Sotomayor, who, hearing Lynch's troops going into action, realized that the fighting had already started. Anxious to join the battle, Sotomayor ordered his troops to run toward the sounds of the cannon. Fortunately, they arrived at roughly the same time that Martínez's troops joined the battle against Iglesias's men, thus protecting Lynch's flank from a Peruvian riposte.[83] Just before going into action with the Third Division, the journalist turned army subaltern Justo Rosales inexplicably stopped to look around, as if to imprint on his memory the battle that he would soon join. "In all directions," he noted, "we saw large platoons of cavalry, sabers in hand, advancing; the artillery located on some hills firing on the enemy's fortifications and we entering the battle at a trot, in assault columns, followed by the other units of the division, each one of whom had their beautiful standards unfurled."[84]

The Chilean Second Division's First Brigade, led by José Francisco Gana, advanced in company formation and, ignoring the Peruvian artillery fire, attacked Cáceres's Fourth Corps and the San Juan Pass. Unfortunately for Gana, Silva's reserves arrived in time to bolster Cáceres's defenses. Still, after three hours of heavy fighting, the Buin, led by an officer exhorting them to "get the *cholos*," drove the Peruvians from their positions, while the Esmeralda, the Chillán, the Lautaro, the Curicó, and the Victoria captured San Juan's heights and the pass. Resting briefly, they pursued the retreating Peruvians, who had fled to Chorrillos, from where they were driven by early afternoon.[85]

Chile's Second Division's Second Brigade—the Lautaro, the Curicó, and the Victoria—led by Col. Orizmbo Barboza, aimed for the western end of Dávila's position. Attacking in two waves "that mountain that vomits fire [Mount Viva el Perú]" and spurred on by their junior officers, the Chileans took the enemy position at bayonet point.[86] After penetrating the Peruvian lines, the Lautaro and the Curicó circled to the southwest, tracing an arc that brought them to Chorrillos by 2 p.m. Some of the Esmeralda's men remained in San Juan, but Adolfo Holley, on Sotomayor's orders, sent three hundred troopers to capture Chorrillos. Not without some difficulty, the artillery dragged its guns through the sand, only to discover that the Peruvians threatened to overrun them. Thanks to the timely assistance of the Chilean Third Division and the reserves, the gunners escaped, opening fire first on the by now beleaguered Morro del Solar and later on a Peruvian armored train reinforcing Lima. By 2 p.m. General Sotomayor's men controlled San Juan, and his units continued driving southwest to besiege Chorrillos, while the cavalry chased down the fleeing enemy.[87]

The dawdling of Chile's Second Division's prevented Col. Pedro Lagos from moving his men to their assigned position facing the easternmost part of Colonel Dávila's defensive position. Thus, like Sotomayor, upon hearing the sounds of gunfire, Lagos force-marched his units to join the battle. The left of Lagos's division joined Sotomayor's attack on the Peruvian center. Enveloping the Peruvian left, some of Lagos's troops drove north to Monterico Chico; the others moved northwest to the Llano de Pamplona and then southwest, where they entered the fight for Chorrillos. The Second Brigade, however, broke off to reinforce the First

Division's efforts to evict the Peruvians from Morro del Solar. To achieve this objective, Lagos's men had to run from the easternmost end of the Peruvian line to the westernmost point, where the Regimiento Santiago and the Batallones Bulnes and Valdivia attacked the Morro del Solar's rear while their comrades of the Regimientos Caupolicán and Concepción stormed the mountain's left flank.

The participation of the Chilean Third Division proved providential, since Lynch's men had begun to pull back from the Morro del Solar. The arrival first of Martínez's units, then the recently resupplied mountain artillery, and finally Lagos' troops permitted the Chileans to regain the momentum. When one soldier of the Colchagua hesitated to attack, Lagos is reputed to have said, "Kill this son of a bitch." In addition, he ordered his adjutants, "If anyone, be he a colonel, an officers, or a soldier, falters, kill him." The Morro del Solar came under fire from all sides: the Coquimbo and the Melipilla attacked on the east, and the Valdivia's Captain Tronocoso led three bayonet charges of his troops. When the Regimiento Santiago ran out of ammunition, Lagos, who earlier refused to dismount from his very large, very prominent red horse, rode among his men, screaming, "Use your bayonets boys . . . victory is yours. Forward, forward!" By the late afternoon, the Chileans had vanquished their foes.[88]

In many respects, the fighting at Chorrillos resembled the struggle for Arica. Again the Peruvians had sowed the battlefield with improvised mines; they also had booby-trapped items, such as watches, hoping to maim as many Chileans as possible. Curiously, the mines did not injure many Chileans, in part, perhaps, because stray dogs inadvertently detonated these explosive devices. Baquedano's men also fashioned a crude mine detector: they tied a Peruvian officer on a horse sending him ahead to clear any minefield. Sometimes these devices backfired: a Peruvian subaltern, Lizardo Benavides, for example, mistakenly stepped on one of his own mines, which tore off his leg, fatally wounding him.[89] Although these explosive devices did not inflict that many casualties, they so infuriated the Chileans that, in retaliation for sowing the battlefield with mines, they rarely took prisoners. Father Salvador Donoso reported that the Chileans preferred to use their bayonets and, to judge by the number of crushed Peruvian skulls, their rifle butts to finish off their wounded or captured enemies.[90]

Panic overcame the Peruvians. A young Peruvian reservist and future journalist, Alberto Ulloa, noted how quickly his countrymen's enthusiasm waned once confronted with the seasoned Chilean troops. The road to Chorrillos, he reported, "was sown with the separated [stragglers] who fled in the most horrible disorder: some of the wounded dragging themselves, others begging for help, some with weapons, others without; covered with blood, wearing torn uniforms, presenting the most wrenching spectacle."[91] Not surprisingly, newly created Peruvian units like the Huanuco 17, the Paucarpata 19, or the Libertad became some of the first to disintegrate, despite the efforts of Piérola's pistol-wielding commanders—Colonels Cáceres, Canevero, Valle, Carrillo, and Dávila—to rally them. Still, thanks to the skill of Colonels Suárez and Dávila, a substantial number of Peruvian troops did retreat in good order to the temporary safety of Lima.

The fighting did not end after the Chileans had broken through the Peruvian line. Many of those who survived the battle for the Morro del Solar holed up in Chorrillos, where the Chileans had to drive them from each house.[92] As Gen. Marcos Maturana noted, the "battle in the streets was stubborn and without mercy, something that the combatants from either side neither gave nor sought." Even if Baquedano's men were inclined to pity, the Peruvian penchant of shooting Chilean officers who tried to encourage them to capitulate hardened their hearts. Consequently, as one French observer noted, some Peruvian soldiers elected to remain inside a burning house rather than risk surrender.[93] These same fires that the Chileans had set to make the city's defenders yield quickly spread, ultimately engulfing Chorrillos. Indeed, during the night the flames detonated so many unexploded ammunitions and explosives that it sounded as if another battle were taking place.[94]

Unfortunately, after vanquishing the Peruvians, the Chilean troops began to battle one another over Peruvian women, booty, or liquor. One officer described the soldiers like ants "loaded down by whatever they found in the houses, while others searched fenced in yards and gardens for something to eat."[95] Regrettably, the level of violence grew as men, many drunk, began to pillage homes, even those of neutrals, as well as rob or rape their inhabitants. The situation became so dangerous that Chilean officers feared to intervene.[96] A Dane serving as a Chilean army engineer noted, "The atmosphere became indescribably tainted with the odor of roasting bodies and hot blood and the smell of powder and smoke from the burning houses." Officers riding through the streets passed over "a mire of human flesh, intermixed with fragments of all kinds."[97]

Eventually, General Baquedano had to send in some troops, who, in the process of quelling the rioting, killed perhaps three hundred Chileans. Colonel Cáceres, well aware of the utter collapse of Chilean discipline, wanted to lead a counterattack on Chorrillos while his foes concentrated on sacking the city. Piérola, however, refused to authorize such a response because the plan, the dictator claimed, "involved a sterile and useless sacrifice because the Chilean army is already arrayed in the outskirts of Chorrillos, and those involved in the looting are only a few." Piérola was, as usual, misinformed.[98]

Although Baquedano shattered the Peruvian contingents at Chorrillos, Piérola was not without resources. He still commanded a reserve army of some twelve thousand men, plus approximately eight thousand indifferently trained troops. These were not elite units: the most senior had but two years' training; the majority, such as light infantry columns, had been organized literally days before the battle. Worse, many of the troops, particularly those from the altiplano, had not mastered "the most basic rudiments of tactics, because they cannot speak the language of instruction." Similar problems afflicted the artillery: José Diez lamented that 20 percent of his 121 gunners were untrained; the small cavalry contingents generally rode substandard horses and carried a variety of different types of weapons.[99]

Piérola shuffled the survivors of Chorrillos and the reservists into the First, Second, and Third corps, controlled by Colonels Cáceres, Suárez, and Dávila, respectively. These officers commanded an eight-mile line of still incomplete redoubts, each separated by six hundred to one thousand yards of trenches, running west to northeast. Consisting of sandbags piled seven feet high, these breastworks protected the infantry, as well as the forty artillery pieces and machine guns, placed in pits eight feet deep. Those redoubts at most northern end of the line fronted on the Surco River. Those on the extreme Peruvian right faced the Chileans across the seventy-foot-deep Almendariz Ravine. Judging from an *El Co-*

mercio article, not all these redoubts merited the name of fortifications. Batallón Cuatro, for example, unable to finish constructing its fortified position, used the money it raised in the aristocratic Club Nacional to hire some Chinese workers to complete the emplacement. Unfortunately, they ran out of funds before the Asians could finish, forcing the battalion's members, consisting of some of "the most select classes of our capital," to conclude the job.[100]

Piérola did possess one substantial advantage: he could command the various heavy guns batteries, what the American Lt. Theodorus Mason called Lima's "crescent of steel," to fire on any Chilean positions located up to a distance of ten thousand yards to the south, west, or east. The Peruvian authorities had also constructed a new gun position on the edge of the ocean, the *Alfonso Ugarte*, whose heavy coastal defense cannon should have given the Chilean fleet pause. Still, looking behind the facade of impressive forts, Lima's defenders, a mixed bag of unevenly trained troops, confronted about twenty-one thousand better-equipped, better-trained, and better-led Chileans plus their eighty-eight artillery pieces.[101]

Lima's diplomatic community viewed the Chilean approach with more than a little trepidation. The sacking of Chorrillos had given them ample cause for worry. Foreign envoys, for example, requested permission to move their various merchant and naval ships closer to shore, so their citizens could take refuge on board; some six hundred women and children begged for and received asylum in the British embassy. Eventually, most of the foreign ministers requested that Piérola grant their nationals safe passage out of the city.

While willing to negotiate peace terms with Piérola, General Baquedano first demanded that the dictator surrender Callao and abandon his line of forts defending Miraflores. The European diplomats, noting that Peru had suffered so much, urged the dictator to end the war. But Piérola refused, even after Baquedano offered to grant the Peruvians safe conduct. Unable to stop the fighting, the foreign envoys convinced both sides to accept a temporary truce: the Chileans promised not to attack the Peruvians, but they reserved the right to move their troops around. Although Piérola's obstinacy angered the Europeans, Baquedano's behavior had not endeared him to the neutral diplomats. Indeed, the British admiral, in conjunction with the commanders of the French and Italian naval vessels, warned the Chilean that they would destroy his fleet if his troops attacked their respective embassies. That message imparted, the diplomats returned to Piérola to discuss surrender terms, when, at approximately 10 a.m., fighting erupted.[102]

The Second Act: The Battle of Miraflores

No one is any more sure who started the Battle of Miraflores than who fired first at Dolores. The Chileans were shuffling their troops around when a group of them, including General Baquedano, apparently approached to within five hundred yards of the Peruvian lines. A Peruvian colonel, Mariano Ceballos, informed Cáceres that the Chileans fired first and that the naturally nervous Peruvians had responded.[103] In truth, the Chileans were hardly in a position to confront the Peruvians: Baquedano's four divisions occupied positions, beginning at the ocean's edge, that ran from west to east. The element closest to the Peruvians and slightly north of Barranco, Colonel Lagos's Third Division, held a line that ran from the waters of the Pacific to the rail line connecting Lima with Chorrillos. To Lagos's left and to the rear, stood Col. Arístides Martínez's Regimientos Tercero de la Línea, Zapadores, and Movilizado de Valparaíso, plus the artillery. Only the Third Division and the reserves faced to the east, toward Redoubts One and Two. A substantial distance to the southeast, Colonel Lynch's battered division—his command lost 442 dead and 1,400 wounded—held the ground roughly opposite Redoubts Three and Four.[104] Colonel Barboza's Second Brigade of the Second Division was stationed south of Lagos, Lynch, and Martínez. Gana's First Brigade and most of Baquedano's artillery and cavalry were closest to Chorrillos and hence the most distant from Miraflores.

Of all the Chilean divisions, only those of Lagos and perhaps Martínez were in a position to respond. And respond they did by assembling their men into their respective units and then manning the line. Not surprisingly, mass confusion resulted as officers tried to form men from disparate detachments into cohesive units. But even if all the errant Chileans returned, the combined strength of Colonels Suárez and Cáceres's corps, consisting of six to seven thousand men and twelve cannon occupying the five redoubts, clearly outnumbered Lagos's three to four thousand soldiers. The Chileans, however, could call upon the naval guns of the *Blanco*, the *Huáscar*, the *O'Higgins*, and the *Pilcomayo*, which rained almost three hundred shells on the Peruvian positions until a Chilean counterattack forced the fleet to cease firing.

Peru's Colonel Cáceres, sensing Lagos's vulnerability, attacked his left flank, hoping to outflank Barceló's brigade while simultaneously moving on Lagos's center, thus preventing the division commander from shoring up his beleaguered comrades. To make Barceló's situation worse, Suárez's corps also attacked, concentrating on the Chilean's right flank. The combination of these two units eventually drove Chileans back, leading Cáceres to claim later that had he more troops, he might have carried the day.[105]

The appearance of reinforcements, which began around ninety minutes after the battle's onset, stanched the Chilean flight. Lynch's tattered division plus Martínez's men—the Third Regiment of the Line—arrived, taking up positions on Lagos's right. Slowly the balance of power tilted toward the Chileans, whose thirteen thousand men began engaging the Peruvians. Soldiers from other brigades took their places on the once-exposed Chilean right. At approximately 4 p.m. General Baquedano's divisions counterattacked. Now it was Colonel Cáceres's turn to steel his men as Lynch smashed into his flanks. Supported by the Third Regiment of the Line, the Chileans attacked and captured Fort Alfonso Ugarte, although not before its commander had time to destroy his supplies, while Lagos and Martínez struck at Suárez's right flank.[106] Thirty minutes later, the Chileans launched a frontal assault all along the Peruvian front, including Colonel Dávila's four thousand troops. Under this pressure Colonel Cáceres's Batallones Concepción and 28 de Julio and Colonel Suárez's Manco Cápac abandoned their positions and, ignoring their commanders' orders, bolted for the rear. Some Peruvian troops fled because they had run out of ammunition. In Gen. Pedro Silva's case, his forces lacked the means to bring these crucially needed supplies to the front.

Some of the battle's participants doubted that shortages had precipitated flight. Indeed, Ambrosio del Valle, a Peruvian naval officer serving in the army, claimed that some soldiers threw away their bullets and then used this as an excuse to flee. But often their commanders behaved no more heroically. Del Valle reported that most of the general staff officers, after shouting either "Each man to his house" or "Save yourself if you can," also bolted. When the commanders of line units, such as Gens. Ramón Machuca and Andrés Segura, fell wounded and others, like Silva, had their horse shot out from beneath them, the Peruvian retreat became a rout. After ninety minutes, the Chileans had over overrun Piérola's lines, putting to flight his men.[107]

The fighting had been brutal. Father Salvador Donoso reported finding a Chilean soldier of the Buin impaled on a Peruvian bayonet, who apparently spent his dying breath to spilt open his enemy's head.[108] Miraflores, like most Chilean battles, exacted a heavy toll from the victors: 502 dead and 1,622 wounded. Among the deceased was Brigade Commander Col. Juan Martínez, who had survived every battle beginning with Pisagua. Predictably, Lagos's Third Division paid the highest blood tax: 28 percent of its men suffered wounds or died. Gen. Cornelio Saavedra, a veteran of countless battles with the army's inspector general said that with a few more casualties the Battle of Miraflores "lacked very little for us to have had another [bloody battle like] Tarapacá."[109]

As the Chileans prepared to enter Lima, Piérola abandoned the capital for the interior. His decision to flee, made, he asserted, so he could lead the resistance, did not endear him to his brothers in arms. A soldier of the reserve criticized Piérola, claiming that he never had a "plan or any order except the wish to sacrifice a certain number of victims" to ensure that the dictator could "preserve his post until the last moment." That Piérola failed did not surprise the Peruvian journalist J. Quimper, who blamed the Chorrillos debacle not simply on the "seminarian general's" inadequate martial skills but also on his "vanity and personal ineptitude," which prevented him from properly utilizing his remaining military assets. Other Peruvians laid the onus on less temporal forces: the dean of Arequipa's main church saw Chile's victories as God's punishment for Peru's sins, although the cleric did indicate that he believed that the Almighty's punitive anger had limits.[110] The two Argentine officers serving with Piérola's army attributed the defeat at Lima to the Peruvian troops' wretched discipline and poor training. Deficient though they might be, however, the Argentines still considered the Peruvian enlisted men vastly superior to their officers, who lacked "valor, patriotism, and education" and who were "the first to flee shamefully at the first enemy shots."[111]

Peru's lengthy casualty lists, however, belie these charges of cowardice. Estimates of the total number of Peruvian dead and wounded, which rest on anecdotal evidence, seem quite high. A Chilean correspondent for *El Ferrocarril* calculated that, out of an army of approximately seventeen thousand, four thousand Peruvians perished at Chorrillos and that the Chileans captured another two thousand. Supposedly, an additional six thousand fell at Miraflores, while three thousand suffered wounds and another three thousand became prisoners.[112] Thus, while it is true that some units fled, like the men of the Batallón Libertad, who took the Ayacucho with them, not all Peruvian soldiers reacted so cravenly. Elements like the Ancachs and Jauja, commanded by Col. Issac Recabarren, who suffered a wound at Chorrillos, fought until almost overrun.[113] Even some of the hastily formed reserve units resisted tenaciously: approximately 51 percent of Batallón Seis fell. Among the mortally wounded volunteers was Lt. Adolfo Gosdinski, perhaps the first Jewish man to be born in modern Peru, who, along with his brother and cousin, served his new homeland.[114] Nor were all dead and wounded impressed highland Indians: Batallón Cuatro, which consisted of the capital's judges, ex-legislators, and former high-ranking civil servants, lost 90 percent of its complement, many of whom perished.[115]

In truth, it is a testimony to the bravery of the generally ill equipped and poorly trained Peruvian troops that they performed as well as they did. Nor did their officers funk. Colonels Cáceres and Canevaro, for example, valiantly tried to rally their men when some began to flee. Often these leaders paid a high price for this bravery: 17 colonels died at Chorrillos, almost 10 percent of the 180 officers who perished on 13 January, while 3 generals, 11 colonels, and 106 other officers suffered wounds. A Chilean correspondent noted that the "Peruvians, far from withdrawing, . . . fought desperately, as they defended the last bulwarks that stood between the Chilean Army and its victorious march on the old capital of the Incas and the Viceroys."[116]

Anticipating a wave of rapine vandalism, thousands of Lima's citizens, particularly the women and children, fled to the protection of foreign consulates. Some two thousand camped out on the beaches of Ancón, under the benevolent cannon of the British Navy; twenty-six hundred filled the French Embassy.[117] Foreign merchants hung their nations' flags on their storefronts in hopes that it would deter the looters. (It did not.) Eventually the ministers of Britain and France demanded that Lima's mayor declare the capital an open city. General Baquedano, after deliberately ignoring the peace delegation—in part because the Chileans were still furious over Peru's use of mines—finally agreed that they would wait for twenty-four hours before entering the capital and that they would send only three thousand carefully selected men to occupy the capital on the proviso that the Peruvians disarm and disband their army. The hours between Piérola's departure and Baquedano's entry proved trying for Lima's *gente decente*: the capital's *léperos* (rabble), later joined by angry armed soldiers, began pillaging stores, particularly those of owned by the Chinese, and setting fires. More than one observer likened the scene to the Paris Commune. Only the intervention of Lima's *guardia urbana*, which adopted the policy of shooting anyone it caught looting or carrying a weapon, restored a modicum of order.[118]

As the smoke from the gutted city rose, the Peruvian authorities burned the fleet's remaining naval vessels and destroyed the coastal artillery fortresses that had failed to stop the Chileans. The captain of the *Unión* sailed Peru's last warship to the center of Callao Bay, where he set it afire; the *Atahualpa* succumbed to a torpedo. The Peruvians so thoroughly wrecked the transports *Rimac*, *Tumbes*, *Limeña*, *Chalaco*, and *Talismán* that the Chileans had to auction off the remains as scrap metal.[119]

Thus, on the summer afternoon of 22 January 1881, the first Chilean troops entered the former viceregal capital. An Italian cleric noted that "the splendid Queen of the Pacific resembled in those moments the sad majesty of a cemetery," confirming a Chilean soldier's judgment that the city looked as if it were commemorating Good Friday.[120] This must have been a bitter moment for the journalist A. A. Aramburú, who had earlier proclaimed that "Lima was invincible" and predicted, correctly in some cases, that its loyal sons would imitate Bolognesi by fighting to their last bullet. Still, some may have regarded the capitulation as a blessing. Since early January "communist machinations" had driven up the price of food and services, in part due to the declining value of the paper *billete fiscal* printed by the Prado government and Piérola's inca, about which a French visitor noted, "These rectangles of dirty paper, held only by the tips of the fingers, are for the present the principal means of interchange."[121]

Initially the transfer of power went smoothly. A Colombian resident of Lima noted, "The army of Chile made its entrance [into the capital] with a moderation that plainly shows the discipline of the soldiers and the sensitivity of its officers." Robert Ramsay, a Scotsman, agreed: "The bands," he remarked, "played very tranquil music, no national anthem nor anything that might offend, and after the march around the plaza, the soldiers calmly went to their barracks."[122] After watching the parade of Baquedano's men, preceded by a band, thirty Krupp guns, and their cavalry, some foreign observers reported that they now grasped why the Chilean army defeated Piérola's makeshift legions. A sailor from the *Garibaldi* was so moved that he claimed, "They are men just like we." Even the Peruvians agreed, one Limeño even telling the British minister, "We can now understand our defeats!"[123]

Regrettably, the discipline that allowed the Chileans to triumph quickly disappeared. The Spanish consul Merlé bitterly observed that "a few days earlier, Lima was a model city in terms of the security enjoyed within their homes and even the most isolated places. With the exception of the town's most central streets, there is no safety either during the day or night."[124] Both Peruvians and Chileans looted from the living and the dead. Additional factors made the city close to unbearable: the thousands of flies, the sight of seven hundred wild dogs feasting on the remains of the glorious dead, the aroma of the "still scattered, half-burned, decomposing, and putrifying bodies" of the soldiers, as well as their horses, made worse by the summer heat that filled the capital's air with an "unbearable stench."[125]

The Chilean authorities tried to respond: they limited the sale of liquor because Lima's residents dare not venture out at night for fear of being attacked by drunken Chilean troops. To restore the rule of law, Colonel Lynch, who became Lima's Chilean ruler, created a court composed of military officers to hear both criminal and civil cases. The authorities also ordered the cremation of the dead soldiers and their mounts—whose remains people feared to remove from the battlefield because of the danger of detonating unexploded mines—to prevent an epidemic.[126]

The British minister to Peru reported that given the recent excesses, people of property might "desire that the Chileans should prolong the occupation of the country."[127] This opinion quickly changed as the Chileans helped themselves, and their nation, to Lima's treasures. The National Library, created in 1821, as well as other educational institutions, lost thousands of books and scientific instruments. Federico Stuven urged the minister of war to send the new machines that produced Peruvian money to Santiago's mint.[128] The victors uprooted Peruvian coastal cannon, which they sent south. Cultural objects enjoyed no exemptions: Peru's books, art objects, printing presses, and even the animals from the zoo found new homes in Santiago. Lynch once suggested that his men dismantle for shipment to the south a monument erected in honor of Columbus.[129]

Not surprisingly, the resentment against the Chileans grew. Lynch tried to limit friction by confining his troops to barracks during Chile's Independence Day. But with General Baquedano's troops swaggering through the streets, each day saw other incidents occur. Sometimes these disputes escalated to the point that Peruvians killed Chilean troopers. When these deaths occurred, Lynch's minions reacted quickly and brutally, generally executing the supposed criminals. If the Chilean authorities could not catch those who actually committed the murder, they put to death any eyewitnesses—at a ratio of three Peruvians for each dead Chilean—either to convince the assassin to surrender or to cause someone to denounce the real criminal.[130] Occasionally, the Chileans satisfied the condemned last wishes: before shooting him, they allowed Manuel Rolán, to marry his paramour, so she would inherit his estate.[131] Eventually, the Chilean military's relations with Lima's inhabitants softened. Florentino Salinas, a Chilean soldier in the Aconcagua, initially had found the capital's citizens unfriendly, apparently because some tobacco chewing and drunken black women had insulted him. But within a few weeks, he described Lima's life "an uninterrupted carnival" and its womenfolk so generous that by September 1881 300 of the Aconcagua's approximately 590 men suffered from venereal disease.[132] The relationships between Chilean soldiers and Peruvian women became so congenial that the intellectual Ricardo Palma denounced Lima's citizens as "men without faith and women without shame."[133]

The victorious General Baquedano would depart Lima with great ceremony, returning to Chile and to a raucous welcome in Valparaíso and Santiago, where as many as one hundred thousand people attended the capital's victory celebration. The general's wartime popularity did not translate into a victory in the 1881 presidential election. Throughout the political campaign, Baquedano's opponent, Domingo Santa María, reminded the Chilean public of the general's failures: his political inexperience, his alliance with the conservatives and the Church, and, not the least, his inept handling of the war, which cost so many lives. The political contest became so cruel that the general might have wished to return to the quiet of the battlefield. Rather than endure his enemies' vicious personal attacks, he withdrew from the race, allowing Santa María to triumph.

Peru's new de facto viceroy was Adm. Patricio Lynch, the sailor turned soldier, the toast of the recently emancipated Chinese. He would rule Peru until 1884. Tragedy marked his last years. In 1883 Santa María informed Lynch that he would try to promote him to the rank of vice admiral, a rare honor. In the same letter the president informed the Red Prince that his son Luis was fatally ill. Lynch had the misfortune to outlive his son by three years, dying, perhaps appropriately, at sea as he returned to Chile from Spain, where he served as Santa María's minister to Madrid.[134]

The loss of Lima caused Peruvians to debate, yet again, the causes of their defeat. Ricardo Palma blamed the loss of Lima on Peru's Indians, "who had no concept of the motherland . . . regarding the Chileans just like a Turk." "Although it pains us to say it," he noted, "one has to agree that the Araucanian race was more virile because it tenaciously resisted the conquest."[135] Palma was not the only one to foist responsibility for the defeat onto the shoulders of the nation's most humble. Manuel González Prada noted that when someone asked the Indian troops arriving in Lima why they had come to the capital, they replied, "To kill a Chilean, an enormous animal with boots." Others believe the conflict was simply a civil war between "General Chili and Piérola," certainly not worth being "shot for the sake of the white men."[136] But a modern scholar, Nelson Manrique, rejects these disparaging judgments: "Embarked in the defense of objectives that were alien to them; transported like cattle to an unknown land to fight against enemies as strange as were the officers of an army in which they served . . . [and] used like cannon fodder to die . . . in San Juan and Miraflores," Peru's Indians had performed magnificently.[137] They simply could not overcome the better-trained, -equipped, and -led Chilean forces.

In fairness, González Prada did recognize the Indians' humanity. While serving alongside these men, he saw one commander beat an Indian for trying to insert a bullet in the muzzle of his rifle. Such men, he noted, deserved "compassion instead of blows."[138] Even Palma, unlike many of his contemporaries, eventually realized that the fault lay not with Peru's indigenous population but with their white and mestizo rulers. "Because in our unhappy country there is neither virility nor patriotism, because anarchy rots us and because corruption has entered not merely in the men of our generation but in the veins of the generation called upon to replace ours." The painful truth was, as Palma noted, that in Peru "patriotism is a myth."[139]

Baquedano had again triumphed, albeit at great cost to his army. The dug-in Peruvians, enjoying the support of their artillery, should have annihilated the Chilean formations long before they reached the parapets of Chorrillos's defensive works. Instead, they allowed the Chileans to advance, in close formations, with their divisional flags flying, before launching a final bayonet charge. Perhaps the Peruvians did not have enough breech-loading rifles; perhaps they did not know how to use these and their artillery to winnow the attacking Chileans. Most likely, even if they had both the proper weapons and the artillery, they could not deploy them to best advantage. Had Baquedano faced experienced Peruvians troops, he might not have triumphed.

Ironically, the war became more deadly after Lima's fall. Rather than swallow a Chilean-dictated peace, some Peruvians did precisely what a foreign visitor warned they might do: they made the Andean highlands "into a bulwark from which they would war against the invader."[140] This prolonged and brutal guerrilla campaign would provide subsequent generations of Peruvians with examples of patriotism. The Chileans, of course, came to view Peruvian resistance as a campaign of terrorism and banditry.

9. The Dirty War

Contrary to many Chileans' expectations and hopes, Lima's capture did not inspire the Peruvians to sue for peace. It was not, however, for want of politicians. Peru was, after all, awash in *caudillos*, presidential aspirants, and presidents, none of whom in fact actually governed the entire nation. Nicolás Piérola, who lacked constitutional legitimacy and, after the fall of Lima, a capital, desperately hoped to remain Peru's de facto albeit not its de jure leader. (One opponent called him "governor of Peru by divine right.")[1] The beached admiral Lizardo Montero, who after 1881 directed Peru from his headquarters in the Andean city of Arequipa, would serve as a provisional vice president and then president. Two others, Juan Martín Echenique and Pedro del Solar, controlled the Army of the Center and the Army of the South, respectively. Finally, a new player, the one who ironically seemed the least interested in ruling Peru, appeared: Col. Andrés Cáceres. Wounded in the battle for Lima, the colonel hid while recovering from his injuries. Once cured, a mufti-clad Cáceres rode the train from the capital to Chiclayo, whereupon he promptly disappeared into the countryside, only to emerge as the leader of an irregular, but nonetheless potent, army. Piérola would subsequently promote Cáceres to general and name him to command the Army of the Center. Unlike his colleagues, Cáceres had but one obsession: expelling the Chileans. With so many leaders each pursuing their own agenda, the war sputtered on for two additional years.

Any of these aspiring leaders could have ended the conflict simply by ceding Tarapacá to Chile. But even Piérola's mania for power had limits. And if he had favored transferring his nation's southernmost province to Santiago, which he did not, Admiral Montero and especially General Cáceres would never have concurred. Aníbal Pinto's ministers, therefore, had to find someone other than Piérola, whom they loathed and distrusted, who would be willing to abandon Tarapacá. Until then, an occupation army would remain in place to make Peru feel "all the weight of our virtues" and to oblige the vanquished nation to pay the war taxes that Chile needed to defray the cost of occupation as well as to finance a campaign to eradicate the remnants of Peruvian resistance.[2] This campaign would last approximately eighteen months, draining Chile's coffer and manpower reserves while subjecting the residents of Peru's altiplano to a brutal war of counterinsurgency and the rest of that hapless nation's citizens to an equally brutal occupation.

Peace Feelers

Curiously, Piérola and Pinto earlier tried to negotiate an end to the war. In October 1880 U.S. Secretary of State William Evarts ordered his ministers Newton Pettis in Bolivia, Thomas Osborn in Chile, and Isaac Christiancy in Peru to arrange a peace conference aboard the uss *Lackawanna*, a gunboat anchored in Arica's harbor. Washington took this unusual step largely to forestall British or French intervention on behalf of their citizens who owned either Peruvian bonds or shares in the nationalized nitrate mines. Earlier Christiancy had traveled to Santiago to discuss the negotiations with Pinto. At that time, the Chilean president told the U.S. envoy that under no circumstances would Chile accept anything less than the cession of Tarapacá. Thus, although the American minister knew that the Chilean government had categorically refused to return to the status quo ante bellum, Christiancy lied: he reported to Washington and Lima that President Pinto had not set any preconditions for holding the talks. Given this crucial piece of information, any witling could have predicted that the conference would fail.

And the negotiations did collapse. The Chileans demanded that Bolivia cede Atacama, that Peru surrender Tarapacá plus pay an indemnity of twenty million dollars, return Chilean owned property, including the *Rimac*, abrogate the 1873 alliance, and promise not rebuild Arica's defenses. Since the Bolivians and the Peruvians expected the Chileans to settle for monetary reparations, Pinto's demands seemed Carthaginian. As the Peruvian delegate Antonio Arénas noted, his nation would not cede part of its territory, particularly one that constituted the "principal source of its wealth."[3] Recognizing that they were at an impasse, the participants ended the negotiations on 27 October, five days after the discussions began. In one artless move, Washington had failed to bring peace to the Pacific while simultaneously alienating the belligerents.

Only three months had elapsed since the abortive 1880 Arica conference, but the military and the diplomatic situation had changed dramatically. Having spent additional blood and treasure to capture Lima, the Chileans upped the ante: Pinto now demanded that Peru disarm, that it cede Arica as well as Tarapacá, that it grant Santiago trade concessions, and that it permit Chilean troops to occupy Peru until its administration fulfilled its obligations. Pinto, moreover, still required Bolivia to surrender the Atacama.

Chile's demand for territory, while perhaps draconian, was predictable. Since Lima and La Paz lacked the financial resources to pay reparations, most Chileans insisted that only the annexation of Tarapacá and Atacama could compensate them for their human and financial losses. Geopolitics also influenced Chile's decision: owning the two provinces would buffer Chile from its revanchist neighbors. But Peru and Bolivia adamantly rejected the notion of surrendering the most valuable parts of their patrimony solely to gratify Chilean cupidity and allay its sense of insecurity. Clearly, the belligerents had reached an impasse.

By 1881, however, it seemed that a bankrupt Peru might accept Chile's terms. In February the members of the congress elected during the pre-Piérola government of Mariano Prado met in Lima, where they reinstated the 1860 Constitution. This rump congress also agreed to select a provisional president who could negotiate a peace settlement. The man they chose was Francisco García Calderón. Hoping that he would be pliable, the Chileans quickly recognized García Calderón's regime, giving him a capital in Magdalena and even donating weapons to his newly forged army. García Calderón, in the meantime, went about the business of restoring the pre-Piérola government: he convened the legislature—all of whose members' terms of office had expired—and restored the judiciary. He also called for elections to fill congressional vacancies.

The new assembly responded by electing García Calderón permanent president and granting him the authority to negotiate a peace treaty with Chile.

But if President Pinto's ministers expected García Calderón to accede supinely to their territorial demands, they received a shock: instead of cooperating, the new president demanded an armistice and called for Chile either to leave Lima or to allow his regime to administer the capital. García Calderón, moreover, became increasingly difficult, pointedly refusing to discuss the matter of territorial cession. Given his utter lack of military and particularly economic resources, García Calderón's resistance seemed almost quixotic. As we shall see, however, Washington's maladroit attempts to resolve the war stiffened García Calderón's backbone, thereby almost precipitating a conflict with Chile.

James Garfield assumed the presidency of the United States in early 1881. Although highly competent, James G. Blaine proved controversial as Garfield's choice for secretary of state. A former senator from Maine, Blaine possessed great intelligence, charm, and ambition, relatively elastic morals, and, paradoxically, "an inexhaustible capacity for making enemies."[4] The new secretary of state, whom various diplomatic historians would subsequently credit for bringing great energy to his post, wanted to advance America's economic presence throughout the world, particularly in Latin America. But recognizing that political unrest discouraged economic investment, he urged Washington to resolve the War of the Pacific before Europeans became involved.

Blaine, however, was anything but evenhanded. The Anglophobic secretary of state believed that Britain had prodded Chile into war in order to protect England's investments. Consequently, his proposed peace treaty called for Chile to accept monetary indemnities rather than demand annexation of the Atacama and Tarapacá. If successful, Blaine's policy would accomplish two goals: by limiting Santiago's gains, Washington would blunt British economic influence and, by guaranteeing Peru's and Bolivia's prewar boundaries, Latin America would escape the curse of revanchism that bedeviled post-1871 Europe after France's cession of Alsace and Lorraine. Chileans, of course, found it difficult to comprehend Blaine's antipathy to Santiago's demand for land. The United States, many Chileans plaintively noted, had also used war to expand its boundaries. Thus, if Washington could demand territory, why not Chile? As we shall discover, consistency may have been the hobgoblin of ordinary minds but not of Blaine's.

Regrettably, Blaine's selection of envoys to Chile and Peru complicated an already complex situation. The U.S. representative in Lima, Stephen Hurlburt, was not a diplomatic neophyte: earlier, he had served for three years as U.S. minister to Peru. But the ex–Civil War general was also a drunkard, a mountebank, and, based on his corrupt misuse of his military command, utterly venal. Washington's envoy to Chile, former general Judson Kilpatrick, enjoyed a much better reputation. Also a career diplomat and a former general, he had served in Chile during the ill-fated Spanish war. Married to a prominent Chilean woman, his reassignment to Santiago constituted a sort of homecoming. Kilpatrick, however, suffered from poor health. Normally this issue would not have mattered, but as he became more infirm, Kilpatrick's wife apparently began acting as the de facto minister, presumably using her influence to advance her nation's cause, not that of the United States. It is a mark of his popularity that after his death in December 1881 the Chilean government gave Kilpatrick a state funeral. Whatever their vices or virtues, neither diplomat could persuade the Chile to accept monetary damages instead of territory.[5]

In his zeal to settle the dispute, Hurlburt unilaterally recognized the García Calderón administration and then proclaimed that the United States would tolerate Chilean annexation only if Peru lacked the funds to pay reparations. Hurlburt, again acting without Washington's permission, also convinced the García Calderón administration to grant the United States some railroad concessions plus a coaling station in the port of Chimbote. When it became known that Hurlburt would personally profit from this arrangement, Chile correctly concluded that the U.S. minister was complicating, not facilitating, the diplomatic process.

Hurlburt's unfortunate endorsement of the Peruvian agenda doubtless reinforced García Calderón's resistance to ceding Tarapacá. And the sudden appearance of two previously unknown corporations—the Credit Industriel and the Peruvian Company, representing European and American creditors—simply strengthened García Calderón's resolve not to surrender any territory to Chile. These corporations offered to lend Peru the money that it required to pay reparations to Chile, but in return the Peruvian government would have to grant mining concessions in Tarapacá to these corporations. Having won García Calderón's acquiescence, the Credit Industriel and the Peruvian Company hired the services of a cabal of seedy politicians, influence peddlers, and greedy lawyers to advance their respective claims in America's courts and to convince the U.S. Congress to support Blaine's hard-line policy vis-à-vis Santiago. Buoyed by Hurlburt's actions and the promises of funds, García Calderón emphatically rejected Chile's territorial demands. His obstinacy infuriated Chile's new president, Domingo Santa María, who had dramatically changed the diplomatic equation by demanding that Peru surrender Arica as well as Tarapacá. When García Calderón temporized, Chile's representative in Peru first confiscated his treasury, then disbanded his army, and finally arrested the now lame-duck president before sending him to a Chilean exile, not aboard a warship, but, for reasons of economy, on a squalid transport.[6]

The collapse of García Calderón's government chafed the already raw Chilean-American diplomatic relations. Painfully aware that he could trust neither the infirm Kilpatrick nor the monumentally maladroit, if not blatantly dishonest, Hurlburt, Secretary Blaine ordered his son, Walker, as well as a professional diplomat, William Trescot, to Chile. The men had two missions: to determine if Chile's jailing of García Calderón constituted an affront to Washington's honor—which could have given Blaine an excuse to urge President Garfield to declare war—and to offer U.S. mediation of the Chilean-Peruvian dispute. Should President Santa María continue to obstruct Washington's efforts, Blaine hinted that the United States might use its strength to bring peace to the Pacific.

In truth, Blaine's threats rang hollow: Chile possessed a navy so vastly superior to that of the United States that it was Washington, not Santiago, that should have feared a conflict. Fortunately, the dispute did not ripen into war. Following the unexpected death of James Garfield, President Chester Alan Arthur appointed James Frelinghuysen to replace Blaine. In early 1882 the new U.S. secretary of state, realizing that the United States was "on the highway to war for the benefit of about as nasty a set of people as ever gathered about a Washington department," publicly disavowed Blaine's policy while abandoning any notion of intervening militarily in Chile's dispute with Peru.[7] Regrettably for them, Trescot and Walker Blaine learned of their nation's policy change only when they arrived in Chile. Still, although the somewhat chastened Trescot managed to heal the U.S.-Chilean breach, he could not bring Chile or Peru closer to peace.

The Endless War

Lima's capture, while felicitous, did not confer complete mastery of Peru upon President Pinto or his successor. Indeed, in early 1881 General Baquedano asked for reinforcements, so he could finish the job of crushing isolated pockets of Peruvian resistance. A prominent member of the Chilean government, José Francisco Vergara, demurred: simply occupying Lima, Callao, and certain other key cities would suffice. The nation's sons, he observed, "will be much more useful to Chile harvesting wheat or working the land than learning now how to use a rifle" in order to annihilate the remnants of Peru's army. In the end, the decision became a matter of simple arithmetic: cowing Peru required only 8,000 soldiers and sailors; eradicating the last vestiges of resistance would consume at least 22,000 troops. Vergara's logic carried the day: the government ordered Baquedano and most of his soldiers back to Chile before the combination of Peru's deadly climate and occupation duty ruined the army's health and eroded its discipline.[8] It would fall to Adm. Patricio Lynch's 12,700- to 15,000-man Army of the North to keep order until Peru accepted Chile's terms.[9]

Clearly, the War of the Pacific had entered a new stage. Each of the belligerents pursued different objectives: the Santa María regime hoped that its imposition of heavy taxes would pay for Chile's army of occupation and that Santiago's refusal to accept cash reparations would eventually compel Peru's citizens to cede Tarapacá. Conversely, Peruvian patriots like Cáceres advocated waging a defensive war of "exhaustion,"—one that would "slowly erode and weaken the invader in the highlands of the Center [of Peru]" through a mixture of strategic retreats and "counterattack when and where there are the possibilities of success"—to defeat Santa María's legions.[10] In other words, consume so much of Chile's blood and treasure that the country's leaders abandon their demand for territory, settling instead for monetary damages.

Thanks to Cáceres, the plight of Chile's occupation army became increasingly difficult. Guerrilla bands, the *montoneros*, began to harass Lima's occupying garrison. The situation reached such a point that Admiral Lynch had to station his troops on the capital's outskirts to protect it as well as to interdict the flow of military supplies and intelligence to Cáceres from the Junta Patriótica, a clandestine Peruvian resistance organization created in September 1881 and staffed by civilians to serve as a shadow government and to support the guerrilla war.[11]

It quickly became apparent to the red-haired Lynch that squatting in Lima would never eradicate the montoneros. The Peruvian irregulars, many of them survivors of Piérola's army, took refuge in a series of valleys located 11,500 to 13,200 feet above sea level and sandwiched between two branches of the Andes. Even veteran Chilean troops blanched at the prospect of entering this uncharted maze of mountain ridges and cul-de-sacs. The altiplano's primitive roads, often just narrow paths gouged from the mountains' sides that bordered deep ravines, hampered movement. Montonero bands sometimes included the Indian inhabitants of the altiplano hamlets, who demonstrated great skill attacking and harassing the Chilean columns. Their most lethal weapon was the *galga*, a boulder or a large rock, which the guerrillas rolled down upon unsuspecting Chilean soldiers, either crushing them or hurtling them into the abyss below. The Indians also used slings and spears to kill or wound Chilean soldiers, whom they then decapitated or whose bodies they mutilated.[12]

Besides the montoneros, the Chileans' most effective foes were the seemingly endless population of venomous insects and reptiles and endemic diseases—respiratory failures, smallpox, dysentery, and sundry fevers, including typhoid, typhus, and particularly altitude sickness (*sorroche*), which crippled or killed hundreds of Chileans. In short, the Sierra campaign, which many considered a strategic afterthought, cost Chile dearly in terms of its wealth and its men.

Letelier's Folly

The Peru of 1881, like Caesar's Gaul, was defended by three distinct military organizations. The Army of the North was commanded by Adm. Lizardo Montero and his assistant, Gen. Miguel Iglesias. The Army of the

South was originally controlled by a politician, Pedro del Solar, and his military commander, Col. José La Torre. These forces paled in size and power before the Army of the Interior, Cáceres's three thousand troops who would terrorize the Chileans on Peru's roads and in its highlands, as well as in its capital.

Ironically, Chile encountered more difficulties pacifying the Peruvian interior than it did vanquishing the Allies during the War of the Pacific's first two years. The Chilean army's medical and supply corps, which barely functioned during the first phase of the conflict, virtually collapsed when confronted with the task of provisioning or caring for the troops fighting in the altiplano. The army simply could not deliver food, clothing, or medical care, in large part because it lacked adequate transport. And even if the Chileans had the necessary pack animals and mounts, Peruvian irregulars constantly menaced the road network as well as the railways. Consequently, Lynch's soldiers had to live off the land of an increasingly sullen and unrelenting enemy. And each foraging expedition, whether successful or not, so alienated the local Indians, who could barely feed themselves, that they joined the resistance movement.

After January 1881 Lynch concentrated his efforts on pacifying the province of Junín. Squeezed between the Andes' western flank, sometimes called the Andes Negro (Black Andes), and the Andes Blanco (White Andes), the Mantaro, or Oroya, River valley runs on a northwest-to-southeast axis. To reach this basin, the Chileans first had to ride the railroad from Lima through Chosica to Chicla, a 12,300-foot-high town lying on the Black Andes' western flank. Once they detrained, the troops had to march up to and then through a pass nearly 13,600 feet above sea level before descending into the Mantaro Valley. Those moving southeast through the Mantaro Valley discovered that the towns' altitudes declined to about 10,500 feet. Conversely, as the Chileans trudged toward to the northwest, the elevation increased. The mining center of Cerro de Pasco, for example, was 14,200 feet above sea level.

In February 1881 Lynch launched his first punitive expedition, ordering Lt. Col. Ambrosio Letelier to lead a column of seven hundred soldiers into the Peruvian interior. Letelier had three missions: to annihilate the local guerrilla bands so that they would cease attacking Lima, to protect the crucial Lima to La Oroya railway as well as a military hospital in Chosica, and to levy enough taxes to defray the cost of the occupation. Virtually from the beginning, the Letelier expedition encountered difficulties. Within two days the lieutenant colonel noted that *sorroche* had incapacitated one hundred of his men. Two days after the onset of the expedition, another commander, reporting that ninety of his troops were ill, requested medical assistance, beds, and the means to keep the sick warm. Others grumbled about poor or nonexistent rations, the lack of livestock, too few horses or mules, wretched boots, and inadequate clothing and blankets. The situation degenerated to such a point that one officer described the men of the Regimiento Santiago as "basically naked."[13]

Militarily the expedition achieved very little. Initially, Letelier declared martial law in Junín, Jauja, and Tarma, demanding that the local population surrender any weapons or property belonging to the Peruvian government.[14] While he moved north to Cerro de Pasco, he wisely left part of his army in the south to ensure that the Peruvian irregulars could not cut the vital bridge spanning the Mantaro River at Oroya, thereby denying the Chilean forces access to the mountain pass, which constituted the only way out of the valley. Letelier's forces also pushed north to Huanuco, which they captured on 30 April. Thus, within three weeks of leaving, Letelier's troops held a strip of land extending from Huanaco in the north to Junín in the south.

But waging a campaign in the altiplano taxed the expeditionary force's stamina and resources. At fourteen thousand feet above sea level, the cold mountain air ravaged the soldiers' noses and ears; oxygen deprivation forced Letelier's gasping troops to rest every few minutes simply to catch their breath. In this climate, once described as suitable only for a consumptive, the soldier's rifle became not merely a weapon but also a means of support, as many soldiers leaned on their rifles. Poverty, like disease, was endemic: with the exception of the mining center of Cerro de Pasco, the Andean towns consisted of a collection of *chozas*, ramshackle huts inhabited by "filthy and ragged Indians," who predictably refused to share their limited food supply with the Chilean interlopers. Thus, after weeks of marching, the weather and terrain had shredded the uniforms of Letelier's troops, while the shortages of food and a lack of air taxed their bodies.[15]

By mid-May, Lynch ordered Letelier and his men to return to Lima, supposedly because he wished to reorganize the army. In fact, Letelier had developed a reputation for brutality—his soldiers often beat the local population to discover the location of their valuables—and for despoiling property, including that owned by neutrals, which turned the Peruvians against the occupation government.[16] But while Lynch ordered Letelier to abandon the altiplano, he did not direct him to take the most direct route to Lima. Instead, he instructed Letelier's troops first to evacuate Cerro de Pasco, then march southwest, crossing the mountains through Huallay Pass before proceeding to Canta, a town that lay on a main highway, northeast of Lima and north of the Lima-Chicla railway. Lynch selected this convoluted path because he wanted Letelier's men to punish Canta's civilian population for helping the guerrilla bands harass Lima.[17] Letelier shared Lynch's desire to eradicate Canta's montoneros: he ordered his troops to push southwest from the Mantaro Valley while those stationed in Chilca and Casapalca moved northwest. Together they would envelop the irregulars that had been plaguing Lima.[18]

The Peruvians, however, had plans of their own. The Indians of Cajamarquilla and Vilcabamba rebelled, besieging Chilean garrisons. These uprisings were more than pinpricks: in Huanuco, for example, eighty Chileans had to fight for three days repulsing a montonero attack even as the Indians heaved galgas, which with great noise "swept all before it as if it were a movement of the earth," upon the relief column rushing to save the Chilean garrison. While Letelier's men inflicted heavy losses on the Peruvians, their situation became increasingly perilous when they began to run out of ammunition.[19]

The most epic of the battles occurred at Sangra. Letelier ordered a company of the Regimiento Buin to occupy Cuevas in order to protect those Chileans moving on to Canta. Fifteen of these troops remained in Cuevas; the remainder dug in at the nearby Hacienda Sangra. The Chilean commander, Capt. José Araneda, had just sent some foragers into the countryside when between 140 and 700 Peruvian troops plus Indian irregulars led by Col. Manuel Vento attacked. The first wave consumed the rations party and the men in Cuevas; those remaining in Sangra managed to repel their attackers until 2 a.m. of 27 June, when Vento ended the assault, but not before killing twenty-four Chileans and wounding eighteen.[20] Eventually, the expeditionary force managed to fight its way to the Chicla railhead and safety.

Letelier's expedition failed, in part, because it poisoned the well from which it wished to drink. Foreign nationals complained, for example, that the Chileans stole their property and abused their persons. Letelier's imposition of taxes, payable either in kind or in cash, antagonized everyone. Perhaps the Chileans mistakenly believed that the Indians, long habituated to abuse, would passively accept these imposts without protest.[21] In truth, the highland Peruvians did not bear the Letelier's taxes any more graciously than they tolerated the Chilean habit of executing prisoners or anyone caught carrying firearms or ammunition. Hilarión Bouquet, a Chilean officer, agreed that these harsh punishments alienated the local inhabitants, but, he observed, the Chileans had little choice: heavily outnumbered, Letelier's troops had to use draconian penalties in hopes of cowing the Peruvians.[22] Their reprisals had the opposite effect: instead of being intimidated, the Indians first resisted and then rebelled.

Lynch shared the Peruvian disdain of Letelier. Certainly the arrival in Lima of Letelier's disheveled army proved disappointing. The troops' uniforms were in tatters, and those horses that the soldiers had not eaten were as decrepit as their saddles were shoddy. Curiously, though unkempt, undisciplined, and demoralized, these men, as well as their officers, carried large sums of money, leading Lynch to note, "Pecuniary result favorable for the expeditionary troops, nothing for the state." This financial imbalance aroused official curiosity because although the expedition collected $2 million in taxes, Letelier reported that he had, in fact, raised far less and that he had to spend some of these funds for food and clothing.[23] A subsequent court-martial revealed that Letelier as well as many of his subordinates illegally diverted $102,000 into their own pockets. Consequently, the court stripped Letelier of his rank, sentenced him to six years in jail, and demanded restitution.[24] (In an unusual step, Letelier appealed the sentence of court-martial to the Council of State, which overturned the military tribunal's original decision.)

Lynch faced more pressing problems than disciplining Letelier. Guerrilla bands had begun to move from their foothill sanctuaries to occupy some of Peru's coastal valleys and seaports: Peruvian colonels Pedro Mas and Octavio Bernasola, for example, terrorized the Ica Valley; Col. Manuel Negrón led irregulars in Piura, as did Col. Gregorio Relaize in Lambayeque. Lynch, however, lacked the troops to pursue all these enemies:

more than 60 percent of his 15,429-man army protected Lima, Callao, and Chorrillos.[25] Perhaps he was correct to stress controlling the nation's capital and its principal seaport: the two cities, in addition to containing approximately 120,000 people, generated a large portion of the revenues that Chile needed to support its army of occupation, and they also served as the conduit through which passed the supplies and the troops to equip and staff Lynch's units. Finally, Lima's elites possessed most of Peru's liquid assets, which the Chileans periodically taxed to assuage the occupation army's economic demands.[26]

But the stationing the majority of his troops in Lima still did not guarantee the safety of Lynch's army of occupation. Limeños waylaid Chilean soldiers on the capital's streets, at haciendas barely thirteen miles away, as well as in the nearby mountain towns of Chosica, San Jeronimo, and Santa Elena.[27] In truth, few places in Peru seemed safe: Chileans had to struggle to prevent the sabotage of the rail lines and the commandeering of trains, to end assaults on haciendas, as well as fight pitched battles with montonero bands.[28] In an attempt to show the flag, Chileans landed at Paita to pursue Colonel Negrón.[29] Lynch also sent men of the Batallón Victoria south to Cerro Azul in hopes of collecting money from the local customs house as well as reviving the sugar economy of Cañete. As one officer noted, however, the expedition walked into a cockpit, battling 1,000-man-strong montonero bands that scorched the earth by torching haciendas and destroying bridges when required to retreat. In the north, the Chileans of the Lautaro and the Zapadores repulsed an attack by more than 200 irregulars under the command of a local guerilla chieftain.[30] Thus, when Lynch described as "completely tranquil" large stretches of the Peruvian coast, from its northern border with Ecuador to Paracas, south of Lima, he misspoke.[31] Guerrilla units operated freely in Peru's north, in Libertad, Lambeyque, Trujillo, and Chancay, and in its south, in the Cañete and Ica valleys. Montoneros even compelled the Chileans to revisit their earlier victories in the south: in September 1881 Lynch's men moved inland from Tacna to destroy 250 to 300 irregulars commanded by Pachecho de Céspedes headquartered in Tarata.[32]

By the end of 1881 Lynch's counterinsurgency program became almost as ritualized as a ballet: Peruvian irregulars would seize territory; the Chileans would respond by sending an expedition to expel the guer-

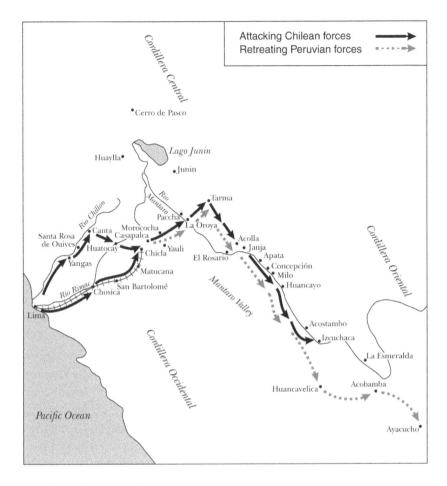

10a. The 1882 Sierra Campaign

rillas, restore order, and impose taxes, which they often could not collect. Then, facing an uprising in another area, the Chileans would depart, allowing the montoneros to reoccupy the recently vacated territory. As the Chilean Col. Eulojio Robles lamented, with his troops spread so thinly, he lacked the manpower to ensure even the safety of the rail lines, let alone protect an entire region.[33]

The 1882 Sierra Campaign

Vexing though they were, the guerrilla bands were like mosquitoes: they irritated the occupying forces, but they did not threaten Chilean hege-

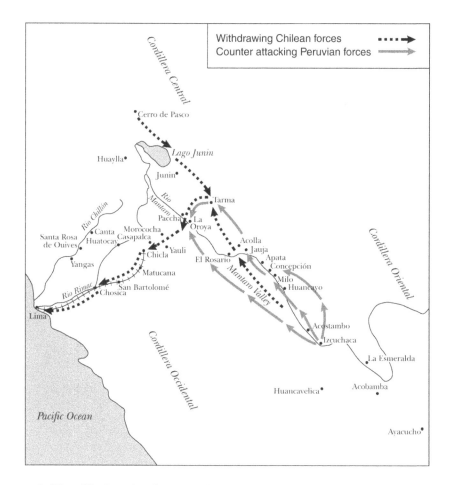

10b. The 1882 Peruvian Counteroffensive

mony. Lynch's principal foe remained General Cáceres, and thus, on 1 January 1882 the naval officer authorized a second expedition into the Andes with orders to annihilate the Peruvian's elements. The Chilean offensive consisted of two columns: two thousand men under Colonel Gana would march parallel to the Lima-Chicla railroad to attack frontally General Cáceres's Army of the Center. Meanwhile, Lynch's three thousand troops, who departed Lima on 5 January, would drive first northeast through the Chillón River valley to Canta. Once they had reached that objective, the Chileans would turn south to southeast. If all went according to plan, as the Chileans attacked from the south, Lynch's contingents

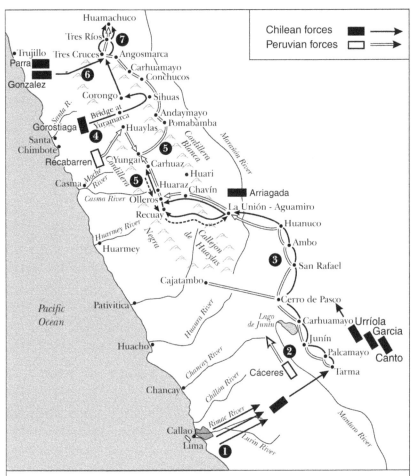

Chilean forces ■ ➝
Peruvian forces ☐ ⇒

Huamachuco
Tres Ríos ⑦
Trujillo Tres Cruces Angosmarca
Parra
Gonzalez Carhuamayo Conchucos
⑥
Corongo Sihuas
Bridge at Andaymayo
Gorostiaga Yuramarca Pomabamba
④ Huaylas
Santa ⑤
Chimbote
Récabarren Yungai Carhuaz
⑤ Huari
Casma Huaraz Chavín
Casma River Olleros La Unión - Aguamiro Arriagada
Recuay Huanuco
Huarmey River Ambo
Huarmey ③ San Rafael
Cajatambo
Pacific Pativitica Cerro de Pasco
Ocean Lago
de Junín Carhuamayo Urríola
Junín Garcia
Huacho Palcamayo Canto
Cáceres Tarma
②
Chancay
Callao ①
Lima

1. In early 1882, the Chileans launch a three-pronged attack on Cáceres. The Chilean commanders are Leon Garcia, who departs on 6 April; Colonel Canto who leaves on 25 April, and Urríola.

2. Cáceres retreats northwest.

3. Cáceres, believing that General Issac Recabarren is near Aguamiro/Union, goes there. Arriagada tries to capture Cáceres, who tricks the Chilean into believing that he retreated south. When Arriagada tries to follow him, Cáceres escapes to the north.

4. Gorostiaga left Trujillo on 10 May hoping to prevent Recabarren from joining Cáceres' forces. When the Chilean failed to accomplish this mission, Lynch, in late June, ordered him to Sihuas in order to block Cáceres' army which was moving northwest. Realizing that he could not reach his objective in time, Gorostiaga counter-marched on Corongo, in hopes of intercepting Cáceres' men.

5. To avoid being caught in a vise, Cáceres crosses the Cordillera Blanca at Arguaychancha, entering the Callejon de Huaylas. Cáceres proceed northwest to Yungai where he links up with Recabarren's forces on 19 June.

5. Cáceres, to avoid Gorostiaga, recrosses the Cordillera Blanca at 5,574 meter pass at Llanganuco. Arraiagada erroneously believing that Cáceres has retreated, moves southeast to La Unión. Cáceres, in the interim, marches to, Pomabamba.

6. Gorostiaga receives reinforcements from González and Parra, both of whom leave Trujillo on 29 and 5 June, respectively. Gorostiaga moves northwest to protect Iglesiàs's forces.

7. Cáceres, hoping to prevent González's troops from reinforcing Gorostiaga, unsuccessfully tries to intercept them at Tres Cruces. González, however, links up with Gorostiaga forcing Cáceres to fight them at Humanchuco.

11. The 1883 Sierra Campaigns and the Battle of Huamachuco

would strike from the north, smashing Cáceres's army on Gana's anvil.

The Chilean offensive caught Cáceres at a vulnerable moment: an outbreak of typhus killed so many of his troops, between eight and ten men per day, that the epidemic sidelined his Batallón Tarma. Cáceres had other problems: the constant rain destroyed his few supplies; a subordinate, Colonel Vento, defected, exposing Cáceres's flank; and a cavalry unit, the Cazadores del Perú, mutinied twice, forcing Cáceres to execute the uprisings' leaders. Thus, by the time that Cáceres reached Huancayo, the combination of disease, summary executions, and exhaustion had reduced his army from five thousand to thirteen hundred men.[34]

It quickly became clear that Lynch had learned some of the lessons of Letelier's botched mission. According to his new orders, commanders should use narrow roads and mountain passes only with great care; they also had to maintain strict march discipline to prevent the montoneros from picking off stragglers. Aware that disease incapacitated more men than the enemy's bullets, the Chileans tried to ensure that the troops were well fed, rested, and healthy. Realizing that their mission depended on the good will of the local Peruvians, Lynch instructed his commanders to respect neutral property as well as that of Peruvian citizens. If Chileans had to impose taxes to purchase necessities like food, they should try to collect these without antagonizing the local Peruvian residents. Lynch's sensitivity, however, had its limits: labeling armed irregulars as bandits, he explicitly authorized his men to "exterminate" all montoneros. He even sanctioned the seizing of hostages as well as taking reprisals to deter future attacks on Chilean troops.[35]

Alerted by his intelligence network, Cáceres was not caught unawares by Lynch's offensive. Indeed, by the time Gana's men reached Chicla, their prey already had retreated, albeit somewhat sloppily, to the northeast. Ordering some of his troops to guard the rear, Gana pursued Cáceres's command, estimated at two thousand men, through the mountains. Although Cáceres managed to remain just out of reach, achieving this feat came at the cost of leaving behind a "trail of dead, and of soldiers and officers dying of illness and misery, whom they [the Chileans] had to collect and help."[36]

The Chileans seemed only marginally more fortunate: poor weather and worse roads forced Lynch to order his artillery units to return to

Lima, leaving his exhausted infantry to push forward through the rain and three- to four-day-long snowstorms. The troops suffered enormous hardships: the Regimiento Maule, Lynch's rearguard, spent a night exposed to a snowstorm at 14,600 feet. Fortunately for the column, Gana ordered the unit to go back to Lima, but not before two of the Maule's men succumbed to the frigid temperatures.[37]

A dispute erupted between Lynch and Chile's officials in Lima. Citing the terrible conditions and the weather, Lynch begged the government to abort the expedition. When on 20 January President Santa María's local officials spurned Lynch's request, the officer turned his command over to Gana. Leading his men over a sixteen-thousand-foot-high pass, Gana occupied Oroya on 22 January and Tarma two days later. On 1 February, however, the government recalled Gana, who assigned Col. Estanislao del Canto to command the Chilean expedition. The ever-enthusiastic del Canto divided his men into two contingents of five hundred men, who advanced southeast on either side the Mantaro River.

Initially, Cáceres avoided the Chilean leviathan, but on 5 February his luck ran out. Del Canto's troops caught up with and attacked Cáceres's rearguard at Pucara. The Peruvians tried to resist, but eventually they had to retreat. During the withdrawal, a storm swept four hundred of Cáceres's men, many screaming for help, plus their mounts and equipment off the mountain trails and into a gorge below. By the time Cáceres reached Ayacucho in late February, his army numbered only four hundred starving and exhausted troops.[38] Ironically, both the Chileans and the Peruvians would celebrate the second Sierra campaign: Cáceres for managing to retreat to Ayacucho and del Canto for winning control of the Mantaro Valley from Cerro de Pasco in the north to Huancayo in the south.[39] The Chilean commander would savor his victory for but a short time.

Between February and July, Cáceres managed to raise, reorganize, and equip a band of fifteen hundred. Capitalizing on their anger over having to pay taxes and provide food to the Chileans, Cáceres also incorporated the local Indians into the army. Although sometimes armed with old rifles, harquebusses or blunderbusses, and pistols, the majority served in three different units: *rejoneros* (spearmen), *galgueros* (those who threw the rocks), and *honderos* (slingmen).

Beginning in April, the Peruvian attacks on Chilean units, particularly those traveling in small groups on isolated roads, increased; elements of the Chilean Lautaro and the Second Line Regiment also came under fire. On 8 April some of the Indians in the Jauja Valley demonstrated their opposition to paying taxes or contributing food by cutting the local bridge. The newspaper *El Coquimbo* reported that Indians rebelled on both sides of the Mantaro River, killing the tax collector and ambushing a group of Chilean soldiers sent to restore order.[40] Increasingly, Chilean units had to endure sniper fire and ambushes, compelling them to fight their way back to their camps. The Chilean commanders had not realized it, but the nature of the struggle with Peru had fundamentally changed: Cáceres abandoned the notion of fighting a traditional war. Henceforth, he observed, his campaign would be a "combination of local actions; stratagems, traps, ambushes, skirmishes, and raids, in which surprise, speed of movement, astuteness, guile, skill and artifice more than force, will compensate for the disadvantages of our numerical inferiority and ways of fighting."[41] Paradoxically, the Chileans, having learned to fight a "modern war," had to relearn some of the lessons so they had so painfully mastered battling the Araucanians of the south.

By the end of May, the Chileans suffered the loss of three hundred men. Isolated in a sea of hatred, the lice-covered troops suffered enormous privations. When his one-eyed horse died, Marcos Ibarra, a volunteer enlisted man in the Second of the Line, had to slog through mountain snow in straw-stuffed boots. Clothed in patched uniforms and existing on vegetables, worm-eaten beef jerky, llama meat, and biscuits so hard that the men had to use their rifle butts to break them into pieces, the Chileans barely survived. The monthly or bimonthly butchering of an ox became cause for joy, providing the men fresh meat for their stomachs and hides to cover their feet.[42] Diseases such as typhus and smallpox ravaged the ill-clad and hungry Chileans. One unit, the Third Line Regiment, lost 193 of its 600 men. Realizing that Cáceres's approximately 5,000-man army, including 3,000 Indians, outnumbered the Chileans, Gana secretly ordered his men to retreat. Inexplicably, he had sent this message en clair via a telegraph service staffed by Peruvians. Forewarned of the Chilean retreat, Cáceres launched an offensive in early July to pursue his enemies as they tried to flee from the Mantaro Valley.[43]

Cáceres unleashed a series of attacks, which, coupled with the constant harassment by the Indian auxiliaries, compelled Canto to spread out his units, thus increasing their vulnerability. Meanwhile, the Peruvian commander divided his men into three columns. The first, under Col. Juan Gastó, headed north along the Mantaro Valley's eastern heights. The second, led by Col. Máximo Tafur, moving on the valley's western flank, hoped to cut or capture the crucial bridge over the Oroya River. Meanwhile, Cáceres, at the head of the third column, would advance up the Mantaro Valley, pushing the Chileans before him. If all went according to plan, Cáceres would drive the Chilean occupation army toward the Oroya Bridge, which his men would have already either destroyed or captured. Once his soldiers controlled this crucial choke point, Cáceres could seal del Canto's men in the Mantaro Valley as effectively, and with the same result, as a scientist's killing bottle. The Chileans would then face a choice: death or capitulation.[44]

Del Canto may not have known Cáceres's precise strategy, but he realized that he had to escape from the Mantaro Valley. The Chilean's retreat from Huancayo called for his men to move north, passing through Concepción and Jauja. Once they reached Tarma, they would turn west, cross the Mantaro River at Oroya, and then march first to Chicla and beyond to Lima. As elements of del Canto's army moved north, those Chileans garrisoning Cerro de Pasco and Junín would withdraw to the south until they too reached Tarma, where they would also cross the Mantaro River bridge. Unfortunately for del Canto, Cáceres's troops and his Indian auxiliaries increased the pressure by waylaying Chilean units as they retreated.[45] Already slowed by more than 150 wounded and the sick, many in litters, each ambush further delayed the six-mile column.[46] Del Canto's exodus out of the Mantaro Valley became Chile's *via crucis*. Arturo Benavides of the Lautaro described his sick, malnourished, and poorly shod companions, sometimes supported by a comrade, riding a horse, or borne on a litter, running a gauntlet of stone-throwing montoneros.[47] Stumbling down mountain trails under an avalanche of boulders and rocks, an officer of the Batallón Santiago noted that the Peruvians were inflicting casualties on "victorious soldiers, whom enemy bullets have known how to respect from Antofagasta to Lima."[48] By mid-July del Canto reported that his men needed rations and his mounts forage, that the smaller garrisons begged for reinforcements, and that his soldiers required between fifty and one hundred thousand rounds of ammunition. Illness inflicted perhaps more casualties than the montoneros: 237 of 473 sick Chileans died.[49] The lack of food became so acute that some troops slaughtered and ate their unit's llama mascot.[50] As the men force-marched north toward Tarma and the Oroya Bridge, the Chileans' plight became desperate. "Absolutely without provisions," del Canto's animals devoured the thatch roofs of houses, and his troops burned parts of homes to keep warm. The freezing weather turned the constant rain into snow, killing not just the wounded but even the supposedly acclimated Indian bearers.[51] "The battle we are waging here," noted del Canto, "is not against the enemy but against the elements that besiege us."[52] "If the supplies and ammunition do not arrive," del Canto wrote, "the army's situation will be desperate."[53]

For some Chileans, the war had already ended. On 10 July del Canto's men reached the town of La Concepción, where they discovered the mutilated bodies of its seventy-seven-man garrison commanded by Capt. Ignacio Carrera Pinto and its three cantineras, as well as those of two children, including an infant. The day before, some three hundred Peruvian troops plus fifteen hundred irregulars had attacked the town. Although outgunned and outmanned, the Chileans, many ill with typhus, refused to surrender. For twenty hours Carrera Pinto's men, some firing from buildings the Peruvians set ablaze, fought until they exhausted their ammunition. Then they fixed their bayonets, charging the Peruvians for one last time. No Chilean survived. The Peruvians butchered Carrera Pinto's men, often skewering body parts, including severed heads, on their lances like kabobs on a spit. The noncombatants suffered a more gruesome fate: the Peruvian apparently dragged the cantineras into the main plaza where they stripped the women naked and then cut them to pieces. The same fate also befell the two children. The Peruvians characterized the slaughter as retribution, because, as Cáceres observed, "there are no crimes which [the Chileans] have not [already] committed." M. F. Horta, a Peruvian journalist writing in *El Eco de Junín*, concurred: the Peruvians were legitimately retaliating for past Chilean atrocities. Del Canto could ill afford to mourn his martyred men. After burying the dead and removing the hearts of the officers, which he placed in glass bottles for shipment to Chile, del Canto razed Concepción, killing so many that he stained the town's soil red with blood, before resuming his march.[54] Cáceres, who believed he was on the verge of winning his first victory over the Chileans, reveled in del Canto's grief. "The confusion in the enemy is terrible," he gloated, "and it is hoped that not one returns to Lima."[55]

Cáceres's plan to trap the Chileans foundered when Lt. Francisco Meyer and seventy men of the Chilean Third Line Regiment repulsed the Peruvian assault on the Oroya Bridge; the door to del Canto's road of salvation still remained ajar.[56] But it was unclear how long a handful of beleaguered men could keep this vulnerable escape route open. Del Canto had to speed the movement of his men through the pass at Oroya before Cáceres managed to seal it. Although del Canto's contingent arrived at Tarma on 13 July, the commander of the Chilean units occupying Cerro de Pasco, Col. José Antonio Gutiérrez, had not. The longer del Canto delayed, of course, the more he risked his men, particularly those trying to keep open the transportation and communications lines.[57] Tired of enemy ambushes, without sleep, hungry, beset by a cold so fierce it killed the sick and the wounded in their stretchers, one unknown Chilean feared that his unit might suffer the same fate as those of La Concepción. "I have never seen a retreat like ours. Given our present condition," he noted, just reaching the Oroya Bridge "would be a victory."[58] Harsh though the trek might be, the Chileans had no choice but to persevere. After discovering the bodies of their naked, often decapitated comrades, some stabbed more than five hundred times, the Chilean soldiers realized that either they endured or they had better save their last bullet for themselves.[59]

Finally, Gutíerrez's men reached Tarma. Then, just after midnight on 17 July, del Canto's units, under strict orders not to smoke or speak loudly, began their tramp through the twelve-thousand-foot-high pass. The eight-mile-long string of men, largely unshod, their uniforms shredded, and carrying seventy-two litters, cleared the mountain passage by 6:30 a.m.[60] When Cáceres learned two hours later that del Canto's men had escaped, he unsuccessfully tried to chase them down. But fleeing the Mantaro Valley, no matter how miraculous, did not end del Canto's problems: his troops, who for days had subsisted on meat, water, and salt, still desperately needed food, while smallpox, typhus, dysentery, and typhoid, as well as other fevers, scourged them. Del Canto had to wait for assistance to arrive.

Lynch publicly praised del Canto for carrying out a retreat "whenever possible, . . . according to the security and health needs of our army," but privately he faulted him for taking so long to evacuate the altiplano.[61] The naval officer also criticized del Canto for carping that he had not received needed ammunition and transport, which, in fact, Lynch had sent.[62] The Red Prince had yet another cause for distress: the Sierra expedition consumed 534 soldiers—154 died in combat, 277 succumbed to disease, and 103 deserted—without snaring Cáceres.[63] Perhaps angry at del Canto for sustaining these losses or for charging that his superiors had maltreated him and his men, Lynch replaced him with Col. Martiniano Urriola.

Having pulled back, Lynch could station his troops in easily defensible areas: Callao and Lima as well as Cañete, Ica, and Chinca. To Lynch's great disappointment, these regions often lacked the financial or agricultural resources to support the occupation army. The Chilean admiral tried to levy new taxes, but since the Chileans could not tax neutral-owned property, which was often the most valuable, his occupation government's future seemed particularly bleak. Bankrupted by the old taxes, Peru simply could not pay the new levies Lynch needed to prosecute the war.[64] Given the miserable results of the second Sierra campaign, an Arequipa newspaper questioned whether Lynch would continue fighting in Peru at the cost of ruining Chilean agriculture and industry.[65]

Lynch also discovered that Peru's coastal provinces were almost as turbulent as those in the Sierra. In the spring of 1882, for example, Chileans had to blunt an assault of 500 men led by Col. Miguel Iglesias, who, as part of a larger scheme to expel the Chileans from Libertad Province, attacked the northern city of San Pablo. The assault failed, triggering a Chilean counteroffensive that captured Cajamarca, Admiral Montero's headquarters, and collected forty-five thousand silver pesos.[66] Lynch's troops had to return yet again to Pisco to levy taxes and to purge the Ica Valley of Colonel Mas's forces as well as other montonero bands.[67] Though Lynch was seemingly successful, in July a band of 400 irregulars compelled Maj. Máximo Correa of the Lontue Battalion to retreat to Tambo de Mora, where, thanks to the presence of the warship *Angamos*, they escaped.[68] Within weeks Col. Marco Arriagada returned with reinforcements, but their presence still did not deter montonero raids.[69] On the contrary, attacks on the railroad, the telegraph line, and the population centers convulsed the Ica Valley through October. The situation became so precarious that no sooner had Arriagada and his troops departed Ica to lead a punitive expedition into the interior than Colonel Mas attacked the poorly defended town. The 240 men of the Lontue held off 700 Peruvians for sixteen hours, until their comrades assaulted Mas's rear, killing perhaps as many as 230 men.[70]

Unrest also bedeviled Cañete, a rich sugar cane–producing southern valley. Lynch had hoped to bring "order and work" to Cañete by resuscitating the sugar exporting economy, thereby defraying the cost of occupation; he also wanted to encourage the production of foodstuffs to feed his men.[71] Conversely, Chilean occupation of Cañete would deny the montoneros a source of provisions and revenues, as well as a port through which they could import war materiel. Pacifying the Cañete Valley, however, proved extremely complicated. In 1879 the area's blacks, many of whom remained de facto slaves, began slaughtering the local indentured Chinese workforce.[72] This bloodshed continued into the 1880s. Apparently some montoneros participated in the carnage, murdering as many as one thousand Asians in just one day.[73] Clearly, if Lynch hoped to revive the valley's economy, his troops would have to remain in Cañete, because without Chinese labor the local hacendados could not cultivate their sugar cane plantations or staff their mills, and without the Chilean troops to protect them, the Asians would not stay.[74]

In May 1882, for example, when Vicente Ruíz's Batallón Curicó arrived at Tambo de Mora to liberate the Cañete Valley, revive its agriculture, and raise thirty to forty thousand silver pesos, they encountered opposition almost upon landing.[75] Braving montonero snipers, the Curicó pushed inland, only to discover that most local inhabitants had fled Cañete and that the guerrillas had taken refuge in the heights as well as along the heavily forested banks of a nearby river. Fearful of assaulting the well-entrenched Peruvians, Ruíz returned to Cañete almost empty-handed. (He did extract five thousand pesos from a nearby town's remaining inhabitants in return for not imprisoning them.) The episode depressed Ruíz: the montoneros, he reported, kill "our soldiers with impunity in the passes. We cannot pursue them because the river cannot be forded, because we cannot scale the mountains to outflank them, because of crossfire, and finally . . . we cannot see the enemy and only know he exists when he fires his weapon."[76]

Thus, Cañete remained anything but pacified. In December Arriagada led yet another expedition into the valley's interior in order to eradicate the local montonero bands.[77] He too failed. The Peruvian irregulars, heeding Gen. Miguel Iglesias's advice not to attack the Chileans, "except in the case when you have the greatest possibilities of triumphing," went to ground.[78] Fighting against a hidden enemy clearly frustrated the Chileans. Florentino Salinas angrily described how the montoneros, who escaped by using "routes unknown to their pursuers," invariably managed "to thwart the goals of those who pursue them." Conversely, the exhausted Chileans upon "returning to reoccupy their positions . . . do not know if they can sleep tranquilly or if they have to wait for an attack."[79]

Throughout Peru, the montoneros disrupted the transportation network, sabotaged the local economies, and raided towns. Lynch responded by sending troops to Ancón, Chancay, Huacho, Chimbote, Lambayeque, Trujillo, Chiclayo, Eten, Pimental, and Piura, ports or cities north of Lima, and to Cerro Azul, Pisco, and Tambo de Mora to the south.[80] This almost frenetic movement of men and supplies in and out of the countryside nonetheless failed to subdue Peru: stalwarts such as Colonels Mas and Bernasola still operated in Ica, while Iglesias continued to rule Cajamarca.

The reason for this failure is quite simple: the Chileans lacked manpower not only to capture but also to hold the enemy's territory. Theoretically, or at least according to the official table of organization, Lynch commanded an army of approximately 21,700 men. In fact, as noted earlier, his forces numbered only 15,499. (And after deducting for the sick and the deserters, this figure dropped to 13,090.) Of these, approximately 4,100 garrisoned the towns in the Sierra and 8,270 guarded Callao and Lima, leaving Lynch fewer than 1,000 troops to control Peru's northern and southern provinces.[81] Lacking the troops to take and occupy strategic locations, Chile's soldiers, particularly those in the south, became the equivalent of military firemen who rushed from one disaster to another in the vain hope restoring peace.

The outnumbered Chilean authorities had to try a variety of alternatives to revitalize Peru's economy, rather than stationing troops permanently in an area. Santiago's officials, for example, attempted to guarantee a ready supply of labor by encouraging refugees to return to their old jobs while prohibiting anyone from leaving the area without authorization. Fearing that vagrants might set a bad example, Chile's Col. Alejandro Gorostiaga ordered the unemployed to work on public works projects until they found permanent employment.[82]

Lynch also attempted to win support among the Peruvians. The Red Prince, for example, urged his soldiers to impose only those imposts that were necessary to defray the costs of occupation. In an attempt to impose equitable taxes, Lynch took into consideration local conditions, even reducing the financial burden if a regional economy was weak.[83] He also exhorted his officers to rule fairly any occupied area. The Lontue's Leóncio Tagle echoed these sentiments, indicating that he "would not hesitate to punish either [his] officers or enlisted men . . . [in order] to curb the most insignificant fault."[84] This tough but fair discipline paid dividends: the Peruvians and various foreign residents, according to Chilean reports, appreciated the exemplary conduct of Tagle's men, particularly when contrasted to the behavior of the Peruvian irregulars. Similarly, a Chilean officer noted that the townspeople approved his decision to execute one José Emiliano del Castillo for murdering a Spanish citizen.[85] The supposedly generous treatment of civilians did not mean that Chileans abjured the use of force. Tagle considered it perfectly reasonable, for example, to order a Peruvian official lashed five hundred times for refusing to divulge the location of some stolen goods and the whereabouts of local montonero bands.[86]

But Lynch's attempt to win the Peruvians' hearts and minds often had to yield to the demands of war. Some considered any harsh conduct quite proper. *El Comercio*, alleging that Peruvians would interpret Chilean generosity as a sign of weakness, advocated that Lynch's men to act more punitively. The Peruvians "are savages," the newspaper remarked, "and they have to be exterminated."[87] Certainly occupation officials enjoyed a great deal of leeway to do precisely that. Officers could summarily execute anyone belonging to a rebel group.[88] Col. Waldo Díaz, for example, sanctioned the shooting of individuals fomenting rebellion.[89] He also authorized his subordinates to execute any captured Peruvian officers if they made "the slightest effort to launch an uprising."[90] As noted earlier, Admiral Lynch also encouraged his men to take hostages and, if necessary, to execute even prominent citizens or former officers.[91]

Countless offences triggered the death penalty, including supporting montonero activity and carrying weapons or ammunition.[92] Chileans shot people who looked suspicious as well as those who failed to denounce them for looking suspicious.[93] Manuel J. Jarpa, the commander of the Zapadores, ordered his men to kill anyone who did not possess identification, who entered an area without reporting to the authorities, who tried to leave the same area without authorization, or who attempted to extort money.[94] In some places the authorities demanded that hacendados post a bond and then issue all agricultural workers papers that would serve as a safe conduct pass.[95] Even minor offenses sometimes proved fatal. When five Peruvians gave confusing responses to questions, for example, the authorities shot them all "as punishment and an example."[96] To underscore the folly of resisting, the army left twenty montonero bodies dangling from telegraph poles. In Ica, Díaz made a similar point by publicly displaying the corpses of five montoneros to local residents.[97]

Predictably, Peruvian-owned property also suffered. Lynch's men burned any home that harbored a montonero sniper.[98] Chileans even torched entire towns, such as Guadalupe, Carmen, and Collazo, for supposedly sheltering the guerrillas who destroyed two railroad bridges as well as raided nearby haciendas.[99] Troops of Maj. Daniel Silva Vergara set ablaze the northern town of Chota for serving as a base for attacking San Pablo; they also incinerated two churches upon learning that the montoneros had used them to store ammunition. Sunape's chapel went up in flames because the Peruvians utilized its tower as a lookout post to warn the population of approaching Chileans and because "it is necessary that this little town should not be left even its foundations, so it will stop cooperating with the bandits and cease giving refuge to the montoneros."[100] Some Chileans seemingly relished scorching the earth: the Zapadores' Jarpa proudly reported that his men had made a tabla rasa of one area in order to deprive the insurgents of supplies.[101] But eventually fighting against irregulars disenchanted many soldiers. The use of collective punishments, reprisals, arson, hostage taking, and summary executions, as well as battling the montoneros, somehow cheapened the

Chilean army. As Captain Saravia of the Rengo noted, "It would have been an honor to fall in Chorrillos or Miraflores but a shame now to die from these savages' bullet."[102]

Those Chileans stationed in Chiclayo, Trujillo, Libertad, and Lambayeque confronted a more deadly enemy: yellow fever. The authorities tried a variety of measures to prevent the onset of the disease, including cleaning up towns, changing the troops' rations, and ordering them to bathe in the ocean. When these measures did not stanch this epidemic, some units lost half their number. By May 1882, 743 men had fallen ill and 137 had died; four months later, Lynch reported that 419 soldiers had perished. Chilean authorities acknowledged that moving the troops out of the infected areas might improve their health, but they feared that shifting the men could have adverse political or military consequences. It appears that only the death of Lt. Col. José Urrutia, the commander of the Zapadores, and the division surgeon, Dr. Ismael Merino, convinced the Chileans to evacuate troops from the infected zone and to send them to the supposedly more benign cities of Eten, Pimentel, and San José.[103]

Throughout the summer, fall, and even winter of 1883, the Chilean army reploughed the same fields: its troops revisited Chincha Alta, Sama, Eten, Pisco, Tambo de Mora, Cañete, and Huaco. Unrest even erupted in the Locumba area, where a Cuban-born guerrilla leader, Juan Pacheco de Céspedes, operated. Described as the "worst executioner of the very people he should protect," Céspedes attacked Tacna in November. Thanks to the bravery of Lt. Enrique Strange, the local garrison managed to hold off the insurgents until a relief column arrived.[104] That the Peruvians could threaten Tacna, which the Chileans had controlled since 1880, indicated how little authority Lynch's men in fact exercised over supposedly pacified areas. Ending the attacks on the fringes of the Chilean empire, however, would not resolve the war: Santiago would have to subjugate Peru's heartland, not just its coastal regions, if it wished to emerge victorious from the war.

The Diplomacy of Defeat

Ending the war became as much a matter of domestic Peruvian politics and international diplomacy as of military action. Simply put, neither of those vying for the post of president of Peru—Piérola or García Calderón—would sign a peace treaty that ceded Tarapacá to Chile. Ironically, once Lynch arrested and deported him to the south of Chile, García Calderón, whom many Peruvians earlier excoriated as a Chilean puppet, became a symbol of resistance to Santiago. Before he left Peru, García Calderón appointed Adm. Lizardo Montero his vice president. Meanwhile, without the support of Col. José La Torre in the south, Montero in the north, or Cáceres in the center, Piérola quit. But before departing Lima in November 1881, the old caudillo urged his followers to transfer their loyalties to Cáceres. The general, however, refused to become involved in politics. Instead, he announced his support of Montero, who moved from Cajamarca to Arequipa, which became the seat of his government. In the few years since 1879, five men had ruled Peru. The landlocked admiral would not be the last.

President Garfield's death marked a sea change in Washington's foreign policy vis-à-vis Chile: in February 1882 President Chester Alan Arthur recognized Chile's right to annex Tarapacá, although he seemed less enthusiastic about the Chilean demand for Tacna and Arica. To implement these new policies, Frederick Frelinghuysen, Arthur's first secretary of state, sent James Partridge and Dr. Cornelius Logan as his ministers to Peru and Chile, respectively. These seasoned diplomats not only had to convince García Calderón and Montero to accept the loss of Tarapacá but also at least to consider ceding Tacna and Arica. They would also have to persuade Santa María to grant compensation to Peru for its lost territories. Initially, neither side appeared particularly accommodating. Chile's costly 1882 Sierra campaign, however, disenchanted many Chileans. Elements of Chile's press and its legislature urged the government to moderate its peace terms. If the war continued, warned *El Independiente*, it will "be the cancer of our prosperity."[105] Consequently, the president did soften his demands: Peru had to cede Tarapacá, but Santa María might agree to accept the temporary occupation, not the annexation, of Tacna.

Fortunately for Chile, changes had also occurred in Peru's political elites: a new contender, Gen. Miguel Iglesias, appeared. A veteran of the war's earlier battles, Iglesias became a Chilean prisoner after Chorrillos. Paroled, he replaced Montero as head of the Army of the North when the admiral moved his headquarters to Arequipa. Iglesias initially continued to oppose the Chileans, unsuccessfully trying to drive them from San Pablo in Cajamarca. Iglesias's defeat apparently became an epiphany: he finally realized that Peru could not militarily overwhelm the Chileans and that Lima would have to surrender Tarapacá if it wished to return to normality. Hence, on 31 August 1882 Iglesias used his hacienda at Montán to announce that he would sign a peace treaty that ceded territory to Chile. The general even convened a congress, the Asamblea del Norte, that granted him the power to negotiate with the Chileans.

Montero and Cáceres may have regarded Iglesias as a renegade, but Santa María hailed him as his messiah: the Chilean government dispatched an emissary to negotiate a peace treaty with Iglesias's representative, José de Lavalle, Peru's former envoy in 1879. The ensuing agreement, eventually enshrined as the Treaty of Ancón, ceded Tarapacá to Chile. It also permitted Chile to occupy Tacna and Arica for a period of ten years, when a plebiscite would presumably resolve whether these lands would remain in Santiago's hands or revert to Peru. In fact, the plebiscite was merely a device to gull the Peruvian public while allowing the Chileans to annex the two provinces.[106] Not only did General Cáceres reject Iglesias's proposal, he immediately launched an offensive to destroy him.

1883: The Second Sierra Campaign

The Chileans, who saw Iglesias as their way out of the war, began to nurture the supposed turncoat, while Cáceres tried to eradicate him. Hence, in early 1883 the Chileans launched another offensive to drive the montoneros from Lurín, Canta, and Chosica while simultaneously destroying Cáceres. The 1883 attack closely resembled the 1882 offensive; only the participants had changed. The plan called for Col. Juan León García to depart Lima in early April and head northeast, roughly parallel to the Chillón River, to Canta. Once in the altiplano, he was to engage and pursue Cáceres until he had destroyed him. Meanwhile Colonel Urriola would advance via train from Chosica to Chilca, while del Canto would depart from Lurín and move on the Chilean right flank via Oroya, also arriving in Chicla. Once they had reached that city, Urriola and del Canto would turn northwest in order to drive Cáceres north, right into the troops of García, who by that time would have advanced southeast from Canta to Chicla.[107] Ideally, the Chileans would snare their foe. Should that strategy fail, the Chileans had orders to hunt down and destroy Cáceres by other means.

As usual, nothing went as planned: montonero resistance slowed the Chilean offensive, costing one of the Buin's officers fourteen of his fifty men. Again the usual problems—exhaustion, poor animals, bad roads, and too little knowledge of the terrain—limited the Chileans' advance. Complaints about the lack of food, boots, and blankets again resurfaced. The outbreak of another typhus epidemic compounded the problems. The shortage of ammunition became so acute that the Coquimbo's officers decided to save 108 bullets (135 including the coup de grâce) by hanging, not shooting, twenty-seven captured montoneros.[108] Meanwhile, Cáceres eluded his pursuers and headed for the high Andes.

Many Chileans saw their mission as doomed: by mid-May, rumors abounded that the Buin, tired of all the sterile sacrifices, might mutiny.[109] Although the battalion remained loyal, the general situation degenerated: men continued to perish from disease as well as inadequate supplies of clothing, boots, and food. By the end of May García's most senior subordinates, tired of his brutal treatment of the men, indicated that they might cease obeying his orders. Eventually the relations became so acrimonious that del Canto relieved García of his command. This would not be the last personnel change: Admiral Lynch eventually decided to replace del Canto with Gen. Marco Arriagada.[110]

While he still retained his command—Arriagada did not assume command until mid-June—del Canto pursued General Cáceres, who retreated from Canta to Tarma and then moved northwest to Cerro de Pasco. As usual, the Peruvian troops, acclimated to the altiplano's altitude and, enjoying the support of the local populations, easily outdistanced the Chileans. The Peruvians moved northwest across the ridges of the Andes, first swerving slightly northeast to Huanuco and then turning northwest through Aguamiro before descending from the mountains until they reached Yungay. At this site of an historic Chilean victory, Cáceres's troops rendezvoused with Col. Issac Recabarren, whose fourteen hundred men increased the size of the insurgent army to thirty-four hundred.

Originally, Colonel Recabarren had been ordered to attack the seat of Iglesias's government in Cajamarca. However much he might wish to help, Arriagada, committed to destroying Cáceres, could not divert any troops to protect Iglesias. This task would fall to Chilean Col. Alejandro Gorostiaga, Trujillo's military and political head. In late May Admiral Lynch, ordered Gorostiaga to march into the interior so that he could prevent Recabarren's contingents from reaching Cajamarca. Should Recabarren still manage to link up with Cáceres, the combined Peruvian army would be too great for Gorostiaga's small task force to oppose. In that eventuality, Lynch instructed Gorostiaga to retreat to the north and to request reinforcements, all the while interposing his men between Iglesias and the advancing Peruvians.[111] At the head of approximately one thousand men, Gorostiaga departed Trujillo, reaching the Andean foothills in mid-May. The poor weather, however, delayed by four days his traversing a twelve-thousand-foot-high pass, and additional time would elapse before Gorostiaga reached his objective, Huamachuco, on 21 May 1883.

By then the Chileans learned that Colonel Recabarren had successfully rendezvoused with Cáceres. In need of reinforcements, Colonel Gorostiaga, as per his instructions, requested that Maj. Herminio González and his 581 men march from Trujillo to meet him at Angasmarca. González would depart on 29 June, a few weeks after Maj. Sofanor Parra, leading a 180-man task force, had also left Trujillo to join Gorostiaga.[112] If all went according to plan, Cáceres army, fleeing from Arriagada in the south, would rush headlong to the north, only to collide with Gorostiaga's recently reinforced army. Lynch made it explicitly clear that he would not accept "climate, bad weather, or difficult roads as an excuse, mitigation, and even less as a justification" for failing to fulfill his mission. Gorostiaga had to triumph, or else.[113]

After two months of marching through snow and rain, of wading through rivers up to their necks in icy water, of enduring altitude sickness—which felled two hundred men—Arriagada's column appeared finally to have caught Cáceres.[114] Sandwiched between the Andes Negro and the Andes Blanco, with Gorostiaga blocking the north as Arriagada pushed from the south, the Peruvians' position seemed hopeless. But rather than surrender, Cáceres audaciously moved northeast, through the 18,800-foot-high Llanganuco Pass and across the Cordillera Blanca. Cáceres's decision bordered on desperate. Subsisting on maize and cocoa and bedeviled by *sorroche*, the Peruvian soldiers trekked over the Andean mountain on trails so narrow that the troops, not the pack animals, had to carry the artillery.[115] Not all who struggled to reach to reach Pomabamba on the Cordillera Blanca's eastern slope on 26 June survived: men and beasts regularly slipped off the paths snaking up the cordillera. Just to ensure that Arriagada could not follow them, Cáceres ordered his engineers to dynamite the trails they had used.[116]

The Peruvians could have saved the explosives. Fed misinformation by the local population, Arriagada believed that Cáceres had turned not north but south. Thus, the Chilean ordered his army to reverse direction in hopes of overtaking the fleeing Peruvians. Initially Lynch supported Arriagada's decision, fearing that a Cáceres breakout to the south would have "rendered fruitless so much effort . . . [while] demeaning our forces' enterprise and good leadership."[117] But in late June Gorostiaga informed Lynch that Cáceres had used an Indian uprising to divert Arriagada while he escaped to the north.[118] This news infuriated and perhaps even frightened the Red Prince because all that stood between Iglesias and Cáceres was Gorostiaga's small command. Lynch, of course, quickly informed Arriagada that Cáceres had turned to the north, but neither a warning nor a threatened letter of reprimand could convince the colonel to pursue the Peruvian.[119]

Meanwhile, as Colonel Gorostiaga, still hoping to block Cáceres's drive on Miguel Iglesias's troops, continued to retreat, the Peruvian had turned to the northwest and, after descending from the Cordillera Blanca's western flank, emerged near Angasmarca. Although successful, the Peruvian odyssey "had been extraordinarily painful because of the lack of forage for the animals, the scant rations provided to the troops, the impenetrability of the roads, crossed by the high and numerous mountain spurs, and the rigor of the temperature." In truth, the expedition had become a convoy of the ill and the lame. Officers no longer rode, because their horses had died, as had 70 percent of the Peruvians' pack animals.[120]

Cáceres could ill afford to rest his exhausted men: a captured Chilean dispatch revealed that González had departed Trujillo in order to reinforce Gorostiaga's ranks. Anxious to intercept his relief column before it could rendezvous with Gorostiaga at Huamachuco, Cáceres planned to ambush the Chileans when they marched through a particularly narrow pass located between the towns of Tres Ríos and Tres Cruces. Reaching Tres Ríos in time, however, proved difficult. Burned by the frigid altiplano winds and subsisting largely on coca tea, the Peruvian commander force-marched his men at night on mountain paths illuminated only by torchlight. His heroic efforts failed to achieve their mission: Cáceres reached Tres Cruces just in time to watch the Chileans proceed north. Recabarren, not Cáceres, was responsible for this failure: his decision to make an example of some deserters by publicly flogging them delayed by approximately an hour the column's departure, just enough time to allow the Chileans to clear the pass. (Supposedly Cáceres did not appear too distressed, noting, "I will have time to devour these Chileans.") Praying that González might rest his men en route, however, Cáceres ordered his men to march through the dark in hopes of catching them unawares. But the Chileans, aware of the Peruvian presence, did not halt for the night, reaching Huamachuco on 7 July. Cáceres had suffered a double disaster: not only did he fail to stop González, whose troops plus those of Parra increased the size of Gorostiaga's army to fifteen hundred men, but he lost six hundred of his soldiers, who, cloaked by the night, deserted.[121]

On 8 July as Cáceres's men approached Huamachuco, they learned that the Chileans had abandoned the town. Realizing that Peruvian artillery, which held the high ground overlooking the hamlet, could easily shell his troops, Gorostiaga moved his men to Cerro Sazón, a more defensible position to the north. Separated from Cáceres's troops by a flat plain, the Llano de Purrubamba, Gorostiaga placed the Batallón Talca plus two guns on his east, two companies of the Zapadores with four guns in the center, and the Batallón Concepción with one last artillery piece on the west. The Chilean's cavalry, supply and medical sections remained at the rear, behind a stone wall.

Cáceres recognized that the coming battle might be decisive: defeating Gorostiaga's army would leave General Iglesias defenseless. And with his foe gone, Cáceres doubtless prayed that a discouraged Chilean president would realize the futility of continuing the struggle and abandon

Table 21. Battle of Huamachuco, 10 July 1883

Chile

Rgt. Cazadores a Caballo	Lt. Col. Alberto Novoa	183
Rgt. Zapadores	Capt. Ricardo Canales	222
Btn. Concepción	Lt. Col. Hermino González	532
Btn. Talca	Lt. Col. Alejandro Cruz	620
Brigada de Artillería	Maj. Gumecindo Fontecilla	115
	Total	1,672

Peru

Army of the Center	Col. Francisco Secada
1a. División	Col. Manuel Cáceres
Btn. Gloriosa Tarapacá, N. 1	Col. Mariano Espinosa
Btn. Zepita, N. 2	Col. Justiniano Borgoño
2a. División	Col Juan Gastó
Btn. Marcavalle, N. 6	Col. Felipe Crespo
Btn. Concepción, N. 7	Col. Pedro Carrión
3a. División	Col. Maximo Tafur
Btn. Junín N. 3	Col. Juan Vizcarra
Btn. Cazadores de Jauja, N. 9	Col. Miguel Luna
4a. División	Capt. de Navío Jermán Astete
Btn. Cazadores de Apata, N. 8	Col. Diego Goizueta
Btn. San Jerónimo, N. 10	Col. Melchor González
Es. Cazadores del Perú	Maj. Santiago Zavala
Es. Tarma	Maj. Agustín Zapatel
Artillería	Col. Federico Ríos
Army of the North	Col. Isaac Recabarren
1a. División	Col. Mariano Aragonez
Btn. Pucará, N. 4	Lt. Col. Ponde de León
Btn. Pisagua, N. 5	Col. Mariano Aragonez
2a. División	
Btn. Tarma, N. 11	Lt. Col. Julio Aguirre
Btn. Huallaga, N. 12	
Es. Húsares	Lt. Col. J. Cabrera
Artillería	Col. Federico Rios
13 cannon	

Sources: Machuca, *Cuatro campañas*, 4:398; *El Eco de Junín*, June 1883, in Ahumado Moreno, *Guerra del Pacífico*, 7:209–10; Cáceres, *Guerra del 79*, 218–19.

his demand for Tarapacá. Consequently, the Peruvian commander took particular care to place his men in the foothills of Mount Cuyurca so that they would not simply defeat but destroy Gorostiaga's army.[122] Clearly the Chileans appeared quite vulnerable. In their haste to evacuate Huamachuco, they had fled with only the clothes on their backs. Worse, Gorostiaga's men had not eaten until they managed to capture four head of cattle, which they devoured almost raw. On the night of 9 July, the first anniversary of the Battle of Concepción, some Chileans doubtless feared they might suffer the same fate as their martyred countrymen.

The Battle of Huamachucho began slowly. The adversaries spent 9 July desultorily exchanging rifle and artillery fire as well as various vulgar insults without inflicting any damage, real or psychic. The following morning, a fog cloaked the valley floor when Gorostiaga sent Capt. Ricardo Canales of the Zapadores to discover the Peruvians' strength and positions. Forming two skirmish lines, about two hundred Zapadores moved toward the Peruvians. The Chileans had advanced about 250 paces when Cáceres's Batallón Junín fired a volley and then attacked. As some Peruvian units moved toward the Chileans others began probing Gorostiaga's flanks. After approximately fifteen minutes, the Zapadores, running low on ammunition, received orders to retreat. As they did so, the Peruvians counterattacked, trying to destroy the Chileans before they could reach their own lines. Fearing for the safety of Canales's men, four companies from the Batallón Concepción moved to protect the Chileans' flank and center. Cáceres upped the ante, committing the Batallón Jauja as well as the Junín, which attacked in a long skirmish line. Threatening to envelop both flanks of Gorostiaga's infantry, the Peruvians, urged on by their bands' music and bugle calls, pushed the Chileans back toward their trenches on Cerro Sazón. At the same time, Cáceres's artillery moved toward the battlefield to provide close fire support for the Peruvian offensive.

The men of the Concepción managed to halt the Peruvian assault, but the Talca on the Chilean flank encountered more resistance. Consequently, Gorostiaga ordered Parra's cavalry to disrupt the enemy advance by charging, but the rocky hills prevented the mounted Chileans from dispersing the Peruvian infantry. Meanwhile, the Chilean artillery fired first on the Peruvian right to prevent it from overrunning Gorostiaga's men and then on Cáceres's artillery. To provide the advancing Peruvians close fire support, Cáceres ordered his cannons forward. Having almost scaled Cerro Sazón, it seemed as if Cáceres had triumphed. Suddenly, the Peruvians lost their momentum: deprived of artillery support—the guns were still being moved forward—and having exhausted their ammunition and without bayonets, Cáceres's men began to fall back. The Chilean infantry, sensing their advantage and yelling a variety of racial and homophobic slurs, charged, as did Parra's cavalry. Calling for the Peruvian troopers' heads and yelling "take no prisoners," the Chilean horsemen scattered their dispirited foes, who began fleeing for their lives. By 12:30 p.m. the fighting had ceased, leaving approximately sixty dead Chileans and one hundred wounded. The Zapadores and the Concepción suffered the heaviest losses, although the latter's mascot, a goat, survived a battlefield wound to return, uneaten, to Trujillo with its masters.[123]

The battle cost the Peruvians perhaps twelve hundred dead, together with thirty-three of its most senior officers, including a general. Not all fell in the course of the battle: the Chileans shot those captured officers who, because they violated their parole, were considered montoneros. Nor did Gorostiaga's troops spare the Peruvian enlisted men, including the wounded. Among the most famous to perish was Col. Leóncio Prado, who suffered such a serious wound that he was abed when the Chileans captured him. In enormous pain, Prado appealed for mercy to those Chilean officers who were his brother Masons. When that tactic failed, he accepted his fate with calm, only begging his executioners to spare his eyes. Still seated in his bed, he first finished a cup of coffee and then signaled that his executioners should open fire. Cáceres did not share Prado's fate: thanks to his horse, Elegante, he escaped. Few, if any, of Huamachuco's inhabitants enjoyed Cáceres's good fortune: according to an eyewitness those residents of Huamachuco whom the vanquished Peruvians and the victorious Chilean did not rape, they murdered, and that which they did not loot, they destroyed.[124]

Revolted by the stench of decomposing bodies and the sight of scavengers and birds of prey feasting on rotting corpses and animal carcasses, Gorostiaga and his troops happily departed Huamachucho, hoping that they had finally defeated Cáceres.[125] But fearing that the Peruvians might still cause them mischief, the Chileans dared not leave the area. Only after having dedicated most of July to pursuing the enemy, did Gorostiaga's "weakened [and] exhausted" troops return to Lima.[126]

Lynch, perhaps in retaliation for Arriagada's failure to catch Cáceres, ordered him to remain in the highlands until he was sure that General Iglesias was safe and the area was pacified. Then and only then did he and his men return to the coast.[127] By the time he reached Lima, 22 percent of his 3,334-man army had died, suffered from wounds or disease, or deserted.[128] Col. Martiniano Urriola, complaining about the lack of supplies, particularly food, the "alien" climate that sapped the men's health, and the pack animals so decrepit that the horses walked more slowly than the infantry, also wished to end his Andean purgatory.[129] Lynch concurred: the severe weather and food shortages had already felled so many of his troops that he urged the minister of war to withdraw the men before the onset of the rainy season further compromised their health.[130] The Chilean government agreed: Peruvian participation in the War of the Pacific had ended. Still, in the war's last eighteen months, Lynch's 15,000-man army suffered 2,407 illnesses or wounds. In that same time, 142 died from combat injuries, 593 died from disease, and 674 deserted.[131]

The Final Days of the Peruvian War

Many Chilean officers hoped that the defeat at Huamachuco might have so damaged "Cáceres's prestige and power and with it his criminal ambitions" that he would capitulate. He did not. Accompanied by a handful of officers and collecting survivors from Huamachuco along the way, Cáceres managed to elude Chilean patrols, reaching Ayacucho by 12 August. After informing Montero of his defeat, the general raised yet another army, which eventually numbered approximately five hundred men.

Cáceres was not the only thorn in Lynch's side. At the end of August 1883, the Chilean had ordered Colonel Urriola "to destroy Pastor Dávila's montonero band [also consisting mainly of the survivors of Huamachuco] and to prevent Cáceres from organizing, with the help of the people of this *departamento*, any new montoneros."[132] The Chileans also wished to eradicate other anti-Iglesias caudillos such as Becerra and Bar-reneche in Lambayeque and the perennially dangerous Pacheco Ces-pedes in Tacna. Suppressing regional caudillos did not always involve bloodshed. Lynch indicated, for example, that Chile would happily grant montonero leaders, like Dávila, political favors if they would but come in from the cold. Sometimes the Chileans managed to convince local chiefs, like Fernando Seminario of Piura as well as others, to turn their coats.[133] While politically astute, these arrangements sometimes bordered on the surreal: after years of trying to destroy him, the Chil-eans turned over control of Chincha Alta to the former guerrilla leader Col. Octavio Bernasola.[134]

With Cáceres nursing his losses in Ayacucho, Lynch could finally con-front Montero's four-thousand-man army in Arequipa. Eradicating the admiral's mountain redoubt could have proved costly. But Santa María, perhaps following the Union's "Anaconda strategy" in the U.S. Civil War, decided to starve the Andean city into submission. The president called for one portion of his army to capture Mollendo, thus severing supply lines between that port and Arequipa. Another contingent would ad-vance from Tacna either through Ilo or Pacocha to seize Moquegua, thereby severing the rail line to Arequipa and effectively cutting off Mon-tero from the south and west. Meanwhile, a Chilean attack on Ayacucho would limit access from the north. Montero's only contact with the world would have been northeast to Puno and Bolivia.

Thus, a few days before the anniversary of Chile's independence, on 18 September, Col. José Velásquez departed Tacna leading twenty-two hundred men—that number subsequently increased—to capture Mo-quegua. The colonel departed but not in high spirits: in a private letter he indicated that he had tired of a "war of guerrillas, of gorges, of defiles, of galgas, coming and going, etc., . . . of the pointless marches and coun-termarches that always, in my judgment, then as now, will be the cause of the complete disorganization of the most disciplined armies."[135]

As Colonel Velásquez moved from Tacna to Moquegua, del Canto, commanding another three thousand men, sailed from Callao on 3 Oc-tober. Landing at Pacocha, he immediately marched inland to join Ve-lásquez, whose men had reached Moquegua at the end of September. Following del Canto's arrival, Velásquez divided his army in two, assigning two thousand men to Col. Victor Ruíz and three thousand to Canto. The march inland, while difficult, did not take a heavy toll on the men because the Chileans finally had learned the logistical lessons of their earlier desert campaigns. Meanwhile, Colonel Tagle's Batallón Lontue sailed from Ica, landing at Islay to occupy Mollendo on 23 October, thereby severing any supply lines connecting the port to Montero's headquarters.

Thus, almost two months after Chile's victory at Huamachuco, Colonel Urriola's men departed Huancayo to invest Ayacucho. Within four hours, his troops came under enemy sniper fire. Del Canto had been wise enough to avoid errors of earlier marches through the deserts, but not so Colonel Urriola: the trek proved taxing as the Chileans had to struggle up steep mountain trails, beset by rain, the piercing cold, *sorroche*, and a lack of food, all the while dodging rock-hurling Indians. As before, the montoneros picked off Chilean stragglers.[136]

Increasingly, it appeared that the nature of the conflict had changed. The Indian irregulars, fighting not solely the Chilean invaders but "white men from all parties," looted towns and seized the land of local property owners. Urriola ignored these anti-white *jacqueries* as long as they confined themselves to attacking Peruvians: fighting the Indians, as he once observed, produced "little profit and no glory." Still, if the Indian violence compromised his mission to destroy Cáceres's legions, Urriola could not permit them to interdict supplies, attack Chilean patrols, or sack towns.[137]

By 18 September, the Chileans entered Huancavelica, where they camped before moving on to Acobamba. Eight days later, Huanta, a town seven leagues from Ayacucho, fell. Welcomed by most of Huanta's inhabitants, who had suffered at the hands of pro-Cáceres Indians, Urriola's troops rested until 30 September, when they completed the last phase of the march, taking Ayacucho on 1 October without having to do battle. With Urriola still in Ayacucho and Velásquez in Monquegua, Arequipa was now effectively isolated from all except Bolivia.

After forty days of living in a sea of hostile Indians, of paying exorbitant prices for food, of encountering increasingly greater difficulty finding forage for his mounts, and of running low on ammunition, Urriola requested permission to abandon his mountain redoubt. Having learned that Arequipa had fallen and thus sure that abandoning Ayacucho would not compromise Lynch's plans, Urriola unilaterally decided to move his men toward Huancayo.

The march north through the Mantaro Valley proved more painful than the journey south: Urriola might have professed no animus toward the Indians, but apparently they did not feel similarly. Ambushes and falling gaglas picked off Urriola's men, and the Indians' destruction of bridges drove the Chileans to ford fast-moving rivers, which consumed troops, their equipment, and their pack animals.[138] Despite the hardships, Urriola's people reached Huancayo on 26 October and then, after passing through Chicla Pass, arrived in Lima on 12 December. Urriola's expedition accomplished little: Cáceres reoccupied Ayacucho and then marched to Huancayo, which became his provisional capital.[139]

Everyone in Arequipa expected that the Chileans would move on the Andean citadel. Chile's prospects were daunting: Montero had improved the city's defenses by mounting naval guns on earthen parapets, and the Bolivian leader, Narciso Campero, had also sent the local seven-thousand-man garrison—two thousand regulars and five thousand unruly national guardsmen—and a large number of new rifles as well as fifteen Krupp field guns.[140] With his army increasing in size and his arsenals filled with weaponry, Montero melodramatically vowed that "he would fight in the country and in the city, in the streets and in the plazas, and even in Church" before he would surrender.[141] The admiral's bellicose rhetoric may not have impressed the Chileans, but it certainly terrified Arequipa's burghers. Fearing the damage that a battle might inflict on Arequipa, the town's elites demanded that the admiral make his last stand anywhere but inside their city.[142] Consequently, Montero ordered his men to dig emplacements on Huasacachi and Jamta, two ridges that guarded the southern approaches to the city.

But on 22 October, the Chileans, using a little-known path, outflanked the position's defenders at Huasacachi. At dawn of 23 October, realizing that Velásquez's men controlled both their flanks, the Peruvians retreated. Some took up a position at Puquina, the high ground dominating the road to Arequipa. If defended properly, the Chileans might not have been able to scale Puquina's heights without incurring enormous casualties. But the defenders of Puquina were anything but resolute.

When the Chileans launched their offensive, Arequipa's stalwarts threw down their weapons and ran.[143]

It quickly became clear that the Chilean troops would soon capture Arequipa. Curiously, few of the city's residents believed Montero's bombastic declarations. As one cynic noted, for the admiral to fulfill his promise of fighting from house to house, "it would be necessary for him to be a superior man, and General [*sic*] Montero was not cast in the mold of superior men."[144] Events proved the doubters correct: when Arequipa's church bells signaled the impending Chilean attack, the admiral bolted to board a train to Puno. Obviously dismayed at this betrayal, a furious national guard unit marched to the station, where it compelled Montero to sneak back to the city.

With the admiral hiding, more guard units rebelled. Only the arrival of the regular troops, who sometimes had to fire on the unruly militiamen, restored a modicum of order. When mutineers murdered one of Montero's aides and the mob killed a local government official, Montero and Gen. César Canevaro fled a second time for the Bolivian border, which they managed to cross. Once the admiral had decamped, the local municipal government arranged for the consular corps to declare Arequipa an open city. By now the city's elites yearned for the Chileans to restore order. On 29 October, some of Colonel Velásquez's men entered Montero's former citadel.[145] They would later march on Puno to collect any abandoned weapons and to ensure that no Peruvian aspirant to power would use the area to regroup his forces.[146]

Unsurprisingly, Montero defended his decision to flee to Bolivia. Writing Cáceres, he claimed that the citizens of Arequipa had refused to wage a guerrilla war, and rather than turn his army's guns on the volatile national guard units, he quit. Ensconced in exile, the admiral urged Cáceres to continue battling against the "conqueror colluding with the traitors."[147] His attitude stands in sharp contrast with that of his companion Canevaro, who yearned to see Peru end the war and begin to rebuild a government.[148]

In 1883 Iglesias accepted the Treaty of Ancón, which surrendered Tarapacá and permitted Chile to occupy Tacna and Arica for ten years, at which time a plebiscite would determine which nation would retain these provinces. Regrettably for Iglesias, the agreement only ended the state of war with Chile; he still had to battle Cáceres. But the resistance leader, following "an anguished internal struggle, . . . decided to accept the Treaty of Ancón, as an accomplished fact." His good will, however, did not extend to "the government that Chile firmly established."[149] Thus, the general returned to fighting Iglesias, who, after months of struggle, resigned the presidency in favor of Cáceres.

Cáceres was not the only Peruvian officer to continue the impromptu war: in November 1883 Pacheco led a surprise attack on Pachia. Although he managed to inflict some damage, the Chileans forced him to retreat. This time he did not stop running until he reached Bolivia, where the authorities, citing his disruptive behavior, wisely rejected his offer of assistance.[150]

The War's Finale

Bolivia had not fought since its defeat at Tacna. And as long as the Chileans concentrated on destroying the remnants of Peruvian resistance, Narciso Campero knew that he and his nation could rest easy. Bolivia's leaders wisely used their de facto armistice to purchase modern weapons, reform the army, and recruit new men, whom they schooled in the latest tactics. The results of these reforms delighted the Bolivian government. The Bolivian soldier, the minister of war intoned, "has been converted into a citizen armed to defend the law instead of an instrument destined to enthrone usurpation and tyranny."[151]

The new leaders might have created a new soldier, but the army in which he served was still too small: only thirty-five hundred troops to oppose the five thousand battle-tested Chileans garrisoned in the Puno. Engaging Lynch's army would require at least ten thousand troops, far more than the Bolivian treasury could support.[152] Like it or not, the Bolivian statesman Nataniel Aguirre concluded, the nation would have to accept any treaty, "however onerous," providing it did not jeopardize the nation's independence.[153]

Some Bolivians still argued that signing a separate peace treaty would constitute a betrayal of its alliance with Peru. But Maríano Baptista, one of the leaders of the propeace faction, rejected this notion: "We want peace because the country is tired of this passive and incomprehensible state of war, which serves only to absorb the nation's resources and to labor in favor of militarism." To settle for less would, in essence, indenture Bolivia to Peru.[154]

Bolivians, of course, hoped that Chile might return the Atacama Desert or, barring that, at least give La Paz a piece of Tacna or Arica to compensate for losing its seacoast. But even had they wished to do so, the Chileans could not gratify this desire: the Treaty of Ancón specified that only the 1893 plebiscite would definitively determine the ownership of Tacna and Arica. Obviously, President Santa María could not cede Bolivia land that his government did not legally own. Besides, he saw no reason for being so generous to Bolivia. Given this situation, it became increasingly clear that the two nations would have to negotiate a truce, not a permanent peace treaty. Yet, from Chile's perspective, Bolivia seemed to pursue contradictory goals, speaking of negotiating a settlement while simultaneously taking delivery of weapons and trying to raise money to pursue the war option.

After three years, Chileans had tired of the war. Thus, when the propeace faction in Bolivia won the legislature's support, Chile agreed to parley with its two envoys, Belisario Suárez and Belisario Boeto. The negotiations that began in November 1883, however, dragged on for months. Eventually, Bolivia's wrangling infuriated President Santa María. Never the most patient of men, he ordered Dublé de Almeida, commander of the Puno region, to mass his troops on the Bolivian border and to end all shipping on Lake Titicaca. In one of the more picturesque episodes of the war, the minister of the navy told the navy to send by train the torpedo boat *Colo Colo* first to Arequipa and then Puno, where it would sweep any Bolivian or Peruvian ships from the 12,500-foot-high lake.[155] Bolivia got the message: in April 1884 it granted Chile the right to occupy its littoral in return for peace, however temporary, and a share of the revenues that the local customs house would generate. Five years to the month from its start, the War of the Pacific had ended.

Certain factors favored the waging of a guerrilla war. Chile's attempt to impose taxes failed both fiscally as well as politically. Beset by bad weather, which reduced their harvests, Peru's rural poor deeply resented the occupiers' attempts to live off the land, which in this case meant living off the Indians' sweat equity. Thus, each Chilean foraging expedition or military reprisal simply drove more Indians into Cáceres's army or his montonero bands.

Scholars like Nelson Manrique claim that racism motivated Chilean behavior, that they regarded the Peruvian Indian as "organically a coward" and that, fundamentally, Chile's policies sought to subjugate Peru by annihilating its indigenous population. This same disdain supposedly led the Chileans to indulge in the wide-scale rape of Indian women, a policy that allegedly inspired the Peruvians to mutilate the genitalia of Chilean wounded or dead.[156] Conversely, the Quechua-speaking Cáceres became the Indians' savior when he abolished the Indian tribute and levied taxes only on the wealthy. Contrast that behavior with that of the Chileans, who, the Peruvians claimed, went through the highlands like an Araucanian *malon* or raid.[157] Perhaps threatened by an increasingly radicalized Indian population, Cáceres accepted the Ancón treaty. He still continued his vendetta against Iglesias, whose regime, a British diplomat noted, "will only last while he has the support of Chilean bayonets."[158] Meanwhile, Bolivia, facing the possibility of an attack on its heartland, also capitulated. Peace, however tenuous, had finally arrived.

Conclusion

In 1879 the armies of Bolivia, Chile, and Peru were, to varying degrees, unsophisticated, even primitive, organizations consisting mainly of infantry units supported by smaller contingents of artillery and cavalry. These armed forces contained no medical, quartermaster, signal, supply, or transportation corps, and what the combatants proudly called their general staffs were often ad hoc creations, formed on the spur of the moment and often staffed by the army's dross, certainly not its intellectual elites. At the conflict's conclusion, Peru's prewar army no longer existed, and that of Bolivia had changed. And, because of existing flaws—the Moneda still allowed the wealthy to buy command of militia units—some foreigners argued that "the Chilean army could not be considered as such, at least if considering it in the European sense of the word."[1]

New technology—the breech-loading rifle, the machine gun, the steel-barreled artillery, the armored warship, the torpedo, and the land mine—may have influenced the outcome of the hostilities that convulsed the United States during its civil war and Europe during the Franco-Prussian conflict, but not so much the struggle between Chile and the Allies. Certainly the conduct of the naval side of the war, though it involved ironclads, seems remarkably devoid of innovation. The Peruvian and Chilean fleets, like two bare-knuckled fighters, inelegantly traded blows until one had obliterated the other. The few conclusions emerging from the maritime side of the conflict appeared to prove more negative than positive propositions: the naval ram did not work, and deploying a spar, or even a Lay torpedo, seemed to endanger the attacker as much as his supposed foe.

Table 22. Estimated Chilean combat casualties

Battle	Date	Killed in Action	Wounded
Calama	23 March 1879	7	6
Iquique	21 May 1879	51	6
Arica - naval	28 August 1879	9	12
Angamos	8 October 1879	1	9
Pisagua	2 November 1879	58	155
Pisagua - naval	12 November 1879	8	20
San Francisco	19 November 1879	61	176
Tarapaca	27 November 1879	546	212
Arica - naval	27 February 1880	10	10
Los Angeles	22 March 1880	4	40
Alianza/Tacna	26 May 1880	434–58	1,373–509
Arica	7 June 1880	117	355
Chorrillos	13 January 1881	797	2,522
Miraflores	15 January 1881	502	1,622
Arriagada	1883 Expedition	130	574
Huamachuco	10 July 1883	56–66	101–19

Sources: E. Ramírez to Commanding Officer, Operations of the North, Calama, 24 March 1879, 1:126, Iquique Nicolás Redolés, "Relación nominal i clasificada del personal," Iquique, 5 June 1879, 1:323–25, C. Condell to Admiral Williams, Antofagasta, 6 June 1879, 1:297, "Muertos y heridos durante la espedición sobre Moquegua y acción de Los Anjeles," 2:438, "Razon de las bajas del Ejercito de Chile en la batalla del Campo de la Alianza," 2:598–99, Manuel Baquedano to Minister of War, Arica, 21 June 1880, 3:178, "Anexo al parte oficial," in Ahumada Moreno, *Guerra del Pacífico*, 8:193, J. F. Merino to Commander-in-Chief, Division of the North, Huamachuco, 11 July 1883, 8:214, Alejandro Gorostiaga to Commander-in-Chief of the Army, Huamachuco, 12 July 1883, 8:212, Cárlos Vargas Clark [Gorostiaga's divisional surgeon] to Aniceto Vergara A., Humachuco, 14 July 1883, 8:224–25, in Ahumada Moreno, *Guerra del Pacífico*; G. Riveros to Commanding Officer of the Fleet, Antofagasta, 10 October 1879, Chile, Ministry of War, *Memoria de Guerra y Marina, 1879,* 20; E. Escala to Minister of War, Hospicio, 10 November 1879 and n.d., 47–48, 65, Luis Arteaga to Commander-in-Chief, Santa Catalina, 4 December 1879, 75–79, Manuel Baquedano to Commander-in-Chief of the Army, Moquegua, 27 March 1880, 88, José Goñi to Minister of the Navy, Valparaíso, 8 September 1879, 159, Luis Castillo to Minister of the Navy, 27 February 1880, 200–201, in Chile, Ministry of War, *Memoria de Guerra y Marina, 1880*; Adolfo Silva, "El estado que manifiesta el número de Jefes, Oficiales e individuos de tropa muertos i heridos en las batallas de Chorrillos i Miraflores, los dias 13 i 15 de enero de 1881," Chile, Ministry of War, *Partes oficiales*; Molinare, *Historia*, 274.
The statistics on battlefield deaths are inaccurate because they do not provide follow up information on those who subsequently died of their wounds.

The military side of the War of the Pacific should have reinforced the lessons of the recent American and European conflicts: if doubling the range of the newer muzzle-loading rifles gave an enormous advantage to entrenched troops defending against an attack, then the introduction of the modern breech-loading small arm, such as the Comblain II, particularly when used in conjunction with the breech-loading and rifled artillery pieces, made it virtually suicidal to attack in massed formations over

Table 23. Allied casualties

Battle	Date	Killed in Action	Wounded	Killed in Action and Wounded	Prisoners of War
Calama	23 March 1879	16			30
Iquique	21 May 1879	2	19		
Angamos	8 October 1879	31	3		162
Pisagua	2 November 1879			567	56
San Francisco	19 November 1879	135–500	88	400–6,000	87
Tarapaca	27 November 1879	236	261		76
Los Angeles	22 March 1880	14–28	20–25	100	64
Alianza/Tacna	26 May 1880	600–1,500	1,300	2,500–3,000	1,300
Arica	7 June 1880	700–1,200	200		1,328
Chorrillos	13 January 1881	4,000–7,500	3,000		2,000–3,000
Miraflores	15 January 1881	6,000	3,000		3,000
Huamachuco	10 July 1883	1,200		800	

Sources: "Lista nominal de jefes, oficiales, i tropa pows," 1:131, Santiago Tavora, "Razon de heridos y muertos," Iquique, 21 May 1879, 1:325–26, Luis A. Castillo, Antofagasta, 10 October 1879, 1:500–501, El Ayudante del Estado Mayor Boliviano, 2:86, Telegramas, Caldera, 9 November 1879, 2:122, Erasmo Escala to Minister of War, 25 November 1879, 2:135, "Relacion de los muertos y heridos peruanos," 2:201–2, Andrés Gamarra to General, Second Army of South, Omate, 4 April 1880, 2:440, Julio C. Chocano to General, First Division of Second Army of the South, Omate, 31 March 1880, 2:441–42, Martin Alvárez to Lieutenant Colonel, Chief of Staff of First Division of Second Army of South, Omate, 28 March 1880, 2:442–43, Pedro J. Armayo to Narciso Campero, La Paz, 12 June 1880, 2:590, El Ferrocaril (Santiago), 6 June 1880, and El Nacional (Lima), 26–28 June 1880, 2:617–20, Manuel Baquedano to Minister of War, Arica, 21 June 1880, 3:178, Manuel C. de la Torre to Secretary of State, Arica, 9 June 1880, 3:186, Eulogio Altamirano to President, Iquique, 19 January 1881, 4:409, Eduardo Henoekm, El Ferrocarril (Santiago), 4:512, 528, in Ahumada Moreno, Guerra del Pacífico; Correspondent for El Mercurio, 15 June 1880, 676, José Francisco Vergara to President, 19, 20 January 1881, 922, Manuel Baquedano to Minister of War, Lima, 18 January and 20 February 1881, 970, in Chile, Boletín de la Guerra del Pacífico; Dellepiane, Historia militar, 2:45, 100, 140, 163, 218, 258, 258, 366; Ochoa, Diario, 203–4; Buendía, Guerra con Chile, 39; Ekdahl, Historia militar, 2:398; Manuel Baquedano to Commander-in-Chief, Moquegua, 27 March 1880, Chile, Ministry of War, Memoria, 1880, 88.

open terrain. But none of the War of the Pacific's battles appeared to validate these principles. Indeed, but for the presence of the new small arms and the steel-barreled artillery, veterans of Napoleon's campaigns would have felt at home on the battlefields of the War of the Pacific.

In truth, the South American hostilities should not have resembled the wars that occurred seventy years earlier. After all, officers such as Chile's Dublé Almeidas and Bolivia's Eliodoro Camacho studied abroad, and upon their return they tried to introduce the new tactics and technology to their brother officers. A Bolivian colonel, Miguel Aguirre, even wrote a manual explaining how to use open order tactics at the battalion level.[2] Because Aguirre's book, a revised edition of an earlier work, appeared after Bolivia had dropped out of the war, it could not influence Nicolás Campero's direction of the hostilities. But, as this study demonstrates, Aguirre and the Dublé Almeidas seemed to be voices in the wilderness. The Allied and Chilean armies steadfastly failed to apply many of the lessons of the earlier conflagrations.

The waging of the late-nineteenth-century wars in Europe and the United States differed radically from Napoleonic conflicts: the commanders of the larger, conscript armies needed railroads to concentrate their troops, quartermasters to feed, clothe, and arm them, medics to maintain the soldiers' health and to evacuate the wounded from the battlefield, engineers to construct fortifications, and signalers to maintain contact between the armies in the field and the headquarters. And towering above this mélange of the combat and technical units should loom the general staff, that organization that became the hallmark of late-nineteenth-century European armies and had guaranteed von Moltke's 1871 triumph, that highly trained elite tasked with directing the efforts of the various technical and combat organizations to prosecute the war.

But the competing South American belligerents did not contain these specialized supply and technical units, in part because the civilian societies they hoped to protect had only recently, if at all, savored these fruits of the Industrial Revolution. In many respects, these nations appeared rooted in a preindustrial age. Without railroads, a telegraph system, or even decent roads, Bolivia's army relied on mules to move materiel and, in some cases, on runners to transmit messages. Obviously an underdeveloped Bolivia could not integrate technology that did not exist within its borders.

To a lesser degree, a similar lack of resources also plagued the armed forces of Peru and Chile, thereby denying them desperately needed services. The Chilean and Peruvian armies, for example, had to hire civilians to run the rail and telegraph systems because the military lacked the expertise to operate these instruments. Medical problems bedeviled both sides. Chile, which contained only 350 doctors in 1881, did not have enough trained physicians to attend to the nation's civilian ills, let alone to staff its armed forces' embryonic medical corps. Consequently, the Pinto government had to recruit medical students or rely upon the generosity of foreign naval surgeons to treat their wounded. Similarly, the Peruvian and Bolivian armies had appeal to civilians to finance, found, staff, supply, and administer newly created ambulance units. Santiago would also have to depend on civilians to staff its Intendencia General el Ejército y Marina en Campaña, which supervised the acquisition and distribution of food, clothing, and supplies to the army and the navy. In short, without organic supply or technical units, the Bolivian, Chilean, and Peruvian military came to depend on civilians to provide the skills, and sometimes the funds, to enable the armed forces to function. These omissions continued long after the war: Chile's officer corps, for example, still pestered the government to fund the construction of a longitudinal railroad, so it could send troops overland to defend the north.[3] Chile's army did not create a railroad or signal unit until 1911 and 1906 respectively. The War of the Pacific, in short, evolved into a mixed state-civilian enterprise, hardly a model to delight General von Moltke.

Since the armies that fought the War of the Pacific failed to assimilate the technical lessons of the American Civil War and Franco-Prussian War, it should not surprise us that they also botched their attempts to embrace the new tactical doctrine that soldiers, when facing new long range small arms and artillery, should advance in small groups rather than massed units, that those on the defensive and the offensive should dig in because, as Eliodoro Camacho so tersely noted, lying "down on the ground when enemy fire is perceived does not demonstrate cowardice but more properly vigilance and foresight," and that armies should use maneuver to envelop their foes' flanks to defeat them rather than rely on the shock of a frontal assault.[4]

In fairness, it was not so much a lack of interest but the want of opportunity that dictated Allied choice of tactics. With the exception of the Battle of Dolores, the Bolivian and Peruvian forces devoted their efforts to defending, not attacking, entrenched positions. Consequently, these armies rarely had the chance to practice maneuvering. Even when the Allies seized the offensive, they could not advance in dispersed order: many of their troops still carried short-range, muzzle-loading rifles or, worse, muskets. Hence the Allied soldiers had to attack in large formations to maximize the effect of their massed volleys. The fact that disaffected conscripts comprised most of their armies certainly limited the

Peruvian and Bolivian choice of tactics. The closed formation, with all its defects, provided the only way for commanders to control imperfectly trained and often singularly unenthusiastic soldiers.

The Chilean army had to reject the tactics of maneuver for many of the same reason as the Allies. At half of its battles—Pisagua, Tarapacá, Los Angeles, and Arica—Chile's troops had to scale mountains before closing with their enemy. Obviously these conditions limited the Chileans' ability to maneuver or to attack in dispersed order. Defending their positions atop San Francisco Sur and San Francisco Norte severely restricted movement. In short, only twice, at Tacna, or Campo de la Alianza, and at Chorrillos, did the Chilean army have the chance to apply the new tactics. (Chile's attack at Miraflores did not occur as a consequence of prearranged plan but in response to Peru's unexpected attack.) Yet, on both occasions the army's commander, Manuel Baquedano, refused to use maneuver and dispersal to crush his enemies.

Baquedano had two options at Tacna and Chorrillos: he could have followed the advice of those who had urged avoiding the frontal assault, what some defined as "the emetic of a battle," by utilizing Prussia's doctrine of maneuver. This approach, which involved enveloping the Allies' flank, might have not merely routed them but also led to their capture. Instead, Baquedano embraced Marshal Ney's "antiquated tactics," by attacking in massed units across a wide front.[5] Tacna's casualty lists should have warned Baquedano that he had to change his tactics when he invested Lima. Instead, the general rejected the advice of Gens. Marcos Maturana and José Vergara, who had advocated that Baquedano try to envelop the enemy's flank at Chorrillos. What motivated the commanding general remains unclear. Having entered the army at fifteen, Baquedano had learned to soldier not by attending the Escuela Militar, as did Maturana, but in the field. Consequently, he may have spurned his subordinate's suggestions, precisely because they appeared, in a sense, almost cowardly. Or perhaps he, a self-trained soldier, did not care to heed the advice of his more academic colleague. Thus, Baquedano may have preferred the frontal assault, in part because it was so simple but also because it was more virile than Maturana's advocacy of the effete maneuver. But regardless of what motivated his choice, as the esteemed Chilean military historian Guillermo Ekdahl, acerbically noted, "We cannot speak here of the influence of the tactics [Baquedano] used, since the Chilean army evidently did not know another at this time."[6]

The Anatomy of Chile's Victory

Given Arteaga's incipient senescence, Escala's obsessive ultramontanism, and Baquedano's primitive tactics, one may well wonder how Chile vanquished Peru and Bolivia. Some cynics might suggest that Aníbal Pinto's and Domingo Santa María's forces won by default, that the Allied military house of cards simply collapsed under the weight of accumulated Bolivian and Peruvian incompetence. That answer, however, ignores reality.

Not all Allied units performed poorly on the battlefield. Depending on the battle, if some contingents bolted, others fought tenaciously. Bolivia's Batallón Victoria and its Batallón Dalence strenuously resisted the Chileans at Pisagua and Dolores, respectively. Similarly, in the mid-1880 Bolivia's Colorados and the Amarillos preferred to immolate themselves on the plains of Campo de Alianza rather than retreat. The same was true of Peru's Batallón Zepita and the Columna de Artesanos, which defended Tacna, Arica's garrison, and many of the elements defending Lima. Simply put, certain Bolivian and Peruvian units often refused to capitulate. Then why did the armies of Peru and Bolivia ultimately fail?

Unfortunately for them, the Allied armies suffered from a chronic paucity of skilled leaders. This problem began in early 1879, when the Bolivian and Peruvian high commands had to assign some of their most seasoned officers, both commissioned and noncommissioned, to staff the newly formed Peruvian Army of the South or, in the case of Bolivia, the soldiers raised to retake its littoral. Unfortunately, the manpower problem worsened: the unsuccessful defense of Pisagua, Tarapacá, Tacna, and Arica consumed so many Allied senior officers and noncommissioned officers that their loss degraded the quality of Peru's and Bolivia's armed forces. In short, virtually from the onset of the conflict, the Allied military began to bleed to death: each defeat, or even their only victory, consumed so many officers—one general and seven Peruvians of field grade rank died at Tarapacá—that the Allies increasingly came to depend on novice company grade officers, noncommissioned officers (NCOs), and the newly impressed recruit. What is surprising, given the lack of skilled officers, is not that the newly forged Allied contingents bolted but that so many resisted for as long as they did. Whether acting on pride, fear, anger, or patriotism, certain units continued to resist the Chileans even after it became clear that the battle or the war had ended. Thus to attribute Chile's victory solely to Allied ineptitude unfairly diminishes the resistance of heroes such as Col. Francisco Bolognesi, Gen. Andrés Cáceres, and Adm. Miguel Grau, as well as the countless unknown officers, both commissioned and noncommissioned, and the thousands of private soldiers and montoneros who tenaciously resisted Chile's might. It also demeans Santiago's efforts to overcome these men. Still, if both sides fought well, why did the Chileans triumph?

Chile vanquished its foes thanks to its geographical location, its superior civilian infrastructure as well as its political institutions—which managed to function even during the stress of war—and, most important, the intellectual skills and practical experience of its officer corps. Chile's geographical location contributed greatly to its victory. Santiago's access to the Strait of Magellan facilitated its importation of weapons, clothing, and military equipment. In 1879 and 1880 Pinto's ministers purchased more than forty thousand rifles, thirty-six machine guns, and seventy-eight artillery pieces, mainly from Krupp, materiel which Chile needed to defeat the Allies. Conversely, even when Grau's ships dominated the sealanes, Peru's supply process not only was more complicated than Chile's but it also depended upon the good will of the Colombian authorities to ship materiel across the Isthmus of Panama. Of course, after the capture of the *Huáscar* off Punta Angamos in October 1879, Santiago's control of the eastern South Pacific drastically hampered Peru's supply efforts.[7]

By connecting Santiago to the nation's south and then to Valparaíso, the Chilean rail system facilitated the massing of men and supplies and their movement to the northern battlefields. Conversely, Peru's main rail line stopped at Chicla, short of some of the nation's most inhabited regions. And although the Mollendo to Arequipa rail line tapped into the more densely populated Arequipa and Puno regions, it did not necessarily enhance the war efforts. The government lacked the facilities to train or equip those junior officers, NCOs, and recruits who reached Mollendo, particularly once the Chilean fleet won naval supremacy. Lima's army, as one Peruvian author acutely observed, "was at the mercy of whoever dominated the sea, since the railroads began there."[8]

Clearly Chile's internal stability contributed enormously to its military success. And, just as clearly, the lack of order handicapped the Allied effort. Of the Allies, Bolivia appeared the most insecure, enjoying only eighteen years of political calm in the years between 1826 and 1879. "Politics in Bolivia," noted the English visitor Edward Mathews, "are best described as purely personal, for the different political parties seem to spring up, change, and die out according as some ambitious leader comes to the front, and soon gives place to a newer man."[9] Bolivia lived in such a state of insecurity that its capital, noted one Bolivian, "is the haunch of the horse which the President of the Republic rides."[10]

Peru suffered from the same affliction. Just during Manuel Pardo's presidency (1872–76), Lima endured nine coups. President Pardo's successor, Mariano Prado (1876–79), not only failed to restore tranquility, but his impromptu abdication plunged the nation into a maelstrom of unrest during which as many as five men febrilely vied for power. Conversely, in the almost fifty years after 1830, only two civil wars, the last in 1859, roiled Chile.

The same lack of order that prevented the creation and perpetuation of stable political institutions also crippled the Allied armed forces. Only in 1877, for the first time in ten years, did Peru's Colegio Militar graduate some junior officers. Eliodoro Camacho, who had seen European military schools in operation, bemoaned the fact that Bolivia lacked similar institutions, a condition that a retired officer attributed to "the convulsive state, the result of personal or partisan grudges, in which the nation had always lived."[11] Thus, many Bolivians and Peruvians, without access to formal training, became officers like many a self-ordained preacher: they responded the call to an inner or divine force. By shattering the armed forces' chain of command, moreover, the constant *pronunciamientos* and domestic upheavals splintered the integrity of the military's hierarchy. Consequently, the Peruvian and Bolivian armed forces that emerged from this chronic domestic turmoil appeared to consist of a haphazard jumble of officers who won their commissions, postings, and promotions not through seniority or merit but by participating in their nations' countless coups or civil wars. The same internecine conflicts also consumed the military's assets, forcing the Allied armies to begin the war employing weapons salvaged from the domestic battlefields.

Because Chile escaped much of the hurly-burly of civil unrest, its armed forces did not become a force vying for political ascendancy. This does not mean that Chile's officer corps refrained from appealing to political cronies for favors. We saw, for example, how Admiral Williams Rebedollo used his political connections to retain his command. But Chile's officers did not win their commissions or promotions fomenting or crushing the *cuartelazos*. By the 1870s most of the officer corps had studied at Chile's Escuela Militar which, despite its limitations, provided its graduates with at least some knowledge of their craft. Nor did graduation mark the end of professional training. And as early as the 1850s, the army's high command insisted that its officers attend a series of unit-level military miniseminars, where they practiced war games. Some senior officers tried to reform training by incorporating new technical manuals, including some written by Europeans. The army's commissioned ranks, moreover, had ample opportunities to exercise their profession on the Indian frontier. Fighting Araucanians—clearly not a task for the faint-hearted—might not educate an officer to direct a set-piece battle, but it nonetheless provided combat experience. And by 1878 the army had promulgated a set of regulations establishing the criteria for promotion based upon seniority and merit.

Similarly, the Chilean navy bested the Peru fleet thanks to the quality of its personnel. Most naval officers attended the Escuela Naval; and more than a few served with foreign flotillas, including the vaunted Royal Navy. Once the government extirpated the dead wood, such as the hypochondriacal Williams Rebedollo and the alcoholic Simpson, Riveros and a host of well-trained junior officers quickly drove the Peruvians from the sea-lanes. Conversely, on the Peruvian side, many of country's naval officers, commanded literally by ancient mariners, lacked either any formal training or, thanks to the government's penury and fear, sufficient practical experience. Unlike Peru, the Chilean government could trust its navy enough that it did not have to hide crucial engine parts to prevent renegade officers from using the ships to support a rebellion. In short, Chile began the War of the Pacific with a smaller but better-educated officers corps, leading a cadre of professional noncommissioned officers as well as common soldiers and sailors. In the end, of course, Chile's superior armed forces defeated their enemies.

Embracing the Future

Although it had triumphed, Chile's leaders, and many of its officer corps, recognized that the country could ill afford to rest upon its military laurels. In 1885 the army's young Turks founded a military journal, the *Revista Militar de Chile*, to convert the obdurate or the nostalgic to the cause of change. (Ironically, some of its first articles argued for the adoption of open or dispersed order.)[12] The reforms did not end with the publication of the *Revista Militar*. Facing the possibility of post-1884 revanchist wars and an increasingly hostile Argentina, President Santa María realized he had to achieve military parity, if not superiority, over his nation's neighbors. Thus in 1885, impressed by Prussia's victory over France, the Santa María administration hired the services of the German artilleryman and general staff officer Capt. Emil Körner to modernize its army. He arrived in Chile the next year, and later, at the head of a German military mission, he restructured, reequipped, and reeducated the Chilean army. Within a few years, Chile became the paladin of German military culture and technology in Latin America. Chile's fleet also embarked upon an impressive modernization program, modeling itself on the Royal Navy.

Chile was not the only country to revamp drastically its armed forces. The Peruvians also sought foreign military assistance, albeit after Chile had done so and from a different source: acting perhaps out of a desire to be contrary, Lima chose to cloak its army not the mantle of Germany's victorious legions but in those of France. In 1895 Capt. Paul Clemént and three other officers—each representing a different combat arm— arrived in Lima. They would remain until 1914 and would return to Lima after World War One. Bolivia's Eliodoro Camacho, one of those who recognized the impact of technology on military tactics also hired some French officers to restructure his nation's army. But La Paz did not accept a formal military mission until 1911, when it too turned to Berlin, engaging the services Maj. Hans Kundt and a team of German officers. While all the members of these missions left for Europe at the outbreak of the war, some returned: Kundt, accompanied by the scar-faced sadist and future SA leader Ernst Rohm—who would perish in the Night of Long Knives—reappeared and would later direct Bolivia's disastrous participation in the Chaco War.

Although various foreign military observers provided their respective nations detailed reports reinforcing the lessons of the U.S. Civil War or the Franco-Prussian conflict, the United States and Europe did not seem to pay much attention to the War of the Pacific. Racism or an unwarranted sense of cultural superiority might have engendered this disdain. As a British colonel, Lonsdale Hale, once noted, "An officer who has seen service [in non-European countries] must sweep from his mind all recollections of that service, for between Afghan, Egyptian, or Zulu warfare and that of Europe, there is no similarity whatever. To the latter the former is merely the play of children."[13] Indeed, using words that might have served as a fitting epitaph for the Twenty-fourth Foot at Isandlwana, another British officer remarked, "Man for man, the fanatic or cut-throat, the hardy nomad or the reckless savage may match or be more than a match for the European soldier; in the aggregate irregular warriors fail."[14]

In retrospect, it should not surprise us that none of the War of the Pacific's combatants assimilated many of the lessons either of the American Civil War or the Franco-German conflict. If the supposedly more advanced Great Britain and Russia ignored these wars—as their performance in the Boer War or Russo-Turkish conflict painfully demonstrated—then so could the nations of Latin America. Ironically, the same armies whose battlefield experiences shaped the development of tactics, the French, Germans, and the Americans, also forgot what they had so painfully gleaned from the battlefield. Even after the slaughter of the French cavalry in 1870, a German officer still defended mounted assaults: "No technology comes to our aid. We have only that which our ancestors had a thousand years ago: a man, a steed, and iron."[15]

Clearly, officers from other nations shared this nostalgia for the past tactics: in initial stages of the Boer War in 1899, the British launched frontal assaults—at Stormberg, Colenso, Modder River, and Magersfontein—losing hundreds of men each time, before it dawned on them to adopt alternatives. Similarly, the Japanese and Russians flung men at each other in the approaches to Port Arthur, before losing their zeal for massed attack across open fields. Even the vaunted German army failed to assimilate this lesson: at Langemarck in late October 1914 massed troops, many singing their national anthem or other patriotic songs, some accompanied by bands and led by flag-bearing officers, assaulted dug-in British regulars. Their enemy, as a German historian noted, "reaped a great harvest": seven thousand dead and thirteen thousand wounded.[16] If the French and Germans had to relearn in 1914 what they had so painfully discovered earlier, then what could one expect of nations that had not fought for decades? Twentieth-century Bolivia and Peru would again go to war, not so Chile, which apparently absorbed some of history's most important lessons: that the methods employed by the victorious in one war do not always lead to a triumph in subsequent conflicts and that sometimes the appearance of military superiority achieves the same result as having gone to war.

Notes

Introduction

1. John Spurling, "And the Winners Shall Be Losers," *Times Literary Supplement*, 14 January 2000. When asked why he robbed banks, Sutton explained, "That's where the money was."

2. Greene, *Report of the Russian Army*, 421, 545; Emory Upton cited in Jamieson, *Crossing the Deadly Ground*, 10, 71–72, 128.

3. Qtd. in Spiers, *Late Victorian Army*, 245.

4. Callwell, *Small Wars*, 388.

5. Greene, *Report of the Russian Army*, 64, 436; McElwee, *Art of War*, 200–201.

6. Howard, Franco-Prussian War, 175.

7. Qtd. in Fuller, *Military History*, 2:105.

8. Qtd. in Fuller, *War and Western Civilization*, 99; cited in Luvaas, *Military Legacy*, 126.

9. For a general overview of the evolution of warfare, see van Creveld, *Command in War*; Howard, *Franco-Prussian War*; and Black, *Western Warfare*.

10. Greene, *Report of the Russian Army*, 30, 34–36; Menning, *Bayonets before Bullets*, 114; Mitchell, *Victors and Vanquished*, 62–63.

11. Bowman, *Andes*, 113; Bowman, *Desert Trails*, 90.

12. Bowman, *Andes*, 187.

13. Paz Soldán, *Narración histórica*, 111.

14. Boyd, *Chili*, 186.

15. Blakemore, "Chile," 522.

16. Ugarte, *Efemérides*, 12.

17. Blakemore, "Chile," 521.

18. Boyd, *Chili*, 175, 178.

19. Boyd, *Chili*, 179; Urquieta, *Recuerdos de la vida*, 1:89.

20. Weiner, "La guerra en Sud America."

21. Vicuña Mackenna, *Historia de la campaña de Tarapacá*, 1:54–55; *El Constituyente* (Copiapó), 27 November 1876, 26 January 1877; *El Ferrocarril* (Santiago), 20, 25 January 1877. *El Ferrocarril*, 20 January 1877, claimed that La Patria was a mutual aid society.

22. Mathews, *Up the Amazon*, 259.

23. Bresson, *Una visión francesa*, 82–83, 96.

24. There is a disagreement about Bolivia's size and population. A contemporary geographer, L. V. Doll, estimated that the nation covered 1.3 million square kilometers and that its population numbered 2,325,000. "Jeografía de Bolivia," in Ahumada Moreno, *Guerra del Pacífico*, 1:144–45.

25. Caviano, *Historia de la guerra*, 2:143, 145; José Clavero, "Perú, Bolivia, y Chile," in Ahumada Moreno, *Guerra del Pacífico*, 1:144–45, 146.

26. A. T. Edelmann qtd. in Smith, "Central Andes," 321; Querejazu Calvo, *Guano*, 224.

27. Caviano, *Historia de la guerra*, 2:137; Dunkerley, "Politics," 24.

28. Fellmann Velarde, *Historia*, 2:269.

29. Dennis, *Documentary History*, 53.

30. *El Ferrocarril* (Santiago), 25 January 1877; *The Chilian Times* (Valparaíso), 27 January 1877.

31. Weiner, "La guerra en Sud America," 270; Spangler, *Civilization in Chili*, 43.

32. Bonilla, "Peru and Bolivia," 3:548.

33. Qtd. in Arguedas, *Historia general*, 65; Mathews, *Up the Amazon*, 270; Klein, *Parties and Political Change*, 25; Aranzaes, *Revoluciones*.

34. Chile, *Diario Oficial*, 8 March 1877.

35. Mayo, *British Merchants*, 170–71; O'Brien, *Nitrate Industry*, 10–11.

36. Barros, *Historia diplomática*, 293.

37. *El Constituyente* (Copiapó), 27 November 1876.

38. Chile, House of Representatives, *Sesiones ordinarias*, 725, 738; *El Constituyente*, 26 January 1877.

39. Phillips, "Bolivia in the War," 93.

40. Caviano, *Historia de la guerra*, 2:143–45; Alba, *Diario*, 120; Claros, *Diario*, 28. Alba notes that there were additional troops garrisoning other areas.

41. Qtd. in Travers, "Offensive," 531; Arnold, "French Tactical Doctrine," 66. Eric Brose argues, for example, that the German refusal to accept that the new tactics had virtually nullified the role of the cavalry's habit of attacking in massed formations. *Kaiser's Army*, 102, 156, 188, 195–96, 201.

42. Querejazu Calvo, *Guano*, 224.

1. The Prewar Maneuvers

1. Emilio Sotomayor to Minister of War and Navy, Antofagasta, 20 February 1879, 2:36, Sotomayor to Minister of War and Navy, Antofagasta, 18 February 1879, 6:3, in Ahumada Moreno, *Guerra del Pacífico*; Sotomayor to Minister of War, Calama, 26 March 1879, in Chile, Ministry of War, *Memoria de guerra, 1879*, 9–11.

2. *La Opinión Nacional* (Lima), 3 March 1879, qtd. in *El Mercurio* (Valparaíso), 22 March 1879.

3. Rafael Sotomayor Valdés to Minister of Foreign Relations, Cochabamba, 25 November 1879, in Sotomayor Valdés, *Legación de Chile*, 359.

4. Querejazu Calvo, *Guano*, 255; Peñaloza, *Historia económica*, 2:169; *El Heraldo* (Cochabamba), 22 January and 31 March 1879; *El Industrial* (Sucre), 11 January 1879, cited in *El Mercurio* (Valparaíso), 12, 15 February 1879; Fellmann Velarde, *Historia*, 1:267.

5. Pedro Videla to Minister of Foreign Relations, La Paz, 2 July 1878, in Ahumada Moreno, *Guerra del Pacífico*, 2:15–16; Dennis, *Documentary History*, 70.

6. Pedro Videla to Minister of Foreign Relations, La Paz, 2 July 1878 and 5 February 1879, 1:15–16, 35, Alejandro Fierro to Videla, Santiago, 8 November 1878, 1:16, in Ahumada Moreno, *Guerra del Pacífico*.

7. Serapio Réyes Ortíz to Minister of Foreign Relations, La Paz, 11 December 1878, in Ahumada Moreno, *Guerra del Pacífico*, 1:17–18.

8. Martín Lanza to Pedro Videla, La Paz, 26 December 1878, in Ahumada Moreno, *Guerra del Pacífico*, 1:20.

9. Salvador Reyes to Alejandro Fierro, Antofagasta, 31 December 1878, in Ahumada Moreno, *Guerra del Pacífico*, 1:29.

10. Alejandro Fierro to Pedro Videla, Santiago, 8 November 1878, in Ahumada Moreno, *Guerra del Pacífico*, 1:16.

11. Alejandro Fierro to Pedro Videla, Santiago, 3 January 1879, in Ahumada Moreno, *Guerra del Pacífico*, 1:29, 31–32.

12. Alejandro Fierro to Salvador Reyes, Santiago, 16 January 1879, 1:29, Martín Lanza to Pedro Videla, La Paz, 27 January 1879, Videla to Lanza, La Paz, 27 January 1879, 1:34–35, in Ahumada Moreno, *Guerra del Pacífico*.

13. Severino Zapata to Administrator of the Aduana, Antofagasta, 11 January 1879, 1:28, Pedro Videla to Minister of Foreign Relations, 20 January 1879, 1:33–34, Martín Lanza to Videla, La Paz, 6 February 1879, 1:35 in Ahumada Moreno, *Guerra del Pacífico*.

14. Hilarión Daza to Severino Zapata, La Paz, 6 February 1879, qtd. in Querejazu Calvo, *Guano*, 219.

15. Martín Lanza to Pedro Videla, La Paz, 6 February 1879, in Ahumada Moreno, *Guerra del Pacífico*, 1:35.

16. Pedro Videla to Minister of Foreign Relations, La Paz, 14 February 1879, in Ahumada Moreno, *Guerra del Pacífico*, 1:39.

17. Pedro Videla to Minister of Foreign Relations, La Paz, 8 February 1879, in Ahumada Moreno, *Guerra del Pacífico*, 1:35–36; Hilarión Daza to Severino Zapata, La Paz, 6 February 1879, in Querejazu Calvo, *Guano*, 219.

18. Querejazu Calvo, *Guano*, 259.

19. Markham, *War between Peru and Chile*, 71; Mathews, *Up the Amazon*, 274–75; Uriburu, *Guerra del Pacífico*, 79; Ochoa, *Semblanzas*, 60–66; *El Constitucional* (Cochabamba), 18 June 1884, qtd. in Irurozqui Victoriano, *"A bala, piedra, y palo,"* 238; Phillips, "Bolivia in the War," 63; Cristi, *Antecedentes históricos*, 41.

20. De Lavalle, *Mi misión en Chile*, xxxiv; Ahumada Moreno, *Guerra del Pacífico*, 1:94.

21. Mathews, *Up the Amazon*, 274.

22. Díaz Arguedas, *Historia*, 200, 202.

23. Agustin Blanco to Minister of Foreign Relations, La Paz, 10 May 1879, in Ahumada Moreno, *Guerra del Pacífico*, 2:18; Peralta Ruiz and Irurozqui Victoriano, *Por la concordia*, 189.

24. Arguedas, *Historia general*, 361; Querejazu Calvo, Guano, 197.

25. Hilarión Daza to unknown recipient, in Ahumada Moreno, *Guerra del Pacífico*, 1:93–94.

26. Villar Cordova, "Situación del Perú," 143.

27. Qtd. in Querejazu Calvo, *Guano*, 317.

28. Gibbs to William Evarts, Lima, 19 February 1879, Manuel Irigoyen, "Counter Manifest," Lima, 1 May 1879, in United States of America, *Message from the President*, 196, 232–32; Spenser St. John to Marquis of Salisbury, Lima, 20 March 1879, Foreign Office, General Correspondence, Peru (FO 61), 1879–84, Public Records Office, London, Great Britain (hereafter cited as FO 61); Paz Soldán, *Narración histórica*, 43; de Lavalle, *Mi misión en Chile*, 68–69.

29. Sater, *Chile and the War of the Pacific*, 9–10, 15.

30. De Lavalle, *Mi misión en Chile*, 96–100, 111–12, 120.

31. Jobet, Ensayo crítico, 63–65; Segal, Desarrollo del capitalismo, 140; Vitale, *Interpretación marxista*, 4:120, 128, 133; Amayo, *Política británica*; Sater, *Chile and the War of the Pacific*, 13; O'Brien, *Nitrate Industry*, 49.

32. Greenhill and Miller, "Peruvian Government," 117.

33. According to the *Tercera memoria del directorio e informe de la administración Jeneral de Huanchaca*, Concha y Toro and his brothers owned approximately 12 percent of the company's stock. *Las Novedades* (Santiago), 5, 22 March 1879; *The Chilian Times* (Valparaíso), 1 February 1879; Lorenzo Claro to Aníbal Pinto, 26 December 1879, Fondos Varios, vol. 838, Archivo Nacional, Santiago, Chile; Miller to Gibbs, 14 January 1879, Gibbs Papers 11:470, Gibbs Archive, London, Great Britain; Concha y Toro telegram to Belisario Prats, 2 February 1879, vol. 902, Archivo de Ministerio del Interior, Santiago, Chile; Peñaloza, *Historia económica*, 2:170. Among the mines expropriated were those of Corocoro, Socavón de la Virgen de Oruro.

34. Baron Gülich to von Bülow, Santiago, 23 September 1879, in *Informes inéditos*, 31.

35. Consul General Packenham to Marquis of Salisbury, Santiago, 20 April 1879, Foreign Office, General Correspondence, Chile (FO 16), 1875–84, Public Records Office, London, Great Britain (hereafter cited as FO 16); Perolari-Malmignati, *Il Perú*, 277; Greenhill and Miller, "Peruvian Government," 123–24.

36. *El Indpendiente* (Santiago), 8, 13 March and 4, 19, 22 April 1879. See also *El Ferrocarril* (Santiago), 2 April 1879; *El Constituyente* (Copiapó), 25 January

1879; *The Chilian Times* (Valparaíso), 15, 29 March 1879; *La Tribuna* (Lima), qtd. in *El Mercurio* (Valparaíso), 26 March 1879. *El Mercurio* considered *La Tribuna* the only neutral paper in Lima.

37. Consul General Packenham to Marquis of Salisbury, Santiago, 20 April 1879, FO16/202; *Las Novedades* (Santiago), 8 February 1879.

38. Spenser St. John to Marquis of Salisbury, Lima, 20 March 1879, FO 61.

39. De Lavalle, *Mi misión en Chile*, 15.

40. Spangler, *Civilization in Chile*, 202–3.

41. Baron d'Avril to Waddington, Santiago, 28 March 1879, in *Informes inéditos*, 258; Thomas Osborn to William Evarts, Santiago, 20 February 1879, in United States of America, *Message from the President*, 74; Chile, House of Representatives, *Discurso de S. E. el Presidente*, 7–8.

42. De Lavalle, *Mi misión en Chile*, 69, 85; Spenser St. John to Marquis of Salisbury, Lima, 20 March 1879, FO 61; Antonio Varas to Aníbal Pinto, qtd. in Barros, *Historia diplomática*, 322; Belisario Prats to Minister of War, n.d., in Bulnes, *Historia*, 1:122; Subercaseaux, *Memorias*, 1:369.

43. Chile, *Diario Oficial*, 19, 27, 28 August 1878.

44. Chile, *Diario Oficial*, 21 August, 24 September, and 6 November 1878. Chile's exports to Bolivia declined 5.5 percent between 1877 and 1878. Chilean imports from Bolivia also fell, doubtless due to the collapse of the silver mines at Caracoles. Herrmann, *Producción*, 41.

45. *El Curicano* (Curicó), 1 November 1879; *El Telegrafo* (Chillán), 2 May 1879; *Las Novedades* (Santiago), 1 March 1879.

46. De Lavalle, *Mi misión en Chile*, 25.

47. Ricardo Becerra to Nicolás Piérola, 17 March 1879, in Basadre, *Historia*, 5th ed., 5:296.

2. Comparing the Armies

1. Peru, Ministry of War and the Navy, *Memoria del ramo de guerra*, 3–4.

2. Grieve, *Historia*, 327–28; *El Peruano* (Lima), 2 September 1879; Segundo Leiva to Colonel War, Arequipa, 7 May 1880, in Ahumada Moreno, *Guerra del Pacífico*, 7:70; Dellepiane, *Historia militar*, 2:328.

3. Dellepiane, *Historia militar*, 2:77, 79; Körner and Boonen Rivera, *Estudios*, 2:29; Grieve, *Historia*, 323–25; Le León, *Recuerdos*, 23.

4. *El Peruano* (Lima), 5 February 1879.

5. Markham, *War between Peru and Chile*, 68; *El Peruano* (Lima), 5 February 1879.

6. Dellepiane, *Historia militar*, 2:66; Peru, Directorate of Statistics, *Estadística*, 225–30. Körner and Boonen Rivera, *Estudios*, 2:291, claimed Peru's army contained 5,700 men; Markham, *War between Peru and Chile*, 183, placed the number at 4,500; Spangler, *Civilization in Chile*, 204, put the figure at 9,000; and Mariano

Felipe Paz Soldán, a contemporary of the war, stated the number as 5,241 (*Narración histórica*, 109).

7. Clavero listed Bolivia's peacetime forces as 2,000 with a militia numbering 54,000, while those of Chile were 3,516 and 48,170, respectively. In Ahumada Moreno, *Guerra del Pacífico*, 1:147–48.

8. Peru, Ministry of War and the Navy, *Memoria del ramo de guerra, 1878*, 69; "El Ejército del Perú," Chile, *Boletín de la Guerra del Pacífico*, 4 July 1879, 229; Spila de Subiaco, *Chile*, 81.

9. Caviano, *Historia de la guerra*, 1:194–96.

10. Peru, Ministry of War and the Navy, *Memoria del ramo de guerra, 1878*, 11.

11. *Historia de la escuela militar del Perú*, 18–26.

12. Caviano, *Historia de la guerra*, 1:195; Tauro, "Defensa de Lima," 104; Ricardo Palma to Nícolas Piérola, 27 June and 12 August 1881, in Palma, *Cartas a Piérola*, 51–52, 62.

13. *El Peruano* (Lima), 5 February 1879.

14. Körner and Boonen Rivera, *Estudios*, 2:270; Peru, Ministry of War and the Navy, *Memoria del ramo de guerra, 1878*, 4, 15–16.

15. *El Mercurio* (Valparaíso), 23 April 1879.

16. Spencer St. John to Marquis of Salisbury, Lima, 19 July 1879, FO 16; Perolari-Malmignati, *Il Perú*, 307.

17. Spila de Subiaco, *Chile*, 68; *El Comercio* (Lima), 5 November 1879, in *El Mercurio* (Valparaíso) 18 November 1879.

18. El Profesor to Justo Arteaga, Guayaquil, 7 August 1879, in Ahumada Moreno, *Guerra del Pacífico*, 2:45.

19. Santini, *Viaggio*, 125.

20. *El Nacional* (Lima), 17 April 1880, cited in *El Mercurio* (Valparaíso), 30 April 1880.

21. Perolari-Malmignati, *Il Perú*, 313.

22. Holguin, "Toma de Lima," 5–6; Lt. Reginald Carey-Brenton, in Tauro, "Defensa de Lima," 102–13.

23. Emilio Bonifaz to Minister of Foreign Relations, Guayaquil, Secret, 19 November 1879, 3:58, Miguel Riofrio to Manuel Irigoyen, Lima, 27 March and 19 September 1879, 3:59, 60, in Ahumada Moreno, *Guerra del Pacífico*; Manrique, *Guerrillas indígenas*, 59.

24. *El Mercurio* (Valparaíso), 23 April 1879; Spenser St. John to Marquis of Salisbury, Lima, 19 July and 7 August 1879, FO 16; El Profesor to Justo Arteaga, Guayaquil, 7 August 1879, in Ahumada Moreno, *Guerra del Pacífico*, 2:45.

25. *El Nacional* (Lima), cited in *El Mercurio* (Valparaíso), 27 March 1879; Díaz Arguedas, *Historia*, 28, 71; Bolivia, Ministry of War, *Memoria, 1882*, 9.

26. Díaz Arguedas, *Historia*, 30.

27. Aranzaes, *Revoluciones*, 269–72; Bolivia, Ministry of War, *Memoria, 1877*, 7–8, 11, 13.

28. Juan S. Lizárraga to Minister of Foreign Relations, La Paz, 23 January 1879, 7:42, Juan Fernández to Minister of Foreign Relations, Potosí, 27 June 1879, 2:25, Gustavo, *El Nacional* (Lima), 9 November 1879, 2:106–7, Agustin Blanco to Peru's Minister in Bolivia, Potosí, 1 July 1879, 2:26, in Ahumada Moreno, *Guerra del Pacífico.*

29. Díaz Arguedas, *Historia,* 30.

30. Bolivia, Ministry of War, *Memoria, 1883,* 23; Phillips, "Bolivia in the War," 64.

31. "Cuadros de la vida militar," in Ahumada Moreno, *Guerra del Pacífico,* 1:95.

32. Counsul J. D. Hay to the Earl of Derby, Valparaíso, 6 November 1875, enclosure in Despatch No. 41, Confidential, FO 16.

33. Díaz Arguedas, *Historia,* 54–58; Bolivia, Ministry of War, *Informe,* 9–10, and *Memoria, 1883,* 22.

34. Ballivián, *Colorados de Bolivia,* 9.

35. Arguedas, *Obras completas,* 2:641.

36. Bolivia, Ministry of War, *Informe,* 16.

37. Bolivia, Ministry of War, *Informe,* 16; Caviano, *Historia de la guerra,* 1:197.

38. Bolivia, Ministry of War, *Informe,* 17, 28.

39. Bolivia, Ministry of War, *Memoria, 1883,* 24.

40. *El Mercurio* (Valparaíso), 22 April 1879.

41. Díaz Arguedas, *Historia,* 607, 609, 623; Bolivia, Ministry of War, *Memoria, 1877,* Sección de Inspección, nos. 1 and 2. The difference in size is due to the fact that these figures did not include some groups as physicians, bandsmen, or cadets.

42. *El Mercurio* (Valparaíso), 28 February and 14 April 1879; Bulnes, *Historia,* 1:599; Wilde, *Historia militar,* 137–38; Quiróz, "Epistolario inédito," 84.

43. Claros, *Diario,* 38–39.

44. Mason, *War on the Pacific Coast,* 12; Dellepiane, *Historia militar,* 2:84; Bolivia, Ministry of War, *Memoria, 1877,* 7, 16, 21, and *Memoria, 1883,* 24.

45. Bolivia, Ministry of War, *Memoria, 1877,* 19–23.

46. Zolio Flores to Manuel Irigoyen, Lima, 28 October 1878, Irigoyen, 22 November 1878, Flores to Irigoyen, Lima, 23 January 1879, 3:3–4, Juan Fernández to Peru's Minister in Bolivia, Potosí, 18 July 1879, 2:27, Flores to Irigoyen, Lima, 20 August 1879, 2:28, in Ahumada Moreno, *Guerra del Pacífico;* Bolivia, Ministry of War, *Informe,* 7.

47. Gen. Manuel Othón Jofré to Prefects, October 1879, in Ochoa, *Diario,* 252.

48. Bolivia, Ministry of War, *Memoria, 1877,* 18.

49. Bolivia, Ministry of War, *Memoria, 1877,* 18, and *Memoria, 1883;* Mariano Bladez to General, Chief of the Departments of the South, 24 April 1880, 2:530, N. Flores to Subprefect of Cinti, Potosí, 26 April 1880, 2:530, N. Flores to Prefect

of Chuquisaca, Potosí, 26 May 1880, 3:157, Arístedes Moreno, Potosí, 23 May 1880, 3:158, in Ahumada Moreno, *Guerra del Pacífico*.

50. *La Patria* (La Paz), 30 April 1880.

51. *El Civilista* (La Paz), cited in *El Mercurio* (Valparaíso), 10 March 1880; Narciso Campero to Chief of the Army's General Staff, Potosí, 6 June 1879, in Díaz Arguedas, *Historia*, 44.

52. Pedro Urquidi noted that he had to reject 126 of 200 recruits as unfit. Urquidi to Narciso Campero, Camargo, 8 August 1879, in *Documentos relativos a la organización*, 164. See also Campero to Chief of the Army's General Staff, Potosí, 6 June 1879, and Francisco Buitrago to Campero, Potosí, 19 August 1879, in *Documentos relativos a la organización*, 45, 87.

53. D. Calbimonte to Narciso Campero, Potosí, 25 September 1879, and L. Morales to Campero, Vitichi, 22 June 1879, in *Documentos relativos a la organización*, 154, 166; Bolivia, Ministry of War, *Informe*, 7.

54. Querejazu Calvo, *Aclaraciones históricas*, 135–36.

55. Ochoa, *Diario*, 254.

56. Juan Fernández to Peru's Minister in La Paz, Peruvian Consulate in Potosí, 27 June 1879, in Ahumada Moreno, *Guerra del Pacífico*, 2:25.

57. Querejazu Calvo, *Aclaraciones históricas*, 135–36.

58. Ochoa, *Diario*, 102.

59. Díaz Arguedas, *Historia*, 272.

60. Ochoa, *Diario*, 254; Díaz Arguedas, *Historia*, 319–20.

61. Narciso Campero, La Paz, 31 January 1881, in Ahumada Moreno, *Guerra del Pacífico*, 5:144–45.

62. Bolivia, Ministry of War, *Memoria, 1883*, 25; Narciso Campero to Jefe de Personal, Potosí, 6 June 1879, in *Documentos relativos a la organización*, 44.

63. Bolivia, Ministry of War, *Memoria, 1877*, 19–20. Not all Chileans agreed. *El Mercurio*'s Bolivian correspondent described the regular Bolivian line units as "vicious and corrupt" and claimed that the rest of the army suffered from the same vices that afflicted all of Bolivian society. *El Mercurio* (Valparaíso), 14, 22 April, 1879; Körner and Boonen Rivera, *Estudios*, 2:264; Bolivia, Ministry of War, *Memoria, 1877*, 18–19, and *Memoria, 1883*, 25; Agustin Blanco to Peru's Minister in Bolivia, Potosí, 1 July 79, in Ahumada Moreno, *Guerra del Pacífico*, 2:26.

64. Bolivia, Ministry of War, *Informe*, 13, 14, 16, 23–25, 27.

65. Commander-in-Chief of the Division to Narciso Campero, in Alba, *Diario*, 40.

66. Ochoa, *Diario*, 102; Bolivia, Ministry of War, *Informe*, 16.

67. *El Titicaca* (La Paz), 23 May 1879.

68. Spangler, *Civilization in Chili*, 52; Chile, House of Representatives, *Sesiones ordinarias*, 3 August 1876, 423.

69. Sater, Chile and the War of the Pacific, 75–82.

70. Estado Mayor General, *Historia*, 5:21, 35, 39; Chile, Ministry of War, *Memoria, 1878*, vi, 105, 110; *The Chilian Times* (Valparaíso), 7 October 1876.

71. Medina, *Excusión a Tarapacá*, 12; Barrientos Gutiérrez, *Artillería*, 161; Jose Antonio Varas, "Inspección Jeneral del Ejército," in Chile, Ministry of War, *Memoria, 1878*, anexo 24.

72. Chile, Ministry of War, *Memoria, 1878*, 101, 105–6.

73. Bedregal, *Militares en Bolivia*, 31.

74. The text was translated by José Silva Chávez in 1867. Pérez, Santiago, 3 May 1867, in Risopatrón Cañas, *Legislación militar*, 1:453; Luvaas, *Military Legacy*, 149–50. Chilean officers also studied *Le Secq de Crepy Táctica de Artillería*, translated in 1848.

75. Mason, *War on the Pacific Coast*, 21; Emilio Sotomayor to Minister of War and Navy, Antofagasta, 1 April 1879, in Ahumada Moreno, *Guerra del Pacífico*, 6:8.

76. Bedregal, *Militares en Bolivia*, 31.

77. Körner and Boonen Rivera, *Estudios*, 2:257–58. Gen. Justo Arteaga wrote the study *Táctica de Artillería*, which the army adopted in 1874. Errázuriz, Santiago, 18 December 1874, in Risopatrón Cañas, *Legislación militar*, 1:453; Mason, *War on the Pacific Coast*, 11.

78. Chile, Ministry of War, *Memoria, 1878*, 110.

79. Maj. José Francisco Gana studied in France and England, Col. Emilio Sotomayor in France and Belguim, Maj. Benjamín Viel at St. Cyr, and Majs. Diego Dublé Almeida and Baldomero Dublé Almeida in France and Belgium. Barrientos Gutiérrez, *Estado Mayor General*, 157.

80. Dublé Almeida, "Diario de Campaña," 100, 104–5, 109; Ricardo Santa Cruz to Joaquín Santa Cruz, 22 June 1879, in Fernández Larraín, *Santa Cruz y Torreblanca*, 9; Mason, *War on the Pacific Coast*, 21.

81. Estado Mayor General, *Historia*, 6:389; Chile, Ministry of War, *Memoria, 1878*, 110.

82. Estado Mayor General, *Historia*, 5:44; Körner and Boonen Rivera, *Estudios*, 2:257–60; Poblete, "Desarrollo histórico," 240, and "Nuestro ejército," 255; González, "Alrededor," 892; Querejazu Calvo, *Guano*, 523; *El Peruano* (Lima), 12 August 1879.

83. Estado Mayor General, *Historia*, 5:34.

84. Estado Mayor General, *Historia*, 5:29, 32, 46, 51.

85. Estado Mayor General, *Historia*, 5:29.

86. Estado Mayor General, *Historia*, 5:46, 51, 56.

87. González Salinas, *Reseñas históricas*, 49. Surprisingly, the nation's crime rate did not surge. Thanks to the government policy of press-ganging society's least favored, the number of crimes fell until 1881, when the process of demobilization released the criminal elements back into their native habitat.

88. Aníbal Pinto, Valparaíso, 20 January 1879, in Risopatrón Cañas, *Legislación militar*, 1:135–36.

89. Estado Mayor General, *Historia*, 5:29, 34, 46, 51, 53; Barrientos Gutiérrez,

Artillería, 158–59, 173. In 1869 the regiment was placed under the authority of the general staff. Henceforth, its personnel served as coastal defense gunners as well as in Chile's south.

90. Estado Mayor General, *Historia*, 5:52–53, 57; Chile, Ministry of War, *Memoria, 1880*, 119.

91. Chile, Ministry of War, *Memoria, 1880*, 120–22.

92. Aníbal Pinto, Valparaíso, 20 January 1879, in Risopatron Cañas, *Legislación militar*, 1:135–36.

93. González Salinas, *Reseñas históricas*, 59; Emilio Sotomayor to Minister of War and Navy, Antofagasta, 18 February 1879, 6:4, José 2. Soto, "Fuerza del Ejército del Norte," Antofagasta, 23 May 1879, 6:17, Raimundo Ansieta, "Estado Mayor General," Antofagasta, 16 June 1879, 6:20, Luis Arteaga, Antofagasta, 7 August 1879, 6:27–28, Luis Arteaga, "Estado que manifiesta la fuerza, etc.," 14 June 1879, 6:24, in Ahumada Moreno, *Guerra del Pacífico*; Chile, Ministry of War and Navy, *Memoria de guerra, 1880*, 132–33.

94. "Estado que manifiesta el número de las fuerzas del ejército y Guardia Nacional mobilizada . . . diciembre del año de 1880," Santiago, 28 June 1882, in Ahumada Moreno, *Guerra del Pacífico*, 7:41; Chile, Ministry of War, *Memoria, 1881*, 61; Estado Mayor General, *Historia*, 5:227; Chile, Ministry of War, *Memoria, 1884*, 119–20.

95. Díaz Arguedas, *Historia*, 275–76, 326.

96. Díaz Arguedas, *Historia*, 535–36, 560–61, 577–78, 590.

97. Dellepiane, *Historia militar*, 2:76–77; Díaz Arguedas, *Historia*, 609.

98. Wilhelm Ekdahl makes the point that the Peruvian military did not know with any certainty the location and number of the enlisted militia. Still, one can get some idea from the number of guard officers serving in each area. *Historia militar*, 2:58–61.

99. Paz Soldán, *Narración histórica*, 426, 455.

100. Vargas Hurtado, *Batalla de Arica*, 121; Ochoa, *Semblanzas*, 134; Dellepiane, *Historia militar*, 2:68.

101. Manuel Othón Jofré to Narciso Campero, Tacna, 13 August and 6 September 1879, in *Documentos relativos a la organización*, 35–36, 39; Campero, *Informe*, 48; Díaz Arguedas, *Historia*, 320.

102. Dunkerley, "Politics," 30.

103. Entry of 28 March 1879 in Claros, *Diario*, 32; Ochoa, *Diario*, 281; Querejazu Calvo, *Aclaraciones históricas*, 183; Campero, *Informe*, 49.

104. *El Mercurio* (Valparaíso), 22 May and 6, 16 October, 1879.

105. Ochoa, *Diario*, 309; Hilarión Daza, "Manifesto del Jeneral Hilarión Daza a sus conciudadanos," Paris, 1881, 4:158, Juan Fernández to Peru's Minister in La Paz, Peruvian Consulate in Potosí, 27 June 1879, 2:25, Issac Tamayo to Minister of the Government, Tacna, 12 May 1879, 2:21, in Ahumada Moreno, *Guerra del Pacífico*.

106. Vargas Hurtado, *Batalla de Arica*, 122.

107. By the end of 1880 the Bolivian army consisted of twelve infantry battalions, three cavalry regiments, and one artillery regiment. Díaz Arguedas, *Historia*, 492.

108. Bolivia, Ministry of War, *Informe*, 8.

109. Manuel Othón to Narciso Campero, Tacna, 29 June 1880, in *Documentos relativos a la organización*, 31.

110. Ballivián, *Colorados de Bolivia*, 3; *La Patria* (La Paz), 4 May 1880.

111. Alba, *Diario*, 54; Claros, *Diario*, 47–48, 52; Díaz Arguedas, *Historia*, 200.

112. *La Patria* (La Paz), 4 May 1880.

113. Bolivia, Ministry of War, *Informe*, 15, and *Memoria, 1882*, 12.

114. Arguedas, *Historia general*, 221–24.

115. Narciso Campero, La Paz, 1 February 1881, in Ahumada Moreno, *Guerra del Pacífico*, 5:145.

116. Manuel Othón Jofré, 31 December 1879, in Ochoa, *Diario*, 252.

117. Narciso Campero to Minister of War, San Cristóbal, 6 November 1879, in *Documentos relativos a la organización*, 186.

118. Narciso Campero to Chief of the Army's General Staff, Cotagaita, 1, 7 August 1879, 49–51, Francisco Buitrago to Campero, Potosí, 3 September and 2 October 1879, 133, 183, Francisco Velasco to Campero, 27 December 1879, 186, Francisco Benavente to Campero, San Cristóbal, 3 September 1879, 194, E. Apocada to Campero, San Cristóbal, 24 December 1879, 198–99, in *Documentos relativos a la organización*; Manuel Landaeta to Peru's Minister to Bolivia, Sucre, 26 September 1879, 2:31, Zolio Flores to Pedro J. Calderón, Lima, 6 February 1880, 2:367, in Ahumada Moreno, *Guerra del Pacífico*; Alba, *Diario*, 46; Claros, *Diario*, 14–15, 59.

119. *La Patria* (La Paz), 4 May 1880; Ballivián, *Colorados de Bolivia*, 4; *La Patria* (Lima), 24 December 1879, in Ahumada Moreno, *Guerra del Pacífico*, 2:237; Alba, *Diario*, 54; Claros, *Diario*, 23, 48; Díaz Arguedas, *Historia*, 200, 205; Ochoa, *Diario*, 312; Francisco Benavente to Narciso Campero, San Cristóbal, 31 August 79, in *Documentos relativos a la organización*, 129–30; Alba, *Diario*, 54; Birbuet España, *Recuerdos*, 47; Claros, *Diario*, 59–60.

120. Entry of 13 May 1879 in Claros, *Diario*, 14–15.

121. Alba, *Diario*, 54, 66–67; Claros, *Diario*, 8; Narciso Campero to Hilarión Daza, Potosí, 6 June 1879, 14, Campero to Chief of the Army's General Staff, Cotagaita, 27 July 1879, 47, Francisco Buitrago to Ministry of Property and War, Potosí, 22 August 1879, 88, Campero to Buitrago, San Cristóbal, 3 September 1879, 97, Francisco Velasco to Campero, 27 December 1879, 198–99, *Documentos relativos a la organización*.

122. M. González Prada, *Impresiones*, 213–14; Le León, *Recuerdos*, 24–25; Markham, *War between Peru and Chili*, 99–100; Perolari-Malmignati, *Il Perú*, 307.

123. Rivas and Rivas, *Mantilla y Huancavilca*, 88–90; Manrique, *Guerrillas indígenas*, 201, 203; Moreno de Cáceres, *Recuerdos*, 43.

124. Luis Guzmán Palomino, "La resistencia de fuerzas irregulares que precedío a la victoriosa contraofensiva de Julio de 1882," in Peru, Ministry of War, *Guerra del Pacífico*, 2:400, 478.

125. Juan Buendía to Mariano Prado, Iquique, 29 October 1879, in Buendía, *Guerra con Chile*, 143; Belisario Suárez, Tarapacá, 23 November 1879, 2:142–44, Guillermo Zilveti to Political and Military Superior Chief of the Departments of the South, 15 April 1880, 2:531, in Ahumada Moreno, *Guerra del Pacífico*.

126. Mariano Prado to Juan Buendía, Arica, 22 September 1879, in Buendía, *Guerra con Chile*, 152; Juvenal Zorrilla et al. to Prefect of Ica, Huayuri, 1 April 1880, 8:63–64, Segundo Leiva to Colonel War, Arequipa, 7, 13, 16, May 1880, 8:70, José Martínez to Secretary of Guerra, Ica, 6 April 1880, 8:65, in Ahumada Moreno, *Guerra del Pacífico*.

127. Andrés Cáceres to Prefect, Departament of Ayacucho, Izcuchaca, 28 June 1882, in *Diario Oficial* (Lima), and 11 August 1882, in Guzmán Palomino, *Campaña de la Breña*, 173; Segundo Leiva to Colonel War, Arequipa, 7 May 1880, 8:70, Benito Neto, *La Patria* (Lima), Arica, 24 December 1879, 2:237, in Ahumada Moreno, *Guerra del Pacífico*.

128. Guillermo Zilveti to Political and Military Superior Chief of the Departments of the South, 15 April 1880, 2:531, José Mariano Jiménez, circular, Cuzco, 12 June 1880, 3:217–18, Agustín Gamarra to Piérola, Arequipa, 11 February 1880, 7:86–88, in Ahumada Moreno, *Guerra del Pacífico*.

129. Medina, Excusión a Tarapacá, 12; Pizarro, *Abastecimeintos militares*, 35.

130. Justo Arteaga to Minister of War and Navy, Antofagasta, 1 May 1879, 6:10, Vicente Dávila Larraín to Minister, Valparaíso, 9 January 1880, 2:321–22, Decree, Santiago, 8 December 1879, 2:244, in Ahumada Moreno, *Guerra del Pacífico*.

131. J. Brand[s] to Emilio Valverde, Pisco, 16 August 1881, in *Huáscar*, 84; *La Patria* (Valparaíso), 1 July 1880.

132. Eleutario Ramírez to Minister of War and Navy, Calama, 30 April 1879, in Ahumada Moreno, *Guerra del Pacífico*, 6:12.

133. Rosales, *Mi campaña*, 129.

134. Sepúlveda Rojas, *Así vivieron y vencieron*, 164.

135. Ibarra Díaz, *Campaña de la Sierra*, 76–77. See also Ibarra Díaz's unpublished manuscript "El rigor de la Sierra," qtd. in Rodríguez Rautcher, *Problemática*, 50–51, 56.

136. Roberto Souper to Cornelio Saavedra, 26 June 1879, Fondos Varios, vol. 559, Archivo Nacional.

137. Benavides Santos, *Seis años*, 35–36; 39; Basilio Urrutia to Commander, Army of the North, Santiago, 10 June 1879, in Ahumada Moreno, *Guerra del Pacífico*, 2:39.

138. Poblete, "Servicio sanitario," 38, no. 39:485.

139. Castro E., *Diario de Campaña*, 43; S. Urízar Gárfias (Batallón Talca) to Commander-in-Chief of Arms, Trujillo, 8 February 1882, in Ahumada Moreno, *Guerra del Pacífico*, 6:467–48.

140. Ruperto Marchant Pereira to Jorge Montes, Antofagasta, 18 March 1879, in Marchant Pereira, "Correspondencia del capellán," 354; *El Censor* (San Felipe), 10 February 1880; *El Mercurio* (Valparaíso), 20 January 1880; *La Revista del Sur* (Concepción), 24 February 1880; Benavides Santos, *Seis años*, 95.

141. Acland, *Six Weeks*, 16; Acland, "Descripción," 71; Benavides Santos, *Seis años*, 201.

142. *La Discusión* (Chillán), 8 January 1880.

143. Francisco Echaurren to Minister, Valparaíso, 2 August 1879, 6:26, Wenceslao Díaz to Quatermaster of Army and Navy, Santiago, 1 August 1879, 6:26, Erasmo Escala to Minister of War and Navy, Antofagasta, 7 July 1879, 6:25–26, in Ahumada Moreno, *Guerra del Pacífico*.

144. Urquieta, *Recuerdos de la vida*, 2:12; Juan Martínez (CO, Batallón Atacama) to General, Alto de la Villa, Moquegua, 25 March 1880, in Ahumada Moreno, *Guerra del Pacífico*, 2:434–35; "Juana López, cantinera," 21.

145. *Los Tiempos* (Santiago), 2 April 1880; *El Telégrafo* (Chillán), 16 May 1879; *El Lota* (Lota), 1 June 1879; *La Esmeralda* (Lota), 16 April 1882; *El Maipo* (San Bernardo), 18 April 1880.

146. Flint, *Memories*, 85.

147. De Secada, "Arms, Guano, and Shipping," 612.

148. Manuel Irigoyen to Ramón Vallarino, Secret, Lima, 14 April 1879, 4:24, Luis E. Márquez to Minister of Foreign Relations, Panama, 5 May 1879, 3:26–27, Irigoyen to Peru's Minister in Centra America, Secret, Lima, 28 May 1879, 4:30, Márquez to Minister of Foreign Relations, Panama, 18 June, 4, 29 July, 13 August, 17 September, and 1 October 1879, 3:27, 28, 32–33, 35, 39, 40, 41, Vallarino to Minister of Foreign Relations, 18, 23 June 1879, 3:46, 47, Statement by Columbian Government, Panama, 27 June 1879, 3:47–48, Vallarino to Minister of Foreign Relations, 19 November 1879, 3:49, A. V. de la Torre to Minister of Foreign Relations, Buenos Aires, 5 June and 31 July 1879, 4:75–76, M. M. Rivas to Minister of Foreign Relations, Panama, 27 July 1880, 4:102, in Ahumada Moreno, *Guerra del Pacífico*.

149. Juan M. Echenique, Bando, Lima, 21 January 1880, 2:344, Andrés Cáceres, Tarma, 22 July and 29 November 1882, 7:247, 387–88, in Ahumada Moreno, *Guerra del Pacífico*.

150. Alberto Blest Gana to Minister of War, Paris, 6 March 1879, 7:6, C. Morla Vicuña to Blest Gana, Amberes, 5 March 1879, 7:6–7, Blest Gana to Minister of War, Paris, 21 March, 18 April, 29 May, 11 July, 8 August, and 29 December 1879, 7:7–9, 11–12, 14–17, 20–21, Morla Vicuña to Minister of War, Paris, 17 May 1879, 7:10–11, Blest Gana to Minister of War, Paris, 28 January and 20 April 1880, 7:21–22, 26, in Ahumada Moreno, *Guerra del Pacífico*.

151. Alberto Blest Gana to Minister of War, London, 20 April 1880, 7:25, C. Morla Vicuña to Minister of War, Hamburgo, 12 April 1880, 7:25–26, in Ahumada Moreno, *Guerra del Pacífico.*

152. Another sutler, Alejandro Fraser, also refused to deliver bullets until he received his payment. Telmo Ichaso to Narciso Campero, Tupiza, 5 October 1879, 110, Hilarión Daza to Campero, Tacna, 21 August 1879, Campero to Chief of Staff, Cota, 1, 5 August 1879, 6, 49–50, in *Documentos relativos a la organización*; Agustin Blanco to J. L. Quiñones, Cochabamba, 12 September 1879, 2:30–31, Manuel Landaeta to Peru's Minister in Bolivia, Sucre, 26 September 1879, 2:31, in Ahumada Moreno, *Guerra del Pacífico*; Alba, *Diario,* 33.

153. Francisco Buitrago to Narciso Campero, Potosí, 1 August 1879, in *Documentos relativos a la organización,* 78; Bolivia, Ministry of War, *Memoria, 1883,* 21; Peru, Ministry of War and the Navy, *Memoria del ramo de guerra, 1878,* 6–7, 9; Chile, Ministry of War, *Memoria, 1878,* 107; Le León, *Recuerdos,* 23; *El Peruano* (Lima), 9 June 1879.

154. Benedicto, "Servicio," 63–64.

155. "Sinopsis estadística de la República de Chile," in Chile, *Diario Oficial,* 5 January 1880; Markham, *War between Peru and Chile,* 42–43; Basadre, *Historia,* 5th ed., 5:2061.

156. Villalobos, *Historia,* 159.

157. Chile, *Diario Oficial,* 30 August 1880.

158. Lynch, *Memoria,* 82–83.

159. Sinopsis estadística, in Chile, *Diario Oficial,* 5 January 1880.

160. Peru, Ministry of War, Permanent Commission, *Gesta de Lima,* 30–31.

161. Peru, Ministry of War and the Navy, *Memoria de guerra y marina, 1878,* 69, notes that the medical corps consisted of fifty-seven men.

162. Lastres, *Historia,* 3:239, 243; Plácido Garrido Mendivilto to Presidente Junta Central de Ambulancias, Arica, 3 December 1879, in Ahumada Moreno, *Guerra del Pacífico,* 8:50–51.

163. Dalence, *Informe histórico,* 2, 56; Díaz Arguedas, *Historia,* 171; Manuel Othón Jofré to Prefects, La Paz, October 1879, in Ochoa, *Diario,* 256.

164. Poblete, "Servicio sanitario," 33, no. 37:470.

165. Chile, Ministry of War, *Memoria, 1879,* 7; Poblete, "Servicio sanitario," 33, no. 37:468–69.

166. Dalence, *Informe histórico,* 5, 22.

167. Federico Granier and Luis Salinas Vega to Archbishop Juan de Dios Bosque, Tacna, 6 August 1880, 3:403–4, Archbishop to Granier, La Paz, 17 August 1880, 3:404, Dr. Zenon Dalence to Bishop, Tacna, 16 August 1880, 3:405–6, in Ahumada Moreno, *Guerra del Pacífico.*

168. Plácido Garrido Mendivil to Presidente de Junta Central de Ambulancias, Arica, 3 December 1879, in Ahumada Moreno, *Guerra del Pacífico,* 8:50–51.

169. Poblete, "Servicio sanitario," 35, no. 39:475.

170. Plácido Garrido Mendivil to Presidente de Junta Central de Ambulancias, Arica, 3 December 1879, 8:50–51, Garrido Mendivil to Chief, Chilean Army, Oficina Huáscar, 20, 21 November 1879, 8:51, in Ahumada Moreno, *Guerra del Pacífico*.

171. Erasmo Escala to Plácido Garrido Mendivil, Dolores, 21 November 1879, in Ahumada Moreno, *Guerra del Pacífico*, 8:51.

172. Dr. Zenon Dalence to Archbishop, Tacna, 16 August 1880, 3:405–6, Eliodoro Camacho to Chief, Chilean Army, Tacna, 25 August 1880, 3:406, in Ahumada Moreno, *Guerra del Pacífico*.

173. Dalence, *Informe histórico*, 23.

174. R. Torrico, Lima, 4 December 1880, in Ahumada Moreno, *Guerra del Pacífico*, 4:353.

175. Browne, "Growing Power," 56, 74; "Growing Power," 114.

176. Markman, *The War*, 207–8.

177. *El Mercurio* (Valparaíso), 15 April 1879; Curtis, "South American Yankee," 566; Uriburu, *Guerra del Pacífico*, 154; Paz Soldán, *Narración histórica*, 476–77, 495; Molina, *Hojas*, 26; Caviano, *Historia de la guerra*, 2:69; *El Correo de Quillota* (Quillota), 13 June 1880.

178. *El Mercurio* (Valparaíso), 5, 10, 13 December 1879, J. Martínez to Alejandro Gorostiaga, 20 December 1879, in *El Mercurio*, 18 January 1880; D. Zañartu to President, 21 January 1881, in Ahumada Moreno, *Guerra del Pacífico*, 5:103; Grieve, *Historia*, 341.

179. Manrique, *Guerrillas indígenas*, 147, 201; Palma, *Crónicas*, 217; Bulnes, *Historia*, 3:24–25.

180. Greene, *Report of the Russian Army*, 110; Spiers, *Late Victorian Army*, 73–74; Coffman, *Old Army*, 196–97; McCann, *Soldiers*, 72. It should be noted that such practices, however bloodthirsty, were beginning to fall out of favor. The British, Russian, and U.S. armies employed similar punishments. In addition to the whip, whose use the English did not outlaw until 1881, the Victorian army even branded deserters, a practice it halted in 1871. The Americans, who after 1833 mandated flogging for only one offense—desertion—abandoned the lash in 1861. The Russians, as of 1879, continued to rely on the whip as did the Brazilians ten years later.

181. Mercado Moreira, *Guerra del Pacífico*, 263; Claros, *Diario*, 19.

182. Benavides, *Historia*, 35; del Solar, *Diario*, 44, 69–70; Acland, *Six Weeks*, 10; Rosales, *Mi campaña*, 25, 99, 138; Chaparro White, *Recuerdos*, 48.

183. Ochoa, *Diario*, 263; Alba, *Diario*, 61, 81, 82; Piérola, 14 June 1881, in Ahumada Moreno, *Guerra del Pacífico*, 5:439; Ibarra Díaz, *Campaña de la Sierra*, 72; Rosales, *Mi campaña*, 138, 145–46.

184. Palma, *Crónicas*, 56, 67, 72.

3. Comparing the Navies

1. Grez, "Supuesta preparación," 111–39; Civati Bernasconi, *Guerra del Pacífico*, 1:117, 123; Dellepiane, *Historia militar*, 2:27–30, 65.

2. Fuenzalida Bade, *Marinos*, 27–29, 55–57, 151–52, 160, 227–30, 265–71.

3. Alberto Blest Gana to Aníbal Pinto, Paris, 8 March 1878, Fondos Varios, vol. 413, Archivo Nacional; Arosemena Garland, *Armamentismo*, 147, 154–60.

4. Clowes, *Modern Naval Campaigns*, 105.

5. Mason, *War on the Pacific Coast*, 14.

6. Mason, *War on the Pacific Coast*, 15; Clowes, *Modern Naval Campaigns*, 77.

7. For reasons of economy, the navy sold the *Abtao* prior to the outbreak of the conflict. When the war began, it managed to repurchase the ship. García Castelblanco, *Estudio*, 155.

8. Chile, Ministry of War and Navy, *Memoria de guerra, 1878*, xvi, 190. Prior to 21 May, the navy added two nine-pound guns.

9. López Urrutia, *Historia*, 407; Chile, Ministry of War and Navy, *Memoria de guerra, 1880*, 6.

10. Mason, *War on the Pacific Coast*, 17.

11. The specifications are largely taken from the 1878 *Memoria*, reprinted in López Martínez, *Historia marítima*, 252–62. Mason, *War on the Pacific Coast*, 20; Valdizán Gamio, *Historia naval*, 4:191–93. Any differences may be due to the fact that the 1878 *Memoria* appeared prior to the onset of the war, while Mason published his study in 1883 after various repairs and additions had been made.

12. The Peruvians required fourteen anxiety-filled months to tow these unwieldy vessels from New Orleans to Callao. Mason, *War on the Pacific Coast*, 18–20.

13. Chile, Central Office of Statistics, *Estadística*, 364.

14. Vargas Valenzuela, *Tradición naval*, 40–43.

15. Hilarión Daza, Decree, La Paz, 26 March 1879, Chile, *Boletín de la Guerra del Pacífico*, 29 May 1879.

16. Manuel Irigoyen to Peru's Minister in London, Lima, 16 September 1879, in Ahumada Moreno, *Guerra del Pacífico*, 4:45.

17. Draft, Law Offices, 12 July 1879, Archivo Nacional, Foreign Office, General Correspondence, 16/205, 163–64.

18. Draft of Letter from Marquis of Salisbury to Lord Commissioners of the Admiralty, 15 August 1879, FO 16 205, 266; Thomas Osborn to William Evarts, Santiago, 11 June 1879, no. 101 in United States of America, *Message from the President*, 88.

19. William Evarts to Newton Pettis, Washington, 23 June 1879, in United States of America, *Message from the President*, 1; John Holker to Lord Salisbury, 19 July, 28 July 1879, Archivo Nacional, Foreign Office, 205.

20. Evaristo Gómez Sánchez to Secretary of State in the Foreign Ministry, Montevideo, 19 August 1880, in Ahumada Moreno, *Guerra del Pacífico*, 4:89. The Bolivian government subsequently suggested that its minister in Argentina give mercenaries letters of marque to attack Chilean ships sending nitrate to Europe.

21. Ochoa, *Diario*, 74. Apparently a group of Peruvian sailors purchased another ship, the *Laura*, which, like the *Antofagasta*, participated in the war until the Peruvian government forced its captain to quit. Sapunar Peric, "Cosario boliviano *Laura*," 72–75.

22. Chile, Ministry of War and Navy, *Memoria de guerra, 1878*, xx, 187–88.

23. Uribe, *Combates*, 9; García Castelblanco, *Estudio*, 158.

24. Uribe, *Combates*, 9.

25. Chile, Ministry of War and Navy, *Memoria de guerra, 1878*, 190, 224–27, 229, 232, 234–35.

26. Chile, Ministry of War and Navy, *Memoria de guerra, 1878*, 231–32; Echaurren, "Marinería de la Escuadra," Valparaíso, 7 August 1872, and "Desertores de la Armada," Valparaíso, 17 March 1875, in Chile, Ministry of the Navy, *Manual de Marino*, 2:196–97, 260–61.

27. Cornelio Saavedra to Eulogio Altamirano, 29 October 1878, Archivo Nacional, Fondos Varios, vol. 559.

28. Chile, Ministry of the Navy, *Memoria, 1882*, x.

29. Chile, Ministry of the Navy, *Memoria, 1883*, 72–73, and *Memoria, 1884*, 174.

30. Chile, Ministry of the Navy, *Memoria, 1884*, 243–44.

31. Chile, Ministry of the Navy, *Memoria, 1884*, 243–44; Dr. Manuel Ramírez to Quartermaster General, 22 June 1879, in Chile, *Diario Oficial*, 28 June 1879; Dr. Alexis Scherbakoff to Chief Surgeon of the Department of the Navy, Valparaíso, 1 April 1881, in Chile, Ministry of the Navy, *Memoria, 1880*, 158, 261.

32. Chile, Ministry of the Navy, *Memoria, 1880*, 262.

33. Dr. Alexis Scherbakoff to Chief Surgeon of the Department of the Navy, Valparaíso, 1 April 1881, in Chile, Ministry of the Navy, *Memoria, 1880*, 159.

34. Chile, Ministry of the Navy, *Memoria, 1882*, x–xi, Javier Villanueva to Commander-in-Chief of the Navy, Valparaíso, 29 April 1882, *Memoria, 1882*, 76, *Memoria, 1884*, xviii, 178, 191.

35. Javier Villanueva to Commander-in-Chief of the Navy, Valparaíso, 29 April 1882, in Chile, Ministry of the Navy, *Memoria, 1882*, 75–76.

36. "Cirujano mayor del departamento," 29 April 1882, in Chile, Ministry of the Navy, *Memoria, 1882*, 76.

37. Chile, Ministry of War and Navy, *Memoria de guerra, 1878*, xvi, xviii, 228, 232, 241.

38. Chile, Ministry of War and Navy, *Memoria de guerra, 1878*, 241.

39. Parkenham to Salisbury, Santiago, 7 April 1879, Archivo Nacional, Foreign Office, 16, vol. 202, no. 14.

40. Qtd. in Barros Arana, *Histoire*, 62.

41. Peru, Ministry of War and the Navy, *Memoria de guerra y marina*, 2:9–10, 12.

42. Prado's inaugural address was reprinted in Chile's *Diario Oficial*, 28 August 1878.

43. López Martínez, *Historia marítima*, 10:757.

44. López Martínez, *Historia marítima*, 10:776–77.

45. Peru, Ministry of War and the Navy, *Memoria de guerra y marina*, 2:13. More than 120 years later, Adm. Melitón Carvajal Pareja (ret.) concluded that the Peruvian navy's ships were quite seaworthy. *Historia marítima*, 1:98, 108–9, 110, 158.

46. Alejandro Fierro to Minister of War and Navy, Santiago, 25 March 1879, in Ahumada Moreno, *Guerra del Pacífico*, 5:4.

47. López Martínez, *Historia marítima*, 10:72–73.

48. López Martínez, *Historia marítima*, 10:23, 76–78.

49. *El Comercio* (Lima), 14 March 1879, and *La Opinión Nacional* (Lima), qtd. in López Martínez, *Historia marítima*, 10:779–90. The material in *La Opinión Nacional* was a letter to the newspaper, which was republished in *El Comercio*, 28 March 1879.

50. Romero Pintado, *Historia marítima*, vol. 8, no. 2, 132–47; López Martínez, *Historia marítima*, 10:105–6; Peru, Ministry of War and the Navy, *Memoria de guerra y marina*, 2:5.

51. López Martínez, *Historia marítima*, 10:112.

52. Vegas G., *Historia*, 189; Peru, Ministry of War and the Navy, *Memoria de guerra y marina*, 2:5; Mason, "War between Chile, Peru, and Bolivia," 55.

53. *El Comercio* (Lima), 3 March 1879, qtd. in López Martínez, *Historia marítima*, 10:778.

54. *El Comercio* (Lima), 20 March 1877, qtd. in López Martínez, *Historia marítima*, 10:67.

55. Mason, "War between Chile, Peru, and Bolivia," 555.

56. López Martínez, *Historia marítima*, 10:115, 117, 118.

57. *La Opinión Nacional* (Lima) qtd. in Vegas G., *Historia*, 184.

58. Antonio 2. Marazzi to J. Frederick, Iquique, 10 April, 1879, in Ahumada Moreno, *Guerra del Pacífico*, 8:76.

59. Mason, *War on the Pacific Coast*, 18; López Martínez, *Historia marítima*, 10:70.

60. Juan Moore to Commander-in-Chief of the First Naval Division, Iquique, 22 May 1879, in Paz Soldán, *Narración histórica*, 172, 174.

61. *El Peruano* (Lima), 29 April 1879.

62. Antonio de la Haza to Miguel Grau, Callao, 15 July 1879, in Ahumada Moreno, *Guerra del Pacífico*, 1:597.

63. Vegas G., *Historia*, 184.

64. *El Peruano* (Lima), 27 March 1879.

65. "Nómina de los prisoneros i muertos a bordo del *Huáscar*," in Ahumada Moreno, *Guerra del Pacífico*, 1:500, also Chile, *Boletín de la Guerra del Pacífico*, 20 October 1879; Luis A. Castillo, Antofagasta, 10 October 1879, in Ahumada Moreno, *Guerra del Pacífico*, 1:500.

66. Meigs, "War in South America," 462; Mason, *War on the Pacific Coast*, 13, 21; Karsten, *Naval Aristocracy*, 300, 303.

67. Meigs, "War in South America," 461–62.

68. Uribe, *Combates*, 10.

4. Chipana to Iquique

1. Leigh, "Peruvia, Bolivia, and Chile," 539; Bonilla, *Gran Bretaña*, 1:176, 194.

2. "Grau: El marino epónimo del Perú," in *Fuentes para el estudio del historia naval del Perú*, 2:761–62.

3. Basadre, *Historia*, 8:95.

4. Fuenzalida Bade, *Marinos*, 267–71.

5. Williams Rebolledo, *Operaciones*, 12–13.

6. Rafael Sotomayor to Aníbal Pinto, 5, 7, 12 May 1879, Correspondencia de Pinto, vol. 1, Fondos Varios, Archivo Nacional, also in Sotomayor, "Correspondencia," 285–94.

7. Rafael Sotomayor to Aníbal Pinto, Secret, Antofagasta, 4 June 1879, in Sotomayor, "Correspondencia," 292–93; Sotomayor to Antonio Varas, Iquique, 5 June 1879, in Varas, *Correspondencia*, 128, 155–56; Domingo Santa María to Pinto, 25 June 1879, Correspondencia de don Domingo Santa María a don Aníbal Pinto, vol. 416, Fondos Varios, Archivo Nacional.

8. Williams Rebolledo, *Operaciones*, 20–21.

9. Merlet Sanhueza, *Juan José Latorre*, 29, 31.

10. During the battle, the *Magallanes*'s 115–pound cannon tore loose from it deck and might have fallen into the ocean had the Chileans not stopped firing it. But it was faulty workmanship, not Peruvian skill, that caused this incident. Similarly, the Chileans did lose a steam launch but, again, not because it was damaged by shellfire. The *Magallanes*'s crew had to throw it overboard because it obstructed the ship's field of fire. "Combate de Chipana," 17 April 1879 (Report from the correspondent of *El Mercurio* [Valparaíso]), Manuel José Vicuña to Eulogio Altamirano, Caldera, n.d., Juan José Latorre, "Partes oficiales," 1 April 1879, Aurelio García y García, "Parte del Comandante García y García," Loa, 12 April 1879, "Parte de Comandante Portal", At Sea, 12 April 1879, "Parte de Comandante de la Guerra," At Sea, 12 April 1879, Onofre Peréz to Eloi T. Cavidez, n.d., J. M. Villarreal C. to Daniel, Iquique, 14 April 1879, Vicente Zegers to father, Iquique, 13 April 1879, in Ahumada Moreno, *Guerra del Pacífico*, 1:218–21; Melo, *Historia*, 1:323.

11. Melo, *Historia*, 1:323.

12. Remo, "La espedición de la 'Unión' i el 'Pilcomayo,'" in Ahumada Moreno, *Guerra del Pacífico*, 1:224–25.

13. *El Independiente* (Santiago), 19 April 1879; *El Ferrocarril* (Santiago), 30 April 1879.

14. Rafael Sotomayor to Aníbal Pinto, 27 April 1879, in Sotomayor, "Correspondencia," 192. Antonio Marazzi said it more tersely: the *Magallanes* escaped thanks to "its good speed and the cold blood of its commander." Antonio 2. Marazzi to Jorge Frederick, Iquique, 12 April 1879, in Ahumada Moreno, *Guerra del Pacífico*, 8:76.

15. Rafael Sotomayor to Belisario Prats, qtd. in Bulnes, *Historia*, 1:213.

16. "Telegramas oficiales perúanos," 1:230, Oscar Viel telegram to Minister of War, Caldera, 23 April 1879, 1:230–31, in Ahumada Moreno, *Guerra del Pacífico*.

17. Eulogio Altamirano to Minister of the Navy, Valparaíso, 27 April 1879, in Ahumada Moreno, *Guerra del Pacífico*, 1:232–33.

18. Williams Rebolledo, *Operaciones*, 28–29; Mason, *War on the Pacific Coast*, 29.

19. Williams Rebolledo, *Operaciones*, 31.

20. Enrique Simpson, "Partes oficiales," Iquique, 1 May 1879, in Ahumada Moreno, *Guerra del Pacífico*, 1:233–35.

21. Andrés Bustamante to Coronel, Prefect of Tarapacá, Mejillones del Perú, 1 May 1879, *El Peruano* (Lima).

22. Antonio Varas to Juan Williams Rebolledo, Santiago, 25 April 1879, in Ahumada Moreno, *Guerra del Pacífico*, 5:6–7.

23. *La Patria* (Valparaíso), 9, 10, 16 April 1879; *El Ferrocarril* (Santiago), 13 April 1879.

24. Rafael Sotomayor to Aníbal Pinto, June 1879, in Sotomayor, "Correspondencia," 415.

25. Juan Williams Rebolledo to Minister of Foreign Relations, Iquique Harbor, 9 May 1879, in Ahumada Moreno, *Guerra del Pacífico*, 5:8; Williams Rebolledo to Aníbal Pinto, Iquique, 15 May 1879, and to Antonio Varas, Iquique, 15 May 1879, Fondos Varios, vol. 838, Archivo Nacional.

26. *El Peruano* (Lima), 23 May 1879.

27. Paz Soldán, *Narración historica*, 121, 155–60; Bulnes, *Historia*, 1:219.

28. Aurelio García y García to Commander-in-Chief of the Second Naval Division, Callao, 25 May 1879, in Ugarte Chamorro, *Diario*, 127; Mariano Ignacio Prado to Minister of State in the Office of War and Navy, Arica, 24 May 1879, in Ahumada Moreno, *Guerra del Pacífico*, 1:383.

29. "Plan frustrado," in Ahumada Moreno, *Guerra del Pacífico*, 1:385.

30. Porras had ample reason to believe that some mines protected the *Esmeralda*. According to a survivor of the ship, midshipman and later admiral Arturo Wilson, the Chileans had experimented with making a mine to defend them-

selves. Under the direction of either an engineer or electrician, they filled a can with powder, which they electrically detonated. Seeing the explosion from shore, the Peruvians naturally believed that the Chileans had more of these weapons. Arturo Wilson to G. Bulnes, in Bulnes, *Historia*, 1:292–93.

31. A Peruvian sailor present at the battle claimed that he and his shipmates carried Prat to Grau's cabin, where he subsequently died. Chile, *Boletín de la Guerra del Pacífico*, 29 October 1879.

32. *El Independiente*, 23 April 1879.

33. Del Campo, *Campaña Naval*, 15–25.

34. Juan G. Moore to Commander-in-Chief of the First Naval Division, Iquique, 22 May 1879, "Partes Oficial," in Ahumada Moreno, *Guerra del Pacífico*, 1:299–300. Moore denied that he struck his colors, while Condell claims that he did.

35. *El Peruano* (Lima), 2 September 1879.

36. Justo Arteaga to Minister of War, Antofagasta, 30 May 1879, in Ahumada Moreno, *Guerra del Pacífico*, 1:390; del Campo, *Campaña naval*, 34–50.

37. Miguel Grau to Director of the Navy in the Ministry of Ramo, At Anchor, Ilo, 31 May 1879, in *Correspondencia general*, 178–80.

38. Eluogio Altamirano to Antonio Varas, 29 May 1879, in Varas, *Correspondencia*, 108.

39. Sater, *Heroic Image*, 48–68.

40. Domingo Santa María to Aníbal Pinto, 25 June 1879, Fondos Varios, vol. 415, Archivo Nacional.

41. Juan Moore to Carlos Condell, Arica, 14 June 1879, in Ahumada Moreno, *Guerra del Pacífico*, 1:306.

42. *El Peruano* (Lima), 26 May 1879.

43. Torres Lara, *Recuerdos*, 87; *El Peruano* (Lima), 26 May and 18 July 1879.

44. *El Peruano* (Lima), 29 May 1879.

45. *El Peruano* (Lima), 18 July 1879; Mariano Ignacio Prado to Minister of State in the Office of War and Navy, Arica, 24 May 1879, in *Diario de la campaña naval*, 116.

46. Julio O. Reyes, "Informaciones de Julio O. Reyes, corresponsal a bordo del 'Huáscar' de la 'Opinión Nacional' de Lima, sobre el combate de Iquique," in *Diario de la campaña naval*, 152.

47. Mason, *War on the Pacific Coast*, 32–33; Vegas G., *Historia*, 211.

48. Roberto Souper to Cornelio Saavedra, Antofagasta, 29 May 1879, Fondos Varios, vol. 559, Archivo Nacional.

49. García Castelblanco, *Estudio*, 175.

50. Roberto Souper to Cornelio Saavedra, Antofagasta, 4 June 1879, Fondos Varios, vol. 559, and José Alfonso to Aníbal Pinto, Antofagasta, 13 June 1879, vol. 414, Archivo Nacional; Birkedal, "Late War," 88. Jaime Puig, an Ecuadorian diplomat stationed in Iquique, noted that the blockading Chilean fleet spoke to each mail ship of the Pacific Steam Navigation Company as it proceeded south

and that most people of Iquique were aware that the Peruvians had left Callao. Puig y Veraguer, *Memorias*, 48–49.

51. Rafael Sotomayor to Aníbal Pinto, Antofagasta, 4 June 1879, in Sotomayor, "Correspondencia," 292–93; Sotomayor to Antonio Varas, Iquique, 5 June 1879, Domingo Santa María to Varas, Antofagasta, 27 June 1879, in Varas, *Correspondencia*, 128, 155–56.

52. José Alfonso to Aníbal Pinto, Antofagasta, 23 May 1879, Fondos Varios, vol. 414, Archivo Nacional.

53. *Los Tiempos* (Santiago) 25, 27, 29 May 1879; *El Ferrocarril* (Santiago), 24 May 1879; *La Patria* (Valparaíso), 30 May and 14 August 1879; *Las Novedades* (Santiago), 23, 30 May 1879; *El Independiente* (Santiago), 24 May 1879.

54. Juan Williams Rebolledo to Aníbal Pinto, Iquique, 15 May 1879, Fondos Varios, vol. 838, Archivo Nacional; Williams Rebolledo, *Operaciones*, 45–46.

55. Melo, *Historia*, 1:337.

5. Angamos and Beyond

1. Melo, *Historia*, 1:349.

2. Ejército del Perú, "Apuntes para la historia: Díario de la campaña," 2:99–100, Archivo Nacional.

3. Roberto Souper to Cornelio Saavedra, June 28 and 9 July, 1879, Antofagasta, Fondos Varios, vol. 559, Archivo Nacional.

4. Domingo Santa María to Antonio Varas, Antofagasta, 20 July 1879, in Varas, *Correspondencia*, 189–90.

5. Sater, "Chile during the First Months," 149, 153.

6. Domingo Santa María to Antonio Varas, 20 July 1879, in Varas, *Correspondencia*, 191; Roberto Souper to Cornelio Saavedra, June 28, 1879, Antofagasta, Fondos Varios, vol. 559, Archivo Nacional.

7. Miguel Grau to Minister of War, Ilo, 31 May 1879, in Ahumada Moreno, *Guerra del Pacífico*, 1:392.

8. Mason, *War on the Pacific Coast*, 34–35; George Robinson to Rear Adm. A. F. R. de Horsey, HMS *Turquoise*, Callao, 11 June 1879, FO 16/205/195. See also Miguel Grau to Commander-in-Chief of the Navy, 7 June 1879, 1:557, and Grau to Supreme Director of the War, 18 June 1879, 1:558, in Ahumada Moreno, *Guerra del Pacífico*.

9. "Llegada del *Huáscar* a Mollendo," 31 May 1879, in Ahumada Moreno, *Guerra del Pacífico*, 1:399.

10. Williams Rebolledo, *Operaciones*, 73; Fuenzalida Bade, *Armada*, 3:803.

11. Williams Rebolledo, *Operaciones*, 71.

12. "Encuentro del Huáscar con el Blanco Encalada," *La Opinión Nacional* (Lima), in Ahumada Moreno, *Guerra del Pacífico*, 1:398.

13. Juan Williams Rebolledo to Commander-in-Chief of the Navy, Iquique

Bay, 2 June 1879, in Ahumada Moreno, *Guerra del Pacífico*, 5:11–12; Williams Rebolledo, *Operaciones*, 79; J.R.C., "La campaña del 'Huáscar,'" *El Comercio* (Lima), 8 June 1879, in del Campo, *Campaña naval*, 34–50.

14. Miguel Grau to Director General of the War, 4 June 1879, in *Correspondencia general*, 35.

15. Miguel Grau to Commander-in-Chief of the Navy, 7, 9, 19 June 1879 in *Correspondencia general*, 38, 40, 41, 53.

16. Luciano Benjamín Cisneros to Minister of State, Paris, 15 July 1879, in Ahumada Moreno, *Guerra del Pacífico*, 7:75; Mason, *War on the Pacific Coast*, 35; Miguel Grau to Commander-in-Chief of the Navy, 7, 9 June 1879, in *Correspondencia general*, 38–39, 41.

17. Arosemena Garland, *Almirante Grau*, 195–97; Fuentes para el estudio del historia naval del Perú, 1:398, 434.

18. Roberto Souper to Cornelio Saavedra, Antofagasta, 29 May and 4 June 1879, Fondos Varios, vol. 559, Archivo Nacional.

19. Rafael Sotomayor to Cornelio Saavedra, Iquique, 9 April 1879, Fondos Varios, vol. 559, Archivo Nacional; Sotomayor to Aníbal Pinto, 4 June 1879, in Sotomayor, "Correspondencia," 411–18; Valdizan Gamio, *Historia naval*, 5:12; Personal Conversation with Dr. Joel Shulman, 5 May 1999, Los Angeles CA.

20. Domingo Santa María to Aníbal Pinto, 25 June 1879, Fondos Varios, vol. 415, Archivo Nacional; Sater, *Chile and the War of the Pacific*, 40–41.

21. Mason, War on the Pacific Coast, 36–37.

22. Juan Williams Rebolledo to Minister of War, Aboard the *Blanco Encalada*, Iquique Bay, 15 June 1879, in Ahumada Moreno, *Guerra del Pacífico*, 5:13–14.

23. Ochoa, *Diario*, 70.

24. Basilio Urrutia to Juan Williams Rebolledo, Santiago, 24 June 1879, in Ahumada Moreno, *Guerra del Pacífico*, 5:14.

25. Juan Williams Rebolledo to Commander-in-Chief, Antofagasta, 12 July 1879, in Ahumada Moreno, *Guerra del Pacífico*, 5:14–15; *El Comercio* (La Paz), 13 July 1879.

26. There is some debate over the status of the *Matías Cousiño*. Mason, *War on the Pacific Coast*, 36, claimed that Grau had actually captured the collier when he spied a ship that turned out to be the *Magallanes*. Unable to take the collier as a prize, Grau tried to destroy it. Juan José Latorre, Iquique, 10 July 1879, in Ahumada Moreno, *Guerra del Pacífico*, 1:422. The Peruvians claimed that the *Huáscar* fired on the collier. *El Mercurio*, 15 July 1879, 1:423–24, *El Comercio* (Lima), 11 July 1879, 1:424–26, Latorre to Command of the Blockade Division of Iquique, Iquique, 10 July 1879, 1:422–23, in Ahumada Moreno, *Guerra del Pacífico*.

27. Miguel Grau to Supreme Director of the War and Director of the Navy, 10 July 1879, in *Correspondencia general*, 84.

28. Mason, *War on the Pacific Coast*, 37; Juan José Latorre to Commanding Officer, *Cochrane*, Iquique, 10 July 1879, Enrique Simpson to Commanding Offi-

cer, Blockade Division of Iquique, Iquique, 10 July 1879, in Ahumada Moreno, *Guerra del Pacífico*, 1:422.

29. Miguel Grau to Augusto Castleton, Arica, 14 August 1879, qtd. in Arosemena Garland, *Almirante Grau*, 202–3.

30. Prefect of the Departament of Tarapacá, Iquique, 17 July 1879, in Ahumada Moreno, *Guerra del Pacífico*, 1:427.

31. Domingo Santa María to Antonio Varas, Antofagasta, 20 July 1879, in Varas, *Correspondencia*, 191.

32. Miguel Grau to Commander-in-Chief of the First General Division, Arica, 25 July 1879, 1:439–40, Aurelio García y García, Arica, 25 July 1879, 1:440–41, in Ahumada Moreno, *Guerra del Pacífico*.

33. Domingo Santa María to Antonio Varas, Antofagasta, 20 July 1879 in Varas, *Correspondencia*, 191; Santa María to José V. Lastarria, 6 October 1879 [*sic*], in Santa María, "Cartas," 255–60.

34. Miguel Grau to Supreme Chief of the Main Directorate of the War, Director of Navy, and Commander-in-Chief of the Batteries and Existing Forces in the Seat of Arica, 25 July 1879, in *Correspondencia general*, 90.

35. Basilio Urrutia to Commanding Officer of the Navy, Santiago, 30 July 1879, in Ahumada Moreno, *Guerra del Pacífico*, 5:18.

36. Basilio Urrutia to Commanding Officer of the Navy, Santiago, 30 July 1879, in Ahumada Moreno, *Guerra del Pacífico*, 5:19.

37. Basilio Urrutia to Commanding Officer of the Navy, Santiago, 30 July 1879, 4:18, Urrutia to Commanding Officers of the Squadron, Santiago, 30 July 1879, 5:19, in Ahumada Moreno, *Guerra del Pacífico*.

38. Bulnes, *Historia*, 1:394; J.R.C., "Capture del 'Rímac' e buques mercantes y el regimiento Yungay," *El Comercio* (Lima), 29 July 1879, in del Campo, *Campaña naval*, 67–83.

39. J.R.C., "Captura del 'Rímac' e buques mercantes y el regimiento Yungay," *El Comercio* (Lima), 29 July 1879, in del Campo *Campaña naval*, 83.

40. Ignacio Luis Gana to Commanding Officer of the Navy, Arica, 25 July 1879, in Ahumada Moreno, *Guerra del Pacífico*, 1:435–36, Lathrup to Commanding Officer, *Rímac*, 1:436–37, Gonzalo Bulnes, "Relación de don Gonzalo Bulnes sobre la captura del 'Rímac,'" 1:437–38, in Ahumada Moreno, *Guerra del Pacífico*.

41. Sentencia dada por el Consejo de Oficiales Jenerales en el proceso seguido al capitán de fragata Ignacio Gana, Valparaíso, 5 November 1880, in Ahumada Moreno, *Guerra del Pacífico*, 4:200–201.

42. Samuel Márquez to José Rafael de Izcue, Arica, 2 June 1879, in Ahumada Moreno, *Guerra del Pacífico*, 7:85.

43. Roberto Souper to Cornelio Saavedra, Antofagasta, 29 July 1879, Fondos Varios, vol. 559, Archivo Nacional, and Eulogio Altamirano to Aníbal Pinto, 6 August 1879, vol. 415.

44. Juan José Latorre to Benjamín Vicuña Mackenna, Iquique, 27 July 1879, published in *El Nuevo Ferrocarril* (Santiago), 20 October 1879.

45. Miguel Grau to Supreme Chief of the Main Directorate of the War, Director of Navy, and Commander-in-Chief of the Batteries and Existing Forces in the Seat of Arica, 25 July 1879, in *Correspondencia general*, 92.

46. Miguel Grau to Supreme Chief of the War and Director of the Navy, 10 August 1879, in *Correspondencia general*, 83-84.

47. J.R.C., "El viaje de la 'Unión' a 'Magallanes,'" *El Comercio* (Lima), 19 September 1879, in del Campo, *Campaña naval*, 111.

48. Aurelio García y García to Commander-in-Chief of the Second Naval Division, Punta Arenas, 14 September 1879, 1:476-77, Carlos Wood to Minister of the Navy, Magallanes, 19 August 1879, 1:475-76, Baslilio Urrutia to Governor, Magallanes Colony, Santiago, 4 August 1879, 5:19, Rafael Sotomayor to Commander, *Blanco Encalada*, Antofagasta, 2 September 1879, 5:32, in Ahumada Moreno, *Guerra del Pacífico*; Chile, Ministry of War and Navy, *Memoria de guerra, 1880*, 7.

49. El Mercurio qtd. in Vicuña Mackenna, Historia de la campaña de Tarapacá, 2:94.

50. Williams Rebolledo, *Operaciones*, 103; Basilio Urrutia to Commander of Squadron, Santiago, 30 July 1879, 5:19, Francisco Echaurren, Valparaíso, 16 August 1879, 5:20-24, in Ahumada Moreno, *Guerra del Pacífico*.

51. Williams Rebolledo to Minister of the Navy, Tocopilla, 3 August 1879, Antofagasta, 4 August 1879, in Ahumada Moreno, *Guerra del Pacífico*, 5:17-18.

52. Williams Rebolledo to Minister of the Navy, Iquique Bay, 28 July and 3, 4 August 1879, 5:16-18, Basilio Urrutia to Commanding Officer of the Navy, Santiago, 5 August 1879, 5:18, in Ahumada Moreno, *Guerra del Pacífico*.

53. *El Peruano* (Lima), 2 September 1879.

54. The quotation originated in Strachey's description of his fellow Apostle John Maynard Keynes's wartime work in the British government. *The Times Literary Supplement*, 24 December 1999.

55. The Lay torpedo, invented by an American, John Lay, was a wire-guided explosive directed to the target and exploded by a gunner. Gray, *Nineteenth-Century Torpedoes*, 41-61.

56. Curiously, neither Grau's official account of the battle nor that of Julio Octavio Reyes, a journalist for a Lima paper who sailed on the *Huáscar*, lauded Diez Canseco for saving the ship from the errant torpedo. Nor did Melitón Carvajal, who served aboard the *Huáscar* at that time, refer to this incident. Diez Canseco, moreover, had served on the *Huáscar* when it engaged the *Esmeralda* at Iquique. Sir William Laird Clowes also noted that he was "unable to verify it [the story of Diez Canseco's exploits] to my entire satisfaction, owing to the unusual reticence of the official eye-witnesses." *Modern Naval Campaigns*, 90. Yet, by 1883 Diez Canseco's feat had made him a Peruvian war hero. Markham, *War between*

Peru and Chile, 119. That Grau, Reyes, and Carvajal failed to mention Diez Canseco raises the question whether the incident actually occurred. On the other hand, a report by Patricio Iriarte, 12 July 1880, praises Diez Canseco while criticizing the manner in which the Lay torpedo was deployed. Melo, *Historia*, 1:355. Certainly the American naval observer Lt. Theodorus B. M. Mason seemed initially skeptical: "The following account of what next happened [the description of Diez Canseco's heroism] is generally accepted," the officer noted, "but I have been unable to verify it to my entire satisfaction, owing to the unusual reticence of the official eye-witnesses." Mason, *War on the Pacific Coast*, 38. In a sense, it did not matter if the incident truly occurred: Diez Canseco had provided Peru with one of its few naval victories. Recent research offers evidence that Diez Canseco did indeed prevent the torpedo from sinking the *Huáscar*. Carvajal Pareja, *Historia marítima del Perú*, Tomo 11, 2:392–93n143, 811–12.

57. Miguel Grau to Commander-in-Chief of the Batteries and Existing Forces in the Seat of Arica and Director of the Navy, 31 August 1879, in *Correspondencia general de la comandencia general*, 104, 106; Mariano Prado to La Puerta, 1 September 1879, qtd. in Grieve, *Historia*, 120; Mason, *War on the Pacific Coast*, 39; Clowes, *Modern Naval Campaigns*, 91.

58. Miguel Grau to Commander-in-Chief of the Batteries and Existing Forces in the Seat of Arica and Director of the Navy, 31 August 1879, in *Correspondencia general*, 104–11.

59. *El Peruano* (Lima), 6 October 1879.

60. Qtd. in Bulnes, *Historia*, 1:439–40.

61. Domingo Santa María to Galvarino Riveros, "Instrucciones para el Comandante en Jefe de la Escuadra, capitán de navío don Galvarino Riveros," Santiago, 18 September 1879, in Ahumada Moreno, *Guerra del Pacífico*, 1:474–75.

62. Domingo Santa María to Erasmo Escala, Santiago, 8 September, in Ahumada Moreno, *Guerra del Pacífico*, 2:50.

63. Scheina, *Latin America*, 34.

64. Fuenzalida Bade, *Armada*, 3:827–28.

65. Bulnes, *Historia*, 1:438.

66. C. Aguirre to Quartermaster, Caldera, 21 September 1879, Domingo Santa María to Quartermaster of Copiapó, 22 September 1879, Intendencia de Atacama, vol. 513, Archivo Nacional.

67. Domingo Santa María to Guillermo Matta, Moneda, 26, 27, 28 August 1879, Rafael Sotomayor to Quartermaster of Atacama, Antofagsta, August 1879, Intendencia de Atacama, vol. 528, Archivo Nacional; Sotomayor to Minister of War, Antofagasta, 3 September 1879, in Ahumada Moreno, *Guerra del Pacífico*, 5:31.

68. Galvarino Riveros et al., Minutes of the Navy Council of War, Mejillones, 1, 5 October 1879, in Ahumada Moreno, *Guerra del Pacífico*, 1:576–77, Galvarino Riveros to Commanding Officer of the Navy, Antofagasta, 10 October 1879, 1:486–87, in Ahumada Moreno, *Guerra del Pacífico*.

69. Guillermo Matta to Minister of the Interior, Copiapó, 5 October 1879, J. Walton to Quartermaster, Ovalle, 5 October 1879, Rafael Sotomayor to A. Gandarillas, Antofagasta, 5 October 1879, Gomez Solar to Minister of the Interior, Coquimbo, 5 October 1879, Sotomayor to Domingo Santa María, Antofagasta, 7 October 1879, Sotomayor to Minister of War, Antofagasta, 7 October 1879, Ministerio del Interior, vol. 910, Archives Nacional. Addition annal information on this topic can be found in Intendencia de Atacama, vol. 528, Archivo Nacional.

70. Grieve, *Historia*, 245–50.

71. Mason, *War on the Pacific Coast*, 42–43; Manuel M. Carvajal to Rear Admiral Commander-in-Chief of Arica, San Bernardo, 16 October 1879, 1:495–96, Pedro Gárezon to Melitón Carvajal, Antofagasta, 10 October, 1:497, Samuel MacMahon to Commanding Officer, *Huáscar*, Antofagasta, 10 October 1879, 1:497, in Ahumada Moreno, *Guerra del Pacífico*; *El Mercurio* (Valparaíso), 12 October 1879.

72. Pedro Gárezon to CF Melitón Carvajal, Antofagasta, 10 October 1879, in Ugarte Chamorro, *Diario*, 105; *El Corresponsal*, "Conversación con los prisioneros del "Huáscar,'" in Ahumada Moreno, *Guerra del Pacífico*, 1:520.

73. Rafael Sotomayor to Antonio Varas, Santiago, 17 October 1879, Fondos Varios, vol. 838, Archivo Nacional. Today the *Huáscar* rests in Talcahuano Harbor.

74. Federico Landaeta to Peru's Minister, Potosi, 24 October 1989, 2:108, J. L. Quiñones to Minister of Foreign Relations, La Paz, 7 November 1879, 2:118, in Ahumada Moreno, *Guerra del Pacífico*.

75. Fuenzalida Bade, *Armada*, 3:857.

76. Carlos Ferreyros to Minister of War and Navy, Pisagua, At anchor, 22 November 1879, 2:127–28, Galvarino Riveros to Minister of War and Navy, Pisagua, 20 November 1879, 2:126–27, Manuel Villavicencio to Capitán de Navío Mayor de Órdenes del Departamento, Aboard the *Chalaco*, 20 November 1879, 2:128–29, in Ahumada Moreno, *Guerra del Pacífico*.

77. Armstrong, *Torpedoes*, 72.

78. *El Peruano* (Lima), 25 August 1879.

79. Galvarino Riveros to Minister of War and Navy, Callao, 12 May 1880, in Ahumada Moreno, *Guerra del Pacífico*, 2:536–37. The Peruvians claimed that these were McEvoy drifting torpedoes. *Marino italiano*, 105.

80. Galvarino Riveros to Minister of War and Navy, Callao, 12 June 1880, in Ahumada Moreno, *Guerra del Pacífico*, 5:59.

81. *La Patria* (Lima), 26 April, 1880; *La Sociedad* (Lima), 7 May 1880, in *El Mercurio* (Valparaíso) 5, 21 May 1880.

82. Eduardo de la Barra to Augusto Matte, Valparaíso, 22, 26 April 1880, Fondos Varios, vol. 826, Archivo Nacional.

83. Galvarino Riveros to Minister of War and Navy, Aboard the *Blanco Encalada*, Pisagua, 26 November 1879, in Ahumada Moreno, *Guerra del Pacífico*, 5:37–38.

84. Orden del Día, 4 July 1880, in Ahumada Moreno, *Guerra del Pacífico*, 5:72. Vicuña Mackenna claims that the source of this torpedo was the Englishman Harris, who ran a torpedo factory on San Lorenzo Island. *Historia de la Campaña de Lima*, 433–34.

85. Cuadros's first attempt at manufacturing torpedoes supposedly misfired, killing an officer plus eight sailors. His second creation may have been designed to destroy the *O'Higgins*. Vegas G., *Historia*, 260.

86. Aníbal Pinto to José V. Lastarria, Santiago, 12 June 1880, in Pinto, "Hundimiento," 249.

87. Leoncio Señoret to Minister of the Navy, Callao Bay, 4 July 1880, 3:291–92, Ernesto Turenne, Ancón Bay, 23 July 1880, 3:293–96, Sumario indagatoria para averiguar la pérdida del crucero 'Loa' en la rada del Callao, el día 3 de julio de 1880," 3:301, in Ahumada Moreno, *Guerra del Pacífico*.

88. *El Ferrocarril* (Santiago), 15 August and 14 September 1880.

89. Manuel Baquedano to Aníbal Pinto, 9 July 1880, Fondos Varios, vol. 415, Archivo Nacional; Victor Bianchi to Benjamín Vicuña Mackenna, Callao, 17 July 1880, Archivo Benjamín Vicuña Mackenna, vol. 357; *El Mercurio* (Valparaíso), 12 July and 11 August 1880.

90. *El Mercurio* (Valparaíso), 10 July 1880.

91. *La Estrella de Panama* (Panama), 6 July 1880, 3:297, José Casimir Ulloa, *El Peruano* (Lima), 3 July 1880, 3:350–51, in Ahumada Moreno, *Guerra del Pacífico*.

92. Galvarino Riveros to Minister of War and Navy, Callao, 4 July 1880, in Ahumada Moreno, *Guerra del Pacífico*, 5:62.

93. Galvarino Riveros to Minister of War and Navy, Callao, 11 July 1880, in Ahumada Moreno, *Guerra del Pacífico*, 5:64.

94. *La Patria* (Lima), 15 September 1880, in Ahumada Moreno, *Guerra del Pacífico*, 3:441–42.

95. *La Esmeralda* (Coronel), 22 September 1880. Vicuña Mackenna claims that Peru's minister of development, Echegaray, had hired the services of two foreign adventurers, Pedro Beausejour and Aquiles Canti, to build more infernal machines. Their payment was based on what they managed to sink: an ironclad would earn six hundred thousand gold pesos. Sinking the *Huáscar* or any other ship would fetch one million dollars, or eight hundred thousand gold pesos. Vicuña Mackenna, *Historia de la Campaña de Lima*, 461.

96. A. Alfonso to President, Iquique, 17 September 1880, 3:433, Enrique T. Gutierrez to Chief of the Squadron (Riveros), Aboard the *Blanco Encalada*, 14 September 1880, 3:434, Report of the *El Mercurio* Correspondent, Arica, 18 September 1880, 3:435, "Como fué echada a pique la 'Covadonga': Descripción documentada por Benjamín Vicuña Mackenna," 3:442–43, "Sumario seguido para averiguar las causas de la pérdida de la goleta 'Covadonga' en Chancai, el 13 de Setiembre de 1880," 3:443–48, in Ahumada Moreno, *Guerra del Pacífico*.

97. *El Independiente* (Santiago), 18 September 1880.

98. Juan José Latorre to Minister of the Navy, Callao, 13 October 1880, Chile, *Boletín de la Guerra del Pacífico*, 6 November 1879; Vegas G., *Historia*, 261.

99. Stewart, "Peruvian Submarine," 468–78.

100. Ernesto Turenne to Benjamín Vicuña Mackenna, Ancon Bay, 23 July 1880, in Ahumada Moreno, *Guerra del Pacífico*, 3:295.

101. Markham, *War between Peru and Chile*, 221; M. García de la Huerta to Commanding Officer of the Fleet, Santiago, 27 October 1880, 5:80, Galvarino Riveros to Minister of War and Navy, Arica, 12 December 1880, 5:81, in Ahumada Moreno, *Guerra del Pacífico*; Spencer St. John to Earl of Granville, Lima, 6 October 1880, Captain Stephens, HMS *Tetis*, to Spenser St. John, Callao, 11 October 1880, FO 61/92.

102. Galvarino Riveros to Minister of War, Callao, 26 December 1880, in Ahumada Moreno, *Guerra del Pacífico*, 5:77.

103. M. García de la Huerta to Commanding Officer of the Fleet, Santiago, 27 October 1880, in Ahumada Moreno, *Guerra del Pacífico*, 5:80.

104. R. Amengual to Commanding Officer, *Cochrane*, Callao, 16, 17 September 1880, 3:448–50, R. Osorio to Commanding Officer of the Squadron, Callao, 16 September 1880, 3:448, in Ahumada Moreno, *Guerra del Pacífico*.

105. José Francisco Vergara to Commanding Officer of the Squadron, Santiago, 17 September 1880, 5:73, Galvarino Riveros to the Dean of the Diplomatic Corps, Callao Harbor, 21 September 1880, 5:73, Riveros to Aníbal Pinto, 6 October 1880, 3:471, Juan José Latorre to Commanding Officer of the Fleet, Callao, 22 September 1880, 3:472–73, Luis A. Castillo to Riveros, 24 September 1880, 3:473, Carlos Moraga to Commanding Officer of the Fleet, Arica, 25 September 1880, 3:473, Correspondencias i descripción de los puertos bombardeados, Las últimas operaciones marítimas, Arica, 8 October, 1880, 3:477–78, in Ahumada Moreno, *Guerra del Pacífico*.

106. Melo, *Historia*, 1:328, 331.

107. Caviano, *Historia de la guerra*, 1:259.

108. Conducta del García y García, Arica, 9 October 1879, in Ahumada Moreno, *Guerra del Pacífico*, 7:85–86. For the court-martial proceedings, see *Corbeta "Union."*

109. "Capture of the 'Huáscar'," 454.

110. Riveros, *Angamos* and *En la escuadra*.

6. The Land War Begins

1. Erasmo Escala to Minister of War and Navy, Antofagasta, 9 August 1879, in Ahumada Moreno, *Guerra del Pacífico*, 6:26.

2. Junta de Antofagasta, 28 June 1879, in Ahumada Moreno, *Guerra del Pacífico*, 3:80–82.

3. "Orden en que salío el convoi de Antofagasta i distribución del ejército," Ahumada Moreno, *Guerra del Pacífico*, 2:64–65.

4. Isiodoro Errázuriz to Minister of War, Antofagasta, 27 October 1879, in Ahumada Moreno, *Guerra del Pacífico*, vol. 7.

5. Bulnes, *Historia*, 1:527.

6. Humberstone, *Huida de Agua Santa*, 14; *El Comercio* (Lima), 2:95–96, *El Nacional* (Lima), 9 November 1879, 2:93–94, in Ahumada Moreno, *Guerra del Pacífico*.

7. Manuel T. Thomson to Commander-in-Chief of the Navy, Pisagua, 3 November 1879, 24–26, Patricio Lynch to General of the Navy, 7 November 1879, 40–42, in Chile, Ministry of the Navy, *Memoria, 1880*; Erasmo Escala to Minister of State, Hospicio, 10 November 1879, in Chile, Ministry of War and Navy, *Memoria, 1880*, 48.

8. Erasmo Escala to Minister of War, Campamento de Hospicio, 10 November 1879, in Ahumada Moreno, *Guerra del Pacífico*, 2:73–76.

9. Machuca, *Cuatro campañas*, 1:263.

10. Issac Recabarren to Chief of the Army of the South, Agua Santa, 4 November 1879, 2:84–85, Ezequiel de la Peña to Gen. Pedro Villamil, Agua Santa, 4 November 1879, 2:85–86, "El Ayudante del Estado Mayor Boliviano," 2:86, *El Nacional* (Lima), Pozo Almonte, 9 November 1879, 2:93–94, Modesto Molina, "Sangriento Combate de Pisagua," *El Comercio* (Lima), 2:95–96, in Ahumada Moreno, *Guerra del Pacífico*; Estado Mayor General, *Historia*, 5:228; Juan Granier to Hilarión Daza, Agua Santa, November 1879, Jorge Salinas Vega to Luis Salinas Vega, Carmen Bajo, 9 November 1879, in Ochoa, *Diario*, 202–3.

11. Emilio Valverde to Commanding Officer, *Acidental*, Pisagua, 3 November 1879 in Chile, Ministry of the Navy, *Memoria, 1880*, 36–37.

12. Matte Varas, "Informe," 195.

13. José Alfonso to Aníbal Pinto, Valparaíso, 12 November 1879, Fondos Varios, vol. 414, Archivo Nacional, Eduardo de la Barra to Augusto Matte, 14 November 1879, vol. 826, and Pío Puelma to Maríano Guerrero Bascuñán, 5 November 1879, vol. 826.

14. Bulnes, *Historia*, 1:511.

15. Telegram, Caldera, 9 November 1879, in Ahumada Moreno, *Guerra del Pacífico*, 2:1, 22; Vergara, "Memorias," 39.

16. José Francisco Vergara, Combate de Agua Santa, Dolores, 8 November 1879, Chile, Ministry of War, *Memoria, 1879*, 50–53.

17. Bulnes, *Historia*, 1:512.

18. *El Titicaca* (La Paz), 23 November 1879.

19. Ochoa, *Diario*, 186; Mercado Moreira, *Guerra del Pacífico*, 54, 57.

20. Camacho, *Tratado sumario*, 392–93; Gamarra Zorrilla, *Guerra del Pacífico*, 114.

21. Díaz Arguedas, *Historia*, 203; Mercado Moreira, *Guerra del Pacífico*, 157; Gamarra Zorrilla, *Guerra del Pacífico*, 118.

22. Hilarión Daza, "Manifesto," Paris 1881, in Ahumada Moreno, *Guerra del Pacífico*, 4:157-58.

23. Mercado Moreira, *Guerra del Pacífico*, 157-59, 177-78; Juan José Pérez, *El Comercio* (Lima), in Ahumada Moreno, *Guerra del Pacífico*, 2:163.

24. Hilarión Daza, "Manifesto," in Ahumada Moreno, *Guerra del Pacífico*, 4:158; Mercado Moreira, *Guerra del Pacífico*, 57.

25. Urquieta, *Recuerdos de la vida*, 1:190-91; Amunátegui, 2:137, Juan Martínez to José Amunátegui, Dolores, 21 November 1879, 2:138-39, in Ahumada Moreno, *Guerra del Pacífico*.

26. Cáceres, *Guerra del 79*, 25. The number of Allied troops is adjusted for losses.

27. Dellepiane, *Historia militar*, 2:124-25.

28. Buendía, *Guerra con Chile*, 30; Belisario Suárez, Tarapacá, 23 November 1879, in Ahumada Moreno, *Guerra del Pacífico*, 2:142-44.

29. Ladislao Cabrera, *La Democracia*, in Ahumada Moreno, *Guerra del Pacífico*, 2:157.

30. Camacho, *Tratado sumario*, 404.

31. Cáceres, *Guerra del 79*, 26; Paz Soldán, *Narración histórica*, 322; Belisario Suárez to Juan Buendía, Puno, 12 August 1885, in Cáceres, *Guerra del 79*, 193.

32. Luis Felipe Rosas to Major General, La Angostura, 5 November 1879, in Buendía, *Guerra con Chile*, 182.

33. Cáceres, *Guerra del 79*, 26-27; Buendía, *Guerra con Chile*, 41-42; Belisario Suárez to Juan Buendía, Puno, 12 August 1885, in Cáceres, *Guerra del 79*, 191-92; Gamarra Zorrilla, *Guerra del Pacífico*, 99.

34. Armaza, *Verdad*, 5; Molina, *Hojas*, 37.

35. Erasmo Escala to Minister of War and Navy, Dolores, 25 November 1879, 2:134, Emilio Sotomayor to Escala, Dolores, 3 November 1879, 2:135, in Ahumada Moreno, *Guerra del Pacífico*.

36. Pedro Bustamante, *La Patria* (Lima), 19 January 1880, in Ahumada Moreno, *Guerra del Pacífico*, 2:216; Cáceres, *Guerra del 79*, 27; Dellepiane, *Historia militar*, 2:136.

37. Cáceres, *Guerra del 79*, 27; Belisario Suárez, Tarapacá, 23 November 1879, in Ahumada Moreno, *Guerra del Pacífico*, 2:142-44.

38. Belisario Suárez, Tarapacá, 23 November 1879, in Ahumada Moreno, *Guerra del Pacífico*, 2:142-44.

39. Remijo Morales Bermúdez to Chief of Staff, División de Vanguardia, Aguada de Ramírez, 20 November 1879, 2:145, Ladislao Cabrera, *La Democracia*, 2:156-57, in Ahumada Moreno, *Guerra del Pacífico*,.

40. José Amunátegui, Dolores, November 1879, 2:137, Emilio Sotomayor to Erasmo Escala, Campamento de Dolores, 3 November 1879, 2:135-36; José

Martínez to José Amunátegui, Campamento de Dolores, 21 November 1879, 2:138–39, in Ahumada Moreno, *Guerra del Pacífico*.

41. Belisario Suárez, Tarapacá, 23 November 1879, 2:142–44, Manuel Isaac Chamorro to Chief of Staff, Division of Vanguard, n.d., 2:144; Remijo Morales Bermúdez to Chief of Staff, Division of Vanguard, Aguada de Ramírez, 20 November 1879, 2:144–45, in Ahumada Moreno, *Guerra del Pacífico*.

42. Martiniano Urriola to Emilio Sotomayor, Campamento de Dolores, 20 November 1879, in Ahumada Moreno, *Guerra del Pacífico*, 2:139.

43. Donato Vásquez to Prefect and Commander of the Department, Oruro, 12 December 1879, in Ahumada Moreno, *Guerra del Pacífico*, 2:159.

44. Cáceres, *Guerra del 79*, 28.

45. Donato Vazquez to Prefect and Commander of the Department, Oruro, 12 December 1879, 159; Ladislao Cabrera, *La Democracia*, in Ahumada Moreno, *Guerra del Pacífico* 2:157; Molina, *Hojas*, 44.

46. *El Nacional* (Lima), 29 November 1879, in Ahumada Moreno, *Guerra del Pacfico*, 2:177.

47. *El Comercio* (Lima), 18 November 1879, in Ahumada Moreno, *Guerra del Pacífico*, 2:155.

48. Molina, *Hojas*, 33.

49. *El Nacional* (Lima), cited in *El Mercurio* (Valparaíso), 10 December 1879; *La Opiníon Nacional* (Lima), 29 December 1879, cited in *El Mercurio* (Valparaíso), 2 January 1880; Armaza, *Verdad*, 13.

50. *El Independente* (Santiago), 23 April 1879; *La Reforma* (La Paz), 2 December 1879, in *El Mercurio* (Valparaíso), 15 January 1880; Ladislao Cabrera, *La Democracia*, in Ahumada Moreno, *Guerra del Pacífico*, 2:156–57. There is some difference of opinion about this young woman's age. Alberto del Solar described her as an eighteen year old, thereby elevating the general's status from pedophile to lecher. *Diario*, 65.

51. Dublé Almeida, "Diario de Campaña," 111–12; Vergara, "Memorias," 56; *El Mercurio* (Valparaíso), 23 February 1880; Marchant Pereira, *Crónica*, 31.

52. Buendía, *Guerra con Chile*, 39; Ladislao Cabrera, *La Democracia*, in Ahumada Moreno, *Guerra del Pacífico*, 2:158; Poblete, "Servicio sanitario," 38, no. 39:480; Erasmo Escala to Minister of War and Navy, n.d., in Chile, Ministry of War and Navy, *Memoria de guerra, 1880*, 65.

53. Molina, *Hojas*, 26–27.

54. Alejandro Gorostiaga to Editor of *Los Tiempos*, Dolores, 31 December 1879, in Ahumada Moreno, *Guerra del Pacífico*, 2:302.

55. Ladislao Cabrera, *La Democracia*, in Ahumada Moreno, *Guerra del Pacífico*, 2:156–57; Molina, *Hojas*, 46.

56. Ladislao Cabrera, *La Democracia*, 2:157, Erasmo Escala to Minister of War, Pisagua, 2, 24 December 1879, 6:33, Emilio Sotomayor to Commander-in-Chief, Pisagua, 29 November 1879, 2:166–67, José Martínez to José Amunátegui, Camp

at Dolores, 21 November 1879, 2:139, in Ahumada Moreno, *Guerra del Pacífico*; Estado Mayor General, *Historia*, 5:362. Buendía, *Guerra con Chile*, 38;

57. Pinochet U., *Guerra del Pacífico*, 174.

58. Cáceres, *Guerra del 79*, 30–31; *La Patria* (Lima), 24 December 1879, 2:236–38, *La Democracia*, 2:157, in Ahumada Moreno, *Guerra del Pacífico*; Molina, *Hojas*, 44–45, 47.

59. Molina, *Hojas*, 49–50; Dellepiane, *Historia militar*, 2:154; Roberto, *El Nacional* (Lima), 8 December 1879, in Ahumada Moreno, *Guerra del Pacífico*, 2:216; Guzmán, *Apuntes*, 8–9.

60. José Echeverría to Chief of Staff, San Francisco, 25 November 1879, in Ahumada Moreno, *Guerra del Pacífico*, 3:90–91.

61. Erasmo Escala to Minister of War, Santa Catalina, 5 December 1879, in Chile, Ministry of War and Navy, *Memoria de guerra, 1879*, 68–71.

62. Ricardo Santa Cruz to Vicente Santa Cruz, Iquique, 24 December 1879 in *El Mercurio* (Valparaíso), 7 January 1880.

63. Bulnes, *Historia*, 1:681.

64. Ricardo Santa Cruz to Colonel Chief of Operations, Dibujo, 29 November 1879, in Ahumada Moreno, *Guerra del Pacífico*, 2:191–92.

65. Luis Arteaga to Commander of the Army of the North, Santa Catalina, 29 November 1879, Chile, Ministry of War and Navy, *Memoria, 1879*, 72–74; Ricardo Villagrán to Arteaga, n.d., in Ahumada Moreno, *Guerra del Pacífico*, 2:192–93.

66. O. Liborio Echanes to Luis Arteaga, Santa Catalina, 1 December 1879, in Ahumada Moreno, *Guerra del Pacífico*, 2:189–90.

67. "Importante correspondencia," in Ahumada Moreno, *Guerra del Pacífico*, 2:208–9.

68. Guzmán, *Apuntes*, 20.

69. Luis Arteaga to Commander-in-Chief, Santa Catalina, 4 December 1879, 2:189, O. Liborio Echanes to Arteaga, Santa Catalina, 1 December 1879, 2:190, Ricardo Santa Cruz to Chief of the Division, Dibujo, 29 November 1879, 2:191–92, in Ahumada Moreno, *Guerra del Pacífico*.

70. Dellepiane, *Historia militar*, 2:163; Molina, *Hojas*, 63; Guzmán, *Apuntes*, 15.

71. O. Liborio Echanes to Luis Arteaga, Santa Catalina, 1 December 1879, in Ahumada Moreno, *Guerra del Pacífico*, 2:190; Guzmán, *Apuntes*, 19–20; Ochoa, *Diario*, 237.

72. José Vidaurre, Quillasguasa, 25 January 1880, in Ahumada Moreno, *Guerra del Pacífico*, 2:347–348.

73. Pinochet U., *Guerra del Pacífico*, 213; Francisco Bolognesi, Parte del comandante de la tercera división, in Ahumada Moreno, *Guerra del Pacífico*, 2:199–200.

74. Juan Buendía to Secretary General of the South and Supreme General Director of the War, n.d., 2:196, Belisario Suárez to Lizardo Montero, Mocha, 30 November 1879, 2:197, in Ahumada Moreno, *Guerra del Pacífico*.

75. Claros, *Diario*, 26; Buendía, *Guerra con Chile*, 36; Benito Neto, *La Patria* (Lima), Arica, 24 December 1879, in Ahumada Moreno, *Guerra del Pacífico*, 2:236–38; de Varigny, *Guerra del Pacífico*, 105; Guzmán, *Apuntes*, 27.

76. Lizardo Montero, Arica, 27 November 1879, in Ahumada Moreno, *Guerra del Pacífico*, 2:219–20.

77. *El Nacional* (Lima), 20 December 1879, qtd. in *El Mercurio* (Valparaíso), 20 January 1880.

78. J. L. Quiñones to Manuel Irigoyen, La Paz, 26 October 1879, in Ahumada Moreno, *Guerra del Pacífico*, 2:35.

79. Zolio Flores to Hilarión Daza, Lima, 8 December 1879, in Ahumada Moreno, *Guerra del Pacífico*, 2:261.

80. *La Reforma* (La Paz), 2 December 1879, in *El Mercurio* (Valparaíso), 15 January 1880.

81. Juan Granier to Hilarión Daza, Tacna, 20 December 1879, in Ahumada Moreno, *Guerra del Pacífico*, 2:263.

82. Rafael Velarde to Minister of War and Navy, Secret, Lima, 26 November 1879, 4:57, Zolio Flores to Hilarión Daza, Lima, 8 December 1879, 2:261, in Ahumada Moreno, *Guerra del Pacífico*.

83. Zolio Flores to Hilarión Daza, Lima, 8 December 1879, 2:261–62; J. L. Quiñones to Manuel Irigoyen, La Paz, November 1879 Ahumada Moreno, *Guerra del Pacífico* 2:259, Juan Granier to Daza, Tacna, 20 December 1879, 2:262–63, in Ahumada Moreno, *Guerra del Pacífico*; *El Comercio* (La Paz), 19 December 1879, qtd. in Phillips, "Bolivia in the War," 164.

84. Claros, *Diario*, 28; Daza, in Ahumada Moreno, *Guerra del Pacífico*, 4:158.

85. Juan José Pérez, "Quien con los traidores?" *El Comercio* (Lima), 16 December 1879, in Ahumada Moreno, *Guerra del Pacífico*, 2:164.

86. Vidaurre Retamoso, *Presidente Daza*, 312.

87. *La Revista del Sur* (Tacna), 2:280–81, Juan José Pérez, *El Comercio* (Lima), 16 December 1879, 2:164–65, in Ahumada Moreno, *Guerra del Pacífico*.

88. *La Patria* (Lima), 27 November 1879, in *El Mercurio* (Valparaíso), 10 December 1879.

89. *La Tribuna* (Lima), 7 October 1879, cited in *El Mercurio* (Valparaíso), 29 October 1879.

90. *El Nacional* (Lima), 9 December 1879; *El Comercio* (Lima), 29 November and 5 December 1879, in *El Mercurio* (Valparaíso), 22 December 1879; *The South Pacific Times* (Callao), 13 December 1879, in *El Mercurio* (Valparaíso), 24 December 1879.

91. R. M. Espiell to General, Lima, 23 December 1879, 8:54–55, N. Beingolea to Nicolás Piérola, 8:52, J. de Osma to Minister of War, Lima, 23 December 1878, 8:53, Ramon Vargas Machuca to Osma, Ancon, 22 December 1879, 8:52, in Ahumada Moreno, *Guerra del Pacífico*.

92. *La Patria* (Lima), 7 February 1880, and *El Nacional* (Lima), 27 December

1879, cited in *El Mercurio* (Valparaíso), 9 January and 24 February 1880; Decree of 26 December 1879, in Ahumada Moreno, *Guerra del Pacífico*, 2:272.

93. Decree, Ministry of Government, La Paz, 8 April 1881, in *El Mercurio* (Valparaíso), 2 June 1881.

7. The Tacna and Arica Campaigns

1. Erasmo Escala to Minister of War, Camp Santa Catalina, 1 January 1880, in Ahumada Moreno, *Guerra del Pacífico*, 3:92.

2. Erasmo Escala to Minister of War, Camp Santa Catalina, 1 January 1880, in Ahumada Moreno, *Guerra del Pacífico*, 3:93; *El Nuevo Ferrocarril* (Santiago), 10 June 1880.

3. Domingo Santa María, Miguel Luis Amunátequi, Augusto Matte, José Gandarillas to Commander-in-Chief, Pisagua, 31 December 1879, 2:285–86, Rafael Sotomayor to Commander-in-Chief, Pisagua, 25 January 1880, 2:346, Galvarino Riveros to Minister of War and Navy, Aboard the *Blanco Encalada*, Pisagua, 26 November 1879, 5:37–38, in Ahumada Moreno, *Guerra del Pacífico*.

4. Rafael Sotomayor to Minister of War, Pisagua, 14 December 1879, in Ahumada Moreno, *Guerra del Pacífico*, 5:38.

5. José Goñi to Minister of the Navy, Valparaíso, 14 December 1879, 2:275, Oscar Viel to Prefect, Arica, 26 November 1879, 2:221, in Ahumada Moreno, *Guerra del Pacífico*.

6. Rafael Sotomayor to Aníbal Pinto, Ilo, 2, 28 February 1880, Fondos Varios, vols. 412, 416, Archivo Nacional.

7. Gustavo Rodríguez to Director, *El Nacional* (Lima), 9 March 1880, in Ahumada Moreno, *Guerra del Pacífico*, 3:391–92.

8. Galvarino Riveros to Minister of the Navy, Pacocha, 1 March 1880, Riveros to Minister of the Navy, Ilo, 1 March 1880, 195–98, Emilio Valverde to Carlos Condell, Arica, 27 February 1880, 199–201, Combate del Carlos Condell to Head of Fleet, Arica, 27 February 1880, 201–2, Rafael Sotomayor to Minister of the Navy, Ilo, 1 March 1880, 203, in Chile, Ministry of the Navy, *Memoria, 1880*; Fuenzalida Bade, *Armada*, 3:886.

9. Galvarino Riveros to Commander-in-Chief of the Navy, Pacocha, 10 March [*sic*] 1880, 209, Juan José Latorre, 19 March 1880, 209–10, Carlos Condell, Pacocha, 19 March 1880, 210–11, in Chile, Ministry of the Navy, *Memoria, 1880*.

10. Melo, *Historia*, 1:390; Storace, *Diario*, 94–96; Galvarino Riveros to Minister of the Navy, Pacocha, 26 March 1880, Chile, Ministry of the Navy, *Memoria, 1880*, 211–12.

11. Rafael Sotomayor to Galvarino Riveros, Ilo, 28 February 1880, in Ahumada Moreno, *Guerra del Pacífico*, 2:336.

12. Galvarino Riveros to Minister of War and Navy, Pacocha, 5 April, 1880, Chile, Ministry of the Navy, *Memoria, 1880*, 213.

13. José Gandarillas to Quartermaster General of the Active Army, Santiago, 19 April 1880, in Ahumada Moreno, *Guerra del Pacífico*, 5:51.

14. Correspondent for *El Comercio* on the *Unión*, 22 December 1879, in Ahumada Moreno, *Guerra del Pacífico*, 2:274–75.

15. Galvarino Riveros to Minister of War and Navy, Callao, 19 June and 1, 10 July 1880, in Ahumada Moreno, *Guerra del Pacífico*, 5:61–63.

16. Manuel Orella to Commanding Officer of the Fleet, 12 September 1880, in Ahumada Moreno, *Guerra del Pacífico*, 5:70–71.

17. Chile, Ministry of War and Navy, *Memoria de los trabajos*, 8.

18. "Segunda espedición i de ocupación de Ilo," in Ahumada Moreno, *Guerra del Pacífico*, 2:371; Galvarino Riveros to Minister of the Navy, Pachoca, 28 February 1880, 190–91, Luis A. Castillo to Minister of the Navy, 191–93, in Chile, Ministry of the Navy, *Memoria, 1880*.

19. José Francisco Vergara to Aníbal Pinto, 10 March 1880, qtd. in Gonzalo Bulnes, *Historia*, 2:145.

20. José Gandarillas to Commanding Officer of the Fleet, Santiago, 5 April 1880, 5:48 (although Barboza commanded the expedition, the report was written by José Gandarillas), Galvarino Riveros to Minister of War, Callao, 26 April 1880, 5:48–49, in Ahumada Moreno, *Guerra del Pacífico*; Rafael Torreblanca to Manuel Torreblanca, Pacocha, 27 February 1880, in Fernández Larraín, *Santa Cruz y Torreblanca*, 180.

21. Bonilla, *Gran Bretaña*, 4:5.

22. Rafael Torreblanca to Manuel Torreblanca, Ilo, 12 March 1880, in Fernández Larraín, *Santa Cruz y Torreblanca*, 184.

23. Del Canto, *Memorias militares*, 91–93; Máximo Lira to Isabel Errázuriz, Pacocha, 13 March 1880, in Claro Tocornal, "Cartas," 73.

24. Rafael Torreblanca to Manuel Torreblanca, Ilo, 12 March 1880, in Fernández Larraín, *Santa Cruz y Torreblanca*, 187; Máximo Lira to Isabel Errázuriz, Pacocha, 25 March 1880, in Claro Tocornal, "Cartas," 76.

25. Máximo Lira to Isabel Errázuriz, Pacocha, 13 April 1880, in Claro Tocornal, "Cartas," 76.

26. Manuel Baquedano to Commander-in-Chief, Moquegua, 27 March 1880, Chile, Ministry of War, *Memoria, 1880*, 86–89; Juan Martínez to General, Alto de la Villa, Moquegua, 25 March 1880, 2:434–35, Mauricio Muñóz to General, On march, Molino, 22 March 1880, 2:435, Lisandro Orrego to General of Infantry, Alto de la Villa, Moquegua, 25 March 1880, 2:436, Feliciano Echeverría to General, Moquegua, 25 March 1880, 2:436, José Novoa to Colonel, Pacocha, 28 March 1880, 2:437, José Velásquez to Colonel, Commanding Officer, Second Division, Alto de la Villa, Moquegua, 24 March 1880, 2:436–37, Simon Barrionuevo to Colonel, Commanding Officer of the Division, Omate, 4 April 1880, 2:439–40, Andrés Gamarra to General, Second Army of South, Omate, 4 April 1880, 2:440–41, Julio C. Chocano to General, First Division of Second Army

of the South, Omate, 31 March 1880, 2:441–42, Martin Alvárez to Lieutenant Colonel, Chief of Staff of First Division of Second Army of South, Omate, 28 March 1880, 2:442–43, in Ahumada Moreno, *Guerra del Pacífico; El Mercurio* (Valparaíso), 19 April 1880.

27. *La Opinión Nacional* (Lima), 1 April 1880; *El Mercurio* (Valparaíso), 14 April 1880.

28. Bonilla, *Gran Bretaña*, 4:260.

29. Poblete, "Servicio sanitario," 35, no. 39:467; Manuel Baquedano to Minister of War and Navy, Ilo, 17 April 1880, 3:112, Dr. Ramón Allende Padín to Quartermaster General of Army and Navy in the Field, Tacna, 5 July 1880, 3:342–43, in Ahumada Moreno, *Guerra del Pacífico;* Máximo Lira to Isabel Errázuriz, Pacocha, 20 April and 3 May 1880, in Claro Tocornal, "Cartas," 78.

30. Gutiérrez, *Crónica*, 43.

31. Letters of Tristán Chacón and Manuel Salas in Vicuña Mackenna, *Historia de la campaña de Tacna y Arica*, 651–54; Benavides Santos, *Seis años de vacaciones*, 53–57.

32. Gutiérrez, *Crónica*, 47.

33. Florencio del Mármol, "Descripción de la Batalla de Tacna," in Ahumada Moreno, *Guerra del Pacífico*, 3:355.

34. Narciso Campero, "Informe del Jeneral Narciso Campero ante la convención nacional de Bolivia, como jefe del ejército aliado," in Ahumada Moreno, *Guerra del Pacífico*, 2:592–93.

35. Narciso Campero, "Informe," in Ahumada Moreno, *Guerra del Pacífico*, 2:593.

36. Machuca, *Cuatro campañas*, 2:246, 263–65; Toro Dávila, *Síntesis histórico militar*, 288; "Cuadro demonstrativo," in Ahumada Moreno, *Guerra del Pacífico*, 3:121. Various Peruvian and Bolivian scholars have claimed that the Allied army was, in fact, much smaller. Some, like Roberto Querajazu Calvo, put it as low as eighty-five hundred. *Aclaraciones históricas*, 540. Conversely, José Jiménez wrote his father that, as of 24 April, the Allied army numbered sixteen thousand. Tacna, 24 April 1880, in Ahumada Moreno, *Guerra del Pacífico*, 7:50.

37. Aguirre, *Lijeras*, 10.

38. Claros, *Diario*, 48.

39. Alba, *Diario*, 97.

40. Del Canto, *Memorias militares*, 103–4.

41. Marchant Pereira, *Crónica*, 41, 43.

42. Urquieta, *Recuerdos de la vida*, 2:8.

43. Machuca, *Cuatro campañas*, 2:271.

44. Gutiérrez, *Crónica*, 50–51.

45. Benavides Santos, *Seis años*, 68–71.

46. Del Canto, *Memorias militares*, 105.

47. *El Nacional* (Lima), 26, 27, 28 June 1880, in Ahumada Moreno, *Guerra del*

Pacífico, 2:618, Pedro Vargas to Severino Zapata, La Paz, 18 June 1880, 2:590, in Ahumada Moreno, *Guerra del Pacífico*, Claros, *Diario*, 52–53.

48. Ballivián, *Colorados de Bolivia*, 14.

49. Del Mármol, *Recuerdos*, 102.

50. Alba, *Diario*, 100.

51. Ballivián, *Colorados de Bolivia*, 10.

52. Dalence, *Informe histórico*, 20; *Armada Boliviana*, http://www.armada.mil.bo; Alba, *Diario*, 98.

53. Alba, *Diario*, 99; Dalence, *Informe histórico*, 34, 56; Campero, *Informe*, 17.

54. Camacho, *Tratado sumario*, 436–37.

55. Ekdahl, *Historia militar*, 2:297.

56. Mason, "War between Chile, Peru, and Bolivia," 557.

57. Chaparro White, *Batalla de Tacna*, 25; Santiago Amengual to General, Tacna, 2 June 1880, in Ahumada Moreno, *Guerra del Pacífico*, 2:562–63.

58. Barrientos Gutiérrez, *Artillería*, 192.

59. Urquieta, *Recuerdos de la vida*, 2:9.

60. Alba, *Diario*, 100; Ildefonso Murguia to Minister of War, Oruro, 13 August 1880, in Ahumada Moreno, *Guerra del Pacífico*, 8:73.

61. Adolfo Holley to Santiago Amengual, Tacna, 29 May 1880, 2:564, Narciso Campero, "Informe," 2:595, in Ahumada Moreno, *Guerra del Pacífico*.

62. Claros, *Diario*, 35.

63. Florencio del Mármol, "Descripción de la Batalla de Tacna," in Ahumada Moreno, *Guerra del Pacífico*, 3:357; Ildefonso Murgia to Minister, Oruro, 13 August 1880, in Ahumada Moreno, *Guerra del Pacífico*, 8:73–75.

64. Ildefonso Murgia to Minister, Oruro, 13 August 1880, in Ahumada Moreno, *Guerra del Pacífico*, 8:74.

65. Benedicto, "Servicio," 66.

66. Vicuña Mackenna, Historia de la Campaña de Tacna y Arica, 1014.

67. Ildefonso Murgia to Minister, Oruro, 13 August 1880, in Ahumada Moreno, *Guerra del Pacífico*, 8:74.

68. Benavides Santos, *Seis años*, 73.

69. Narciso Campero, "Informe," 2:595, Florencio del Mármol, "Descripción," 3:357, in Ahumada Moreno, *Guerra del Pacífico*; Urquieta, *Recuerdos de la vida*, 2:70; Abraham Quiróz to Leoncio Quiróz, Tacna, 14 June 1880, in Quiróz, "Epistolario inédito," 80. Del Mámol, "Descripción," Ahumada Moreno, *Guerra del Pacífico*, 3:357.

70. A. Quiróz to Leoncio Quiróz, Tacna, 14 June 1880 in Dos Soldados en la Guerra del Pacífico (Buenos Aires, 1976), p. 80; F. Mármol, "Descripción," AM, III, p. 357.

71. Del Mármol, *Recuerdos*, 103.

72. Narciso Campero, "Informe," in Ahumada Moreno, *Guerra del Pacífico*,

2:595; Claros, *Diario*, 55; Abraham Quiróz to Luciano Quiróz, Tacna, 14 June 1880, in Quiróz, "Epistolario inédito," 79.

73. Andrés Cáceres to Commander-in-Chief of First Army's Chief of Staff, n.d., in Ahumada Moreno, *Guerra del Pacífico*, 2:580.

74. *El Comercio* (Lima), 1 July 1880, 2:622, Florencio del Mármol, "Descripción," 3:355, in Ahumada Moreno, *Guerra del Pacífico*; Ochoa, *Diario*, 313.

75. Florencio del Mármol, "Descripción," in Ahumada Moreno, *Guerra del Pacífico*, 3:355.

76. Claros, *Diario*, 53.

77. Gutiérrez, *Crónica*, 56.

78. Paz Soldán, *Narración histórica*, 477; Venegas Urbina, *Sancho en la Guerra*, 192.

79. "Razón de las bajas del Ejercito de Chile en la batalla del Campo de la Alianza," in Ahumada Moreno, *Guerra del Pacífico*, 2:598–99. Vicuña Mackenna puts the figure for deaths higher. *Historia de la Campaña de Tacna y Arica*, 1084.

80. Poblete, "Servicio sanitario," 35, no. 39:477.

81. Urquieta, Recuerdos de la vida, 2:24–25; Greene, Report of the Russian Army, 145.

82. Vicuña Mackenna, *Historia de la Campaña de Tacna y Arica*, 997.

83. Dalence, *Informe histórico*, 25, 29; Pedro J. Armayo to Narciso Campero, La Paz, 12 June 1880, in Ahumada Moreno, *Guerra del Pacífico*, 2:590.

84. Narciso Campero, "Informe," 2:595, Pedro Vargas Severino Zapata, La Paz, 18 June 1880, 2:590, Pedro Armayo to Narciso Campero, La Paz, 12 June 1880, 2:590; Ballivián, *Colorados de Bolivia*, 24–25, in Ahumada Moreno, *Guerra del Pacífico*; Pedro Vargas (Btn. Padilla 6) to Gen. 2 Division of Bolivian Army, Severino Zapata, La Paz, 12 June 1880 in Ahumada Moreno, *Guerra del Pacífico*, 2:590; Machuca, *Cuatro compañas*, 3:290–91; *El Mercurio* (Valparaíso), 8 July 1880.

85. Cáceres, *Guerra del 79*, 59; Díaz Arguedas, *Historia*, 275, 468; Pedro P. Vargas to Severino Zapata, La Paz, 18 June 1880, in Ahumada Moreno, *Guerra del Pacífico*, 2:590.

86. "Relación de los principales bajas del ejército peruano en la batalla Campo de Alianza," in Ahumada Moreno, *Guerra del Pacífico*, 2:599–600.

87. Severino Zapata to the Supreme Director of the War, La Paz, 18 June 1880, in Ahumada Moreno, *Guerra del Pacífico*, 3:120; .

88. Ballivián, *Colorados de Bolivia*, 31–33.

89. Felipe Ravelo to Senón Zamora, Tacna, 2 June 1880, qtd. in Querejazu Calvo, *Guano*, 575.

90. Cáceres, *Guerra del 79*, 59; Lizardo Montero to Minister of State in the Office of War, Tarata, 1 June 1880, in Ahumada Moreno, *Guerra del Pacífico* 2:578.

91. Del Solar, *Diario*, 175–77; Rosales, *Mi campaña*, 168; Cáceres, *Guerra del 79*, 59; Paz Soldán, *Narración histórica*, 476; del Canto, *Memorias militares*, 105.

92. Dalence, *Informe histórico*, 17–21, 24, 27, 30, 47–49; Ramón Allende Padín to Quartermaster General of Army and Navy in the Field, Tacna, 5 July 1880, 3:339–44, Manuel Baquedano to Minister of War and Navy, Ilo, 17 April 1880, 3:112, in Ahumada Moreno, *Guerra del Pacífico*.

93. *El Nacional* (Lima), 22 May 1880, cited in *El Mercurio* (Valparaíso), 16 June 1880.

94. *La Opinión Nacional* (Lima), 2 June 1880, cited in *El Mercurio* (Valparaíso), 18 June 1880.

95. *La Tribuna* (La Paz), 12 June 1880, in Ahumada Moreno, *Guerra del Pacífico*, 3:144–45.

96. Salazar, *Batallas*, 25; Justo Dávila to Chief of Staff, First Army of South, Tarata, 29 May 1880, in Ahumada Moreno, *Guerra del Pacífico*, 2:578; Cáceras, *Guerra del 79*, 57.

97. Vicuña Mackenna, Historia de la Campaña de Tacna y Arica, 1063–64.

98. Bonilla, *Gran Bretaña*, 4:291; Alberto del Solar to Nicolás Piérola, Torata, 3 June 1880, in Ahumada Moreno, *Guerra del Pacífico*, 3:149.

99. Manuel de la Torre to Secretary of State in Charge of War, Aboard the *Limari*, Arica, 9 June 1880, in Ahumada Moreno, *Guerra del Pacífico*, 3:185; Dellepiane, *Historia militar*, 2:276.

100. Estado Mayor General, *Historia*, 6:115–16.

101. Ricardo O'Donovan, Census of 1 May 1880, in Machuca, *Cuatro campañas*, 2:307–8. This figure does not include some of the troops manning the artillery, some of whom had served as crewmembers of the *Independencia*.

102. José Inclan to Jefe de la Plaza, Arica, 1 June 1880, 3:227, El Jefe de la Torre to Nicolás Piérola, 29 May and 6 June 1880, 3:227, in Ahumada Moreno, *Guerra del Pacífico*.

103. Rafael Vargas (Cazadores a Caballo) to Father, Arica, 11 June 1880, in Ahumada Moreno, *Guerra del Pacífico*, 3:199–200. Elmore categorically denied this charge and published his version, as well as a variety of letters supporting him in Elmore, *Defensa de Arica*.

104. Machuca, *Cuatro campañas*, 2:390; Dellepiane, *Historia militar*, 2:284.

105. Patricio Lynch, Santiago, 7 June 1880, in Ahumada Moreno, *Guerra del Pacífico*, 3:174.

106. Ekdahl, *Historia militar*, 2:391.

107. Marcelino Varela to Secretary of State in the Ministry of War, Tacna, 10 August 1880, in Vargas Hurtado, *Batalla de Arica*, 367.

108. Marcelino Varela, in Vargas Hurtado, *Batalla de Arica*, 368.

109. Dellepiane, *Historia militar*, 2:292.

110. Dellepiane, *Historia militar*, 2:293; Ricardo Castro to Pedro Lagos, Pocollai, 9 June 1880, in Ahumada Moreno, *Guerra del Pacífico*, 3:180.

111. Benavides Santos, *Seis años*, 81.

112. Manuel Espinosa to Lieutenant Colonel, Aduana de Arica, 7 June 1880, in Ahumada Moreno, *Guerra del Pacífico*, 3:186.

113. José Sánchez Lagomarsino to Jefe de la Plaza, Arica, 7 June 1880, in Ahumada Moreno, *Guerra del Pacífico*, 3:188.

114. Vicuña Mackenna, *Historia de la Campaña de Tacna y Arica*, 1158; Bulnes, *Historia*, 2:388; Ekdahl, *Historia militar*, 2:398.

115. See the declarations of various eyewitnesses in Ahumada Moreno, *Guerra del Pacífico*, 3:336-39.

116. Dr. Bertonelli (Chief Surgeon of Army of the South) to Chief Surgeon of Army, Tacna, 4 June 1880, 3:330, Plácido Garrido Mendivil to Presidente de Junta Central de Ambulancias Civiles de la Cruz Roja, Lima, 14, 27 July 1880, 3:330-31, Felipe Duran (Head of 4 Ambulance Unit) to Roja [*sic*] Presidente de Junta Central de Ambulancias civiles de la Cruz Roja, Lima, 14 July 1880, 3:332, Claudio Aliaga to Plácido Garrido Mendivil (Presidente) Junta Central de Ambulancias Civiles de la Cruz Roja, Lima, 16 July 1880, 3:333-34, Vicente Dávila Larraín to Minister of War, Valparaíso, 16 July 1880, 3:343, in Ahumada Moreno, *Guerra del Pacífico*; Vargas Hurtado, *Batalla de Arica*, 227-29.

117. Paz Soldán, *Narración histórica*, 494-96.

118. Maximo Lira to I. Errázuriz, in Claro Tocornal, "Cartas," 81; Patricio Lynch, in Ahumada Moreno, *Guerra del Pacífico*, 3:175.

119. Capt. Manuel Barahona to N. N., Arica, 9 June 1880, in Ahumada Moreno, *Guerra del Pacífico*, 3:198-99.

120. Carta de un oficial del 3, in Ahumada Moreno, *Guerra del Pacífico*, 3:200-201; Dellepiane, *Historia militar*, 2:193.

121. *El Mercurio* (Valparaíso), 19 June 1880.

122. Ricardo Silva Arriagada, Tacna, 23 June 1880, in Ahumada Moreno, *Guerra del Pacífico*, 3:201-2.

123. Vargas Hurtado, *Batalla de Arica*, 206, 249.

124. Markham, *War between Peru and Chile*, 207-8; Spangler, *Civilization in Chile*, 214; Uriburu, *Guerra del Pacífico*, 154; Mason, *War on the Pacific Coast*, 64.

125. Benavides Santos, *Seis años*, 83; Rafael Vargas to Father, Arica, 11 June 1880, in Ahumada Moreno, *Guerra del Pacífico*, 3:200.

126. *La Estrella de Panama* qtd. in *El Mercurio* (Valparaíso), 2 August 1880; *El Mercurio*, 19 June 1880.

127. Castro, *Opúsculo*, 9, 22-23;.

128. *La Patria* 5, 9 June 1880, cited in *El Mercurio* (Valparaíso), 26 June 1880; *El Nacional* (Lima), 10 July 1879, in *El Mercurio* (Valparaíso), 2 August 1880.

8. Investing Lima

1. De Irizarri, *Carta a propósito*, 34.

2. Bulnes, *Historia*, 2:553-54.

3. Patricio Lynch to Aníbal Pinto, Iquique, 26 June 1880, in Ahumada Moreno, *Guerra del Pacífico*, 4:141-42.

4. José Francisco Vergara to Patricio Lynch, 24 August 1880, 2:554, Lynch to Aníbal Pinto, n.d., 2:556, in Bulnes, *Historia.*

5. Ignacio Santa María to Minister of War, 20 September 1880, in Ahumada Moreno, *Guerra del Pacífico,* 3:507.

6. Orbegoso, Lima, 11 September 1880, in Ahumada Moreno, *Guerra del Pacífico,* 3:528.

7. Patricio Lynch to Arturo Derteano, Chimbote, 13 September 1880, in Ahumada Moreno, *Guerra del Pacífico,* 3:529.

8. José M. Aguirre to Patricio Lynch, Monsefu, 24 September 1880, in Ahumada Moreno, *Guerra del Pacífico,* 3:535.

9. Adolfo Salmon to Nicolás Piérola, Chocope, 14 October 1880, 3:540–41, Piérola to Prefect of Libertad, Lima, 15 October 1880, 3:541, Luis Albrecht to Patricio Lynch, Hacienda Casa Grande, 16 October 1880, 3:541, S. C. Montjoy to Lynch, Casa Grande, 18 October 1880, 3:542, N. Orbegoso to Piérola, Lima, 2 November 1880, 3:542–43, Salmon to Lynch, Chocope, 9, 14 October 1880, 3:543, 544, Lynch to Salmon, San Pedro, 14 October 1880, 3:544, Orbegoso, Lima, 18 November 1880, 3:544, in Ahumada Moreno, *Guerra del Pacífico.*

10. Spencer St. John to Patricio Lynch, Lima, 13 September 1880, 3:520, E. de Vorges to Lynch, Lima, 12 September 1880, 3:520–21, Isaac Christiancy to Lynch, Lima, 14 September 1880, 3:521, Christiancy to Lynch, Lima, 17 September 1880, 3:522, G. Viviani to Lynch, Lima, 16 September 1880, 3:522, in Ahumada Moreno, *Guerra del Pacífico.*

11. A. Blacker, Paita, 21 September 1880, Luis Gualterio Gyton, Quilca, 6 November 1880, in Ahumada Moreno, *Guerra del Pacífico,* 3:532.

12. Patricio Lynch to Minister, Aboard the *Itata,* Quilca, 1 November 1880, 3:508–11, Lynch to Minister of War, Paita, 22 September 1880, 3:530–31, Manuel Frias to Minister of War, Piura, 28 September 1880, 3:531, Federico Stuven to Capitán de Navio, Commander of Operations, Aboard the *Itata,* 31 October 1880, 3:514–15, Manuel J. Soffia, *Itata* on the high seas, 30 October 1880, 3:512–13, in Ahumada Moreno, *Guerra del Pacífico;* Chile, Ministry of War, *Memoria, 1881,* 425–32.

13. Aspillaga Hermanos to Aspirllaga Hermanos, Hacienda Cayalti, 13 September 1880, in Ahumada Moreno, *Guerra del Pacífico,* 3:536–37.

14. Espedición Lynch al Norte del Perú: Telegramas i partes oficiales, 3:507, Purpose of Mission, Telegram, Commander of Forces to Minister of War, Santiago, 20 September 1880, 3:507, Patricio Lynch, "Partes oficiales," Aboard the *Itata,* 1 November 1880, 3:509–11, O. Viel "Comandancia de la Corbeta 'Chacabuco'" Arica (Quilca), 10 November 1880, 3:515–16, Federico Stuven to Lynch, *Itata,* 31 October 1880, 3:514–15, Ahumada Moreno, *Guerra del Pacífico;* Chile, Ministry of War and Navy, *Memoria de guerra, 1880,* 423–32.

15. J. Chaparro et al., Chimbote, 13 September 1880, 3:517, J. R. Lira, Aboard

the *Itata*, 26 October 1880, 3:517, F. Caces, Aboard the *Copiapó*, 3:518, Manuel Soffia et al., Aboard the *Itata*, Paita, 29 September 1880, 3:518-19, J. R. Lira, Aboard the *Itata*, 30 October 1880, 3:518-19, in Ahumada Moreno, *Guerra del Pacífico*.

16. Aníbal Pinto to Eulogio Altamirano, Santiago, 24 July 1880, in Jofre Alvarez, "Don Eulogio Altamirano," 74; José Francisco Vergara to Ministros del Estado, Tacna, 30 October 1880, in Ahumada Moreno, *Guerra del Pacífico*, 4:224; Pinto to Esubio Lillo, 2 July 1880, 2:418, José Alfonso to Altamirano, 16 July 1880, 2:425, in Bulnes, *Historia*.

17. Aníbal Pinto to Eulogio Altamirano, Santiago, 20 September 1880, in Pinto, "Apuntes," 125. See also Vicente Dávila Larraín to Domingo Santa María, 28 July 1880, in Bulnes, *Historia*, 2:429.

18. Marcos Maturana to Minister, Tacna, 3 November 1880, in Ahumada Moreno, *Guerra del Pacífico*, 4:227-28.

19. Aníbal Pinto to José Francisco Vergara, Santiago, 29 September 1880, 4:223, Hermójenes Pérez de Arce, Arica, "Decreto and reglamentos sobre provisión de víveres, vestuario y equipo al ejército espedicionario," 6 November 1880, 4:234-36, in Ahumada Moreno, *Guerra del Pacífico*; Machuca, *Cuatro campañas*, 2:178-80, 182.

20. Hermójenes Pérez de Arce, "Memoria del Delegado de la Intendencia Jeneral del Ejército y Armada, Hermójenes Pérez de Arce," Callao, June 1881, in Ahumada Moreno, *Guerra del Pacífico*, 6:123-33.

21. Telegrams from Marcos 2. Maturana to Minister of War, Tacna, 16 October to 23 November 1880, 4:224-36, Quartermaster of the Army, Delegado de la Intendencia, 4:223-25, José Francisco Vergara to Minister of War and Minister of State, Tacna, 30 October and 22 November 1880, 4:224, Vergara to Quartermaster General of the Army, Tacna, 4 December 1880, 4:288, Vincente Dávila Larraín to Minister of War in the Field, Valparaíso, 6 December 1880, 4:288, Maturana to Commander-in-Chief, Tacna, 7 December 1880, 4:289, Maturana to Delegado de la Intendencia, Tacna, 5 November 1880, 4:225, Hermójenes Pérez de Arce, "Memoria del Delegado de la Intendencia Jeneral del Ejército y Armada, Hermójenes Pérez de Arce," Callao, July 1881, 6:123-33, in Ahumada Moreno, *Guerra del Pacífico*; Machuca, *Cuatro campañas*, 2:206, 208.

22. Aníbal Pinto to Vicente Dávila Larraín, 26, 29 November 1880, in Bulnes, *Historia*, 2:612; Machuca, *Cuatro campañas*, 2:208, 249; Telegrams from Marcos Maturana to Minister of War, Tacna, 23 November and 11 December 1880, in Ahumada Moreno, *Guerra del Pacífico*, 4:286-89.

23. Hermójenes Pérez de Arce, "Instructions para maestres de Víveres," 4:233, 235, Marcos Maturana, "Organización de Parque," Tacna, 3 November 1880, 4:228, Pérez de Arce to Quartermaster General of Army and Navy in the Field, "Memoria del Delegado de la Intendencia Jeneral del Ejército y Armada don

Hermójenes Pérez de Arce," Callao, June 1881, 6:124, in Ahumada Moreno, *Guerra del Pacífico*; Machuca, *Cuatro campañas*, 2:259.

24. Véliz, *Historia*, 226–29; Chile, Ministry of War and Navy, *Memoria de los trabajos*, 6–9; José Francisco Vergara to Minister of War in the Field, Tacna, 2 November 1880, in Ahumada Moreno, *Guerra del Pacífico*, 4:224 ; Bulnes, *Historia*, 2:594; Machuca, *Cuatro campañas*, 2:206; Ekdahl, *Historia militar*, 3:30.

25. José Francisco Vergara to Minister of War in the Field, Tacna, 2 November 1880, 4:224, Manuel Baquedano to José Antonio Villagrán, Tacna, 12 November 1880, 4:231, in Ahumada Moreno, *Guerra del Pacífico*; Machuca, *Cuatro campañas*, 2:209; Ekdahl, *Historia militar*, 3:32; Bulnes, *Historia*, 2:596.

26. Machuca, *Cuatro campañas*, 2:211.

27. *El Heraldo* (Santiago), 16 November 1880; Hermójenes Pérez de Arce, Arica, 6 November 1880, 4:230, 232–36, Manuel Baquedano, "Proclama a la 1 División a su llegada a Pisco," 13 November 1880, 4:231, in Ahumada Moreno, *Guerra del Pacífico*.

28. Hermójenes Pérez de Arce, "Decreto," in Ahumada Moreno, *Guerra del Pacífico*, 4:235; Machuca, *Cuatro campañas*, 2:254; Benavides Santos, *Seis años*, 101–2.

29. *El Mercurio*, Pisco, 22 November 1880, in Ahumada Moreno, *Guerra del Pacífico*, 4:237–41; Machuca, *Cuatro campañas*, 2:227.

30. Machuca, *Cuatro campañas*, 2:211, 227–28; *El Mercurio* (Valparaíso), 22 November 1880.

31. Lucio Gutiérrez to Juan José Pinillos, Humai, 16 October 1880, in Ahumada Moreno, *Guerra del Pacífico*, 4:248.

32. H. Camino to Executive Office, Escuadrón del Valle de Chuchanga, Pisco, 13 November 1880, 4:248–49, H. Fernández to Prefect and Commanding Officer of the Department, 8 November 1880, 4:249, Manuel de la Guardia et al. to Superior Commander, Political and Military Departments of the South and Prefect of Arequipa, 9 November 1880, 4:249, in Ahumada Moreno, *Guerra del Pacífico*.

33. Juan José Pinillos, General Order, Pisco, 17 November 1880, in Ahumada Moreno, *Guerra del Pacífico*, 4:248.

34. Bello, Pisco, 19 November 1880, *La Patria* (Lima), in Ahumada Moreno, *Guerra del Pacífico*, 4:243. Ships appeared at 9 a.m. (4:244).

35. Villena to Dr. Solar Cañete, 21 November 1880, in Ahumada Moreno, *Guerra del Pacífico*, 4:243.

36. Zamudio to Sr. Pisco, 19 November 1880, 4:242, [Agustin] Matute [the subprefect of Pisco felt so much remorse that he cut his throat with his straight razor] to Secretary of Government, Chincha, 19 November 1880, 4:242, Chincha, 20 November 1880, 4:244, in Ahumada Moreno, *Guerra del Pacífico*.

37. Vicente Dávila Larraín to Minister of War in the Field, Valparaíso, 6 December 1880, 4:289, Telegrams of Marcos 2. Maturana to Minister of War,

Tacna, 23 November to 11 December 1880, 4:286–89, José Francisco Vergara to Quartermaster General of the Army, Tacna, 4 December 1880, 4:288, Maturana to Commanding General of Forces, Tacna 7, 11 December 1880, 4:289, in Ahumada Moreno, *Guerra del Pacífico.*

38. José Francisco Vergara to Aníbal Pinto, 8 December 1880, in Bulnes, *Historia*, 2:615; Machuca, *Cuatro campañas*, 2:243; Ekdahl, *Historia militar*, 3:38.

39. Alfonso to President, Lurín, 24 December 1880, 4:295–96, Manuel J. Jarpa, 24 December 1880, 4:293, in Ahumada Moreno, *Guerra del Pacífico*; Rosales, *Mi campaña*, 187–88.

40. José Antonio Villagrán to José Francisco Gana, Tambo de Mora, 17 December 1880, in Ahumada Moreno, *Guerra del Pacífico*, 4:254–55.

41. Manuel Baquedano to José Antonio Villagrán, Pisco, 19 December 1880, in Ahumada Moreno, *Guerra del Pacífico*, 4:298.

42. Manuel Baquedano to José Antonio Villagrán, San Pedro de Lurín, 25 December 1880, in Ahumada Moreno, *Guerra del Pacífico*, 4:298.

43. *El Ferrocarril* (Santiago), 29 December 1880, in Ahumada Moreno, *Guerra del Pacífico*, 4:303–5.

44. Manuel Baquedano to President, Carayaco, 24 December 1880, 5:295, Alfonso to President, 24 December 1880, 4:295–96, in Ahumada Moreno, *Guerra del Pacífico.*

45. Spencer St. John to Earl of Granville, Lima, 2 August 1880, FO 61/326; Manuel Zanutelli Rosas, "Semblanza antologica de la época," 23–32, Héctor Valenzuela Ricardo, Chorrillos, Miraflores y Lima, antes de 1881," in Peru, Ministry of War, Permanent Commission, *Gesta de Lima*, 43.

46. Spencer St. John to Earl of Granville, Lima, 2, 14 August 1880, FO 61, no. 76.

47. Nicolás Piérola, Decree, Lima, 27 June 1880, 3:266, Luis Jermán Astete, Callao, 29 November 1880, 4:352–53, in Ahumada Moreno, *Guerra del Pacífico.*

48. *Deustche Nachricten* qtd. in *Los Tiempos* (Santiago), 7 September 1880.

49. Juan Martín Echenique, "Alistamiento militar," Lima, 9 July 1880, 2:320–21, Echenique, Lima, 17 July 1880, 2:321–22, in Ahumada Moreno, *Guerra del Pacífico.*

50. Spencer St. John to Earl of Granville, Lima, 16 July 1880, FO 61, no. 68.

51. Miguel Iglesias, Lima, 30 November 1880, 4:352, Nicolás Piérola, Lima, 5 August 1880, 3:402–3, in Ahumada Moreno, *Guerra del Pacífico.*

52. Juan Peña y Coronel, Lima, 26 November 1880, 4:352, Lucio Gutiérrez to Juan José Pinillos, Humai, 16 October 1880, 4:248, in Ahumada Moreno, *Guerra del Pacífico.*

53. Lt. Reginald Carey-Brenton, in Tauro, "Defensa de Lima," 102–34; Francisco [Archbishop of Lima] Pastoral, 25 December 1880, in Ahumada Moreno, *Guerra del Pacífico*, 4:329–30. *La Estrella de Panama* qtd. in *El Mecurio* (Valparaíso), 19 August 1880.

54. *El Mercurio* (Valparaíso), 31 August 1880; Francisco [Archbishop of Lima] Pastoral, 25 December 1880, 4:329–30, Manuel Jesus Obin, "Vencer o Morir," *La Patria* (Lima), 23 December 1880, 4:334–35; M. G. de la Fuente Chávez, "La muerte de Chile o sea la muerte chilena," 23 December 1880, 4:335–36, in Ahumada Moreno, *Guerra del Pacífico*.

55. Manuel Jesus Obin, "Sacrificios," *La Patria* (Lima), 20 November 1880, 4:273, Cesáro Chacaltana, *El Nacional* (Lima), 22 November 1880, 4:273–74, in Ahumada Moreno, *Guerra del Pacífico*.

56. Spencer St. John to Earl of Granville, Lima, 20 November 1880, Office, FO 61, no. 101.

57. Sevilla, Humai Huaya Grande, 26 November 1880, in Ahumada Moreno, *Guerra del Pacífico*, 4:246–47.

58. Mariano Felipe Paz Soldán to Romero, Lima, 18 December 1880, in Ahumada Moreno, *Guerra del Pacífico*, 4:247.

59. Mariano Felipe Paz Soldán to Romero, 18 December 1880, 4:247, Peña y Coronel Subprefect, 19 December 1880, in Ahumada Moreno, *Guerra del Pacífico*, 4:361.

60. *El Peruano* (Lima), 22 November 1880.

61. A. A. Aramburú, "Deberes de Actualidad," *La Opinión Nacional* (Lima) 21 November 1880, in Ahumada Moreno, *Guerra del Pacífico*, 4:272.

62. Marcos Maturana, "Plan de operaciones sobre Lima," 4:385, Miguel Iglesias, Lima, 22 December 1880, 4:397, Ahumada Moreno, *Guerra del Pacífico*; Peru, Ministry of War, Permanent Commission, *Gesta de Lima*, 152; Holguin, "Toma de Lima," 5.

63. Miguel Iglesias, Lima 22 December 1880, 4:396, 398, Luis Jermán Astete, Callao, 25 December 1880, 4:398, Emeterio Pareja, Lima, 28 December 1880, 4:398, in Ahumada Moreno, *Guerra del Pacífico*, 4:398.

64. Juan Miranda, Lima, 27 December 1880, in Ahumada Moreno, *Guerra del Pacífico*.

65. Manuel Yarlequé, "El ejército peruano en campaña," *La Opinión Nacional* (Lima), 3 January 1881, in Ahumada Moreno, *Guerra del Pacífico*, 4:402.

66. Lt. Reginald Carey-Brenton, in Tauro, "Defensa de Lima," 104; Alberto Tauro, "Preparación de la defensa: Marco histórico," in Peru, Ministry of War, Permanent Commission, *Gesta de Lima*, 142; Cáceres, *Guerra del 79*, 65; Caviano, *Historia de la guerra*, 2:38, 40, 51.

67. Alberto Tauro, in Peru, Ministry of War, Permanent Commission, *Gesta de Lima*, 143; Dellepiane, *Historia militar*, 2:318.

68. Alejandro Seraylán L., "La campaña de Lima," in Peru, Ministry of War, Permanent Commission, *Gesta de Lima*, 156.

69. Cáceres, *Guerra del 79*, 69.

70. *El Ferrocarril* (Santiago), 3 May 1880; Manuel Señoret to Commanding Officer, Division of the North, Iquique, 4 March 1882, in *Huáscar*, 97.

71. "Orden General de la Escuadra," Callao, 16 January 1881, in Ahumada Moreno, *Guerra del Pacífico*, 5:101; Alberto Tauro, in Peru, Ministry of War, Permanent Commission, *Gesta de Lima*, 143.

72. Marcos Maturana, "Plan de Operaciones sobre Lima," Tacna, 30 November 1880, 4:385–89, Maturana, Lurín, 9 January 1881, 4:390–91, in Ahumada Moreno, *Guerra del Pacífico*.

73. Ekdahl, *Historia militar*, 3:74–76.

74. Manuel Baquedano to President, Received 19 September 1881, in Ahumada Moreno, *Guerra del Pacífico*, 4:411–12, qtd. in del Canto, *Memorias militares*, 136.

75. Memoirs of Capt. Elias Casa, Regimiento Esmeralda, Diary, in Ahumada Moreno, *Guerra del Pacífico*, 7:36–39.

76. Le León, *Recuerdos*, 102.

77. Urquieta, *Recuerdos*, 2:154–55; del Canto, *Memorias militares*, 136, 139.

78. Benavides Santos, *Seis años*, 112; Acland, *Six Weeks*, 49; Rosales, *Mi campaña*, 209; Julio Lucas Jaimes, "La versión del aliado," in López Martínez, *Piérola*, 125–33.

79. Arnaldo Panizo to Chief of Staff of the Armies, Lima, 9 February 1881, 4:488–90, Manuel Baquedano to Minister of War, Lima, 12 February 1881, 4:416–17, Marcos Maturana to Baquedano, 4:424–26, in Ahumada Moreno, *Guerra del Pacífico*.

80. Patricio Lynch to General, Chief of Staff, in Ahumada Moreno, *Guerra del Pacífico*, 4:430; del Canto, *Memorias militares*, 136.

81. Del Canto, *Memorias militares*, 141.

82. Patricio Lynch to General, Chief of Staff, 4:429–30, J. D. Amunátegui to Lynch, Callao, 23 January 1881, 4:430–31, Luis Solo Zaldívar to Commanding Officer, Second Brigade of First Division, Chorrillos, 14 January 1881, 4:431, Artemon Arellano to Colonel, Chief of the Brigade, Callao, 22 January 1881, 4:433, S. Urízar Gárfias to Colonel, Chief of the Brigade, Callao, 25 January 1881, 4:434–35, Emilio Gana to Lynch, Callao, 20 January 1881, 4:436, V. Balmaceda to Unk, Callao, 23 January 1881, 5:171–72, in Ahumada Moreno, *Guerra del Pacífico*; del Canto, *Memorias militares*, 140.

83. Machuca, *Cuatro campañas*, 3:347, 351; Manuel Baquedano to Minister of War, Lima, 12 February 1881, in Ahumada Moreno, *Guerra del Pacífico*, 4:417–18.

84. Rosales, *Mi campaña*, 209.

85. José Francisco Gana to Commanding General, Second Division, Chorrillos, 23 January 1881, 4:440–41, Emilio Sotomayor to Commanding General, San Borja, 25 January 1881, 4:439, Adolfo Holley to Colonel, First Brigade, Second Division, Chorrillos, 18 January 1881, 4:441–42, in Ahumada Moreno, *Guerra del Pacífico*; Rosales, *Mi campaña*, 207.

86. Ruben Guevara to Colonel, Second Brigade, Second Division, San Borja, 20 January 1881, in Ahumada Moreno, *Guerra del Pacífico*, 4:443; Benavides Santos, *Seis años*, 115.

87. Manuel Jarpa to Colonel, First Brigade, Second Division, Lima, 20 January 1881, 4:444–45; Pedro Soto Aguilar to Commanding Officer of Cavalry, Lima, 23 January 1881, 4:446–47, Adolfo Holley to Colonel, First Brigade, Second Division, Chorrillos, 18 January 1881, 4:441–42, in Ahumada Moreno, *Guerra del Pacífico*.

88. Pedro Lagos to General, C. Staff, Lima, 31 January 1881, 4:447–48, Francisco Barceló to Colonel, Chief of Third Division, Lima, 20 January 1881, 4:449, Demofilo Fuenzalida to Commanding Officer, Second Brigade, Third Division, Lima, 18 January 1881, 4:450, Lucio Martínez to Commanding Officer, Second Brigade, Third Division 4:450, in Ahumada Moreno, *Guerra del Pacífico*; Pérez, *Apuntes biograficos*, 78–79.

89. Temistocles to Basilio Urrutia, Callao, 20 January 1881, 5:172–73, Diego to Shanklin, Chorrillos Cem., 13 January 1881, 5:173–74, Juan Matta to Valentin Letelier, Arica, 27 January 1881, 5:174–75, in Ahumada Moreno, *Guerra del Pacífico*; Le León, *Recuerdos*, 115.

90. Perolari-Malmignati, *Il Perú*, 317; Father Salvador Donoso to Carlos Irarrázaval, Lima, 19 January 1881, in Ahumada Moreno, *Guerra del Pacífico*, 5:177–79.

91. Alberto Ulloa, "Lo que yo ví: Apuntes de un reservista sobre las jornadas de 13 y 15 de enero de 1881," in López Martínez, *Piérola*, 90–91.

92. Pedro Silva to Capitán de Navío, Secretario Jeneral de S.E. el Jefe Supremo de la Republica, Lima, 28 January 1881, in Ahumada Moreno, *Guerra del Pacífico*, 4:482–83; del Solar, *Diario*, 218.

93. Marcos Maturana to Manuel Baquedano, in Ahumada Moreno, *Guerra del Pacífico*, 4:425–26; Le León, *Recuerdos*, 121.

94. Le León, *Recuerdos*, 126.

95. Rosales, *Mi campaña*, 213.

96. John Spenser to Earl of Granville, Confidential, Lima, 22 January 1881, in Wu Brading, *Testimonios*, 140–48.

97. Birkedal, "Late War," 119, and *Peru-Bolivia-Chile*, 1.

98. Cáceres, *Guerra del 79*, 78–79.

99. General Pedro Silva to Capitán de Navío, Secretario Jeneral de S.E. el Jefe Supremo de la Republica, Lima, 28 January 1881, 4:479–85, José Diez to Minister, 16 January 1881, 4:490, in Ahumada Moreno, *Guerra del Pacífico*.

100. *El Comercio* (Lima), in Ahumada Moreno, *Guerra del Pacífico*, 5:186–87.

101. Mason, *War on the Pacific Coast*, 57; Ekdahl, *Historia militar*, 3:177; José Díez to Ministro, 16 January 1881, in Ahumada Moreno, *Guerra del Pacífico*, 4:490; Seraylán L., "Campaña," 167; Dellepiane, *Historia militar*, 2:380–82.

102. Spencer St. John to Earl of Granville, in Wu Brading, *Testimonios*, 147.

103. Cáceres, *Guerra del 79*, 82. Some spell his name as Cevallos.

104. B. Maturana, "Ejército Espedicionario del Norte," Lima, 31 January 1881, in Ahumada Moreno, *Guerra del Pacífico*, 4:479.

105. Cáceres, *Guerra del 79*, 84.

106. José Diez to Minister, 16 January 1881, in Ahumada Moreno, *Guerra del Pacífico*, 4:490.

107. Pedro Silva to Capitán de Navío, Secretario Jeneral de S.E. el Jefe Supremo de la República, Lima, 28 January 1881, 6:484, G. Ambrosio del Valle to Capitán de Navío, Secretario Jeneral de S.E. el Jefe Supremo de la República, Lima, 5 February 1881, 4:487–88, in Ahumada Moreno, *Guerra del Pacífico*; Le León, *Recuerdos*, 143.

108. Father Salvador Donoso to Carlos Irarrázaval, Lima, 19 January 1881, in Ahumada Moreno, *Guerra del Pacífico*, 5:177.

109. Cornelio Saavedra to J. Besa, 27 January 1881, Fondos Varios, vol. 183, Archivo Nacional.

110. Un Soldado de la Reserva, Herido en Miraflores, to Piérola, Lima, 8 March 1881, 5:223, J. M. Quimper, "Manifiesto," Lima, 25 May 1881, 5:223–28; *La Bolsa* (Arequipa), 13 January 1881, 5:219, in Ahumada Moreno, *Guerra del Pacífico*.

111. Ramón Rodríguez and Valentin Espejo to Unknown recipient, Lima, 20 January 1881, *La Pampa* (Buenos Aires), in Ahumada Moreno, *Guerra del Pacífico*, 5:196–97.

112. Eduardo Hempel, "La Batalla de Chorrillos," in Ahumada Moreno, *Guerra del Pacífico*, 4:512.

113. Pedro Silva Capitán de Navío, Secretario Jeneral de S.E. el Jefe Supremo de la Republica, Lima, 28 January 1881, in Ahumada Moreno, *Guerra del Pacífico*, 4:483.

114. J. M. Quimper, "Manifiesto," Lima, 25 May 1881, in Ahumada Moreno, *Guerra del Pacífico*, 5:523, 528; Böhm, *Judios en el Perú*, 74.

115. "Las batallas de Chorrillos y Miraflores descritas por los Peruanos," *El Comercio* (Lima), 5:186, 188, Silva, "Partes oficiales peruanos de las batallas de Chorrillos y Miraflores," 4:483, 485–86, "Relación nominal de los jefes I oficiales peruanos muertos, heridos y prisioneros," *El Comercio* (Lima), 4:491–93, in Ahumada Moreno, *Guerra del Pacífico*; Vicuña Mackenna, *Historia de la Campaña de Lima*, 2:1173, 1177.

116. Silva, "Partes oficiales peruanos de las batallas," in Ahumada Moreno, *Guerra del Pacífico*, 4:483, 486, Hempel, 4:512, in Ahumada Moreno, *Guerra del Pacífico*.

117. Bulnes, *Historia*, 2:692–93.

118. *La Actualidad* (Lima), 5:106, *La Estrella de Panamá* (Panama), Lima,

21 January 1881, 5:115, A. A. Aramburú, " A las armas," *La Opinión Nacional* (Lima), 4:382, Father Salvador Donoso to Carlos Irarrázaval, Lima, 19 January 1881, 5:178, in Ahumada Moreno, *Guerra del Pacífico*; Vicente Holguin, "Toma de Lima," 26.

119. Galvarino Riveros to Minister of Army and Navy in the Field, Callao, 16 February 1881, 5:246–7, José Francisco Vergara, Lima, 25 February 1881, 5:247, Ahumada Moreno, *Guerra del Pacífico*.

120. Caviano, *Historia de la guerra*, 2:119; Riquelme, *Expedición*, 157.

121. Perolari-Malmignati, *Il Perú*, 306; A. A. Aramburú, "A las armas," *La Opinión Nacional* (Lima), 4:382, Pedro José Calderón to Nicolás Piérola, Lima, 7, 11 January 1881, 5:94–95, Ahumada Moreno, *Guerra del Pacífico*; Holguin, "Toma de Lima," 11. Davin, *Chile y Peru en tiempos de la Guerra del Pacífico*, 83.

122. Robert Ramsay to Catherine Sturrock, Lima, 18 January 1881, in Peri, *Batallones*, 165.

123. Perolari-Malmignati, *Il Perú*, 313; "Otra Carta de Lima," Lima, 17 January 1881, in Ahumada Moreno, *Guerra del Pacífico*, 5:176; Spencer St. John to Earl of Granville, 22 January 1881, in Wu Brading, *Testimonios*, 147–48.

124. Qtd. in Guerra Martiniere, *Ocupación de Lima*, 143.

125. Perolri-Malmignati, *Il Perú*, 315; Holguin, "Toma de Lima," 13–14; Larraín, *Impresiones*, 362–63; Witt, *Diario*, 318.

126. Gmo. Carvallo, Ancón, 23 January 1881, 5:120, Patricio Lynch, Callao, 15 February 1881, 5:124–25, in Ahumada Moreno, *Guerra del Pacífico*; Holguin, "Toma de Lima," 13.

127. Spencer St. John to Earl of Granville, 22 January 1881, FO vol. 61.

128. Federico Stuven to Minister of War, Lima, 8 February 1881, in Ahumada Moreno, *Guerra del Pacífico*, 5:122; Isaac Christiancy to James G. Blaine, Lima, 16 March 1881, in United States of America, *Message from the President*, 465.

129. Patricio Lynch, Cablegrams of 30 May and 6, 8 June 1881, in "Cablegramas del Cuartel Jeneral de Lima, 1881–1882." In possession of the author.

130. Palma, *Crónicas*, 56, 80.

131. Manuel Zanutelli Rosas, "Lima durante la ocupacion chilena," in Peru, Ministry of War, *Guerra del Pacífico*, 1:116–17.

132. Salinas, *Representantes*, 242, 257, 261.

133. Ricardo Palma to Nicolás Piérola, Lima, 5 April 1881, Palma to Piérola, Lima, 27 June 1881, in Palma, *Cartas a Piérola*, 33, 51.

134. Domingo Santa María to Patricio Lynch, Santiago, 7 August and 23 November 1883, Fondos Varios, vol. 414, Archivo Nacional.

135. Ricardo Palma to Nicolás Piérola, Lima, 8 February 1881, in Palma, *Cartas a Piérola*, 20.

136. Qtd. in A. González Prada, *Mi Manuel*, 83; Lt. Reginald Carey-Brenton qtd. in Tauro, "Defensa de Lima," 104.

137. Manrique, *Guerrillas indígenas*, 59.

138. Manuel González Prada, *Impresiones*, 218.

139. Ricardo Palma to Nicolás Piérola, Lima, 27 June and 11 October 1881, in Palma, *Cartas a Piérola*, 51, 79.

140. Bossi, *Vapor Oriental*, 46.

9. The Dirty War

1. García Calderón, *Memorias*, 89.

2. M. García de la Huerta to Minister of War in the Field, Santiago, 7 February 1881, Ahumada Moreno, *Guerra del Pacífico*, 5:228.

3. Conferencias diplomáticas, 14.

4. Justus D. Doenecke qtd. in Healy, *James G. Blaine*, 5–9.

5. Lash, Politician Turned General, 212; Millington, American Diplomacy, 93–94.

6. Sater, *Empires in Conflict*, 31–50; García Calderón, *Memorias*, 92.

7. Qtd. in Pletcher, *Awkward Years*, 42.

8. Chile, Ministry of War, *Memoria, 1881*, 6, 55; Manuel Baquedano to José Francisco Vergara, Lima, 6, 9 February 1881, 5:230–31, Vergara to Baquedano, Lima, 7, 9 February 1881, 5:230–31, in Ahumada Moreno, *Guerra del Pacífico*.

9. Estado Mayor General, *Historia*, 6:226–30; R. Riquelme, Callao, 28 May 1881, in Ahumada Moreno, *Guerra del Pacífico*, 5:489.

10. Cáceres, *Guerra del 79*, 97.

11. Guerra Martiniere, *Ocupación de Lima*, 304.

12. Tomás Patiño to Col. Prefect Ayacucho, Huancavelica, 30 June and 11 July 1882, in Ahumada Moreno, *Guerra del Pacífico*, 7:186–87.

13. Ambrosio Letelier to Daniel Silva Vergara, 17 April 1881, 6:94, José Echeverría to Commanding officer, Chicla, 19 April 1881, 6:95, V. Méndez to C. Staff, Casapalca, 8 May 1881, 6:97, Méndez to Adolfo Silva, 8 May 1881, 6:97, in Ahumada Moreno, *Guerra del Pacífico*.

14. Ambrosio Letelier, Decree, Cerro de Pasco, 29 April 1881, in Ahumada Moreno, *Guerra del Pacífico*, 5:454–55.

15. "Detalles sobre la espedición Letelier," Junín, 20 May 1881 [taken from a letter], in Ahumada Moreno, *Guerra del Pacífico*, 5:456.

16. "Detalles sobre la espedición Letelier," Junín, 20 May 1881 [taken from a letter], in Ahumada Moreno, *Guerra del Pacífico*, 5:456.

17. Telegram, Patricio Lynch to Ambrosio Letelier, 28 May 1881, in Bulnes, *Historia*, 3:36.

18. Ambrosio Letelier to Commanding Officer, Army of Lima, Cerro de Pasco, 13 May 1881, 6:34–35, Letelier to General in Charge of Operations, Cerro de Pasco, 9 June 1881, 5:482, in Ahumada Moreno, *Guerra del Pacífico*.

19. Duarte, *Exposición*, 32–33; Ambrosio Letelier, Telegram, Cerro de Pasco, 11 June 1881, 5:482–83, Letelier to Commander-in-Chief, Chicla, 21 June 1881,

5:483, Letelier to Commander-in-Chief, Lima, 14 June 1881, 5:483–84, Hilarión Bouquet to Letelier, Huánuco, 13 June 1881, 5:487–89, Letelier to Commander-in-Chief, Lima, 14 July 1881, 6:37–38, in Ahumada Moreno, *Guerra del Pacífico*.

20. One of the problems was that both sides over- or underestimated the size of their forces and those of the enemy. Thus, Carlos Dellepiane claimed that Vento's men numbered 140. *Historia militar*, 2:412; Estado Mayor General, *Historia*, 6:251. Admiral Montero said Vento commanded only 70; see Lizardo Montero to Prefects, Cajamarca, 16 August 1881, in Ahumada Moreno, *Guerra del Pacífico*, 6:174. Vicuña Mackenna claimed there were in excess of 600 *Sangra*, 18.

21. Bulnes, *Historia*, 3:28–40.

22. Hilarión Bouquet to Ambrosio Letelier, Huánuco, 13 June 1881, in Ahumada Moreno, *Guerra del Pacífico*, 5:489; Peru, Ministry of War, *Guerra del Pacífico*, 1:57–58.

23. Patricio Lynch to Eulogio Altamirano, 13 July, Cablegramas; "Detalles sobre la espedición Letelier," Junín, 20 May 1881 [taken from a letter], in Ahumada Moreno, *Guerra del Pacífico*, 5:455–456.

24. Patricio Lynch, Lima, 4 February 1882, in Ahumada Moreno, *Guerra del Pacífico*, 6:392.

25. José Francisco Gana to Patricio Lynch, Lima, 17 May 1882, in Ahumada Moreno, *Guerra del Pacífico*, 7:145–53.

26. Giesecke, "Las clases sociales," 68–69; López Martínez, *Piérola*, 25.

27. Demofilo Fuenzalida et al., Lima, 22 July 1881, 5:512–13, Estanislao del Canto et al., Lima, 29 September 1881, 6:240–41, Patricio Lynch to Minister of War, Lima, 24 October 1881, 6:284–85, J. M. Alcérreca to Adolfo Silva, Chosica, 9 April 1881, 6:7, in Ahumada Moreno, *Guerra del Pacífico*.

28. Patricio Lynch to Minister of War, Lima, 1, 24 October 1881, in Ahumada Moreno, *Guerra del Pacífico*, 6:221, 283–84.

29. Patricio Lynch to Minister of War, Lima, 16 October 1881, in Ahumada Moreno, *Guerra del Pacífico*, 6:221–22.

30. Patricio Lynch to Minister of War, Lima, 21 June 1881, 5:473, Enrique Baeza to General, Chief of Staff, Pueblo Nuevo, 24 June 1881, 5:473–74, Sofanor Parra to Commanding Officer, Cañete Division, Cañete Nuevo, 24 June 1881, 5:474–75, Enrique Baeza to Wife, Cañete, 21 June 1881, 5:476–77, Lynch to Minister of War, Lima, 10 September 1881, 6:215, Manuel Novoa to Commanding Officer, Army of North, Trujillo, 31 October 1881, 6:216, in Ahumada Moreno, *Guerra del Pacífico*.

31. Lynch to Minister of War, Lima, 17, 18 June 1881, in Ahumada Moreno, *Guerra del Pacífico*, 6:79.

32. Luis Arteaga to President of the Republic, Tacna, 3, 13 September 1881, in Ahumada Moreno, *Guerra del Pacífico*, 6:179.

33. Patricio Lynch to Minister of War, Lima, 24 October 1881, in Ahumada Moreno, *Guerra del Pacífico*, 6:283–84.

34. Cáceres, *Guerra del 79*, 114, 118, 119, 121, 123, 133–35, 139, 141.

35. Patricio Lynch to José Francisco Gana, Lima, 1 January 1882, 6:367–68, Lynch, "Instrucciones al Jefe de la Division que marcha a Jauja, Tarma y otros puntos del Peru," Lima, 1 January 1882, 6:368–69, Gana to Lynch, Chilca, 10 January 1882, 6:366, in Ahumada Moreno, *Guerra del Pacífico*.

36. José Francisco Gana to Patricio Lynch, Chilca, 10 January 1882, in Ahumada Moreno, *Guerra del Pacífico*, 6:366.

37. W. Castillo to Lynch, Callao, 17 January 1882, in Ahumada Moreno, *Guerra del Pacífico*, 6:366–67.

38. Cáceres, *Guerra del 79*, 141, 148–49.

39. Del Canto, *Memorias militares*, 171–75.

40. *El Coquimbo* (Coquimbo), 12 April 1882, in Ahumada Moreno, *Guerra del Pacífico*, 6:496–97.

41. Cáceres, *Guerra del 79*, 112.

42. Ibarra Díaz, *Campaña de la Sierra*, 72, 77.

43. Lynch, *Segunda memoria*, 2:75–76; Estanislao del Canto to General, Huancayo, 4 June 1882, in del Canto, *Memorias*, 225, 234; Benavides Santos, *Seis años*, 176; de la Barra Fontecilla, *Historia*, 153; Palma, *Crónicas*, 125.

44. Cáceres, *Guerra del 79*, 177–78; Andrés Cáceres to Delegate of Supreme Government in Lima, Tarma, 22 July 1882, in Ahumada Moreno, *Guerra del Pacífico*, 7:209–10.

45. Estanislao del Canto to Patricio Lynch, Oroya, 18, 19 July 1882, in Ahumada Moreno, *Guerra del Pacífico*, 7:211–12.

46. Estado Mayor General, *Historia*, 6:283; Ravest Mora, "*Memorias íntimas*," 330.

47. Benavides Santos, *Seis años*, 190–99.

48. "Carta," 25 June 1882, in Ahumada Moreno, *Guerra del Pacífico*, 7:187–88.

49. Domingo Castillo to Colonel of the Division, Zapallanga, 29 June 1882, 7:183–84, Estanislao del Canto to Patricio Lynch, Huancayo, 10 July 1882, 7:175, in Ahumada Moreno, *Guerra del Pacífico*; H. Latapiat to Commanding Officer, Army of the Center, Jauja, 10 July 1882, in del Canto, *Memorias militares*, 226, 238.

50. Benavides Santos, *Seis años*, 199.

51. Estanislao del Canto to Patricio Lynch, La Oroya, 18, 19 July 1882, 7:211–12; del Canto to Chief of Staff, La Oroya, 18 July 1882, 7:212, in Ahumada Moreno, *Guerra del Pacífico*, 7:212.

52. Estanislao del Canto to Patricio Lynch, La Oroya, 19 July 1882, in Ahumada Moreno, *Guerra del Pacífico*, 7:212.

53. Del Canto, *Memorias militares*, 239.

54. Duarte, *Exposición*, 57–58; Ravest Mora, "Combate de Conceción," 7–13; Marcial Pinto Agüero to Commanding Officer, Division of the Center, Jauja, 12 January 1882, 7:189–90, Andrés Cáceres to Prefect of Ayacucho, Apata, 13 July

414 NOTES TO PAGES 322–324

1882, 7:192, M. F. Horta, *El Eco de Junín* (Junín), 26 August 1882, 7:192–96, José Francisco Gana to Francisco Barceló, Lima, 2 August 1882, 7:202–3, in Ahumada Moreno, *Guerra del Pacífico.*

55. Andrés Cáceres to Remijio Morales Bermudes, Huancayo, 11 July 1882, in Ahumada Moreno, *Guerra del Pacífico*, 7:187.

56. Francisco Meyer to Commanding Officer, Oroya, 3 July 1882, 7:176, José Antonio Gutiérrez to Chief of Staff, Cerro de Pasco, 10 July 1882, 7:177, in Ahumada Moreno, *Guerra del Pacífico.*

57. Estanislao del Canto to Patricio Lynch, Lima, 30 July 1882, in Ahumada Moreno, *Guerra del Pacífico*, 7:215–16.

58. [A Chilean officer], Tarma, 17 July 1882, in Ahumada Moreno, *Guerra del Pacífico*, 7:218–19.

59. Benavides Santos, *Seis años*, 182, 188, 190; Domingo Castillo to Colonel, Commanding Officer, Forces of the Center, Zapallanga, 29 June 1882, in Ahumada Moreno, *Guerra del Pacífico*, 7:183–84.

60. Lynch, *Segunda memoria*, 2:85.

61. Lynch to Minister of War, Lima, 30 August 1882, in Ahumada Moreno, *Guerra del Pacífico*, 7:306.

62. Lynch to Minister of War, Lima, 21 July 1882, in Ahumada Moreno, *Guerra del Pacífico*, 7:213; Benavides Santos, *Seis años*, 210.

63. Estanislao del Canto to C. Staff, Oroya, 29 July 1882, José Francisco Gana to del Canto, Chicla, 20 July 1882, del Canto to Patricio Lynch, 24 July 1882, Lynch to del Canto, Lima, 21 July 1882, in del Canto, *Memorias militares*, 265–68, 282–83; Cáceres, *Guerra del 79*, 180–81; Basadre, *Historia*, 5th ed., 6:2591.

64. Patricio Lynch to Minister of War, Lima, 30 August 1882, in Ahumada Moreno, *Guerra del Pacífico*, 7:306–7.

65. *El Diario de Arequipa* (Arequipa), 8 August 1882, in Ahumada Moreno, *Guerra del Pacífico*, 7:232.

66. Chile, Ministry of War, *Memoria, 1882*, ix; Patricio Lynch to Minister of War, Lima, 27 September 1882, 7:282, Ramón Carvallo Orrego to Commander-in-Chief, San Pedro, 17 July 1882, 7:205, in Ahumada Moreno, *Guerra del Pacífico.*

67. Patricio Lynch to Minister of War, Lima, 19 January and 23 February 1882, in Ahumada Moreno, *Guerra del Pacífico*, 6:397, 399–400.

68. Waldo Díaz to Chief of Operations of the Army, Ica, 31 July 1882, in Ahumada Moreno, *Guerra del Pacífico*, 7:253.

69. Patricio Lynch to Marco Arriagada, Lima, 26 September 1882, in Ahumada Moreno, *Guerra del Pacífico*, 7:351.

70. Horacio de Nordenflict to General, Commanding Officer, Operations, Pisco, 3 October 1882, 7:352–53, Máximo Correa to Chief of Staff, Ica, 4 October 1882, 7:354, Marco Arriagada to Chief of Operations of the Army of the North, Ica, 12 October 1882, 7:353–54, in Ahumada Moreno, *Guerra del Pacífico.*

71. Patricio Lynch to Jefe, "Ocupación de Cañete," Lima, 29 May 1882, in Ahumada Moreno, *Guerra del Pacífico*, 7:153–54.

72. Chile, Ministry of War, *Memoria, 1882*, xi; Aranda de los Rios and Sotomayor Rogguero, "Subelevación negra," 1:243, 245.

73. Vicente Ruíz to Patricio Lynch, La Quebrada, 30 June 1882, in Ahumada Moreno, *Guerra del Pacífico*, 7:155.

74. Manuel Jarpa, Cañete, 9 August 1882, 7:273–74, Jarpa to Patricio Lynch, La Quebrada, 17 August 1882, 7:274–76, Jarpa to Lynch, La Quebrada, 30 August 1882, 7:276–77, Jarpa to Lynch, Cañete, 17 August and 5 September 1882, 7:277–78, Jarpa to Commander-in-Chief, Cañete, 2 October 1882, 7:349–50, in Ahumada Moreno, *Guerra del Pacífico*.

75. Patricio Lynch to Chief, Occupation of Cañete, Lima, 29 May 1882, 7:153–54, Lynch to Minister War, Lima, 5 June 1882, 7:154, Lynch to Military Chief, Cañete, Lima, 29 July 1882, 7:271–72, in Ahumada Moreno, *Guerra del Pacífico*.

76. Vicente Ruíz to Patricio Lynch, La Quebrada, 30 June 1882, in Ahumada Moreno, *Guerra del Pacífico*, 7:155.

77. Patricio Lynch to Minister of War, Lima, 23 December 1882, 7:455–56, Julio Salcedo to Commanding Officer, Army of the Center, El Arenal, 28 December 1882, 7:456–58, in Ahumada Moreno, *Guerra del Pacífico*.

78. Miguel Iglesias to Subprefect of Chiclayo, Cajamarca, 22 July 1882, in Ahumada Moreno, *Guerra del Pacífico*, 7:210.

79. Salinas, *Representantes*, 274.

80. Chile, Ministry of War, *Memoria, 1882*, x; Patricio Lynch to Minister of War, Lima, 27 September 1882, 7:283, Lynch to Minister of War, Lima, 24 October 1881, 6:283–84, in Ahumada Moreno, *Guerra del Pacífico*.

81. Patricio Lynch to Minister of War, Lima, 19 April 1882, 6:498, José Francisco Gana to Lynch, Lima, 17 May 1882, 7:145–52, in Ahumada Moreno, *Guerra del Pacífico*; Lynch, *Memoria*, 226–37. These figures do not add up to 13,090, perhaps because they were published at different times.

82. Gabriel Alamos, Bando, Chincha, Alta, 4 August 1882, 7:267, Ramón Carvallo Orrego, Cañete, 12 November 1882, 7:427, Alejandro Gorostiaga, Trujillo, 30 November 1882, 7:427, in Ahumada Moreno, *Guerra del Pacífico*. Lynch approved of this policy of forcing vagrants to work. Patricio Lynch to Chief, Departments of the North, Lima, 9 December 1882, in Ahumada Moreno, *Guerra del Pacífico*, 7:487.

83. Patricio Lynch to Manuel Jarpa, Lima, 19 January 1882, in Ahumada Moreno, *Guerra del Pacífico*, 6:397.

84. Patricio Lynch, Lima, 31 July 1882, 7:272, Leóncio E. Tagle to Commanding Officer, Palpa Expedition, Ica, 27 January 1882, 7:105, in Ahumada Moreno, *Guerra del Pacífico*.

85. Patricio Lynch to Minister of War, Lima, 23 February 1882, in Ahumada Moreno, *Guerra del Pacífico*, 6:399–400.

86. Leóncio E. Tagle to Commanding Officer, Ica, 9 February 1882, in Ahumada Moreno, *Guerra del Pacífico*, 6:399.

87. *El Comercio* (Lima), Pisco, 28 July 1882, in Ahumada Moreno, *Guerra del Pacífico*, 7:255–56.

88. Patricio Lynch to Commanding Officer of Forces in Ica, Lima, 24 July 1882, Ahumada Moreno, *Guerra del Pacífico*, 7:215; Lynch to Military Chief of Cañete, Lima, 29 July 1882, Ahumada Moreno, *Guerra del Pacífico*, 7:271–72; Lynch to Manuel Jarpa, Lima, 31 July 1882, Ahumada Moreno, *Guerra del Pacífico*, 7:272.

89. Waldo Díaz, Ica, 27 July 1882, Ahumada Moreno, *Guerra del Pacífico*, 7:251–52.

90. Waldo Díaz to Chief of Staff, Ica, 31 July 1882, in Ahumada Moreno, *Guerra del Pacífico*, 7:254.

91. Patricio Lynch to Political and Military Chief of Ica, Lima, 31 July 1882, in Ahumada Moreno, *Guerra del Pacífico*, 7:252.

92. Patricio Lynch to Political and Military Chief of Ica, Lima, 31 July 1882, in Ahumada Moreno, *Guerra del Pacífico*, 7:252.

93. Waldo Díaz to Jefe Ejército de Operaciones, Ica, 12 August 1882, 6:256–57, Leóncio Tagle, Ica, 24 September 1882, 6:262, in Ahumada Moreno, *Guerra del Pacífico*.

94. Manuel Jarpa, Cañete, 3 August 1882, Ahumada Moreno, *Guerra del Pacífico*, 7:272–73, Waldo Díaz to Chief of Operations, Ica, 31 July 1882, 7:253, in Ahumada Moreno, *Guerra del Pacífico*.

95. Manuel Jarpa, Cañete, 6 October 1882, in Ahumada Moreno, *Guerra del Pacífico*, 7:350.

96. Gabriel Alamos to C. Staff, Chincha Alta, 4, 8, 9 August 1882, in Ahumada Moreno, *Guerra del Pacífico*, 7:267, 268.

97. Leóncio Tagle to General, Chief of Operations, Ica, 25 September 1882, 7:263–64, Waldo Díaz to Commanding Officer, Army of the North, Ica, 31 January 1882, 6:398, in Ahumada Moreno, *Guerra del Pacífico*.

98. Máximo Correa to Commander-in-Chief of Forces, Ica, 12 August 1882, 7:257; Leóncio Tagle, Ica, 24 September 1882, 6:262, in Ahumada Moreno, *Guerra del Pacífico*.

99. Máximo Correa to Colonel, Chief of Forces of the Occupation, Ica, 3 September 1882, 7:259–60, Leóncio Tagle to Chief of Staff, Ica, 4 September 1882, 7:258–59, Tagle to General, Commanding Officer of Operations, Ica, 21 September 1882, 7:261, Tagle to Correa, Ica, 20 September 1882, 7:262, Patricio Lynch to Minister of War, Lima, 12 September 1882, 7:270, Francisco Fuentes to Commanding Officer, Chincha, Chincha Baja, 15 September 1882, 7:271, in Ahumada Moreno, *Guerra del Pacífico*.

100. Patricio Lynch to Minister of War, Lima, 5 September 1881, in Ahumada Moreno, *Guerra del Pacífico*, 7:270.

101. Manuel Jarpa to Patricio Lynch, La Quebrada, 30 August 1882, in Ahumada Moreno, *Guerra del Pacífico*, 7:276–77.

102. *El Comercio* (Lima), 4 October 1882, in Ahumada Moreno, *Guerra del Pacífico*, 7:356–58.

103. S. Urízar Gárfias to Commander-in-Chief of Forces, Trujillo, 8 February 1882, 6:467–68, Patricio Lynch to Minister of War, Lima, 19 April 1882, 6:497–99, Lynch to Minister of War, Lima, 17 May 1882, 6:498–99, Lynch, Lima, 6 September 1882, 7:365–66, Lynch to Ramón Carvallo Orrego, Commanding Officer, Department of the North, Lima, 27 September 1882, 7:366, Lynch to Minister of War, Lima, 23 October 1882, 7:367–68, in Ahumada Moreno, *Guerra del Pacífico*.

104. L. Bysivinger [*sic*] to Patricio Lynch, Chinca Alta, 10 February 1883, 7:481, Lynch to Commanding Officer, Batallón Lautaro, Lima, 1 March 1883, 8:118, Lynch to H. Martínez, Commanding Officer, Chile, Lima, 3 March 1883, 8:118, Lynch to Major Camus, Commanding Officer, Batallón Cañete, Lima, 3 March 1883, 8:118, Lynch to Marco Arriagada, Lima, 24 March 1883, 8:119, Lynch to Minister of War, Lima, 28 February 1883, 8:114–15, Soffia to President, Tacna, 16 March 1883, 7:481, Leóncio Tagle to Commander-in-Chief, Ica, 2 April 1883, 8:120, Ruperto Ovalle to Major, Chincha Alta, 30 March, 8:120, Lynch, Lima, 2 October 1883, 8:323–24, Lynch to Minister of War, Lima, 12 October 1883, 7:324–25, José Velásquez to President, 4 August 1883, Oyarzún to Commanding Officer of Las Heras, Mirabe, 3 August 1883, "La persecución a Pacheco Céspedes," Sama, 6 August 1883, 8:280–82, Basilio Urrutia to Minister of War, Tacna, 12 November 1883, 8:455–56, Velásquez, 4 August 1883, 8:280, Correspondencia del Tacora, 6 August 1883, 8:281, in Ahumada Moreno, *Guerra del Pacífico*; Moreno Guevara, *Combate de Pachia*, 19, 24–25, 29, 32–34; Peru, Ministry of War, Permanent Commission, *Huamachuco y el alma Nacional*, 1:568.

105. *El Independiente* (Santiago), 30 April and 10 August 1882.

106. Fernández Valdés, *Chile y Perú*, 107.

107. Patricio Lynch to Estanislao del Canto, Lima, 24 April 1883, 8:174–75, Lynch to Juan León García, Lima, 5 April 1883, 8:167–68, in Ahumada Moreno, *Guerra del Pacífico*.

108. Machuca, *Cuatro campañas*, 4:352.

109. Martiniano Urriola to Patricio Lynch, Chosica, 28 March 1883, 8:187, Lynch to President, Lima, 3 May 1883, 8:175, Lynch to Minister of War, Lima, 12 April 1883, 8:169, Lynch to Minister of War, Lima, 18 April 1883, 8:170, in Ahumada Moreno, *Guerra del Pacífico*; Florencio Pinto Agüero to Estanislao del Canto, San Mateo, 13 May 1883, in del Canto, *Memorias militares*, 311.

110. Del Canto, *Memorias militares*, 325–26, 333–36.

111. Patricio Lynch to Alejandro Gorostiaga, Lima, 31 May and 10 June 1883, 8:176–77, Lynch to Gorostiaga, Lima, 18 June 1883, 8:178, Lynch to Gorostiaga, Lima, 3 July 1883, 8:188–89 in Ahumada Moreno, *Guerra del Pacífico*.

112. Patricio Lynch to Herminio González, Lima, 2, 3 June 1883, 8:204–5, Lynch to Marco Arriagada, Lima, 16 July 1883, 8:186, Lynch to Alejandro Gorostiaga, Lima, 18 June 1883, 8:178, in Ahumada Moreno, *Guerra del Pacífico*. Gorostiaga wrote that both González and Parra arrived with more men than 130 and 108 men, respectively, as originally believed. Gorostiaga to Commander-in-Chief of the Army, Huamachuco, 12 July 1883, in Ahumada Moreno, *Guerra del Pacífico*, 8:212.

113. Patricio Lynch to Alejandro Gorostiaga, Lima, 18 June 1883, in Ahumada Moreno, *Guerra del Pacífico*, 8:178.

114. Huaráz, 20 June 1883, 8:175, Alejandro Gorostiaga to Patricio Lynch, Huamachuco, 12 July 1883, 8:212–14, Lynch to Minister of War, 25 July 1883, 8:184, Marco Arriagada to Lynch, Lima, 6 August 1883, 8:189–93, in Ahumada Moreno, *Guerra del Pacífico*.

115. Cáceres, *Guerra del 79*, 204–10.

116. Cáceres, *Guerra del 79*, 210–11.

117. Patricio Lynch to Martiniano Urriola, Lima, 3 July 1883, in Ahumada Moreno, *Guerra del Pacífico*, 8:206.

118. Alejandro Gorostiaga to Patricio Lynch, Huamachuco, 12 July 1883, in Ahumada Moreno, *Guerra del Pacífico*, 8:212–14.

119. Patricio Lynch to Martiniano Urriola, Lima, 16 July 1883, 8: 188, Lynch to Marco Arriagada, Lima, 16 July 1883, 8:186, Ahumada Moreno, *Guerra del Pacífico*; Machuca, *Cuatro compañas*, 4:375.

120. Gamazza, *Batalla de Huamachuco*, 34.

121. Molinare, *Historia*, 110, 112; "Batalla de Huamachuco," Lima, 14 July 1883, 7:222–23, [A letter from a Chilean officer], "Gorostiaga en Mollendo," 8:211, Marco Arriagada to Patricio Lynch, Lima, 6 August 1883, 8:189–93, Alejandro Gorostiaga to Lynch, Huamachuco, 12 July 1883, 8:212–14, in Ahumada Moreno, *Guerra del Pacífico*; Cáceres, *Guerra del 79*, 204–10, 213–17.

122. Cáceres, *Guerra del 79*, 224; Andrés Cáceres to Minister of War, "Batalla de Huamachuco," Huancayo, 30 July 1883, Biblioteca Militar Nacional; Guzmán Palomino, *Campaña de la Breña*, 255–57; *Batalla de Huamachuco*, 221–24.

123. Letters of Alejandro Binimelis to Nicanor Molinare, Valdivia, 1 August 1913, in Molinare, *Historia*, 223–24, 274, 302.

124. Andrés Cáceres to Minister of War, "Batalla de Huamachuco," Huancayo, 30 July 1883, Biblioteca Militar Nacional; Guzmán Palomino, *Campaña de la Breña*, 258–59; Carlos Vargas Clark to Aniceto Vergara Albano, Huamachuco, 14 July 1883, 8:224, E. Rioseco Vidaurre, Lima, 18 July 1883, 8:225, in Ahumada Moreno, *Guerra del Pacífico*; Ignacio Prado Pastor, "Leóncio Prado," in *Huamachuco*, 619–48; Gamazza, *Batalla de Huamachuco*, 50–51; Letters of Alejandro Binimelis to Nicanor Molinare, Valdivia, 1 August 1913, in Molinare, *Historia*, 286, 290–94.

125. Gamazza, *Batalla de Huamachuco*, 57; Ruperto Correa to Martiniano Urriola, Cerro, 18 July 1883, in Ahumada Moreno, *Guerra del Pacífico*, 8:310.

126. "Partida de la división Gorostiaga de Huamachuco," Cajabamba, 17 July 1883, 8:226–27, Chile, *Diario Oficial*, 8:242–43; Alejandro Gorostiaga to Patricio Lynch, Cajabamba, 26 July 1883, 8:310–11, in Ahumada Moreno, *Guerra del Pacífico*.

127. Patricio Lynch to Alejandro Gorostiaga, Lima, 19 July 1883, in Ahumada Moreno, *Guerra del Pacífico*, 8:241.

128. Cajabamba, 17 July 1883, 8:226, Marco Arriagada to Patricio Lynch, Lima, 6 August 1883, 8:192, in Ahumada Moreno, *Guerra del Pacífico*.

129. Martiniano Urriola to Patricio Lynch, Jauja, 25 July 1883, 8:311–12, Urriola to Lynch, Jauja, 5 August 1883, 8:312–13, in Ahumada Moreno, *Guerra del Pacífico*.

130. Patricio Lynch to Minister of War, Lima, 1 August 1883, in Ahumada Moreno, *Guerra del Pacífico*, 7:221.

131. Poblete, "Servicio sanitario," 41, no. 45:475.

132. Patricio Lynch to Martiniano Urriola, Lima, 28 August 1883, 7:315, Alejandro Gorostiaga to General, Army of North, Cajabamba, 26 July 1883, 7:310–11, in Ahumada Moreno, *Guerra del Pacífico*.

133. Patricio Lynch to Minister of War, Lima, 12 October 1883, 7:324–25, Lynch to Minister of War, Lima, 27 October 1883, 7:325, Balsilio Urrutia to Minister of War, Tacna, 12 November 1883, 8:455, Correspondencia del Tacora, Sama, 6 August 1883, 8:281–82, Lynch, Lima, 2 October 1883, 8:323–24, Herminio González to Lynch, Chorrillos, 27 October 1883, 8:326, Urrutia to Minister of War, Tacna, 12 November 1883, 8:455, in Ahumada Moreno, *Guerra del Pacífico*.

134. Machuca, *Cuatro compañas*, 4:439.

135. José Velásquez to Domingo Santa María, 8 June 1883, qtd. in Bulnes, *Historia*, 3:535.

136. Tribunal Militar, Quequeña, 24 November 1883, in Ahumada Moreno, *Guerra del Pacífico*, 8:392–93.

137. Duarte, *Esposición*, 51; Martiniano Urriola to Lynch, Huancayo, 17 August 1883, 8:313, Lima, 22 August 1883, 8:314, Ahumada Moreno, *Guerra del Pacífico*.

138. Martiniano Urriola to Lynch, Jauja, 30 November 1883, in Ahumada Moreno, *Guerra del Pacífico*, 7:316. See Favre, "Remarques," 64.

139. Patricio Lynch to Martiniano Urriola, Lima, 28 August and 7 September 1883, 8:315–16, Urriola to Lynch, Jauja, 30 November 1883, 8:316, in Ahumada Moreno, *Guerra del Pacífico*.

140. Parodi Revoredo, *Laguna*, 116–18.

141. Parodi Revoredo, *Laguna*, 43.

142. Parodi Revoredo, *Laguna*, 124.

143. José Velásquez to Minister of War, Arequipa, 31 October 1883, in Ahumada Moreno, *Guerra del Pacífico*, 8:358–61.

144. A. Zevallos, "Notas para la historia," in Ahumada Moreno, *Guerra del Pacífico*, 8:381–83.

145. A. Zevallos, "Notas para la historia," 8:381–83, E. J. Casanave, "La sublevación de Arequipa," 8:383–85, José Goines, Lima, 4 December 1883, 8:385–86, "Memoria prestada por el alcalde del honorable concejo provincial de Arequipa," 31 December 1883, 7:387–91, José Velásquez to Minister of War, Arequipa, 31 October 1883, 8:358–61, in Ahumada Moreno, *Guerra del Pacífico*.

146. José Velásquez, Arequipa, 2 November 1883, Ahumada Moreno, *Guerra del Pacífico*, 8:440.

147. Lizardo Montero to Andrés Cáceres, Aboard the *Yavarí* in Puno, 28 October 1883, in Ahumada Moreno, *Guerra del Pacífico*, 8:365.

148. Cesar Canevaro, Esposición, La Paz, 3 November 1879, in Ahumada Moreno, *Guerra del Pacífico*, 8:366.

149. *Traición de Iglesias*, 4–8, flayed Iglesias as a Quisling who became Lynch's accomplice by trying to eradicate Cáceres. Cáceres, *Guerra del 79*, 257.

150. Basilio Urrutia, "Memoria del jefe de la división de observación de Tacna y Arica," Tacna, 26 May 1884, in Chile, Ministry of the Navy, *Memoria, 1884*, 165; Nataniel Aguirre to General Commanding La Paz, Sucre, 4 August 1884, in Aguirre Lavayen, *1884 pacto*, 240.

151. Bolivia, Ministry of War, *Informe*, 7–8, 16, 26, *Memoria, 1882*, 3, and *Memoria, 1883*, 2, 7, 21,.

152. Acta Primera, sesión del 16 de febrero de 1884, in Aguirre Lavayen, *1884 pacto*, 77–79.

153. Acta Primera, sesión del 16 de febrero de 1884, in Aguirre Lavayen, *1884 pacto*, 82.

154. Qtd. in Querejazu Calvo, *Guano*, 682.

155. Chile, Ministry of War, *Memoria, 1884*, 180.

156. Manrique, *Guerrillas indígenas*, 86, 98–102, 105–7, 146–48.

157. Luis Guzmán Palomino, "La resistencia de fuerzas irregulares que precedío a la victoriosa contraofensiva de Julio de 1882," in Peru, Ministry of War, *Guerra del Pacífico*, 2:42–43.

158. Spencer St. John to Earl of Granville, Lima, 5 June 1884, FO 61/53.

Conclusion

1. William A. Dyke Acland to A. H. Markham, Callao, 27 January 1881, in Tauro, "Defensa de Lima," 70; Consul General Pakenham to Marquis of Salisbury, Santiago, 10 July 1880, FO vol. 16/202.

2. Aguirre, *Instrucción*. Curiously, the author sent a copy of this work to Cáceres.

3. F. J. Díaz, "Estudio sobre la defensa territorial de Chile," in Brahm García, *Preparados*, 69.

4. Camacho, *Tratado sumario*, 24–25, 30.

5. Ekdahl, *Historia militar*, 2:349.

6. Ekdahl, *Historia militar*, 2:349–50, 371.

7. Documento 14 in Chile, Ministry of War and Navy, *Memoria de los trabajos*.

8. Roel, *Perú*, 185.

9. Aranzaes, *Revoluciones*; Mathews, *Up the Amazon*, 270.

10. Qtd. in Pinochet de la Barra, *Misión en Bolivia*, 182.

11. Camacho, *Tratado sumario*, ii–v; Díaz Arguedas, *Historia*, 109.

12. *Revista Militar de Chile*, 15 August 1885, 293, 12 January 1886, 468, 10 January 1887, 168, cited in Brahm García, *Preparados*, 113.

13. Col. Lonsdale Hale qtd. in Spiers, *Late Victorian Army*, 245.

14. Col. C. E. Callwell qtd. in Spiers, *Late Victorian Army*, 279.

15. Brose, *Kaiser's Army*, 13.

16. Beckett, *Ypes*, 76–78, 81; Herwig, *First World War*, 116.

Bibliography

Archival Materials

Archivo Benjamín Vicuña Mackenna, Santiago, Chile.
Archivo de la Intendencia de Atacama, Santiago, Chile.
Archivo de Ministerio del Interior, Santiago, Chile.
Archivo Nacional, Santiago, Chile.
Gibbs Archive, London, Great Britain.
Public Records Office, London, Great Britain.
    Foreign Office. General Correspondence, Chile (FO 16), 1875–84.
    Foreign Office. General Correspondence, Peru (FO 61), 1879–84.

Government Documents

  Bolivia

Ministry of War. *Informe del ministro de la guerra a la Convención Nacional de 1881.* La Paz, 1881.
———. *Memoria del Ministro de la Guerra al Congreso Ordinario de 1883.* La Paz, 1883.
———. *Memoria que presenta el general de División Ministro de la Guerra al Congreso Ordinario de 1882.* La Paz, 1882.
———. *Memoria que presenta el Jeneral Ministro de la Guerra a la Honrable Asamblea Constituyente de 1877.* La Paz, 1877.

  Chile

El Boletín de la Guerra del Pacífico, 1879–81.
Central Office of Statistics. *Estadística comercial de la República de Chile correspondiente al año de 1878.* Valparaíso, 1879.
El Diario Oficial (Santiago), 1879–84.
House of Representatives. *Discurso de S. E. el Presidente de la República en la apertura del congreso constituyente de 1891.* Santiago, 1891.
———. *Sesiones ordinarias y estraordinarias*, 1876–82.
Ministry of the Navy. *Manual de Marino.* 5 vols. Santiago, 1883.

————. *Memoria del ministro de marina presentada al congreso nacional en 1881–1884.* Santiago, 1881–84.

Ministry of War. *Memoria de guerra y marina presentada al congreso nacional en 1876, 1877, 1878, 1879, 1880.* Santiago, 1876–1880.

————. *Memoria del Ministro de la Guerra correspondiente al año de 1881, 1882, 1883, 1884.* Santiago, 1881–84.

————. *Partes oficiales de las batallas de Chorrillos i Miraflores libradas por el ejército chileno contra el Peruano en los dias 13 i 15 de enero de 1881.* Santiago, 1881.

Ministry of War and Navy. *Memoria de los trabajos ejecutados de la intendencia jeneral del ejército y armada en campaña, 1879–1880.* Santiago, 1880.

————. *Memoria de los trabajos ejecutados de la intendencia jeneral del ejército y armada en campaña 1880–1881.* Santiago, 1882.

Peru

Directorate of Statistics. *Estadística del estado del Peru.* Lima, 1879.

Ministry of War. *La Guerra del Pacífico 1879–1883: La resistencia de la Breña.* 3 vols. Lima, 1981–83.

————. Permanent Commission of the History of the Army of Peru. *La Gesta de Lima.* Lima, 1981.

————. *Historia de la escuela militar del Perú.* Lima, 1962.

————. *Huamachuco y el alma nacional, 1882–1884.* 3 Vols. Lima, 1983.

Ministry of War and the Navy. *Memoria de guerra y marina.* 2 vols. Lima, 1878.

————. *Memoria del ramo de guerra que presenta a la legislatura de 1876 y 1878.* Lima, 1876, 1878.

————. *Memoria del ramo de Marina que presenta a la legislatura de 1876.* Lima, 1876.

————. *Memoria que el Ministro de Estado en el despacho de Guerra y Marina General D. Javier de Osma presenta a la Asamblea Constituyente de 1884.* Lima, 1884.

United States

Message from the President of the United States Transmitting Papers Relating to the War in South America, and Attempts to Bring about a Peace. Washington DC, 1882.

Primary Materials

Acland, William Alison Dyke. *Six Weeks with the Chilian Army: Being a Short Account of a March from Pisco to Lurin and of the Attack on Lima.* Norfolk Island, Melanesian, Mission, 1881.

————. "Descripción del ejército del norte." In Tauro, "Defensa de Lima," 70–101.

Aguirre, Miguel Aguirre. *Instrucción de batallón en el orden abierto para los cuerpos de infantería de Bolivia.* La Paz, 1881.

————. *Lijeras reminiscencias del Campo de la Alianza*. Cochabamba, 1880.

Ahumada Moreno, Pascual. *Guerra del Pacífico: Recopilación completa de todos los documentos oficiales, correspondencias, y demás publicaciones referentes a la guerra que a dado a luz la prensa de Chile, Perú, y Bolivia*. 9 vols. Valparaíso, 1884–92.

Alba, Manuel V. *Diario de la campaña de la 5 division del ejército boliviano: Comandante general de la división el General Narciso Campero*. Sucre, 1882.

Armaza, Miguel. *La verdad sobre la campaña de San Francisco*. La Paz, 1897.

Ballivián, Daniel. *Los Colorados de Bolivia: Recuerdos de un Subteniente*. Valparaíso, 1919.

Barra Fontecilla de la, Tomás. *Historia del Batallón No. 3 de Infantería de Chile*. Santiago, 1901.

Barros Arana, Diego. *Histoire de la Guerre de Pacifique, 1879–1881*. Paris, 1881.

La batalla de Huamachuco ante la historia. Lima, 1886.

Benavides Santos, Arturo. *Seis años de vacaciones*. 3rd ed. Buenos Aires, 1967.

Birkedal, Holger, "The Late War in South America." *The Overland Monthly* 5, no. 2 (January 1884): 77–94; (February 1885): 113–19.

————. *Peru-Bolivia-Chile*. Chicago, 1884.

Birbuet España, Miguel. *Recuerdos de la campaña de 1879*. La Paz, 1986.

Bonilla, Heraclio, ed. *Gran Bretaña y el Perú: Informes de los cónsules: Islay, Mollendo, Arica e Iquique, 1855–1913*. 5 Vols. Lima, 1976.

Bossi, B. *El Vapor Oriental "Chaurrua" en el Pacífico y Regiones Magallanicas con algunos datos sobre el Perú y Chile en la presente guerra*. Buenos Aires, 1880.

Boyd, R. Nelson, *Chili: Sketches of Chili and the Chilians during the War*. London, 1881.

Bresson, André. *Una visión francesa del litoral boliviano*. Translated by Teresa Bedoya de Ursic. La Paz, 1997. Originally published as *Bolivia Sept Annés d'Explorations, de Voyages et de Séjours dans l'Amerique Australe*. Paris, 1886.

Browne, Albert G., Jr. "The Growing Power of the Republic of Chile." *American Geographical Society of New York* (July 1880): 1–88.

Buendía, Juan. *Guerra con Chile: La campaña del Sur. Memoria del General Juan Buendía y otros documentos inéditos*. Lima, 1967.

Cáceres, Andrés. *La Guerra del 79*. Lima, 1973.

Camacho, Eliodoro. *Tratado sumario del arte militar seguido de una reseña crítica de la historia militar de Bolivia*. La Paz, 1897.

Campero, Narciso. *Informe del General Narciso Campero ante la Convención Nacional de Bolivia como general en jefe del Ejército Aliado*. La Paz, 1880.

"The Capture of the 'Huáscar'." *Engineering*, 12 December 1879, 454–55.

Carrasco, Rufino. *Manifesto del Coronel Rufino Carrasco sobre la expedición al Litoral boliviano en 1879*. 1880.

Carvajal, Melitón. "Reseña de la campaña del Huáscar contra Chile en 1879," *Revista Chilena* 15 (1922): 79–88.

Castro, N. *Opúsculo sobre la guerra I dictadura en el Perú*. Lima, 1880.

Castro E., Guillermo. *Diario de Campaña, 1880–1881*. Santiago, 1986.

Caviano, Tomás. *Historia de la guerra de America entre Chile, Perú, y Bolivia*. Translated by Arturo de Ballesteros y Contin. 2 vols. Iquique, 1904.

Chaparro White, Guillermo. *Batalla de Tacna*. Santiago, 1911.

———. *Recuerdos de la Guerra del Pacífico*. Santiago, 1910.

Claros, Manuel P. *Diario de un excombatiente de la guerra del Pacífico*. La Paz, 1962.

Claro Tocornal, Regina. "Cartas de don Máximo R. Lira a doña Isabel Errázuriz desde los campamentos chilenos durante la Guerra del Pacífico (1879–1881)." *Historia* 36 (2003): 61–88.

Compañía de minería de Huanchaca. *Tercera memoria del directorio e informe de la administración jeneral Huanchaca*. Valparaíso, 1878.

Conferencias diplomáticas de Arica entre los plenipotenciarios de Bolivia, Chile y el Perú con motivo de la mediación de Estados Unidos. La Paz, 1880.

La Corbeta "Unión" el 8 de Octubre de 1879. Lima, 1880.

Correspondencia jeneral de la Comandancia Jeneral de la 1 División Naval bajo el mando del Contra-Almirante don Miguel Grau, comandante del "Huáscar." Santiago, 1880.

Cristi, Eduardo H. *Antecedentes históricos de la guerra con Bolivia e importancia de este pais*. Valparaíso, 1879.

Curtis, William Elroy. "The South American Yankee." *Harper's Magazine* 75 (1887): 556–71.

Dalence, Zenon. *Informe histórico del servicio prestado por el cuerpo de ambulancias del ejército boliviano*. La Paz, 1881.

Davin, Albert. *Chile y Peru en tiempos de la guerra del Pacifico*. Translated by Fernando Casanueva Valencia. Santiago, 1992. Originally published as *Noirs et Jaunes, Pasages cermonies, traités 50,000 milles dans l'ocean Pacifique*. Paris, 1886.

de Irizzarri, Hermójenes. *Una carta a propósito de la guerra entre Chile i las repúblicas del Perú i Bolivia*. Santiago, 1880.

de Lavalle, José Antonio. *Mi misión en Chile en 1879*. Lima, 1979.

del Campo, José Rodolfo. *Campaña Naval: Correspondencia a "El Comercio." Año de 1879*. Lima, 1920.

del Canto, Estanislao. *Memorias militares*. Santiago, 1927.

del Mármol, Florencio. *Recuerdos de viaje y de guerra*. Buenos Aires, 1880.

del Solar, Alberto. *Diario de Campaña*. 3rd. ed. Buenos Aires, 1967.

Diario de la campaña naval escrito a bordo del Huáscar: El combate de Iquique. Lima, 1984.

Documentos relativos a la organización y campaña de la 5a División, Año 1879. La Paz, 1884.

Duarte, Luis E. *Exposición que dirije el Coronel Duarte a los hombres de bien*. Lima, 1884.

Dublé Almeida, Diego. "Diario de Campaña." In *Guerra del Pacífico*, edited by Fernando Ruz Trujillo, 77–135. Santiago, 1979.

Elmore, Teodro. *Defensa de Arica la improvisada fortificación*. Arica, 1902.

Flint, Charles. *Memories of an Active Life*. New York, 1923.

Fuentes para el estudio del historia naval del Perú. 2 vols. Lima, 1960.

Gamazza, Abelardo. *La batalla de Huamachuco*. Lima, 1983.

García Calderón, Francisco. *Memorias del cautiverio*. Lima, 1949.

González, José Antonio. "Un soldado de la Guerra del Pacífico: Apuntes y espisodios de José Ramon Lira." *Revista Chilena de Historia y Geografía* 150 (1982): 14–28.

González Prada, Adriana de. *Mi Manuel*. Lima, 1947.

González Prada, Manuel. *Impresiones de un reservista*. Lima, 1976.

"The Growing Power of the Republic of Chile." *Atlantic Monthly* 54 (July 1884): 110–16.

Gutiérrez, Hipólito. *Crónica de un soldado en la Guerra del Pacífico*. Santiago, 1956.

Guzmán, Trinidad. *Apuntes para la historia: La división Rios, en la campaña, batalla y retirada de Taracpacá*. Cochabamba, 1882.

Holguin, Vicente. "La toma de Lima (correspondencia)." *Revista Chilena* 10 (November–December 1926): 1–33.

Huáscar: Las cartas perdidas. Santiago, 2002.

Humberstone, J. F. (Santiago). *Huida de Agua Santa en 1879*. Santiago, 1980.

Ibarra Díaz, Marcos. *Campaña de la Sierra*. La Serena, 1985.

Informe histórico del servicio prestado por el Cuerpo de Ambulancias del Ejército boliviano. La Paz, 1881.

Informes inéditos de diplomáticos extranjeros durante la Guerra del Pacífico. Santiago, 1980.

Larraín, José C. *Impresiones y Recuerdos sobre la campaña al Peru*. Santiago, 1910.

Leigh, J. Studdy, "Peruvia [*sic*], Bolivia, and Chile." *The Overland Monthly* 3, no. 5 (May 1884): 527–41.

Le León, M. *Recuerdos de una misión en el ejército chileno*. Buenos Aires, 1969.

Lynch, Patricio. *Memoria que el vice-almirante D. Patricio Lynch jeneral en jefe del ejército de operaciones en el norte del Perú presenta al supremo gobierno de Chile*. Lima, 1882.

———. *Segunda memoria que el vice-almirante D. Patricio Lynch jeneral en jefe del ejército de operaciones en el norte del Perú presenta al supremo gobierno de Chile*. 2 vols. Lima, 1884.

Marchant Pereira, Ruperto, "Correspondencia del capellán de la Guerra del Pacífico Pbro. D. Ruperto Marchant Pereira." *Historia* 18 (1983): 345–66.

———. *Crónica de un capellán de la Guerra del Pacífico*. Santiago, 1959.

———. *Testimonios de un capellán castrense en la Guerra del Pacífico*. Santiago, 2004.

Un marino italiano en la guerra de 1879. Lima, 1971.

Markham, Clements. *The War between Peru and Chile, 1879–82.* London, 1883.

Mason, Theodorus B. M. "The War between Chile, Peru, and Bolivia: Shakings from the Log-Books of a Lieutenant." *The United Service* 2 (May 1880): 553–74.

―――. *The War on the Pacific Coast of South America between Chile and the Allied Republics of Peru and Bolivia, 1879–81.* Washington DC, 1883.

Mathews, Edward. *Up the Amazon and Madeira Rivers through Bolivia and Peru.* London, 1879.

Matte Varas, Joaquín. "Informe del capellán de la Guerra del Pacífico J. Valdés Carrera." *Revista Chilena de Historia y Geografía* 151 (1983): 187–99.

Medina, José Toribio. *Una excusión a Tarapacá: Los juzgados de Tarapacá, 1880–1881.* Santiago, 1952.

Meigs, J. F. "The War in South America." *The Record of the United States Naval Institute* 5 (1879): 461–78.

Molina, Modesto. *Hojas del Proceso: Apuntes para un libro de historia.* Arica, 1880.

Moreno de Cáceres, Antonia. *Recuerdos de la campaña de la Breña.* Lima, 1974.

Molinare, Nicanor. *Historia de la batalla de Huamachuco, 10 Julio de 1883.* Santiago, 1913.

Moreno Guevara, Anjel. *Combate de Pachia (11 de Noviembre de 1883).* Tacna, 1913.

Ochoa, José Vicente. *Diario de la Campaña del Ejército Boliviano en la Guerra del Pacífico.* Sucre. 1899.

―――. *Semblanzas de la Guerra del Pacífico.* La Paz, 1881.

Palma, Ricardo. *Cartas a Piérola (Sobre la ocupación chilena de Lima).* Lima, 1964.

―――. *Crónicas de la Guerra con Chile.* Lima, 1984.

Paz Soldán, Mariano Felipe. *Narración histórica de la guerra de Chile contra el Perú y Bolivia.* Buenos Aires, 1884.

Pérez, I. *Arica: Sus fortificaciones, asalto, defensa por un testigo y autor.* Lima, 1880.

Pérez, José Antonio. *Apuntes biograficos sobre el mui ilustre jeneral de brigada don Pedro Lagos.* (Santiago) 1884.

Perolari-Malmignati, Pietro. *Il Perú e I suoi tremendi giornia (1878–1881); pagine d'uno spettatore.* Milano, 1882.

Pinto, Aníbal. "Apuntes." *Revista Chilena* 14 (1922): 112–22.

―――. "El hundimiento del trasporte *Loa* en *1880.*" *Revista Chilena* 11, no. 8 (1917): 247–49.

Puig y Veraguer, Jaime. *Memorias del bloqueo de Iquique.* Santiago, 1954.

Quiróz, Abraham. "Epistolario inédito de su campaña como soldado raso durante toda la Guerra del Pacífico." In *Dos Soldados en la Guerra del Pacífico.* Buenos Aires, 1976. 143–229.

Ravest Mora, Manuel, "Combate de Concepción: Narración del soldado Marcos Ibarra." *Revista Chilena de Historia y Geografía* 150 (1982): 7–13.

————. "*Memorias íntimas* del General Estanislao del Canto (1840–1923)." *Boletín de la Academia Chilena de la Historia* 80, no. 113 (2004): 315–31.

Risopatron Cañas, D. *Legislación militar de Chile.* 3 vols. Santiago, 1882.

Riquelme, Daniel. *La expedición a Lima.* Santiago, 1967.

Rivas, E. A., and V. M. Rivas. *Mantilla y Huancavilca: Episodios heroicos de la Guerra del Pacífico, 1879–1883.* Lima, 1927.

Riveros, Galvarino. *Angamos.* Santiago, 1882.

————. *En la escuadra.* Santiago, 1882.

Rosales, Justo Abel. *Mi campaña al Peru, 1879–1881.* Concepción, 1984.

Salazar, Francisco Javier. *Las batallas de Chorrillos y Miraflores y el arte de la guerra.* Lima, 1882.

Salinas, Florentino, *Los representantes de la Provincia de Aconcagua en la Guerra del Pacífico 1879–1884.* Santiago, 1893.

Santa María, Domingo. "Cartas de don Domingo Santa María a don José Victorino Lastarria" *Revista Chilena* 6 (1918): 255–60.

Santini, Felice. *Viaggio della "Garibaldi," Intorno al mondo a bordo della regia corvetta "Garibaldi" (anni 1879–90–81–82): Memorie di viaggio.* Roma, 1895.

Sotomayor, Rafael. "Correspondencia de don Rafael Sotomayor con don Aníbal Pinto sobre la Guerra del Pacífico." *Revista Chilena* 6, no. 57 (1922): 178–94; 15 (1922): 285–94; 17 (1924): 410–30.

Sotomayor Valdés, R. *La legación de Chile en Bolivia desde Setiembre de 1867 hasta principios de 1871.* 2nd ed. Santiago, 1912.

Spangler, J. M. *Civilization in Chili: Past and Present.* San Francisco, 1885.

Spila de Subiaco, P. Benedicto, *Chile en la Guerra del Pacífico.* 2nd ed. Roma, 1887.

Storace, Pedro Luis. *Diario personal del maquinista italiano.* Lima, 1971.

Subercaseaux, Ramón. *Memorias de ochenta años.* 2nd ed. 2 vols. Santiago, 1936.

Tauro, Alberto. "La defensa de Lima." *Revista San Marcos* 20 (1979): 1–128.

Tercera memoria del directorio e informe de la administración jeneral de Huanchaca. Valparaíso, 1878.

Torres Lara, José T. *Recuerdos de la guerra con Chile.* Lima, n.d.

La traición de Iglesias: Documentos para el proceso. Guayaquil, 1884.

Ugarte, Ricardo. *Efemérides de la Guerra del Pacífico.* La Paz, 1882.

Ugarte Chamorro, Guillermo. *Diario de la campaña a bordo del "Huscar." El combate de Iquique.* Lima, 1984.

Uribe, Luis. *Los combates de la Guerra del Pacífico.* Valparaíso, 1886.

Uriburu, D. E. *Guerra del Pacífico: Episodios 1879–1881.* Buenos Aires, 1899.

Urquieta, Antonio. *Recuerdos de la vida de campaña en la Guerra del Pacífico.* 2 vols. Santiago, 1907.

Varas, Antonio. *Correspondencia de don Antonio Varas sobre la Guerra del Pacífico.* Santiago, 1918.

Varigny, Charles de. *La Guerra del Pacífico.* 2d ed.; Buenos Aires, 1971.

Venegas Urbina, L. Lucio. *Sancho en la Guerra: Recuerdos del ejército en la campaña al Perú y Bolivia.* Santiago, 1885.

Vergara, José Francisco. "Memorias de José Francisco Vergara," in *Guerra del Pacífico,* edited by Fernando Ruz Trujillo, 11–74. Santiago, 1979.

Vicuña Mackenna, Benjamín. *Historia de la Campaña de Lima, 1880–1881.* 2 vols. Santiago, 1880–81.

———. *Historia de la campaña de Tacna y Arica.* 2d ed. Santiago, 1881.

———. *Historia de la campaña de Tarapacá.* 2 vols. Santiago, 1881.

———. *Sangra: La jornada heróica.* Santiago, 1915.

Weiner, Charles. "La guerra en Sud America." *Boletín de la Guerra del Pacífico,* 6 August 1879, 270–75, and 19 August 1879, 287–89. Originally published as *XIX Siécle.* Paris, n.d.

Williams Rebolledo, Juan. *Operaciones de la escuadra chilena miéntras estuvo a las órdenes del contra-almirante Williams Rebolledo.* Valparaíso, 1882.

Witt, Heinrich. *Diario y Observaciones sobre el Perú (1824–1890).* Lima, 1987.

Wu Brading, Celia. *Testimonios británicos de la ocupación chilena de Lima.* Lima, 1986.

Secondary Materials

Aguirre Lavayen, Joaquín. *1884 pacto de tregua Guerra del Pacífico.* La Paz, 1987.

Amayo, Enrique. *La política británica en la Guerra del Pacífico.* Lima, 1988.

Aranda de los Rios, Ramón, and Carmel Sotomayor Rogguero. "Una subelevación negra en Chincha: 1879." In Reategui, *Guerra del Pacífico,* 243–53.

Aranzaes, Nicanor. *Las revoluciones en Bolivia.* La Paz, 1992.

Arguedas, Alcídes. *Historia general de Bolivia, 1809–1921.* La Paz, 1922.

———. *Obras completas.* 2 vols. Buenos Aires, 1959.

Armada Boliviana. http://www.armada.mil.bo.

Armstrong, G. E. *Torpedoes and Torpedo Boats.* London, 1896.

Arnold, Joseph C. "French Tactical Doctrine, 1870–1914." *Military Affairs* 42, no. 2 (1878): 61–67.

Arosemena Garland, Geraldo. *El Almirante Grau.* 7th ed. Lima, 1979.

———. *Armamentismo antes de 1879.* Lima, 1972.

Barrientos Gutiérrez, Pablo. *Historia del Estado Mayor General del Ejército, 1811–1944.* Santiago, 1947.

———. *Historia de la Artillería de Chile.* Santiago, 1946.

Barros, Mario. *Historia diplomática de Chile.* Barcelona, 1970.

Barros Arana, Diego. *Histoire de la Guerre de Pacifique, 1879–1880.* Paris, 1881.

Basadre, Jorge. *Historia de la República del Perú,* 10 vols. 5th corrected and revised ed. Lima, 1962.

———. *Historia de la República del Perú.* 12 vols. Lima, 1969.

Beckett, Ian F. W. *Ypes.* Harlow, 2004.

Bedregal, Guillermo. *Los militares en Bolivia.* La Paz, 1971.

Benedicto, A. "Servicio de alimentación y amunicionamiento en la guerra de 1879–1884." *Memorial del Ejército de Chile* 13, no. 2 (1918): 137–54.

Black, Jeremy. *Western Warfare.* 2 vols. Bloomington, 2001.

Blakemore, Harold. "Chile." In *Latin America Geographical Perspectives*, edited by Harold Blakemore and Clifford Smith, 465–566. London, 1971.

Böhm, Günter. *Judios en el Perú durante el siglo XIX.* Santiago, 1985.

Bonilla, Heraclio. "Peru and Bolivia from Independence to the War of the Pacific." In Leslie Bethell, *The Cambridge History of Latin America.* 20 vols. 3:539–82. Cambridge, 1985.

Bowman, Isaiah. *The Andes of Southern Peru.* New York, 1916.

———. *Desert Trails of Atacama.* New York, 1924.

Brahm García, Enrique. *Preparados para la guerra: Pensamiento militar chileno bajo influencia alemana, 1885–1930.* Santiago, 2003.

Brose, Eric. *The Kaiser's Army.* New York, 2001.

Bulnes, Gonzalo. *Historia de la Guerra del Pacífico.* 3 vols. Valparaíso, 1911–17.

Callwell, C. E. *Small Wars.* 3rd ed. London, 1976.

Carvajal Pareja, Melitón. *Historia marítima del Perú: La República 1879 a 1883.* Tomo 11, vol. 1. Lima, 2004.

———. *Historia marítima del Perú: La República 1879 a 1883.* Tomo 11, vol. 2. Lima, 2006.

Civati Bernasconi, Edmundo H. *La Guerra del Pacífico.* 2 vols. Buenos Aires, 1946.

Clowes, William Laird. *Four Modern Naval Campaigns.* London, 1902.

Coffman, Edward M. *The Old Army.* New York, 1986.

Conways, A. *All the World's Fighting Ships, 1860–1905.* London, 1979.

Dellepiane, Carlos. *Historia militar del Perú.* 2 vols. Buenos Aires, 1941.

Dennis, William Jefferson. *Documentary History of the Tacna-Arica Dispute.* Port Washington NY, 1971.

de Secada, C. Alexander G. "Army, Guano, and Shipping: The W. R. Grace Interests in Peru, 1865–1885." *Business History Review* 59 (Winter 1985): 597–621.

Díaz Arguedas, Julio. *Historia del ejército de Bolivia, 1825–1932.* La Paz, 1971.

Dunkerley, James. "The Politics of the Bolivian Army: Institutional Development to 1935." PhD diss. University of Oxford, 1979.

Ekdahl, Wilhelm. *Historia militar de la Guerra del Pacífico entre Chile, Peru, i Bolivia.* 3 vols. Santiago, 1917–19.

Estado Mayor General. *Historia del ejército de Chile.* 10 vols. Santiago, 1981–82.

Fellmann Velarde, José. *Historia de Bolivia.* 2 vols. La Paz, 1970.

Fernández Larraín, Sergio. *Santa Cruz y Torreblanca: Dos héroes de las campañas de Tarapacá y Tacna.* Santiago, 1979.

Fernández Valdés, Juan José. *Chile y Perú: Historia de sus relaciones diplomáticas entre 1879 y 1929.* Santiago, 2004.

Fuenzalida Bade, Rodrigo. *La armada de Chile.* 4 vols. N.p., n.d.

———. *Marinos ilustres y destacados del pasado.* Concepción, 1985.

Fuller, J. F. C. *A Military History of the Western World.* 3 vols. New York, 1957.

———. *War and Western Civilization, 1832–1932.* London, 1932.

Gamarra Zorrilla, José. *La Guerra del Pacífico: Breve bosquejo y reflexiones.* La Paz, 1998.

García Castelblanco, Alejandro. *Estudio crítico de las operaciones navales de Chile.* Santiago, 1929.

Giesecke, Margarita. "Las clases sociales y los grupos de poder." In *Reflexiones en torno a la guerra de 1879,* edited by Jorge Basadre et al. Lima, 1979.

González Salinas, Edmundo. *Reseñas históricas de las unidades e institutos del Ejército de Chile.* Santiago, 1987.

Gray, Edwyn. *Nineteenth-Century Torpedoes and Their Inventors.* Annapolis, 2004.

Greene, Francis V. *Report of the Russian Army and Its Campaign in Turkey, 1877–1878.* New York, 1879.

Greenhill, Robert G., and Rory M. Miller. "The Peruvian Government and the Nitrate Trade, 1873–1879." *Journal of Latin American Studies* 5, no. 1 (1973): 107–31.

Grez, Carlos. "La supuesta preparación de Chile para la Guerra del Pacífco." *Boletin de la Academia Chilean de la Historia* 3, no. 5 (1935): 111–39.

Grieve, Jorge. *Historia de la artillería y de la marina de guerra en la Contienda del 79.* Lima, 1981.

Guerra Martiniere, Margarita. *La ocupación de Lima, 1881–1883.* Lima, 1999.

Guzmán Palomino, Luis. *Campaña de la Breña: Colección de documentos inéditos.* Lima, 1990.

Healy, David. *James G. Blaine and Latin America.* Columbia MO, 2001.

Herrmann, Alberto. *La producción en Chile de los metales i minerales mas importantes . . . hasta fines del año 1902.* Santiago, 1903.

Herwig, Holger. *The First World War: Germany and Austria-Hungary, 1914–1918.* London, 1997.

Historia de la escuela militar del Peru. Lima, 1962.

Howard, Michael. *The Franco-Prussian War.* New York, 1962.

Irurozqui Victoriano, Marta. *"A bala, piedra, y palo": La construcción de la ciudadanía política en Bolivia, 1826–1952.* Seville, 2000.

Jamieson, Perry D. *Crossing the Deadly Ground.* Tuscaloosa AL, 1994.

Jobet, Julio C. *Ensayo crítico del desarrollo económico-social del Chile.* Santiago, 1955.

Jofre Alvarez, Luis. "Don Eulogio Altamirano." *Revista Chilena de Historia y Geografia* 65, no. 69 (1930): 63–81.

Johnson, George B., and Hans Bert Lockhoven. *International Armament.* 2 vols. Cologne, 1965.

"Juana López, cantinera." *Revista de Historia Militar* 3 (2004): 20–22.

Karsten, Peter. *The Naval Aristocracy.* New York, 1972.

Klein, Herbert. *Parties and Political Change in Bolivia, 1880–1952.* Cambridge, 1969.

Körner, Emilio, and J. Boonen Rivera. *Estudios sobre historia militar.* 2 vols. Santiago, 1887.

Lastres, Juan. *Historia de la medicina peruana.* 3 vols. Lima, 1951.

López Martínez, Héctor. *Historia marítima del Perú: La república, 1876 a 1879.* Lima, 1988.

———. *Piérola y la defensa de Lima.* Lima, 1981.

López U., Carlos. *Historia de la marina de Chile.* Santiago, 1969.

Luvaas, Jay. *The Military Legacy of the Civil War: The European Inheritance.* Lawrence KS, 1988.

Machuca, Francisco. *Las cuatro campañas de la Guerra del Pacífico.* 4 vols. Santiago, 1926–30.

Manrique, Nelson. *Las guerrillas indígenas en la guerra con Chile.* Lima, 1981.

Mayo, John. *British Merchants and Chilean Development, 1851–1886.* Boulder, 1987.

McCann, Frank D. *Soldiers of the Pátria.* Stanford CA, 2004.

McElwee, William. *The Art of War.* Bloomington IN, 1974.

Melo, Rosendo. *Historia de la marina del Perú.* 2nd ed. 2 vols. Lima, 1980.

Menning, Bruce W. *Bayonets before Bullets.* Bloomington IN, 2004.

Mercado Moreira, Miguel. *Guerra del Pacífico: Nuevos esclarecimientos.* La Paz, 1956.

Merlet Sanhueza, Enrique. *Juan José Latorre: Héroe de Angamos.* Santiago, 1997.

Millington, Herbert. *American Diplomacy and the War of the Pacific.* New York, 1948.

Mitchell, Allan, *Victors and Vanquished: The German Influence on Army and Church in France after 1870.* Chapel Hill NC, 1984.

O'Brien, Thomas F. *The Nitrate Industry and Chile's Crucial Transition, 1870–1891.* New York, 1982.

Parodi Revoredo, Daniel. *La laguna de los villanos: Bolivia, Arequipa, y Lizardo Montero en la Guerra del Pacífico, 1881–1883.* Lima, 2001.

Peñaloza, Luis. *Historia económica de Bolivia.* 2 vols. La Paz, 1954.

Peralta Ruiz, Victor, and Marta Irurozqui Victoriano. *Por la concordia, la fusión, y el unitarismo estado y caudillismo en Bolivia, 1825–1880.* Madrid, 2000.

Peri, René. *Los Batallones Bulnes y Valparaíso.* N.p., n.d.

Phillips, Richard. "Bolivia in the War of the Pacific, 1879–1884." PhD diss. University of Virginia, 1973.

Pinochet U., Augusto. *La Guerra del Pacífico: Campaña de Tarapacá.* Santiago, 1980.

Pinochet de la Barra, Oscar. *Misión en Bolivia de C. Walker Martínez y R. Sotomayor Valdés.* Santiago, n.d.

Pizarro, Rafael. *Los abastecimientos militares en la Guerra del Pacífico.* Santiago, 1967.

Pletcher, David. *The Awkward Years: American Foreign Policy under Garfield and Arthur.* Columbia MO, 1962.

Poblete, Rafael. "Desarrollo histórico de la organización de nuestra ejército." *Memorial del Ejército de Chile* 1st semestre (1916): 213–20.

———. "Nuestro ejército al estallar la Guerra del Pacífico." *Memorial del Ejército de Chile* 1st semestre (1918): 227–52.

———. "El servicio sanitario en el ejército de Chile durante la Guerra del Pacífico." *Revista Chilena de Historia y Geografía,* 33, no. 37 (1920): 465–79; 35, no. 39 (1920): 463–89; 38, no. 39 (1920): 469–99; 39, no. 43 (1921): 474–96; 41, no. 45 (1922): 456–82.

Querejazu Calvo, Roberto. *Aclaraciones históricas sobre la Guerra del Pacífico.* La Paz, 1995.

———. *Guano, salitre, sangre.* La Paz, 1979.

Lash, Jeffrey N. *A Politician Turned General: The Civil War Career of Stephen Augustus Hurlburt.* Kent OH, 2003.

Reátegui, Wilson, et al., eds. *La Guerra del Pacífico.* 2 vols. Lima, 1979.

Rodríguez Rautcher, Sergio. *Problemática del soldado durante la Guerra del Pacífico.* Santiago, nd.

Roel, Virilio. *El Perú en el siglo XIX.* Lima, 1986.

Romero Pintado, Fernando. *Historia marítima del Peru: La Republica, 1850–1870.* Tomo 8, vols. 1–3. Lima, 1984.

Sapunar Peric, Pedro. "El cosario boliviano *Laura.*" *Revista de Marina* 1, no. 95 (1995): 72–75.

Sater, William F. *Chile and the War of the Pacific.* Lincoln, 1986.

———. "Chile during the First Months of the War of the Pacific." *The Journal of Latin American Studies* 5, no. 1 (1972): 133–58.

———. *Empires in Conflict.* Athens GA, 1990.

———. *The Heroic Image in Chile.* Los Angeles, 1973.

Scheina, Robert L. *Latin America: A Naval History, 1810–1987.* Annapolis, 1987.

Segal, Marcello. *Desarrollo del capitalismo en Chile.* Santiago, 1953.

Sepúlveda Rojas, Arturo. *Así vivieron y vencieron, 1879–1884.* Santiago, 1980.

Seraylán L., Alejandro. "La campaña de Lima." In *La Gesta de Lima.* Lima, 1981. 156–74.

Smith, Clarence. "The Central Andes." *Latin American Geographical Perspectives.* London, 1971.

Smith, W., and Joseph Smith. *The Book of Rifles.* 3rd ed. Harrisburg, PA 1963.

Spiers, Edward S. *The Late Victorian Army, 1868–1902.* Manchester, 1992.

Stewart, Watt "Federico Blume's Peruvian Submarine." *Hispanic American Historical Review* 28, no. 3 (1948): 468–78.

Tarnstrom, Ronald. *French Arms.* Lindsborg KS, 2001.

Toro Dávila, Agustín. *Síntesis histórico militar de Chile.* Santiago, 1976.

Travers, T. E. "The Offensive and the Problem of Innovation in British Military Thought 1870–1915." *Journal of Contemporary History* 13 (1978): 531–53.

Valdizán Gamio, José. *Historia naval del Perú.* 5 vols. Lima, 1987.

van Creveld, Martin. *Command in War.* Cambridge, 1985.

Vargas Hurtado, Gerardo. *La batalla de Arica.* 2nd ed. Lima, 1980.

Vargas Valenzuela, José. *Tradición naval del pueblo boliviana.* La Paz, 1974.

Vegas G., Manuel. *Historia de la marina de guerra del Peru.* 3rd ed. Lima, 1978.

Véliz, Claudio. *Historia de la Marina Mercante de Chile.* Santiago, 1961.

Vial Correa et. al. Gonzalo. *La sudamericana de vapores en la historia de Chile.* Santiago, 1997.

Vidaurre Retamoso, Enrique. *El Presidente Daza.* La Paz, 1975.

Villalobos, Sergio, et al. *Historia de la ingeniería en Chile.* Santiago, 1990.

Villar Cordova, Socrates. "Situación del Perú: 1868–1878." In Reátegui, *Guerra del Pacífico,* 1:14–78.

Vitale, Luis. *Interpretación marxista de la historia de Chile.* 5 vols. Frankfurt, 1975.

Wilde, Fernando. *Historia militar de Bolivia.* La Paz, 1963.

Index

Angamos, Battle of, 157–60; Allied response to, 159; Chilean conduct at, 156–57; Chilean preparation for, 154–55; Chilean reaction to, 159; impact of, 159, 169; naval offensive preceding, 155–56; Peruvian participation in, 156–59

Antofagasta: attack on, 151–52; blockade of, 118

Arequipa, Chilean assault of, 339, 341–42

Arica: atrocities at, 255–56; bombardment of, 214; casualties at, 254; Chilean advance on, 250; Chilean attack on, 252–53; Chilean brutality at, 253; Chilean troops at, 249; description of battle for, 247; and failed attempts at negotiations, 250–51; impact of capture of, 256–57; initial Chilean assault on, 250; naval blockade of, 251; Peruvian defenses of, 247–49; Peruvian garrison of, 249–50; sinking of *Manco Cápac* at, 254; strategic importance of, 247–48; strategy for attacking, 251–52

armies of Bolivia: acquisitions of, 86–87; communications within, 87; conditions in, 58–59; discipline of, 53–54, 93; domestic production of, 87; evaluation of, 52–54, 58–59; logistics in, 75, 76–77; medical care of, 89–90; morale of, 52–53, 57; officer corps of, 50–51, 54; prewar preparation of, 55; prewar size of, 51–52, 54–55; races of, 57; recruitment practices of, 45, 56–58; reforms in, 54, 56; role of Militia in, 44, 57, 73–74; role of rabonas in, 54–55, 75–76, 178–80; size of, 176, 178–80; stamina of, 55; supply of, 75–77, 87; tactics of, 53, 70; training of, 53; units of, 51–52, 55, 57, 72–74; unrest in, 51–52, 73; weapons and uniforms of, 55–56, 62, 66–67

armies of Chile: acquisitions of, 85–86; arms of, 61; atrocities committed by, 61, 191–92; communications and transportation within, 87–88; condition of, 70; discipline in, 74, 93–94; domestic production of, 87; equipment of, 59, 61; health of, 81; logistics in, 79–81, 87–88; medical service in, 89–91; nature of, 59; and occupation policy of Peru, 94; officer corps of, 44, 61, 68–70; political involvement of, 61; prewar preparation of, 44, 68–70; prewar strength of, 59; professionalism of, 68; purchases of, 63–65, 85–86; recruitment practices of, 44–45, 60; role of *cantineras* in, 82–84; role of militia in, 44, 60–61, 72–74; size of, 44, 59–60, 70–72; tactics of, 68–69; training of, 69–70; units of, 60–61, 71–73; weapons of, 61–62, 63–65

armies of Peru: acquisitions of, 84–85; atrocities of, 92; communications within, 88; domestic production of, 87; equipment of, 46–47; evaluation of, 38; logistics in, 78–79, 87–88; medical care of, 89–90; militias in, 44, 73; officer corps of, 48; prewar preparation of, 45; prewar size of, 45, 47–48; races of, 47; recruitment practices of, 45, 49–50; role of rabonas in, 48, 77–78; size of, 47; supply of, 78–79; tactics of, 70; transportation of, 88; units of, 72; weapons of, 46–47, 62, 66

Arriagada, Gen. Marco A.: and Sierra Campaign, 325; and views of Chilean Army, 70

Arteaga, Col. Luis, role in Tarapacá, 198–99

Arteaga Cuevas, Gen. Justo: character of, 170; manual by, 69; military training of, 68; resignation of, 170

Ayacucho, Chilean capture of, 340

Baquedano, Gen. Manuel: and attempts to negotiate armistice, 291; and conflict with Maturana and Vergara, 279, 281; disciplinary policies at Tacna of, 221; humanitarian gestures of, 90; military training of, 68; and plans for capturing Lima, 265, 278–79, 283, 285; and plans for capturing Tacna, 235–36; and plan to cross desert, 225; and prepara-

Studies in War, Society, and the Military

Lightning Source UK Ltd.
Milton Keynes UK
UKHW010606050419

340534UK00001B/154/P